P9-DDN-037

LIVERMORE PUBLIC LIBRARY
1188 S. LIVERMORE AVE.
LIVERMORE, CA 94550

NEVADA

SCOTT SMITH

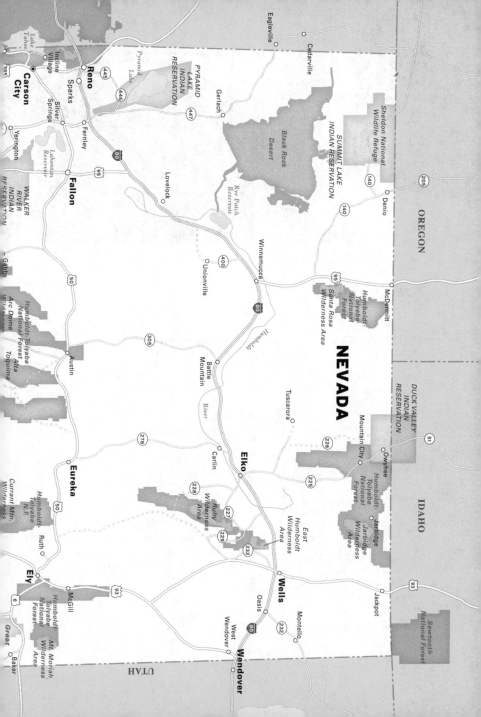

Contents

DISCOVER

Nevada

Nevada is no pushover. Its geography, history, and culture will challenge you to reconsider your sensibilities, push your limits, and press your luck.

The Silver State is still a frontier setting, straddling the line between the rough-hewn and the sophisticated, always with one foot planted firmly in the past, but ever poised to take the next step forward. The independent spirit found in the Native American's respect for the land, the pioneer's sense of adventure, the prospector's optimism, and the immigrant Basque's industriousness still abides here. There's also an air of anticipation . . . that something exciting will happen on the next roll of the dice, with the next cast of your trusty fly rod, or around the next curve on the Loneliest Road in America.

To discover Nevada is to embrace its idiosyncrasies and incongruities: the urbanity of Las Vegas balanced by Fallon's agrarian idyll; the forbidding barrenness of the desert counterpointed by fruit trees and grapevines. While cowboy conservatism is prevalent in much of the state, Nevada remains the only place in the country where not only gambling but also rural prostitution and recreational marijuana are both legal and vital to the economy.

Clockwise from top left: International Car Forest of the Last Church in Goldfield; the famous Las Vegas sign; Joshua tree; Alien Research Center in Hiko; Bellagio Conservatory in Las Vegas; Artist's Drive in Death Valley.

There's plenty of opportunity for vice and consumption in Nevada, but there's more to it than bright lights and unchecked hedonism. Dance along with the neon on the Las Vegas Strip, Reno's casino row, and the main street of just about any Nevada town big enough to have a stoplight. But far from the neon jungle, you will find some of the darkest skies in the United States, perfect for gazing at the stars. Plunge deep into Nevada's backcountry to explore hundreds of river tributaries where you can cast a fly, battle your own rainbow, and celebrate victory with a hard-won meal grilled over a campfire. Experience home-spun pleasures like farmers markets, local art shows, and balloon festivals.

The Vegas Strip, Reno, and Lake Tahoe shine like nuggets in a gold pan, but Nevada's real treasures lie just below the surface. And like the miners of the past, you too will be rewarded if you're willing to dig a little.

Clockwise from top left: Heavenly Mountain Resort overlooking Lake Tahoe; entrance to Boulder City's historic downtown; Charles Albert Szukalski's *Ghost Rider* at the Goldwell Open Air Museum near Rhyolite; Cathedral Gorge State Park.

10 TOP
EXPERIENCES

1 **Las Vegas Glitz:** Think flashing neon, luxury resorts, and feathered showgirls. It doesn't get any glitzier than Vegas (page 31).

2 **Outdoor Recreation in Tahoe:** Surrounded by majestic peaks, this bluest of lakes makes the ideal setting for hiking, camping, and of course, skiing (pages 26 and 152).

>>>

3 **Fun in Reno:** Even beyond the slot machines, cocktails, and floor shows, Reno offers serious fun, including the Truckee Riverwalk and an emerging art scene (page 120).

>>>

THE BIGGES

^
^
^

4 **Scenic Drives:** Nevada was made for road trips, from the Loneliest Road (page 28) to the Extraterrestrial Highway (page 184).

^
^
^

5 **Otherworldly Landscapes:** Explore lunar craters, valleys of death, and eerily quiet prairies beneath star-strewn blackness. Choose the Black Rock Desert (page 278), Cathedral Gorge (page 181), Pyramid Lake (page 275), the Lunar Cuesta (page 201)—or all of the above.

6 **Wild West History:** Relive the Gold Rush era with visits to ghost towns (page 29) as well as still thriving cities like Carson City (page 212) and Virginia City (page 233).

<<<

7 **Hot Springs:**
Relax and rejuvenate with a natural mineral bath (page 23).

>>>

8 **Ruby Mountains:**
Nevada is filled with gorgeous landscapes, but this series of 10,000-foot peaks may be its most stunning backdrop (page 306).

<<<

9 **Great Basin National Park:**
This hallowed temple of the wilderness range contains permanent glacier-like ice, limestone corridors, and 4,000-plus-year-old trees (page 263).

>>>

10 **Small-Town Charm:** Friendly, rustic communities bring a touch of civilization to Nevada's rugged terrain (page 30).

Planning Your Trip

Where to Go

Las Vegas

Las Vegas has a way of winning people over. Even nongamblers horrified at the thought of throwing away hard-earned cash break down and slide $20 into a **slot machine**—hey, you never know, right? Even strict dieters simply *must* sample a seafood buffet. Wallflowers gyrate under pulsing strobes. **Dine, drink, dance,** and double down, then do it all again tomorrow. Some 36 million visitors a year can't be wrong. **Gambling** is Nevada's lifeblood, and Vegas is its heart.

Reno and Tahoe

While showgirls and Elvis impersonators live here too, somehow Reno seems like a real town. Just a few blocks from the **casinos**, the **Truckee River** meanders right through town alongside **museums, parks, fine restaurants,** and **upscale**

boutiques. Not far away are the **pristine waters** and rugged, tree-lined shoreline of Lake Tahoe. Its **ski resorts** beckon with plentiful runs, from bunny slopes to the blackest of black diamonds.

Central Nevada

Central Nevada is home to quintessential icons of the American West. Rainbow Canyon's **Native American petroglyphs** and Goldfield and Rhyolite's **boomtown relics** shed light on the lives of our ancestors; the hauntingly beautiful **caves and spires** at **Cathedral Gorge** take travelers even further back to primordial times. Perhaps it's this rich past that drives restless spirits to haunt its **historic towns.**

The Loneliest Road

To some, US 50's miles of solitary roadway

Cathedral Gorge State Park

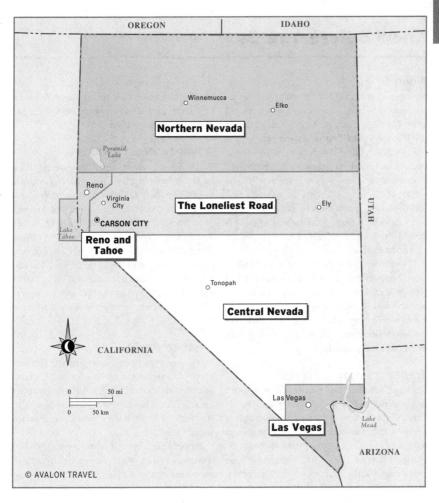

OREGON   IDAHO

Winnemucca   Elko

Northern Nevada

Pyramid
Lake

Reno

Virginia
City   **The Loneliest Road**   Ely   UTAH

CARSON CITY

Lake
Tahoe   **Reno and
Tahoe**

Tonopah

Central Nevada

CALIFORNIA

0   50 mi

0   50 km

Las Vegas

Lake
Mead

Las Vegas

ARIZONA

© AVALON TRAVEL

feel like heaven. The trip starts at **state capital Carson City,** continues through **Virginia City** (the state's first boomtown), and pushes on to **Great Basin National Park** and the state line, tempting road-trippers with soothing **hot springs,** venerable **watering holes,** and **quaint motels.**

Northern Nevada

Northern Nevada's Humboldt River Valley is your high school geography and history lessons come to life—only more interesting. **Pyramid Lake,** with its perfect triangular rock jutting through the placid surface, is one of the most beautiful desert waterways in the world. The **Black Rock Desert,** an expanse of playa at turns spiritually calm and eerily still, comes alive during the annual **Burning Man festival.** On the other side of the state, the **Ruby Mountains** reign from some 10,000 feet above, offering adventure recreation.

Know Before You Go

When to Go

Nevada makes a great **winter escape,** whether you want to shred the manicured slopes around **Lake Tahoe** or enjoy sunny mild temperatures (60°F or so) in **Las Vegas.** Expect high season rates in Tahoe, but enjoy bargains in Vegas—especially between Thanksgiving and Christmas.

In **summer,** these big destinations still draw plenty of visitors. In Tahoe, the hiking's fine and the lake is just as blue. In Vegas, the blackjack odds never change, the swimming pool is always open, and casinos and hotel rooms are air-conditioned.

If you're headed to Nevada to enjoy outdoor recreation, **spring** and **fall** are perhaps the best times to visit. The spring sun is bright but not too hot, showers bring out desert wildflowers, and the fish are biting in lakes and rivers. Fall sees the baking heat abate in time for picnics, outdoor events, and camping trips.

Transportation

Las Vegas's **McCarran International Airport** is one of the busiest in the country, and **Reno-Tahoe International** knows a little something about handling visitors as well. Most air visitors will make use of one of these state-of-the-art facilities. However, the resort cities receive huge percentages of their clientele from California. Starting on Thursday nights, the eastbound **traffic** on **I-80** and **I-15** can be murder; it's more of the same in the other direction beginning on Sunday afternoon. Those visitors at least have the advantage of having their cars with them, a must for exploring beyond the resort corridors. However, the big cities are well provided with rental-car companies, and public transportation and taxis are easy to find.

Advance Reservations

While Vegas is always open for business, it's a good idea to make a few calls to Las Vegas hotels or to the **Las Vegas Convention and Visitors Authority** (702/892-0711) *before* you confirm your dates of your vacation to find out if there's a convention, event, or holiday. While **Vegas shows** are quite popular, if you're flexible, you shouldn't have any trouble seeing your favorite production or headliner. Guaranteeing attendance at major boxing matches and music festivals may require some planning and advance purchases.

What to Pack

You'll need copious amounts of **sunscreen** and **water,** but you can stock up when you get here. Summer nights in all but the highest elevations are mild. But in late fall, even when daytime highs flirt with 90°F, you'll often need a sweater when the sun goes down.

Nevada has a bit of a split personality when it comes to attire. Most restaurants are **casual,** but some—even in the most out-of-the-way places in the state—may require jackets. On the other hand, men often attend southern Nevada church services in shirt sleeves and even shorts. The trendy clubs usually enforce **dress codes,** most disallowing jeans, tank tops, and tennis shoes.

Leaving Las Vegas

Aside from being one of the world's premier destinations, Las Vegas also serves as a handy base camp for exploring southern Nevada's natural and recreational attractions. With flights arriving from around the country and around the world. the city's **McCarran International Airport** makes it an easy gateway to the state. Including a day or two in Vegas at the beginning or end of your trip rounds it out to a full week. For suggestions on how to spend your time in Vegas itself, see page 36.

Day 1
HOOVER DAM AND LAKE MEAD
33 MILES / 45 MINUTES

Head south on I-515 to **Boulder City** (about a 30-minute drive), gateway to Lake Mead and Hoover Dam. You will burn a lot of calories today, so treat yourself to breakfast at the **Southwest Diner.** Park at the Mike O'Callaghan-Pat Tillman Memorial Bridge, downstream from **Hoover**

Dam, and walk across, pausing to read the interpretive signs and take in a fine view of the engineering marvel. Next drive to the **visitors center** and **tour** the bowels of the dam. Check out the visitors center until lunchtime. Restaurant choices in the Lake Mead National Recreation Area are slim, so pick up a few snacks and rent a pontoon boat at **Lake Mead Marina.** Spend the afternoon exploring the lake's coves and enjoying a floating picnic. The marina also sells fishing gear and licenses in case you want to match wits with the lake's legendary striped bass.

Return to the marina before sundown and head back up the hill to Boulder City for some window shopping and an evening stroll through the historical downtown, full of curiosity shops and boutiques housed in 1930s Spanish Colonial Revival buildings. On the way back to Vegas, stop again at the Southwest Diner for a home-style dinner of meatloaf, pot roast, or grilled ham steak, but make it an early night.

Hoover Dam

Day 2
CALIENTE, PANACA, AND PIOCHE
180 MILES / 2.75 HOURS

After exploring some of humanity's greatest creations in Boulder City, today you'll head out on a jaunt through nature's handiwork. Order coffee and muffins to go and head out on US 93 for the roughly 90-minute drive to arrive at **Pahranagat National Wildlife Refuge.** Get there early to catch a glimpse of deer, foxes, cougars, egrets, and tortoises, which are most active in the early morning. Continue north on US 93 for lunch at Caliente's **J&J Fast Food** for fried finger food made from scratch but served in minutes.

Spend the afternoon looking up at the eerie spires and spindles at **Cathedral Gorge State Park,** then drive up to Pioche for dinner at the **Silver Café,** the best of the sparse offerings in this part of the state. Head back to Panaca and settle in with a good book and a restful night's sleep at the **Pine Tree Inn and Bakery.**

Day 3
THE EXTRATERRESTRIAL HIGHWAY
210 MILES / 3.25 HOURS

Dig into the Pine Tree Inn's full breakfast for the fuel you will need for a full day of chasing extraterrestrials. Drive the 65 miles from Panaca to **Hiko** (following US 93 south). Pick up a Martian coffee cup and take a selfie with the 30-foot-tall metallic spaceman standing guard at the **Alien Research Center.** Then head west on the Extraterrestrial Highway (NV 375) to **Rachel** for an Alien Burger lunch at the **Little A'Le'Inn.** Explore the perimeter of **Area 51**—carefully—including the "Use of Deadly Force Authorized" sign. Reach the end of the ET Highway at Warm Springs and head on to **Tonopah** for a spicy, cheesy dinner at **El Marques.**

If you don't mind sharing a room with the ghosts of miners and working girls, book the night's stay at the Comstock-opulent **Mizpah Hotel.** But don't turn in before a **star party** with the Tonopah Astronomical Society under the dark, dark canopy illuminated by thousands of stars.

Day 4
BOOMTOWNS AND GHOST TOWNS
93 MILES / 1.5 HOURS

You won't need a pick or pan for today's lesson in Nevada's mining history. Start the day with the Miner's Breakfast amid Comstock-era decor at the **Stage Shop Café** at Tonopah Station casino. Peer into the shaft of Burro Tunnel and peruse the hoists and works at the **Tonopah Historic Mining Park.** Visit the **Central Nevada Museum** to gain some perspective into mining's place in life in the Old West. The faithful boomtown re-creation outside includes a saloon, blacksmith shop, and stamp mill.

Head 30 minutes south on US 95 to stretch your legs with a wander around **Goldfield.** Its turn-of-the-20th-century hotel, fire station, and courthouse serve as apt selfie backgrounds. Finish with burgers and fries at **Dinky Diner,** then continue another hour south to **Beatty** and onto NV 374 to see the surreal plaster cast sculptures and other modern art at the **Goldwell Open Air Museum.** Head next door to check out the Bottle House, railroad depot, bank building, and other relics at **Rhyolite** ghost town before beating it back to Beatty for a casual alfresco dinner at **KC's Outpost.** Load up on jerky and trail mix at **Death Valley Nut & Candy Co.** for tomorrow's adventure, then hit the hay at the retro-cool **Atomic Inn.**

Day 5
INTO DEATH VALLEY
220 MILES / 4 HOURS

Leave Beatty early for the drive southwest along NV 374 into Death Valley toward Stovepipe Wells Village (roughly 40 minutes), planning to arrive at **Mesquite Flat Sand Dunes** to see the sunrise. Climb a dune to watch the play of light and shadow on the sand and rock formations. Backtrack slightly through the Titus Canyon Narrows and follow the signs to **Scotty's Castle** for a guided tour of the iconic Spanish-style residence. The landmark castle was damaged during flooding in 2015, but the National Park Service offers a limited number of tours to witness its

Hot Springs Hot Spots

LAS VEGAS AND VICINITY

- **Arizona Hot Springs:** Part of Lake Mead National Conservation Area, this series of three graduated pools lies midway through a six-mile loop that's perfect for a day hike or weekend camping getaway (page 110).

- **Gold Strike Hot Springs:** The area around the springs is ripe for cliff-launched cannonballs into the Colorado River and even features a natural slide for a thrilling plunge (page 110).

THE LONELIEST ROAD

- **Carson Hot Springs:** Upscale accommodations and a variety of soaking options draw guests to this resort just west of Carson City Airport. The pool, hot tub, and in-room mini spas are fed from natural 121-degree springs (page 217).

- **Spencer Hot Springs:** The Toquima Mountains silhouette against a huge sky, providing a fitting and tranquil backdrop for a relaxing soak (page 253).

NORTHERN NEVADA

- **Trego Hot Springs:** Hot only in pockets, these "warm springs" are nevertheless soothing for hikers and off-roaders traveling the playa of Black Rock Desert (page 283).

- **Soldier Meadows Hot Springs:** Over the years, this life-giving water has been a destination drawing in Native Americans, Oregon- and California-bound immigrants, cavalry soldiers, and prospectors (page 283).

- **12-Mile Hot Springs:** Temperatures in this three-foot-deep, gravel-bottomed pool near Wells range from a barely bearable 105°F to a tepid 99° opposite the source (page 312).

recovery, planned for completion in 2020. Either way, it's worth a stop.

Head back south on CA 190 (60 miles, 75 minutes) for lunch at the **Ranch at Death Valley,** fuel for the **Golden Canyon/Gower Gulch trail.** Park at the trailhead on Badwater Road, two miles south of the junction with CA 190. The trail encompasses Zabriskie Point and views of Red Cathedral, Manly Beacon, and wave after wave of basalt ridges.

Returning to your car, drive the scenic **Artist's Drive** loop through Artist's Palette. The scenic route, lined with canyon walls stained green, yellow, pink, and white by minerals in the rock, starts three miles south of the Golden Canyon trailhead on Badwater Road. Nine miles and 22 minutes later, the drive returns to Badwater Road, four miles south of the embarkation point. From here, go north on Badwater Road and take CA 190 and NV 373 to **Amargosa Valley** (61 miles, 1 hour). Enjoy a late dinner at the **Nebraska Steakhouse,** a little slot play, and a room for the night.

Return to Las Vegas via US 95 or NV 160 (roughly 120 miles; a two-hour drive).

Lamoille Canyon

Reno to the Rubies

The road trip from the Biggest Little City in the World to the Alps of Nevada is a real slice of Americana. You'll experience the Code of the West as it's lived by cattlemen, shepherds, and farmers. Stretch your muscles and imagination communing with snowy peaks, mountainous trails, trout-filled streams, and verdant valleys. **Reno-Tahoe International Airport** offers an easy gateway to this section of the state.

Day 1
RENO

There's plenty to see and do even before you start your drive across Nevada's northern frontier. It may be much smaller than Las Vegas, but Reno can wine, dine, and entertain with the best of them. Start with a history and culture lesson at the **Wilbur D. May Museum and Arboretum,** which displays the magnate's collections of Western gear, hunting trophies, Africana, and more. More evidence of how the other half lived is on offer at the **W. M. Keck Earth Science and Mineral Engineering Museum,** highlighted by mining millionaire John Mackay's 1,250-piece Tiffany silver service—enough to accommodate a tea party of 24. Lunch on enchiladas and beer at one of **Miguel's** two locations, then hit your favorite casino and spend some quality time with the one-eyed jacks and one-armed bandits. Top off the evening with a stroll along the **Riverwalk,** tasting wines and browsing art galleries along the way.

Day 2
DAY TRIP TO VIRGINIA CITY
26 MILES / 35 MINUTES

A living, breathing tribute to early American ingenuity, hard work, and hedonism, Virginia City places visitors in the roles of hardscrabble miner and silver baron, schoolmistress and soiled dove. Strollers along C Street encounter new insights on boomtown life on every corner. Start at **The Way It Was Museum** to see how the silver went from mine to mill to amalgamation to bullion to mint. A short film puts the town in historical perspective. Before lunch, stop into the **Mark Twain Museum.** Twain's original desk is as characteristically messy as he kept it at the *Territorial Enterprise.* You'll see state-of-the-art 19th-century printing technology: It's all hot type and primitive binding machines.

If you're here in summer, escape the midday heat on a guided tour deep into **Chollar Mine.** Rough timbers and old-time equipment will make you want to grab a pick and try your luck at finding a rich vein. Imagine you've struck it rich and celebrate with barbecue and brews at the **Firehouse Restaurant & Saloon.** Cap off your visit riding the rails of the **Virginia & Truckee Railroad** past mines, over trestle bridges, through tunnels, and back through time. Head back to Reno to bunk down for the night.

Day 3
RENO TO WINNEMUCCA
166 MILES / 2.5 HOURS

Grub up with a skillet breakfast at **Peg's Glorified Ham & Eggs** in Reno, then head northwest on I-80. In less than two hours, you'll be in Lovelock. If you're traveling with your significant other, stop and hang a padlock in **Lovers Lock Plaza** to symbolize your unbreakable love in the Chinese tradition. Throw away the key, of course. Load up on picnic supplies, then continue to **Rye Patch State Recreation Area.** Depending on the weather, go for a swim, watch the shore anglers, or hike into the western hills to search for ammonite fossils, agate, tourmaline, and other specimens.

Enjoy your picnic lunch, then continue another hour to Winnemucca and a perusal of the **Buckaroo Hall of Fame,** a tribute to the stylish wranglers who keep the area's ranches running. You're in for a real treat at the **Martin Hotel,** one of the best authentic Basque restaurants in the country. Order the lamb and enjoy a full complement of side dishes: fries, beans, salad, soup, and more. The clean, quiet, quaint, no-frills rooms at the **Town House Motel** will provide the rest you'll need for tomorrow's leg of the journey.

Day 4
WINNEMUCCA TO ELKO
124 MILES / 1.5 HOURS

Plan for today to be the third Thursday of the month, April-October, and take Newmont Mining's **Phoenix Mine** tour. It starts at 9am, so you'll need to get up early to make the 50-minute drive from Winnemucca.

After the three-hour tour, the 71-mile, 70-minute drive on I-80 to Elko gets you there in time for a late lunch of pot stickers and hot and sour soup at **Chef Cheng's Chinese Restaurant.** Fill the afternoon checking out the **Northeastern Nevada Museum's** eclectic collection—animals, mining, railroads, printing, Native American history, etc.—and the cowboy culture, ethics, and heritage at the **Western Folklife Center.**

For dinner, dig into Basque cuisine at the **Star Hotel,** or go for the south-of-the-border seafood at **Dos Amigos.**

Day 5
LAMOILLE SCENIC BYWAY
45 MILES / 75 MINUTES

Nevada's canyon, valley, and mountain beauty takes center stage today. Just 20 minutes from Elko on NV 227 in the village of Lamoille, start with the **Lamoille Canyon Scenic Byway,** a winding 12-mile interpretive drive along Lamoille Creek. Stop to read the interpretive signs and gape at 11,249-foot Ruby Dome. For a closer look, park at the byway turnaround and pick up the **Ruby Crest National Scenic Trail.** Hike the trail as far as stamina and daylight will allow, past Dollar and Lamoille Lakes and elevation changes from 8,780 to 10,893 feet. It's an 8-mile round-trip to Liberty Lake.

Head back to the village of Lamoille for dinner at the **Pine Lodge Dinner House,** and overnight at the **Hotel Lamoille.**

Day 6
LAMOILLE TO RUBY LAKE AND ELY
160 MILES / 3.25 HOURS

Pick up some road food as you drive through **Spring Creek** and head south on NV 228. On

Best Skiing and Snowboarding

The first dusting of snow in late October sends Nevada residents scurrying for the ski wax and the mountain resorts fielding reservations calls. Most Tahoe slopes open around Thanksgiving, but you can bet the lifts will be running any time an early cold front dumps a foot or so of the white stuff. Ski season lasts until mid-April—or until temperatures rise high enough for all the snow to melt.

Here's a look at Nevada's best powder destinations.

LAKE TAHOE

- **Mt. Rose Ski Tahoe:** The closest ski area to Reno, Mt. Rose is perhaps the best overall resort on the Nevada side, considering cost and variety of runs. With a base elevation of 8,260 feet, it's positively arctic at the top and chilly enough along the runs to keep the snow in optimal shape even when the sun beats down. Families will find something for everyone, with 43 runs evenly divided among beginner, intermediate, and expert. The 16 chutes—all black diamond or double diamond—are favorites for advanced snowboarders (page 157).

- **Diamond Peak:** This resort is family-oriented, with special touches for children, such as private and group lessons, indoor and outdoor play areas, and all-day ski and day-care packages (page 157).

- **Northstar California:** With lots of tree-lined runs sheltered somewhat from the wind, Northstar boasts perfectly groomed corduroy conditions. One of the most upscale of resorts, it's nevertheless a fine choice for families. The slopes are not particularly steep or challenging, and there are plenty of beginner and intermediate trails and terrain (page 157).

- **Squaw Valley Alpine Meadows:** This resort spans six summits with more than 270 trails and 43 lifts. Two-thirds of the runs are rated for beginners and intermediates, but as befitting the former host of Olympic alpine events, it challenges experts as well. Open bowls abound above the tree line, but the resort makes a name for itself with gnarly steeps and innovative terrain parks (page 158).

- **Heavenly:** Downhill junkies rejoice, as more than one-third of Heavenly's trails are rated for experts, and the more than 40 intermediate runs will challenge even the most proficient of alpine aficionados. The undulating, swaying blue runs are long and wide, perfect for snowboarders (page 166).

- **Kirkwood:** It's all about the powder at Kirkwood; the shopping is mundane compared to other ski villages, and you can't see the lake from here. But you can see challenging runs, ridges, and cornices hotdoggers love. More than two-thirds of the trails are rated advanced and expert (page 167).

RUBY MOUNTAINS

- **Ruby Mountain Heli-Skiing:** Virtually inaccessible other than by helicopter, the Ruby Mountain backcountry slopes guarantee pristine snow and awe-inspiring precipices. Choose your own terrain: steep drops, narrow tree-lined corridors, glades, open bowls, and more (page 306).

LAS VEGAS AND VICINITY

- **Lee Canyon:** A welcome respite from the heat and bad beats, Lee Canyon is just an hour north of Las Vegas. Pending an environmental impact study, the resort will begin expanding in 2019, adding three lifts and dozens of runs—many in Mount Charleston's upper elevations—that will double the amount of skiable terrain. The $35 million addition also would see installation of mountain bike trails, zip lines, and a "mountain coaster" thrill ride (page 75).

Great Basin National Park

your way out of the canyon, drive the auto tour at **Ruby Lake National Wildlife Refuge,** which encompasses a network of dikes that provide fine in-vehicle viewing of waterfowl and other wildlife. Spend some time roaming the station, engine yard, and maintenance shop, as well.

It's a rough 65 miles on White Pine County Road 3 to US 50, and another 30 luxurious-by-comparison miles to Ely. Head over the **Nevada Northern Railway** for a 90-minute steam excursion through tunnels, up steep grades, and into mining territory. In keeping with the railroad theme, walk the two blocks to **All Aboard Cafe & Inn** for a salad bar or lobster roll lunch. Book a night's stay while you're at it. The inn is a B&B, so you've got tomorrow's breakfast covered.

Day 7
GREAT BASIN NATIONAL PARK
67 MILES / 70 MINUTES
Spend the day at Great Basin National Park, an hour east of Ely, off the Baker exit. If you have not purchased tickets for the **Lehman Caves tour,** drive past the park visitors center to the caves visitors center to make reservations. Walk the one-third mile to the 100-year-old apricot trees. They ripen in mid-August; pluck one and enjoy! Before or after your cave tour, backtrack to the park visitors center and spend a quality hour with the orientation exhibits and videos there.

Drive the **Wheeler Peak Scenic Drive** along Lehman Creek, closer and closer to the looming peak. Park at the trailhead and prepare for the 3,000 feet you'll gain in elevation to the top of 13,063-foot Wheeler Peak via **Summit Trail.** Bunk at the **Stargazer Inn** in Baker and dine at **Kerouac's** on-site.

From Baker, you can pick up US 93 south to Las Vegas or head back to Reno via US 50, following the route of the Loneliest Road Trip (see page 28) in reverse order.

The Loneliest Road Trip

The stark landscape along US 50 is the origin of its famed solitude, but it has given rise to some of the best recreational activities Nevada has to offer. From hot springs to mountain-biking trails to sand drifts just begging for a dune buggy ride, the Loneliest Road in America is the perfect route for outdoor enthusiasts.

Day 1
CARSON CITY AND LAHONTAN STATE RECREATION AREA
91 MILES / 2 HOURS

If you're based in Reno, slide down to **Carson City** on I-580 and share the antipasti plate and crab and tomato salad at **Café at Adele's,** a candidate for best restaurant in the state. Although it's not the typical tourist attraction, tours of the old **Nevada State Prison** encompass the world's first gas chamber and the most brutal solitary-confinement cell in the country. After a visit, you'll want to shake the feeling of confinement

with an exhilarating flight over lake, ridges, or treetops in **Hang Gliding Tahoe**'s motorized ultralight aircraft.

Recover from the rush by communing with wild horses, foxes, herons, and Nevada's only nesting bald eagles at **Lahontan State Recreation Area,** a little over halfway on the 90-mile drive to **Fallon.** For dinner, order soup and egg rolls at **Vn Pho** in Fallon.

Day 2
HIDDEN CAVE AND SAND MOUNTAIN
125 MILES / 2 HOURS

Start your day in Fallon at the **Churchill County Museum,** checking out the re-creations of frontier dwellings and a Native American tule shelter. At the museum, get directions to **Hidden Cave,** where generations of local indigenous people stored tools, weapons, and food. Hike a mile from the caves to **Grimes Point,** containing fine examples of Native American petroglyphs.

Continue east on US 50 to spend the rest of

Sand Mountain

Ghost Towns

Following the lure of a big strike, miners, gamblers, and entrepreneurs have been betting big on Nevada for 175 years. More than 100 ghost towns testify to the Silver State's boom-and-bust cycles. A few of these towns were mere flashes in the pan, burning brightly for only a few years before the silver played out. Others prospered for decades before finally petering out.

- **Rhyolite:** One of only a few "ghost cities," Rhyolite, near Beatty and Death Valley, at one time boasted a population of more than 10,000. In addition to the famous Bottle House, with 10,000 barroom empties encrusting the walls, the ruins of several other buildings fitting such a metropolis still stand, including the three-story concrete bank, the jail, and the train depot (page 192).

- **Gold Point:** You can spend the night in a restored miner's cabin while immersing yourself in an authentic Wild West atmosphere. Gold Point features a 1909 pool table, a well-appointed saloon, historical lectures from "Sheriff Stone," museum artifacts, and about 40 lovingly restored buildings (page 193).

- **Belmont and Manhattan:** Though it meted out its last justice in 1905, Belmont's imposing courthouse still holds an air of judicial authority. Shortly after Belmont's mines played out, the focus of mining operations shifted to Manhattan, 50 miles north, where photo-worthy structures include the Sacred Heart Mission. The Manhattan Bar & Motel has been updated since pioneer days but still stands ready with cold beer and comfortable beds (page 201).

- **Berlin:** This classic boomtown was founded in 1897, reached its peak in 1905, and was abandoned by 1914. It's the best-preserved mining town in Nevada, and Berlin's structures—the shell of its 30-stamp mill, the machine shop, a stagecoach station, etc.—beg to have their pictures taken (page 252).

- **Unionville:** Unsuccessful miner Mark Twain left town before Unionville boomed from 1865 to 1880, but the remnants of his vandalized cabin are still here. Some 1,500 people settled here during the town's heyday, leaving behind a well-preserved classic one-room schoolhouse (central pot-bellied stove and student desks intact), a few cabins, and other structures (page 290).

- **Jarbidge:** In the state's remote northeast corner is the site of one of America's last gold rushes (1929) and last stagecoach robbery (1916). The robber murdered the stage driver, and the villain's jail cell still stands in Jarbidge, only 10 miles from the Idaho line. Miners' cabins still line Main Street, and former brothels are tucked away off side streets. The community center is housed in one of the town's original structures (page 305).

---

the day at **Sand Mountain.** Wax up your sandboard and hurtle down 500-foot inclines, dodging OHVs along the way. If the ATVs and motorcycles don't drown them out, listen for the whistling moans of the "singing sand" as the wind blows through the grains.

Stop at **Cold Springs Station** for comfort food and a Pony Express history lesson, then cruise the final 50 miles to bunk down at **Union Street Lodging** in **Austin.**

Day 3
MOUNTAIN BIKING
136 MILES / 3.5 HOURS

After loading up on coffee and carbs at Union Street's complimentary breakfast, break out the mountain bikes and pedal some of the varied trails scattered throughout the Toiyabe Range. **Castle Loop,** a 4.5-mile ride, is a moderate place to start. (More seasoned cyclists may want to take the time to test their mettle on the steep climbs of the 27.5-mile **Gold Venture Loop.**)

Morning exercise out of the way, take the scenic drive south along NV 21, flanked by the Toiyabe and Shoshone Ranges. It takes nearly two

Small-Town Charm

With just four metropolitan areas with populations over 200,000, Nevada is virtually all small towns. For visitors, that means neighborly hospitality, home-style cooking, fenceless wilderness, and live-and-let-live sensibilities. So kick your shoes off at the state line and take a load off your mind in small-town Nevada.

- **Pioche** offers a community park as unassuming as the town's residents. It includes a target-shooting range, a motorcycle course, a lassoing field, and a nine-hole golf course built and maintained by volunteers (page 183).

- **Hawthorne** has been supporting our troops since long before yellow-ribbon bumper stickers, with a patriotism rooted in the townsfolk's appreciation of their sacrifices (page 202).

- **Ely** is a microcosm of Nevada history, from ancient Native American populations to the Pony Express and the mining and railroad days. It's a great base for exploring Great Basin National Park (page 257).

- **Winnemucca** was there at the birth of Nevada's hospitality industry in the 1850s, when entrepreneurs established trading posts, ferries, and other businesses to cater to travelers along the Humboldt Trail. Today visitors still come here in search of fiery opals, messes of crappie, and peace of mind (page 290).

- **Elko** invites visitors to enjoy the view at the end of a hike in the Ruby Mountains, a lunker pulled from a Lamoille Canyon stream, or a well-turned phrase at the National Cowboy Poetry Gathering (page 298).

hours to cover the 50 miles to Ione Pass through the southern Shoshones, but your destination, **Berlin-Ichthyosaur State Park,** is at the end of the pass. Spend a few hours strolling among the well-preserved mining town relics and check out the ichthyosaur fossil beds and interpretive displays that describe the life and times of the ancient marine lizard that once plied the seas covering Nevada.

Take the easier route back through Austin via NV 844, NV 361, and US 50. Your bike-addled bones and muscles will thank you for continuing the 20 miles southeast to **Spencer Hot Springs,** one of the most visitor-friendly hot springs in Nevada.

From Austin, you can retrace your route back to Reno or continue eastward to **Great Basin National Park.** Better yet, jump on NV 305 north for 95 miles (1 hour 25 minutes) and take I-80 back to Reno through **Winnemucca** and **Lovelock.**

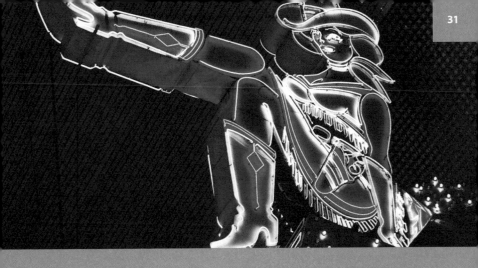

Las Vegas

Highlights

★ **Caesars Palace:** Caesars Palace carries on the Roman Empire's regality and decadence with over-the-top excess (page 42).

★ **Gondola Rides:** Just like the real Grand Canal, only cleaner, The Venetian's waterway meanders along the Strip, with gondoliers providing the soundtrack (page 53).

★ **Secret Garden and Dolphin Habitat:** At The Mirage's twin habitats, the tigers, lions, and leopards can be seen playing impromptu games, and the bottlenose dolphins never resist the spotlight (page 54).

★ **High Roller:** The world's largest observation wheel overwhelms the senses with driving music, videos, and unmatched views of the Strip (page 55).

★ **Fremont Street Experience:** Part music video, part history lesson, the six-minute shows are a four-block-long, 12-million-diode, 550,000-watt burst of sensory overload (page 57).

★ **Mob Museum:** Explore what some old-timers still refer to as "the good old days," when wiseguys ran the town, meting out their own brand of justice (page 59).

★ **Las Vegas Springs Preserve:** The city's birthplace, these natural springs now display the area's geological, anthropological, and cultural history along with what may be its future: water-conserving "green" initiatives (page 60).

★ **Atomic Testing Museum:** Visit a fallout

shelter and measure your body's radioactivity at this museum, which traces the military, political, and cultural significance of the atomic bomb (page 61).

★ **Love:** Cirque du Soleil's magical mystery tour features artistry, acrobatics, and Beatles music in a surreal examination of the Fab Four's legacy (page 64).

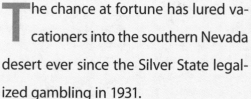

The chance at fortune has lured vacationers into the southern Nevada desert ever since the Silver State legalized gambling in 1931.

At first, the "sawdust joints"—named for the stuff spread on the floor to sop up spilled beer (and perhaps a few tears)—that popped up along downtown's Fremont Street were the center of the action, but they soon faced competition from a resort corridor blooming to the south on NV 91. The burgeoning entertainment district reminded Los Angeles nightclub owner Billy Wilkerson of Sunset Boulevard in Hollywood, so he dubbed it "The Strip," and together with Bugsy Siegel built the Flamingo, the first upscale alternative to frontier gambling halls. Their vision left a legacy that came to define Las Vegas hotel-casinos. Las Vegas has gone through many reinventions in the decades since—from city of sleaze to Mafia haven, family destination, and upscale resort town. Today, Las Vegas is known for its fine restaurants, music festivals, and people-watching as much as for its slot machines and craps tables.

So pack your stilettos, string bikini, money clip, and favorite hangover remedy, and join the 35 million others who trek to Sin City every year to experience as many of the Seven Deadlies as they can cram into their vacation time. No one back home has to know you've succumbed to the city's siren song.

PLANNING YOUR TIME

If you only have a few days to spend, head straight to the **Strip**—a moderately priced resort is a fine option, as long as it makes up in location what it may lack in amenities. Soak up the Vegas vibe with intense gambling sessions, lavish shows, and bass-heavy dance clubs by night, followed by rejuvenating spa treatments and poolside lounging by day.

If you have more than a couple of days, mix in a little exercise: biking through **Red Rock Canyon,** hiking a tree-line trail at **Mount Charleston,** or paddling through **Black Canyon** on the Colorado River. Better yet, rent a houseboat at **Lake Mead** and see the basin's sheer walls and colorful mineral-stained boulders in style. The lake's deep, wide bays and inlets offer boaters access to slot canyons, backcountry camping sites, and secret

Previous: classic example of Las Vegas neon; Bellagio Conservatory. **Above:** statue at Hoover Dam.

Las Vegas

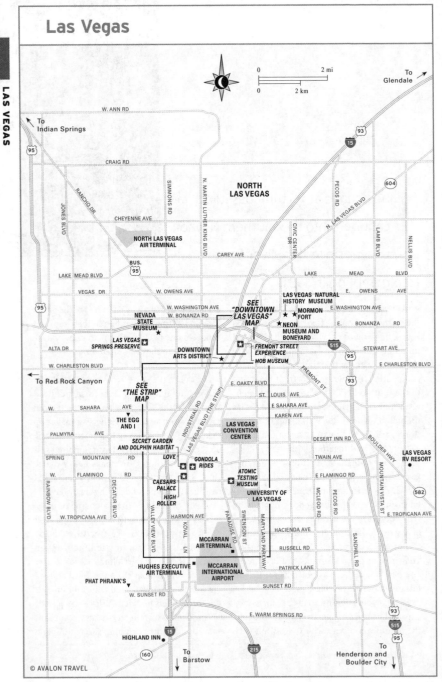

© AVALON TRAVEL

fishing holes. Marinas within the Lake Mead National Recreation Area and the stores in Boulder City and Overton have all the supplies you'll need.

If you've chosen the Overton Arm of Lake Mead, don't miss the **Lost City Museum**, where you'll learn about the Ancestral Puebloan people, the valley's first residents. The Boulder Basin is a more common option, where of course you'll visit **Hoover Dam**. The best view is from the recently completed bypass bridge, just downstream. Park at the bridge and stroll across (there's a protected pedestrian walkway), learning about the arch bridge's fascinating construction process and taking full advantage of its dam photo ops. A tour of the dam and exploration of the visitors center make for an afternoon well spent.

Always a major-league entertainment destination, Sin City is now an official major-league sports town, with the Vegas Golden Knights joining the NHL in 2018 and the Oakland Raiders relocating here for the 2020 (or possibly 2019) season. Out-of-town visitors can schedule their vacations to include their favorite teams' road games.

ORIENTATION

Las Vegas Boulevard South—better known as the **Strip**—is the city's focal point, with 14 of the 25 largest hotels in the world welcoming gamblers and hedonists from around the world. Six of the world's 10 biggest hostelries line a four-mile north-south stretch between Tropicana and Sahara Avenues. Running parallel to I-15, this is what most folks think of when someone says "Vegas."

Major east-west thoroughfares include Tropicana Avenue, Harmon Avenue, Flamingo Road, Spring Mountain Road, Desert Inn Road, and Sahara Avenue. Koval Lane and Paradise Road parallel the Strip to the east, while Frank Sinatra Drive does likewise to the west, giving a tour of the loading docks and employee parking lots of some of the world's most famous resorts.

I-15 also mirrors the Strip to the east, as both continue north-northeast through **downtown** and its casino and arts districts. Main Street juts due south at Charleston Boulevard and joins Las Vegas Boulevard at the Stratosphere. The Strip and I-15 continue parallel southeast and south out of town.

Casinos

UPPER STRIP

Ranging from Spring Mountain Road to the Stratosphere, the **Upper Strip** is known for its throwback swagger, but has something for everyone. Visitors can opt for world-class art, celebrity chef creations, midway games, stand-up comedy—and friendly rates at old standby casinos.

Stratosphere Casino, Hotel, and Tower

Restaurants: Top of the World, McCalls, Nunzio's Pizzeria, Fellini's, Stratosphere Buffet, Roxy's Diner, Mookies, Tower Creamery, Starbucks, McDonald's, El Nopal Mexican Grill, Wok Vegas, Chicago Hot Dog Construction Co.
Entertainment: MJ Live, Spy Escape & Evasion, World's Greatest Rock Show, L.A. Comedy Club
Attractions: SkyJump, Top of the Tower thrill rides, Elation Pool, Radius Pool, Observation Deck, Roni Josef Spa, Tower Shops, Fitness Center
Nightlife: Margarita Bay, Sin City Hops, Air Bar, CBar, 107 Sky Lounge

It's altitude with attitude at this 1,149-foot-tall exclamation point on the north end of the Strip. The **Stratosphere Tower** (2000 Las Vegas Blvd. S., 702/380-7777, www.stratospherehotel.com, $103-146) is the brainchild of entrepreneur, politician, and professional poker player Bob Stupak. Daredevils will delight in the 40-mph quasi-freefall at SkyJump, along with the other vertigo-inducing thrill rides on the tower's observation deck. The more faint-of-heart may want to steer clear

Two Days in Las Vegas

DAY 1

Pick a hotel based on your taste and budget. We suggest **The Linq** (page 43), close to the High Roller observation wheel, fine dining, hip watering holes, and rocking live music venues.

Get your gambling fix for a few hours before heading across the street for brunch at The Mirage's **Cravings Buffet** (page 41). It operates on a familiar theory, with separate stations highlighting different cuisines. After the gorge-fest, you'll be ready for a nap, and you'll need it. This is Vegas; no early nights for you!

Couples should start the evening off with a romantic dinner at Paris's **Mon Ami Gabi** (page 82). For a more modest meal, the eponymous offering at The Venetian's **B&B Burger & Beer** (page 39) hits the spot. If you only have time for one show, make it **Love** (page 64) at The Mirage. The show is a loose biography of the Beatles' creative journey, told by tumblers, roller skaters, clowns, and the characters from John, Paul, George, and Ringo's songs—Eleanor Rigby, Lucy in the Sky, and Sgt. Pepper.

DAY 2

Celebrate the kitsch and class of vintage Vegas. Head downtown to stock up on Elvis sideburns and Sammy Davis Jr. sunglasses before loading up on eggs Benedict and 1970s flair at the **Peppermill Restaurant & Fireside Lounge** (page 79). While it's daylight, make your way to the **Neon Museum and Boneyard** (page 58), the final resting place of some of Las Vegas's iconic signage. And while you're in the neighborhood, witness the rise and fall of the Mafia in Las Vegas at the **Mob Museum** (page 59).

Back at the hotel, change into your glad rags and beat it over to the Tuscany's Copa Room. Order up a neat bourbon and watch Sinatra try to make it through a rendition of "Luck Be a Lady" while Dino and Sammy heckle and cut up from the wings in **The Rat Pack Is Back** (page 66). Then get out there and gamble into the wee hours! For a chance to rub elbows with celebrities, head over to **XS** (page 39) at the Wynn. Expect celebrity DJs, a major party, and steep prices.

not only of the rides but also the resort's double-decker elevators, which launch guests to the top of the tower at 1,400 feet per minute. But even acrophobes should conquer their fears long enough to enjoy the views from the restaurant and bars more than 100 floors up, where the **Chapel in the Clouds** can also ensure a heavenly beginning to married life.

If the thrill rides on the observation deck aren't your style, get a rush of gambling action on the nearly 100,000-square-foot ground-floor casino. Or perhaps the two swimming pools (one is tops-optional) and the dozen bars and restaurants are more your speed.

Spot-on impersonators and elaborate choreography make the Stratosphere's two tribute shows among the best in town. Each night, one of two Michael Jackson impersonators takes the stage at *MJ Live* (7pm daily, $61-90), backed by a full cast of dancers, a live band,

and a dazzling array of lighting effects in the Stratosphere Theater. Similarly, the *World's Greatest Rock Show* (Tues.-Sun., $35-45) captures classic artists' sounds and mannerisms, with doppelgangers of Van Halen, Journey, Bruce Springsteen, Kiss, and other arena rock gods.

Roxy's Diner (24 hours daily, $10-15) is a trip back to the malt shop for comfort food, red vinyl booths, checkered floors, and wise-cracking waitstaff.

Lucky Dragon

Restaurants: Pearl Ocean, Phoenix, Cha Garden, Dragon's Alley, Bao Now
Attractions: Sothys Spa
Nightlife: Pagoda Bar, Atrium Bar

Swathed in red for good fortune and surrounding a pagoda-shaped bar, the 27,000-square-foot casino floor at the **Lucky**

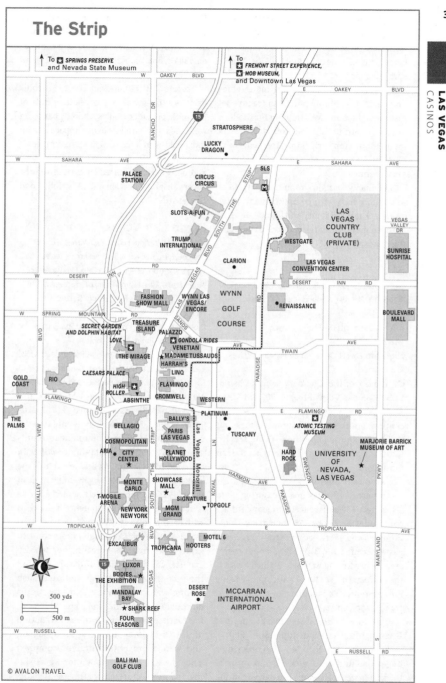

The Strip

To ⭐ SPRINGS PRESERVE and Nevada State Museum

To ⭐ FREMONT STREET EXPERIENCE, ⭐ MOB MUSEUM, and Downtown Las Vegas

W OAKEY BLVD
E OAKEY BLVD

RANCHO DR

15

STRATOSPHERE
LUCKY DRAGON

W SAHARA AVE
THE STRIP
SLS
E SAHARA AVE
M

VEGAS VALLEY DR

PALACE STATION

CIRCUS CIRCUS

LAS VEGAS COUNTRY CLUB (PRIVATE)

SUNRISE HOSPITAL

SLOTS-A-FUN

WESTGATE

TRUMP INTERNATIONAL

LAS VEGAS CONVENTION CENTER

LAS VEGAS BLVD SOUTH

CLARION

W DESERT INN RD
E DESERT INN RD

BOULEVARD MALL

FASHION SHOW MALL

WYNN LAS VEGAS/ENCORE

WYNN GOLF COURSE

RENAISSANCE

W SPRING MOUNTAIN RD

SECRET GARDEN AND DOLPHIN HABITAT

TREASURE ISLAND

SANDS

PALAZZO

TWAIN AVE

LOVE

⭐ GONDOLA RIDES
VENETIAN

THE MIRAGE

⭐ MADAME TUSSAUDS
HARRAH'S

PARADISE RD

GOLD COAST

RIO

CAESARS PALACE

LINQ

HIGH ROLLER

FLAMINGO

ABSINTHE

CROMWELL

WESTERN

THE PALMS

W FLAMINGO RD

BELLAGIO

BALLY'S

PLATINUM

E FLAMINGO RD

ATOMIC TESTING MUSEUM

COSMOPOLITAN

PARIS LAS VEGAS

TUSCANY

MARJORIE BARRICK MUSEUM OF ART

ARIA

CITY CENTER

PLANET HOLLYWOOD

Las Vegas Monorail

HARD ROCK

UNIVERSITY OF NEVADA, LAS VEGAS

VALLEY VIEW

MONTE CARLO

SHOWCASE MALL

HARMON AVE

SWENSON ST

T-MOBILE ARENA

SIGNATURE

KOVAL LN

NEW YORK NEW YORK

MGM GRAND

TOPGOLF

W TROPICANA AVE
E TROPICANA AVE

MARYLAND

EXCALIBUR

TROPICANA
MOTEL 6
HOOTERS

15

LUXOR

BODIES... THE EXHIBITION

DESERT ROSE

PARADISE RD

0   500 yds

MANDALAY BAY

McCARRAN INTERNATIONAL AIRPORT

0   500 m

⭐ SHARK REEF

FOUR SEASONS

W RUSSELL RD
E RUSSELL RD

BALI HAI GOLF CLUB

© AVALON TRAVEL

Dragon (300 W. Sahara Ave., 702/889-2018, www.luckydragonlv.com, $108-228) spreads Eastern-style games such as pai gow and baccarat, with only the occasional blackjack table sprinkled in.

Strip views and dainty, intimate tables and chairs resembling porcelain teacups set just the right mood for sampling the modern and adventurous Chinese fare at **Phoenix** (5pm-10pm Mon.-Fri., 5pm-11pm Sat.-Sun., $28-40). Dare you order the deer tendon or sea cucumber?

The Lucky Dragon's rooms are largish at 415 square feet, with complimentary water and tea. The decor is airy and light; the cherry blossom murals over the bed add to the relaxing atmosphere.

SLS

Restaurants: Katsuya, Bazaar Meat, Cleo, Umami Burger, 800 Degrees, Northside Café & Chinese Kitchen, The Perq
Entertainment: The Foundry, Sayers Club
Attractions: Foxtail Pool
Nightlife: Foxtail, Center Bar, Monkey Bar, W Living Room

On the site of the legendary Sahara Casino, **SLS** (2535 Las Vegas Blvd. S., 702/761-7000, www.slslasvegas.com, $139-249) draws 21st-century Frank and Sammy wannabes and the rest of the swanky sophisticate set. It's Rat Pack cool, filtered through modern hipsterism.

Two towers offer standard rooms of 325-360 square feet, with suites measuring up to a spacious 730 square feet. All standard accommodations boast 55-inch televisions, minibars and snacks at no extra charge, soft pastel accents, and 310-thread-count sheets atop BeautyRest mattresses. A third tower is the independent **W Hotel,** where guests in the European-accented rooms enjoy their own entrance, pool, and spa.

Chef Jose Andres doesn't want guests at **Bazaar Meat** (5:30pm-10pm Sun.-Thurs., 5:30pm-11pm Fri.-Sat., $65-140) ordering a huge bone-in rib eye, rack of lamb, or inch-thick tuna steak. He wants you to try them all.

His Spanish-influenced meat-centric dishes are meant to be shared. The restaurant's decor reinforces that aim with long communal tables, open cooking stations, and a small gaming area.

Sayers Club (10pm-2am Thurs.-Sat.) bills itself as a live-music venue. There's plenty of live indie pop, folk, and psychobilly bands on weekends, but with lots of open space and an industrial-warehouse feel, it's a natural environment for DJs. The go-go cages, platforms, and poles seem imported en masse from the Sayers' original location on L.A.'s Hollywood Boulevard.

Wynn Las Vegas/Encore

Restaurants: Andrea's, Costa Di Mare, Lakeside Seafood, Mizumi, Sinatra, SW Steakhouse, Tableau, Wing Lei, The Buffet, Allegro, La Cave, Drugstore Café, Jardin, Red 8 Asian Bistro, Wazuzu, Terrace Point Cafe
Entertainment: Le Rêve, Encore Theater
Attractions: Lake of Dreams, Wynn Golf Course, Esplanade shopping, Wynn Salon and Spa, Encore Salon and Spa, fitness center, pools
Nightlife: XS, Surrender, Intrigue, Encore Beach Club, Eastside Lounge, Lobby Bar, Players Bar, Parasol Up, Parasol Down, Tower Suite Bar, Encore Players Lounge

Named after casino mogul Steve Wynn, ★ **Wynn** (3131 Las Vegas Blvd. S., 702/770-7000 or 888/320-9966, www.wynnlasvegas.com, $200-450) is a monument to indulgence, a $2.5 billion invitation to wallow in the good life. Gaze at Wynn's art, one of the best and most valuable private collections in the world. The appropriately named **Encore** is next door. The twins' opulence is matched with casino areas awash in red—carpet, tapestries, and neon. Although guests come to explore the privileges of wealth, they can also experience the wonders of nature without the inconvenience of bugs and dirt. Lush plants, waterfalls, lakes, and mountains dominate the pristine landscape. Plans call for further growth with the construction of **Paradise Park,** a 20-acre sandy lagoon and waterfront entertainment complex. The lake will be big enough for water-skiing and nonmotorized boating, while bars,

That Fabulous Sign

When someone says "Las Vegas," what image pops into your mind? Watch any movie or television show set in Las Vegas, and you're sure to see it; drive past it at any time of day or night and somebody—road-tripping buddies or a bachelorette party—will be having their picture taken in front of it.

"It" is The Sign, a beacon that has guided thrill seekers to the Strip since 1959. Its message is simple: "Welcome to Fabulous Las Vegas Nevada." But Betty Willis's creation at 5100 Las Vegas Boulevard South—the design, imagery, colors, and vocabulary—epitomizes a trip to the most exciting city in the world. Silver dollars, harkening back to a time when slot players actually plunked coins into the machines and paying homage to the precious metal that put Nevada on the map, back the letters in "Welcome." The message's only adjective, "Fabulous," is a distinctly Vegas word. L.A. may be hip; New York is cosmopolitan; Miami is trendy; but Vegas is "fabulous"—spoken with jazz hands and Liberace enunciation. Bold primary colors and neon flash hint at the visual explosion lying just behind the sign. "Las Vegas" is bold and unapologetic, like the city itself. The sign's diamond shape is a subtle reminder that riches can be yours if Lady Luck smiles. The red-and-gold star promises fun at all hours in the city that never sleeps.

The 25-foot-tall sign even performs double duty; the back reminds motorists to "Drive Carefully; Come Back Soon."

Willis, whose parents were among the first settlers in Las Vegas, considered the sign's design her gift to the city; as a result, she never copyrighted it, and it's in the public domain. You'll see the sign appropriated for souvenirs and event announcements—especially when out-of-towners hold conventions, trade shows, and other happenings in Las Vegas.

boutiques, ice cream stands, and nightly fireworks will tempt beachcombers.

In addition to the gourmet offerings, don't miss the dim sum and Hong Kong barbecue at **Red 8 Asian Bistro** (11:30am-midnight Sun.-Thurs., 11:30am-1am Fri.-Sat., $20-40). Then party to excess at **XS** ($20-50) where Skrillex, David Guetta, or some other world-class DJ is likely to be spinning this weekend.

The formal sophistication belies the hotels' location on the site of the old Desert Inn, with the unselfconscious swagger Frank, Dino, and Sammy brought to the joint. Both towers boast some of the biggest guest rooms and suites on the Strip, with the usual (although better-quality) amenities, including 55-inch TVs, and a few extra touches, like remote-controlled drapes, lights, and air-conditioning.

Wynn's guest rooms are appointed in wheat, honey, and other creatively named shades of beige. Encore's all-suite accommodations are more colorful, with the color scheme running toward dark chocolate and cream.

CENTER STRIP

The **Center Strip** is between Harmon Avenue and Spring Mountain Road. The casinos are packed tight, and though the sidewalks can become masses of humanity on weekend nights, all the temptations are within walking distance.

The Venetian

Restaurants: AquaKnox, B&B Burger & Beer, B&B Ristorante, Bouchon, Bouchon Bakery, Café Presse, Chica, Delmonico Steakhouse, Grand Lux Café, Juice

Farm, Noodle Asia, Public House, Sugarcane, Yardbird, Zio Gelato, Buddy V's Ristorante, Canaletto, Canonita, Carlo's Bakery, Casanova, Cocolini, Lobster ME, Mercato Della Perscheria, Otto Enoteca Pizzeria, Tao Asian Bistro, Coffee Bean and Tea Leaf, Trattoria Reggiano, Food Court

Entertainment: *Human Nature Juke Box*

Attractions: Madame Tussauds Las Vegas, gondola rides, Streetmosphere, Grand Canal Shoppes

Nightlife: Tao Nightclub, Bellini Bar, The Dorsey, Sin City Brewing Co., Rockhouse, Fat Tuesday, Rosina

The Venetian (3355 Las Vegas Blvd. S., 702/414-1000 or 866/659-9643, www. venetian.com, $209-349) comes close to capturing the elegance of Venice. An elaborate faux-Renaissance ceiling fresco greets visitors in the hotel lobby, and the sensual treats just keep coming. A life-size streetscape—with replicas of the Bridge of Sighs, Doge's Palace, the Grand Canal, and other treasures—gives the impression that the best of the Queen of the Adriatic has been transplanted in toto. Tranquil rides in authentic **gondolas** with serenading pilots are perfect for relaxing after a hectic session in the 120,000-square-foot casino. Canal-side, buskers entertain the guests in the **Streetmosphere** (St. Mark's Square, noon-6pm daily on the hour, free), and the **Grand Canal Shoppes** (10am-11pm Sun.-Thurs., 10am-midnight Fri.-Sat.) entice strollers, window-shoppers, and serious spenders.

World-class DJs, A-list celebrities, and wall-to-wall hardbodies pack **Tao Nightclub** (10:30pm-5am Thurs.-Sat.) at the end of each week to groove to thumping house and hip-hop. Reservations and advance tickets are recommended, as this is one of the hottest party spots in town, with a powerful light and sound system, two dance rooms, and open architecture. Scattered throughout, bathing beauties luxuriate, covered (more or less) only by rose petals.

After you've shopped till you're ready to drop, **Madame Tussauds Las Vegas** (10am-8pm Sun.-Thurs., 10am-9pm Fri.-Sat., adults $30, ages 4-12 $20, under age 4 free) invites stargazers for hands-on experiences with their favorite entertainers, superheroes, and athletes.

Fine dining options abound. Try the lobster ravioli or traditional pizza and pasta dishes in the bistro setting of **Trattoria Reggiano** (10am-midnight daily, $20-30). Or step away from the Italian theme and go French at Thomas Keller's **Bouchon** (702/414-6200, 7am-1pm and 5pm-10pm Mon.-Thurs., 7am-2pm and 5pm-10pm Sat.-Sun., $30-65). Try the sensational croque madame sandwich with its rich Mornay sauce, or climb a tower of French fries to recover from a night in Sin City. The luxe setting features high ceilings, wood columns, and tile floors.

The Venetian spares no expense in the hotel department. Its 4,027 suites are tastefully appointed with plum accents and Italian (of course) marble, and at 650 square feet, they're big. They include sunken living rooms and Roman tubs.

The Palazzo

Restaurants: Carnevino, Coffee Bean and Tea Leaf, Cut, Grand Lux Café, Hong Kong Café, Illy Coffee, Juice Farm, Lagasse's Stadium, Lavo, Morels Steakhouse & Bistro, Café Presse, Grimaldi's Pizzeria, Sushisamba

Entertainment: *Baz—Star Crossed Love*

Attractions: Grand Canal Shoppes, Atrium Waterfall

Nightlife: Fusion Latin Mixology Bar, Lavo Lounge, Double Helix Wine and Whiskey Bar

An 80-foot domed skylight illuminates a faux-ice sculpture, bronze columns, and lush landscaping surrounding the lobby at **The Palazzo** (3325 Las Vegas Blvd. S., 702/607-7777 or 866/263-3001, www.palazzo.com, $239-349). Motel 6 this ain't. A big chunk of the 100,000-square-foot casino is smoke-free, embodying the casino's efforts toward energy efficiency and environmentally friendly design.

The Palazzo is a gourmand's dream, with a handful of four-star establishments dominated, as you would expect, by Italian influences. **Carnevino** (5pm-11pm daily, $40-75) is light and bright, with snootiness kept to a minimum, especially during the Taverna lunch (noon-midnight daily, $20-40). That does not mean the chefs skimp on quality. They select the best cuts and refrain from overwhelming them in preparation. Wine shares top billing in the restaurant's name, so you know the cellar is excellent.

Accommodations are all suites, measuring even larger than The Venetian's, with Roman tubs, sunken living rooms, and sumptuous beds that would make it tough to leave the room if not for the lure of the Strip.

The Mirage

Restaurants: Tom Colicchio's Heritage Steak, Fin, Otoro, Portofino, Cravings Buffet, Carnegie Delicatessen, Paradise Café, Samba, Pantry, LVB Burger, Stack, Paradise Café, California Pizza Kitchen, Blizz Frozen Yogurt, The Roasted Bean
Entertainment: *Love,* Terry Fator, Boys II Men, Aces of Comedy
Attractions: Secret Garden and Dolphin Habitat, Aquarium, Mirage Volcano, Atrium
Nightlife: 1 Oak, Rhumbar, The Still, The Sports Bar, Lobby Bar, Parlor Cocktail Lounge, Heritage Steak Lounge, Stack Lounge, Otoro Lounge, Portofino Lounge

The Mirage (3400 Las Vegas Blvd. S., 702/791-7111 or 800/627-6667, www.mirage. com, $140-300) was the first "understated" megaresort, starting a trend that brought Vegas full circle to the mature pursuits it was built on—gourmet dining, lavish production shows, hip music, and hard liquor. This Bali Hai-themed paradise lets guests bask in the wonders of nature alongside the sophistica-tion and pampering of resort life. More an oasis than a mirage, the hotel greets visitors with exotic bamboo, orchids, banana trees, secluded grottoes, and peaceful lagoons. Dolphins, white tigers, stingrays, sharks, and a volcano provide livelier sights.

The Mirage's guest rooms have tasteful appointments and some of the most com-fortable, down-comforter beds in town. The standard 396-square-foot rooms emit a mod-ern and relaxing feel in golds, blacks, and splashes of tangerine, mauve, and ruby.

Bump and grind at **1 Oak** (10:30pm-4am Wed., Fri., Sat.), an urban space with lots of hip-hop and gritty, socially aware artwork. Two separate rooms have bars, DJs, and crowded dance floors. With dark walls and sparse lighting, it's a sinful, sexy venue for the beautiful people to congregate.

The Mirage commands performances by the world's top headliners, but Cirque du Soleil's Beatles show *Love* packs 'em in every night for a celebration of the Fab Four's music.

Harrah's

Restaurants: Ruth's Chris Steak House, Flavors the Buffet, Oyster Bar, Ben & Jerry's, Toby Keith's I Love This Bar & Grill, Fulton Street Food Hall, Starbucks
Entertainment: *Tenors of Rock, Menopause the Musical,* Mac King Comedy Magic Show, Big Elvis, *X Country*
Nightlife: Carnaval Court, Numb Bar, Piano Bar, Signature Bar

Adjacent to the happening Linq, ★ **Harrah's** (3475 Las Vegas Blvd. S., 800/214-9110, www. caesars.com/harrahs-las-vegas, $115-201) sud-denly finds itself on the cutting edge of the Las Vegas party scene. The venerable prop-erty has taken a few baby steps toward hipster-ism, booking the topless *X Country* revue and the raunchy *Menopause, the Musical.* Still, conservative habits are hard to break, and the family-friendly **Mac King Comedy Magic Show** remains one of the best afternoon of-ferings in town.

Carnaval Court, outside on the Strip's sidewalk, capitalizes on the street-party atmo-sphere with live bands and juggling bartend-ers. Just inside, Vegas icon **Big Elvis** (2pm, 3:30pm, and 5pm Mon., Wed., and Fri., free) performs in the **Piano Bar,** which invites as-piring singers to the karaoke stage Monday through Wednesday evenings, and dueling twin sister keyboardists take over each night at 9pm. The country superstar lends his name and unapologetic patriotism to **Toby Keith's I Love This Bar & Grill** (11:30am-2am Sun.-Thurs., 11:30am-3am Fri.-Sat., $15-25). Try the fried bologna sandwich.

For the best experience, book a room in the remodeled (2016) and renamed Valley Tower. Its 600 rooms and 72 suites feature subtle blues and grays along with traditional Harrah's purple in geometric designs and artwork throughout. Backlighted vanities, big windows, and modern lights and fixtures add to the sleek design.

★ Caesars Palace

Restaurants: Bacchanal Buffet, Gordon Ramsay Hell's Kitchen, Gordon Ramsay Pub & Grill, Restaurant Guy Savoy, Brioche by Guy Savoy, Stripside Café & Bar, Beijing Noodle No. 9, Mesa Grill, Old Homestead Steakhouse, Rao's, Mr. Chow, Searsucker, Nobu, Pronto, Café Americano, Forum Food Court (Smashburger, Halal Guys, Earl of Sandwich, Tiger Wok & Ramen, Difara Pizza, La Gloria, Romaine Empire), Starbucks
Entertainment: Absinthe, Cocktail Cabaret
Attractions: *Fall of Atlantis*, aquarium, Appian Way Shops, Forum Shops
Nightlife: Omnia, Fizz, Cleopatra's Barge, Spanish Steps, Numb Bar, Alto Bar, Lobby Bar, Vista Lounge, Montecristo Cigar Bar

The Roman Empire probably would look a lot like Las Vegas had it survived this long. **Caesars Palace** (3570 Las Vegas Blvd. S., 866/227-5938, www.caesars.com, $175-300) has incorporated all of ancient Rome's decadence while adding a few thousand slot machines. Caesars opened with great fanfare in 1966 and has ruled the Strip ever since. Like the empire, it continues to expand and innovate, now boasting 3,348 guest rooms in six towers and 140,000 square feet of gaming space accented with marble, fountains, gilding, and royal reds. Wander the grounds searching for reproductions of some of the world's most famous statuary, including Michelangelo's *David*.

Cleopatra's Barge (7pm-2am Tues.-Wed., 8pm-3am Thurs.-Sat.), a floating lounge, attracts the full spectrum of the 21-and-over crowd for late-night bacchanalia. Local rockers and pop-choral fusionists are the current house bands, with occasional forays from touring groups taking the stage for acoustic performances in the intimate, 170-seat venue.

Guests luxuriate in the **Garden of the Gods Pool Oasis,** with each of several distinct water-and-sun shrines catering to a different proclivity. Gamblers can play at a swim-up blackjack table at Fortuna; beach bunnies can flaunt it toplessly at Venus; tanners can roast in peace at Apollo; kids can frolic at Temple; and the wealthy can splurge on cabanas at Bacchus. What, no aqueduct?

All roads lead to the **Forum Shops** (10am-11pm Sun.-Thurs., 10am-midnight Fri.-Sat.), a collection of famous designer stores, specialty boutiques, and restaurants. An hour here can

Caesars Palace

do some serious damage to your bankroll. You'll also find the *Fall of Atlantis* show (hourly 11am-11pm Sun.-Thurs., 11am-11pm Fri.-Sat., free), a multisensory, multimedia depiction of the gods' wrath.

Caesars is the center of the world for celebrity chefs, with culinary all-stars lending their names to multiple eateries. At **Gordon Ramsay Hell's Kitchen** (11am-10pm Sun.-Thurs., 11am-11pm Fri.-Sat., $40-65), epicureans and fans of Ramsay's TV show *Hell's Kitchen* (also fans of the F-word, we presume) can dine in a setting reminiscent of the show's studio set. Guests can also get their British on at **Gordon Ramsay Pub & Grill** (11am-11pm Sun.-Thurs., 11am-midnight Fri.-Sat., $25-40). Sip a Guinness while munching on shepherd's pie, bangers and mash, and fish-and-chips among the iconic red phone booths straight out of *Doctor Who*.

With so many guest rooms in six towers, it seems Caesars is always renovating somewhere. Most newer guest rooms are done in tan, wood, and marble. Ask for a south-facing room in the Augustus or Octavius tower to get commanding vistas of both the Bellagio fountains and the Strip.

The Linq

Restaurants: Guy Fieri's Vegas Kitchen and Bar, Chayo Mexican Kitchen & Tequila Bar, Hash House a Go Go, Nook Café, Off the Strip

Entertainment: Mat Franco's *Magic Reinvented*, Frank Marino's *Divas Las Vegas*

Attractions: High Roller, VR Adventures, Club Tattoo, Brooklyn Bowl

Nightlife: 3535, Catalyst, O'Shea's, Tag Lounge and Bar

Rooms at **The Linq** (3535 Las Vegas Blvd. S., 800/634-6441, www.caesars.com/linq, $99-249) are sleek, stylish, and smallish, at 250-350 square feet. Pewter and chrome are accented with eggplant, orange, or aqua murals depicting vintage Vegas in all its neon glory. Other amenities include marble countertops, 47-inch flat-screen TVs, and iPod docks. But the hotel is really just a way to stay close to all the Gen X-focused boutiques,

bars, and restaurants in the adjacent outdoor promenade.

The high point of this pedestrian-friendly plaza is the **High Roller** ($22-32, age 4-12 $9-19), the highest observation wheel in the world, but there's plenty more to warrant a stop. **Brooklyn Bowl** (5pm-1am Sat.-Thurs., 5pm-2am Fri., $15-25) has you covered on eat, drink, and be merry, combining tenpin excitement with dozens of beer taps, delectable finger foods, and live entertainment. The spicy diablo shrimp highlights the modern fare at **Chayo Mexican Kitchen & Tequila Bar** (9am-midnight Sun.-Thurs., 9am-3am Fri.-Sat., $16-28), but the menu takes a back seat to the tequila-fueled party. There's a mechanical bull in the middle of the dining room, for goodness sake. Patio seating puts diners and drinkers in prime people-watching territory. Vegas icon and local favorite **O'Shea's** (24 hours daily) brings back the lowbrow frivolity of the kegger party with cheap drafts, heated beer pong matches, and a rockin' jam band that keeps the festivities raging well into the wee hours.

America's Got Talent winner **Mat Franco** (7pm Thurs.-Mon., 4pm Sat., $48-88) combines jaw-dropping production illusions with how'd-he-do-that close-up tricks. His easygoing banter and anything-to-please attitude ensure it's never the same show twice.

Flamingo

Restaurants: Center Cut Steakhouse, Paradise Garden Buffet, Jimmy Buffett's Margaritaville, Carlos N Charlie's, Beach Club Bar & Grill, Club Cappuccino, Café Express Food Court (Bonanno's Pizza, Johnny Rockets, L.A. Subs, Pan Asian Express)

Entertainment: Donny & Marie, Piff the Magic Dragon, *Legends in Concert*, *X Burlesque*

Attractions: Wildlife Habitat

Nightlife: It's 5 O'Clock Somewhere Bar, Garden Bar, Bugsy's Bar

Named for Virginia "Flamingo" Hill, the girlfriend of Benjamin "don't call me Bugsy" Siegel, the **Flamingo** (3555 Las Vegas Blvd. S., 702/733-3111, www.caesars.com/flamingo-las-vegas, $109-219) has at turns embraced and shunned its gangster ties, which stretch back to the 1960s. After Bugsy's (sorry, Mr. Siegel's) Flamingo business practices ran afoul of the Cosa Nostra and led to his untimely end, Meyer Lansky took over. Mob ties continued to dog the property until Hilton Hotels bought the Flamingo in 1970, giving the joint the legitimacy it needed. Today, its art deco architecture and pink-and-orange neon conjure images of aging Mafiosi lounging by the pool in a Vegas where the mob era is remembered almost fondly. At the **Flamingo Wildlife Habitat** (8am-dusk daily, free), ibis, pelicans, turtles, koi fish, and, of course, Chilean flamingos luxuriate amid riparian plants and meandering streams.

Guests can search for their lost shaker of salt at **Jimmy Buffett's Margaritaville** (702/733-3302, 8am-1am Sun.-Thurs., 8am-2am Fri.-Sat., $20-30).

Piff the Magic Dragon (8pm, days vary, $69) performs mind-boggling card tricks with deadpan delivery and the help of adorable Chihuahua Mr. Piffles. Most of the humor is family-friendly, but the venue recommends audience members be age 13 and over.

The Flamingo transformed many of its guest rooms into Fab Rooms in 2012, but the older Go Rooms are actually more modern, dressed in swanky mahogany and white. The rooms are only 350 square feet but boast high-end entertainment systems and 42-inch TVs, vintage art prints, padded leather headboards, and all the other Vegas-sational accoutrements. Fab Rooms are more boldly decorated, incorporating swatches of hot pink.

Rio

Restaurants: VooDoo Steakhouse, Carnival World & Seafood Buffets, Royal India Bistro, Wine Cellar & Tasting Room, KJ Dim Sum & Seafood, All-American Bar & Grille, Hash House a Go Go, Pho Da Nang Vietnamese Kitchen, Guy Fieri's El Burro Borracho, Sports Deli, Smashburger
Entertainment: Penn & Teller, Chippendales, *X Rocks*, WOW—World of Wonder
Attractions: VooDoo Beach, VooDoo Zip Line, Kiss by Monster Mini Golf, Masquerade Village, Count's

Tattoo Company
Nightlife: VooDoo Rooftop Nightclub & Lounge, IBar, Flirt Lounge, Masquerade Bar, Purple Zebra Daiquiri Bar

This Carnival-inspired resort of more than 2,500 all-suite accommodations just off the Strip keeps the party going with terrific buffets, beautiful people-magnet bars, and steamy shows. "Bevertainers" at the **Rio** (3700 W. Flamingo Rd., 866/983-4279, www.caesars.com/rio-las-vegas, $99-199) take breaks from schlepping cocktails by jumping on mini stages scattered throughout the casino to belt out tunes or shimmy to the music. Dancers and other performers may materialize at your slot machine to take your mind off your losses.

While topless dancers and hard rock are the premise of every strip club in town, the focus at *X Rocks* (10pm Thurs.-Sat., $48-73, 18 and over) is on the music, costumes, choreography, and props, rather than the flesh (yeah, right!). Comedian John Bizarre yuks it up between routines. Rio has an equal-opportunity policy when it comes to titillation, with the famous **Chippendales** (8:30pm and 10:30pm daily, $60-70) flashing pecs and crooning ballads. There's more beefcake at **Flirt Lounge** (6:30pm-midnight Sun.-Thurs., 6:30pm-1am Fri.-Sat.) in the form of easy-on-the-eyes waiters.

Rio suites measure about 600 square feet. The hotel's center-Strip location and room-tall windows provide middle-of-the-action sights. A dressing area separate from the bathroom makes night-on-the-town preparations easy.

VooDoo Beach is a complex comprising four pools, a maze of waterfalls, cabanas, and more. Kids are welcome everywhere but Voo Pool, which attracts the over-21 crowd with a bar, spa treatment tables, and topless bathing.

LOWER STRIP

The **Lower Strip**—roughly between the "Welcome to Fabulous Las Vegas" sign and Harmon Avenue—is a living city timeline. The Tropicana is here, providing a link to the mobbed-up city of the 1960s and 1970s.

The Next Big Things

With new shows, new clubs, and new restaurants opening every month, you really can't visit the same Las Vegas twice. Two major changes loom on the Strip.

NOMAD/PARK MGM

MGM is spending nearly a half billion dollars to transform the rather staid Monte Carlo into two new luxurious resorts opening in 2018. The top three floors of the new building will carry the NoMad Hotel brand, with the chic restaurants, pampering amenities, and opulent guest rooms (292) made famous by the New York City original. The pool area promises to be the place to be seen on the Strip, and the gaming floor will be one of the swankiest in town.

Below, Park MGM takes a more traditional Las Vegas megaresort approach: 2,700 rooms, European styling including Italian marble and continental restaurants, and 100,000 square feet of convention space. Reflecting the sensibilities of the young demographic the resort targets, many restaurants will feature to-go counters and locally sourced ingredients.

The project includes Park Theater, a 5,300-seat theater that opened in late 2016 with a concert by The Pretenders and Stevie Nicks. Intimate seating (none more than 150 feet from the stage), projection screens, and multimedia motion graphics add to the experience. Lady Gaga is set to begin her residency in December 2018.

RESORTS WORLD

Yet another delay—this one owing to a rethinking of the design to attract affluent young Chinese and Chinese American gamblers—has pushed the projected opening of Resorts World Casino to 2020. To be built on the former site of the Stardust Casino, Resorts World will focus on a 100,000-square-foot casino full of Asian games, as well as Eastern-themed restaurants, shops, and shows.

Camelot-themed Excalibur, completed in 1990, and the Egyptian-inspired Luxor, which opened in 1993, serve as prime examples from the city's hesitant foray into becoming a "family" destination in the early 1990s. Across from the Tropicana, the emerald-tinted MGM Grand opened in 1993 as a salute to *The Wizard of Oz*. City Center puts the mega in megaresort—condos, boutique hotels, trendy shopping, a huge casino, and a sprawling dining and entertainment district—and cemented the city's biggest-is-best trend. The Lower Strip seems made for budget-conscious families. Rooms are often cheaper than mid-Strip, and there are plenty of kid-friendly attractions (even a roller coaster).

The Palms

Restaurants: Nove Italiano, 24 Seven Café, Bistro Buffet, Café 6, A.Y.C.E. Buffet, The Eatery (Earl of Sandwich, McDonalds, Panda Express, Nathan's Famous, Famous Famiglia Pizzeria, Blizz Frozen Yogurt, Chronic Tacos, Coffee Bean and Tea Leaf)

Entertainment: Pearl Theater, Brendan Theater

Nightlife: Rojo, Tonic, Moon, Rain

The expression "party like a rock star" could have been invented for **The Palms** (4321 W. Flamingo Rd., 866/942-7777, www.palms. com, $110-175). Penthouse views, uninhibited pool parties, lavish theme suites, and starring roles in several televised parties have brought notoriety and stars to the clubs, concert venue, and recording studio. The 2,500-seat **Pearl Concert Theater** regularly hosts rock concerts.

The Palms' Fantasy Tower houses the fantasy suites, where you can choose from rooms with bowling lanes, erotic rotating beds, pool tables, basketball courts, and more. The original Ivory Tower offers large guest rooms. They're sleek, with geometric shapes and custom artwork, but their best features are the feathery beds and luxurious comforters. The rejuvenating shower and "spa-inspired" stone, glass, and chrome bathrooms help get the day started. The newest tower, Palms Place, has 599 studios and one-bedrooms with suite views, gourmet kitchens, and nearby restaurant, spa, and pool.

Bellagio

Restaurants: Lago, Yellowtail, Harvest by Roy Ellamar, Jasmine, Fix, Michael Mina, Picasso, Prime Steakhouse, Le Cirque, Noodles, The Buffet, Café Bellagio, Jean Philippe Patisserie, Starbucks, Café Gelato, Palio, Snacks, Pool Café
Entertainment: Cirque du Soleil's O
Attractions: Fountains at Bellagio, Bellagio Conservatory & Botanical Garden, Bellagio Gallery of Fine Art, public art
Nightlife: The Bank, Hyde, Lily Bar & Lounge, Petrossian Bar, Baccarat Bar, Pool Bar, Sports Bar Lounge

With nearly 4,000 guest rooms and suites, ★ **Bellagio** (3600 Las Vegas Blvd. S., 702/693-7111 or 888/987-6667, www.bellagio. com, $199-349) boasts a population larger than the village perched on Lake Como from which it borrows its name. To keep pace with its Italian namesake, Bellagio created an 8.5-acre lake between the hotel and Las Vegas Boulevard. The views of the lake and its **Fountains at Bellagio** (3pm-midnight Mon.-Fri., noon-midnight Sat., 11am-midnight Sun.) are free, as is the 80,000-flower aromatic fantasy at **Bellagio Conservatory & Botanical Garden** (24 hours daily). The **Bellagio Gallery of Fine Art** (10am-8pm daily, $18) would be a bargain at twice the price—you can spend an edifying day at one of the world's priciest resorts (including a cocktail and lunch) for less than $50. Even if you don't spring for gallery admission, art demands your attention throughout the hotel and casino. The 2,000 glass flower petals in Dale Chihuly's *Fiori di Como* sculpture bloom from the lobby ceiling, foreshadowing the opulent experiences to come. Masatoshi Izumi's *A Gift from the Earth*, comprising four massive basalt sculptures representing wind, fire, water, and land, dominates the hotel's main entrance.

The display of artistry continues but the bargains end at **Via Bellagio** (10am-midnight daily), the resort's shopping district, including heavyweight retailers Armani, Prada, Chanel, Gucci, and their ilk.

Befitting Bellagio's world-class status, intriguing and expensive restaurants abound. **Michael Mina** (5:30pm-10pm Mon.-Sat., $70-100) is worth the price. Restrained decor adds to the simple elegance of the cuisine,

Bellagio fountains

The "Black Book": A Very Exclusive Club

For much the same reason that Willie Sutton robbed banks ("because that's where the money is"), plots are continually being hatched to rip off Nevada's casinos. Modern plots are rarely as sophisticated as an *Ocean's 11* caper, and the culprits are rarely as engaging as Frank Sinatra or George Clooney. But while slot-machine technology and casino security have foiled token counterfeiters, card markers, and loaded-dice artists, the villains have used technology as well.

Those who get caught often wind up in a most exclusive club—the Nevada Gaming Commission's List of Excluded Persons. The "Black Book" is full of geniuses and the not-so-bright who designed and used mechanical devices, sabotage, bribery, or their inside position to steal from the casinos. The book—which is silver, not black—also contains names of known organized-crime figures and other unsavory characters whose affiliation or association with gambling parlors would give the appearance of impropriety. Eleven mob associates made up the book's first class in 1960. Dozens have been added since, although more than a few have wriggled off the hook for various reasons. Today 39 people grace the book's pages. The newest additions are two slot cheaters added in 2004.

Anyone with a felony conviction, a rap sheet that includes a crime of moral turpitude or violation of any state's gaming laws, an interest in a gaming establishment that they did not disclose to authorities, or a history of willfully evading taxes is eligible for Black Book membership. Excluded persons face gross misdemeanor charges if they're caught entering a gaming establishment (stores, airports, bars, and other places with no gambling tables and only a few slot machines are not included in the ban).

Perhaps the most intriguing Black Book member is Ronald Dale Harris. For 12 years he was an employee of the Nevada Gaming Control Board, where he evaluated the security of gaming machines. He used his familiarity to rig several Nevada machines, winning several small payouts over three years before he and an accomplice got greedy. Harris gaffed a video keno game's random-number generator and sent the accomplice to Atlantic City to win a $100,000 jackpot. Casino authorities became suspicious because—well, because nobody ever wins at video keno—and the investigation led back to Harris.

---

which is mostly seafood with European and Asian influences.

Bellagio's tower rooms are the epitome of luxury, with Italian marble, oversize bathtubs, remote-controlled drapes, Egyptian-cotton sheets, and 510 square feet in which to spread out. The sage-plum and indigo-silver color schemes are refreshing changes from the goes-with-everything beige and the camouflages-all-stains paisley often found on the Strip.

Paris Las Vegas

Restaurants: Burger Brasserie, Mon Ami Gabi, Martorano's, Hexx, Gordon Ramsay Steak, Eiffel Tower Restaurant, Café Belle Madeleine, La Creperie, JJ's Boulangerie, Beef Park, Café Belle Madeleine, Sekushi, La Creperie, Le Café Ile St. Louis, Le Village Buffet, Yong Kang Street

Entertainment: *Sex Tips for Straight Women from a*

Gay Man, Anthony Cools
Attractions: Eiffel Tower
Nightlife: Napoleon's Lounge, Le Cabaret, Le Central, Le Bar du Sport, Gustav's, Chateau Nightclub & Rooftop

Designers used Gustav Eiffel's original drawings to ensure that the half-size tower that anchors **Paris Las Vegas** (3655 Las Vegas Blvd. S., 877/242-6753, www.caesars.com/paris-las-vegas, $149-276) conformed—down to the last cosmetic rivet—to the original. That attention to detail prevails throughout this property, which works hard to evoke the City of Light, from large-scale reproductions of the Arc de Triomphe, Champs Élysées, and Louvre to more than half a dozen French restaurants. The tower is perhaps the most romantic spot in town to view the Strip; you'll catch your breath as the elevator whisks you to the observation deck 460 feet up, then have it taken away again by the lights from one of the most famous skylines in the world. Back at street level, the cobblestone lanes and brass streetlights of **Le Boulevard** (8am-2am daily) invite shoppers into quaint shops and patisseries. The casino offers its own attractions, not the least of which is the view of the Eiffel Tower's base jutting through the ceiling. Paris is one of the first casinos to test "skill-based" gaming, which combines video poker with video games. It also offers a variation of fantasy football during the NFL season.

Entertainment veers toward the bawdy, with **Anthony Cools—The Uncensored Hypnotist** (9pm Tues. and Thurs.-Sun., $49-82) cajoling mesmerized subjects through very adult simulations. The same venue hosts the Broadway export *Sex Tips for Straight Women from a Gay Man* (7pm and 11pm, Sun.-Thurs., $39-69), in which the audience and flamboyant Dan help uptight Robyn shed her bedroom inhibitions.

You'll be wishing you had packed your beret when you order a beignet and cappuccino at **Le Café Ile St. Louis** (6pm-11pm Sun.-Thurs., 6am-midnight Fri.-Sat., $12-20). While the checkered tablecloths and streetlights scream French sidewalk café, the menu tends toward American comfort food.

Standard guest rooms in the 33-story tower are decorated in a rich earth-tone palette and have marble baths. There's nothing Left Bank bohemian about them, however. The guest rooms exude little flair or personality, but the simple, quality furnishings make it a moderately priced option. Book a Red Room if modern decor is important to you.

Cosmopolitan

Restaurants: Scarpetta, Rose. Rabbit. Lie., E by Jose Andres, STK, Beauty & Exxex, Blue Ribbon Sushi Bar & Grill, China Poblano, D.O.C.G., Secret Pizza, Eggslut, Estiatorio Milos, The Henry, Holsteins, Jaleo, The Juice Standard, Milk Bar, Momofuku, Overlook Grill, Starbucks
Entertainment: Opium
Attractions: public art

Nightlife: Marquee, Bond, The Chandelier, Clique, The Study, Vesper Bar

Modern art, marble bath floors, and big soaking tubs in 460-square-foot rooms evoke urban penthouse living at ★ **Cosmopolitan** (3708 Las Vegas Blvd. S., 702/698-7000, www.cosmopolitanlasvegas.com, $220-380). The hefty rates do nothing to harsh the NYC vibe. Because it's too cool to host production shows, the resort's entertainment schedule mixes DJs of the moment with the coolest headliners.

That nouveau riche attitude carries through to the dining and nightlife. **Rose. Rabbit. Lie.** (6pm-midnight Wed.-Sat., $80-150) is equal parts supper club, nightclub, and jazz club. Bluesy, jazzy torch singers, magicians, tap and hip-hop dancers, and a rocking sound system keep the joint jumping. If you go for dinner, order 5-6 small plates per couple. **Vesper Bar** (24 hours daily), named for James Bond's favorite martini, prides itself on serving hipster versions of classic cocktails. Possibly the best day club in town, **Marquee** (11am-sunset daily Apr.-Oct.), on the roof, brings in the beautiful people with DJs and sweet bungalow lofts. When darkness falls, the day club becomes an extension of the pulsating Marquee nightclub (10:30pm-5am Mon. and Fri.-Sat.).

Aria

Restaurants: Bardot, Sage, Herringbone, Tetsu, Blossom, Jean Georges Steakhouse, BarMasa, Carbone, Jean Philippe Patisserie Javier's, Lemongrass, The Buffet, Julian Serrano Tapas, Aria Café, Five50 Pizza Bar, Bobby's Burger Palace
Entertainment: Cirque du Soleil's *Zarkana*
Attractions: public art, Crystals
Nightlife: Jewel, Alibi, Baccarat Lounge, High Limit Lounge, Lift Bar, Lobby Bar, Pool Bar, Sports Bar

All glass and steel, ultramodern ★ **Aria** (3730 Las Vegas Blvd. S., 702/590-7757, www.aria.com, $210-379) would look more at home in Manhattan than Las Vegas. Touch pads control the drapes, the lighting, the music, and the climate in Aria's fern- or grape-paletted guest rooms. Program the "wake up scene" before bedtime, and the room will gradually summon you from peaceful slumber at the appointed time. A traditional hotel casino, Aria shares the City Center umbrella with **Vdara,** a Euro-chic boutique hotel with no gaming.

Guests are invited to browse an extensive public art collection, with works by Maya Lin, Jenny Holzer, and Richard Long, among others. **Crystals,** a 500,000-square-foot mall, lets you splurge among hanging gardens. Restaurants fronted by Julian Serrano and Michael Mina take the place of Sbarro's and Cinnabon.

Culinary genius Masa Takayama guarantees that the bluefin at **BarMasa** (5pm-10pm Thurs.-Tues., $40-80) goes from the Sea of Japan to your spicy tuna roll in less than 24 hours.

Hard Rock

Restaurants: MB Steak, Culinary Dropout, Fu Asian Kitchen, Mr. Lucky's, Nobu, Pink Taco, Oyster Bar, Fuel Café, Goose Island Pub, Pizza Forte, Juice Bar, Dunkin' Donuts
Entertainment: *Magic Mike Live, Raiding the Rock Vault,* Vinyl, Soundwaves
Nightlife: The Joint, Rehab Pool Party, Breathe, Vanity, Center Bar, Sidebet Draft Bar, Luxe Bar, Midway Bar

Young stars and the media-savvy 20-somethings who idolize them contribute to the frat party mojo at the **Hard Rock** (4455 Paradise Rd., 800/473-7625, www.hardrockhotel.com, $129-275). While the casino is shaped like an LP, if your music collection dates back to wax records, this probably isn't the place for you. The gaming tables and machines are located in the "record label," and the shops and restaurants are in the "grooves."

Contemporary and classic rockers regularly grace the stage at **The Joint** and party with their fans at **Rehab Pool Parties** (11am-dusk Fri.-Sat.). The provocatively named **Pink Taco** (11am-10pm Sun.-Thurs., 11am-2am Fri.-Sat., $15-25) dishes up Mexican and Caribbean specialties.

The 1,500 sleek guest rooms include stocked minibars, Bose CD sound systems, and 55-inch plasma TVs, a fitting crib for wannabe rock stars.

New York New York

Restaurants: Tom's Urban, Il Fornaio, Nine Fine Irishmen, Gallagher's Steakhouse, America, MGM Grand Buffet, New York Pizzeria, Chin Café & Sushi Bar, Broadway Burger Bar & Grill, Gonzalez y Gonzalez, Shake Shack, 48th and Crepe, Greenberg's Deli,

New York New York

Fulton's Fish Frye, Village Bakery, Times Square to Go, Nathan's Famous, Starbucks

Entertainment: Cirque du Soleil's *Zumanity*, Brooklyn Bridge buskers, dueling pianos, The Park **Attractions:** Hershey's Chocolate World, Big Apple Coaster & Arcade, T-Mobile Arena **Nightlife:** Coyote Ugly, The Bar at Times Square, Center Bar, Pour 24, Big Chill, High Limit Bar, Lobby Bar, Chocolate Bar

One look at this loving tribute to the city that never sleeps and you won't be able to fuhgedaboutit. From the city skyline outside (the skyscrapers contain the resort's hotel rooms) to laundry hanging between crowded faux brownstones indoors, **New York New York** (3790 Las Vegas Blvd. S., 702/740-6969 or 866/815-4365, www.newyorknewyork.com, $130-255) will have even grizzled Gothamites feeling like they've come home again.

The **Big Apple Coaster** (11am-11pm Sun.-Thurs., 10:30am-midnight Fri.-Sat., $15, all-day pass $26) winds its way around the resort, an experience almost as hair-raising as a New York City cab ride, which the coaster cars are painted to resemble.

Dueling pianists keep **The Bar at Times Square** (1pm-2:30am Mon.-Thurs., 11am-2:30am Fri.-Sun.) rocking into the wee hours, and the sexy bar staff at **Coyote Ugly** (6pm-3am daily) defy its name.

The Park takes dining, drinking, and strolling to new heights. The plaza surrounding T-Mobile Arena, where the NHL's Vegas Golden Knights and the hottest musical acts play, incorporates responsible landscaping and artistic, if man-made, shade structures.

New York New York's 2,023 guest rooms are standard size, 350-400 square feet. The roller coaster zooms around the towers, so you might want to ask for a room out of earshot.

MGM Grand

Restaurants: Morimoto, Joël Robuchon, Tom Colicchio's Craftsteak, Michael Mina Pub 1842, Emeril's New Orleans Fish House, L'Atelier de Joël Robuchon, Wolfgang Puck Bar & Grill, Hakkasan, Grand Wok and Sushi Bar, Hecho En Vegas, Crush, MGM Grand Buffet, Fiamma Trattoria & Bar, Stage Deli, Tap Sports Bar, Blizz,

Pieology, Avenue Café, Cabana Grill, Corner Cakes, Starbucks, Subway, Pan Asian Express, Bonanno's New York Pizzeria, Häagen-Dazs, Nathan's Famous, Original Chicken Tender, Tacos N 'Ritas, Johnny Rockets **Entertainment:** Cirque du Soleil's *Kà*, David Copperfield, Jabbawockeez, Brad Garrett's Comedy Club, MGM Garden Arena **Attractions:** Topgolf, Level Up, CSI: The Experience, CBS Television City Research Center **Nightlife:** Wet Republic, Hakkasan, Whiskey Bar, Losers Bar, Centrifuge, Lobby Bar

Gamblers enter **MGM Grand** (3799 Las Vegas Blvd. S., 888/646-1203, www.mgmgrand.com, $130-250) through portals guarded by MGM's mascot, the 45-foot-tall king of the jungle. The uninitiated may feel like a gazelle on the savanna, swallowed by the 171,000-square-foot casino floor, the largest in Las Vegas. But the watering hole, MGM's 6.5-acre pool complex, is relatively predator-free. MGM capitalizes on the movie studio's greatest hits. Even the hotel's emerald facade evokes the magical city in *The Wizard of Oz.*

Boob tube fans can volunteer for studies at the **CBS Television City Research Center** (10am-8:30pm daily, free), where they can screen pilots for shows under consideration. If your favorite show happens to revolve around solving crimes, don some rubber gloves and search for clues at **CSI: The Experience** (9am-8pm daily, age 12 and up $32, not recommended for children under 12). Three crime scenes keep the experience fresh.

MGM Grand houses enough top restaurants for a week of gourmet dinners. You can take your pick of celebrity chef establishments, but **L'Atelier de Joël Robuchon** (5pm-10pm daily, $75-200) offers the most bang for the buck. Counter service overlooks kitchen preparations, adding to the anticipation.

Standard guest rooms in the Grand Tower are filled with the quality furnishings you'd expect. The West Tower guest rooms are smaller, at 350 square feet, but exude swinging style with high-tech gizmos; the 450-square-foot rooms in the Grand Tower are more traditional.

Tropicana

Restaurants: Bacio Italian Cuisine, Biscayne, Chef Irvine, Beach Café, South Beach Food Court, Starbucks
Entertainment: Men of the Strip, Rich Little, Laugh Factory
Attractions: Xposed!
Nightlife: Tropicana Lounge, Lucky's Sports Bar, Coconut Grove Bar

When it opened at in 1959, the **Tropicana** (3801 Las Vegas Blvd. S., 702/739-2222, www.troplv.com, $140-200) was the most luxurious, most expensive resort on the Strip. It has survived several boom-and-bust cycles since then, and its decor reflects the willy-nilly expansion and refurbishment efforts through the years. Today, the rooms have bright, airy South Beach themes with plantation shutters, light wood, 42-inch plasma TVs, and garden views.

The beach chic atmosphere includes a two-acre pool complex with reclining deck chairs and swim-up blackjack. After a slow start, Las Vegas is now quite LGBTQ friendly. On summer Saturdays (noon-7pm) the pool deck hosts **Xposed!,** a gay-friendly pool party with sand volleyball, go-go dancers, and trendy DJs.

While it features hard-bodied singers and dance routines by world-renowned choreographers, the sultry **Men of the Strip** (9pm Thurs.-Sun., $50-80) promises a more risqué version of the male revue. Think more bump and grind than flex and flirt. The producers note that both women and men are welcome in the audience.

Luxor

Restaurants: Tender Steak & Seafood, Rice & Company, Public House, T&T Tacos & Tequila, More Buffet, Pyramid Café, Backstage Deli, Blizz, Burger Bar, Ri Ra Irish Pub, Slice of Vegas, Hussong's Cantina, Bonanno's Pizzeria, Johnny Rockets, LA Subs, Nathan's Famous, Original Chicken Tender, Starbucks
Entertainment: Criss Angel *Mindfreak Live,* Carrot Top, Blue Man Group, *Fantasy*
Attractions: *Bodies … the Exhibition, Titanic* artifacts
Nightlife: Centra, Aurora, Flight, High Bar, PlayBar

Other than its pyramid shape and name, not much remains of the Egyptian theme at the

Luxor (3900 Las Vegas Blvd. S., 702/262-4000, www.luxor.com, $99-220). In its place are upscale and decidedly post-pharaoh nightclubs, restaurants, and shops. Many are located in the **Shoppes at Mandalay Place,** on the sky bridge between Luxor and Mandalay Bay. The huge base of the pyramid houses a cavernous 120,000-square-foot casino, while the slanted walls and twin 22-story towers contain 4,400 guest rooms. Luxor also has the largest atrium in the world, an intense light beam that is visible from space, and inclinators—elevators that move along the building's oblique angles.

Carrot Top's (8pm Wed.-Mon., $50-82) rapid-fire prop comedy fills the Atrium Showroom, while Criss Angel performs his skull-crushing illusions in *Mindfreak Live* (7pm and 9:30pm Wed.-Sun., $72-173) in the Luxor Theater. The theater also hosts the comely and talented singers and dancers in the topless *Fantasy* (10:30pm nightly, $49-66), as well as comedians, jugglers, and other specialty acts.

Staying in the pyramid makes for interesting room features, such as a slanted exterior wall. Stay on higher floors for panoramic views of the atrium below. Tower rooms are newer and more traditional in their shape, decor, and amenities.

Mandalay Bay

Restaurants: Aureole, Red Square, Lupo by Wolfgang Puck, Charlie Palmer Steak, Fleur by Hubert Keller, Rick Moonen's RM Seafood, Kumi, Stripsteak, Libertine Social, Border Grill, Rx Boiler Room, Rivea, Ri Ra Irish Pub, Della's Kitchen, Hussong's Cantina, Citizens Kitchen & Bar, Slice of Vegas, Seabreeze Café, Burger Bar, Bayside Buffet, Noodle Shop, Bonanno's Pizzeria, Nathan's Famous, Pan Asian Express, Johnny Rockets, Subway
Entertainment: House of Blues, *Michael Jackson One*
Attractions: Shark Reef, Mandalay Place
Nightlife: Foundation Room, Light, Daylight Beach Club, Skyfall, Mizuya, Press, Minus 5 Ice Bar, Eyecandy Sound Lounge, Orchid Lounge, Evening Call, Fat Tuesday, Bikini Bar, Verandah Lounge, 1923 Bourbon Bar

The South Pacific behemoth ★ **Mandalay**

Bay (3950 Las Vegas Blvd. S., 877/632-7800, www.mandalaybay.com, $150-300) has one of the largest casino floors in the world at 135,000 square feet. An 11-acre paradise comprises eight pools, including a lazy river, a 1.6-million-gallon wave pool complete with a real beach made of five million pounds of sand, an adults-only dipping pool, and tops-optional sunbathing deck. You could spend your entire vacation in the pool area, gambling at the beach's three-level casino, eating at its restaurant, and loading up on sandals and bikinis at the nearby Pearl Moon boutique. The beach hosts a concert series during summer.

House of Blues (hours vary by event) hosts live blues, rock, and acoustic sets and a surprisingly good restaurant. It's the site of the Sunday **Gospel Brunch** (702/632-7600, 10am and 1pm Sun., $55), where a gospel choir serenades guest with contemporary spirituals as they dine on Southern delicacies like chicken and waffles, biscuits and gravy, brisket, and more.

Even at 100,000 square feet, **Mandalay Place** (10am-11pm daily), on the sky bridge between Mandalay Bay and the Luxor, is smaller and less hectic than other casino malls. It features unusual shops, such as the Guinness Store, celebrating the favorite Irish stout, and Cariloha, with clothes, accessories, and housewares made of bamboo. The shops share space with eateries and high-concept bars like **Minus 5 Ice Bar** (11am-3am daily), where barflies don parkas before entering the below-freezing (23°F) establishment. The glasses aren't just frosted; they're fashioned completely out of ice.

An urban hip-hop worldview and the King of Pop's unmatched talent guide the vignettes in *Michael Jackson One* (7pm and 9:30pm Fri.-Tues., $69-170). Michael's musical innovation and the Cirque du Soleil trademark aerial and acrobatic acts pay homage to the human spirit.

Sheathed in Indian artifacts and crafts, the **Foundation Room** (5pm-3am daily) is just as dark and mysterious as the subcontinent, with private rooms piled with overstuffed furniture, fireplaces, and thick carpets; a dining room; and several bars catering to various musical tastes.

Vegas pays tribute to Paris, Rome, New York, and Venice, so why not Moscow? Round up your comrades for caviar and vodka as well as continental favorites at **Red Square** (5pm-10pm Sun.-Thurs., 5pm-11pm Fri.-Sat., $35-50). Look for the headless Lenin statue at the entrance.

Standard guest rooms are chic and roomy (550 square feet), with warm fabrics and plush bedding. Get a north-facing room and put the floor-to-ceiling windows to use gazing the full length of the Strip. The guest rooms are big, but nothing special visually, but the baths are fit for royalty, with huge tubs and glass-walled showers. To go upscale, check out the Delano boutique hotel or book at the Four Seasons—both are part of the same complex.

DOWNTOWN
Binion's

Restaurants: Top of Binion's Steakhouse, Binion's Deli, Binion's Café, Benny's Smokin BBQ & Brews
Entertainment: Hypnosis Unleashed
Nightlife: Cowgirl Up Cantina, Whiskey Licker

Before Vegas became a resort city, it catered to inveterate gamblers, hard drinkers, and others on the fringes of society. Ah, the good old days! A gambler himself, Benny Binion put his place in the middle of downtown, a magnet for the serious player, offering high limits and few frills. **Binion's** (128 Fremont St., 702/382-1600, www.binions.com) now attracts players with occasional $1 blackjack tables and a poker room frequented by grizzled veterans. This is where the World Series of Poker began, and the quaint room still stages some wild action on its 10 tables. Players can earn $2 per hour in comps—about double what they can pull down in most rooms. A $4 maximum rake and big-screen TV add to the attraction. The little den on Fremont Street still retains the flavor of Old Vegas.

The hotel at Binion's closed in 2009, but the restaurants remain open, including the

Top of Binion's Steakhouse (5pm-10pm daily, $40-55), famous for its Fremont Street views, aged steaks, and chicken-fried lobster appetizer.

Golden Nugget

Restaurants: Vic & Anthony's, Chart House, Grotto, Lillie's Asian Cuisine, Red Sushi, Cadillac Mexican Kitchen & Tequila Bar, Buffet, The Grille, Claim Jumper, Starbucks
Entertainment: 52 Fridays
Attractions: Hand of Faith, shark tank
Nightlife: Rush Lounge, Gold Diggers, H2O Bar at the Tank, Claude's Bar, Ice Bar, Bar 46, Cadillac Tequila Bar, Stage Bar

The ★ **Golden Nugget** (129 E. Fremont St., 702/385-7111, www.goldennugget.com, $129-249) has been a fixture for nearly 70 years, beckoning diners and gamblers with gold leaf and a 61-pound gold nugget in the lobby. Landry's, the restaurant chain and Nugget owner since 2005, has maintained and restored the hotel's opulence, investing $300 million for casino expansion, more restaurants, and a new 500-room hotel tower. Rooms are appointed in dark wood and warm autumn hues.

If you don't feel like swimming with the sharks in the poker room, you can get up close and personal with their finned namesakes at the **Golden Nugget Pool** (9am-6pm daily, free), an outdoor pool with a three-story waterslide that takes riders through the hotel's huge aquarium, home to sharks, rays, and other exotic marine life. Bathers can also swim up to the aquarium for a face-to-face with the aquatic predators. Waterfalls and lush landscaping help make this one of the world's best hotel pools.

Gold Diggers nightclub (9pm-late Thurs.-Sun.) plays hip-hop, pop, and classic rock for the dancing pleasure of guests and go-go girls. Thursday is Ladies Night, and Sunday features flashbacks to the '80s.

Sights

CENTER STRIP
Madame Tussauds Las Vegas

Ever wanted to dunk over Shaq? Party with the dudes from *The Hangover*? **Madame Tussauds Las Vegas** (3377 Las Vegas Blvd. S., 702/862-7800, www.madametussauds. com/lasvegas, 10am-8pm Sun.-Thurs., 10am-9pm Fri.-Sat., adults $30, age 4-12 $20, under age 4 free) at The Venetian gives you your chance. Unlike most other museums, Madame Tussauds encourages guests to get up close and "personal" with the world leaders, sports heroes, and pop icons immortalized in wax. Photo ops and interactive activities abound. Club Tussauds puts you in the middle of the happening club scene, with A-listers all around. Share a cocktail with Angelina Jolie; hit the dance floor with Channing Tatum; or discuss your screenplay with Will Smith.

★ Gondola Rides

We dare you not to sigh at the grandeur of Venice in the desert as you pass beneath quaint bridges and idyllic sidewalk cafés, your gondolier serenading you with the accompaniment of the Grand Canal's gurgling wavelets. The **indoor gondolas** (Venetian, 3355 Las Vegas Blvd. S., 702/607-3982, www. venetian.com, 10am-11pm Sun.-Thurs., 10am-midnight Fri.-Sat., $29) skirt the Grand Canal Shoppes inside The Venetian under the mall's painted-sky ceiling fresco for a half mile; **outdoor gondolas** (11am-10pm daily, weather permitting, $29) skim The Venetian's 31,000-square-foot lagoon for 12 minutes, giving riders a unique perspective on the Las Vegas Strip. Plying the waters at regular intervals, the realistic-looking gondolas seat four, but couples who don't want to share a boat can pay double.

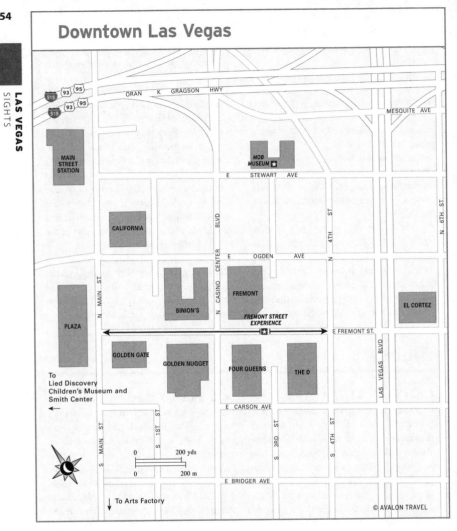

Downtown Las Vegas

★ Secret Garden and Dolphin Habitat

It's no mirage—those really are pure-white tigers lounging in their own plush resort on The Mirage casino floor. Legendary Las Vegas magicians Siegfried and Roy, who have dedicated much of their lives to preserving big cats, opened the **Secret Garden** (Mirage, 3400 Las Vegas Blvd. S., 702/791-7188, www. miragehabitat.com, 10am-6pm daily, adults $22, age 4-12 $17, under age 4 free) in 1990. In addition to the milky-furred tigers, the garden is home to blue-eyed, black-striped white tigers as well as black panthers, lions, and leopards. Although caretakers don't "perform" with the animals, if your visit is well-timed you could see the cats playing, wrestling, and even swimming in their pristine waterfall-fed pools. The cubs in the specially built nursery are sure to register high on the cuteness meter.

Visit the Atlantic bottlenoses at the **Dolphin Habitat** right next door, also in the middle of The Mirage's palm trees and jungle foliage. The aquatic mammals don't perform on cue either, but they're natural hams and often interact with their visitors, nodding their heads in response to trainer questions, turning aerial somersaults, and "walking" on their tails across the water. An underwater viewing area provides an unusual perspective into the dolphins' world. Feeding times are a hoot.

Budding naturalists (age 13 and over) won't want to miss Dolphin Habitat's Trainer for a Day program ($495), which allows them to feed, swim with, and pose for photos with some of the aquatic stars while putting them through their daily regimen. Other interactive activities with the aquatic mammals include painting and yoga.

★ High Roller

Taller than even the London Eye, the 550-foot **High Roller** (The Linq, 3545 Las Vegas Blvd. S., 702/777-2782 or 866/574-3851, www. caesars.com/linq/high-roller, 11:30am-2:30am daily, $25-37, youth $10-20) is the highest observation wheel in the world. Two thousand LED lights dance in intricate choreography among the ride's spokes and pods. The dazzling view from 50 stories up is unparalleled. Ride at night for a perfect panorama of the famous Strip skyline. Ride at dusk for inspiring glimpses of the desert sun setting over the mountains. Forty passengers fit in each of the High Roller's 28 compartments, lessening wait time for the half-hour ride circuit. With **Happy Half Hour** tickets (noon-1am daily, age 21 and up, $52) passengers can board special bar cars and enjoy unlimited cocktails during the ride. Book online to save on tickets.

LOWER STRIP
Showcase Mall

"Mall" is an overly ambitious moniker for the **Showcase Mall** (3785 Las Vegas Blvd. S., 702/597-3117, 9am-5pm Mon.-Sat.), a mini diversion on the Strip. The centerpiece, the original **M&M's World** (702/736-7611, www. mmsworld.com, 9am-midnight daily, free), underwent a 2010 expansion and now includes a printing station where customers can customize their bite-size treats with words and pictures. The 3,300-square-foot expansion on the third floor of the store, which originally opened in 1997, includes additional opportunities to stock up on all things M: Swarovski crystal candy dishes, a guitar, T-shirts, and

gondolas at The Venetian

purses made from authentic M&M wrappers. The addition brings the chocoholic's paradise to more than 30,000 square feet, offering keychains, coffee mugs, lunch boxes, and the addicting treats in every color imaginable. Start with a viewing of the short 3-D film, *I Lost My M in Las Vegas*. A replica of Kyle Busch's M&M-sponsored No. 18 NASCAR stock car is on the fourth floor.

As you might expect, everything inside the **Everything Coca-Cola** store (702/270-5952, 10am-11pm daily, free) is related to the iconic soft drink. The small retail outlet has collectibles, free photo ops, and a soda fountain where you can taste a dozen Coke products from around the world ($7). Look for the giant green Coke bottle facade on the Strip.

Other mall tenants include a food court, an eight-screen movie theater, Adidas, and Hard Rock Café.

Bodies... the Exhibition and Titanic Artifacts

Although they are tastefully and respectfully presented, the dissected humans at *Bodies... the Exhibition* (Luxor, 3900 Las Vegas Blvd. S., 702/262-4400, www.luxor.com, 10am-10pm daily, adults $32, over age 64 $30, age 4-12 $24, under age 4 free) still have a creep factor. That uneasiness quickly gives way to wonder and interest as visitors examine 13 full-body specimens, carefully preserved to reveal bone structure and muscular, circulatory, respiratory, and other systems. Other system and organ displays drive home the importance of a healthy lifestyle, with structures showing the damage caused by overeating, alcohol consumption, and sedentary lifestyle. Perhaps the most sobering exhibit is the side-by-side comparisons of healthy and smoke-damaged lungs. A draped-off area contains fetal specimens, showing prenatal development and birth defects.

Luxor also hosts some 250 less surreal but just as poignant artifacts and reproductions commemorating the 1912 sinking of the *Titanic* (3900 Las Vegas Blvd. S., 702/262-4400, 10am-10pm daily, adults $32, over age

The 550-foot High Roller looms over the Linq entertainment district on the Strip.

64 $30, age 4-12 $24, under age 4 free). The 15-ton rusting hunk of the ship's hull is the biggest artifact on display; it not only drives home the *Titanic*'s scale but also helps transport visitors back to that cold April morning a century ago. A replica of the *Titanic*'s grand staircase—featured prominently in the 1997 film with Leonardo DiCaprio and Kate Winslet—testifies to the ship's opulence, but it is the passengers' personal effects (a pipe, luggage, an unopened bottle of champagne) and re-created first-class and third-class cabins that provide some of the most heartbreaking discoveries. The individual stories come to life as each patron is given the identity of one of the ship's passengers. At the end of tour they find out the passenger's fate.

Luxor offers combination admission to both attractions for $42.

Shark Reef

Just when you thought it was safe to visit Las Vegas. . . . This 1.6-million-gallon habitat proves not all the sharks in town prowl the poker rooms. **Shark Reef** (Mandalay Bay, 3950 Las Vegas Blvd. S., 702/632-4555, www.sharkreef.com, 10am-10pm daily, $25, age 65 and over $23, age 4-12 $19, under age 4 free) is home to 2,000 animals—almost all predators. Transparent walkthrough tubes and a sinking-ship observation deck allow terrific views, bringing visitors nearly face-to-face with some of the most fearsome creatures in the world. Among the 15 species of sharks on display is a sand tiger shark, whose mouth is so crammed with razor-sharp teeth that it doesn't fully close. Other species include golden crocodiles, moray eels, stingrays, giant octopuses, the venomous lionfish, jellyfish, water monitors, and the fresh-from-your-nightmares eight-foot-long Komodo dragon.

Mandalay Bay guests with dive certification can dive in the 22-foot-deep shipwreck exhibit at the reef. Commune with eight-foot nurse sharks as well as reef sharks, zebra sharks, rays, sawfish, and other denizens of the deep. **Scuba excursions** (3pm daily, age 18 and over, $650) include 3-4 hours underwater, a guided aquarium tour, a video, and admission for up to four guests. Wearing chain mail is required. One tour option will prove your love runs deep: Have a reef diver present a surprise proposal at the end of a guided one-hour tour ($100). The price includes a commemorative photo.

DOWNTOWN
★ Fremont Street Experience

With land at a premium and more and more tourists flocking to the opulence of the Strip, downtown Las Vegas in the last quarter of the 20th century found its lights beginning to flicker. Enter the **Fremont Street Experience** (702/678-5600, www.vegasexperience.com), an ambitious plan to transform downtown and its tacky "Glitter Gulch" reputation into a pedestrian-friendly enclave. Highlighted by a four-block-long canopy festooned with 12 million light-emitting diodes 90 feet in the air, the Fremont Street Experience is downtown's answer to the Strip's erupting volcanoes and fantastic dancing fountains. The canopy, dubbed Viva Vision, runs atop Fremont Street between North Main Street and North 4th Street.

Once an hour between dusk and 1am, the promenade goes dark and all heads lift toward the canopy, supported by massive concrete pillars. For six minutes, visitors are enthralled by the multimedia shows that chronicle Western history, span the careers of classic rock bands, or transport viewers to

sea turtle at Mandalay Bay's Shark Reef

fantasy worlds. Viva Vision runs several different shows daily.

Before and after the light shows, strolling buskers sing for their supper, artists create five-minute masterpieces, caricaturists airbrush souvenir portraits, and (sometimes scantily) costumed characters pose for photos. Tipping is all but mandatory ($2-5 is fair). Fremont Street hosts top musical acts, including some A-listers during big Las Vegas weekends such as National Finals Rodeo, NASCAR races, and New Year's. The adjacent Fremont East Entertainment District houses quirky eateries, clubs, and art galleries.

Las Vegas Natural History Museum

Las Vegas boasts a volcano, a pyramid, and even a Roman coliseum, so it's little wonder that an animatronic *Tyrannosaurus rex* calls the valley home, too. Dedicated to "global life forms. . . from the desert to the ocean, from Nevada to Africa, from prehistoric times to the present," the **Las Vegas Natural History Museum** (900 Las Vegas Blvd. N., 702/384-3466, www.lvnhm.org, 9am-4pm daily, adults $10, seniors, military, and students $8, age 3-11 $5) is filled with rotating exhibits that

belie the notion that Las Vegas culture begins and ends with neon casino signs.

Visitors to the Treasures of Egypt gallery can enter a realistic depiction of King Tut's tomb to study archaeological techniques and discover golden treasures of the pharaohs. The Wild Nevada gallery showcases the raw beauty and surprisingly varied life-forms of the Mojave Desert. Interactive exhibits also enlighten visitors on subjects such as marine life, geology, African ecosystems, and more.

The 35-foot-long T. rex and his friends (rivals? entrées?)—a triceratops, a raptor, and an ichthyosaur—greet visitors in the Prehistoric Life gallery. And by "greet" we mean a blood-curdling roar from the T. rex, so take precautions with the little ones and the faint of heart.

Neon Museum and Boneyard

Book a one-hour guided tour of the **Neon Museum and Boneyard** (770 Las Vegas Blvd. N., 702/387-6366, www.neonmuseum.org, 8:30am-10pm daily, adults $19-26, students, seniors, and veterans $15-22) and take a trip to Las Vegas's more recent past. The boneyard displays 200 old neon signs that were used to advertise casinos, restaurants, bars, and even a flower shop and a dry cleaner. Several have been restored to their

Fremont Street Experience

former glory and are illuminated during the more costly nighttime tours. The boneyard is not open for self-guided exploration, but the visitors center, housed in the scallop-shaped lobby of the historical La Concha Motel, offers a prime example of Googie architecture and can serve as a base for a do-it-yourself tour of restored neon displayed as public art. A word of caution: The neighborhood surrounding the museum and public neon signs is a bit sketchy after dark.

Lied Discovery Children's Museum

Voted Best Museum in Las Vegas by readers of the local newspaper for 21 out of the last 25 years, **Lied Discovery Children's Museum** (360 Promenade Pl., 702/382-3445, www.discoverykidslv.org, summer 10am-5pm Mon.-Sat., noon-5pm Sun., winter 9am-4pm Tues.-Fri., 10am-5pm Sat., noon-5pm Sun., $14.50) near the Smith Center in the cultural corridor presents more than 100 interactive scientific, artistic, and life-skill activities. Children enjoy themselves so much that they forget they're learning. Among the best permanent exhibits is *It's Your Choice,* which shows kids the importance of eating right and adopting a healthy lifestyle. Exhibits show kids creative ways to explore their world: drama, cooperation, dance, and visual arts. *The Summit* is the playground jungle gym on steroids—three levels of slides, ladders, tubes, and interactive experiments. *Solve It! Mystery Town* lets junior CSI agents gather evidence and practice the scientific method.

Mormon Fort

The tiny **Mormon Fort** (500 E. Washington Ave., 702/486-3511, http://parks.nv.gov, 8am-4:30pm Tues.-Sat., $1, under 12 free) is the oldest building in Las Vegas. The adobe remnant, constructed by Mormon missionaries in 1855, was part of their original town site, the first permanent non-native settlement in the valley, which they abandoned in 1858. It then served as a store, a barracks, and a shed

on the Gass-Stewart Ranch. After that, the railroad leased the old fort to various tenants, including the Bureau of Reclamation, which stabilized and rebuilt the shed to use as a concrete-testing laboratory for Hoover Dam. In 1955 the railroad sold the old fort to the Elks, who in 1963 bulldozed the whole wooden structure (except the little remnant) into the ranch swimming pool and torched it.

Now a state park, the museum includes a visitors center, a re-creation of the original fort built around the remnant, and a re-creation of the little spring-fed creek that enticed the Mormons to put down roots here in the first place. A tour guide presents the history orally while display boards provide it visually. Your visit will not go unrewarded—it's immensely refreshing to see some preservation of the past in this city of the ultimate now.

★ Mob Museum

The **Museum of Organized Crime and Law Enforcement** (300 Stewart Ave., 702/229-2734, http://themobmuseum.org, 9am-9pm daily, $24, seniors, military, law enforcement, and teachers $18, age 11-17 $14, under age 11 free) chronicles Las Vegas's Mafia past and the cops and agents who finally ran the wiseguys out of town. The museum is inside the city's downtown post office and courthouse, appropriately the site of the 1951 Kefauver Hearing investigating organized crime.

Displays include the barber chair where Albert Anastasia was gunned down while getting a haircut, as well as an examination of the violence, ceremony, and hidden meanings behind Mafia "hits," all against a grisly background—the wall from Chicago's St. Valentine's Day Massacre that spelled the end of six members of Bugs Moran's crew and one hanger-on. *Bringing Down the Mob* displays the tools federal agents used—wiretaps, surveillance, and weapons—to clean up the town. Another section explores Hollywood's treatment of organized crime. Say hello to my little friend!

Downtown Arts District

Centered at South Main Street and East Charleston Boulevard, the district gives art lovers a concentration of galleries to suit any taste, plus an eclectic mix of shops, eateries, and other surprises. The **Arts Factory** (107 E. Charleston Blvd., 702/383-3133, www.theartsfactory.com), a two-story redbrick industrial building, is the district's birthplace. It hosts exhibitions, drawing classes, and poetry readings. Tenants include a toy shop, a yoga studio, a roller-skate store, a *très chic* bistro, and galleries and studios belonging to artists working in every medium and genre imaginable. One downstairs space, **Jana's RedRoom** (11am-7pm Wed.-Sun. and by appointment), displays and sells canvases by local artists.

Virtually all the galleries and other paeans to urban pop culture in the district participate in Las Vegas's **First Friday** (https://ffflv.org, 5pm-11pm 1st Fri. each month) event, which includes wine receptions, pub crawls, art lessons, and plenty of exhibits. Otherwise galleries keep limited hours, so if there's something you don't want to miss, call for an appointment.

Bringing art to the masses, the nonprofit **City of the World Art Gallery** (1229 S. Casino Center Blvd., 702/523-5306, www.cityoftheworldlasvegas.org, 1pm-5pm Sun. and Wed., 1pm-7pm Thurs., 11am-7pm Fri.-Sat., donation) showcases the works of dozens of local artists and offers classes for children and adults.

OFF THE STRIP
★ Las Vegas Springs Preserve

The **Las Vegas Springs Preserve** (333 S. Valley View Blvd., 702/822-7700, www.springspreserve.org, 10am-6pm daily, adults $19, students and over age 64 $17, age 5-17 $11, under age 5 free) is where Las Vegas began, at least from a Eurocentric viewpoint. More than 100 years ago, the first nonnatives in the Las Vegas Valley—Mormon missionaries from Salt Lake City—stumbled on this clear artesian spring. Of course, the native

A replica of a mammoth fossil uncovered in the state greets visitors to the Nevada State Museum.

Paiute and Pueblo people knew about the springs and exploited them millennia before the Mormons arrived. You can see examples of their tools, pottery, and houses at the site, now a 180-acre monument to environmental stewardship, historical preservation, and geographic discovery. The preserve is home to lizards, rabbits, foxes, scorpions, bats, and more. The nature-minded will love the cactus, rose, and sage gardens, and there's even an occasional cooking demonstration using the desert-friendly fruits, vegetables, and herbs grown here.

Las Vegas has become a leader in water conservation, alternative energy, and other environmentally friendly policies. The results of these efforts and tips on how everyone can reduce their carbon footprint are found in the Sustainability Gallery.

Nevada State Museum

Visitors can spend hours studying Mojave and Spring Mountains ecology, southern Nevada wildlife (both contemporary and prehistoric), and local mining and railroad history at the **Nevada State Museum** (309 S. Valley View Blvd., 702/486-5205, http://nvculture.org, 9am-5pm Tues.-Sun., $19, included in admission to the Springs Preserve, college students and ages 65 and over $17, age 5-17 $11, under age 5 free). Permanent exhibits on the 13,000-square-foot floor describe southern Nevada's role in warfare, mining, and atomic weaponry and include skeletons of a Columbian mammoth, which roamed the Nevada deserts 20,000 years ago, and the ichthyosaur, a whale-like remnant of the Triassic period. The *Nevada from Dusk to Dawn* exhibit explores the nocturnal lives of the area's animal species. Other exhibits trace the contributions of Las Vegas's gaming, marketing, and business communities.

★ Atomic Testing Museum

Members of the "duck and cover" generation will find plenty to spark Cold War memories at the **Atomic Testing Museum** (755 E. Flamingo Rd., 702/794-5151, www.nationalatomictestingmuseum.org, 10am-5pm Mon.-Sat., noon-5pm Sun., adults $22). Las Vegas embraced its role as ground zero in the development of the nation's atomic and nuclear deterrents after World War II. Business leaders welcomed defense contractors to town, and casinos hosted bomb-watching parties as nukes were detonated at the Nevada Test Site, a huge swath of desert 65 miles away. One ingenious marketer promoted the Miss Atomic Bomb beauty pageant in an era when patriotism overcame concerns about radiation.

The museum presents atomic history without bias, walking a fine line between appreciation of the work of nuclear scientists, politicians, and the military and the catastrophic consequences their activities and decisions could have wrought. The museum's best permanent feature is a short video in the Ground Zero Theatre, a multimedia simulation of an actual atomic explosion. The theater, a replica of an observation bunker, is rigged for motion, sound, and rushing air.

One gallery helps visitors put atomic energy milestones in historical perspective, along with the age's impact on 1950s and 1960s pop culture. Another permanent exhibit explains the effects of radiation and how it is tracked and measured. Just as relevant today are the lectures and traveling exhibits that the museum hosts.

Computer simulators, high-speed photographs, Geiger counters and other testing and safety equipment, along with first-person accounts, add to the museum's visit-worthiness.

Marjorie Barrick Museum of Art

The **Marjorie Barrick Museum of Art** (4505 S. Maryland Pkwy., 702/895-3381, www.unlv.edu/barrickmuseum, 9am-5pm Mon.-Fri., noon-5pm Sat., donation), on the University of Nevada, Las Vegas (UNLV) campus, is a good place to bone up on renowned artists such as Llyn Foulkes, Richard Tuttle, and Edda Renouf, as well as artists with ties to southern Nevada.

Other displays include collections of pre-Columbian native baskets, kachinas, masks, weavings, pottery, jewelry, and urban art in various media, along with an auditorium offering screenings of independent and experimental film.

The **Donald H. Baepler Xeric Garden** is adjacent.

Entertainment

HEADLINERS AND PRODUCTION SHOWS

Production shows are classic Las Vegas-style diversions, the kind that most people identify with the Entertainment Capital of the World. An American version of French burlesque, the Las Vegas production show has been gracing various stages around town since the late 1950s. Recently, however, these variety shows have evolved from distinct acts—a juggler, followed by a contortionist, magician, acrobat, etc. Today, many shows incorporate these talented performers, but in the context of a connected story. The Cirque du Soleil franchise is a good example. Most other variety shows have given way to more one-dimensional, specialized productions of superstar imitators, jukebox musical revues, and striptease acts masquerading as song-and-dance programs. Most of these are large-budget, skillfully produced and presented extravaganzas, and they make for highly entertaining nights on the town.

As Las Vegas has grown into a sophisticated metropolis, with gourmet restaurants, trendy boutiques, and glittering nightlife, it has also attracted Broadway productions to compete with the superstar singers—many now signing extended-engagement mini residencies—that helped launch the town's legendary status.

Since they're so expensive to produce, the big shows are fairly reliable, and you can count on them being around for the life of this book's edition. They do change on occasion; the smaller shows come and go with some frequency, but unless a show bombs and is gone in the first few weeks, it'll usually be around for at least a year. All this big-time entertainment is centered, of course, around Las Vegas's casino resorts, with the occasional concert at the Thomas & Mack Center on the UNLV campus.

Absinthe

As great as they are, the world-class singers and dancers and specialty acts featuring astounding acts of balance, athleticism, magic, striptease, and other vaudeville- and cabaret-inspired performances aren't even the main attraction in **Absinthe** (Caesars Palace, 3570 Las Vegas Blvd. S., 800/745-3000, www.absinthevegas.com, 8pm and 10pm Wed.-Sun., $99-139). That distinction goes to The Gazillionaire, the show's foul-mouthed, sleaze ball ringmaster, and his female counterpart.

If you go, leave your inhibitions and prudishness at home, lest you find yourself the target of the Gazillionaire's barbs. In-the-round audience configuration ensures there's not a bad seat in the house, but with VIP tickets, the performers are, sometimes literally, right in your lap.

Avengers S.T.A.T.I.O.N.

Immerse yourself in one of the most enduring entertainment franchises going at **Avengers S.T.A.T.I.O.N.** (Treasure Island, 3300 Las Vegas Blvd. S., 702/894-7722, www.stationattraction.com, 10am-10pm daily, $34, age 4-11 $24). You can train to become a Marvel Avenger at this interactive Scientific Training and Tactical Intelligence Operative Network center, full of movie props like a life-size Iron Man suit and David Banner's laboratory. Guests will be tested on their Marvel superhero knowledge with trivia questions throughout. The same creative team is developing a similar museum/experience (not yet open at the time of writing) based on the **Transformers.**

Baz—Star Crossed Love

Baz—Star Crossed Love (Palazzo, 3325 Las Vegas Blvd. S., 702/414-9000, www.venetian.com, 7pm Tues.-Sun., $64-86) reimagines love songs from the films of director Baz Luhrmann. Performers sing and dance their way through highlights from *Moulin Rouge*, *The Great Gatsby*, and *Romeo and Juliet*.

Tables placed on the stage and banquettes arranged in a semicircle give the production a theater-in-the-round feel, evoking a cabaret floor show. It's almost as if Luhrmann had this show in mind when he selected the songs that appeared in his films. Despite the movies' historical settings, the soundtracks feature contemporary pop songs rather than mood music or stereotypical musical theater standards. As a result, the songs evoking doomed love affairs play well with the show's polished choreography.

Blue Man Group

Bald, blue, and silent (save for homemade PVC musical instruments), **Blue Man Group** (Luxor, 3900 Las Vegas Blvd. S., 702/262-4400 or 877/386-4658, www.blueman.com, 7pm and 9:30pm daily, $69-128) was one of the hottest things to hit the Strip when it debuted in 2000 after successful versions in New York, Boston, and Chicago. It continues to wow audiences with its thought-provoking, quirkily hilarious gags and percussion performances. It is part street performance, part slapstick, and all fun.

Carrot Top

With fresh observational humor, outrageous props, and flaming orange hair, Scott Thompson stands alone as the only true full-time headlining stand-up comic in Las Vegas. He's also better known as **Carrot Top** (Luxor, 3900 Las Vegas Blvd. S., 702/262-4400 or 800/557-7428, www.luxor.com, 8pm Wed.-Mon., $55-76). His rapid-fire, stream-of-consciousness delivery ricochets from sex-aid props and poop jokes to current events, pop culture, and social injustice, making him the thinking person's class clown.

Chippendales

With all the jiggle-and-tease shows on the Strip, **Chippendales** (Rio, 3700 W. Flamingo Rd., 702/777-7776, www.chippendales.com, 8:30pm and 10:30pm Thurs.-Sat., 8:30pm

Sun.-Wed., $55-90) delivers a little gender equity. Tight jeans and rippled abs bumping and grinding with their female admirers may be the main attraction, but the choreography is more tasteful than most similar shows, and the guys really can dance. The "firefighters," "cowboys," and other manly man fantasy fodder boys dance their way through sultry and playful renditions of "It's Raining Men" and other tunes with similar themes. They occasionally stroll through the crowd flirting and lap-sitting. However, there is a hands-off policy (wink, wink).

Circus 1903

Feats of strength, daring, comedy, and skill recall the golden age of the big top at **Circus 1903** (Paris, 3655 Las Vegas Blvd. S., 702/777-2782, 7pm Tues.-Sun., some 3pm matinees Sat.-Sun., $55-129). This circus is turn-of-the-century authentic, from its top-hatted, handlebar-mustachioed ringmaster to its precariously perched acrobats. State-of-the-art sound and lighting and comfortable theater seats are the only bow to modern production values—other than the elephants. Named Queenie and Peanut, the pachyderms are actually realistic life-sized puppets, created by the same geniuses who brought *War Horse* to the stage.

Donny and Marie

A little bit country, a little bit rock-and-roll, **Donny and Marie Osmond** (Flamingo, 3555 Las Vegas Blvd. S., 702/733-3333, www. caesars.com, 7:30pm Tues.-Sat., $116-134) manage a bit of hip-hop and soul as well, as they hurl affectionate put-downs at each other between musical numbers. The most famous members of the talented family perform their solo hits, such as Donny's "Puppy Love" and Marie's "Paper Roses," along with perfect-harmony duets, while their faux sibling rivalry comes through with good-natured ribbing.

Terry Fator

America's Got Talent champion **Terry Fator** (Mirage, 3400 Las Vegas Blvd. S.,

702/792-7777, www.terryfator.com, 7:30pm Mon.-Thurs., $65-142) combines two disparate skills—ventriloquism and impersonation—to channel Elvis, Garth Brooks, Lady Gaga, and others. Backed by a live band, Fator sings and trades one-liners with his foam rubber friends. The comedy is fresh and mostly clean, the impressions spot-on, and the ventriloquism accomplished with nary a lip quiver.

Fear the Walking Dead

Because Las Vegas naturally will be the Armageddon of the zombie apocalypse, guests can receive their basic training at **Fear the Walking Dead** (425 Fremont St., 702/947-8342, www.vegasexperience.com, 1pm-1am Sun-Thurs., 1pm-2am Fri.-Sat., $30), in the Fremont Street Experience. Only the most intrepid and dexterous will escape the brain-eaters by negotiating this part haunted house, part escape room, part video game attraction.

Kà

Cirque du Soleil's *Kà* (MGM Grand, 3799 Las Vegas Blvd. S., 702/531-3826, www.mgmgrand.com, 7pm and 9:30pm Sat.-Wed., $75-209) explores the yin and yang of life through the story of separated twins journeying to meet their shared fate. Martial arts, acrobatics, puppetry, plenty of flashy pyrotechnics, and lavish sets and costumes bring cinematic drama to the variety-show acts. Battle scenes play out on two floating, rotating platforms. The show's title was inspired by the ancient Egyptian belief of *ka*, in which every human has a spiritual duplicate.

Legends in Concert

The best of the celebrity impersonator shows, *Legends in Concert* (Flamingo, 3555 Las Vegas Blvd. S., 702/777-2782, www.legendsinconcert.com, 7:30pm and 9:30pm Mon., 9:30pm Tues., 4pm and 9:30pm Wed.-Thurs. and Sat., 7:30pm Sun., $53-82), brings out the "stars" in rapid-fire succession. Madonna barely finishes striking a pose

before Janis Joplin gives us another little piece of her heart. Each show features four acts; two generally rotate, while Elvis and Michael Jackson appear in almost every show.

Le Rêve

All the spectacle we've come to expect from the creative geniuses behind Cirque du Soleil is present in the aquatic stream-of-unconsciousness *Le Rêve* (Wynn, 3131 Las Vegas Blvd. S., 702/770-9966, www.wynnlasvegas.com, 7pm and 9:30pm Fri.-Tues., $115-175). The loose concept is a romantically conflicted woman's fevered dream (*rêve* in French). Some 80 perfectly sculpted specimens of human athleticism and beauty flip, swim, dive, and show off their muscles around a huge pool/stage. More than 2,000 guests fill the theater in the round, with seats all within 50 feet; those in the first couple of rows are in the "splash zone." Clowns and acrobats complete the package.

★ Love

For Beatles fans visiting Las Vegas, all you need is *Love* (Mirage, 3400 Las Vegas Blvd. S., 866/983-4279, www.cirquedusoleil.com/love, 7pm and 9:30pm Thurs.-Mon., $86-196). This Cirque du Soleil-produced journey down Penny Lane features dancers, aerial acrobats, and other performers interpreting the Fab Four's lyrics and recordings. With the breathtaking visual artistry of Cirque du Soleil and a custom sound-scape using the original master tapes from Abbey Road Studios, John, Paul, George, and Ringo have never looked or sounded so good.

Magic Mike Live

Is it hot in here, or is it just the 13 studs parading around the *Magic Mike Live* stage (Hard Rock, 4455 Paradise Rd., 800/745-3000, www.magicmikelivelasvegas.com, 7pm and 10pm Wed.-Sun., $49-139)? Based on the wildly popular movies, the show features baby oil-slathered hunks in tight jeans, tear-away T-shirts, and less strutting around a facsimile of Club Domina.

Mystère

Celebrating the human form in all its beauty, athleticism, and grace, *Mystère* (Treasure Island, 3300 Las Vegas Blvd. S., 702/894-7722 or 800/392-1999, www.cirquedusoleil.com/mystere, 7pm and 9:30pm Sat.-Wed., $76-149) is the Vegas Cirque du Soleil production that most resembles a traditional American circus. But among the trapeze artists, feats of strength, and clowning around, Mystère also plays on other performance archetypes, including classical Greek theater, Kabuki, and surrealism. The first Cirque show in Las Vegas, *Mystère* continues to dazzle audiences with its revelations of life's mysteries.

O

Bellagio likes to do everything bigger, better, and more extravagant, and *O* (Bellagio, 3600 Las Vegas Blvd. S., 866/983-4279, www.cirquedusoleil.com/O, 7:30pm and 9:30pm Wed.-Sun., $107-187) is no exception. This Vegas Cirque du Soleil incarnation involves a $90 million set, 80 artists, and a 1.5-million-gallon pool of water. The title comes from the French word for water, *eau,* pronounced like the letter O in English. The production involves both terrestrial and aquatic feats of human artistry, athleticism, and comedy.

Penn & Teller

The oddball comedy magicians **Penn & Teller** (Rio, 3700 W. Flamingo Rd., 702/777-2782, www.pennandteller.com, 9pm Sat.-Wed., $77-97) have a way of making audiences feel special. Seemingly breaking the magicians' code, they reveal the preparation and sleight-of-hand involved in performing tricks. The hitch is that even when forewarned, observers still often can't catch on. And once they do, the verbose Penn and silent Teller add a wrinkle no one expects.

Raiding the Rock Vault

Join rock archaeologists as they unearth the treasures of the 1960s, '70s, and '80s in *Raiding the Rock Vault* (Hard Rock, 4455 Paradise Rd., 800/745-3000, www.raidingtherockvault.com, 8pm Sat.-Wed., $69-109). Each room of the vault brings a rock era to life, with members of music's hit-makers—Bon Jovi, Quiet Riot, Whitesnake, Guns N' Roses, Heart, and more—performing the best arena anthems.

Tournament of Kings

Pound on the table with your goblet and let loose a hearty "huzzah!" to cheer your king to victory over the other nations' regents at

entrance to *Love*

the *Tournament of Kings* (Excalibur, 3580 Las Vegas Blvd. S., 702/597-7600, www.excalibur.com, 6pm and 8:30pm Sat.-Mon. and Wed.-Thurs., $76). Each section of the equestrian theater rallies under separate banners as their hero participates in jousts, sword fights, riding contests, and lusty-maid flirting at this festival hosted by King Arthur and Merlin. A regal feast, served medieval style (that is, without utensils), starts with a tureen of dragon's blood (tomato soup). But just as the frivolity hits its climax, an evil lord appears to wreak havoc. Can the kings and Merlin's magic save the day? One of the best family shows in Las Vegas.

Zumanity

Cirque du Soleil seems to have succumbed to the titillation craze with the strange melding of sensuality, athleticism, and voyeurism that is *Zumanity* (New York New York, 3790 Las Vegas Blvd. S., 866/983-4279, www.cirquedusoleil.com/zumanity, 7pm and 9:30pm Tues.-Sat., $75-145). The cabaret-style show makes no pretense of story line, but instead takes audience members through a succession of sexual and topless fantasies—cellmates, sexual awakening, bathing beauties, ménage-à-trois, and more for the uninhibited over-18 crowd.

SHOWROOM AND LOUNGE ACTS

Showrooms are another Las Vegas institution, with most hotels providing live entertainment—usually magic, comedy, or tributes to the big stars who played or are playing the big rooms and theaters under the same roofs.

The Vegas lounge act is the butt of a few jokes and more than one satire, but they offer some of the best entertainment values in town—a night's entertainment for the price of a few drinks and a small cover charge. Every hotel in Las Vegas worth its salt has a lounge, and the acts change often enough to make them hangouts for locals. These acts are listed in the free entertainment magazines and the *Las Vegas Review-Journal*'s helpful website (www.lvrj.com), but unless you're familiar with the performers, it's the luck of the draw: They list only the entertainer's name, venue, and showtimes.

The Rat Pack Is Back

Relive the golden era when Frank, Dean, Sammy, and Joey ruled the Strip with *The Rat Pack Is Back* (Tuscany, 255 E. Flamingo Rd., 702/947-5981, www.ratpackisback.com, 7:30pm Mon.-Sat., $60-66). Watch Sinatra try to make it through "Luck Be a Lady" amid the others' sophomoric antics. Frank plays right along, pretending to rule his crew with an iron fist, as the crew treats him with the mock deference the Chairman of the Board deserves.

All Shook Up: A Tribute to the King

A swivel-hipped, curled-lip journey through his career, *All Shook Up* (Planet Hollywood, 3667 Las Vegas Blvd. S., 702/260-7200, www.vtheaterboxoffice.com, 6pm daily, $60-70) is the only all-Elvis impersonator show on the Strip. Both rotating impressionists bear a strong resemblance to the King, capturing not only his voice but also his mannerisms, as they recount Elvis's hits from rock-and-roll pioneer to movie idol. The intimate 300-seat showroom makes every seat a good one.

Mac King Comedy Magic Show

The quality of afternoon shows in Las Vegas is spotty at best, but **Mac King Comedy Magic Show** (Harrah's, 3475 Las Vegas Blvd. S., 866/983-4279, www.mackingshow.com, 1pm and 3pm Tues.-Sat., $36-47) fits the bill for talent and affordability. King's routine is clean both technically and content-wise. With a plaid suit, good manners, and a silly grin, he cuts a nerdy figure, but his tricks and banter are skewed enough to make even the most jaded teenager laugh.

Divas Las Vegas

Veteran female impersonator Frank Marino has been headlining on the Strip for 25 years, and he still looks good—with or without eye shadow and falsies. Marino stars as emcee

Joan Rivers, leading fellow impersonators who lip-synch their way through cheeky renditions of tunes by Lady Gaga, Katy Perry, Madonna, and others in *Divas Las Vegas* (The Linq, 3535 Las Vegas Blvd. S., 702/777-2782 or 866/574-3851, www.caesars.com, 9:30pm Sat.-Thurs., $26-98).

Gordie Brown

A terrific song stylist in his own right, **Gordie Brown** (Hooters Casino Hotel, 115 E. Tropicana Ave., 702/483-8056, www.hooterscasinohotel.com, 7:30pm Wed.-Thurs. and Sat.-Mon., $45-55) is the thinking person's singing impressionist. Using his targets' peccadilloes as fodder for his song parodies, Brown pokes serious fun with a surgeon's precision. Props, mannerisms, and absurd vignettes add to the madcap fun. But make no mistake—behind the gimmicks, Brown is not only a talented impressionist but a gifted singer in his own right, no matter whose voice he uses.

Comedy

Comedy in Las Vegas has undergone a shift in recent years. Nearly gone are the days of top-name comedians as resident headliners. Those gigs increasingly go to singers and production shows. In fact, Carrot Top, at the Luxor, is about the only long-term funnyman left. However, **The Venetian** (3355 Las Vegas Blvd. S., 866/641-7469, www.venetian.com) regularly books funny females for its *Lipshtick* shows (nights and times vary, $54-118), such as Lisa Lampanelli, Joy Behar, and other A-listers. The other biggies—Daniel Tosh, Jay Leno, and Ron White, among others—still make regular appearances as part of the **Aces of Comedy** (Mirage, 3400 Las Vegas Blvd. S., 702/791-7111, www.mirage.com, 7:30pm-10pm Fri.-Sat., $50-60). But most of the yuks nowadays come from the talented youngsters toiling in the comedy club trenches.

The journeymen and up-and-coming have half a dozen places to land gigs when they're in town. Among the best are **Brad** **Garrett's Comedy Club** (MGM Grand, 3799 Las Vegas Blvd. S., 866/740-7711, www.bradgarrettcomedy.com, 8pm daily, $43-65, plus $22 when Garrett performs), **L.A. Comedy Club** (Stratosphere, 2000 Las Vegas Blvd. S., 702/380-7777 or 800/998-6937, www.thelacomedyclub.com, 8pm daily, 6pm and 10pm shows some nights, $47-64), **Laugh Factory** (Tropicana, 801 Las Vegas Blvd. S., 702/739-2222, www.laughfactory.com, 8:30pm and 10:30pm daily, $38-55), **Las Vegas Live** (Planet Hollywood, 3667 Las Vegas Blvd. S., 702/260-7200, www.lasvegaslivecomedyclub.com, 9pm daily, $56-67), and **Jokesters** (The D, 301 Fremont St., 702/388-2111, www.jokesterslasvegas.com, 10:30pm daily, $30-40).

Magic

Magic shows are nearly as ubiquitous as comedy, with the more accomplished, such as Penn & Teller at Rio and **David Copperfield** (MGM Grand, 3799 Las Vegas Blvd. S., 866/740-7711, www.davidcopperfield.com, 7pm and 9:30pm Sun.-Fri., 4pm, 7pm, and 9:30pm Sat., $78-123), playing long-term gigs in their own showrooms.

The best smaller-scale magicians also have the distinction of being kid-friendly. In addition to Mac King at Harrah's, two other clean prestidigitators have taken up residency at Planet Hollywood. Both are *America's Got Talent* alumni. **Nathan Burton Comedy Magic** (Planet Hollywood, 3663 Las Vegas Blvd. S., 866/932-1818, www.nathanburton.com, 4pm Tues., Thurs., and Sat.-Sun., $50-60) serves up epic disappearing acts, while **Murray the Magician** (Planet Hollywood, 3663 Las Vegas Blvd. S., 866/932-1818, www.murraymagic.com, 4pm Sat.-Mon. and Thurs., $60-80) mixes comedy banter with his sleight of hand.

LIVE MUSIC

With all the entertainment that casinos have to offer—and the budgets to bring in the best—there's some surprising talent lurking in the dives, meat markets, and neighborhood pubs around Las Vegas. Locals who don't want to deal with the hassles of a trip to the Strip and visitors whose musical tastes don't match the often-mainstream pop-rock-country genre of the resort lounges might find a gem or two by venturing away from the neon.

The newest, best, and most convenient venue for visitors, **Brooklyn Bowl** (The Linq Promenade, 3545 Las Vegas Blvd. S., Ste. 22, 702/862-2695, www.brooklynbowl.com, 5pm-late daily) replicates its successful New York City formula with 32 lanes, comfortable couches, beer, and big-name groups sprinkled among the party band lineup. Elvis Costello, Wu-Tang Clan, Jane's Addiction, and the Psychedelic Furs are among the notables that have played the Brooklyn. Showtimes range from noon to midnight, often with several acts slated throughout the day.

The best indie bands in Las Vegas, as well as touring jammers, electropoppers, and garage bands, make it a point to play the **Bunkhouse Saloon** (124 S. 11th St., 702/982-1764, www.bunkhousedowntown.com, 5pm-1am Sun.-Mon. and Wed.-Thurs., 5pm-2am Fri.-Sat.). **Count's Vamp'd** (6750 W. Sahara Ave., 702/220-8849, www.vampdvegas.com, 11am-2am daily) books a mix of tribute bands and '80s metal icons appearing solo or with their newest project. Progressive metal and punk fans should check out **Backstage Bar & Billiards** (601 Fremont St., 702/382-2227, www.backstagebarlv.com, 8pm-3am Tues.-Sat.).

With more than 20,000 square feet of space and a 2,500-square-foot dance floor, **Stoney's Rockin' Country** (6611 Las Vegas Blvd. S., Ste. 160, 702/435-2855, http://stoneysrockincountry.com, 7pm-2am Wed.-Sat.) in the Town Square mall could almost *be* its own country. It is honky-tonk on a grand scale, with a mechanical bull and line-dancing lessons. Muddy Waters, Etta James, B. B. King, and even Mick Jagger have graced the stage at the reopened **Sand Dollar** (3355 Spring Mountain Rd., 702/485-5401, http://thesanddollarlv.com, 7pm-3am Tues.-Sun.), where blue-collar blues and smoky jazz rule. Bands start around 10pm weekends. The

people your mama warned you about hang out at the never-a-cover-charge **Double Down Saloon** (4640 Paradise Rd., 702/791-5775, www.doubledownsaloon.com, 24 hours daily), drinking to excess and thrashing to the punk, ska, and psychobilly bands on stage.

THE ARTS

With so much plastic, neon, and reproduction statuary around town, it's easy to accuse Las Vegas of being a soulless, cultureless wasteland, and many have. But Las Vegans don't live in casino hotels and eat every meal in the buffet. We don't all make our living as dealers and cocktail waitresses. Las Vegas, like most others, is a city built of communities. So why shouldn't Las Vegas enjoy and foster the arts? As home to an urban university and many profitable businesses just itching to prove their corporate citizenry, southern Nevada's arts are as viable as those of any city of comparable size in the country.

The local performing arts are thriving, thanks to the 2012 construction of the **Smith Center for the Performing Arts** (361 Symphony Park Ave., 702/749-2012, www.thesmithcenter.com), a major cog in the revitalization of downtown, along with the development of 61 acres of former Union Pacific Railroad land the city has been working to turn into a pedestrian-friendly park and showplace. It is home to the Las Vegas Philharmonic, the Nevada Ballet Theatre, the Cabaret Jazz series, local and school performances and classes, and the best professional theatrical touring companies.

Classical Music

The **Las Vegas Philharmonic** (702/258-5438, http://lvphil.org) presents a full schedule of pops, masterworks, holiday, and youth performances at the Smith Center. The Phil also works with the local school district to develop music education classes.

Ballet

With a 36,000-square-foot facility, **Nevada Ballet Theatre** (702/243-2623, www.

nevadaballet.org) trains hundreds of aspiring ballet, jazz, tap, hip-hop, and other dancers age 18 months through adults and provides practice and performance space for its professional company. The company presents classical and contemporary performances throughout the year at the Smith Center. The **Las Vegas Ballet Company** (702/240-3262, www.lasvegasballet.org) was founded by former Nevada Ballet Theatre principal dancers as a performance outlet for students. Advanced students perform periodically throughout the valley.

Theater

Theater abounds in Las Vegas, with various troupes staging mainstream plays, musical comedy, and experimental productions. **Las Vegas Little Theatre** (3920 Schiff Dr., 702/362-7996, www.lvlt.org), the town's oldest community troupe, performs mostly mainstream shows in its Mainstage series and takes a few more chances on productions in its Black Box theater. **Cockroach Theatre Company** (1025 S. 1st St., 702/818-3422, www.cockroachtheatre.com) stages mostly serious productions (think Camus and Albee as well as budding masters like Kristoffer Diaz) in the Art Square building in the arts district.

Focusing on American works new and classic, **Majestic Repertory Theatre** (1217 S. Main St., 702/423-6366, www.majesticrepertory.com) spotlights the issues society faces today, often through the lens of history or via new perspectives on historical "truths." Presenting provocative works and staged readings, **A Public Fit** (100 S. Maryland Pkwy., 702/735-2114, www.apublicfit.org) is all about the story, including audience-led interactive discussions following the performances in order to elicit perspectives, nuances, and shared experiences based on the art.

The highest-quality acting and production values outside the Smith Center can be found at the **University of Nevada, Las Vegas Performing Arts Center** (4505 S. Maryland Pkwy., 702/895-3535, http://pac.

unlv.edu), comprising the Artemus Ham Concert Hall, the Judy Bayley Theater, and the Alta Ham Black Box Theater. The **Nevada Conservatory Theatre,** the university's troupe of advanced students and visiting professional actors, directors, and set designers, performs fall-spring. Shows run from the farcical to the poignant: *The Bomb-itty of Errors* and *Peter Pan* took their place alongside *Macbeth* and *Sense and Sensibility* during the 2016-2017 season. The Performing Arts Center also hosts free lectures, opera, ballet, and modern dance, and even bodybuilding competitions.

Guests become witnesses, sleuths, and even suspects in **Marriage Can Be Murder** (The D, 301 Fremont St., 702/388-2111, www.marriagecanbemurder.com, 6:15pm daily, $66-99), an interactive dinner theater. The first stiff shows up just as you're finishing your salad, and before long the bodies start piling up between the one-liners and slapstick. Dig out your deerstalker and magnifying glass and help catch that killer.

Visual Art

Outside the downtown arts district and the fabulous art collections amassed and displayed at the Cosmopolitan and Wynn/Encore, the **Donna Beam Fine Art Gallery** (4505 S. Maryland Pkwy., 702/895-3893, www.unlv.edu/donnabeamgallery, 9am-5pm Mon.-Fri., noon-5pm Sat., free) at UNLV hosts exhibitions by nationally and internationally known painters, sculptors, designers, potters, and other visual artists. Most of the collection exudes contemporary examples of technical, as well as artistic, expertise, serving as teaching tools for UNLV students and the public. In addition to helping visitors enhance their critical thinking and aesthetic sensitivity, the exhibits teach students the skills needed in gallery management.

Sadly, Las Vegas has not had a municipal art gallery since the modest Las Vegas Art Museum—tucked into a corner of a branch library—closed in 2009. That may be changing, as a private group is raising funds, and the city has pledged to donate land near the Smith Center and the children's museum for **The Art Museum at Symphony Park,** an ambitious project that, if successful, would exhibit contemporary works, old masters, and more in an "architecturally significant" building.

RIDES AND GAMES
Stratosphere Tower

Daredevils will delight in the vertigo-inducing thrill rides on the observation deck at the **Stratosphere Tower** (2000 Las Vegas Blvd. S., 702/383-5210, www.stratospherehotel. com, 10am-1am Sun.-Thurs., 10am-2am Fri.-Sat., $15-120). The newest ride, Sky Jump Las Vegas, invites the daring to plunge into space for a 15-second free fall. Angled guide wires keep jumpers on target and ease them to gentle landings. This skydive without a parachute costs $120. The other rides are 100-story-high variations on traditional thrill rides: The Big Shot is a sort of 15-person reverse bungee jump; X-Scream sends riders on a gentle (at first) roll off the edge, leaving them suspended over Las Vegas Boulevard; Insanity's giant arms swing over the edge, tilting to suspend riders nearly horizontally. These attractions are $25 each, including the elevator ride to the top of the tower. Multiple-ride packages and all-day passes are available but don't include the Sky Jump.

SlotZilla

For an up-close, high-speed view of the Fremont Street Experience canopy and the iconic casino signs, take a zoom on **SlotZilla** (425 Fremont St., 702/678-5780, www. vegasexperience.com, 1pm-1am Sun.-Thurs., 1pm-2am Fri.-Sat., $25-45), a 1,750-foot-long zip line that takes off from the world's largest slot machine (only in Vegas, right?). Riders are launched horizontally, Superman-style, for a 40-mph slide. For the less adventurous, SlotZilla also operates a lower, slower, half-as-long version. Fly before 6pm to save $5 per ride.

SlotZilla

Adventuredome

Behind Circus Circus, the **Adventuredome Theme Park** (2880 Las Vegas Blvd. S., 702/794-3939, www.circuscircus.com, 10am-midnight daily summer, 10am-6pm Sun.-Thurs. and 10am-midnight Fri.-Sat. during the school year, over 48 inches tall $33, under 48 inches $19) houses two roller coasters, a 4-D motion simulator, laser beam mazes, climbing wall, miniature golf, and vertigo-inducing amusement machines—all inside a pink plastic shell. The main teen and adult attractions are the coasters—El Loco and Canyon Blaster, the only indoor double-loop, double-corkscrew coaster in the world, with speeds up to 55 mph, which is pretty rough. The five-acre fun park can host birthday parties. The all-day passes are a definite bargain over individual ride prices, but carnival games, food vendors, and special rides and games not included in the pass give parents extra chances to spend money. It's not the Magic Kingdom, but it has rides to satisfy all ages and bravery levels. Besides, Las Vegas is supposed to be the *adult* Disneyland.

Wet 'n' Wild

With rides conjuring Las Vegas, the desert, and the Southwest, **Wet 'n' Wild** (7055 Fort Apache Rd., 702/979-1600, www.wetnwildlasvegas.com, 10:30am-8pm Sun.-Thurs., 10:30am-10pm Fri.-Sat. June-Aug. and weekends and holidays Apr., May, and Sept., $35, discounts for seniors, guests under 42 inches tall, and entrance after 4pm) provides a welcome respite from the dry heat of southern Nevada. Challenge the Royal Flush Extreme, which whisks riders through a steep pipe before swirling them around a simulated porcelain commode and down the tube. The water park boasts 12 rides of varying terror levels along with a lazy river, wave pool, and Kiddie Cove. Guests must be over 42 inches tall to enjoy all the rides.

Cowabunga Bay

Wet 'n' Wild's competitor on the east side of town, **Cowabunga Bay** (900 Galleria Dr., Henderson, 702/850-9000, www.cowabungabayvegas.com, 11am-7pm Sun.-Thurs., 11am-10pm Fri.-Sat. June-Aug., limited days and hours Apr., May, and Sept., $40, under 48 inches $30) has nine waterslides, four pools, and the longest lazy river in the state.

Driving Experiences

Calling all gearheads! If you're ready to take the wheel of a 600-hp stock car, check out the **Richard Petty Driving Experience** (Las Vegas Motor Speedway, 7000 Las Vegas Blvd. N., 800/237-3889, www.drivepetty.com, days and times vary, $109-3,200). The Rookie Experience ($499) lets NASCAR wannabes put the stock car through its paces for eight laps around the 1.5-mile tri-oval after extensive in-car and on-track safety training. Participants also receive a lap-by-lap breakdown of their run, transportation to and from the Strip, and a tour of the Driving Experience Race Shop. Even more intense—and more

expensive—experiences, with more laps and more in-depth instruction, are available. To feel the thrill without the responsibility, opt for the three-lap ride-along ($109) in a two-seat stock car with a professional driver at the wheel.

Exotics Racing (6925 Speedway Blvd., Ste. C-105, 702/802-5662, www.exoticsracing.com, 7am-8pm Mon.-Fri., 8am-7pm Sat.-Sun., $300-500 for five laps), **Dream Racing** (7000 Las Vegas Blvd. N., 702/599-5199, www.dreamracing.com, $199-500 for five laps), and **Speed Vegas** (14200 Las Vegas Blvd. S., 888/341-7133, www.speedvegas.com, $39-99 per lap) offer similar pedal-to-the-metal thrills in Porsches, Ferraris, Lamborghinis, and more. All offer add-ons such as videos of your drive, passenger rates, and ride-alongs with professional drivers.

EVENTS

Just as Reno crams most of its annual events in the spring-fall months, Las Vegas's event season sidesteps the jarring heat of the summer months. The World Series of Poker, contested in air-conditioned comfort, is the only major southern Nevada event conducted from May through August.

March

Pennzoil 400 Weekend (7000 Las Vegas Blvd. N., 800/644-4444, www.lvms.com) is held in late February or early March, when the Monster Energy NASCAR race, Xfinity Series Boyd Gaming 300, and Camping World Truck Series pack in 140,000 race fans for paint-swapping action.

April

The intimate 2,800-capacity amphitheater at the Clark County Government Center amphitheater (500 S. Grand Central Pkwy.) hosts the **Las Vegas City of Lights Jazz and R&B Festival** (702/221-9771, www.yourjazz.com), an extravaganza of vocal and instrumental music. Funnel cakes, fried Twinkies, and the finest specimens of farmyard physique in southern Nevada gather over the four days of the **Clark County Fair and Rodeo** (1301

Whipple Ave., Logandale, 702/398-3247, www.ccfair.com). The largest rally in the western United States brings 75,000 Harley jockeys, wannabes, and hangers-on to the **Laughlin River Run** (949/502-3434, www.laughlinriverrun.com) to soak up the history with scenic rides through ghost towns and desert landscape, to get rowdy with classic rockers, and to swap road stories.

May

Some 150 race teams rumble over and through rugged desert terrain to claim top honors in the **Laughlin Desert Classic** (702/457-5775, www.bitd.com), sanctioned by the Best in the Desert Racing Series. The 16-mile course for unlimited classes includes high-banking hairpin turns and the "Laughlin Leap," where steely nerved drivers hurtle themselves and their cars off an earthen ramp.

June

Eat, drink, and be funky at **Blues, Brews, & BBQ** (Cannery Casino, 2121 E. Craig Rd., North Las Vegas, 702/507-5700, www.cannerycasino.com). Smokehouses and microbrewers serve up the refreshments, while jazz and blues bands perform throughout the evening.

July

Fortunes are awarded with the turn of the cards at the **World Series of Poker** (Rio, 3700 W. Flamingo Rd., 866/746-7671, wsop.com) as the top pros and lucky amateurs bluff, raise, and go all-in for their shot at poker immortality. The tournament lasts nearly all month, with bracelets awarded to winners of tournaments involving various poker versions and buy-in amounts.

October

Not nearly as wild as Laughlin River Days, **Bikefest** (899 E. Fremont St., 866/247-3337, www.lasvegasbikefest.com) nevertheless includes the requisite beer drinking, rock concert bikini contest, vendor fair, and poker run. Tough guys try to stay on three-quarter tons of meanness for eight seconds and scoop up scads of cash at the **Professional Bull Riders World Finals** (T-Mobile Arena, 3780 Las Vegas Blvd. S., 702/692-1600, www.pbrfinalsweek.com), the culmination of the PBR schedule. Complementary events include the National Barrel Horse Association's Dash for Cash and a Western apparel and gift expo.

November

Thousands run, jog, or walk the Strip and on a downtown course lined with musicians and other entertainers in the **Las Vegas Rock 'n' Roll Marathon** (800/311-1255, www.runrocknroll.com/las-vegas). Fitness supply vendors and pre- and post-race events draw top athletes from around the world. A half marathon and 10K event add to the fun.

December

The whole town polishes its Tony Lamas and slides into Wranglers as the world's best riders and ropers compete for obscene amounts of money over 10 days at the **National Finals Rodeo** (Thomas & Mack Center, 702/739-3267, www.nfrexperience.com). Casinos get into the act, rustlin' up parties, Western trade shows, and concerts by country music royalty. Members of the Lake Mead Boat Owners Association deck the decks of their watercraft and get into the holiday spirit at **Parade of Lights** (7000 Las Vegas Blvd. N., 800/644-4444, www.glitteringlightslasvegas.com). All sizes of floating floats compete for trophies and bragging rights. Businesses and civic organizations build and decorate intricately beautiful holiday displays, creating a **Magical Forest** on the campus of Opportunity Village, a nonprofit outfit that provides occupational training for people with intellectual disabilities. Proceeds help defray the cost of the training.

Sports and Recreation

GOLF

Las Vegas is chock-full of picturesque, world-class courses. All are eminently playable and fair, although the dry heat makes the greens fast, and the city's valley location can make for some havoc-wreaking winds in the spring. Many Las Vegas courses, especially in recent years, have removed extraneous water-loving landscaping, opting for xeriscape and desert landscape, irrigating the fairways and greens with reclaimed water. Still, lush landscaping and tricky water holes abound. Greens fees and amenities range from affordable municipal-type courses to some of the most exclusive country clubs anywhere. The following is a selective list in each budget category. There are bargains, if you're willing to brave the scorching afternoon temperatures. Fees are exponentially higher in the early morning and evening, when temperatures are bearable.

The only course open to the public on the Strip is **Bali Hai** (5160 Las Vegas Blvd. S., 888/427-6678, www.balihaigolfclub.com, $149-189), next to Mandalay Bay on the south end of casino row. The South Pacific theme includes lots of lush green tropical foliage, deep azure ponds, and black volcanic outcroppings. A handful of long par-4s are fully capable of making a disaster of your scorecard even before you reach the par-3 sphincter-clenching 16th. Not only does it play to an island green, it comes with a built-in gallery where others can enjoy your discomfort while dining on Bali Hai's restaurant patio.

There's plenty of water to contend with at **Siena Golf Club** (10575 Siena Monte Ave., 702/341-9200, www.sienagolfclub.com, $85). Six small lakes, deep fairway bunkers, and desert scrub provide significant challenges off the tee, but five sets of tee boxes even things out for shorter hitters. The large, flattish greens are fair and readable. The first Las Vegas course to adopt an ecofriendly xeriscape design, **Painted Desert** (5555 Painted Mirage Rd., 702/645-2570, www. painteddesertgc.com, $45-90) uses cacti, mesquite, and other desert plants to separate its links-style fairways. The 6,323-yard, par-72 course isn't especially challenging, especially if you're straight off the tee, making it a good choice for getting back to the fundamentals. Video tips from the 18-time major winner himself play on an in-cart screen at **Bear's Best** (11111 W. Flamingo Rd., 702/804-8500, www.clubcorp.com, $129-199), a collection of Jack Nicklaus's favorite holes from courses he designed: Castle Pines, PGA West, and more.

RACING

Home to two events (Mar. and Sept.) in the Monster Energy NASCAR Cup Series, the **Las Vegas Motor Speedway** (7000 Las Vegas Blvd. N., 702/644-4444, www.lvms.com) is a racing omniplex. In addition to the superspeedway, a 1.5-mile tri-oval for NASCAR races, the site also brings in dragsters to its quarter-mile strip; modifieds, late models, bandoleros, legends, bombers, and more to its paved oval; and off-roaders to its half-mile clay oval. There's also a motocross track and a road course. A multimillion-dollar renovation project between NASCAR Weekends in 2006 and 2007 created the Neon Garage in the speedway's infield. It brings fans up close with their favorite drivers and their crews, providing an unprecedented interactive fan experience. Neon Garage has unique and gourmet concession stands, live entertainment, and the winner's circle.

BOXING AND MIXED MARTIAL ARTS

Las Vegas retains the title as heavyweight **boxing** champion of the world. Nevada's legalized sports betting, its history, and the facilities at the MGM Grand Garden, Mandalay Bay Events Center, T-Mobile Arena, and other locations make it a natural for the biggest matches. For the megafights, expect to dole out big bucks to get inside the premier venues. The "cheap" seats at MGM and Mandalay Bay often cost a car payment and require the Hubble telescope to see any action. Ringside seats require a mortgage payment. Check the venues' websites for tickets.

Fight fans can find a card pretty much every month from March to October at either the Hard Rock, Sam's Town, Sunset Station, Palms, or other midsize arena or showroom. The fighters are hungry, the matches are entertaining, and the cost is low, with tickets priced $15-100. **Mixed martial arts** also continues to grow in popularity, with MGM and Mandalay Bay hosting UFC title fights about every other month.

SPECTATOR SPORTS

Southern Nevada's first major league franchise, the **Vegas Golden Knights** (T-Mobile Arena, 3780 Las Vegas Blvd. S., 702/645-4259, www.nhl.com) dropped the puck for the 2017-2018 season as the newest member of the National Hockey League's Western Conference Pacific Division. The team filled its roster with a league expansion draft, selecting one unprotected player from each of the NHL's other 30 teams, as well as free agent signings and participation in the 2017 amateur draft.

Coming quickly on the Golden Knights' heels, the Oakland Raiders announced they would move to Las Vegas for the 2020 season. The Raiders will play in a new, $2 billion retractable-roof stadium across I-15 from Mandalay Bay (though if things do not go well in Oakland, the Raiders may move a year early and play at Sam Boyd Stadium, the decrepit home of UNLV's football team). The new state-of-the-art stadium also would host UNLV football, international soccer, and other events.

Major League Baseball shows no sign of following the NHL and NFL's lead in rushing to Las Vegas. Instead, die-hard baseball fans must settle for the minor-league **Las Vegas 51s** of the Pacific Coast League. The 51s play at outdated **Cashman Field** (850 Las Vegas Blvd. S., 702/943-7200, www.milb.com, $7-26) downtown, though there is talk that a new stadium may be in the works in Summerlin, an affluent community on the west side of town.

OUT OF TOWN
Mount Charleston

As late as mid-May snow still clings stubbornly to 12,000-foot Mount Charleston, the jewel of the Spring Mountain range. Its elevation, resulting cool temperature, and more than 25 inches of precipitation a year, make Mount Charleston a summer oasis. Well-maintained roads allow two-wheel-drive vehicles to ascend to about 8,500 feet, high enough for a day of respite from the July heat or a December afternoon of sledding. Nearly a million Las Vegans and tourists take advantage of the mountain's recreational opportunities by hiking, camping, picnicking, and skiing among its natural wonders. Open season for campgrounds shortens as you climb in elevation, from nearly year-round at Fletcher View to late May through late September at McWilliams in Lee Canyon.

A little more than 10 miles from US 95, NV 157 climbs into the forest and gets canyony. For an alpine lodge honeymoon or just a hot chocolate on your way up or down the mountain, stop at the **Resort on Mt. Charleston** (2275 Kyle Canyon Rd., 702/872-5500, www.mtcharlestonresort.com, $107-126), which has a large, chalet-like lobby complete with roaring fireplace, bar with big TVs, a pool table, video poker machines, and spacious restaurant. Built in 1984, this romantic hideaway received a multimillion-dollar upgrade in 2010, making it a perfect place to propose (you can then return to Las Vegas and get married an hour or two later and come back to check into the resort's bridal suite).

Beyond the hotel, NV 157 continues another four miles. You first pass **Kyle Canyon Picnic Area,** about 5,000 feet higher in elevation than downtown Las Vegas (and at least 20 degrees cooler). A little farther along, **Fletcher View Campground**

(877/444-6777, $25 plus hookups) looms at 7,000 feet, with 12 sites (half can be reserved) for tents and trailers.

The road ends at **Mt. Charleston Lodge** (5375 Kyle Canyon Rd., 702/872-5408, http://mtcharlestonlodge.com, $135-270), the main action on the mountain. This is a funky alpine operation, with rustic one-room cabins and a restaurant. The cabins come in two sizes, single (500 square feet with a king bed) and double (900 square feet and two kings). There's no cell or Internet reception, but the lodge has a DVD library, the bar is open till midnight, and the restaurant serves warming fare (8am-10pm daily, $20-30).

Pull into the parking lot above the lodge for access to the easy half-mile **Little Falls Trail** and moderately more strenuous 0.75-mile **Cathedral Rock Trail,** with sheer drops but great views, as well as the hard nine-mile **North Loop Trail** to the peak.

On NV 157 just before the hotel, NV 158 heads off to the left and connects in six miles with NV 156, the Lee Canyon Road. **Robbers Roost** is a short, easy hike to a large rock grotto that, if you believe the legend, once sheltered local horse thieves. A mile north, **Hilltop Campground** (877/444-6777, $19-23) at 8,400 feet has asphalt pavement for RVs and tent sites up the hill. Access points to the southern loop of the **Charleston Peak Trail** and **Mahogany Grove** and **Deer Creek** picnic areas are up the road, and **Desert View Trail** is two miles farther on.

Back on US 95, about three miles past the Kyle Canyon turnoff to Mount Charleston (if you get to the turnoff for Lee Canyon, you've gone too far), turn right and drive four miles down the well-graded dirt and gravel road to **Desert National Wildlife Refuge** (16001 Corn Creek Rd., 702/879-6110, www.fws.gov/refuge/desert).

Picnic, spy on wildlife, or just stroll in the quiet and clean air and meditate among three spring-fed ponds, woodlands, and pastureland. You might see a great blue heron, red-tailed hawk, badger, or bighorn sheep,

but rabbits, squirrels, and mule deer are more common.

Lee Canyon

Past the Kyle Canyon turnoff on US 95, the Lee Canyon turnoff (NV 156) takes you to the **McWilliams Campground** (877/444-6777, $25), just before you get to the parking lot for the Lee Canyon ski resort. Renovated in 2013, the campground has 75 tent and camper sites. At 8,600 feet, the trees are still tall, but sparse, and there's little undergrowth, so there's lots of room between sites. Amenities include piped drinking water, picnic tables, and heated restrooms but not electricity.

Lee Canyon resort (6725 Lee Canyon Rd., 702/385-2754, www.leecanyonlv.com, 9am-4pm daily, lift tickets adults $70, under 12 and over 60 $30-40) is only 45 miles (and 6,500 feet) away from sizzling Sin City. It includes a terrain park and half-pipe for hotdoggers. Base elevation is 8,500 feet and the top of the chairlift is another 1,000 feet higher, but cliff walls towering above the slope protect skiers from biting westerlies. A beginner chairlift and ski school feed the bunny slope. The resort is open year-round, with disc golf, one-wheeling, and archery in summer.

Red Rock Canyon

West of Las Vegas, umber-, crimson-, lavender-, and rust-tinged sandstone vibrant enough to rival the brightest neon beckons visitors to **Red Rock Canyon National Conservation Area** (1000 Scenic Loop Dr., 702/515-5350, www.redrockcanyonlv.org, 6am-8pm daily Apr.-Sept., 6am-7pm daily Oct.-Mar., cars $7, motorcycles, bicycles, pedestrians $3, dry camping Sept.-Oct. $15).

As you drive on Charleston Boulevard westward 12 miles away from the casinos, the last vestiges of city sprawl give way to desert scrub and Joshua trees, as the mountains rise before you. As you round a final bend, Red Rock Canyon's 200,000 acres of unforgiving yet hospitable wilderness come into view. The large, interactive visitors center teaches about the trails, animals, plants, and recreational activities the park supports. Take in the big picture on the scenic drive that circumnavigates the park, with pullouts at popular trailheads, picnic areas, and scenic overlooks. On many warm, windless days, you'll spot rock climbers clinging to colorful rock faces in designated areas. When you're ready to stretch your legs, find the trail that fits your mood and fitness level.

Spring Mountain Ranch

Wild burros browse the sagebrush along the five-mile stretch of NV 159 between Red Rock Canyon and **Spring Mountain Ranch State Park** (6375 NV 159, 702/875-4141, http://parks.nv.gov, 8am-7pm daily Mar.-Oct., 8am-4:30pm daily Nov.-Feb., cars $9, bicycles $1). Some might be very friendly, but don't feed them. Not only is it bad for the burros, it's against the law.

Formerly a refuge from the desert heat (where Paiute Indians and early explorers found refreshing natural springs), the 530-acre park's later use as a working ranch is evidenced by the still-standing bunkhouse, blacksmith's shop, barn, cemetery, outhouse (a two-holer), and other structures. The main ranch house serves as the visitors center, where you can arrange a guided tour, inquire about picnic areas and campsites, and enroll in living-history programs.

The well-received **Super Summer Theatre** (702/579-7529, www. supersummertheatre.org, 8pm, $18.50, age 5 and under free) takes over the ranch for several weekends during the summer, presenting G-rated theater performances. Families are encouraged to bring lawn chairs, blankets, and picnic dinners to enjoy before the shows begin around dusk.

Floyd Lamb Park

Roughly 15 miles north of downtown Las Vegas on US 95, **Floyd Lamb Park** (9200 Tule Springs Rd., 702/229-8100, www. lasvegasnevada.gov, 8am-8pm daily Apr.-Sept., 9am-5pm daily Oct.-Mar., $6) is one of the most un-desert-looking places in the Las Vegas desert. Once a haven for prehistoric mammals and later to Indians and prospectors, the park contains **Tule Springs Fossil Beds National Monument,** where several remnants of Ice Age lions, mastodons, sloths, and camels have been found. The park's four stocked ponds are favorite local fishing holes.

Shopping

MALLS

The most upscale and most Strip-accessible of the traditional, non-casino-affiliated, indoor shopping complexes, **Fashion Show** (3200 Las Vegas Blvd. S., 702/369-8382, www. thefashionshow.com, 10am-9pm Mon.-Sat., 11am-7pm Sun.), across from the Wynn, is anchored by Saks Fifth Avenue, Dillard's, Neiman Marcus, Macy's, and Nordstrom. The mall gets its name from the 80-foot retractable runway in the Great Hall, where resident retailers put on fashion shows on weekend afternoons. Must-shop stores include Papyrus, specializing in stationery and gifts centering on paper arts and crafts, and The Lego Store, where blockheads can find specialty building sets tied to movies, video games, and television shows. Dine alfresco at a Strip-side café, shaded by "the cloud," a 128-foot-tall canopy that doubles as a projection screen.

If your wallet contains dozens of Ben Franklins, **Crystals at City Center** (3720 Las Vegas Blvd. S., 702/590-9299, www.simon. com, 10am-11pm Mon.-Thurs., 10am-midnight Fri.-Sat.) is your destination for impulse buys like a hand-woven Olimpia handbag from Bottega Veneta for her or a titanium timepiece from Porsche Design for him.

Parents can reward their children's patience with rides on cartoon animals, spaceships, and other kiddie favorites in the carpeted, clean play area at **Meadows Mall** (4300 Meadows Ln., 702/878-3331, www. meadowsmall.com, 10am-9pm Mon.-Sat., 10am-6pm Sun.). There are 140 stores and restaurants—all the usual mall denizens along with some interesting specialty shops. It's across the street from the Las Vegas Springs Preserve, so families can make a day of it. The **Boulevard Mall** (3528 S. Maryland Pkwy., 702/735-8268, www.boulevard-mall.com, 10am-9pm Mon.-Sat., 10am-6pm Sun.) is similar. It's in an older and less trendy setting, but a new facade, family attractions, and better dining are driving a comeback. Oddly, there's a large call center in the space recently vacated by the withdrawal of two anchor tenants.

A visit to **Town Square** (6605 Las Vegas Blvd. S., 702/269-5001, www. mytownsquarelasvegas.com, 10am-9pm Mon.-Thurs., 10am-10pm Fri.-Sat., 11am-8pm Sun.) is like a stroll through a favorite suburb. "Streets" wind between stores in Spanish, Moorish, and Mediterranean-style buildings. Mall stalwarts like Victoria's Secret and Abercrombie & Fitch are here, along with some unusual treats—Tommy Bahama's includes a café. Just as in a real town, the retail outlets surround a central square, which holds 13,000 square feet of mazes, tree houses, and performance stages. Around holiday time, machine-made snowflakes drift down through the trees. Nightlife ranges from laid-back wine and martini bars to rousing live entertainment and the 18-screen Rave movie theater.

Easterners and Westerners alike revel in the wares offered at **Chinatown Plaza** (4255 Spring Mountain Rd., 702/221-8448, http:// lvchinatownplaza.com, 10am-10pm daily). Despite the name, Chinatown Las Vegas is a pan-Asian clearinghouse where Asians can celebrate their history and heritage while stocking up on favorite reminders of home. Meanwhile, Westerners can submerge themselves in new cultures by sampling the offerings at authentic Chinese, Thai, Vietnamese, and other Asian restaurants and strolling the plaza reading posters explaining Chinese customs. Tea sets, silk robes, Buddha statuettes, and jade carvings are of particular interest, as is the Diamond Bakery, with its elaborate wedding cakes and sublime mango mousse cake.

CASINO PLAZAS

Almost two-thirds of the Las Vegas Strip's $19 billion in annual casino revenue comes from non-gaming activities. Restaurants and hotel rooms are the biggest contributors, but upscale shopping plazas—many with tenants that would feel right at home on Rodeo Drive, Ginza, or the Champs-Élysées—increasingly are doing their part to put brass in casino investors' pockets.

Caesars Palace initiated the concept of Las Vegas as a shopping destination in 1992 when it unveiled the **Forum Shops** (3570 Las Vegas Blvd. S., 702/893-3807, www.caesars.com, 10am-11pm Sun.-Thurs., 10am-midnight Fri.-Sat.). Top brand luxury stores coexist with fashionable hipster boutiques amid some of the best people-watching on the Strip. A stained-glass-domed pedestrian plaza greets shoppers as they enter the 175,000-square-foot expansion from the Strip. You'll find one of only two spiral escalators in the United States. The gods come alive hourly to extract vengeance in the *Fall of Atlantis* show, and you can check out the feeding of the fish in the big saltwater aquarium twice daily.

Part shopping center, part theater in the round, the **Miracle Mile** (Planet Hollywood, 3663 Las Vegas Blvd. S., 702/866-0703, www. miraclemileshopslv.com, 10am-11pm Sun.-Thurs., 10am-midnight Fri.-Sat.) is a delightful (or vicious, depending on your point of view) circle of shops, eateries, bars, and theaters. If your budget doesn't quite stand up to the Forum Shops, Miracle Mile could be just your speed. Low-cost shows include an Elvis tribute, the campy *Zombie Burlesque,* and family-friendly animal acts and magicians.

Las Vegas comedy icon Rita Rudner loves the **Grand Canal Shoppes** (Venetian, 3377 Las Vegas Blvd. S., 702/414-4525, www.grandcanalshoppes.com, 10am-11pm

Sun.-Thurs., 10am-midnight Fri.-Sat.) because "Where else but in Vegas can you take a gondola to the Gap?" There's not really a Gap here. It would stick out like a sore thumb among the shops that line the canal among streetlamps and cobblestones under a frescoed sky. Nature gets a digital assist in the photos for sale at Peter Lik gallery, and Armani and Diane von Furstenberg compete for your shopping dollar. The "Streetmosphere" includes strolling minstrels and specialty acts, and many of these entertainers find their way to St. Mark's Square for seemingly impromptu performances.

Hermes, Prada, Rolex, and Loro Piana count themselves among the tenants at the **Esplanade** (Wynn/Encore, 3131 Las Vegas Blvd. S., 702/770-7000, www.wynnlasvegas. com, 10am-11pm Sun.-Thurs., 10am-midnight Fri.-Sat.). Wide, curved skylights, fragrant flowers, and delicate artwork create a pleasant window-shopping experience.

Perfectly situated in the flourishing urban arts district, the **Downtown Container Park** (707 E. Fremont St., 702/359-9982, www.downtowncontainerpark.com, 11am-9pm Mon.-Thurs., 11am-10pm Fri.-Sat., 11am-8pm Sun.) packs 40 boutiques, galleries,

bars, and bistros into their own shipping containers. The Dome ($9-15), an IMAX-like theater with reclining chairs, shows immersive, surround-sound video rock band performances and nature documentaries. Container Park is the centerpiece of the Fremont East District, an ambitious development aimed at reclaiming a formerly dicey area with eateries, bars, and shops.

Unless you're looking for a specific item or brand, or you're attracted to the atmosphere, attractions, architecture, or vibe of a particular Strip destination, you can't go wrong browsing the shopping center in your hotel. You'll find shops just as nice at **Le Boulevard** (Paris, 3655 Las Vegas Blvd. S., 702/946-7000, www.boulevardmall. com, 8am-2am daily), **Grand Bazaar Shops** (Bally's, 3645 Las Vegas Blvd. S., 702/967-4366 or 888/266-5687, http:// grandbazaarshops.com, 10am-10pm Sun.-Thurs., 10am-11pm Fri.-Sat.), **The Linq** (3545 Las Vegas Blvd. S., 702/694-8100 or 866/328-1888, www.caesars.com, shop and restaurant hours vary), and **Mandalay Place** (Mandalay Bay, 3950 Las Vegas Blvd. S., 702/632-7777 or 877/632-7800, www. mandalaybay.com, 10am-11pm daily).

Forum Shops

Food

Las Vegas buffets have evolved from little better than fast food served in troughs to lavish spreads of worldwide cuisine complete with fresh salads, comforting soups, and decadent desserts. The exclusive resorts on the Strip have developed their buffets into gourmet presentations, often including delicacies such as crab legs, crème brûlée, and even caviar. Others, especially the locals' casinos and those downtown that cater to more down-to-earth tastes, remain low-cost belly-filling options for intense gamblers and budget-conscious families. The typical buffet breakfast presents the usual fruits, juices, croissants, steam-table scrambled eggs, sausages, potatoes, and pastries. Lunch is salads and chicken, pizza, spaghetti, tacos, and more. For dinner, buffets add steamed vegetables, mashed potatoes, and several varieties of meat, including a carving table with prime rib, turkey, and pork loin.

Buffets are still a big part of the Las Vegas vacation aura, but when the town's swank and swagger came back in the 1990s, it brought sophisticated dining with it. Las Vegas has come a long way from the coffee-and-sandwich shop shoved in a casino corner so players could recharge quickly and rush back to reclaim their slot machine. Most major hotels still have 24-hour coffee shops (often with a graveyard or gambler's special), a top-line steak/chop/seafood house, and a buffet along with a couple restaurants offering French, Italian, Asian, or Mexican fare. Non-casino restaurants around town are also proliferating quickly. Except for the high-brow and celebrity-chef spots, menu prices, like room rates, are consistently less expensive in Las Vegas than in any other major city in the country.

UPPER STRIP
Breakfast
It's all about the hen fruit at ★ **The Egg & I** (4533 W. Sahara Ave., Ste. 5, 702/364-9686, http://theeggworks.com, 6am-3pm daily, $10-20). They serve other breakfast fare as well, of course—the banana muffins and stuffed French toast are notable—but if you don't order an omelet, you're just being stubborn. It has huge portions, fair prices, and on-top-of-it service. Go!

The retro-deco gaudiness of the neon decor and bachelor pad-esque sunken fire pit may not do wonders for a Vegas-sized headache, but the tostada omelet at the **Peppermill Restaurant & Fireside Lounge** (2985 Las Vegas Blvd. S., 702/735-7635, www.peppermilllasvegas.com, 24 hours daily, $12-20) will give it what-for. For a little less zest, try the French toast ambrosia.

French and Continental
The pink accents at **Pamplemousse** (400 E. Sahara Ave., 702/733-2066, www.pamplemousserestaurant.com, 5pm-10pm daily, $35-56) hint at the name's meaning (grapefruit) and set the stage for romance. The cuisine is so fresh that the menu changes daily. Specialties include leg and breast of duck in cranberry-raspberry sauce and a rosemary and pistachio rack of lamb. Save room for chocolate soufflé.

Italian
Long a hangout for the Rat Pack, athletes, presidents, and certain Sicilian "businessmen," **Piero's** (355 Convention Center Dr., 702/369.2305, http://pieroscuisine.com, 5:30pm-10pm daily, $40-60) still attracts the celebrity set with leather booths, stone fireplace, stellar service, and assurance they won't be bothered by autograph hounds. The menu hasn't changed much since the goodfellas started coming here in the early 1980s; it's heavy (and we do mean "heavy") on the veal, breading, cheese, and sauce.

Wall frescoes put you on an Italian thoroughfare as you dine on authentic cuisine at **Fellini's** (Stratosphere, 2000 Las Vegas Blvd.

S., 702/383-4859, http://fellinislv.com, 5pm-11pm Sun.-Thurs., 5pm-midnight Fri.-Sat., $28-50). Each smallish dining room has a different fresco. The food is more contemporary and Americanized than the classic Italian served at Piero's, but only food snobs could find anything to complain about.

Steak

The perfectly cooked steaks and attentive service that once attracted Frank Sinatra, Nat "King" Cole, Natalie Wood, and Elvis are still trademarks at **Golden Steer** (308 W. Sahara Ave., 702/384-4470, www.goldensteerlasvegas.com, 4:30pm-10:30pm daily, $45-65). A gold rush motif and 1960s swankiness still abide here, along with classics like crab cakes, big hunks of beef, and Caesar salad prepared tableside.

Vegas Views

The 360-seat, 360-degree **Top of the World** (Stratosphere, 2000 Las Vegas Blvd. S., 702/380-7711 or 800/998-6937, www.topoftheworldlv.com, 11am-11pm daily, $50-80), on the 106th floor of Stratosphere Tower more than 800 feet above the Strip, makes a complete revolution once every 80 minutes, giving you the full city panorama during dinner. The view of Vegas defies description, and the food is a recommendable complement. Order the seafood fettuccine or surf-and-turf gnocchi with lobster and beef short rib. It's even money that you will witness (or receive) an offer of marriage during your meal. If you're the one popping the question, ask about their proposal packages.

CENTER STRIP
Asian

You may pay for the setting as much as for the food at **Fin** (The Mirage, 3400 Las Vegas Blvd. S., 866/339-4566, www.mirage.com, 5pm-10pm Thurs.-Mon., $40-60). But why not? Sometimes the atmosphere is worth it, especially when you're trying to make an impression on your mate or potential significant other. The metallic-ball curtains evoke

a rainstorm in a Chinese garden, setting just the right romantic mood. Still, it is difficult to pull off gourmet Chinese. While Fin's prices are not outrageous, the fare isn't much better than you could find at many midpriced restaurants; you can probably find more yum for your yuan elsewhere.

Better value can be had at **Tao Asian Bistro** (Venetian, 3377 Las Vegas Blvd. S., 702/388-8338, www.taolasvegas.com, 5pm-midnight daily, $35-50). Pan-Asian dishes—the roasted Thai Buddha chicken is our pick—and an extensive sake selection are served amid decor that is a trip through Asian history, including imperial koi ponds and a floating Buddha.

At **Wing Lei** (Wynn, 3131 Las Vegas Blvd. S., 702/770-3388, www.wynnlasvegas.com, 5:30pm-9:30pm Sun.-Thurs., 5:30pm-10pm Fri.-Sat., $50-75), French colonialism comes through in chef Ming Yu's Shanghai style. If you order one of the live seafood specialties, be prepared to part with a C-note—two if you opt for the red cod.

Breakfast/Brunch

Bright, airy with a touch of South Beach, **Tableau** (Wynn, 3131 Las Vegas Blvd. S., 702/770-3330, www.wynnlasvegas.com, 7am-2:30pm daily, $20-25), overlooking the pools from the garden atrium, changes its menu to suit the season. Any meal is a treat here, but the salmon eggs Benedict and pineapple coconut pancakes make breakfast the most important meal of the day at Wynn.

Buffets

At Caesars Palace's **Bacchanal Buffet** (3570 Las Vegas Blvd. S., 702/731-7928, www.caesars.com, 7:30am-10pm Mon.-Fri., 8am-10pm Sat.-Sun., $30-60, $15 wine, beer, and mimosa supplement), specialty dishes range from gourmet (smoked pork belly) to pub grub (Bacchanal sliders) and include plenty of international delicacies: curry, dim sum, crepes, and more, prepared in bustling show kitchens and with many presented small-plate style.

Italian

It's no surprise that a casino named after the most romantic of Italian cities would be home to one of the best Italian restaurants around. **Canaletto** (Venetian, 3377 Las Vegas Blvd. S., 702/733-0070, www.venetian.com, 11am-11pm Sun.-Thurs., 11am-midnight Fri.-Sat., $28-40), of course, focuses on Venetian cuisine. The kitchen staff performs around the grill and rotisserie—a demonstration kitchen—creating sumptuously authentic dishes under a high vaulted ceiling. The spicy *salsiccia picante* thin-crust pizza gets our vote.

You can almost picture Old Blue Eyes himself between shows, a bourbon at his elbow, twirling linguini and holding court at **Sinatra** (Encore, 3131 Las Vegas Blvd. S., 702/770-5320 or 888/352-3463, www.wynnlasvegas.com, 5:30pm-10:30pm daily, $40-70). The Chairman's voice wafts through the speakers, and his iconic photos and awards decorate the walls while you tuck into classic Italian food tinged with chef Theo Schoenegger's special touches.

Seafood

Submerge yourself in the cool, fluid atmosphere at **AquaKnox** (Venetian, 3355 Las Vegas Blvd. S., 702/420-2541, http://aquaknox.net, 5:30pm-10pm daily, $40-70). Its cobalt and cerulean tableware offset by chrome, cream, and frosted glass suggest a sea-sprayed embarcadero. The fish soup is the signature entrée, but the pan-seared options—barramundi, halibut, or scallops—are the way to go. Start with the crab cake appetizer.

They serve shrimp, lobster, mussels, and more at **Oyster Bar** (Harrah's, 3475 Las Vegas Blvd. S., 702/369-5000, www.caesars.com, 11:30am-11pm Sun.-Thurs., 11:30am-1am Fri.-Sat., $20-40). But stick with the eponymous bivalve in all its glorious forms—grilled, fried, Rockefeller, or Royale.

Vegas Views

Bellagio's dancing fountains and the majestic Caesars Palace provide the eye candy at

Giada (Cromwell, 3595 Las Vegas Blvd. S., 702/442-3271, www.giadadelaurentiis.com, 8am-2:30pm and 5pm-11pm daily, $45-75), opened in 2014 by Giada De Laurentiis. If that's not enough, watch the chefs hard at work in the open kitchen.

Strip views await at **VooDoo Steakhouse** (Rio, 3700 W. Flamingo Rd., 702/777-7800, www.caesars.com, 5pm-10:30pm daily, $55-80), along with steaks with a N'awlins Creole and Cajun touch. Getting to the restaurant and the lounge requires a mini thrill ride to the top of the Rio tower in the glass elevator. The Rio contends that the restaurant is on the 51st floor and the lounge is on the 52nd floor, but they're really on the 41st and 42nd floors, respectively—Rio management dropped floors 40-49 as the number 4 has an ominous connotation in Chinese culture. Whatever floors they're on, the VooDoo double-decker provides a great view of the Strip. The food and drink are expensive and tame, but the fun is in the overlook, especially if you eat or drink outside on the decks. Diners get free entry into VooDoo nightclub.

LOWER STRIP

Asian

Soft lighting, mauve and teal accents, and intricate wooden screens provide the right balance of privacy and people-watching during your journey into the depths of Chinese cuisine at **Blossom** (Aria, 3730 Las Vegas Blvd. S., 877/230-2742, www.aria.com, 5:30pm-10:30pm daily, $50-70). Much of the menu is exotic, bold, and authentic, but there are plenty of playful American spins on tradiional dishes to appeal to Western palates. Adventuresome diners receive the full benefit of chef Chi Kwun Choi's creative mastery—go for the veal cheek or *jian bo* beef. The sweet-and-sour crisp-fried flounder is a signature dish for the more cautious.

Chinese art in a Hong Kong bistro setting with fountain and lake views makes **Jasmine** (Bellagio, 3600 Las Vegas Blvd. S., 702/693-8865, www.bellagio.com, 5:30pm-10pm daily, $50-70) one of the most visually striking

Chinese restaurants in town. The food is classic European-influenced Cantonese.

Breakfast

The **Veranda** (Four Seasons, 3960 Las Vegas Blvd. S., 702/632-5121, www.fourseasons.com, 6:30am-10pm Mon.-Fri., 7am-10pm Sat.-Sun., $30-45) transforms itself from a light, airy, indoor-outdoor breakfast and lunch nook into a late dinner spot oozing with Mediterranean ambiance and a check total worthy of a Four Seasons restaurant. As you might expect from the name, dining on the terrace is a favorite among well-to-do locals, especially for brunch on spring and fall weekends. Tiramisu French toast? Yes, please! Dinner here, with wine, dessert, and tip, can easily run $100 per person.

Buffets

You're in Las Vegas so it's perfectly reasonable to drop a hundo for breakfast. Head over to Bally's **Sterling Brunch Buffet** (3645 Las Vegas Blvd. S., 702/967-7258, www.caesars.com, 9:30am-2:30pm Sun., $95-125) for the only fine dining buffet in town. All-you-can-eat lobster tails? Yes, please. Also rack of lamb, caviar, truffled potatoes, and Perrier-Jouet champagne. Waiters are standing by to present gruyere popover bread, fetch more lobster bisque and Belgian waffles, refill your glass, and refold your napkin while you're making yet another sortie through the buffet.

On the other hand, for the price of that one brunch at Bally's, you can eat for three days at the **French Market Buffet** (The Orleans, 4500 W. Tropicana Ave., 702/365-7111, www.orleanscasino.com, 8am-9pm daily, breakfast $11, lunch $13, dinner $19-28, Sun. brunch $22, age 16 and under get $5 off; children under 43 inches are free). All-day passes are available ($30 Mon.-Thurs., $36 Fri.-Sun.).

Helical lighting fixtures evoke jellyfish and tuna, so you know the limited seafood offerings at **Wicked Spoon** (3708 Las Vegas Blvd. S., 702/698-7870, www.cosmopolitanlasvegas.com, 8am-9pm Sun.-Thurs., 8am-10pm Fri.-Sat., $28-50, $15 beer, wine, mimosa, bloody Mary supplement) are pretty good. Try the scampi and made-to-order fruits de mer soup.

French and Continental

The steaks and seafood at ★ **Mon Ami Gabi** (Paris, 3655 Las Vegas Blvd. S., 702/944-4224, www.monamigabi.com, 7am-11pm daily, $35-55) are comparable to those at any fine Strip establishment—at about half the price. It's a bistro, so you know the crepes and other lunch specials are terrific, but you're better off coming for dinner. Try the baked goat cheese appetizer.

When you name your restaurant after a maestro, you're setting some pretty high standards for your food. Fortunately, **Picasso** (Bellagio, 3600 Las Vegas Blvd. S., 702/693.8865, www.bellagio.com, 5:30pm-9:30pm Wed.-Mon., $113-123) is up to the self-inflicted challenge. Because of limited seating in its cubist-inspired dining room and a small dining time window, the restaurant has a couple of prix fixe menus. It's seriously expensive, and if you include Kobe beef, lobster, wine pairings, and a cheese course, you and a mate could easily leave several pounds heavier and $500 lighter.

Gastropub

Shed your culinary mores and enjoy as chef Shawn McClain blurs the lines between avant-garde and comfort food at **Libertine Social** (Mandalay Bay, 3950 Las Vegas Blvd. S., 702/632-7558, www.mandalaybay.com, 5pm-10:30pm daily, $35-55). The best dishes revolve around cured meats—the prosciutto and toasted cornbread, artisanal sausages and sauerkraut. Pick one and pair it with roasted cauliflower. Start with the crab and spinach dip.

Michael Mina Pub 1842 (MGM Grand, 3799 Las Vegas Blvd. S., 702/891-3922, www.michaelmina.net, 11:30am-10pm Thurs.-Mon., $20-35) delivers tasty burgers and barbecue. Better yet, order appetizers and sides, then share the joy of smoked salmon dip, soft pretzels and beer cheese, and oniony mac-and-cheese.

Pizza

With lines snaking out its unmarked entrance, in a dark alleyway decorated with record covers, **Secret Pizza** (Cosmopolitan, 3708 Las Vegas Blvd. S., 3rd Fl., 11am-5am Fri.-Mon., 11am-4am Tues.-Thurs., slices $5-6) is not so secret anymore. Located next to Blue Ribbon Sushi on the Cosmopolitan's third floor, it's a great place to get a quick, greasy slice.

Seafood

Rick Moonen is to be commended for his advocacy of sustainable seafood harvesting practices, and ★ **RM Seafood** (Mandalay Bay, 3950 Las Vegas Blvd. S., 702/632-9300, http://rmseafood.com, 11:30am-11pm daily, $45-90) practices what he preaches. You can almost hear the tide-rigging whirr and the mahogany creak in the yacht-club restaurant setting.

Estiatorio Milos (3708 Las Vegas Blvd. S., 877/551-7776, http://milos.ca/restaurants/las-vegas, 11:30am-3pm and 5pm-11pm Mon.-Thurs., 11:30am-3pm and 4pm-midnight Fri., 11:30am-midnight Sat., 11:30am-11pm Sun., $40-60) brings the Mediterranean to Las Vegas, with Greek-, Italian-, and Spanish-influenced presentations—think lemons, olives, and capers.

Partially housed in what looks like a modern-art latticed hornet's nest, **Mastro's Ocean Club** (Crystals and City Center, 3720 Las Vegas Blvd. S., 702/798-7115, www.mastrosrestaurants.com, 5pm-11pm daily, $60-100) is dubbed "The Treehouse." The restaurant inside offers standard top-of-the-line dishes elevated through preparation and atmosphere. The sushi menu is limited but a perfectly viable option.

Steak

The care used by the small farms from which Tom Colicchio's **Craftsteak** (MGM Grand, 3799 Las Vegas Blvd. S., 702/891-7318, www.craftsteaklasvegas.com, 5pm-10pm Sun.-Thurs., 5pm-10:30pm Fri.-Sat., $50-75) buys its ingredients is evident in the full flavor of the excellently seasoned steaks and chops. Spacious with gold, umber, and light woodwork, Craftsteak's decor is conducive to good times with friends and family and isn't overbearing or intimidating.

Tapas

The Cosmopolitan's reinvention of the social club takes diners' taste buds to flavor nirvana. Equal parts supper club, nightclub, and jazz club, ★ **Rose. Rabbit. Lie.** (Cosmopolitan, 3708 Las Vegas Blvd. S., 702/698-7440, www.cosmopolitanlasvegas.com, 6pm-midnight Wed.-Sat., $70-125) serves a mostly tapas-style menu. Sharing is encouraged, with about four small plates per person satisfying most appetites, especially if you splurge on the chocolate terrarium for dessert. The supper club experience includes varied entertainment throughout the evening (mostly singers, but sometimes magicians and acrobats), but no one will blame you for focusing on the food and cocktails.

Vegas Views

Paris's **Eiffel Tower Restaurant** (3655 Las Vegas Blvd. S., 702/948-6937, http://eiffeltowerrestaurant.com, 11:30am-3pm and 4:30pm-10:30pm Mon.-Thurs., 11:30am-3pm and 4:30pm-11pm Fri., 10am-3pm and 4:30pm-11pm Sat., 10am-3pm and 4:30pm-10:30pm Sun., $60-100) hovers 100 feet above the Strip. Your first "show" greets you when the glass elevator opens onto the organized chaos of chef Jean Joho's kitchen. Order the soufflé, have a glass of wine, and bask in the romantic piano strains as the bilingual culinary staff performs delicate French culinary feats, with Bellagio's fountains as a backdrop.

DOWNTOWN
Asian

A perfect little eatery for the budding Bohemia of East Fremont Street, ★ **Le Thai** (523 E. Fremont St., 702/778-0888, www.lethaivegas.com, 11am-11pm Mon.-Thurs., 11am-midnight Fri.-Sat., 4pm-10pm Sun., $10-25) attracts a diverse clientele ranging from ex-yuppies to body-art lovers. Most come for the three-color curry, and you should too. There's nothing especially daring on the menu, but the *pad prik, ga pow,* and garlic fried rice are better than what's found at many Strip restaurants that charge twice as much. Choose your spice level wisely; Le Thai does not mess around.

Buffets

Assuming you're not a food snob, the **Garden Court Buffet** (Main Street Station, 200 N. Main St., 702/387-1896, www.mainstreetcasino.com, 7am-3pm and 4pm-9pm Mon.-Thurs., 7am-3pm and 4pm-10pm Fri.-Sun., breakfast $8, lunch $9, dinner $12-15, Fri. seafood $23-26) will satisfy your taste buds and your bank account. The fare is mostly standard, with some specialties designed to appeal to the casino's Asian and Pacific Islander target market.

At **The Buffet** (Golden Nugget, 129 E. Fremont St., 702/385-8152, www.goldennugget.com, 7am-10pm daily, breakfast $15, lunch $16, dinner $21-28, weekend brunch $22), the food leaves nothing to be desired, with extras like an omelet station, calzone, Greek salad, and a delicate fine banana cake putting it a cut above the ordinary buffet, especially for downtown. Glass and brass accents make for peaceful digestion.

French and Continental

Hugo's Cellar (Four Queens, 202 E. Fremont St., 702/385-4011, www.hugoscellar.com, 5pm-10pm daily, $65-80) is romance from the moment each woman in your party receives her red rose until the last complimentary chocolate-covered strawberry is devoured. Probably the best gourmet room for the money, dimly lit Hugo's is located below the casino floor, in a faux wine cellar, shutting it off from the hubbub above. It is pricey, but the inclusion of sides, a mini dessert, and salad—prepared tableside with your choice of ingredients—helps ease the sticker shock. Sorbet is served between courses. The house appetizer is the Hot Rock—four meats sizzling on a lava slab; mix and match the meats with the dipping sauces.

Italian

Decidedly uncave-like with bright lights and an earthen-tile floor, **The Grotto** (Golden Nugget, 129 E. Fremont St., 702/386-8341, www.goldennugget.com, 11:30am-10:30pm daily, $30-40) offers top-quality northern Italian-influenced sandwiches and pizza with a view of the Golden Nugget's shark tank (ask for a window table). Portions are large and the margaritas refreshing.

Seafood

With prices as refreshing as a dip in the Gulf, **7 Mares** (2000 E. Charleston Blvd., 702/473-5522, 10am-9pm Mon.-Thurs., 10am-10pm Fri.-Sun., $14-25) authentically prepares fish and shrimp in a variety of spices and sauces for any taste.

The prime rib gets raves, but the seafood and the prices are the draw at **Second Street Grill** (Fremont, 200 Fremont St., 702/385-3232, www.fremontcasino.com, 5pm-10pm Sun. and Wed.-Thurs., 5pm-11pm Fri.-Sat., $25-40). The grill bills itself as "American contemporary with Pacific Rim influence," and the menu reflects this Asian inspiration with steaks and chops—but do yourself a favor and order the crab legs with lemon ginger butter. If you can't shake your inner landlubber, the nightly T-bone special ($30) should do the trick.

Steaks and seafood get equal billing on the menu at **Triple George** (201 N. 3rd St., 702/384-2761, www.triplegeorgegrill.com, 11am-10pm Mon.-Fri., 4pm-10pm Sat.-Sun., $25-45), but again, the charbroiled salmon and the martinis are what brings the suave crowd back for more.

Steak

Fronted by ex-mob mouthpiece and Las Vegas mayor Oscar Goodman, **Oscar's** (Plaza, 1 S. Main St., 702/386-7227, www.oscarslv.com, 4pm-10pm daily, $40-70) is dedicated to hizzoner's favorite things in life—beef, booze, and broads. With dishes named, apparently, for former wiseguy clients—Fat Herbie, Crazy Phil, Joe Pig, etc.—you're in for an old Vegas treat, full of the scents of leather, cigars, and broiling steaks.

OFF THE STRIP

The congenial proprietor of ★ **Phat Phrank's** (4850 W. Sunset Rd., 702/247-6528, http://phatphranks.com, 7am-7pm Mon.-Fri., 9am-4pm Sat., $10-15) keeps the atmosphere light and the fish tacos crispy and delicious. Try all three of the house salsas; they're all great complements to all the offerings, especially the flavorful pork burrito and *adobada torta*.

Thai Spice (4433 W. Flamingo Rd., 702/362-5308, www.thaispicelv.com, 11am-10pm Mon.-Thurs., 11am-10:30pm Fri., 11:30am-10:30pm Sat., $10-20) gives Le Thai a run for its baht as best Thai restaurant in town; the soups, noodle dishes, traditional curries, pad thai, and egg rolls are all well prepared. Tell your waiter how hot you want your food on a scale of 1 to 10. The big numbers peg the needle on the Scoville scale, so beware.

Accommodations

Casino accommodations offer the closest thing to a sure bet as you will find in Vegas: the most convenient setting for a vacation that includes gambling, dining, drinking, and show-going. See the *Casinos* section for information on these rooms. That being said, if you don't want to expose yourself or your kids to the smoke or vices on display at casinos, or need proximity to the airport, you will find plenty of choices. Even more affordable digs can be had at smaller motels in locations close to the Strip, downtown, the convention center, the university, and other high-traffic areas.

Even with more than 150,000 rooms, Vegas sells out completely on many three-day weekends, for major sports betting events like the Super Bowl and March Madness, big local events like music festivals, the National Finals Rodeo, and NASCAR week, and over U.S. and international holidays such as Chinese New Year, Cinco De Mayo, New Year's Eve, and Valentine's Day. There are some relative quiet times, such as the three weeks before Christmas and July-August, when the mercury doesn't drop below 100°F. Finding the perfect room should not be a problem then.

If you're just coming for the weekend, keep in mind that many major hotels don't even let you check in on a Saturday night. You can stay Friday and Saturday, but not Saturday alone. It may be easier to find a room Sunday-Thursday, when there aren't as many large conventions, sporting events, or getaway visitors from Southern California. Almost all the room packages and deep discounts are only available on these days.

Most Strip hotels charge **resort fees** of $20-40 per night. These charges are not included in the quoted room rate. Many downtown hotel casinos, as well as the mid-level national chains, have not yet resorted to resort fees.

HOTELS
Hotels within Hotels

Many of the megaresorts have gotten into the boutique hotel business, building or transforming towers into stand-alone, ultra-plush accommodations with the finest amenities and never-lift-a-finger service.

Feel like royalty at City Center's ★ **Mandarin Oriental Las Vegas** (City Center, 3752 Las Vegas Blvd. S., 702/590-8888, www.mandarinoriental.com/lasvegas, $295-399), which looks down on the bright lights of the Strip from a peaceful remove. A master control panel in each of the modern rooms sets the atmosphere to your liking, controlling the lights, temperature, window curtains, music, and more. Once everything is set, sink into the sleek, chrome-and-jade plushness with decorations suggesting silks, pearls, Shoji screens, and other hints of the exotic East. Valet closets allow hotel staff to deliver items to your room without entering your unit. The **Mandarin Bar** (888/881-9367, 4pm-1am Sun.-Thurs., noon-2am Fri.-Sat.) on the 23rd floor offers stunning views of the city skyline and several signature martinis. And it's all environmentally friendly, or at least LEED-certified.

There's even more pampering and more Asian influence at **Nobu** (3570 Las Vegas Blvd. S., 800/727-4923, www.caesars.com, $239-319), Caesars Palace's venture into the boutique market. Reflecting the same style and attention to detail that highlight chef Nobu Matsuhisa's eponymous restaurants, the first Nobu hotel includes teak and cherry blossoms, as well as stylized dragon artwork and traditional Japanese prints. Guests are greeted with hot tea, and the nightly turn-down service includes scented sleep oils and customizable bath and pillow menus. Nobu restaurant and lounge (5pm-11pm Sun.-Thurs., 5pm-midnight Fri.-Sat., $35-65) occupies the ground floor, so the indulgences can continue through the cocktail hour and mealtime.

Every guest room is a suite at the **Signature** (145 E. Harmon Ave., 702/797-6000 or 877/612-2121, www.signaturemgmgrand.com, $159-288) at MGM Grand. Even the standard Deluxe suite is a roomy 550 square feet and includes a king bed, kitchenette, and spa tub. Most of the 1,728 smoke-free guest rooms in the gleaming 40-story tower include private balconies with Strip views, and guests have access to the complimentary 24-hour fitness center, three outdoor pools, a business center, and free wireless Internet throughout the hotel. A gourmet deli and acclaimed room service satisfy noshing needs.

Representing for many the definition of opulence, the **Four Seasons** (Mandalay Bay, 3960 Las Vegas Blvd. S., 702/632-5000, www.fourseasons.com, $199-319) entices guests with vibrant colors, lush landscaping, and an elaborate porte cochere that sets the art-deco lemonade-on-the-veranda mood that induces

a stress-shedding sigh at first sight. Floor-to-ceiling windows command Strip or mountain views from atop Mandalay Bay. The **Spa** (702/632-5302), which includes a nail bar, offers treatments that relax all the senses, from aromatherapy and eucalyptus steam to menthol wraps and citrus infusions.

Farther removed from the Strip, the panoramas from the top floors of the 18-story **Berkley** (8280 Dean Martin Dr., 702/224-7400, www.theberkleylasvegas.com, $159-179) rank among the best you will find. Studio units sleep two, but families can go up to two bedrooms to accommodate six comfortably. Fully equipped kitchens, laundry rooms, and living areas with 49-inch TVs provide a home-away-from-home experience. It's across the street from the Silverton Casino, so there is plenty of gaming action, plus dining options, and a shuttle can whisk you away to primo shopping venues. Still, you will want to rent a car to conveniently take in the whole Vegas experience.

Convention Hotels

The best non-casino, non-chain hotels congregate a mile or so west of the Strip, south of the Las Vegas Convention Center, along Koval Lane and Paradise Road.

Offering sophisticated accommodations and amenities without the hubbub of a rowdy casino, the **Renaissance** (3400 Paradise Rd., 702/784-5700, www.renaissancelasvegas.com, $77-189) has big, bright, airy standard guest rooms that come complete with triple-sheeted 300-thread-count Egyptian cotton beds with down comforters and duvets, walk-in showers, full tubs, 42-inch flat-panel TVs, a business center, and high-speed Internet. Upper-floor guest rooms overlook the Wynn golf course. The pool and whirlpool are outside, and the concierge can score show tickets and tee times. Onyx- and burgundy-clad **Envy Steakhouse** (6:30am-11am and 5pm-10pm daily, $40-70) has a few poultry and seafood entrées, but the Angus beef gets top billing.

Catering to families and vacationers seeking a more "residential" stay, **Platinum** (211

E. Flamingo Rd., 702/365-5000 or 877/211-9211, www.theplatinumhotel.com, $113-194) treats both guests and the environment with kid gloves. The resort uses the latest technology to reduce its carbon footprint through such measures as low-energy lighting throughout, ecofriendly room thermostats, and motion sensors to turn lights off when restrooms are unoccupied. Guests also can use PressReader to access thousands of digital publications. Standard suites are an expansive 910 square feet of muted designer furnishings and accents, and they include all modern conveniences, such as high-speed Internet, high-fidelity sound systems, full kitchens, and oversize tubs. **Kil@watt** (6am-2pm daily, $12-20), with sleek silver decor accented with dark woods, is a feast for the eyes and the palate for breakfast and lunch.

The one- and two-bedroom condominium suites at **Desert Rose** (5051 Duke Ellington Way, 702/739-7000 or 888/732-8099, www.shellhospitality.com, $142-249) are loaded, with new appliances and granite countertops in the kitchen as well as private balconies or patios outside. One-bedrooms are quite large, at 650 square feet, and sleep four comfortably. Rates vary widely, but depending on your needs and travel dates, you might find a deal within walking distance of several casinos and the monorail.

Royal Resort (99 Convention Center Dr., 702/735-6117 or 800/634-6118, www.royalhotelvegas.com, $124-229) is part timeshare, part hotel, so its amenities are top-notch. Its outdoor pool area nestles against tropical landscaping, private cabanas, and a hot tub.

West of the Strip

No matter your political bent, you're in for a "yuge" helping of extravagance at **Trump International** (2000 Fashion Show Dr., 702/892-0000, www.trumphotels.com, $120-220). With shimmering gold windows and a foyer with more marble than a quarry, the Trump sets high expectations even before guests arrive in their rooms. Then it sets about exceeding them. No whim will go unfulfilled.

Standard rooms open onto an Italian marble entryway leading to floor-to-ceiling windows with the requisite magnificent views. In-room amenities include European kitchens with dual sinks and marble countertops, flat-screen TVs, and luxury appliances. Feather comforters and Italian linens ensure heavenly restfulness. The pool deck stars, with its cabana and daybed rentals 100 feet above the Strip. Enjoy tasty chicken *katsu* sliders from the poolside restaurant **H2 (EAU)** (7am-sunset daily, weather permitting) delivered straight to your private cabana; a full bar completes a perfect day of splashing or sunbathing. **DJT** (6:30am-3pm and 5pm-10pm daily, $25-45) is a classy steakhouse, but the food is more style than substance. **The Spa at Trump** offers unique packages such as the Las Vegas Oxygenating Facial, to give your pores a breath of fresh air.

No two rooms are the same at the **Artisan** (1501 W. Sahara Ave., 702/214-4000, $99-179), located a mile northwest of the convention center. Most include playful, classic-style prints in baroque frames, dark wood, and bold colors; schemes range from burgundy to gold to emerald. The **Artisan Lounge** hosts one of the best early-night parties in town. And you can nix the tan lines at the European-style (read: topless) pool.

MOTELS

Many of Las Vegas's resort casinos have shifted their business models to diversify toward maximizing non-gaming revenues. Mostly gone are the days of easy-to-earn gourmet restaurant comps and cheap, "anything-to-keep-'em-on-property" room rates. This policy change should open a niche for comfortable, independent, close-to-the-action motels both downtown and on the Strip.

Alas, it hasn't happened yet.

There are several low-cost motels north of the Strip resorts and downtown, scattered along Las Vegas Boulevard and east of downtown along Boulder Highway. Few are recommendable. One exception is the **Downtowner** (129 N. 8th St., 702/384-1441, www.downtownerlv.com, $68-125).

Its modern, minimalist rooms are sparkling white with red, gray, and black accents. The pool and lounge areas are luxuries in this neighborhood and price range, and the Downtowner even has a few cottages for rent. Another viable choice, **City Center Motel** (700 Fremont St., 702/382-4766, http://citycenterlv.com, $69-89) is near the Fremont Street Experience, an outlet mall, and the transitioning Fremont East district. Its pastel walls and busy bedspreads reveal the motel's age, but it's clean and rooms include the standard amenities: coffeemaker, mini fridge, hair dryer, etc. There's a microwave at the front desk for guest use. **Roulette Motel** (2019 Fremont St., 702/910-4637, http://roulettemotel.com, $65-85) features dark wood furnishings, tasteful bedding, and artwork on the walls. A bit east of the downtown arts district, it may provide the best bang for the buck. Right in the middle of the arts district, the building exterior of the **Star Motel** (1418 S. 3rd St., 702/383-9770, $80) is not much to look at, but the grounds are meticulously maintained. The lush landscaping is more in keeping with room interiors, which include wood and tile laminate flooring rather than stiff, is-it-design-or-is-it-a-stain carpeting.

The best non-chain motel south of the Strip resorts, **Highland Inn** (8025 Dean Martin Dr., 702/896-4333, www.highlandinnlasvegas.com, $90-120) is convenient to both the casinos and the airport. There's free coffee and doughnuts each morning in the office.

Motels along the Lower Strip, from Bally's below Flamingo Avenue all the way out to the Mandalay Bay at the far south end of the Strip, are well placed to visit all the new big-brand casino resorts. Prices here are much lower than at the resorts but higher than those to the north, reflecting premium real estate costs. Those costs also all but price out independent motels, but you can take your pick of established brands like **Travelodge Las Vegas Center Strip** (3735 Las Vegas Blvd. S., 702/736-3443, www.travelodgevegasstrip.com, $59-99), which gets a top rating for its reasonable prices; location near the MGM Grand and City Center; and little extras like free continental breakfast, free parking, and a heated swimming pool.

The supersize **Super 8** (4250 Koval Ln., 702/794-0888, www.super8vegas.com, $69-109), just east of Bally's and Paris, is the chain's largest in the world. It offers a heated pool but no other resort amenities; on the other hand, it doesn't charge resort fees. There's free Internet access but not much of a budget for decor in the guest rooms or common areas. Stop at Ellis Island Casino & Brewery next door for ribs and microbrews.

Another group of motels clings to the south side of the convention center on Paradise and Desert Inn Roads as well as the west side between Paradise Road and the Strip on Convention Center Drive. If you're attending a convention and plan well in advance, you can reserve a very reasonable and livable room at any of several motels within a five-minute walk of the convention floor. Most of them have plenty of weekly rooms with kitchenettes, which can save you a bundle. It's a joy to be able to leave the convention floor and walk over to your room and back again if necessary—the shuttle buses to the far-flung hotels are very often crowded, slow, and inconvenient. Even if you're not attending a convention, this is a good part of town to stay in, off the main drag but in the middle of everything.

You won't find whirlpool tubs, white-beach pools, or Egyptian cotton at **Siegel Suites Select** (220 Convention Center Dr., 702/735-4151, www.siegelsuitesselect.com, $45-60), but you will find everything the budget traveler could ask for at this ex-Rodeway Inn: hot showers, clean beds, toaster, coffeemaker, refreshing pool, and studio suite accommodations that seem larger than their 340 square feet.

HOSTELS

It's hard to beat these places for budget accommodations. They offer rock-bottom prices for no-frills "rack rooms," singles, and doubles. Closest to the Strip, **Hostel Cat** (1236 Las

Vegas Blvd. S., 702/380-6902, http://hostelcat. com, $23-40) puts the focus on group activities, organizing pub crawls, beer pong and video game tournaments, movie nights, and more. There's even a 24-hour party table where there are always interesting fellow travelers to talk to.

Sin City Hostel (1208 Las Vegas Blvd. S., 702/868-0222, www.sincityhostel.com, $23-26) is reserved for international, student, and out-of-state travelers only (ID required). Perfect for the starving student's budget, rates include breakfast. The hostel features a barbecue pit, a basketball court, and Wi-Fi. A recent check of Sin City's website revealed current guests included visitors from England, France, the Netherlands, and Singapore.

Six blocks east of the downtown resorts, **Las Vegas Hostel** (1322 Fremont St., 702/385-1150 or 800/550-8958, http://lasvegashostel.net, $16-51) has a swimming pool and a hot tub. The rates include a make-your-own pancake breakfast, billiards and TV room, and wireless Internet connections. The hostel also arranges trips to the Strip and visits to the Grand Canyon and other outdoorsy attractions. Or you can borrow a bike and explore the area on your own.

RV PARKS

A number of casinos have attached RV parks. Other casinos allow RVs to park overnight in their parking lots but have no facilities.

The best bet on the Strip, thanks almost exclusively to its location, the **RV Park at Circus Circus** (2880 Las Vegas Blvd. S., 702/794-3757 or 800/444-2472, www.circuscircus.com, $41-46) is big (170 spaces, all paved, including more than 70 pull-throughs), with a few grassy islands and shade trees. RVing families will appreciate the hotel/casino amenities and entertainment. The convenience store is open 24 hours daily. Ten minutes spent learning where the Industrial Road back entrance is will save hours of sitting in traffic on Las Vegas Boulevard. The free dog wash in the off-leash park is a nice touch.

Again, convenience and amenities, rather than lush surroundings, are the attraction at **Main Street Station RV Park** (200 N. Main St., 702/387-1896, $24-28). The showers and laundry have *hot* water, and the Fremont Street casinos are an easy walk away. Downtown has some sketchy areas after dark, but Main Street's security patrol is diligent, and safety is not an issue. Highway noise and Vegas's famous flashing neon, however, may be, come bedtime.

Boulder Highway, which connects downtown with Lake Mead to the southeast, is RV park central. The cleanest and best-maintained along this road, ★ **Las Vegas RV Resort** (3890 S. Nellis Blvd., 866/846-5432, www.lasvegasrvresort.com, $33-51) has level asphalt pads and palm tree landscaping. A guard is on-site 24 hours, and the laundry, restrooms, pool area, and fitness center are spotless. **Las Vegas KOA at Sam's Town** (5225 Boulder Hwy., 702/454-8055, https://koa.com, $36-45) has nearly 300 spaces for motor homes, all with full hookups and 20-, 30-, and 50-amp power. It's mostly a paved parking lot with spacious sites, a heated (if a bit dated) pool, and a spa; the rec hall has a pool table and a kitchen. And, of course, it's near the bowling, dining, and movie theater in the casino. **Arizona Charlie's Boulder** (4445 Boulder Hwy., 702/951-5911, www.arizonacharliesboulder.com, $32) has 239 spaces and weekly rates. The clubhouse contains a large-screen TV, fitness room, and pool table. Spaces at the back are quieter and closer to the dog run but farther from the laundry room and pool area.

South of the airport, **Oasis RV Resort** (2711 W. Windmill Ln., www.oasislasvegasrvresort.com, 800/566-4707, $52-74) is directly across I-15 from the Silverton Casino. Opened in 1996, Oasis has more than 800 snug spaces with huge date palms and a cavernous 24,000-square-foot clubhouse. Each space is wide enough for a car and motor home but not much else and comes with a picnic table and patio. The foliage is plentiful and flanks an 18-hole putting course with real grass greens along with family and adult swimming pools. The resort features a full calendar of poker tournaments, movies, karaoke, and bar and restaurant specials. Wheelchair-accessible restrooms have flush toilets and hot showers; other amenities include a laundry, a grocery store, an exercise room, and an arcade.

Information and Services

INFORMATION BUREAUS

The **Las Vegas Convention and Visitors Authority** (LVCVA, 3150 Paradise Rd., 702/892-0711 or 877/847-4858, www.lvcva. com, 8am-5pm daily) maintains a website of special hotel deals, show tickets, and other offers at www.lasvegas.com. One of LVCVA's priorities is filling hotel rooms. You can also call the same number for convention schedules and entertainment offerings. The **Las Vegas Chamber of Commerce** (575 Symphony Park Ave., Ste. 100, 702/641-5822, www.lvchamber.com) has a bunch of travel resources and fact sheets on its website. For-profit **Vegas.com** is a good resource for up-to-the-minute show schedules and reviews.

VISITORS GUIDES AND MAGAZINES

Nearly a dozen free periodicals for visitors are available in various places around town—you will find them in racks in motel lobbies and by the bell desks of the large hotels. Others are available online. They all cover basically the same territory—showrooms, lounges, dining, dancing, buffets, gambling, sports, events, coming attractions—and most have numerous ads that will transport coupon clippers to discount heaven.

Anthony Curtis's monthly *Las Vegas Advisor* (www.lasvegasadvisor.com) ferrets out the best dining, entertainment, gambling, and hotel room values, shows, and restaurants, and presents them objectively. A year's subscription is only $50 ($37 for an electronic subscription) and includes exclusive coupons worth more than $3,000. Sign up online.

The articles in *Las Vegas Magazine* (www.lasvegasmagazine.com) are more in-depth and fan-magazine-y. Features include Q&A interviews with touring headliners, celebrity chefs, and pop culture mavens.

Las Vegas Weekly (www.lasvegasweekly. com), the town's alternative newspaper, mixes in political and social commentary as well as inside info on the soon-to-be-happenin' nightspots, restaurants, and hipster trends.

The annual publication *Las Vegas Perspective* (www.lvgea.org) is chock-full of area demographics as well as retail, real estate, and community statistics, updated every year.

MEDICAL AND EMERGENCY SERVICES

If you need the police, the fire department, or an ambulance in an emergency, **dial 911.**

The centrally located **University Medical Center** (1800 W. Charleston Blvd., at Shadow Ln., 702/383-2000) has 24-hour emergency service, with outpatient and trauma-care facilities. Hospital emergency rooms throughout the valley are open 24 hours, as are many privately run urgent care centers.

Most hotels will have lists of dentists and doctors, and the **Clark County Medical Society** (2590 E. Russell Rd., 702/739-9989, www.clarkcountymedical.org) website lists members based on specialty. You can also get a physician referral from **Desert Springs Hospital** (702/733-8800).

Getting Around

CAR

Downtown Las Vegas crowds around the junction of I-15, US 95, and US 93. I-15 runs from Los Angeles (272 miles, 4-5 hours' drive) to Salt Lake City (419 miles, 6-8 hours). US 95 meanders from Yuma, Arizona, on the Mexican border, up the western side of Nevada, through Coeur D'Alene, Idaho, all the way up to British Columbia, Canada. US 93 starts in Phoenix and hits Las Vegas 285 miles later, then merges with I-15 for a while only to fork off and shoot straight up the east side of Nevada and continue due north all the way to Alberta, Canada.

Car Rental

When you call around to rent, ask what the *total* price of your car is going to be. With sales tax, use tax, airport fees, and other miscellaneous charges, you can pay as much as 60 percent over and above the quoted rate. Typical shoulder-season weekly rates run from about $170 total for economy and compact cars to $280 for vans and $500 for luxury sedans, but prices increase by one-third or more during major conventions and holiday periods. One recent holiday week saw economy car rates at about $230 across the board. Parking is free in casino surface lots and garages. Check with your insurance agent at home about coverage on rental cars; often your insurance covers rental cars (minus your deductible), and you won't need the rental company's. If you rent a car on most credit cards, you get automatic rental-car insurance coverage.

Most of the large car-rental companies have desks at the **McCarran Rent-A-Car Center** (702/261-6001). Dedicated McCarran shuttles leave the main terminal from outside exit doors 10 and 11 about every five minutes bound for the Rent-A-Car Center. International airlines and a few domestic flights arrive at Terminal 3. Here, the shuttle picks up outside doors 51 through 58. Taxicabs are also available at the center. Companies represented at the center include **Advantage** (800/777-9377), **Alamo** (800/462-5266), **Avis** (800/331-1212), **Budget** (800/922-2899), **Dollar** (800/800-4000), **E-Z** (800/277-5171), **Enterprise** (800/736-7222), **Firefly** (888/296-9135), **Hertz** (800/654-3131), **National** (800/227-7368), **Payless** (800/729-5377), **Thrifty** (800/367-2277), and **Zipcar** (866/494-7227). Others will pick up customers at the center.

When arriving, follow the "Ground Transportation" signs to the "Rental Car Shuttle" staging area. A blue-and-white bus will pick you up in less than five minutes for the three-mile trip to the Rent-A-Car Center. Of course, the buses will ferry you from the rental drop-off area back to the airport when it's time to go home.

RV Rental

Travelers using Las Vegas as their base or departure point can rent virtually any type of recreational vehicle, from pickup truck-mounted coaches to 40-foot Class A rolling mansions. **El Monte RV** (13001 Las Vegas Blvd. S., Henderson, 702/269-0704 or 888/337-2214), south of town (take I-15 South, exiting at St. Rose Parkway, then head east to Las Vegas Boulevard and drive south), deals primarily in Class C "cab-over" models and Class A rock-star tour bus behemoths. Base prices for the Class C cab-overs start at about $600-800 per week, but miles—bundled in 100-mile packages—and incidentals such as kitchenware, pillows, coffeemakers, and toasters, can easily increase the total by 75 percent. El Monte's big dog, an EMW AF34 Slideout, goes for $1,800 per week before mileage and extras.

Cruise America (551 N. Gibson Rd., Henderson, 702/565-2224 or 888/980-8282), on the southeast side (take US 93 South to the Sunset Road exit east and turn right on Gibson Road), touts its exclusively cab-over fleet as having more ready-to-use sleep space and maneuverability. Its RVs range 19-30 feet, suitable for parties of 3-7 people. Seven-night rentals average $430-900. The company adds a mileage estimate (at about 35 cents per mile) at the time of rental and adjusts the charges based on actual miles driven when you return the vehicle. Common extra charges include linens, kitchen equipment, and generator use.

Road Bear's (4730 Boulder Hwy., 866/491-9853) Class C models sleep 4-7 and go for 42 cents per mile (at $60-85 per day, plus $200 initiation fee and other extras such as kitchen and linen kits).

MONORAIL

Since 2004, the site of the SLS Casino on the north end of the Strip and the MGM Grand near the south end have been connected via the **Las Vegas Monorail** (702/699-8200, 7am-midnight Mon., 7am-2am Tues.-Thurs., 7am-3am Fri.-Sun., $5, 24-hour pass $12), with stops at the SLS, Westgate, Convention Center, Harrah's/The Linq, Flamingo/Caesars Palace, Bally's/Paris, and MGM Grand. More than 30 major resorts are now within easy reach along the Strip without a car or taxi. Reaching speeds up to 50 mph, the monorail glides above traffic to cover the four-mile route in about 14 minutes. Nine trains with four air-conditioned cars each carry up to 152 riders along the elevated track running on the east side of the strip, stopping every few minutes at the stations. Tickets are available at vending machines at each station as well as at station properties.

BUS

Citizen Area Transit (CAT, 702/228-7433, www.rtcsouthernnevada.com), the public bus system, is managed by the Regional Transportation Commission. CAT runs 39 routes all over the Las Vegas Valley. Fares are $6 for 2 hours, $8 for 24 hours, free under age five when riding with a guardian. Call or access the ride guide online. Bus service is pretty comprehensive, but even the express routes with fewer stops take a long time to get anywhere.

TAXI

Except for peak periods, taxis are numerous and quite readily available, and drivers are good sources of scuttlebutt (not always accurate) and entertainment (not always wholesome). Of course, Las Vegas operates at peak loads most of the time, so if you're not in a taxi zone right in front of one of the busiest hotels, it might be tough to get one. The 16 companies plying the streets of Las Vegas charge $3.45 for the flag drop and $2.68 per mile. Waiting time is $0.54 per minute.

LIMO

Offering chauffeur-driven domestic and imported sedans, shuttle buses, and SUVs in addition to stretch and superstretch limos, **Las Vegas Limousines** (702/888-4848, www.lasvegaslimo.com) can transport up to 15 people per vehicle to and from sporting events, corporate meetings, airport connections, bachelor and bachelorette parties, sightseeing tours, and more. Rates are $60 per hour for a 6-seat stretch limo, $80 and up for a 10-seat superstretch.

Presidential Limousine (702/438-5466, www.presidentiallimolv.com) charges $69 per hour for its stretch six-seater, $80 per hour for the superstretch eight-seater; both include TVs and video players, mobile phones, sparkling cider, and roses for the women. They don't include a mandatory fuel surcharge or driver gratuity. **Bell Limousine** (866/226-7206, www.belllimousine.com) has similar rates and fleets.

TOURS

Several companies offer the chance to see the sights of Las Vegas by bus, helicopter, airplane, or off-road vehicle. There are plenty of tour operators offering similar services. Search the Internet to find tours tailored for your needs, the best prices, and the most competent providers.

The ubiquitous **Gray Line** (702/739-7777

or 877/333-6556, www.graylinelasvegas. com) offers air-conditioned motor coach tours of the city by night as well as tours of Hoover Dam and the Grand Canyon. City tours (7pm Thurs.-Sat., $69) visit the major Vegas free sights: the Bellagio Fountains and Conservatory, the "Welcome to Las Vegas" sign, the Fremont Street Experience, and some of the more opulent hotels. The Hoover Dam tour ($66) includes a buffet lunch and a stop at Ethel M's chocolatier for a self-guided tour and a free sample. Travelers can add a 15-minute helicopter flight over Lake Mead and the dam ($99 extra) or a riverboat cruise on the lake ($31 extra).

To book a lake cruise directly, contact **Lake Mead Cruises** (866/292-9191, www. lakemeadcruises.com, noon and 2 pm daily Apr.-Oct., days and times vary Feb.-Mar. and Nov., $26 adults, $13 children 2-11, Sun. 10am champagne brunch cruise $45 adults, $19.50 children 2-11, Sun., Tues., Thurs. dinner cruise $61.50 adults, $25 children 2-11).

Vegas Tours (866/218-6877, www.vegastours.com) has a full slate of outdoor, adventure, and other tours. Some of the more unusual ones include trail rides and full-day dude ranch tours ($120-350) and a visit and tour of the Techatticup gold mine ($113-189). Tours of the Grand Canyon and other nearby state and national parks are available as well.

All Las Vegas Tours (702/233-1627 or 800/566-5868, www.alllasvegastours.com) has all the usual tours: zip-lining over the desert or between hotel towers (weight must be between 75 and 250 pounds, $30-159), tandem skydiving (age 18 and over, less than 240 pounds, $229), and ATV sand-duning (18 and over with valid driver's license, $185).

Pink Jeep Tours (702/895-6778 or 888/900-4480, www.pinkjeeptourslasvegas.com) takes visitors in rugged but cute and comfortable 10-passenger ATVs to such sites as Red Rock Canyon, Valley of Fire, and Hoover Dam.

For history, nature, and entertainment buffs looking for a more focused adventure, themed tours are on the rise in Las Vegas. **Haunted Vegas Tours** (702/677-6499, www. hauntedvegastours.com, 9:30pm Thurs.-Mon., $85) takes an interesting if macabre trip to the "Motel of Death," where many pseudo-celebrities have met their untimely ends. Guides dressed as undertakers take you to the Redd Foxx haunted house, a creepy old bridge, and an eerie park. The same company offers the **Las Vegas Mob Tour** ($85), taking visitors to the sites of Mafia hits. Guides, dressed in black pin-striped suits and fedoras, tell tales of the 1970s, when Anthony "The Ant" Spilotro ran the city, and give the scoop on the fate of casino mogul Lefty Rosenthal. A pizza party is included in both tours.

Hoover Dam and Lake Mead

Hoover Dam began detaining the Colorado and Virgin Rivers in 1935. By 1938, Lake Mead was full of three years' worth of river water braced by the monolithic buttress at Black Canyon. The largest artificial lake in the West, Lake Mead measures 110 miles long and 500 feet deep, has 822 miles of shoreline, and contains 28.5 million acre-feet of water (just over 9 trillion gallons), a little less than half the water stored along the entire Colorado River system. The reservoir irrigates 2.25 million acres of land in the United States and Mexico and supplies water for more than 14 million people. Nine million people use Lake Mead each year as a recreational resource; it's one of the most-visited National Park Service-managed areas in the country.

For all this, Lake Mead is only incidental to the dam's primary purpose: flood and drought control. In addition, Lake Mead is only the centerpiece of the 1.5-million-acre Lake Mead National Recreation Area, which includes Lake Mojave and the surrounding desert from Davis Dam to the south, Grand Canyon National Park to the east, all the way north to Overton—the largest U.S. Department of the Interior recreational acreage in the Lower 48.

HENDERSON

Founded to process magnesium for the Allied war effort, Henderson is now home to 285,000 residents. Henderson during the 2000s was one of the fastest-growing cities in the fastest-growing state in the country, and it is consistently named among the nation's most livable communities thanks to its varied economy, parks, relatively low crime rate, and the development of several new casinos in the Green Valley subdivision. Its excellent location is undeniable—only 15 minutes from Lake Mead, and close enough to Las Vegas to enjoy that city's benefits while far enough away to outdistance the disadvantages.

Clark County Museum

The extensive and fascinating **Clark County Museum** (1830 S. Boulder Hwy., 702/455-7955, www.clarkcountynv.gov, 9am-4:30pm daily, $2 adults, $1 seniors and children) is a rare Las Vegas bargain. Changing exhibits have included casino souvenirs, Native American pottery, the Southern Nevada Gunnery School, a celebration of American headwear and footwear, and more.

The permanent exhibit includes fine displays tracing Native American cultures from the prehistoric to the contemporary and chronicling nonnative exploration, settlement, and industry: Mormons, the military, mining, ranching, railroading, riverboating, and gambling up through the construction of Hoover Dam and the subsequent founding of Henderson.

The old depot that houses the railroad station and rolling-stock collection has been restored. Also be sure to stroll down to the Heritage Street historical residential and commercial buildings: the **Townsite House,** built in Henderson in the 1940s; the

1890s **Donald W. Reynolds Print Shop;** the **Candlelight Wedding Chapel;** the **Babcock and Wilcox House,** one of 12 original residences built in Boulder City in early 1933; and the pièce de résistance, **Beckley House,** a simple yet stunning example of the still-popular California bungalow style, built for $2,500 in 1912 by Las Vegas pioneer and entrepreneur Will Beckley.

Other displays include a ghost town trail, a nature trail with a simulated Paiute village, a general store, a jailhouse, and a blacksmith. The gift shop sells some interesting items—books, magazines, minerals, jewelry, beads, pottery, textiles, and even Joshua tree seeds.

Henderson Bird Viewing Preserve

Southern Nevada's natural side isn't always easy to find, but when you peel back the neon, the discoveries are often surprisingly rich. The **Henderson Bird Viewing Preserve** (2400 Moser Dr., near Boulder Hwy. and Sunset Rd., 702/267-4180, www.cityofhenderson.com, 6am-2pm daily Mar.-May, 6am-noon daily June-Aug., 6am-2pm daily Sept.-Nov., 7am-2pm daily Dec.-Feb., free) is a good example. Situated on 140 acres at the city's water treatment center, the preserve is home to hundreds of hummingbirds, ibis, ducks, eagles, roadrunners, and numerous other migratory species. The park, which is managed by the City of Henderson, offers nine ponds with both paved and dirt paths. Don't feed the wildlife.

Casinos

Classing up the accommodations offerings in Henderson is the **Green Valley Ranch** (2300 Paseo Verde Pkwy., 702/871-7777, http://greenvalleyranch.sclv.com, $160-260). Located on I-215 just west of town, the property offers a lavish spa and attractive rooms packed with amenities such as a terrific pool complex, including one pool just for adults. Though the resort has a vaguely Mediterranean vibe, **Borracha** (4pm-10pm Sun.-Thurs., 4pm-11pm Fri.-Sat., $15-25) is the best of the resort's eight restaurants. With

Hoover Dam and Lake Mead

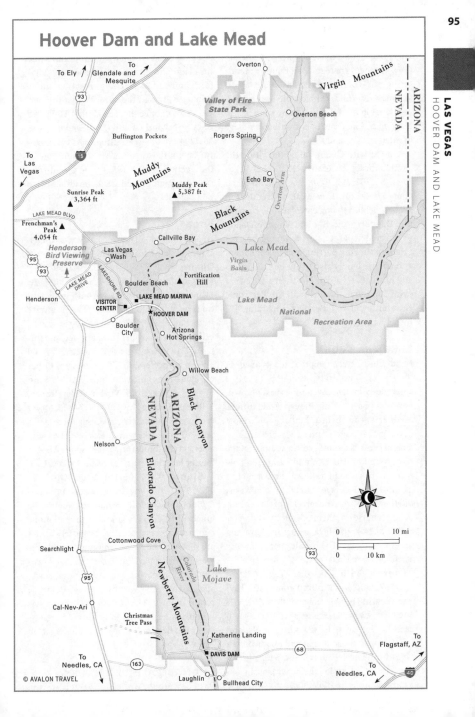

To Ely
Glendale and
Mesquite

To

Overton

Virgin Mountains

NEVADA
ARIZONA

93

Valley of Fire
State Park

Overton Beach

To
Las
Vegas

15

Buffington Pockets

Rogers Spring

Echo Bay

Overton Arm

Muddy Mountains

Muddy Peak
5,387 ft

Sunrise Peak
3,364 ft

LAKE MEAD BLVD

Black
Mountains

Frenchman's
Peak
4,054 ft

95

Henderson
Bird Viewing
Preserve

93

Callville Bay

Lake Mead

Las Vegas
Wash

Virgin
Basin

LAKE MEAD DRIVE

LAKESHORE RD

Boulder Beach

Fortification
Hill

Lake Mead

Henderson

LAKE MEAD MARINA

VISITOR
CENTER

HOOVER DAM

National

Recreation Area

Boulder
City

Arizona
Hot Springs

Willow Beach

Nelson

NEVADA
ARIZONA

Black Canyon

Eldorado Canyon

Searchlight

Cottonwood Cove

95

Newberry Mountains

Colorado River

Lake
Mojave

Cal-Nev-Ari

Christmas
Tree Pass

10 mi

10 km

93

Katherine Landing

68

To
Flagstaff, AZ

To
Needles, CA

163

Davis Dam

To
Needles, CA

Laughlin   Bullhead City

40

© AVALON TRAVEL

a Day of the Dead motif, the restaurant is a virtual fiesta, offering 40 varieties of tequila, street tacos, and a Baja fish burrito to die for. GVR's lounges are regular stomping grounds for up-and-coming musicians and comedians—the resort has carved a niche as a semi-regular stop for TV talent show runners-up. Next door, The District is a walkable village of eateries, bars, and shops.

On par with Green Valley Ranch on the ritziness scale, **M Resort** (12300 Las Vegas Blvd. S., 702/797-1000, www.themresort.com, $150-220), way west of Henderson proper, fields a strong entertainment schedule. Daughtry and Big Bad Voodoo Daddy performed separate shows during one recent month. Pool parties, muscle car shows, and tribute bands also bring out the locals and hotel guests alike. The rooms are a spacious 550 square feet with all the electronic entertainment you'd expect, including 42-inch TVs.

Lake Las Vegas

Henderson's latest attempt to shed its image as the grittier, dowdier stepsister of Las Vegas is a new development seven miles east of town. Lake Las Vegas, the ambitious, ultraluxurious Mediterranean-themed housing and resort development centered on a 320-acre artificial lake, experienced some growing pains, but the playground for the rich and pampered now seems to be on solid footing. There is no live gaming in the village, though a few taverns offer slots and video poker. One of three original golf courses is still in operation, and water activities, from paddleboarding and kayaking to jetpacking and flyboarding, are focusing attention on the lake.

Hilton (1610 Lake Las Vegas Pkwy, 702/567-4700, www.hilton.com, $109-129) and **Westin** (101 MonteLago Blvd., 702/567-6000, www.westinlakelasvegas.com, $125-160) each have great spas, sparkling pools, and top dining options. Bright and airy, **Marssa** (Westin, 5:30pm-9:30pm Tues.-Sat., $45-65) carries on the lakeside theme with sushi and Pacific Rim-inspired seafood.

Railroad Pass

US 93/95 continues southwest up and over a low gate between the River Mountains and the Black Hills known as Railroad Pass (2,367 feet), named for the Union Pacific route to Boulder City and the dam. With a full-service casino, coffee shop, and buffet, **Railroad Pass Hotel and Casino** (2800 Boulder Hwy., 702/294-5000, www.railroadpass.com, $95-145) sits at the top of the pass. Just beyond is the junction where US 95 cuts right, south and west of Laughlin, and US 93 heads east into Boulder City.

Food

Henderson is no match for Las Vegas when it comes to haute cuisine, but **Todd's Unique Dining** (4350 E. Sunset Rd., 702/259-8633, 4:30pm-10pm Mon.-Sat., $30-45) holds its own against any in Sin City, with unpretentious decor and food. The seafood is always fresh, but the short ribs are the way to go. The cellar always has just the right accompaniment. From the kitchen to the waitstaff, you'll always be professionally catered to. Other top gourmet choices include **Hank's Fine Steaks & Martinis** (Green Valley Ranch, 2300 Paseo Verde Pkwy., 702/617-7515, http://greenvalleyranch.sclv.com, 5pm-10pm daily, $60-80) for steaks with juices sealed in with a perfect charbroil and a sweet South African lobster tail; start with the crabmeat cocktail.

Studio B (12300 Las Vegas Blvd. S., 702/797-1000, www.themresort.com, 11am-8:30pm daily, $17-40) brings gourmet to the lunch buffet. Live cooking demonstrations by culinary experts preparing the buffet's dishes are shown on huge video monitors inside the main buffet room. You'll see dedicated professionals preparing delicate pastries, sushi, and Asian cuisine worthy of the top Chinese rooms in town. The beef on the carving station is tender enough to be cut with a plastic knife. Beer and wine are included at no extra charge.

Information and Services

Past downtown on Water Street are the

convention center, city hall, a library, and a park; Water Street runs around to the left and joins Major Street, which heads right back out to Boulder Highway. The **Chamber of Commerce** (590 S. Boulder Hwy., 702/565-8951, www.hendersonchamber.com) is right at the corner.

BOULDER CITY

In 1930, when Congress appropriated the first funds for the Boulder Canyon Project, the Great Depression was in full swing, the dam was to be one of the largest single engineering and public works construction tasks ever undertaken, and urban architects were increasingly leaning toward the social progressiveness of the community planning movement. Boulder City was born of these unique factors and remains the most unusual town in Nevada. In 1930 Saco R. DeBoer, a highly regarded 35-year-old landscape architect from Denver, developed the Boulder City master plan. He set the government buildings at the top of the site's hill. The town radiated out like a fan, and parks, plazas, and perimeters enclosed the neighborhoods in pleasant settings. Construction of the town began in March 1931, only a month before work started at the dam site. The increasing influx of workers, most of whom were housed in a cluster of temporary tent cabins known as Ragtown, forced the government to accelerate construction, and most of DeBoer's more grandiose elements (neighborhood greenbelts, large single-family houses) were abandoned in favor of more economical and expedient dormitories and small cottages. Still, Boulder City became a prettified all-American oasis of security and order in the midst of a great desert and the Great Depression.

Boulder City is the only place in Nevada where gambling is illegal.

Sights

Coming into Boulder City on US 93 (Nevada Highway) is more like entering a town in Arizona or New Mexico: The downtown streets are lined with Indian and Mexican gift shops, galleries, and shops selling crafts, jewelry, antiques, and collectibles, and businesses catering to the lake-bound crowd. Boulder City has no casinos.

Stop at the **Boulder Dam Hotel** (1305 Arizona St., 702/293-3510, www.boulderdamhotel.com, $90-135) for a glimpse at dam-construction and divorce-era Las Vegas. This darling, built in 1933 to accommodate visitors to the construction site, found new life as divorce tourists booked accommodations to wait out Nevada's residency requirements for ending their marriages, and the lobby is now home to the **Boulder City/Hoover Dam Museum** (702/294-1988, www.bcmha.org, 10am-5pm daily, $2 adults, $1 seniors and children). The colonial-style interior looks exactly as it did in 1933 when it was constructed, as you can see in the black-and-white photos that grace the walls. Inside are interesting photos from the 1930s of the Six Companies' rec hall and high scalers working high up on the canyon walls. Hear the inspiring stories of the dam workers' families making do and setting up households in the forbidding landscape. You can also see the high-scaler chair and pick up Dennis McBride's excellent book on Boulder City, *In the Beginning*. The restaurant is open for breakfast (included for hotel guests) and lunch. And the hotel is available for tea parties, reunions, and other special events.

Get a walking tour brochure at the hotel (or stream it on your tablet at https://walkbc.oncell.com/en/index.html) and stroll up Arizona Street then down Nevada Highway to get a feel for the history and design significance of downtown. Then continue on the residential and public-building walks to get an intimate glimpse of DeBoer's plan for the town as modified by the practicalities of government work. You can also head back toward Henderson on Nevada Highway to the **Frank T. Crowe Memorial Park** (www.bcnv.org, named for the chief dam engineer, immortalized in the book *Big Red*) and take a right onto Cherry Street to see the fine row of bungalows from the 1930s built for dam workers, Boulder City's first residents.

At the Boulder City branch of the **Nevada State Railroad Museum** (601 Yucca St., 702/486-5933, www.nevadasouthern.com, 9am-2pm Mon.-Fri., 9am-3pm Sat.-Sun.), railroad buffs can take a train ride on the **Nevada Southern Railway** ($10 adults, $5 ages 4-11, free under age 4); get a discount coupon online. The renovated historical cars make treks along the old Boulder Branch Line departing at 10am, 11:30am, 1pm, and 2:30pm Saturday-Sunday. The Pullman coaches, some of which date back to 1911, take passengers for a seven-mile, 45-minute round-trip journey across the stark Mojave Desert. All the cars and engines have been refurbished, and the enclosed cars have been retrofitted with air-conditioning. The spur used for the excursion was donated to the Nevada State Railroad Museum in 1985, and the train still chugs along the original tracks. The ride goes as far as the Railroad Pass Casino, and along the way passengers can expect to see jackrabbits, the occasional bighorn sheep, desert plant life, and a few historic sites.

Food and Accommodations

Except for the Boulder Dam Hotel, Boulder City has a handful of motels, all strung along Nevada Highway (US 93) as you enter town. Coming from the west, bypass the first several inns you come to. The first recommendable motel, the retro **Sands** (809 Nevada Way, 702/293-2589, http://motelbouldercity.com, $79-109), is clean and comfortable. Furnishings are utilitarian and sparse but include small fridges and microwaves. Boaters will appreciate the extra-large parking lot. A block farther, you'll be greeted by the impeccable landscaping and the retro-chic sign of the **El Rancho** (725 Nevada Hwy., 702/293-1085, $60-110). The spotless grounds mirror the accommodations. Sparkling microwaves and refrigerators, spacious rooms, quilts on the beds, and ceiling fans give the El Rancho a homey feel. Save even more with a cookout on barbecue grills outside, near the solar-heated pool, but be sure to eat at least one meal at the **Southwest Diner** (761 Nevada Hwy., 702/293-1537, www.southwestdinerbouldercity.com, $8-15) right next door.

Boulder City's only bed-and-breakfast, **Milo's Cellar & Inn** (534 Nevada Way, 702/294-4244, www.milosbouldercity.com, $129-149) offers four rooms evoking French and Italian wine country. Cozy comforters, plush linens, rich woodwork, and whirlpool tubs invite relaxation. The restaurant (11am-10pm daily, $14-20) mostly delivers bistro-style small plates but also has a nightly full dinner special.

If you're craving some nearby gaming action, you could continue even farther, almost to the shore of Lake Mead, to **Hoover Dam Lodge** (18000 US 93, 702/293-5000, http://hooverdamlodge.com, $100-150) inside Lake Mead National Recreation Area. The hotel is pet-friendly, with rooms decorated in bold oranges and reds reminiscent of the sunset on the rocks surrounding the lake. Other fun activities include panning for semiprecious gems and fossils at the **Hoover Dam Lodge Mining Co.,** browsing the general store, and testing your skill in the arcade.

Canyon Trail RV Park (1200 Industrial Rd., 702/293-1200, http://canyontrailrvparknv.com, $45) has plenty of overnight spots among its 242 sites. There's no shade and precious little greenery, but craggy sandstone mountains rise from the rear of the place. To get there, from the traffic light in Boulder City, take the truck route one block to Canyon Road. Turn left, drive to the end of Canyon Road, and turn left on Industrial Road.

Information and Services

The **Chamber of Commerce** (465 Nevada Way, 702/293-2034, www.bouldercitychamberofcommerce.com) has all the local brochures and can answer questions about the town, the dam, and the lake.

HOOVER DAM

The 1,400-mile Colorado River has been carving and gouging great canyons and valleys with red sediment-laden waters for 10 million years. For 10,000 years Native Americans, the Spanish, and Mormon settlers coexisted with the fitful river, rebuilding after spring floods and withstanding the droughts that often reduced the mighty waterway to a muddy trickle in fall. But in 1905 a wet winter and abnormal spring rains combined to drown everything in sight: Flash floods deepened the artificial canal and actually changed the course of the river to flow through California's low-lying valley. The message was clear to federal overseers: The Colorado had to be tamed, and over the next 15 years the Bureau of Reclamation began to "reclaim" the West, primarily by building dams and canals. By 1923, equitable water distribution for the Colorado River had been negotiated among the states and Mexico, and six years later Congress passed the Boulder Canyon Project Act, authorizing funds for Boulder Dam to be constructed in Black Canyon; the dam's name was eventually changed to honor Herbert Hoover, then Secretary of Commerce.

Today, the Colorado River system has several dams and reservoirs, storing roughly 60 million acre-feet of water. An acre-foot is just under 326,000 gallons, about as much water as an average U.S. household uses in two years.

California is allotted 4.4 million acre-feet, Arizona gets 2.8 million, Nevada 300,000, and Mexico 1.5 million. Hoover Dam, meanwhile, supplies 4 billion kilowatt-hours of electricity annually, enough to power 500,000 homes.

Visitors Center and Tours

The **Lake Mead visitors center** (702/494-2517, www.usbr.gov/lc/hooverdam, 9am-6pm daily summer, 9am-4:45pm daily winter, $8, free under age 4, parking $7) includes some exhibits, a movie about the Colorado River, and elevators that take you into the bowels of the dam. The 44,000-square-foot facility accommodates some 700,000 visitors each year. You can buy tickets for the 35-minute **Power Plant Tour** ($15 adults, $12 over age 61, ages 4-16, and military, free for military in uniform and children under age 4), which focuses on the dam's construction and engineering through multimedia presentations, exhibits, and a docent talk. Get in line as early as possible to shorten the wait time. The 53-story descent into the dam's interior takes more than a minute. Tunnels lead you to a monumental room housing the monolithic turbines. Next, you step outside to look up to the top of the dam and the magnificently arched bypass bridge downstream. The tour

Hoover Dam

ends with a walk through one of the diversion tunnels, a 30-foot-wide water pipe. The guides pack extensive statistics and stories into the short tour. The one-hour **Dam Tour** (every 30 minutes 9:30am-3:30pm daily, ages 8 and over, $30) is a more comprehensive version of the Power Plant Tour, so no need to do both. Both tours include admission to the visitors center. Tickets to the Dam Tour cannot be purchased in advance; Power Plant Tour tickets are available online at www.usbr.gov/lc/hooverdam.

Getting There

The Hoover Dam makes an interesting half-day escape from the glitter of Las Vegas. The bypass bridge diverts traffic away from Hoover Dam, saving time and headaches for both drivers and dam visitors. Still, the 35-mile drive from central Las Vegas to a parking lot at the dam will take 45 minutes or more. From the Strip, I-15 South connects with I-215 southeast of the airport, and I-215 East takes drivers to US 93 in Henderson. Remember that US 93 shares the roadway with US 95 and I-515 till well past Henderson. Going south on US 93, exit at NV 172 to the dam. A parking garage ($10) is convenient to the visitors center and dam tours, but free parking is available at turnouts on both sides of the dam for those willing to walk.

LAKE MEAD NATIONAL RECREATION AREA

Three roads provide access to Lake Mead from the Las Vegas area. From the north, take NV 147 (Lake Mead Blvd.) as it runs east from North Las Vegas. Turning left at the intersection with NV 167 takes drivers to several access roads leading to coves (Government Wash, Crawdad, Boxcar, etc.) in Las Vegas Bay via unpaved access roads. The highway parallels the lake up to the Overton Arm and Valley of Fire State Park before rejoining I-15. Turning right at the NV 147/167 junction leads to Northshore and then Lakeshore Roads. Several popular destinations can be reached along this road.

From Henderson and points south, you can follow NV 564 (Lake Mead Dr.) northeast past Lake Las Vegas, where it ends at NV 147. Turn left to hook up with Northshore Road or right to Lakeshore Road. You can also take US 93 to Boulder City, where it takes on an additional name: Nevada Highway. If you stay on this road, you'll wind through canyons and eventually reach Hoover Dam, but if you turn left in town, you'll be on Lakeshore Road heading north along the western shore.

From Boulder City, stay on Nevada Highway through town for eight miles. You enter **Lake Mead National Recreation Area** (www.nps.gov/lake) and arrive at the junction of US 93 and NV 166 (Lakeshore Rd.). Taking a left on the state route brings you right to the **Alan Bible Visitor Center** (702/293-8990, 8:30am-4:30pm daily) and park headquarters for the recreation area. Named for a popular U.S. senator from Nevada, the center has maps, brochures, knowledgeable rangers, and a 15-minute movie on the lake and its ecosystem.

Across Lakeshore Road from the visitors center is a parking lot for the trailhead to the **U.S. Government Construction Railroad Trail.** The 2.6-mile one-way route follows an abandoned railroad grade along a ledge overlooking the lake. It passes through four tunnels blasted through the hills and ends at the fifth tunnel, which is sealed. This is an enjoyable level stroll that anyone can do. Mountain bikers can get on the **Bootleg Canyon Mountain Bike Trail,** which has 36 miles of cross-country and downhill runs (the "Elevator Shaft" has a 22 percent grade). Trailhead access is off Yucca or Canyon Street.

Another trail to consider in Boulder City is the **River Mountain Hiking Trail,** a five-mile round-trip hike originally built by the Civilian Conservation Corps in 1935 and recently restored. It has good views of the lake and the valley. The trailhead is on the truck bypass, just beyond the traffic light in downtown Boulder City, on the left as you're heading toward the dam.

Lakeshore Road

On Lakeshore Road about two miles north of the Nevada Highway ingress to the recreation area is the **Lake Mead RV Village** (288 Lakeshore Rd., 702/293-2540, www.lakemeadrvvillage.com, $34-44), which has many permanent mobiles and trailers but has 115 spaces dedicated to transient RVers, including many pull-throughs (register at the office near the entrance). Laundry facilities and groceries are available. Turn right off Lakeshore Road into the entrance and right into the trailer village. If you take a left at the entrance, you enter **Boulder Beach Campground** ($10), a sprawling and somewhat rustic site with water, grills, a dump station, and plenty of shade under cottonwoods and pines, but no hookups. There are 150 campsites for tents or small self-contained motor homes. Find a spot then return to the entrance; pay with cash in an envelope and take your receipt. It's a three-minute walk down to the water, or a half-mile drive north on Lakeshore Road. They don't call it Boulder Beach for nothing: The bottom is rocky and hard on the feet (bring your water shoes), but the water is bathtub warm July-September, around 80°F. Sheltered picnic tables and restrooms are available waterside.

Seven miles beyond Boulder Beach is **Las Vegas Bay Campground** (702/293-8990, $20). Turn right into the Las Vegas Marina, then take your first left; the campground is about one mile down the spur road. The campground sits on a bluff over the lake; it's not quite as shady or as large as Boulder Beach. Also, you have to climb down a pretty steep slope to get to the water, and there's no real beach. There are 86 campsites for tents or self-contained motor homes up to 35 feet. Piped drinking water, flush toilets, picnic tables, grills, and fire pits are provided, and there is a campground host.

Continuing north, follow Lakeshore Road around to the left (northwest), then take a right onto Northshore Road (NV 167). In another few miles, turn right at the intersection with Lake Mead Boulevard (NV 147). In another seven miles is the turnoff for Callville Bay.

Callville Bay

Heading northeast from Las Vegas on NV 167, Callville Bay Road is the next right turn after the Boxcar Cove access road. After rocking and rolling four miles down to the marina, the first left is to **Callville Bay Trailer Village** (702/565-8958, $20), most of which is occupied by permanent mobiles and trailers.

Lake Mead National Recreation Area

There are only five spaces for overnight motor homes, all with full hookups and three with pull-throughs. RVs, along with tent campers, can also park without hookups at the campground across the road.

Callville Bay Campground (702/293-8990, $20) is a little farther down the access road. A beautiful grassy area greets you at the entrance, with stone picnic benches under shelters and a restroom. The sites closer to the front have the taller shade-giving oleanders; those toward the rear are more exposed. A 0.5-mile trail climbs from the dump station near the entrance to a sweeping panorama of the whole area. There are 80 campsites with running water, flush toilets, picnic tables, and grills, and there is a campground host.

The marina has a grocery store with a snack bar, and there is a bar-restaurant with a wall of big picture windows overlooking the lake. Down at the boat launch, you can rent personal watercraft and boats for fishing, skiing, and more—even houseboats from 50 to 75 feet.

Back on NV 167, continue east; it's rugged country out here, with the Black Mountains between you and the lake, and the dark, brooding Muddy Mountains on the left. Eventually the road turns north toward the east edge of the Muddies. The turnoff to Echo Bay, 24 miles from Callville, is on the right.

Back on Northshore Road, continue north, skirting the east edge of the Muddies. Five miles past the turnoff for the abandoned Echo Canyon Marina is **Rogers Spring,** which bubbles up clear and warm in a wash that runs east from the Muddy Mountains into Roger's Bay in the Overton Arm of Lake Mead. The warm turquoise pool, outlined by second-generation palms and cottonwoods, overflows into a bubbling creek that meanders down a tree-lined course toward Lake Mead. Tropical fish, the descendants of the denizens of a failed hatchery from the 1950s, dart in the shallows and thrive in its warm waters. The trailhead for a mile-long trail to an overlook is across the bridge. A mile up the road from Rogers Spring is **Blue Point Spring,** which provides a grand view of Lake Mead on one side and the back of Valley of Fire on the other.

River Tours

Black Canyon River Adventures (800/455-3490, www.blackcanyonadventures.com, 10am daily year-round, $97 adults, $87 youth, $58 children) buses rafters from Lake Mead RV Village to the restricted side of the dam, where they board 35-person motorized craft for a three-hour ride ending at Willow Beach, 13 miles downstream on the Arizona side of the Colorado River. Riders often spot ospreys and bighorn sheep on these trips, and rafters can wade and swim in the chilly water before enjoying the box lunch provided. Round-trip transportation from Strip hotels is $49.

Though trips had been temporarily suspended at press time, the *Desert Princess,* a 250-passenger Mississippi-style stern-wheeler, and its little sister, the 149-passenger side-wheeler *Desert Princess Too,* usually cruise Lake Mead from the **Lake Mead Cruises Landing** (490 Horsepower Cove Rd., 702/293-6180 or 866/292-9191, www.lakemeadcruises.com, noon and 2pm daily Apr.-Oct., days and times vary Feb.-Mar. and Nov., adults $26, ages 2-11 $13). Champagne brunch cruises (10am Sun., adults $45, ages 2-11 $19.50) and dinner cruises (6:30pm Sun., Tues., Thurs., $61.50 adults, ages 2-11 $25) are also offered.

Recreation

Motorized fun is the most obvious recreation on Lake Mead. **Boating** options on the vast lake range from ski boats skipping across the surface to houseboats puttering lazily toward hidden coves to personal watercraft jumping wakes and negotiating hairpin turns. **Las Vegas Boat Harbor** (702/293-1191, www.lasvegasboatharbor.com) and **Lake Mead Marina** (702/293-3484, www.boatinglakemead.com), both at Hemenway Harbor (Hemenway Rd., off Lakeshore Rd. near the junction with US 93, 702/293-1191), rent power boats, pontoons, and WaveRunners for $50-95 per hour; paddleboards and kayaks are $35 per hour, with half-day and daily rates available. **Callville Bay Marina** (off Northshore Rd., 17 miles east of Lake Las Vegas, www.callvillebay.com) has all these and houseboat rentals too.

For **anglers,** largemouth bass, rainbow trout, catfish, and black crappie have been mainstays for decades. These days, however, striped bass are the most popular sport fish. Fishing supplies and fishing licenses can be obtained at the marinas.

Sixty miles south of Boulder City, recreation is also abundant at **Lake Mojave,** created by Davis Dam in 1953. This lake backs up almost all the way to Hoover Dam like a southern extension of Lake Mead. The two lakes are similar in climate, desert scenery, vertical-walled canyon enclosures, and a shoreline lined with numerous private coves. There is excellent trout fishing at Willow Beach on the Arizona side, where the water is too cold for swimming but perfect for serious angling. Stripers, attracted by the fingerling trout planted in the spring, patrol these waters as well. A few over 55 pounds have been caught, and 20-pounders are not at all rare. **Cottonwood Cove Resort** (10000 Cottonwood Cove Rd., Searchlight, 702/297-1464, www.cottonwoodcoveresort. com), 14 miles east of central Searchlight, sits just north of the widest part of the lake. Access is also available on the Arizona side at **Katherine Landing,** just north of Davis Dam. It rents watercraft and has a motel ($90-150) and RV park ($30-45).

Swimming in Lake Mead requires the least equipment—a bathing suit. No lifeguards are on duty. Boulder Beach and Cottonwood Cove offer free life jacket loaners sized for infants through adults. For **divers,** visibility in Lake Mead averages 30 feet, and the water is stable. There is a dive park north of the swimming beach at Boulder Beach. It slopes gently to about 70 feet with placed objects and boats to explore, which makes it a good introduction to the sport for novice divers. The sights of the deep are more spectacular elsewhere: The yacht *Tortuga* rests at a depth of 50 feet near the Boulder Islands; Hoover Dam's asphalt factory sits on the canyon floor nearby; the old Mormon town of St. Thomas, inundated by the lake in 1938, has many a watery story to tell; and Castle Cliffs at Gypsum Reef has drop-offs and irregular formations caused by erosion.

VALLEY OF FIRE STATE PARK

Working with a palette of red-tinged rock for 150 million years, the sun, wind, and rain created the masterpiece that is **Valley of Fire State Park** (29450 Valley of Fire Hwy., 702/397-2088, http://parks.nv.gov). Like Red Rock Canyon, this valley, six miles long and 3-4 miles wide, gets its distinctive color from the oxidizing metals in its Mesozoic-era sandstone. It is part of the Navajo Formation, a rocky block that stretches from southern Colorado through New Mexico, Arizona, Utah, and Nevada, and its monuments—arches and protruding jagged walls in brilliant vermilion, magenta, and gold—epitomize the Southwest.

The highest and youngest formations in the park are mountains of sand deposited by desert winds 140 million years ago. These dunes petrified, oxidized, and were chiseled into psychedelic shapes and colors. Underneath them is a 5,000-foot-deep layer dating back at least 250 million years, when brown mud was uplifted to displace the inland sea. The gray limestone below represents another 200 million years of deposits from the Paleozoic marine environment 550 million years ago.

This stunning valley was venerated by Native Americans, as seen in numerous petroglyphs in the soft rock, and it was part of the old Arrowhead Highway auto trail through southern Nevada.

Exploring the Park

A turnout near the entrance to the park has a self-service fee station: $10 entry, $20 for camping. An information shelter offers a description of **Elephant Rock,** one of the best and most photographed examples of eroded sandstone in the park; a short trail leads to it from the sign. Continue west past signs for the Arrowhead Trail and petrified logs to the **cabins,** built for travelers out of sandstone bricks by the Civilian Conservation Corps in 1935. Farther in, the **Seven Sisters** are stunning sentinels along the road.

The **visitors center** (8:30am-4:30pm daily) has a truly spectacular setting under a mountain of fire. Outside is a demonstration garden, and inside is the finest set of exhibits at any Nevada state park. Signboards by the front window describe the complex geological history of the landscape. You can spend another hour reading all the displays on the history, ecology, archaeology, and recreation of the park as well as browsing the changing exhibit gallery and the bookshelf near the information desk. There is a colorful interpretive signboard describing the most popular features in the Valley of Fire. Don't forget to pick up a map of the park.

From the visitors center, take the spur road to **Petroglyph Canyon Trail** and dig your feet into some red sand. **Mouse's Tank** is a basin that fills with water after a rain. A fugitive Native American named Mouse hid here in the late 1890s. The spur road continues through the towering canyon and peaks

at **Rainbow Vista,** which has a parking area and a spectacular overlook.

The road continues four miles to **Silica Dome,** where you can park and gape at the walls, pillars, and peaks of sparkling white rock.

Head back toward the visitors center and take the through road, NV 169. Driving west, you come to a 0.25-mile loop trail to fenced-in **petrified wood,** the most common local fossil. On the other side of the highway, another spur road leads to the campgrounds and the high staircase up to sheer **Atlatl Rock,** which is inscribed with petroglyphs. This is the tallest outdoor staircase in the state, more than 100 steps up to the face of the rock; you'll wonder how the petroglyphs' creators got up here.

Atlatl Rock is between the two **campgrounds.** Together they total 51 campsites for tents or self-contained motor homes up to 30 feet. Both have piped drinking water, picnic tables under ramadas, grills, and fire rings.

The loop road continues back to the highway. Take a right and continue west to the **Beehives,** which are worth a look. From here you can turn around, return to the east entrance, and take a left on NV 169 toward

Valley of Fire petroglyphs

Overton, or you can head to the west end of the park and back to Las Vegas (55 miles).

BITTER SPRINGS TRAIL AND BUFFINGTON POCKETS

The Bitter Springs Back Country Byway Trail to Buffington Pockets and beyond is a challenging but colorful drive through red and tan sandstone bluffs. The 28-mile drive requires a dependable vehicle with decent ground clearance; four-wheel-drive is not necessary. However, make sure your spare tire and jack are in order and that someone knows where you're headed and when you expect to return. Stay on the main road, and you'll be fine. If you do have four-wheel-drive, you can venture into the many canyons for an even more surreal experience. The beginning of the Bitter Springs Byway is 4.5 miles east of the Valley of Fire exit on I-15; follow the sign for "Bitter Springs" to the left (south).

The trail starts out cutting through the foothills of the Muddy Mountains, then travels through several dry washes and past numerous abandoned mining operations before ending up on Northshore Road. Along the way you have the opportunity to view natural water tanks and geologic formations that are rare in this region. Landforms are colorful, complex, and add to the feeling of isolation. Among the more striking scenes you'll encounter is **Bitter Ridge,** a sweeping arc that cuts across a rolling valley for eight miles. Geology buffs will appreciate the features of this tilt fault, with its rugged vertical southern face looming several hundred feet off the desert floor.

Moving past rolling red, brown, black, and white landforms, you drop into **Bitter Valley,** where red buttes stand on the desert floor. Emerging from the canyon, you'll be captivated by the sight of the brilliantly colored sandstone hills of **Buffington Pockets** and **Color Rock Quarry.**

The trail continues through a field of sandstone boulders, and you'll soon arrive at the entrance to **Hidden Valley,** tucked away a short distance from the road up a deep, winding, boulder-choked canyon. Between the valley walls, which soar hundreds of feet into the desert sky, you'll see sandstone windows, arches, and hoodoos. A short hike up into the valley brings you to a scenic overlook, where—judging by the large number of pictographs—prehistoric visitors were inspired by the view.

Abandoned buildings and other relics and remnants from the American Borax mining operation appear next on ground pocked by 30-foot-deep cisterns that once held water. Mine tunnels and passages are also abundant in the area, along with the debris associated with old mining districts. Be careful around the old mines: Cave-ins, rattlesnakes, and other dangers lurk. Obey all signs and fencing that have been installed for your protection.

There are no services along this isolated road, but maps of the area are available from the local **Bureau of Land Management** office (4701 N. Torrey Pines Dr., Las Vegas, 702/515-5000). Ask for the Nevada Back Country Byway guide for Bitter Springs Trail.

MOAPA VALLEY

Lake Mead terminates at the Muddy River Wash, the outlet of Moapa Valley, along NV 169 (Northshore Rd.) north of Valley of Fire State Park. A thin strip of rich agricultural green lines the road up the river valley. Puebloan ancestors successfully farmed this land 1,000 years ago and built the Pueblo Grande de Nevada, or Lost City, on the fertile delta between the Muddy and Virgin Rivers. The Paiute replaced the Pueblo and still lived in the valley when the Mormons began to colonize it in 1864.

Farther north, seven miles past I-15 exit 90 on NV 168, is the **Moapa Valley National Wildlife Refuge** (www.fws.gov, 9am-3pm Fri.-Sun. Labor Day-Memorial Day). The refuge manages habitat for the Moapa White River springfish and the endangered Moapa dace. The finger-size dace live nowhere else in the world but the waters of Moapa, fed by 88°F springs.

Overton

Overton, 50 miles northeast of Las Vegas, is a compact agricultural community whose downtown is strung along several blocks of NV 169, also known as Moapa Valley Boulevard and Main Street. Surprisingly for such a small town, Overton offers two strong lunch options. **Sugars Home Plate** (309 S. Moapa Valley Blvd., 702/397-8084, www.sugarshomeplate.com, 7am-9pm Tues.-Sun., $13-25) serves $7.50 bacon and eggs, $8-9 burgers such as the Sugar Burger (a cheeseburger with polish sausage), and homemade fish pie. Dinners are traditional: steak, shrimp, halibut, and chicken breast entrées. There's also a sports bar with bar-top video poker and sports memorabilia. The other food pick is just a block away: **Inside Scoop** (395 S. Moapa Valley Blvd., 702/397-2055, 7am-8pm Mon.-Sat., 7am-7pm Sun., $10-20) has 30-plus ice cream flavors and filling sandwiches. The baked potatoes come with a variety of toppings.

North Shore Inn (520 N. Moapa Valley Blvd., 702/397-6000, $90-130) provides basic guest rooms.

Lost City Museum

A glimpse of the Ancestral Puebloan or Anasazi legacy is found at the **Lost City Museum** (721 S. Moapa Valley Blvd., 702/397-2193, 8:30am-4:30pm daily, $5) just south of Overton. The museum houses an immense collection of Pueblo artifacts, including an actual pueblo foundation, and a fascinating series of black-and-white photos covering the site's excavation in 1924. In a November 1976 article in *Nevada* magazine, David Moore made the insightful point that the Lost City wasn't so much lost as simply overlooked; Jedediah Smith mentioned it during his travels through southern Nevada in the 1820s, and another expedition reported these "ruins of an ancient city" in the *New York Tribune* in 1867, but an official excavation was not initiated until 1924. Some of the ruins were drowned by Lake Mead, but in 1975 an entire ancient village was uncovered by workers digging a leach line.

The exterior of the museum, a re-creation of an adobe pueblo like the one the ancient ones built on the site, was constructed of sun-baked adobe by the Civilian Conservation Corps in 1935. It is possible to climb down the log ladder into the authentic pit house in front, and to stroll around back for petroglyphs, more pueblos, picnic tables, and a pioneer monument.

MESQUITE

Thirty miles north on I-15, the reemergence of resorts tells drivers they are nearing the state line. Mesquite gives Nevada's northern Arizona neighbors their closest chance to scratch the casino gambling itch. Mesquite is probably the most upscale of Nevada's border gambling towns, although like the rest of the nation it has not fully recovered from the Great Recession. Still, the city's livability, lush golf resorts, and gambling venues keep it going strong. Thanks to the casinos, the town went from a population of 900 in 1980 to about 17,000 today.

Casinos

Virgin River (100 N. Pioneer Blvd., 702/346-7777 or 800/438-2929, https://virginriver.com, $39-68) is on the east side of town. It's smaller and more crowded, with the usual slots and table games as well as bingo and a sports book, lounge, and bowling alley/arcade. Its 772 guest rooms have gold, brown, and dusty rose color schemes. **Sierra's** (7am-9pm daily, $11-15) is the best buffet and one of the best values in town. Southern barbecue night on Thursday is our favorite.

Formerly Merv Griffin's Player's Island and now the Virgin River's sister casino, **CasaBlanca** (950 W. Mesquite Blvd., 702/346-7529 or 877/438-2929, http://casablancaresort.com, $59-89) has 500 guest rooms, an RV park, an attractive casino, a lounge, a showroom, a coffee shop, a buffet, a steakhouse, and a large pool area. The pièce de résistance is an extensive European-style health spa complete with warm and hot pools, a *watsu* pool, Virgin River mud baths, a steam room and sauna, and all kinds of massage and skin therapies. The "Casablanca Trio" ($160) refreshes mind and body with a scrub, wrap, and massage. The casino hosts free summer outdoor concerts—"Casapooloooza"—poolside, with tribute bands and regional pop and country acts. **Katherine's Steakhouse** (5pm-9pm daily, $35-50) has sumptuous meals and tableside preparation of appetizers, salads, and bananas foster.

Employee-owned **Eureka Casino and Hotel** (275 Mesa Blvd., 702/346-4600 or 800/346-4611, www.eurekamesquite.com, $39-75), up the hill from the Virgin River, draws customers with a 45,000-square-foot casino and several customizable entertainment packages: golf, shooting, massage, etc. **Gregory's Mesquite Grill** (4pm-9pm daily, $32-50) rivals Katherine's at the CasaBlanca for quality. Splurge on the filet Oscar. **Seasons** (24 hours daily) takes bar games to a new level. Corn hole and life-size Jenga blocks take their place beside Ping-Pong on the outdoor patio.

Golf

The architects took great pains to incorporate and accentuate—rather than compete with—Mesquite's natural attractions when constructing the town's championship golf courses. One of the newest courses, **Falcon Ridge** (1024 Normandy Ln., 702/346-6363, http://golffalcon.com, $45-115) is also one of the shortest, at 6,590 yards. It is not, however, short on scenery, with lush, undulating fairways contrasting with stark deserts and bluffs.

One of the top public courses in the country, **Wolf Creek** (403 Paradise Pkwy., 702/346-1670, www.golfwolfcreek.com, $85-200) nestles each hole in its own private canyon, with unique elevation drops and challenging green reads. Even if you don't golf, come for the views and the delectable prime rib at Wolf Creek's **Terrace Restaurant** (702/345-6701, 7am-4pm Sun.-Thurs., 7am-4pm and 5pm-9pm Fri.-Sat., $35-40). Long hitters can try to tame the 7,471-yard **Coyote Springs** course (3100 NV 168, 702/422-1400, www.coyotesprings.com, $90-139), but its 11 water holes place a premium on accuracy off the tee. An hour west of Mesquite, the Jack Nicklaus-designed course lies in a sweeping valley.

Plenty of other courses are well worth checking out: **CasaBlanca** (1100 W. Hafen Ln., 702/346-6764, http://casablancaresort.com, $65-105) and **Conestoga** (1499 Falcon Ridge Pkwy., 702/346-4292, www.conestogagolf.com) are among the most accessible and challenging for any skill level.

The **Mesquite Golf Pass** (www.mesquitegolfpass.com, $125) entitles holders to a round at each of four courses, along with a free sleeve of balls and 15 percent off in the pro shop.

Food

Outside the casinos, Mesquite's top restaurants are of the ethnic variety. **Panda Garden** (2 W. Mesquite Blvd., Ste. 101, 702/346-3028, 11am-9:30pm daily, $10-20) has great lunch specials. For dinner, make your own dim sum from the appetizer menu. You won't be disappointed in the spring rolls, crab puffs, steamed dumplings, and chicken wings. For pasta, go to **Cucina Italiana** (471 W. Mesquite Blvd., 702/346-5117, 11am-2pm and 4pm-9pm daily, $20-35). The homemade vinaigrette will make you want to stuff yourself with salad, but save room for the zesty linguini and veal Marsala. It's worth the search through the office complex in which it's located to find Mesquite's best Mexican joint: **Tacos Tijuana** (340 Falcon Ridge Pkwy., Ste. 402, 702/346-3113, $10-15) earns its stripes for its perfectly prepared pork adobada.

Accommodations

Catering to travel baseball, soccer, and other youth and adult teams, **Rising Star Sports Ranch** (333 N. Sandhill Blvd., 702/346-5678, www.risingstarsportsranch.com, $79-119) offers accommodations with connecting rooms and bunk bed configurations. There's on-site sand volleyball, a putting green, and a swimming pool. Promoting more of a condo feel,

Highland Estates Hotel & Resort (555 Highland Dr., 702/346-0871, www.highland-estatesresort.com, $65-115) touts two pools, a fitness area, a library, a laundry, barbecue pits, and free coffee.

CasaBlanca (702/346-7529, https:// casablancaresort.com/hotel-rv-park, $28) has 45 spaces for motor homes up to 35 feet, all with full hookups; 30 are pull-throughs. Tents are not allowed. **Desert Skies** (350 E. NV 91, Littlefield, AZ, 928/347-6000, http:// desertskiesresorts.com, $50) has 340 large sites, free Wi-Fi, clean facilities, and even a library. The **Solstice Motorcoach Resort** (345 Mystic Dr., 702/346-8522, www.sol-sticemotorcoachresort.com, $35-40) boasts great views of a central pond and its visiting waterfowl. Large sites next door to a full grocery store await at **Sun Resorts RV Park** (400 Hillside Dr., 702/346-6666, http:// sunresortsrv.com, $40).

VIRGIN CANYON

The Virgin River is the only wild river left in southern Nevada. It ends in Lake Mead across from Overton, creating a silted marshland where waterfowl prowl for fish, frogs, and mud-turtles. The headwaters of the Virgin River, one of the main tributaries feeding the Colorado River and Lake Mead, are in Utah's Dixie National Forest, where winter ice and snow and summer rainstorms feed the 300-mile-long river. Occasionally, violent deluges flood out the valleys below Dixie, eroding forests and sending enormous walls of water sweeping through narrow canyons in Zion National Park.

By the time the Virgin reaches the Virgin River Canyon, or Virgin Gorge, as it has come to be known (I-15 runs through it in the far northwest corner of Arizona), its waters are somewhat tamer, but during years with heavy rain, they can still be wild and dangerous. During calmer times of the year, it is possible to explore sections of the Virgin River in canoes, kayaks, inner tubes, and hiking boots.

Among some of the treasures you'll find in the gorge are extensive hikes to places where ancient Native Americans carved petroglyphs into rock walls. When you get tired, you can relax on soft sandy riverbanks under salt cedars and watch the happy birds hunting fat insects, or contemplate what these rock walls have seen during the last 50 million years. Caves abound along the riverbanks; inside some are large tree trunks, pounded into the caves by the force of a raging torrent in times past. In some places the granite walls are polished smooth by water levels dating to thousands of years ago. In other caves, high up on the face of the cliffs, you can see where the campfires of ancient people blackened the ceiling. Deer and other small game abound in the gorge.

BLACK CANYON

The river nearest to Las Vegas flows through Black Canyon. The discharge from Hoover Dam generally creates a current of about 3 mph, making for an easily negotiated upstream paddle even for novices. The dam discharges water from the bottom of Lake Mead, so it comes out at a chilly 53°F all year, warming up as it goes downriver toward Eldorado Canyon, where it widens out and is warm enough for swimming in the summer. Navigational and mile markers are posted on the shores of the river: red triangles with even numbers on the Arizona side, green squares with odd numbers on the Nevada side. These markers indicate the approximate distance, in miles, from Davis Dam at the extreme southern end of Lake Mojave. Also look for bighorn sheep on the cliffs along the river throughout Black Canyon. Sighting them provides the sharp-eyed observer a special opportunity to see these majestic animals in their natural environment. Cormorants, lizards, and small mammals are easier to find as you explore the shoreline.

Remember that the water level in the canyon can fluctuate considerably during the day, sometimes as much as 4-6 vertical feet, depending on releases from Hoover Dam. When stopping to camp, picnic, or explore, small craft should be pulled well up out of the water and tied off; larger craft should be well anchored on shore above any high-water marks to prevent being stranded.

Launching

The launch site is restricted to federal employees and licensed vendors. To put in here, you must make arrangements with one of these contractors to shuttle you and your canoe or kayak to the launch site. The contractor will add the $22 National Park Service permit fee to the bill. The U.S. Department of the Interior's Bureau of Reclamation places strict limits on the number of people allowed to access the canyon from this location. All popular dates, such as weekends and holidays, are booked far in advance. Weekday launches can usually be acquired with a few weeks' notice. The authorized livery services, such as **Desert Adventures** (702/293-5026, http://kayaklasvegas.com), **Desert River Outfitters** (928/736-3033, www.desertriver-outfitters.com), and **Jerkwater Canoe Co.** (928/768-7753, www.jerkwatercanoe.com), also rent canoes and kayaks and can arrange motorized rafting trips through the canyon.

Exploring on the Colorado River
CAVES

Once on the river, there are several exciting places to visit and things to do. You can paddle into two **rain caves** on the west wall that allow warm and cold droplets of water to pour through the grotto roof. During the construction of Hoover Dam, workers started to drill a tunnel at this site, but they encountered 122°F water and had to abandon the work. The partially drilled **Sauna Cave** remains. As you go deeper into the cave, it becomes darker and hotter, and you'll encounter a heavy hot mist. Geothermal activity is high all along the canyon, and you'll find more evidence of it as you drift downstream.

GOLDSTRIKE CANYON

Fifty yards below the entrance to the lagoon on the left is a small, very hot spring near

Goldstrike Canyon. A short walk up the canyon leads to hot pools and a hot waterfall that is about as hot as humanly tolerable—110°F. Algae gives the surrounding rocks a vivid green color. The rock formations are spectacular, and there are many hot pools. The rocks and pebbles in the hot stream are sharp, so wearing shoes is advised. Be aware that *Naegleria fowleri,* an amoeba common in thermal pools, can enter the human body through the nose, causing a rare infection and possible death. Do not allow water from the hot springs or the streams to enter your nose, and never dive into or submerse your head in any thermal water in this recreation area.

Another hot **waterfall** is within a few feet of the river about 100 yards below Goldstrike Canyon on the Arizona side. To ensure you don't drift past it, paddle upstream from Goldstrike Canyon to allow enough space to get across the river. This waterfall is larger and not as hot as the one in Goldstrike Canyon. Just past the waterfall is a palm tree, a non-native species planted around 1970 by G. W. Paulin, who loved these canyons and spent much time exploring the river.

BOY SCOUT CANYON

Back on the Nevada side, **Boy Scout Canyon** is about 0.3 mile south of the mile 62 marker. This sandy beach at the mouth of a large canyon leads to hot springs and hot pools about 0.5 mile up the canyon. The hike involves some climbing, and hand lines have been installed to aid the scramble up some boulders. The stream goes underground before it reaches the river.

RINGBOLT RAPIDS

In the last half of the 19th century, steamboats plied the Colorado River, even this far north. Their engines, however, were insufficient to make the upriver journey without help. Ringbolts were anchored in the riverside boulders, and towropes were threaded through the bolts to assist the boats. You can see one of these bolts on the Arizona side about 50 yards upriver from **Ringbolt Rapids.** The construction of Davis Dam, 60 miles downstream, and the resulting Lake Mojave significantly tamed these rapids, which at one time were some of the most challenging on the Colorado River. The rapids are adjacent to White Rock Canyon and the hot springs on the Arizona side of the river.

ARIZONA HOT SPRINGS

The pools comprising **Arizona Hot Springs** are about 0.5 mile west of the Colorado River and four miles below Hoover Dam on US 93 east. Exit at the sign, park, and walk down the wash to the river and 0.5 mile downstream. The series of three graduated pools lies midway through a six-mile loop that's perfect for a day hike or weekend camping getaway. Despite requiring a bit of scrambling and a 20-foot ladder climb to enter the pools, the springs are quite accessible; expect company if you go. The mineral-rich water cools as it cascades out of the top pool into lower holes.

GOLD STRIKE HOT SPRINGS

Like its sister springs across the river, **Gold Strike Hot Springs** demands some bouldering and scrambling to reach its soothing waters. Pick up the trailhead just off US 93, about a mile east of Hoover Dam Lodge. The trail to the springs is about four miles. Previous soakers have installed ropes to ease the descent into the river valley. The area around the springs is ripe for cliff-launched cannonballs into the Colorado. Look for the natural slide for a thrilling plunge. Intense summer heat in these parts can be deadly. As such, the springs and trail are closed mid-May through September.

GAUGING STATION

An old **Gauging Station** is an interesting remnant of Hoover Dam's construction. It clings to the Nevada canyon wall at mile 54.25. The gauging station was used prior to and during construction of Hoover Dam for monitoring the water level, flow rate, and silt content of the Colorado River. A cable car provided access to the station from the Arizona side. Just across the river on the Arizona side is the trail and catwalk used by the resident engineers (who were responsible for gathering the data at the gauging station) to travel from their residence to the station. The catwalk can be seen high up on the sheer walls above the river; it is unsafe to access. A second cable car across a side canyon enabled the engineers to go from the trail over to the catwalk. The foundations of the engineers' house and garage are just downriver at about mile 53.

WILLOW BEACH FISH HATCHERY

The buildings on the Arizona bank just before mile 52 are the **Willow Beach Fish Hatchery.** The buoys floating on the Arizona shore mark an area that is closed to all watercraft, including canoes and kayaks. The Willow Beach area extends for about 0.5 mile along the Arizona shore. If you're ending your trip at Willow Beach, boat to the south end at the harbor, past the marinas, and bring your vessel to shore at the south end of the parking lot. There is convenient vehicle access to this location, and you will not come into conflict with other boaters as you remove your boat from the water. South of Willow Beach, the river is still narrow and cold; it continues flowing through the deep canyon for about 3.5 miles. Life jackets must still be worn. The hatchery supplies planted rainbow trout to the river, Lake Mead, and other fishing holes nearby. The just-released fingerlings provide monster striped bass with a buffet, and lunkers lurk during plant time. A few rainbows escape to replenish what the stripers and anglers take.

MONKEY HOLE

The point where the river widens is known as **Monkey Hole.** With a bit of imagination, the rock formation high on the Arizona shore kinda sorta resembles a monkey. Just below Monkey Hole and mile 48, the Mead-Liberty power lines cross the river.

WINDY CANYON

The stretch of river between miles 45 and 44A is called **Windy Canyon.** On occasion, up-river winds become quite strong in this area, and the canyon more than earns its name. People in canoes and other small boats are recommended to check the wind currents before venturing below Willow Beach, the last takeout point before Windy Canyon. Below mile 44A, the river spreads out into Copper Basin; several canyons open out in this area, providing good places to camp.

CHALK CLIFFS

Just below Squaw Peaks on the Nevada side are **Chalk Cliffs.** A navigational light and marker 43, high on the Nevada side, mark the mouth of Black Canyon. Life jackets are not required below this point, but their continued use is strongly recommended, as the river current is still strong.

ELDORADO CANYON

Eldorado Canyon is on the Nevada side at about mile 39. The takeout point is a 0.25-mile-long uphill portage to the road. The canyon is a prime spot to see birds and other wildlife, and it's home to the **Techatticup Mine,** once the most productive gold, silver, and copper mine in southern Nevada. The new owners operate a general store and give tours of the mine and remnants of a mill, cabins, and a bunkhouse. Scenes from the movie *3000 Miles to Graceland* were filmed here, and the crashed airplane prop is still here.

For intrepid boaters who want to continue south of Eldorado Canyon, be prepared for open water, possible very windy conditions, and extreme temperature ranges. Cottonwood Cove is 17 miles away, and Katherine Landing is 40 miles downstream, south of Lake Mohave.

Laughlin

Beyond Davis Dam, which contains Lake Mohave, the gaming and river boomtown of Laughlin is one of the hottest spots in the country. In 1994, the official thermometer at Laughlin's Clark County Fire Department station registered a sizzling 125°F, Nevada's highest recorded temperature. In another way, Laughlin is pretty cool: You'll immediately notice how airy and bright the casinos are, thanks to the big picture windows overlooking the river. Their more comfortable and less claustrophobic atmosphere makes you wonder what Las Vegas has against natural light. The hotel rooms can be 50 percent cheaper than comparable ones in Las Vegas. And the food, like the cheap hotel rooms, expansive casinos, cooperative weather, and playful river, is user-friendly.

CASINOS

From the Nevada side of the bridge separating Laughlin from Bullhead City, Arizona,

it's exactly a mile to the traffic light at the Tropicana Laughlin, then another mile exactly to the entrance to Harrah's. March-November, unless you're a camel, it's a long sweaty walk from one end of the Laughlin Strip to the other, even if you take the fine riverwalk behind the casinos between the Riverside and the Golden Nugget. You can take the public bus, the Silver Rider, which runs along the Strip ($1.75). You can also catch a **River Passage Water Taxi** to any of the hotels (www.riverpassagewatertaxi.com, 9am-10pm Mon.-Thurs., 9am-11pm Fri.-Sat., winter hours 9am-9pm daily, $4 one-way, $20 day pass). Or grab a cab to where you want to go. But the easiest way, as always, is to drive. You can park in the Riverside lot to visit that casino, and then park in the Flamingo structure to see the Hilton, Tropicana, Edgewater, Colorado Belle, Pioneer, and Golden Nugget; then drive to River Palms Resort, and on to Harrah's.

Riverside

Start your tour where the town began, at Don Laughlin's front-runner **Riverside Resort** (1650 S. Casino Dr., 702/298-2535, www.riversideresort.com, $79-129) at the northern end of the "mini Strip." The Riverside, being Laughlin's first, has a movie theater, an arcade, a 34-lane bowling alley, supervised child care with video games, pool tables, and a climbing wall, and a **classic car museum** (9am-8pm Sun.-Thurs., 9am-10pm Fri.-Sat., free). It's an older establishment, comparatively speaking, and always crowded with regulars.

In addition to the standard prime rib room, buffet, café, and food court, the affordable French-influenced **Gourmet Room** (4pm-9pm Sun.-Thurs., 4pm-10pm, Fri.-Sat., $30-50) is the Riverside's best dining bet. Start with the bisque or onion soup, but do not bypass the chicken cordon brie.

Rock tribute acts and last-rodeo country stars play **Don's Celebrity Theater,** while **Losers' Lounge** hosts beer pong tournaments under the portraits of some of history's famous failures. Guests take the stage for nightly karaoke in **The Dance Club.**

Aquarius

The 1,907-room **Aquarius** (1900 S. Casino Dr., 702/298-5111, www.aquariuscasinoresort.com, $95-129) invites guests with a striking blue wave facade. It has a 57,000-square-foot casino and olive and gold room designs. **Splash Cabaret** (7pm-midnight, Thurs.-Sun.) is part sports bar, part dance club, part lounge venue, depending on the day and season. Big-time acts such as the Beach Boys, Kid Rock, Kenny Rogers, and ZZ Top play the 1,900-seat **Outdoor Pavilion Amphitheater.**

Windows on the River (7am-3pm and 4pm-10pm daily, $13-24) may be the best buffet in Laughlin, especially the crab and prime rib on Saturday nights or the champagne brunch daily. And we'd trample people in the aisle to get to the berry parfait station.

Edgewater

A Mandalay Resort Group hotel, the **Edgewater** (2020 S. Casino Dr., 702/298-2453, www.edgewater-casino.com, $80-109) grew to nearly 1,500 rooms when the Sedona Tower, right on the river, opened in 1992. Book here for views of the mountains and the river; take the Santa Fe Tower for convenient

Laughlin's casino row

access to parking and entertainment. Both have bold burgundy fabrics and flat-screens.

The casino seems much larger inside than it looks from the outside: sprawling, airy, and bright. Downstairs are the buffet, a 24-hour Coco's Restaurant, and a steakhouse called **Hickory Pit** (702/298-2453, ext. 3716, 4pm-10pm daily, $15-25). The casino level houses a Capriotti's sandwich shop, Wild Style Burgers & Pizza, and Dunkin' Donuts. The Showroom hosts stand-up comedians most weekends.

Colorado Belle

The Edgewater's sister, steamboat-themed **Colorado Belle** (2100 S. Casino Dr., 702/298-4000 or 866/352-3553, www.coloradobelle.com, $18-55) sits right on the river. It features a riverboat theme, with smokestacks soaring 21 stories tall, strobe lights making the paddlewheel appear to turn, and a bridge over a little moat giving access to the main entrance like a real gangway. Red flocked wallpaper, riveted stacks for beams, fancy cut-glass chandeliers, major period murals and paintings, and a sweeping staircase with wood and brass banisters make visitors feel like first-class passengers. You can almost smell the magnolia blossoms. Rock, soul, and country acts perform late into the night at **River Bar Lounge** (8pm-1am Fri.-Sun., free), while acoustic offerings more suitable for dining fill the air from the **Loading Dock Stage.**

Tropicana Express

Across the street sits the **Tropicana Express** (2121 S. Casino Dr., 702/298-4200 or 800/242-6846, https://troplaughlin.com, $25-80), on the west side of the Strip. Its facade illuminated a lime-tree green and its rooms decorated with cool teals and azures, the Trop gives guests their own little island refuge. The sparkling pool is reserved for adults only from 7am to 9am, so get up early and get your laps in. Then enjoy a breakfast of designer coffee, bagels, and pastries at the **Poolside Café** (6am-9pm Mon.-Thurs., 6am-midnight Fri.-Sat., 6am-9pm Sun., $8-15).

For a family dinner, head to **Passagio**

Italian Gardens (5pm-10pm Sun.-Tues., 5pm-11pm Fri.-Sat., $12-15) for New York-style pizza, all-you-can-eat pasta, and appetizers. Top it off with the San Gennaro zeppolis and decadent raspberry dipping sauce. **The Steakhouse** (4pm-9pm Sun. and Wed.-Thurs., 4pm-10pm Fri.-Sat., $30-50) is the place to go for prime rib and lobster tails.

The **Pavilion Theater** is the big room that presents comedians, singers, and variety acts. **Tango's Lounge** hosts smaller acts and danceable DJs.

Pioneer

The name, the waving, winking, cigarette-smoking River Rick marquee, and the adobe hint that the **Pioneer** (220 S. Casino Dr., 702/298-2442 or 800/634-3469, www.pioneerlaughlin.com, $66-99) is a throwback to the sawdust-joint days of early gambling in Nevada. Carpet, not sawdust, covers the casino floor, of course, but dark filigreed wood and glittery chandeliers carry through the Old West theme. Wallpaper and chintz in the rooms complete the picture. There's nothing unique on the **Bumbleberry Flats** menu (24 hours daily, $12-17), but the breakfasts, lunch comfort foods, and dinner entrées like bacon meatloaf are cheap and stick-to-your-ribs hearty.

Golden Nugget

At the **Golden Nugget** (2300 S. Casino Dr., 702/298-7111 or 800/950-7700, www.goldennugget.com, $70-160), you walk in through the familiar tropical rainforest atrium that was inspired by the Las Vegas Mirage: verdant foliage, curvy palms, rocky waterfalls, and a winding alleyway. Have a coconut cocktail at **Gold Diggers Nightclub** (9pm-2am Thurs.-Sun.), which generally showcases lounge acts and DJs spinning hits from the 1980s through today.

Laughlin River Lodge

Freshly updated rooms with peach motifs and a refurbished casino with 500 machines await at the rustic-chic **Laughlin River Lodge**

(2700 S. Casino Dr., 702/298-2242, http://laughlinriverlodge.com, $88-120). There's bingo, too, but no table games. Mellow entertainers perform in the **Lodge Steakhouse** (4pm-10pm Wed.-Sun., $30-45). The buffet and a Denny's are the only other dining options, and there's not much in the way of on-site entertainment. But the lodge is well-positioned for guests to take advantage of venues at other hotels, along with access to the Route 66 museum, Oatman ghost town, and trail rides and hikes.

Harrah's Laughlin

The Mexican Riviera theme at **Harrah's** (2900 S. Casino Dr., 702/298-4600 or 800/221-1306, www.caesars.com, $69-129) is understated, as are the themes at its sister properties in Nevada—a touch of tile here, an adobe bell tower there. The 1,505 guest rooms are a bit more obviously Mexican, with festive comforters, wall accents, and artwork depicting Spanish colonial scenes perking up otherwise basic digs. The casino, with 900 machines and 35 table games, is the most Las Vegas-y in town, with service to match, just the way Bill Harrah would have insisted.

The **Rio Vista Amphitheater** has hosted national comedians and musicians, including Brian Wilson and Chicago. The sandy swimming beach, a rarity at Laughlin casinos, is worth the $12 resort fee, which also includes in-room Wi-Fi. Typical of Harrah's, the nightlife is pretty sedate, but dining is another story. With the hotel's Mexican theme, no matter how vague, it stands to reason that **Guy Fieri's Burro Borracho** (702/298-6898, 5pm-9pm Sun.-Thurs., 5pm-10pm Fri.-Sat., $20-35) would bring south-of-the-border style and preparation to gringo favorites. The Fresh Market Square Buffet is above average, and the food court—located in a family-friendly tower wing along with the arcade and pool—has something for everyone.

Avi Resort and Casino

Way down in the point of Nevada that separates California from Arizona, 10 miles south of Laughlin, is the well-kept 465-room **Avi Resort** (10000 Aha Macav Pkwy., 702/535-5555, www.avicasino.com, $69-139), owned and operated by the Fort Mojave Indians. Avi is a sprawling and scenic resort situated along an attractive stretch of the Colorado River, where you can play on the white-sand, palapa-strewn beach or rent a Jet Ski. A cantina and tiki bar serve both the beach and the sprawling pool area. But the main draw is the **Mojave Resort Golf Club** (www.mojavegolf.com, $35-49), a challenging but fair championship golf course surrounded by purple mountains and sand dunes. Avi fields the usual lineup of resort restaurants—a café, steak and seafood, Italian, a buffet, and a fast food court.

SPORTS AND RECREATION

A smorgasbord of activities await nature lovers at **Big Bend of the Colorado State Park** (702/298-1859, http://parks.nv.gov, $9 day-use, $15 boating, $20 camping, $30 with hookups), five miles south of Laughlin on the Needles Highway. Shoreline and boat fishing holes abound. The wide river channel is popular for speedboaters and Jet Skiers, while kayakers and canoers will find languid backwaters to explore. Herons, hawks, and waterfowl frequent the area, and four miles of hiking trails, plenty of hilly, woody backcountry, and 24 campsites offer pleasant diversions.

Christmas Tree Pass and Grapevine Canyon (Christmas Tree Pass Rd., off NV 163, 7 miles west of Laughlin) is a scenic area for picnicking, hiking, camping, and sightseeing; be on the lookout for petroglyphs on the canyon walls. The area is administered by the **Bureau of Land Management**'s Las Vegas office (4701 N. Torrey Pines Dr., Las Vegas, 702/515-5000).

Fishing

Rainbow trout hang out in the river and Lake Mojave, which is also home to channel catfish, crappie, and carp, but striped bass are the big thing around here—30 pounds isn't uncommon. The world's record inland striper, 59.5 pounds, was landed at Bullhead City. May is the best time to fish for them, when the shad are plentiful and the water is warm enough to stimulate their appetites but not so oppressive as to make them sluggish. They run north from Lake Havasu starting in March.

Anglers age 13 and over must have a license, and you need a trout stamp if you're going after rainbows, cutthroats, or other species. The **Nevada Department of Wildlife** (www.ndow.org/fish) has the information. Laughlin Bay Marina (a couple of miles south of Harrah's), the Avi, and several sites in Bullhead City have boat launch ramps that can be used for a fee. You can launch for free at Fisherman's Access, just north of the Riverside. To boat on Lake Mojave, go across the river to Katherine Landing in Arizona.

Tours

Tour boats cruise the Colorado River, as long as there's enough water downriver—the Bureau of Reclamation controls the levels, often not to the liking of the tour-boat operators. **Laughlin River Tours** (800/228-9825, http://laughlinrivertours.com) runs the *Celebration* from the Aquarius casino dock, offering two-hour dinner cruises (Wed.-Mon., $45-48) and 90-minute narrated scenic tours (12:30pm and 2:30pm, $10, age 4-10 $5, under 4 free). USS *Riverside* cruises (10:30am, 12:30pm, 2:30pm, 4:30pm Sun.-Fri., additional 6:30pm and 8:30pm sailings Sat., $10, age 3-12 $6, under 3 free) are designed to pass under the Laughlin Bridge for a look at Davis Dam during their 80-minute excursions.

Camping and RV Parks

On the Nevada side, there is only one true RV park. **Avi Casino KOA** (10000 Aha Macav Pkwy., 800/430-0721, www.koa.com, $26-29), across the street from the casino, offers free shuttle service to the gaming floor and free access to the hotel's pool and other amenities; tents are not allowed. **Riverside Resort** (1650 S. Casino Dr., 702/298-1859, www.riversideresort.com, $17-24) has large sites of gravel and cement and little shade, but they include full hookups. The $129 weekly special is a bargain, especially with casino breakfast buffet passes included.

SHOPPING

Preferred Outlets (1955 S. Casino Dr., 702/298-3650, www.laughlinoutletcenter.com, 9am-8pm Mon.-Sat., 10am-6pm Sun.) is the big game in town, with 55 stores that include Gap Outlet, Levi's, and Van Heusen stocked with factory-discounted merchandise. Most stores are aimed at the hoi polloi rather than the haute. The mall has a food court and market as well as a nine-screen movie theater.

FOOD

Overall, food outside the casinos in Laughlin is good but not great, plentiful, and cheap, much like Las Vegas of the 1980s and 1990s. Laughlin's buffets are ubiquitous and usually inexpensive, while quality ethnic and specialty restaurants—especially in the casinos—are on the increase.

Outside the casinos, try the **Firehouse Coffee Company** (10200 Aha Macav Pkwy., 702/535-4400, $8-10) for breakfast (Mexican quiche) or lunch (grilled panini). It has a firefighter theme and "coffee" in the name, so you know the joe is always fresh. For steak with all the sizzle and none of the pretense, hit **Daniel's** (Regency Casino, 1950 S. Casino Dr., 702/299-1220, 8am-10pm daily, $14-20), which offers grilled rib eye, a salad, a baked potato, a vegetable, and rolls for $16.95.

The spaghetti and meatballs is a fine selection at **Alberto's Italian Restaurant & Lounge** (3100 Needles Hwy., Ste. 1200, 702/298-2318, 11am-8pm Mon.-Sat., $15-30), but the Mexican specialties are just as good, and you won't find better broasted chicken anywhere in Nevada.

Not only the best Japanese restaurant and best sushi bar in town, **Minato** (2311 S. Casino Dr., Ste. G-1, 702/298-7997, www.minatojapanese.com, noon-10pm Sun. and Tues.-Thurs., noon-11pm Fri.-Sat., 4pm-10pm Mon., $20-35) gets our vote for the best overall place in Laughlin. The sushi is always chilled to just the right temperature to ensure freshness. Grilled and tempura selections are light and never overcooked.

INFORMATION

The local branch of the **Las Vegas Clark County Library** (2840 Needles Hwy., 702/507-4060, www.lvccld.org) is about four miles west of the casinos.

The **visitors center** (1585 S. Casino Dr., 702/298-2214 or 800/227-5245, www.visit-laughlin.com) run by the Laughlin Chamber of Commerce and the Convention and Visitors Authority is right in the heart of the mini Strip.

GETTING THERE

The **Laughlin/Bullhead International Airport** (2550 Laughlin View Dr., Bullhead City, AZ, 928/754-2134, www.flyifp.com) is on the east side of the Colorado River. It is a full-service regional airport with daily flights from numerous cities. Plenty of tour operators offer day trips from Las Vegas to Laughlin. If you want to drive yourself, take US 95 south out of Las Vegas. It's easy to speed on this road, and the Highway Patrol is vigilant. It's also easy to become bored with the drive and let your attention wander, so be careful. After 75 miles, take NV 163 east through winding, hilly country before descending into the river valley and Laughlin. From Southern California or north-central Arizona, take I-40 to US 95 north to NV 163.

Reno and Tahoe

Look for ★ to find recommended sights, activities, dining, and lodging.

Highlights

★ **Truckee Riverwalk:** Wander through idyllic scenes of sophisticated connoisseurs sipping wine and contemplating the new gallery acquisition, fly-fishers making perfect casts, and kayakers challenging swirling white water (page 122).

★ **National Automobile Museum:** Elvis Presley's Caddy and James Dean's Mercury are here, so you know this museum oozes cool (page 125).

★ **Fleischmann Planetarium:** The building is as otherworldly as the one-ton meteorite inside. The theater hosts surreal star shows and larger-than-life nature and space documentaries (page 127).

★ **Wilbur D. May Museum and Arboretum:** Eclectic treasures from the Renaissance man's 40 trips abroad make for an unusual collection: shrunken head, tribal masks, and other frisson-producing oddities (page 127).

★ **Peppermill:** A boisterous flashing rush when you want a night on the town and a quaint boutique resort when you want to get away from it all, the Peppermill casino has it all under one roof (page 135).

★ **Lake Tahoe-Nevada State Park:** This park on the northeastern shoreline offers beach recreation at Sand Harbor, an easy two-mile walk around Spooner Lake, and access to spectacular views from the Tahoe backcountry (page 154).

★ **Thunderbird Lodge:** Ultra-rich George Whittell's opulent summer cottage includes a movie-screening room, quarters for his pet

elephant, and a million-dollar speedboat (page 157).

★ **Mt. Rose Ski Tahoe:** Six lifts and two conveyors whisk skiers to 1,200 acres of runs and trails at a summit elevation of 9,700 feet (page 157).

★ **Tahoe Rim Trail:** Nine trailheads provide access to this remarkable 165-mile wreath around the lake. Depending on which section you take, you'll encounter grueling grades, lakes, wildflowers, and birds (page 163).

O ften mentioned in the same breath, Reno and Tahoe share a geography but represent distinct sensibilities and ambiance.

Once the hub of everything that makes Nevada famous (or infamous), Reno now at least taps the brakes while watching Las Vegas career wildly down the course of excess. The fact is, Reno is the original Las Vegas, which could never have become Sin City if Reno hadn't gotten there first. But Reno has made a deliberate, conscious decision not to emulate, compete with, or—heaven forbid—become Las Vegas.

Once a rambunctious child, born with a silver boom in its mouth, Reno today maintains the characteristics of rebellious adolescence and youthful conquer-the-world exuberance. But it also has mellowed a bit, matured. It still can rock out with the in crowd, but one of the car radio buttons is set to easy listening. Reno continues to run, bike, and hike, but now that after-workout massage is more of a necessity than a luxury. The town still finds inspiration in the raging rapids of the Truckee River, but it also slows down to breathe in the peach and apple aromas at the farmers market, so bitingly tart or subtly sweet you can feel the juice run down your chin. Like all responsible adults, Reno has succeeded in maintaining balance. It remains a mesmerizing resort destination, with the best entertainment, gourmet restaurants, world-class spas, and some of the best outdoor recreation in the United States. But it's also a quaint college town, an art enclave, a riverside community, an industrial hub. In short, a hometown.

Lake Tahoe presents the "fairest picture the whole earth affords," according to Mark Twain, its surface shifting from slate gray to ice blue to navy, depending on the vagaries of the sun and clouds. The water is always 99 percent pure, clear enough to see a dinner plate on the bottom, 75 feet below the surface. Majestic 10,000-foot peaks stand sentinel over this pristine alpine treasure 6,000 feet above sea level. Mackinaw trout—a few tipping the scales at 30 pounds or more, and kokanee (a variety of landlocked sockeye salmon) call the lake home.

Previous: the famous Reno arch; Emerald Bay in Tahoe. **Above:** Northstar California resort.

PLANNING YOUR TIME

Both Reno and Tahoe are popular weekend getaways, and each can be thoroughly explored in five days.

In Reno, there's always enough time: Casino lounges are hopping until the wee small hours, most resorts have at least one 24-hour restaurant, and the gaming floor never closes. An extensive casino crawl is probably a waste of time: Pick the casino that has most of what you enjoy as a home base and do your gambling, dining, and carousing there. The resort hotels on the casino corridor take customer service seriously; rely on the concierge desk for information and insider tips. Taxicabs are always handy, and it's easy to get around, even in winter. Allow some time for art, history, and culture. The Riverwalk district south of downtown is the anti-casino—natural light, fresh air, and open spaces. The gurgling Truckee River makes for a refreshing respite from the clang of the slots.

A similar strategy applies in Tahoe. If you want to spend as much time as possible on the slopes, pick the resort at Incline Village, Stateline, or Zephyr Cove that suits your needs as a home base. All of them are designed with ski bums in mind. Most offer combination room-lift ticket specials throughout the season, and many include free shuttle pickup and drop-off sites throughout the North and South Shores. Nonskiers should visit in summer, when the hiking trails are gorgeous, hotel rooms are cheaper, and the area is less crowded.

A seven-day visit in Reno-Tahoe lets you be as hard-core or as laid-back as you want to be. It's a matter of degrees—both figuratively and literally, with Reno's temperatures running about 15 Fahrenheit ticks higher. Spend five vacation days partaking of your favorite diversion—shredding the slopes in Tahoe or splitting 8s at Reno's blackjack tables. Whichever of the major tourist towns you choose as your base camp, decamp to the other for two days to see how the other half lives. You should still take a stroll on Reno's Riverwalk.

If you have more time, there are enough day-trip destinations close by to provide a break when the powder, backbeats, or wagering grow too intense. At the top of the list are Virginia City and Carson City, along with Washoe and Topaz Lakes (all are covered in the *Loneliest Road* chapter).

Road conditions can change without much notice, particularly during winter. If you're motoring in from California, consult the **Caltrans** website (www.dot.ca.gov); if you're approaching through Nevada, contact the **Nevada Department of Transportation** (877/687-6237, www.nevadadot.com). Officials often declare snow tires a requirement for travel on I-80 and other roads around Lake Tahoe. If you're not sure, check your tires' sidewalls for an M/S (mud/snow) designation. Extreme conditions may call for front-tire snow chains. It's a good idea to have a pair in the trunk. Better yet, use the ski-resort shuttles and public transportation during difficult driving weather.

Reno

TOP EXPERIENCE

Whether you're a serious gambler, a nature lover, a gourmand, a hipster, or a culture freak, you'll want to spend at least a long weekend in Reno. Pick the casino resort that has most of what you're looking for, and do most of your gambling, dining, and carousing there. That doesn't mean you won't want to get out. You'll want to sprinkle a bit of art, history, and culture between the mai tais and inside straight draws. The Riverwalk district south of downtown is the anti-casino—full of natural light, fresh air, and open spaces. The gurgling Truckee River in the background makes for a refreshing respite as

Reno

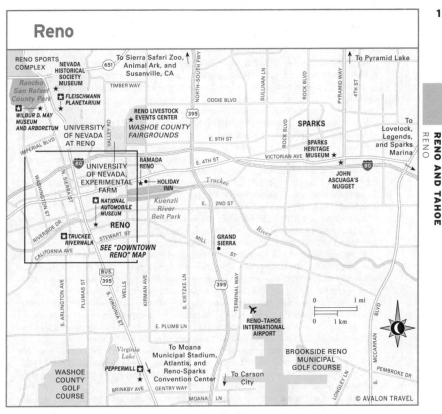

RENO SPORTS COMPLEX
NEVADA HISTORICAL SOCIETY MUSEUM
Rancho San Rafael County Park
FLEISCHMANN PLANETARIUM
WILBUR D. MAY MUSEUM AND ARBORETUM
UNIVERSITY OF NEVADA AT RENO
To Sierra Safari Zoo, Animal Ark, and Susanville, CA
651
TIMBER WAY
ODDIE BLVD
NORTH-SOUTH FWY
RENO LIVESTOCK EVENTS CENTER
395
WASHOE COUNTY FAIRGROUNDS
E. 9TH ST
VALLEY RD
IMPERIAL BLVD
N. SIERRA ST
WASHINGTON ST
80
UNIVERSITY OF NEVADA, EXPERIMENTAL FARM
RAMADA RENO
HOLIDAY INN
Truckee
NATIONAL AUTOMOBILE MUSEUM
Kuenzli River Belt Park
E. 2ND ST
RENO
TRUCKEE RIVERWALK
STEWART ST
SEE "DOWNTOWN RENO" MAP
RIVERSIDE DR
CALIFORNIA AVE
MILL ST
GRAND SIERRA
River
BUS. 395
S. ARLINGTON AVE
PLUMAS ST
WELLS
S. VIRGINIA ST
KIRMAN AVE
S. KIETZKE LN
395
TERMINAL WAY
E. PLUMB LN
RENO-TAHOE INTERNATIONAL AIRPORT
Virginia Lake
WASHOE COUNTY GOLF COURSE
PEPPERMILL
BRINKBY AVE
GENTRY WAY
To Moana Municipal Stadium, Atlantis, and Reno-Sparks Convention Center
To Carson City
MOANA LN
BROOKSIDE RENO MUNICIPAL GOLF COURSE
MCCARRAN BLVD
PEMBROKE DR
LONGLEY LN
SULLIVAN LN
ROCK BLVD
PYRAMID WAY
4TH ST
To Pyramid Lake
SPARKS
SPARKS HERITAGE MUSEUM
VICTORIAN AVE
ROCK BLVD
E. 4TH ST
JOHN ASCUAGA'S NUGGET
80
To Lovelock, Legends, and Sparks Marina
0   1 mi
0   1 km
© AVALON TRAVEL

RENO AND TAHOE

RENO

you study the eclectic styles and media of local and widely renowned artists.

Or, head north of downtown to the pastoral setting of Rancho San Rafael Park and the University of Nevada, Reno (UNR) just across the street. Let the kids blow off some steam at the huge playground, then sneak in some education among the cool exhibits at Wilbur D. May Museum; it's full of treasures the department store scion collected on his dozens of journeys around the world. On the UNR campus you'll find plenty to fire your imagination, whether terrestrial, at the W. M. Keck Earth Science and Mineral Engineering Museum (with ore samples, fossils, and relics from the Comstock Lode), or extraterrestrial, at the Fleischmann Planetarium (with its meteorites, black hole demonstrator, and 3-D solar system shows).

ORIENTATION

Reno sits at the crossroads of I-80, which runs east-west from New York to San Francisco, and US 395, which crosses into Nevada on its way from Oregon to Southern California. The Truckee River parallels I-80, running west-east through the heart of downtown. Downtown is bounded by 1st Street just north of the river, I-80 eight blocks to the north, Wells Avenue to the east, and Keystone Avenue to the west. The intersection of 1st Street and Virginia Street is the hub of the Riverwalk retail district. From this point, addresses are labeled east, west, north, and south. The higher the building number, the farther away you are from downtown. The casino district revolves around 4th and Virginia Streets.

I-80 separates the high-rise downtown

The Famous Arch

Reno's venerable "Biggest Little City in the World" arch received its most environmentally friendly facelift in 2009, when the city replaced its 2,076 incandescent 11-watt lightbulbs with 2.5-watt LED bulbs. Spectators took home a piece of Reno history as the old bulbs were given away as souvenirs. In 2017 city officials were discussing installing color-changing bulbs, adding a digital display, and giving the sign a more modern brushed-steel facade.

If the changes come to fruition, they will be the latest in a string of alterations in the life of one of the world's most recognizable landmarks. The main arch, across North Virginia Street at West 3rd Street, is on the site where the first arch was erected in 1926 to celebrate the completion of the transcontinental Victory and Lincoln Highways. It cost $5,500 and read "Reno Transcontinental Highway Exposition." The arch grew on local residents, who decided to keep it. As the novelty of the highways wore off, Mayor E. E. Roberts announced a contest to create a permanent slogan. The winning slogan was adapted from the ad campaign for the 1910 Jim Jeffries-Jack Johnson prizefight in Reno, which proclaimed Reno the "Biggest Little City on the Map." The sign was composed of nearly 1,000 bulbs and cost $30 a month to operate, which proved too rich for the city's Depression-era budget, so it was shut off in 1932. A great hue and cry erupted over the cost-saving measure, and downtown business owners paid the electric bill to keep the arch lit.

A new improved arch was erected in 1934. Built of reinforced steel and lit with neon, the sign read simply "Reno." This change was again universally condemned, and in 1936 the old slogan was returned to the arch. The next time someone tried to monkey with the archway was in 1956, when Mayor Ken Harris proposed changing the slogan; it nearly cost him his job.

This arch was eventually replaced in 1963, when it was moved to Idlewild Park, the highway exposition site, then to Paradise Park, then into storage. It saw daylight again in 1994 when it was erected over 4th Street to add ambiance to the baseball biopic *Cobb*. In 1995 it traveled to its current spot outside the National Automobile Museum at Lake and Mill Streets.

The 1963 replacement was installed in preparation for Nevada's centennial and reflected the slightly psychedelic sentiments that abounded in northern Nevada and California in the 1960s. This "Hippie Arch" was donated to the town of Willits, California, where it welcomes visitors to California's redwood forests.

The fourth and current arch was unveiled in front of a jam-packed Virginia Street crowd in August 1987. The contemporary design is the creation of Charles Barnard of Ad Art Company in Stockton, California, and the Young Electric Sign Company (YESCO) built the arch for $99,000, charging the city for the materials only. It uses 800 feet of tubing.

hotels from the mostly low-rise buildings of the UNR campus on Virginia Street, which sits on a bluff overlooking downtown. At the northern edge of the campus, Virginia Street, also called Business 395, intersects with North McCarran Boulevard, which circumscribes the valley, encompassing Sparks and Reno-Tahoe International Airport. A trip on the 23-mile loop around Reno-Sparks is a scenic way to get oriented and enjoy superb views of downtown.

Reno and Sparks share a census designation and a chamber of commerce. While Sparks began as a Reno bedroom community in the 1950s, it has grown toward the city so that is difficult to discern where one ends and the other begins. Sparks is, perhaps, a bit slower-paced, with parks and events aimed at local families rather than free-spending tourists.

SIGHTS
★ Truckee Riverwalk

"Pedestrian-friendly" has become a catch-phrase for urban renewal. Reno embraces the concept wholeheartedly with the Raymond I. Smith Truckee Riverwalk (1st St. and Virginia St., www.renoriver.org), a downtown promenade that adds "artist-friendly," "oeno-phile-friendly," and even "kayaker-friendly" to its definition. Named for the founder of

Harold's Club and completed in 1991 at a cost of $7.7 million, the Riverwalk is home to art walks, pub crawls, wine tastings, and many of the city's other social events. The walkway is the centerpiece of Reno's embrace of its history and culture—its "Reno-ssaince"—and now hosts trendy bistros, bars, art galleries, record shops, antiques stores, and clothing boutiques. Waterfalls, idyllic scenes of fly-fishers, rafters and waders, lush riparian landscaping, abstract sculpture, murals, and plentiful waterfowl compete for your attention with strolling performers, Victorian homes, and the snowcapped Sierra Nevada. Try to avoid the metered parking, with its arbitrary and inconsistent rates and enforcement. Instead park in the lot at 1st and Sierra. It's free with validation from any of the shops and restaurants along the Riverwalk. After 5pm and on weekends and holidays, street parking is free around Virginia and Sierra Streets, Mill Street near Museum Drive, and 2nd Street at Arlington Avenue.

Truckee River Whitewater Park

Start your walk of the river at **Wingfield Park** (2 S. Arlington Ave.), a quarter-mile-long island that splits the Truckee into two channels. Smack-dab in the middle of Reno's burgeoning arts scene at 1st Street and Arlington Avenue, the park is home to one of Reno's most unusual and iconic attractions: **Truckee River Whitewater Park**'s Class II and III rapids challenge advanced paddlers while providing a safe environment for beginners, as well as canoeists and rafters. Fed by clear mountain runoff, the rafting course includes 11 drop-in pools and a racing course, so the route never gets old. **Tahoe Whitewater Tours** (775/787-5000 or 800/442-7238, www.gowhitewater.com) or **Sierra Adventures** (775/323-8928 or 866/323-8928, www.wildsierra.com) can set you up.

If you're visiting on a summer weekend, there's a good chance you can catch a classical music, theater, jazz, or children's program at the park's **amphitheater** (775/334-2417). The Wingfield complex includes several other, more traditional parks, with basketball and tennis courts, playgrounds, and softball diamonds. These include **Riverside Park,** with three acres of grass on the banks adjacent to the island.

Walking west along the river leads to **Idlewild Park.** Just under a mile from downtown, this park, originally developed for the

Truckee Riverwalk

Downtown Reno

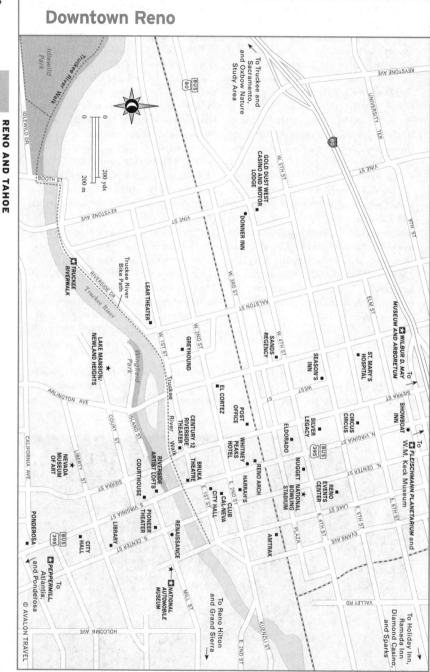

To Truckee and,
Sacramento,
and Oxbow Nature
Study Area

BUS 80

Idlewild Park

Truckee River Walk

IDLEWILD DR

BOOTH ST

KEYSTONE AVE

KEYSTONE AVE

UNIVERSITY TER

VINE ST

80

9TH ST

W. 5TH ST

GOLD DUST WEST CASINO AND MOTOR LODGE

DONNER INN

TRUCKEE RIVERWALK

RIVERSIDE DR

Truckee River Bike Path

Truckee River

LEAR THEATER

VINE ST

W. 3RD ST

RALSTON ST

W. 3RD ST

ELM ST

W. 2ND ST

GREYHOUND

SANDS REGENCY

W. 4TH ST

WEST ST

ST. MARY'S HOSPITAL

MUSEUM AND ARBORETUM

WILBUR D. MAY

To Holiday Inn,

W. 1ST ST

LAKE MANSION/ NEWLAND HEIGHTS

Wingfield Park

SEASON'S INN

SIERRA ST

ARLINGTON AVE

EL CORTEZ

POST OFFICE

SILVER LEGACY

CIRCUS CIRCUS

SHOWBOAT INN

FLEISCHMANN PLANETARIUM and W.M. Keck Museum

CALIFORNIA AVE

COURT ST

ISLAND ST

CENTURY 12 RIVERSIDE THEATER

Truckee River Walk

WHITNEY PEAKS HOTEL

ELDORADO

N. VIRGINIA ST

BUS 395

N. CENTER ST

RENO EVENTS CENTER

E. 6TH ST

NEVADA MUSEUM OF ART

LIBERTY ST

SIERRA ST

RIVERSIDE ARTIST LOFTS

BRUKA THEATRE

RENO ARCH

HARRAH'S

E. 2ND ST

CAL-NEVA

NUGGET

NATIONAL BOWLING STADIUM

LAKE ST

E. 4TH ST

EVANS AVE

PONDEROSA

CITY HALL

LIBRARY

S. VIRGINIA ST

S. CENTER ST

PIONEER THEATER

RENAISSANCE

E. 1ST ST

CITY HALL

E. 2ND ST

PLAZA

AMTRAK

E. 5TH ST

BUS 395

To PEPPERMILL, Atlantis, and Ponderosa

NATIONAL AUTOMOBILE MUSEUM

MILL ST

To Reno Hilton and Grand Sierra

KUENZLI ST

E. 2ND ST

VALLEY RD

To Holiday Inn, Ramada Inn Diamond Casino, and Sparks

HOLCOMB AVE

© AVALON TRAVEL

0 200 yds
0 200 m

Transcontinental Highway Exposition in 1927, is one of the oldest and prettiest city parks in the state. It boasts a large duck pond and outdoor swimming pool, picnic pavilions, stately old trees, a rose garden, and Peter Toth's Nevada sculpture, a *Whispering Giant* looking down from 30 feet to share a special secret with each visitor. The **children's train ride** (11am-3pm Mon.-Fri., 11am-6pm Sat.-Sun. May-Labor Day, 11am-6pm Sat.-Sun. Labor Day-Apr., $2) is pleasant for adults and perfect for preschoolers.

Lake Mansion

Myron Lake charged each horse and rider 10 cents to cross his toll bridge on Virginia Street in the 1860s. All those dimes added up, and in 1879 Lake purchased a stately home at Virginia Street and California Avenue. Though a fitting abode for a city founder, the **Lake Mansion** (250 Court St., 775/826-6100, www.lakemansion.com, 10am-4pm Mon.-Fri., donation optional) never housed Myron Lake. Jane Lake got the home as part of the settlement in her split from Myron, the first of many prominent divorces in Reno. The current address is the mansion's third location. The home is a detailed example of the Italianate style. The veranda traversing the house, carved woodwork, and modern (for the 19th century) sliding parlor doors testify to the quality workmanship Reno's upper crust could afford. Daily self-directed and Friday guided tours provide access to the kitchen, parlor, dining room, master bedroom, and library.

National Bowling Stadium

A bowling alley as a resort destination? A monument to one of America's most popular recreational sports, the **National Bowling Stadium** (300 N. Center St., 800/304-2695, www.gobowlreno.com) is far removed from after-work leagues and beer frames, with a 440-foot video projection screen that would be right at home in any NFL stadium, a computer-driven system to detect even the tiniest flaw in a bowler's delivery, a pro shop with the sophisticated equipment to maximize every frame, and 78 lanes of kegling contentment. Hosting some of the sport's biggest tournaments, the bowling stadium treats pro bowlers like the elite athletes they are, whisking them in twin glass elevators to the fourth-floor Tournament Level.

But bowling isn't the only game in town at the stadium. Striking design features include a 56-foot marble and glass atrium dominated by a life-sized bronze of a 1940s family rushing to a bowling alley. The building's design allows it to be used for conferences, parties, and other functions, and the bowling ball-shaped top-floor Iwerks theater treats up to 172 people to epic 50-foot images and digital sound. The $35 million stadium also hosts a restaurant, gift shop, and Reno information center.

Newland Heights

The lucky, the ruthless, and the professionals and merchants who "mined the miners" during the Comstock boom treated themselves to the spoils of their victories with mansions in Reno. The nouveau riche congregated just after the turn of the 20th century on a bluff overlooking the Truckee River just outside downtown. This **Newland Heights** neighborhood was placed on the National Register of Historic Places in 2017. Frederic DeLongchamps, Nevada's most famous architect, designed many of the homes in this historic district, which you can reach by crossing the river at the Sierra Street Bridge and turning right on Court Street. The **Historic Reno Preservation Society** (775/747-4478, www.historicreno.com, $10) periodically offers walking tours of the neighborhood, with a guide describing the homes' architecture and history.

★ National Automobile Museum

Even the building that houses the **National Automobile Museum** (10 S. Lake St., 775/333-9300, www.automuseum.org, 9:30am-5:30pm Mon.-Sat., 10am-4pm Sun., $10 adults, $8 seniors, $4 ages 6-18, under 5 free) is clad in tinted glass, sleek metallic curves, and glittering chrome. The wide hallways re-create streetscape vignettes depicting 100 years of car culture. The first gallery shows the country's transition from horse to horseless carriage. Another "street" shows the advent of the muscle car. Also among the museum's displays are an Elvis Presley Cadillac, the Mercury driven by James Dean in *Rebel Without a Cause,* and a 22-minute multimedia presentation in which cars roll on and off the screen while video screens project special effects.

The collection is just a small percentage of the 1,000 or so cars amassed by Bill Harrah. After Harrah died and his company was sold, the new owners auctioned off nearly 75 percent of the cars, many of which were bought by Ralph Engelstad, owner of the Imperial Palace in Las Vegas, and displayed in the auto collection there. The remainder were donated to the museum foundation.

A research library houses one of the most extensive collections of literature covering the development of the automobile in the world, including paint chips, photographs, owner's manuals, and even wiring diagrams. Other exhibits include mechanics' tools and car art.

Nevada Museum of Art

The **Nevada Museum of Art** (160 W. Liberty St., 775/329-3333, www.nevadaart.org, 10am-6pm Wed. and Fri.-Sun., 10am-8pm Thurs., $10 adults, $8 seniors and students, $1 ages 6-12) exhibits its 20,000-piece permanent collection in four focus areas, all dealing with the natural, built, and imagined environment. Each focus area might contain works from the 18th century through the present, without regard to artist, style, or period. Feature exhibits focus on the works of American and international artists, and new artists are spotlighted every few months.

The gallery's home was designed by Will Bruder, whose Frank Lloyd Wright inspiration is evident from the first glimpse of the building, which features stark white walls and a black exterior reminiscent of Nevada's Black Rock Desert. With a mission to cultivate "meaningful art and cultural experiences, and foster new knowledge in the visual arts by encouraging interdisciplinary investigation," the gallery is one of the best small art museums in the country.

The museum store sells books, posters, prints, art magnets, jewelry, cards, pottery, T-shirts, and some sculpture. And **Chez Louie** (10am-4pm Wed. and Fri.-Sat.,

vintage cars at the National Automobile Museum

10am-8pm Thurs., 10am-2pm Sun.) is open for light and, of course, creative, meals.

Nevada Historical Society Museum

Nevada's oldest and perhaps best museum, the **Nevada Historical Society Museum** (1650 N. Virginia St., 775/688-1190, http://nvculture. org/historicalsociety, 10am-4:30pm Tues.-Sat., 18 and over $5, under 18 free) resides on the north end of the UNR campus. The museum is dedicated to collecting and preserving Nevada's past, from prehistory through the frontier and Comstock era to its modern position as a resort destination. Its collection includes such diverse and provocative items as mining artifacts, Native American baskets, ranching equipment, slot machine cheating devices, and showgirl costumes.

There is so much history here, you can't possibly absorb even a fraction. If you want to learn more about specific events in Nevada's past, there's sure to be a book about it in the museum's well-stocked gift shop.

The adjoining research library houses half a million historical photographs and huge collections of books, manuscripts, diaries, artwork, relics, and more. It's open to the public, in case you want to track down that long-lost Nevada ancestor to complete your family tree.

★ Fleischmann Planetarium

Next door to the Historical Society Museum, the **Fleischmann Planetarium** (1664 N. Virginia St., 775/784-4812, www.planetarium.unr.nevada.edu, noon-8pm Mon.-Thurs., noon-9pm Fri., 10am-9pm Sat., 10am-6pm Sun., $8, under 12, over 60, and military $6) presents not only out-of-this-world star shows and public stargazing in the observatory, but also large-format documentaries and other educational films in its domed theater. Built in 1964, the planetarium is shaped like a hyperbolic parabola (think: upper half of a floppy flying saucer) and is listed on the National Register of Historic Buildings. Get lost in space among the thought-provoking exhibits: a black hole simulator, globes of the Earth and

moon, man-made satellites, and a collection of meteorites found in Nevada and elsewhere, one weighing more than a ton. Stick a nickel in the gravity well and play (gently) with the instruments in the gift shop. Admission to the main exhibit hall (hours vary) is free.

W. M. Keck Museum

North of the quad on the University of Nevada, Reno campus, the sculpted figure of John Mackay greets visitors to the **W. M. Keck Earth Science and Mineral Engineering Museum** (775/784-4528, www.unr.edu/keck, 9am-4pm Mon.-Fri., free). The generous miner became Bonanza King of the Comstock and later endowed the university. The statue was sculpted by Gutzon Borglum of Mount Rushmore fame. In Borglum's depiction, Mackay holds a pile of mineral-rich Nevada earth and a miner's pick, symbolizing industry and ambition. Originally constructed in 1908, the building today rests an eighth of an inch off the ground on 66 high-tech rubber bearings and 43 Teflon slider plates to make it virtually earthquake-proof.

The museum's pièce de résistance is the 1,250-piece ornate silver service (for 24!) Mackay commissioned from Tiffany and Co. Completed in 1878, the set reportedly required the full-time handiwork of 200 craftsmen tooling the half ton of silver Mackay shipped from his Comstock mines.

The museum also houses several specimens of gold, silver, copper, lead, uranium, turquoise, gypsum, borax, and other minerals Nevada is famous for, and several fossil collections. Historical black-and-white photos of many mining boomtowns grace the walls, and Mackay's own vault houses two dozen rocks from the Comstock itself. Upstairs on the mezzanine is a geological breakdown of minerals and some fossils from around the world, plus miners' tools, machines, scales, and diagrams.

★ Wilbur D. May Museum and Arboretum

Dedicated to the life of the May Company

Reno in Song

Reno's unique history as a frontier town, a Wild West outpost, the original Sin City, and a haven for renegades has been chronicled in songs made famous by everyone from Woody Guthrie to R.E.M. Country and folk seem to be the genres of choice for singers and songwriters setting their musical tales in the Biggest Little City.

Reno's booming divorce trade got the Guthrie treatment. He penned "Reno Blues" in 1937. Rose Maddox recorded it under the title "Philadelphia Lawyer." It tells of the title character's efforts to steal another man's wife: "Come, love, and we will wander / Down where the lights are bright. / I'll win you a divorce from your husband, / And we can get married tonight."

Johnny Cash uses Reno in one of his most popular songs, tabbing the Nevada city as the site of his downfall in "Folsom Prison Blues." The Man in Black was sent up the river after ignoring his mother's plea: "When I was just a baby, my mother told me, "Son / Always be a good boy; don't ever play with guns." / But I shot a man in Reno, just to watch him die."

Reno is the first city mentioned in the "singing" part of the American version of "I've Been Everywhere," originally recorded by Hank Snow and covered by a who's who of country artists: Lynn Anderson, Asleep at the Wheel, Johnny Cash, Willie Nelson, and a dozen more. Incidentally, the song's introduction mentions another Nevada town: "I was totin' my pack along the dusty Winnemucca Road . . ."

Other bands that have found Reno the perfect setting for their tunes include R.E.M. ("All the Way to Reno"), Tom Waits ("Virginia Avenue" mentions the closing of the famous Harold's Club), Rocky Votolato ("Wrong Side of Reno"), and even the Grateful Dead ("Friend of the Devil" includes the line "I set out from Reno / I was trailed by 20 hounds"). Bruce Springsteen's "Reno" is the story of an encounter with a prostitute, and Doug Supernaw's "Reno" laments his bad luck at the gambling tables: "Couldn't roll me a seven / If you gave me loaded dice / I couldn't draw a hand / If I sat here all night."

department store heir, the **Wilbur D. May Museum** (1595 N. Sierra St. at the south end of Rancho San Rafael Park, 775/785-5961, www.maycenter.com, 10am-4pm Wed.-Sat., noon-4pm Sun., adults $5, children and seniors $3.50) chronicles his aesthetic, philanthropic, and adventurous passions.

May overcame physical challenges to become a pilot, adventurer, and financial genius (he sold his investments just before the stock market crash and then bought them back at fire sale prices after Black Monday). A true Renaissance man, his song "Pass a Piece of Pizza, Please" sold 100,000 copies.

And as this gem of a museum amply illustrates, May not only had money, he also had excellent taste; he collected treasures during more than 40 trips around the world. Tour the replicated rooms of the ranch house May lived in on a 2,600-acre spread outside Reno: tack room, living room, trophy room, and bedroom. Watch the 20-minute video of his life showing great travel and wildlife footage. Notice his passports, a spine-chilling shrunken head, and weavings, silver, tribal masks, and ivory from all corners of the globe.

Relax at the indoor **arboretum,** with its ponds (stocked with koi) and waterfall. Then ask at the desk for the attractive brochure with the layout of the arboretum out back and wander through the various gardens: energy conservation, xeriscape, songbird, fragrant, rock, desert, rose, and many others.

Oxbow Nature Study Area

Head west on 2nd Street and bear left on Dickerson Road just before the railroad underpass about two miles west of town. Just when you think the landscape can't get any more urban, the warehouses and body shops part to reveal a most unusual city park: the **Oxbow Nature Study Area** (3100 Dickerson Rd., 775/334-3808, sunrise-sunset daily).

An oxbow is a river channel that has been

diverted from the main flow by sediment deposition. This 30-acre park along the Truckee encompasses a large oxbow area. A flood on New Year's Day 1997 completely changed the face of the park, and it took three years to rebuild. But the park naturalist says the redesigned park is even better now than it was before, sporting a half-mile boardwalk interpretive trail winding through 18 acres of interesting features, including ponds and marshes and a large deck right out over the river, great for bird-watching. Grasses, sedges, tules, cattails, wild rose, alder, and cottonwood dominate the riparian ecosystem.

Take the one-mile loop nature trail that parallels the Truckee River. Make sure you take the time to peruse the interpretive signs and park brochure. Both are chock-full of interesting tidbits about the ecology of the area. But walk softly so you'll not disturb the deer, coyotes, frogs, snakes, beaver, muskrat, waterfowl, and other animals. The trail is wheelchair accessible and an easy hike.

Feathers really fly in the park from early May through late July, when 150 species of migratory birds arrive here to nest and rear their young; this park is a wetlands habitat for nesting on the Pacific Flyway. Hummingbirds are usually the last to leave, in August.

You can spend an enjoyable and relaxing several hours walking the interpretive trail and eating lunch on one of the park benches or picnic tables strategically placed throughout the park.

Sierra Safari Zoo

The **Sierra Safari Zoo** (10200 N. Virginia St., 775/677-1101, www.sierrasafarizoo.org, 10am-5pm daily Apr.-Oct., 10am-3pm Sat.-Sun. and holidays Nov.-Mar., weather permitting, adults $10, children and military $7, seniors $6, 2 and under free) is Nevada's largest self-supporting wild-animal attraction—Las Vegas, incredibly, does not have a zoo. More than 200 animals of more than 40 species call the zoo home, including lemurs, wallabies, zebras, lions, tigers, leopards, lynx, and monkeys.

To get to the zoo, drive eight miles north of Reno on US 395 to exit 76 toward Stead Boulevard; turn left onto Stead Boulevard, then right onto North Virginia Street for 1.5 miles.

Animal Ark

Aaron and Diana Hiibel care for non-releasable wildlife on 38 acres at **Animal Ark** (1265 Deerlodge Rd., 775/970-3111, 10am-4:30pm Tues.-Sun. mid-Mar.-early Nov., $11, seniors $10, children $7.50, age 2 and under free). The Hiibels provide infirm, orphaned, and abandoned creatures permanent care in captivity in as natural a setting as possible. Visitors get a rare glimpse into the lives of exotic cats, raptors, tortoises, and wolves, creating a bridge between humans and animals by increasing the appreciation of the natural world. Come early for the best chance to see nocturnal predators before their nap time. Or time your visit to coincide with 10:30am and 1:30pm bear feedings. Different animals are featured during special events: **Howl Nights** celebrate the wolves' mournful baying and reward the best human imitations, while **Cheetah Runs** let the cats show off their speed.

To get there, take US 395 north to exit 78, turn right on Red Rock Road, drive 11.2 miles to Deerlodge Road, take a right, and go another mile. Animal Ark is on the right.

CASINOS

The everything-under-one-roof nature of Reno's resort casinos means you could spend all week in just one—within a few hundred feet of your hotel room—and still experience a wonderful vacation. You could treat yourself to a café breakfast and then bask in the sun and splash around the resort's fabulous swimming pool all morning. After a salad or grilled chicken sandwich from the poolside grill, you could retire for a short power nap, gearing up for an afternoon of hand-to-hand combat with the dealer or slot machine. Treat yourself to a steak dinner in the hotel's gourmet room, have a couple of drinks in the

Reno Strip Casinos

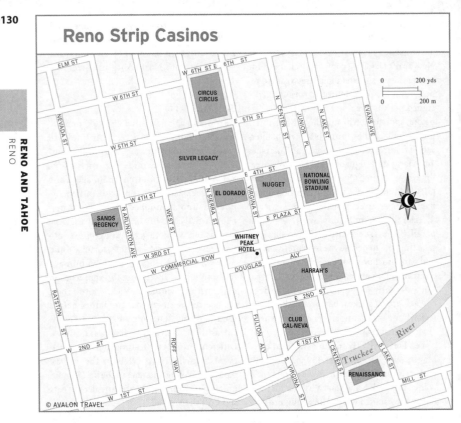

lounge, then enjoy a variety show or musical concert in the showroom.

Next day, trade pool time for shopping in the casino's boutiques, if your gambling session was a success (or just browsing, if it was not). Skip lunch and dinner; gorge yourself at the sumptuous buffets in the middle of the afternoon instead. Recoup your losses and celebrate by dancing the night away in the trendy club. Repeat as often as your vacation lasts and your bankroll holds out. If you exhaust all the entertainment, dining, and drinking options available at your "home" hotel, a dozen more are within walking distance.

Reno casinos generally do not allow pets in their tower rooms. Casinos that still rent their older motel-like rooms in the back, or those with RV parks, usually welcome pets.

Circus Circus

Restaurants: Americana Café, El Jefe's Cantina, Kanpai Sushi, Sips Coffee and Tea, Main Street Deli, Food Court

Entertainment: circus acts, Cabaret Stage

Attractions: midway games

While the family-friendly circus acts and midway remain, the upgrades at **Circus Circus** (500 N. Sierra St., 800/648-5010 or 775/329-0711, www.circusreno.com, $115-135) now exude adult-level elegance. Colorful abstract, slate-gray schemes plus minimalist furnishings and gold accents lead into large bathrooms with lighted mirrors, spa-quality showers, and marble floors.

Perhaps because its neighboring hotels aren't as posh as those in Las Vegas, or maybe because the Reno edition has rounded off the cotton-candy pink decor in favor of more muted tones, the property has found a way to keep pleasing budget-minded families while also giving more sophisticated travelers reasons to visit. Guests in the more than 1,500 rooms in three towers can choose among 900 machines and all the traditional table games, along with several against-the-house gimmicky poker variations.

Following the renovation, the world-class **circus acts** (6pm-11pm daily, free) are visible from both the gaming floor and the midway games area, so everyone has a chance to go home a winner no matter how their luck is running at the tables. The acts themselves have been transformed. They are now less Big Top, more Cirque du Soleil light.

More adult fun abounds on the **Cabaret Stage** (showtimes vary, Fri.-Sat., free), with live music blasted through a state-of-the-art sound system. Classic rock and blues cover bands or karaoke are on tap, with a bar steps away. Shops are scattered throughout the property, in case you've forgotten to pack sundries or sweatshirts, or if you're itching to spend your winnings on some bling.

Two new restaurants, **El Jefe's Cantina** (11:30am-2pm and 5pm-11pm Mon.-Fri., 11:30am-11pm Sat.-Sun., $8-16) and **Kanpai Sushi** (11:30am-2pm and 5pm-11pm Mon.-Fri., 11:30am-11pm Sat.-Sun., $18-25) share cooking and dining space, along with an attitude toward ethnic cuisine. With provocative artwork throughout, the menus both complement and inspire each other in a fusion of Asian and Latin tastes. The raw menu is an example; any of El Jefe's ceviche choices or Kanpai's raw nigiri selections will satisfy.

Silver Legacy

Restaurants: Hussong's Cantina-Taqueria, Café Central, Pearl Oyster Bar and Grill, Flavors the Buffet, Sterling's Seafood Steakhouse, Sips Coffee and Tea, Starbucks

Entertainment: Laugh Factory

Attractions: Grande Exposition Hall, mining machine, health spa, fitness center

Nightlife: Rum Bullions Island Bar, Silver Baron, Aura Ultra Lounge, Drinx, Blender Bar

With a casino housing some 65 table games and 1,200 slot machines in denominations from a cent to a C-note, together with Reno's largest hotel, with 1,700 rooms, the **Silver Legacy** (407 N. Virginia St., 800/687-8733 or 775/325-7401, http://silverlegacyreno. com, $135-165) has the space and resources to provide everything a vacationer desires. Remodeled in early 2010, the 340-square-foot rooms are richly appointed in cream,

Reno at night

gold, and crimson. Upper rooms in the 37-story tower loom over city lights, mountain peaks, or the meandering Truckee River. Spa suites offer all that, along with 50 percent more space and whirlpool tubs.

Take in a show by a big-time entertainer in the 1,600-seat **Grande Exposition Hall.** Performers have included David Crosby, David Spade, and the Gipsy Kings. Then get revved up for a night of partying at one of the Legacy's several bars and lounges. Put yourself on island time and share a flambéed Kava Kava cocktail ($14 for two) at newly renovated **Rum Bullions Island Bar** (4pm-midnight Sun.-Thurs., 4pm-2am Fri.-Sat.). See your favorite late-night talk show guests and rising comics at the **Laugh Factory** (7:30pm Sun. and Tues.-Thurs., 7:30pm and 9:30pm Fri.-Sat., $25).

After a good night's sleep, pamper yourself with a treat from **The Boutique** (women's fashions), featuring Michael Stars, Tribal, and Raviani, or **Tradewinds** (men's), or any of the several other shops carrying everything from wine and jewelry to Harley-Davidson memorabilia.

Oysters, shrimp, clams, and crab get the pan-roasted star treatment at **Pearl Oyster Bar** (775/329-4777 ext. 4335, 11am-10pm daily, $20-30). Rich ambiance and flamboyant tableside preparation make nationally recognized **Sterling's Seafood Steakhouse** (775/325-7573, 5pm-11pm daily, $35-50) a multisensory gastronomic destination. Starched white linen tablecloths contrast pleasingly with the deep red decor as candlelight reflects off polished cherrywood wine racks and crystal stemware. Servers delivering the aged steaks and other beef, chicken, and fish dishes are as professional and proficient as you'd expect from a five-star establishment.

Skywalks connect the Legacy with the Eldorado on one side and Circus Circus on the other, allowing you to walk more than four city blocks in downtown Reno without stepping foot outside.

Eldorado

Restaurants: Roxy, La Strada, Sushi Sake, Pho Mein, Hidden Pizza, The Buffet, Brew Brothers, Eldorado Coffee Company
Entertainment: Eldorado Theatre
Nightlife: NoVi, Roxy's Live Piano Bar, Stadium Bar, Brew Brothers, Cin Cin, Millies24, Bar Centro

The Carano family, which opened the **Eldorado** (345 N. Virginia St., 775/786-5700, www.eldoradoreno.com, $140-180) in 1973 with 282 rooms and a 10,000-square-foot casino, is a testament to hard work and perseverance. Ben Carano, whose Italian immigrant grandfather was a cook during the Comstock silver boom, initiated the family's road to fortune in 1929 with a modest investment in 50 feet of what was to become prime real estate near Virginia and 4th Streets. The clan extended its land holdings, and Ben's son Don opened the Eldorado in 1973, added another 129 rooms in 1978, doubled its size again and extended the casino to 40,000 square feet in 1985.

Located in the heart of the casino district, the Eldorado does a good job of segregating its sometimes-raucous gaming areas from its other resort amenities. With dark wood and marble in the lobby and common areas, the Eldorado instills a quiet elegance. **Brew Brothers** (11:30am-2am Mon.-Fri., 11am-2am Sat.-Sun., $10-15) often continues that sedate theme during dinner (ribs, pizza, and sandwiches), but late at night and on weekends it becomes a boisterous college party with karaoke, battles of the bands, and all-you-can-drink craft beer specials.

The **Eldorado Theatre** is one of the few Reno casino on-site venues delivering Vegas-style production shows and musical theater. Packages are available to combine the show with dinner at several of the casino's better restaurants, including **La Strada** (5pm-9pm Sun.-Thurs., 5pm-10pm Fri.-Sat., $25-35), one of the best Italian restaurants in Nevada. La Strada's northern Italian cuisine includes several veal specialties (we're partial to the Milanese); the pasta is handmade on

Harold's Club or Bust

At 250 North Virginia Street, Harold's Club was once the center of the casino gambling universe. Raymond "Pappy" Smith, a carnival operator, sent his son Harold to Reno to open a little roulette concession (one wheel, two nickel slots) in 1935, a time when gambling, although legal, was still very much a Douglas Alley backroom scam-riddled enterprise. That first little excursion into legal gambling proved profitable, so the Smiths expanded, and in the process changed the face of casino gambling forever. They not only ushered gambling into the daylight of Virginia Street, but they also launched a campaign to improve the image of legalized casino gambling in the national consciousness, which also reflected on the image of Harold's Club and Reno.

In so doing, the Smiths set the ground rules for Nevada's incipient gambling industry by showing the first generation of casino operators how to make gambling palatable to the middle-class masses. Without them, Meyer Lansky and Bugsy Siegel could never have envisioned their own resort hotel in Las Vegas. And it would've been a very different world today.

In the late 1930s the slogan "Harold's Club or Bust" suddenly loomed from billboards, played on the radio, and appeared in newspapers all over the country, introducing locals and non-Nevadans to the novel concept that gambling was good clean fun. The Smiths implemented sophisticated safeguards against cheating on both sides of the table, inventing them as they went along—the original eye-in-the-sky, one-way glass, and the catwalk system, for example. Harold's Club was the first to offer free drinks, comps, and junkets and to charter trains and planes for its customers. Harold's was the first to hire female dealers, during the labor shortage of World War II, further enhancing casino respectability. The whole strategy worked so well that it immediately became standard casino operating procedure and has remained so ever since.

Pappy Smith, who has been called the Henry Ford of Nevada gambling, died in 1967. The Club was sold to Howard Hughes's Summa Corporation in 1970 and expanded in 1979. When Fitzgeralds bought it in 1988, it was the last casino property that Summa had to sell, thereby ending the 20-year presence of Howard Hughes's corporation in Nevada. (Fitzgeralds also bought the Sundance in Las Vegas in 1987, thereby ending Moe Dalitz's nearly 40-year reign as that city's King of Juice.) Fitzgeralds tried to sell the unprofitable casino for years and finally had to shut it down in 1995. Harrah's purchased it in 1999, and the casino's Plaza now occupies the site.

the premises and baked in wood-fired brick ovens.

NoVi (9pm-3am Fri.-Sat.) is part ultra-lounge, part concert venue, and part dance club, spinning country, hip-hop, top 40, and more. Amber and crimson bar lights play off chic leather stools and sensually curved black lacquer furnishings, creating shadowy niches for intimate get-togethers and romantic interludes. **The Buffet** (7:45am-2pm and 4pm-9pm Mon.-Thurs., 7:45am-2pm and 4pm-10pm Fri.-Sun., $12-16) challenges Atlantis's as Reno's best. Another trans-global journey, The Buffet's ravioli and Mexican specialties are epic.

Standard rooms in the towers are an intimate 250 to 275 square feet. Now sporting a clean, light wood and mauve color scheme,

they offer the obligatory mountain and city views. Suites also are available, with escalating levels of luxury and price.

Sands Regency

Restaurants: Copa Bar & Grill, Cabana Café, The Original Mel's Diner, Tacos Tijuana, Sands Buffet

Entertainment: Jester's Theater

Nightlife: Pipeline Lounge, 3rd Street Lounge

While there's much to be said in favor of Nevada's megaresorts, they're definitely not for everyone. If you're one who finds these behemoths leave something to be desired, the **Sands Regency** (345 N. Arlington Ave., 775/347-2200 or 866/386-7829, www. sandsregency.com, $69-99) may be just what you're looking for: low-limit blackjack tables, $2-4 limit hold 'em, and $3 blackjack keep the gaming casual. Skip the snooty maître d' and get your *American Graffiti* on at **The Original Mel's Diner** (24 hours daily, $10-15) with burgers, shakes, and other comfort foods. You'll not find any over-produced and under-costumed reviews at the Sands. You will find quality, affordable shows at **Jester's Theater,** home to the Utility Players improv troupe (8pm Sat. Mar.-May, $15, age 16 and over only).

The Regency's standard rooms weigh in at a generous 377 square feet, among the largest in Reno. They are decorated more boldly than most, with splashes of royal blue, umber, and rose. Just a few blocks off the strip on 4th Street, the Sands has the classic Las Vegas-type look of a casino that's grown up piecemeal, with the original 1964 low-rise motel units surrounding its first pool, towers rising above, and three or four different wings to the casino.

Harrah's

Restaurants: Harrah's Steak House, Ichiban, Hash House A Go Go, Joy Luck Noodle Bar, Carvings, Quiznos, Starbucks
Entertainment: Sammy's Showroom
Nightlife: Sapphire Lounge, The Stage @ The Zone

Gaming icon William Harrah's empire began here with a failed bingo parlor in 1937. Harrah reopened the joint the following year, and within five years, he had acquired five bar-casinos and opened **Harrah's** (219 N. Center St., 775/786-3232 or 800/427-7247, www.caesars.com, $95-150) in 1946. Acquisition and expansion continued with the purchase of the Golden Hotel in 1966 and the addition of a 24-story hotel in 1969. Harrah's legacy of growth continued after his death in 1978: a second tower in 1981, a renovation in 1994 and another in 2006, the incorporation of the 400-room Hampton Inn in 1999. **Sammy's Showroom,** named for the Rat Packer and frequent Harrah's performer, hosts production shows, including a Rat Pack tribute, variety reviews, and Elvis impersonators.

About the only thing that hasn't changed much is **Harrah's Steak House**

(775/788-2929, 5pm-10pm daily, $30-45), which adheres to the attentive service and perfectly prepared dishes Big Bill always insisted upon. The garlicky chicken ravioli is the perfect starter for steak Diane flambéed right at your table. For more tableside culinary magic, visit **Ichiban** (775/323-5550, 5pm-10pm Mon.-Thurs., 4:30pm-10pm Fri.-Sun., $25-35), where theatrical food preparation doesn't overshadow the teppanyaki show-chefs' culinary mastery.

Nightlife at Harrah's is more about relaxation than rowdiness. A well-made martini, some elbow room, and good company are the draws to the **Sapphire Lounge** (6pm-2am Fri.-Sat.). Jazz, blues, top 40, and country bands go on at 9pm.

Harrah's 828 rooms are arranged in its two hotel towers. The West Tower rooms are a bit nicer and a few dollars more per night than their counterparts in the East Tower. Pets can stay in some East Tower rooms for an additional fee.

Club Cal-Neva

Restaurants: Steak & Pasta House, Top Deck, Knockout Grill, Casino Grill
Nightlife: Cabaret Stage karaoke

Not to the confused with the dormant (but not dead, we hope) Cal-Neva Lodge in Lake Tahoe, **Club Cal-Neva** (38 E. 2nd St., 775/323-1046, www.clubcalneva.com) has sold its Nevadan Hotel, and the rooms have been converted to long-term rentals.

The other offerings are still in place, but they're geared strictly to low rollers: The $10 daily poker tournaments; low-limit blackjack, roulette, craps, and pai gow; and hundreds of slots and video poker machines seem more like something to do rather than a shot at riches. Cal-Neva does have a sports book and slot club, however, as well as a weekend table game party pit, with lingerie-clad dealers.

The Cal-Neva does entertainment on a small scale as well. For professional musicians or revue shows, make the walk to the Eldorado, Silver Legacy, Sands Regency, or Circus Circus. Cabaret (8pm-1am

RENO AND TAHOE
RENO

Peppermill hotel and casino

Thurs.-Sun.) and beer pong tournaments (10pm Fri.-Sat.) are the only offerings here. While the **Steak & Pasta House** (5pm-11pm Thurs.-Sun., $15-30) adds some variety with surf, turf, and Italian dishes, the three other restaurants are diners—fast food with dishes and silverware. But you just can't beat the $4.99 steak and eggs at the **Top Deck** on the third floor of the Cal-Neva (6am-11am Sun.-Thurs., 24 hours Fri.-Sat., $5-10). The French toast is a winner, sprinkled with cinnamon and slathered in syrup.

★ Peppermill

Restaurants: Bimini Steakhouse, Chi, Romanza, Oceano, Biscotti's, Island Buffet, Café Milano, Café Espresso

Entertainment: Terrace Lounge, Tuscany Events Center

Attractions: Game Lab, Spa Toscana

Nightlife: Edge Nightclub, Fireside Lounge, Banyan Bar, Sports Bar, Chi Bar, Romanza Bar, Casino Lounge, Lobby Lounge, Sole Poolside

No matter how well hotels appoint their gambling areas with replicas of art masterpieces or carry their casino theme through to their restaurants, nightclubs, and hotel rooms, reconciling the thrills of casino gaming with a desire to project your-whim-is-our-command resort service is never seamless. The **Peppermill** (2707 S. Virginia St., 866/821-9996, www.peppermillreno.com, $89-170) avoids the problem by segregating—both physically and stylistically—its glitter-and-neon gambling den from its more traditional resort amenities. The 100,000-square-foot casino is as flashy, loud, and bright as any in Nevada, but the rest of the property, decked out in marble, leather, and rich wood, might easily be mistaken for a rich-and-famous retreat in the Caribbean or Mediterranean. The Peppermill delivers this best-of-both-worlds scenario using attractions common to most Nevada resorts. It just does them bigger and better than most. A swimming pool is almost a given at resort hotels, but at the Peppermill, two pools—one open year-round—entice swimmers and sun worshippers. Spas are a dime a dozen in Nevada, but the Peppermill's **Spa Toscana** (8am-9pm Mon.-Thurs., 8am-10pm Fri.-Sun.) envelops guests like a terrycloth robe in 30,000 square feet of Roman bath treatments and relaxation in its indoor pool and sundeck.

Top gamers can win video game systems, iPods, and more with a few dexterous flicks of a wrist at **Game Lab** (9am-11pm Sun.-Thurs., 9am-midnight Fri.-Sat.). All that fun is sure to work up an appetite; for breakfast and lunch, you can't go wrong with **Café Espresso** (24 hours daily, $8-10) for gourmet coffee, gelato, and paninis. Northern Italy is featured at **Romanza** (5:30pm-9:30pm Wed.-Sun., $25-50), where chefs show off their chops in a show kitchen and the food is prepared in a massive wood-fired oven. The secluded, classical music-serenaded dining room is made even more intimate with elevated seating. **Oceano**'s (11:30am-9:30pm Sun.-Thurs., 11:30am-10pm Fri.-Sat., $25-35) underwater theme sets the stage for salt-crusted calamari, sushi, and crab-stuffed prawns.

The Peppermill hosts top musical talent and conventions in the **Tuscany Event Center** and live local jazz, rock, and Latin acts amid a garden setting in the **Terrace Lounge** (noon-11:30pm Sun.-Thurs., noon-1am Fri.-Sat.). Speakeasy meets speaker system at **Edge Nightclub** (7pm-1am Thurs., 10pm-2am Fri.-Sat.), an intimate, sophisticated lounge where DJs spin house and hip-hop through 35,000 watts. Put on your swankiest threads and dance the night away, or hole up with a few friends (or one special guy or gal) in the purple shadows.

Standard 350-square-foot rooms in the Peppermill Tower feature lacquer and mirrored accents for a touch of classic elegance. For even more elegance, choose a suite in the Peppermill or 600-room Tuscany Tower with its 550-square-foot accommodations, sweeping views, and old-world charm. Rooms in the north and west wings are a cozy 250 square feet—half the size of Tuscany, and a bit of a chore to reach from the gaming floor and restaurants. But they're also about half the price and include indulgences such as marble tile and mahogany furnishings.

Atlantis

Restaurants: Atlantis Steakhouse, Bistro Napa, Café Alfresco, Chicago Dogs, Gourmet Grind, Manhattan Deli, Oyster Bar, Purple Parrot, Sushi Bar, Toucan Charlie's Buffet and Grille, Java etc.

Entertainment: Center Stage Cabaret, Grand Ballroom

Attractions: Fun Center, Spa Atlantis

Nightlife: Atrium Lounge, Sports Lounge, Sky Terrace Bar, Waterfall Bar

Always on the cutting edge of design, amenities, and hospitality, **Atlantis** (3800 S. Virginia St., 800/723-6500 or 775/825-4700, www.atlantiscasino.com, $180-260) is the first Reno casino to make its race and sports book nonsmoking. **Spa Atlantis** is Reno's first four-star (Forbes) spa, rejuvenating muscles, skin, and mind with treatments such as milk and honey cocoons, hammam baths, and brine inhalation. The 60,000-square-foot casino is striking in blue and gold, housing all the usual tables and machines, along with bars with striking views of the cityscape, mountains, and indoor waterfall. The **Center Stage Cabaret** (8pm-1:30am Sun.-Thurs., 8pm-3:30am Fri.-Sat., free) hosts two musical lounge acts per night, keeping the party going into the wee hours. From classic video games to the latest multimedia and virtual reality, the **Fun Center** (10am-10pm Sun.-Thurs., 10am-midnight Fri.-Sat.) has a "frequent player" card for hard-core gamers.

Can mashed potatoes be a gourmet dish? They can when the staff knows its way around a spud like the chefs at the ★ **Atlantis Steakhouse** (775/824-4460, 5pm-10pm daily, $26-56), possibly the best restaurant in town. With a 4,000-bottle cellar and an experienced sommelier, **Bistro Napa** (775/335-4539, 5pm-9pm Sun.-Thurs., 10am-10pm Fri.-Sat., $25-45) will deliver the perfect pairing for your choice of California cuisine. Bring a friend or a huge appetite if you order the pastrami at **Manhattan Deli** (775/335-3114, 11am-9pm daily, $12-20). Just like the Jewish delicatessen in the old neighborhood, it sells knishes, latkes, lox, chicken salad, and other favorites. The chicken soup is worth catching a cold for. Seafood at a diner often is a 50-50 proposition, but the **Purple Parrot** (775/824-4432, 24 hours daily, $8-15) comes up aces with its shrimp Louie. Fresh off a multimillion-dollar renovation in 2016, **Toucan Charlie's Buffet and Grille** (8am-3pm and 4:30pm-9pm Mon.-Sat., 9am-3pm and 4:30pm-9pm Sun., $16-25, Sun. brunch, Fri. seafood dinner, and Sat. steak and seafood dinner $30-37) follows the trend of international serving stations. But it features several unusual twists, most notably a Mongolian barbecue, where your vegetables and meats are stir-fried on a round grill. Other innovations include a pho station, cotton candy in the dessert station, and kimchi and couscous in the salad bar.

Like its restaurants, Atlantis's rooms run from plush to plain. Standard tower rooms are only average sized, at 375 square feet, but marble and wood accents, city and mountain

The Machine That Started It All

For the second quarter of the 20th century, Reno—not Las Vegas—was the center of the country's gambling culture. And it was all thanks to an ingenious yet unassuming little contraption that has come to symbolize the entire gambling industry.

Charles Fey, a young German immigrant, was tinkering in his San Francisco apartment in 1895 when he created the world's first true slot machine. Today each of the most popular of Nevada's 200,000 slots generate as much as $5,000 per month in revenue. They work 24 hours a day, seven days a week and require little maintenance; they rarely make a mistake, making them the perfect casino "employee."

Although today's machines often include electronics, complicated pay scales, multiple lines, and dozens of symbols, they're easy to play, a feature that has made them popular since Fey placed his first "Liberty Bell" machines in Reno and San Francisco saloons before the turn of the 20th century. During the first half of the 1900s, proprietors of several of Reno's legal and illegal gambling dens installed the simple devices as diversions for wives and mistresses while "serious" gamblers played poker and craps.

Fey drew inspiration from a five-reel poker machine built by a New York company, but the machinist developed several improvements still in use today, including automatic payouts for winning combinations and a "trade check separator" that could distinguish between real nickels and the plug and wooden variety.

The Liberty Bell used three reels, all painted with symbols—hearts, diamonds, spades, and Liberty Bells. For a nickel investment, gamblers could reap a fortune of 10 times their bet by lining up three bells. Fey and the saloons split the profits.

As the popularity of slot machines continued to grow in the early 1900s, competitors copied Fey's design, which he was unable to patent. One of these knock-offs, the Operator Bell, used oranges, lemons, and cherries instead of playing-card suits, thus creating the first "fruit machine."

When Nevada officially outlawed gambling from 1911 to 1930, the halls simply moved their slots to a back room. Other establishments used machines that dispensed cheap gum or candy with each pull, disguising the gambling devices as innocuous vending machines. When the ban was lifted, it didn't take long for slot machines to advance technologically. Electric machines debuted in 1934.

Modern machines are not mechanical. Their wheel sequences are controlled by random number generators. Many offer progressive jackpots, including Megabucks, with machines throughout the state. In 2003 it made one player $39.7 million richer—a far cry from the half-buck that three Liberty Bells were worth to patrons of Fey's original slot machine. The newest slots feature animation, surround sound, and mini-games-within-the-game. One company is test marketing skill-based games. Maybe all those Nintendo hours will pay off.

RENO AND TAHOE
RENO

views, and high ceilings with decorative moldings make them seem bigger. If you want to treat yourself, choose the Concierge Tower. The 450-square-foot digs on the upper floors are tastefully decorated in chocolates, buffs, and creams and include 42-inch televisions with DVD players. Better yet, a stay in the Concierge Tower includes access to the exclusive Concierge Lounge for cocktails, free hors d'oeuvres, continental breakfast, Internet access, and newspapers.

Grand Sierra

Restaurants: Charlie Palmer Steak, Briscola, Rim, Cantina, Grand Buffet, Grand Café, 2nd Street Café Express, Johnny Rockets, Round Table Pizza, Port of Subs, Yogurt Beach, Starbucks
Entertainment: Grand Theatre, The Beach, Bowling Center, Fun Quest, Grand Sierra Cinema, Grand Adventure Land
Attractions: Spa at Grand Sierra, wedding chapel
Nightlife: Reserve Wine Bar, Lex Lounge, Crystal Bar, Rendezvous Bar & Lounge, Butterfly Bar and Cascade Lounge, Race and Sports Bar

Located just outside Reno's casino core, the **Grand Sierra** (2500 E. 2nd St., 775/789-2000 or 800/501-2651, www.grandsierraresort. com, $98-228) has everything the vacationer or conventioneer could want—all under one roof. The aptly named resort is built on a grand scale, from its nearly 2,000-room hotel to its 440-square-foot standard rooms to its 90,000-square-foot casino—larger even than most Las Vegas gambling dens. You could spend a week here and never eat dinner twice in the same restaurant, or shop till you drop and never visit all the boutiques.

With the largest indoor stage in Nevada, the **Grand Theatre** hosts comedy, cover bands, and music headliners ranging from Kiss to Idina Menzel. **The Beach** (May-Sept. weather permitting, $20) is a seaside picnic, with a big sandcastle construction zone, frosty beverages, burger grill, and volleyball pit. When the sun goes down, the pool transforms into a sexy aqua lounge. Excitement of a different stripe is to be had at **Fun Quest** (10am-10pm Sun.-Thurs., 10am-midnight Fri.-Sat.), a state-of-the-art video and virtual reality parlor.

Celebrity chef Charlie Palmer operates two restaurants at Grand Sierra. ★ **Charlie Palmer Steak** (775/789-2458, 5pm-9pm Sun.-Thurs., 5pm-10pm Fri.-Sat., $40-80), which vies with Atlantis Steakhouse for top honors in town, cooks up progressive French preparations and new twists on traditional American favorites. Palmer's Italian entry, **Briscola** (5pm-9pm Sun. and Tues.-Thurs., 5pm-10pm Fri.-Sat., $20-30) is casual and family-friendly, with gooey, cheesy dishes designed with kids in mind. But the caramel decor, Italian pop culture prints, and extensive list of wines and cordials, along with more subtle menu selections, cater to adults. **Grand Buffet** (10:30am-2pm and 4:30pm-9:30pm Mon.-Thurs., 8am-2:30pm and 4:30pm-10pm Fri.-Sat., 9am-2:30pm and 4:30pm-9:30pm Sun., $17-24, Fri.-Sat. seafood dinners $32) ups the ante with tandoori, smoked brisket, cake pops, and a donut maker, as well as one of the most striking buffet interiors in town. Stonework, sleek chrome, innovative lighting, and a colorful entrance provide a feast for the eye while carving-station prime rib and prepared-to-order scampi do the same for the taste buds.

With standard rooms averaging more than 450 square feet, Sierra's standard accommodations meet even the largest family's needs. Suites accommodate larger groups and budgets and come with great views and leather cream furnishings, refrigerators, and microwaves. Rose and burnt orange accents add to the home-away-from-home aura.

Like everything else at the resort, the Grand Sierra's **RV park** ($40-55) is one of the largest in the area. It's something of a concrete jungle, but a handful of the 178 pads (plenty of pull-throughs) overlook the river. Accessible, clean restrooms have flush toilets and hot showers; sewage disposal, laundry, groceries, video rentals, and a heated swimming pool are available. Guests have the full run of the resort's amenities.

Boomtown

Restaurants: Lobster Buffet, Boomtown Steakhouse, Around the World Buffet, Mel's Diner, Baja Mexican, Market Fresh Deli, Peet's Coffee & Tea
Entertainment: Guitar Bar
Attractions: Family Fun Center, Cabela's
Nightlife: Cactus Bar, Six Shooter Saloon

West of Reno in the town of Verdi, the small-ish—at an average of 340 square feet—Best Western rooms at **Boomtown** (2100 Garson Rd., 775/345-6000, http://boomtownreno. com, $90-130) maintain a sleek, clean feel, with starched white linen and varnished wood tables. Amenities include flat-screen TVs, iPod docking stations, and Wi-Fi. Boomtown also is affiliated with a **KOA campground** (775/345-2444, $28-46) with more than 200 spaces on-site. The campground includes a pool, but the Wi-Fi is spotty. It's next to the **Cabela's** (9am-9pm Mon.-Sat., 9am-7pm Sun.), where Grizzly Adams types will be in their element, surrounded by stuffed wildlife, local gamefish in huge aquaria, and a target shooting gallery. There's a deli and a fudge shop, so there's really no reason to ever leave. The **Family Fun Center** (11am-9pm Sun.-Thurs., 10am-10pm Fri.-Sat.) houses a flight simulator, antique carousel, Ferris wheel, and 200 video games in 30,000 square feet.

The Nugget

Restaurants: Steakhouse, Oyster Bar, Rotisserie Buffet, Rosie's Cafe, Noodle Hut & Sushi Bar, Dance Hall & Bar-B-Que, Tailgate Deli and Sports Bar, Starbucks

Entertainment: Celebrity Showroom, Nugget Ballroom, Casino Cabaret

Attractions: atrium pool, health club, Skywalk Arcade, gift shop

Nightlife: Horseshoe Bar, Lobby Lounge, Sports Zone Lounge, Broadway Bar, Game On

East of Reno, in Sparks, John Ascuaga's family operated **The Nugget** (1100 Nugget Ave., 775/356-3300 or 800/648-1177, www.nuggetcasinoresort.com, $93-136) for more than 50 years, beginning in 1960 when the patriarch transformed a coffee shop and slot machine parlor into a full-fledged resort. He built two 29-floor hotel towers in 1984 and 1996. The entrepreneurial Ascuaga even fought not merely City Hall, but the federal government—and won! In the late 1950s, the Nugget commissioned a solid gold rooster to serve as mascot for a new restaurant. But the U.S. Treasury Department claimed the bird ran afowl (sorry) of the law prohibiting private ownership of more than 50 ounces of gold unless it was in the form of an objet d'art. The Nugget won its case that the poultry was indeed art and reclaimed possession. The rooster was removed in 2013 and auctioned for $234,000 when the family sold the resort.

Slightly past-their-prime pop and rock stars perform in the 2,000-seat **Nugget Ballroom.** Pat Benatar, Air Supply, and .38 Special graced the stage in 2017. Slightly less established musical acts entertain in the intimate, 700-seat, pitch-perfect **Celebrity Showroom.**

Many buffets tout their international flavor with stations dedicated to different ethnic foods, but **Rotisserie Buffet** (11am-2pm and 5pm-9pm Mon.-Thurs., 11am-5:30pm Fri., 8:30am-2pm and 5pm-9pm Sat., 8:30am-2pm and 5pm-9pm Sun., $10-24) features a different theme every night. Pick your favorite: Mexican on Monday, Comfort Food on Tuesday, Asian on Thursday, Italian on Sunday, etc.

SPORTS AND RECREATION

Reno is a fantastic recreation destination for cool- and warm-weather sports and activities. It's a great biking town, with close access to some of the best skiing in the country. It also has some surprises—ballooning and urban kayaking (see page 123), for instance, are popular non-casino activities. There's plenty to keep kids entertained, as well, with amusement parks and carnival midways close at hand.

Winter Sports

While several world-class ski alpine resorts are only a couple hours away at Lake Tahoe, **Mt. Rose Ski Tahoe** (22222 Mt. Rose Hwy., 775/849-0704, www.skirose.com) is just a half hour south via I-580 and NV 431, on the way to Incline Village. On the same route, but even closer to town, **Galena Creek Regional Park** (18350 Mt. Rose Hwy., 775/849-4948, www.galenacreekvisitorcenter.org, 9am-6pm Tues.-Sun.) has several trails for cross country skiing and snowshoeing. Between Galena Creek and Mt. Rose, volunteers at **Sky Tavern Ski Area** (21130 Sky Tavern Rd., 775/323-5125, www.skytavern.com) teach basic and advanced skiing and snowboarding skills.

Each winter, the city builds an **ice rink** outside the Reno Aces home park (250 Evans Ave., early Nov.-late Jan., 10am-10pm Mon.-Sat., 10am-7pm Sun., $8, children and seniors $6, skate rental $4). Multi-visit and season passes are available.

Biking and Hiking

The **Truckee River Bike Path** is a paved cycling, jogging, and walking trail nearly the length of Truckee Meadows, right along the river most of the way. It's roughly 12 miles long, stretching between the eastern edge of Sparks (near the Vista Blvd. exit off I-80) through Rock Park (near the west edge of Sparks), Galetti Park (in east Reno), Idlewild Park (in central Reno), and finally to the Mayberry area (at Caughlin Ranch in west Reno). It's an idyllic chain of parks, linked by the murmuring river that snakes right through the middle of the city.

The most popular biking hill climb is to the top of **Geiger Grade** on NV 341 to Virginia City; it's a killer. Cyclists also work out on McCarran Boulevard between 4th and Skyline (though it's somewhat narrow). The streets of Reno-Sparks are in pretty good shape, but mountain bikes are preferred around town for their fat and cushiony tires.

Sierra Adventures (11 N. Sierra St., Ste. 101, 775/323-8928 or 866/323-8928, www.wildsierra.com) is one of a few outfitters in Reno that organize mountain biking tours in addition to renting rides (as well as skis, snowboards, fishing equipment, kayaks, and more). One of the best tours goes down Peavine Mountain, through wild horse and deer habitat and Nevada desert scrub. Other places in Reno rent bicycles: **Sundance Bike Rentals** is based downtown at the Sands Regency (345 N. Arlington Ave., 775/786-0222, www.renoskirent.com). **Snowind Sports** (6275 Sharlands Ave., 775/323-9463, www.snowind.com) is just off I-80 west of downtown on the way to the California ski resorts.

Huffaker Park (south of the airport, just off McCarran) is perfect for the novice hiker. Easy and moderate trails lead to elevations that command panoramic views of the valley: the Reno skyline, Sparks, Peavine Mountain, and more. The **Lookout Trail** around two hills is a just-right 1.7-mile loop.

Ballooning

One of the most popular Reno events of the year is the **Great Reno Balloon Race** (www.renoballoon.com), which takes place in September. More than 100 balloons rise to the occasion from Rancho San Rafael Park, starting very early in the morning. To go up in one yourself at other times of the year, call **Sierra Adventures** (775/323-8928 or 866/323-8928, www.wildsierra.com). This is an experience that's nothing like anything you've ever done before—but it's only for early risers. The balloons take off around 8am in the winter and as early as 6:30am in the summer to avoid being caught in warm thermals as the air heats up. The balloons float 500-1,000 feet

The Truckee River flows through downtown Reno, attracting kayakers and fly-fishers.

up—somewhere between the treetops and the clouds—for about three hours per ride.

Fishing

Northern and central Nevada streams are some of the best trout waters in the country. The Truckee River gives up good-sized browns, especially in the mid- to late spring, as well as cutthroats and stocked rainbows throughout the cooler months. The quantity and diversity of the fish, the variety of habitat, and the ease of access to the river make the Truckee a great all-around fishing destination. Not far away, the forks of the Carson and Walker Rivers are good bets as well.

Idlewild Park has bluegill and stocked rainbows; Virginia Lake has brown trout, and its fishing dock is one of the more easily accessed by people with disabilities. The fishing pier at Sparks Marina Park is another. The 77-acre lake is stocked with rainbow trout.

Nevada fishing licenses are available at most sporting goods stores or at the **Nevada Department of Wildlife** website (www. ndow.org). Visit the website for regulations regarding catch-and-release, bag limits, legal bait and tackle, and more. The site also contains a reliable fishing report, updated weekly. The **Reno Fly Shop** (238 S. Arlington Ave., 775/323-3474, http://renoflyshop.com, 10am-6pm Mon.-Sat.) has a top-notch guide service, rental equipment, and the latest advice and what's catching fish.

Horseback Riding

Rancho Red Rock (15670 N. Red Rock Rd., 30 miles north of Reno, 775/969-3315, www. ranchredrock.com) is open all year, weather permitting. It arranges trail rides and offers riding lessons and pony rides around the ranch. **Sierra Adventures** (775/323-8928 or 866/323-8928, www.wildsierra.com) leads one- and two-day excursions into the Nevada outback.

Golf

The Reno area is golf heaven, with 50 courses within a 90-minute drive of downtown. The Reno-Sparks area has more than a dozen courses, with another dozen courses just to the south in the Carson Valley. Several challenging courses designed by some of the game's legends can be played for less than $50, even at near-peak times, and offer great 19th hole restaurants and other resort amenities. **Wolf Run Golf Club** (1400 Wolf Run Rd., 775/851-3301, www.wolfrungolfclub. com, $30-70) in the foothills has wide fairways, but rolling terrain makes for challenging lies. Elevated tees give great views of the tree-lined valley. **Arrow Creek Country Club** (2905 Arrowcreek Pkwy., 775/850-4653, http://theclubatarrowcreek.com, $40-65) has courses designed by Arnold Palmer and Fuzzy Zoeller. Not only the two courses, but the entire **Resort at Red Hawk** (6590 N. Wingfield Pkwy., Sparks, 775/626-1000, www.redhawk-golfandresort.com, $39-75) is the brainchild of Robert Trent Jones Jr., so you know it's designed for the serious player. It's worth the trip just to stock up in the huge—and very cool—pro shop.

Budget players can rejoice as well. Many of the area's courses are quite playable with fees of less than $25: The walkable course at **Sierra Sage Golf Course** (6355 Silverlake Blvd., 775/972-1564, www.sierrasagegolf.org, $20-27) is less than a dollar a hole most days; **Washoe County Golf Course** (2601 Foley Way, 775/827-6640, www.washoegolf.org, $22-33) opened as a private country club in 1917. It's now a public course with reasonable greens fees.

Information on golf courses and golf packages is available from area visitors centers and chambers of commerce. For a free Reno-Tahoe golf package brochure, contact the **Reno Sparks Convention and Visitors Authority** (800/367-7366, www. visitrenotahoe.com).

Rides and Games

Rivaling the Stratosphere's thrill rides in Las Vegas, the Ultimate Rush at the Grand Sierra resort's **Grand Adventure Land** (2500 E. 2nd St., 775/786-2075, www.

grandsierraresort.com, 10am-9pm Fri., 10am-10pm Sat., 10am-6pm Sun.) plummets riders 185 feet on a swooping, 65 mph swing. The combination bungee jump and hang gliding flight is $25. The attraction also offers mini golf ($6, under 12 $4) and go-kart racing ($6.50) on three different track surfaces. There's also a kiddie track ($4).

The **Wild Island Family Adventure Park** (250 Wild Island Ct., Sparks, 775/359-2927, www.wildisland.com, 10am-10pm Mon.-Thurs., 10am-midnight Fri.-Sat.) is a kid's paradise. The water park (summer only, $35, under 48 inches $25, age 60 and over $10) has slides, pools, waves, lazy rivers, and just all-around splashing. Other attractions include a bowling alley ($3 per game), go-karts ($4.50-6.75), mini golf ($6.75), virtual thrill rides ($6.75), and more. Several ride/game combination tickets and an all-access non-water pass save money.

Spectator Sports

No longer a bush league city, Reno fielded its first triple-A baseball team in 2009. The **Reno Aces** (250 Evans Ave., 775/334-7000, www.renoaces.com, $14-35), the top farm club of the Arizona Diamondbacks, moved into the $50 million, 9,100-seat Greater Nevada Field in the riverfront Freight District to begin the 2009 Pacific Coast League season. The PCL season runs from early April to early September. The Aces share the stadium and ticket facilities with **Reno 1868 FC** (www.reno1868fc.com, $12-75). Named for the year of the city's founding, the United Soccer League expansion franchise debuted in 2017. Their 32-game schedule runs from mid-March through early October.

The **Reno Bighorns** (400 N. Center St., 775/853-8220, www.nba.com/dleague/reno, $24-200) are the NBA D-League affiliate of the Sacramento Kings. The season runs November-April. The Bighorns play their 25-game home schedule at the 7,100-seat Reno Events Center.

The nonprofit Reno Rodeo Foundation hosts the PRCA-sanctioned **Reno Rodeo**

each summer, at the **Reno-Sparks Livestock Center** (1350 N. Wells Ave., 775/688-5752, $8-15), with proceeds benefitting local educational outreach, children's charities, and high school rodeo programs. The 10-day rodeo features a carnival, cattle drive reenactment, kids' sheep riding (mutton bustin'), and Western apparel trade show.

The **University of Nevada, Reno** fields teams in 17 sports (www.nevadawolfpack.com). Competing in the Mountain West Conference as a member of the college football Bowl Championship Subdivision (formerly Division I), the school maintains an intense rivalry with UNLV. The winner of the annual football game takes possession of the Fremont Cannon, the heaviest and most expensive trophy in college athletics. The Wolf Pack football team plays its home games at Mackay Stadium on campus; call 775/347-7225 for tickets. UNR's men's basketball team plays at the Lawler Events Center on campus; call 775/784-4444 for tickets.

Reno's impressive **National Bowling Stadium** (300 N. Center St., 800/304-2695, www.gobowlreno.com) hosts junior, teen, college, international, and professional tournaments throughout the year, including United States Bowling Congress-sanctioned events.

Stead Airport north of the city hosts the **National Championship Air Races** (4895 Texas Ave., 775/972-6663, http://airrace.org, $5-35) each September.

ENTERTAINMENT

Reno has plenty of non-gambling entertainment to offer, and the daily *Reno Gazette-Journal*'s nifty website (www.rgj.com) keeps track of which headliners, big-name bands, comedians, and lounge groups are at which hotels, along with club acts and sporting events in the area. It also has blurbs on parks, museums, outdoor activities, and local recreation. The alternative weekly *Reno News and Review* (www.newsreview.com) is published on Thursday and distributed free on news racks around town. It reviews local art, music, movies, restaurants, and clubs, and prints a weekly calendar of events.

Showrooms and Concerts

Whatever your taste, you're likely to be able to get your fix for the low cost of a few cocktails any night of the week at one of the casinos. For A-list performers, the **RockBar Theater** (211 N. Virginia St., 775/323-5648, http://re.knittingfactory.com), across from Harrah's in the old Knitting Factory, stages concerts by touring bands, as well as karaoke and battles of the local bands.

Mountain Music Parlor (735 S. Center St., 775/843-5500, http://mountainmusicparlor.com) keeps that old-time and ethnic music alive with bluegrass, Irish, chamber, Hawaiian, and more. **Cargo Concert Hall** (255 N. Virginia St., 775/398-5400, www.cargoreno.com) serves as a rung on the ladder of success for rising comedians, rappers, heavy metal bands, and other artists. The dive bar setting at **Studio on 4th** (432 E. 4th St., 775/737-9776, http://studioon4th.com) hosts private and public concerts, mostly by punkers, goths, shoegazers, and other out-of-the-mainstream acts. Local artwork graces the walls and local blues and jazz bands command the stage at **MidTown Wine Bar** (1527 S. Virginia St., 775/800-1960, http://midtownwinebarreno.com). There's craft beer in addition to wine by the glass and bottle and small plates.

Music

Reno and Las Vegas have been accused of being cultural vacuums, but both now boast vibrant arts districts, and Reno, in particular, boasts a long history of embracing the finer things in life.

The 1,500-seat **Pioneer Center for the Performing Arts** (100 S. Virginia St., 775/786-4046, http://pioneercenter.com) stages Broadway musicals and performances of the **Nevada Opera** (775/525-4654, www.nevadaopera.org). Much less pretentious than you might think, the operas include pre-show explanatory discussions, so even if you're a newbie, you'll get the gist of the story. And if you get lost in translation, the theater projects English versions of the lyrics as the performers sing.

The **Reno Philharmonic Association** (775/323-6393, www.renophil.com) performs year-round throughout the region, with indoor concerts fall through spring in the Pioneer Center and outdoor family, festival, and pops shows during summer. The Pioneer is also the primary home of the **Alexander Von Alstyne Ballet Theatre** (775/762-5165, www.avaballet.com), with performances throughout the year. As if these classic entertainments weren't enough, the Pioneer Center also finds time to bring Broadway musicals, standup comedians, and touring musical troupes to Reno.

The **Reno Chamber Orchestra** (775/347-9413, www.renochamberorchestra.org) performs at the **Nightingale Concert Hall** (1335 N. Virginia St.) on the University of Nevada campus. Acoustically perfect, the 615-seat venue also carries several series of student ensemble performances and guest artists from around the globe.

Visual Art

Advocacy, education, and funding are the goals of the **Sierra Arts Foundation** (17 S. Virginia St., Ste. 120, 775/329-2787, www.sierraarts.org), which supports local community-spirited artists and works to develop work, exhibit, and performance space in the community, especially locations in need of beautification and revitalization.

Theater

The **Bruka Theater of the Sierra** (99 N. Virginia St., 775/323-3221, www.bruka.org) brings to its venerable and stark stage everything from Shakespearean drama to contemporary comedy, children's theater to the avant garde. **Reno Little Theater** (147 E. Pueblo St., 775/813-8900, www.renolittletheater.org) educates and exposes adults and children to the world of serious live theater with performances September through June.

Artown

Lots of towns have invested in arts districts to revitalize their downtowns, and many host First Friday or Third Thursday events to show off the resulting urban renewal. But Reno's transformation has been so remarkable that one day a month simply isn't enough time to show it off. The city presents **Artown** (775/322-1538, www.renoisartown.com), a month-long celebration of the visual and performing arts highlighted by visiting world-renowned artists, children's theater performances, gallery events, and cultural experiences. Artown has grown to include some 400 events and attract 350,000 people to Reno's downtown arts district each July.

Recipient of the National Endowment for the Arts' Access to Artistic Excellence grant, Artown boasts that 63 percent of its events are free, with many others costing less than $10. Free offerings in recent years have included family movies, dances, and the wildly popular Discover the Arts children's workshops, where kids 6-12 learn about theater, dance, music, poetry, painting, and sculpture.

"There's an upbeat energy that permeates Reno each July, and we're thrilled that Artown can have that sort of impact," Artown executive director Beth Macmillan said. "To say that we've been able to grow the festival to include so many events and genres and accommodate the number of attendees seen in recent years is phenomenal and speaks to the strength of Artown."

Since its inception in 1996, Artown's annual festival has infused $150 million into the local economy, federal grant funding, and tourism. Just as important, it has fostered the community's appreciation of art and generated valuable partnerships and collaborations among artists, arts organizations, patrons, and local governments.

EVENTS

Maybe it's because Reno enjoys such a mild spring, summer, and fall that it packs in as much entertainment as it can before the winter ski season arrives. Just about any weekend early May through early October will find the city hosting a cultural or athletic festival.

April

The **Reno Jazz Festival** (775/784-4278, www.unr.edu/rjf), sponsored by the University of Nevada, is one of the most respected in the country.

May

White-water paddling is the focus of the **Reno River Festival** (775/784-9400, renoriverfestival.com) at Wingfield Park, but there's also a muddy two-mile obstacle course for runners as well as live bands, food and beer, and an outdoor product trade show.

June

Cowboy up for the 10-day Professional Rodeo Cowboys Association-sanctioned **Reno Rodeo** (775/329-3877, www.renorodeo.com), which draws 140,000 spectators to watch riders and ropers compete through seven go-arounds for the fourth-largest prize pool on the circuit at the Reno Livestock Events Center.

From German brats to Swedish meatballs, Celtic fiddles, and Polish polkas, **EuroFest** (775/348-2200, www.sandsregency.com), at the Sands Regency, celebrates the old world with plenty of beer and wine for good measure.

Bicyclists can strut their stuff at **Tour de Nez** (www.tourdenez.com), a series of races and rallies. The tour includes rides centered at Wingfield Park. A trade show and musical entertainment complete the package. Races for locals, kids, and recumbent bikers, along with food and drink vendors, lend the event a party atmosphere.

July

Reno celebrates its commitment to the visual and performing arts with **Artown** (775/322-1538, www.renoisartown.com), a month-long celebration in the Riverwalk district. The Eldorado Casino hosts the **BBQ, Brews & Blues Festival** (775/325-7401, www.eldoradoreno.com), a journey through some of Reno's best food, the country's best music, and the world's top microbrews. Chicago and Delta blues performers pack two stages throughout the weekend.

Aspiring young local thespians are paired with professional actors to present condensed versions of the Bard's best throughout the area in the **Lake Tahoe Shakespeare Festival** (800/747-4697, www.laketahoeshakespeare.com). If comedy and tragedy aren't your things, the lake hosts a music festival around the same time. Heart-pounding fireworks culminate an Independence Day full of music, cool refreshments, games, and street performers in **Star Spangled Sparks** (775/356-3300, www.cityofsparks.us/event/star-spangled-sparks.com).

August

Part muscle car show, part street party, **Hot August Nights** presents wholesome 1950s and '60s-style entertainment in Reno, Sparks, and Lake Tahoe. Polish up the tailfins and cruise on over. Food, rides, games, a demolition derby, a competition for queen, and livestock—everything that makes Nevada great is at the **Nevada State Fair.** PGA Tour professionals vie for their share of the $3.5 million purse at the **Barracuda Championship** (775/322-3900, https://barracudachampionship.com).

September

John Ascuaga's Nugget in Sparks invites you to gorge yourself on barbecued ribs and other treats at the **Best in the West Nugget Rib Cook-Off** (775/324-6435 www.nuggetribcookoff.com). Free entertainment is presented on several stages, and a children's play area is open daily. Don't miss the professional rib-eating contest—do not try this at home.

The **Great Reno Balloon Race** (www.renoballoon.com) has more than 100 colorful hot-air balloons of all shapes dotting the skies north of Reno. A craft and souvenir show, food, balloon rides, and a student tissue-paper balloon launch add to the excitement. The **National Championship Air Races** (775/972-6663, www.airrace.org) are NASCAR with wings—if stock cars could reach 500 mph.

One of the 10 best and 10 largest bike rallies in the country, **Street Vibrations** (775/329-7469, www.roadshowsreno.com) is a weeklong succession of rides, vendors, and parades, all with a Harley attitude.

October

Bring the oregano and enter your spaghetti sauce in the cook-off at the **Great Italian Festival** (Eldorado Casino, 775/786-5700, www.eldoradoreno.com), or try your hand (foot, rather) in the hilarious grape-stomping contest. Activities include bocce and gelato-eating contests as well as traditional Italian entertainment.

Get the whole clan together to enjoy Scottish and Irish games, music, dances, and food at the **Reno Celtic Celebration** (775/378-0931, www.renoceltic.org) at Bartley Ranch Regional Park.

SHOPPING

Reno has been selling stuff to visitors since before the Civil War. Once Charles Fuller's bridge brought traffic through the area on their way to and from Virginia City, it didn't take long for merchants to spring up, providing food, forage, and supplies for immigrants and their livestock. The vendors' tradition continues today, with eclectic boutiques, massive malls, art and antique treasures, and, of course, trendy shops in every casino.

The **Riverwalk** is a window shopper's paradise. Forty shops—mostly catering to the smart, chic, urban professional—line the shady riverbank and several pedestrian-friendly blocks to the north and south between Barbara Bennett Park and Lake Street. While designer women's resale fashions at **Labels Consignment Boutique** (601 W. 1st St., 775/825-6000, www.labelsreno.com,

10am-6pm Mon.-Fri., 10am-5pm Sat., 11am-4pm Sun.) make a walk to the western edge of the district worthwhile, the largest concentration of shops is around 1st and Sierra Streets, north of the river. That's where you will find **Reno eNVy** (131 N. Sierra St., Ste. C, 775/682-3800, www.renoenvy.com, 10am-6pm daily), purveyor of logo wear so you can represent Nevada and the Biggest Little City in the World, and **Antiques & Treasures** (151 N. Sierra St., 775/327-3121, 10am-6pm daily), with its stash of collectible books, stamps, Coca-Cola signs, Western ephemera, and more. Other don't-miss stores around Riverwalk include **La Terre Verte** (3 N. Virginia St., 775/284-5006, noon-5pm Tues.-Sat.), which sells jewelry created from reclaimed glass, purses with pull-tab accents, and other environmentally friendly fashion accessories.

Edgier than Riverwalk, the **Midtown Shopping District,** extending south of the river along Virginia Street and Holcomb Avenue, caters to a younger, grungier (in a good way) crowd. A tattoo parlor, body-piercing shop, and recycled record, clothing, and furniture vendors hang shingles here, along with boutiques hawking wares for upwardly mobile babies, pampered pets, and appreciators of nontraditional artwork. Midtown's architecture—classic homes turned into storefronts share curb space with modern steel-and-concrete strip malls—is as eclectic as the items for sale. Plenty of museums, tea shops, and urban vibe-y bars break up the marathon shopping sprees.

Reno is home to several shopping malls containing the usual complement of shoe, clothing, and jewelry stores. Locals seem to prefer **Meadowood Mall** (500 Meadowood Mall Cir., 775/827-8450, 10am-9pm Mon.-Sat., 11am-7pm Sun.), off US 395 at McCarran Boulevard, for its mix of large anchor retailers and smaller specialty shops, ample parking, and cleanliness. Pedestrian- and pet-friendly, **The Summit** (13925 S. Virginia St., 775/853-7800, 10am-9pm Mon.-Sat., 11am-6pm Sun.), at Reno's southern tip, is an upscale outdoor plaza with lots of open spaces, fountains, and fire pits. **Outlets at Sparks** (1310 Scheels Dr., 775/358-3800, www.experiencelegends.com, 10am-9pm Mon.-Sat., 11am-6pm Sun.) is a bargain hunter's must-do, with outlets from some of the nation's top sellers of women's clothing, shoes, sporting goods, and more.

FOOD

From the Riverwalk to downtown, the university campus to midtown, to establishments of every stripe in the casinos, Reno supports more, and more varied, restaurants than cities three times its size. The better gambling resort restaurants are reviewed in the *Casinos* section.

Buffets

Nevada's buffets are many things: panaceas for families with finicky eaters, fodder for lounge comedians, and, among the tsk-tsk types, examples of America's gluttony. The best buffets in Reno are based in the casino resorts, such as Toucan Charlie's at Atlantis, The Buffet at Eldorado, and the Grand Buffet at Grand Sierra. Stand-alone buffets are few in Reno, but if you like Indian cuisine, you're in luck, having your pick of two outstanding establishments. We lean toward **Flavors of India** (1885 S. Virginia St., 775/323-4100, www.flavorsofindiarenonevada.com, 11am-10pm daily, $10-13) as the best, as the fresh garlic naan delivers a perfect complement to moist tikka masala and sweet korma. A close second is **India Kabab & Curry** (1091 S. Virginia St., 775/348-6222, www.indiakababcurry.com, 11am-10pm daily, $12-18). As you might expect, the best dishes are vegetarian.

Diners and Delis

Reno's carnivores' eyes glaze over and stomachs begin to rumble at the mention of the Awful Awful Burger at **The Nugget** (233 N. Virginia St., 775/323-0716, www.nugget-casinoresort.com, 24 hours daily, $12-15), a half-pound burger served with enough salty, seasoned fries to choke a horse (or at least clog an artery). It's awful big and awful good—so

School Spirit Writ Large

Those tall whitewashed letters on the hillsides above most of the towns in Nevada—who put them there, and why?

Similar letters are scattered all around the West, but the 38 in Nevada represent the most per capita of any state. Contrary to urban legend, these mountain monograms were not built to help airmail-dropping pilots identify the communities they flew over.

University of California students put the first letter, a C, on a hill overlooking the Berkeley campus in 1905 as an imaginative way to put school spirit ahead of class rivalries. The sentiment found its way to the University of Nevada, Reno, in 1913 when students constructed a huge N on Peavine Mountain above the campus. It consisted of thousands of rocks and hundreds of gallons of whitewash (water and lime) and covered 13,000 square feet. The rage quickly spread to high school students around the state. Elko teens assembled their E in 1916, the Tonopah T went up in 1917, and Carson City (C), Battle Mountain (BM), Virginia City (V), and Panaca (L, for Lincoln County) all had their own letters by 1927. Austin high schoolers finally put up their A in the early 1950s, and Beatty's B dates back to 1971. Other southern Nevada schools are represented as well: Basic, Indian Springs, Boulder City, Eldorado, and Moapa Valley are among those with hillside letters.

Lately, however, liability worries have prevented students from maintaining some of the letters. In places, the task has been taken over by service clubs and alumni groups. In fact, the SV above Smith Valley has gone high-tech and is now kept bright with an air sprayer powered by a portable generator. It'll take more than insurance premiums to jeopardize Nevada's long tradition of sweater letters on hillsides.

good, it's said, that when one entrepreneur opened a restaurant in town, he advertised his joint served "the second-best burger in town," in tribute to the Awful Awful.

A hardworking, hard-playing town like Reno needs plenty of pit-stop joints to keep residents and visitors fueled up. Toss in an always-hungry and perpetually poor college student body, and you end up with a target-rich environment for casual sit-down restaurants, where the gravy's thick, the fry cooker is at the ready, and the coffee's always hot. **Archie's** (2195 N. Virginia St., 775/322-9595, www.archiesreno.com, 24 hours daily, $10-15) has a '50s-style diner menu in a contemporary college setting northwest of campus. The one-third-pound burgers are filling and a bit pricey, but they come with a pound of fries. It's worth the $2 to substitute the beer-battered onion rings. Splurge on a chocolate malt or vanilla shake.

More old-fashioned shakes and burgers await at the **Gold 'N Silver Inn** (790 W. 4th St., 775/323-2696, www.goldnsilverreno. com, 24 hours daily, $10-15). In business for 60

years, it's more popular than ever after being featured on *Diners, Drive-Ins and Dives,* Guy Fieri's Food Network show. Most dishes are traditionally good comfort food, but a few—lemonade pork chops, anyone?—add a little twist. Get to the **Empire Diner** at Baldini's Sports Casino (865 S. Rock Blvd., 775/358-0116, http://baldinissports.com, 24 hours daily, $10-18) for build-your-own omelets and weekend prime rib specials.

Breakfast

If breakfast can ever be considered haute cuisine, **Peg's Glorified Ham & Eggs** (420 S. Sierra St., 775/329-2600, http://eatatpegs.com, 6:30am-2pm daily, $12-15), with four locations in Reno, is about as close as you'll find anywhere. It's no secret—there's often a line out the door, even on frigid mornings. But the locals agree the omelets and eggs Benedict with crab are worth a little frostbite.

A family home renovated into a neighborhood restaurant, **Daughters Cafe** (97 Bell St., 775/324-3447, www.daughterscafe.com,

9am-2pm Tues.-Sun., $14-16) is run by the family matriarch as cook, and her daughters serve as business manager and waitress. Breakfast often evokes French provincial, with crusty baguettes, beignets, and goat-cheese omelets.

Seafood

Rapscallion (1555 S. Wells Ave., 775/323-1211, http://rapscallion.com, 11am-9pm Mon.-Sat., $25-40) has an interesting interior—lots of wood, dimly lit dining alcoves, a lively bar, and stained glass. The cuisine, too, can be fancy, but the simply prepared dishes—grilled or seared fish, garlicky escargot, fried artichokes—make for a satisfying lunch. **Lulou's** (1470 S. Virginia St., 775/329-9979, 5pm-11:30pm Tues.-Sat., $30-42) is much more than a seafood restaurant; the duck and quail are divine, and the sherried crab, citrus-glazed calamari, and other fruits de mer are outstanding. It's a truly world-class restaurant that just happens to be located in Reno. The prices—especially if you spring for wine—are eye-popping as well.

Basque

Come hungry if you visit **Louis' Basque Corner** (301 E. 4th St., 775/323-7203, http://louisbasquecorner.com, 11am-9pm Tues.-Sat., 4pm-9pm Sun.-Mon., $22-32). Traditionally prepared and served family-style, dinner includes soup, salad, beans, French fries, bread, and choice of lamb, steak, or chicken entrée. Ditto for the **Santa Fe Hotel** (235 Lake St., 775/323-1891, 5pm-9pm Tues.-Sun., $14-20), where the steak, pork, and sausage sandwiches with all the fixings ($8-14) are a particular bargain. If you're prepared to sit at tables with strangers and have a good time, you'll leave both downtown Basque restaurants satisfied and socialized—especially after a few glasses of picon punch, a sour brandy concoction popular among Basque shepherds.

Italian

Renaissance art and Tuscan marble are ubiquitous in Reno's casinos, so it's no surprise that just about every hotel resort boasts a stellar *ristorante Italiano*. But Reno is also blessed with a full complement of stand-alone Italian places oozing with atmosphere. **Luciano's** (6135 Lakeside Dr., Ste. 145, 775/828-0400, http://lucianosreno.com, 11am-2pm and 5pm-9pm Tues.-Thurs., 11am-2pm and 5pm-10pm Fri., 5pm-10pm Sat., 5pm-9pm Sun., $17-25), southwest of the airport, delivers authentic food in a neighborhood environment of white linen and red brick.

Hilltop views complement chef Alberto Gazzola's innovative takes on northern Italian cuisine at **La Vecchia** (3005 Skyline Blvd. #160, 775/825-1113, www.lavecchiareno.com, 11am-2pm and 5pm-9pm Mon.-Fri., 5pm-9pm Sat.-Sun., $20-30). At **Mario's Portofino** (1505 S. Virginia St., 775/825-7779, www.mariosportofino.com, 11am-9pm daily, $18-25) the salads, desserts, and wine pairings are almost as tempting as the food. The menu at **Calafuria** (725 S. Center St., 775/360-5175, http://calafuriareno.com, 4:30pm-9pm Tues.-Sat., $22-35) reflects the chef's experience in restaurants of the Tuscan coast.

On the west side, just across the river, you will probably need reservations at **Johnny's Ristorante Italiano** (4245 W. 4th St., 775/747-4511, www.johnnysristorante.com, 5pm-9pm Tues.-Sun., $20-35). Make them, lest you miss out on some of the best veal Marsala and parmesan-crusted sole in town.

Mexican

Cheap and good don't always mix in the dining arena, but that's not the case with Reno's Mexican restaurants. **Los Compadres** (1490 E. 4th St., 775/786-9966, http://loscompadresreno.com, 11am-9pm Mon.-Thurs., 11am-10pm Fri.-Sat., $10-15) is a case in point. For less than $11 you can score virtually any combination of two beef-, chicken-, or veggie-filled tortillas surrounded by rice and beans. Order online and have it delivered, or visit their other location in Sparks (1250 Disc Dr., 775/800-1822).

The oldest Mexican joint in town, **Miguel's** (1415 S. Virginia St., 775/322-2722, www.miguelsmexicanrestaurantreno.com, $10-15) has a large menu, including shrimp—whole fried trout and Mexican shrimp scampi, yum!—as well as breakfast, margaritas, beer, and tequila. Another location on the opposite end of the main drag (13901 S. Virginia St., 775/851-0550) offers a similar menu.

Northern Mexican fare is the specialty at **Bertha Miranda's** (336 Mill St., 775/786-9697, http://berthamirandas.com, 10am-10pm Mon.-Sat., 10am-9pm Sun., $12-20). Bertha also has a second location (7695 S. Virginia St., 775/853-1233). Inside a strip mall adjacent to the airport, at **Albita's** (1280 Terminal Way, Ste. 17, 775/348-7333, 10am-4pm Mon.-Fri., 11am-3pm Sat., $10-15) the red sauce is drinkable (but even better slathering a burrito), and Albita's elevates the humble taco to legendary status.

Other winners include **Casa Grande's** two locations (1655 Robb Dr., Ste. 1, 775/746-0123, and 4796 Caughlin Pkwy., 775/828-7777, www.casagranderestaurant.com, 10am-10pm Sun.-Thurs., 10am-11pm Fri.-Sat., $12-18), for fajitas and seafood burritos Acapulco style, and **La Fuente** (790 Baring Blvd., 775/331-1483, http://lafuentemexicanrestaurantsparks.com, 11am-9pm Mon.-Thurs., 11am-10pm Fri.-Sat., 11am-9:30pm Sun., $14-18) in Sparks's Baring West Center, where they serve carne asada *a la Jalisco*.

Asian

Chef Kwok Nguyen calls upon his vast experience in San Francisco and Reno to find the perfect blend of Asian flavors for American palates at **Jazmine** (9333 Double R Blvd., 775/851-2888, www.jazminereno.com, 11am-9pm Mon.-Thurs., 11am-9:30pm Fri.-Sat., $12-20). The sushi menu is quite serviceable. Despite its reasonable prices, **Palais de Jade** (960 W. Moana Ln., 775/827-5233, http://palaisdejadereno.net, 11am-9pm daily, $18-30) is the most elegant Chinese restaurant in town, in an extremely tasteful room done in mostly black, gold, and white, quite understated and intimate. Authentic Cantonese and Mandarin are prepared by classically trained chefs.

Thai Lotus (6430 S. Virginia St., 775/852-5099, www.thailotusreno.com, 11am-3pm and 4:30pm-9pm Mon.-Fri., 11am-9pm Sat., $12-20) takes top honors for cuisine from The Land of Smiles. Spicy and authentic family recipes punctuate the fresh and delicate menu. Of the dozen or so perfectly good pho restaurants, **Golden Flower** (205 W. 5th St., 775/323-1628, 10am-3am daily, $8-12) is tops for its 25 different varieties of the traditional noodle soup, along with the must-eat imperial egg rolls and pork pot stickers.

German and Austrian

As you might expect, **Bavarian World** (595 Valley Rd., 775/323-7646, www.bavarianworldreno.com, 8am-8:30pm Tues.-Sat., $15-23) is right out of a Black Forest village, with a bakery, deli, and convenience store stocked with German imports: clocks, chocolates, strudel, and schnapps on one side and the Oktoberfestian restaurant on the other. German immigrants Klaus and Lura Ginschel started the bakery so they'd have a steady supply of the heavy rye bread they missed so much when they moved from their native country. Though they lacked restaurant experience, they learned by trial and error. Decades later, their business is still thriving. There are American dishes on the menu, but you'd be remiss if you didn't try the Wurst Wurst Wurst Platter (the German cousin of the Awful Awful Burger offered at The Nugget?). It's heaped with sausages, sauerkraut, and fried potatoes.

The sandwiches and light soups are fine for lunch at **Josef's Vienna Bakery Café & Restaurant** (933 W. Moana Ln., 775/825-0451, www.josefsvienna.com, 8am-3pm daily, $8-12), but you simply must come for the breakfasts and desserts.

ACCOMMODATIONS

Unless you're traveling on a strict budget or prefer solitude over action, there's really no reason not to book your stay at one of Reno's resort casinos.

Hotels

If you insist on staying away from the night-life and gaming, you might find a kindred spirit in **The Renaissance by Marriott** (1 S. Lake St., 775/321-5830, www.marriott.com, $149-199), which also seemingly has tired of blackjack pits and sports books. The former Siena Casino has transformed itself into one of the most luxurious non-gaming hostelries in town, with a rooftop pool, gourmet restaurant with alfresco seating, and even first-class bocce facilities—seriously. The former casino floor now houses seven public courts, along with skee ball lanes and shuffleboard. Upgrades throughout include fresh looks in all 214 guest rooms, with sleek lines, neutral tones, and textures that reflect the nearby mountains and river.

Also at the top of the food chain and price range among non-casino resorts, ★ **Whitney Peak Hotel** (255 N. Virginia St., 775/398-5400, http://whitneypeakhotel.com, $164-234) features rustic cabin-like decor complementing modern amenities. The mountain theme extends to the fitness center, whose centerpiece is a 164-foot climbing wall. The gym also features an extensive bouldering course, with lessons provided. Hotel guests receive discounts on day passes. There's not a bad seat in the house in the hotel's 1,000-seat concert venue, where midlevel acts perform regularly.

Courtyard by Marriott (1 Ballpark Ln., 775/324-0400, www.marriott.com, $125-152) is a lower-priced option with downtown convenience right next to the Aces' home park, great restaurants, and other attractions.

Motels

With reasonable rates available at the casinos, venturing into Reno motel territory is risky. Motels are cheap, but most independent establishments promise nothing more than clean places to park your carcass for the night. Unfortunately, too many motels fail to negotiate even that low threshold. The chains usually come closer, but come up short in the ambiance department. That being said, if

you insist on shoe-stringing it, stick with the boring-but-safe **Seasons Inn** (495 West St., 775/322-6000, www.seasonsinn.com, $50-95), downtown in the shadow of the Circus Circus tower. On the north side, **University Inn** (1001 N. Virginia St., 775/329-3464, $50-65), adjacent to the UNR campus, is a favorite of visiting teams' fans for its convenience to both the football stadium and the basketball arena.

Camping and RV Parks

If your idea of camping means tents and sleeping bags, you'll need to travel 20 miles or so beyond the city's concrete jungle. But once you're beyond the glow of neon, plenty of options are available. By far the best spot to pitch your tent is at **Davis Creek Campground** (south of Reno off US 395 in Washoe Valley, 775/849-0684, $20), a Washoe County facility 19 miles south on US 395. It has 62 rustic sites ringing the perimeter of a small pond and overlooking Washoe Lake and Slide Mountain. Nineteen sites can accommodate larger RVs, but none have hookups. Hot showers are available for a nominal fee. Recreational activities include nonmotorized boating and hiking the well-marked trail system. The campground is only 11 miles from Washoe Lake State Park.

On the other hand, if your idea of roughing it does not include communing too closely with nature or being too far from free Wi-Fi, **Shamrock RV Park** (260 E. Parr Blvd., 775/329-5222, www.shamrockrv.com, $35-40) is a good bet. A few minutes north of downtown, the park includes a small dog park and picnic areas, along with a small pool, laundry, game room, and pristine restrooms. Otherwise the park is paved, with trees and shrubs separating the spaces, which can be a bit snug for larger rigs. Less than a mile to the west, **Bonanza Terrace RV Park** (4800 Stoltz Rd., 775/329-9624, www.bonanzateracervp.com, $34-42) has 80 spaces for RVs up to 45 feet.

Closer to downtown, **Reno RV Park** (735 Mill St., 775/323-3381, www.renorvpark.com, $30-40) has 46 spaces off two narrow alleys, with a few pull-through sites. It's an older part of town near hospitals, medical offices, bus lines, and the police station. No tent camping. Accessible restrooms have flush toilets and hot showers; public phone, sewage disposal, and laundry are available.

★ **River's Edge RV Park** (1405 S. Rock Blvd., Sparks, 775/357-8533 or 800/621-4792, $49) is an idyllic setting for an RV park, right on the Truckee River. Near Idlewild Park and bordered by the Truckee River, its 124 permanent spaces and 28 RV spaces give you immediate access to many miles of paved riverside biking and hiking trails. It's lush and well shaded. It also happens to be right on the eastern landing approach to Reno-Tahoe airport, so big commercial airliners fly 300 feet overhead. But if you can stand an occasional jet engine or two, River's Edge is one of the nicest RV parks around. Formerly Chism's, River's Edge is the oldest private campground in Nevada, opened in 1926.

Northeast of downtown and right on the California state line, **Bordertown Casino and RV Resort** (19575 US 395 N., 775/677-0169 or 800/218-9339, www.bordertowncasinorv.com, $32) is 17 miles northwest of Reno. Fifty paved pull-throughs greet guests with small, colorful trees and patches of grass. Gaming includes 100 slots and video poker machines and a sports book. Two restaurants are on-site: **The Kafana** (6am-10pm daily, $10-12) for American and Mexican favorites and **Border Deli** (24 hours daily, $7-12) for subs and pizza.

Sparks is home to two of the better RV parks in northern Nevada. Top of the line is **Sparks Marina RV Park** (1200 E. Lincoln Way, 775/851-8888, www.sparksmarinarvpark.com, $33-45), thanks to its reasonable rates and proximity to dozens of activities. The park itself features a swimming pool and spa, fitness equipment, pool and Ping Pong tables, a putting green, big-screen TV lounge,

and reading library. It's next door to Sparks Marina Community Park and all the fishing, boating, and other aquatic activities, as well as walking trails. Nearly as opulent, **Victorian RV Park** (205 Nichols Blvd., 775/356-6400, $40-45) has mail service for long-term stays, free bicycle loans, and mature landscaping to provide privacy between sites. Sixty pull-through spaces are roomy enough for the largest rigs.

INFORMATION AND SERVICES

The **Reno Sparks Convention and Visitors Authority** (775/367-7366 or 800/367-7366, www.visitrenotahoe.com) carries loads of useful tourist literature, brochures, a hotel reservation gateway, and itinerary suggestions on its website.

Visitors interested in beginning—or dissolving—a marriage should head to the **County Clerk's office** in the courthouse (1011 E. 9th St., 775/784-7287, 8am-midnight daily, www.washoecounty.us). To get a marriage license, bring your ID, $60 (cash, money order, travelers check, or credit/debit card), and your betrothed, unless he/she is a closer relative than second cousin. If you're under 18, you'll need your parent or guardian to come, too. No blood test or waiting period is required. Then get married in any one of Reno's dozen wedding chapels (prices start at around $150). To just get married for cheap, with no muss and no fuss, go to the **Commissioner of Civil Marriages** (350 S. Center St., Ste. 100, 775/337-4575, by appointment 2pm-4pm Mon., Wed., Fri., $75). If it ultimately doesn't work out, one (or both) of the divorcing parties must be able to prove Nevada residency for six weeks. Several companies advertise fast, cheap divorces. They start at $325 for the filing fee, though many circumstances will drive the cost higher.

Lake Tahoe

TOP EXPERIENCE

Few who have seen it have escaped Lake Tahoe's haunting, spiritual attraction. The Washoe people made pilgrimages to "Da-ow" (Big Water) for millennia, harvesting the teeming trout, partaking in leisurely water sports, and thanking the spirits for their benevolence and abundance.

John C. Frémont and Kit Carson came upon the cobalt waters, tucked amid the Sierra Nevada and Carson Ranges, in 1844. The settlers who followed them appreciated the area less for its majesty than for its practical and commercial potential. The lake's pine-covered shores literally fueled miners' and developers' exploitation of the Comstock Lode. By the 1890s, the lake was nearly fished out, and 50,000 acres of forest had been cut. Those ravages have largely healed, and Tahoe's natural beauty has been restored to its fullest, with chalets, chateaus, boutique hotels, and ski-obsessed villages ringing the lake and surrounding mountains.

ORIENTATION

In Nevada, Incline Village and Crystal Bay hug Lake Tahoe's **North Shore,** serving as gateways to Lake Tahoe State Park and the Tahoe National Forest, which extends a couple miles southward along the ovoid lake. Glenbrook is about midway along the eastern shore on US 50. Along the **South Shore** are Zephyr Cove and Stateline, which sits on the border with California, just at the point where the lakeshore turns westward.

While many of the "organized" recreational opportunities—skiing, golf courses, beaches, water sports, etc.—are in California, Nevada boasts its fair share. Annual snowfall averages 40 feet, with snowpack around 20 feet—perfect skiing and snowboarding conditions. The casinos, of course, are only in Nevada.

Shoreline roads circumscribe Lake Tahoe. The full 72-mile circle can be driven in about 2.5 hours, but with all there is to see and do, you could easily spend a full, enjoyable day circumnavigating the lake.

a snow-covered pier at Lake Tahoe

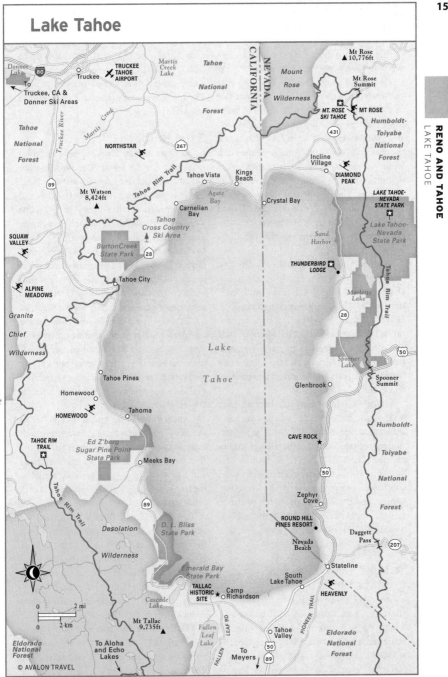

Lake Tahoe

© AVALON TRAVEL

NORTH SHORE

Sitting at high noon on Lake Tahoe's oval clock face, **Crystal Bay** nestles against the California state line on a point jutting into the lake. The actual bay laps against rock-strewn beaches on the Nevada side (the point separates Crystal Bay from Agate Bay in California). Less than 70 years old, the town adheres to its developer's original vision, with mansions on the lake, chalets on the mountainsides, and condos on the flats, all surrounded by dense forest, thanks to second-generation growth and strict tree-cutting regulations. The commercial zones stretch in a thin line along NV 28 and down Southwood Boulevard, a plan designed to prevent congestion and preclude the establishment of a town center.

A bit farther east, prosperous **Incline Village** boasts its own municipal ski resort, Diamond Peak, and boasts a two-mile "millionaires row" of mansions along Lakeshore Drive. All that disposable income supports myriad cultural opportunities. Sierra Nevada College offers degrees in fine arts, humanities, and social sciences, and the community has a thriving arts and historical preservation community.

Incline is said to have the best weather on the lake: 300 days of sunshine a year and the least accumulation of snow. The population more than doubles in the balmy summer months. The Village has more outdoors-related stores—outfitters, ski and ski repair, sportswear, camping, running shoes, cycling, fishing, and the like—than anywhere else in Nevada, and the majority of residents and visitors are decked out in sweats, warm-ups, bike shorts, ski suits, and sailing gear.

★ Lake Tahoe-Nevada State Park

Virtually the entire northeastern Lake Tahoe shoreline is part of **Lake Tahoe-Nevada State Park.** It preserves three miles of shoreline, plus a 10-mile-long stretch of the wooded Carson Range, and adjoins Toiyabe National Forest. There's a lot of wilderness to explore here. Elevations ranges between 6,200 and 8,900 feet. Most flora is second growth, at most 120 years old: Pine, fir, cedar, and aspen grow at elevations up to 7,000 feet, with red fir and lodgepole pine above. Countless birds and rodents live here. The black bear population is increasing, so be careful.

Sand Harbor

Home to an annual **Shakespeare Festival** in August, **Sand Harbor** ($12 mid-Apr.-mid-Oct., $7 mid-Oct.-mid-April) boasts spectacular views year-round. An arm of boulder- and pine-encrusted land five miles south of Incline Village on NV 28, Sand Harbor's eponymous powder (a rarity at Tahoe) gently gives way to clear and surprisingly warm (in summer, anyway) water. While much of the crescent beach gets lapped by gentle wavelets, prevailing winds and currents south of the spit sometimes generate swells high enough to surf, though foam boards work best, as the freshwater is not as buoyant as saltwater. It gets crowded here during warm-weather afternoons because it offers perfect barbecuing, picnicking, tanning, and swimming/snorkeling/scuba opportunities on the north side at Divers' Cove.

Sandy Point at the end of the spit has an excellent 0.75-mile accessible nature trail with interpretive displays in summer (left of the first parking lot). It takes an easy half hour and is well worth the time for the close look at the lake ecology. Pick up free handouts at park headquarters near the entrance.

The **East Shore Bike Trail,** slated for completion in 2018, will provide a paved riding surface for the three miles between Sand Harbor and the Lakeshore Drive bike path, with access to Hidden Beach. It is one component of the Lake Tahoe Bikeway that eventually will encircle the lake. Trails lead to secluded beaches, both sandy and rocky.

The **Sand Harbor Bar and Grill** (10am-5pm daily, $15-25) inside the visitors center has simple sandwiches and refreshing drinks with prices typical of a monopolistic

North and West Shores

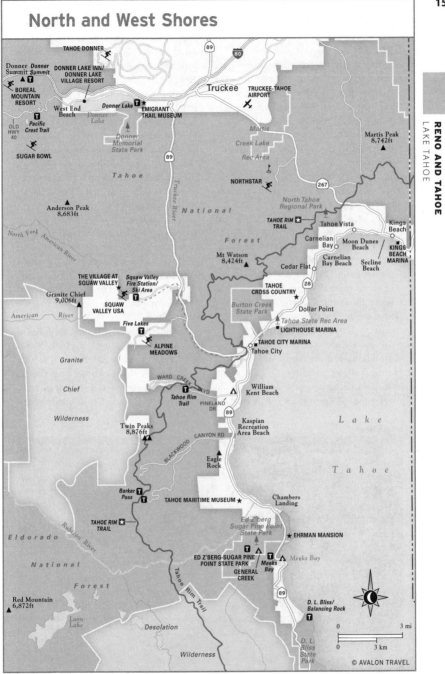

TAHOE DONNER

Donner *Donner*
Summit *Summit*

DONNER LAKE INN/
DONNER LAKE
VILLAGE RESORT

BOREAL
MOUNTAIN
RESORT

West End   Donner Lake
Beach

OLD
HWY
40

Pacific
Crest Trail

SUGAR BOWL

Truckee

TRUCKEE-TAHOE
AIRPORT

89   80

Donner Lake

EMIGRANT
TRAIL MUSEUM

Donner
Memorial
State Park

Martis

Creek Lake

Rec Area

Martis Peak
8,742ft

Tahoe

89

Anderson Peak
8,683ft

N a t i o n a l

Truckee River

NORTHSTAR

267

North Tahoe
Regional Park

Tahoe Vista

Kings
Beach

North Fork American River

F o r e s t

TAHOE RIM
TRAIL

Carnelian
Bay

Moon Dunes
Beach

KINGS
BEACH
MARINA

Mt Watson
8,424ft

Cedar Flat

Carnelian
Bay Beach

Secline
Beach

THE VILLAGE AT
SQUAW VALLEY

Squaw Valley
Fire Station/
Ski Area

TAHOE
CROSS
COUNTRY

28

Granite Chief
9,006ft

SQUAW
VALLEY USA

Burton Creek
State Park

Dollar Point

Tahoe State Rec Area

American   River

Five Lakes

LIGHTHOUSE MARINA

TAHOE CITY MARINA

Tahoe City

Granite

ALPINE
MEADOWS

WARD   CREEK   BLVD

William
Kent Beach

Chief

Tahoe Rim
Trail

PINELAND   DR

89

L a k e

Wilderness

Twin Peaks
8,876ft

CANYON RD

Kaspian
Recreation
Area Beach

American
River

BLACKWOOD

Eagle
Rock

T a h o e

Barker
Pass

TAHOE MARITIME MUSEUM

Chambers
Landing

TAHOE RIM
TRAIL

E l d o r a d o

Ed Z'berg
Sugar Pine Point
State Park

EHRMAN MANSION

Rubicon River

ED Z'BERG-SUGAR PINE
POINT STATE PARK

Meeks
Bay

Meeks Bay

GENERAL
CREEK

N a t i o n a l

89

Red Mountain
6,872ft

F o r e s t

Tahoe Rim Trail

D. L. Bliss/
Balancing Rock

Loon
Lake

Desolation

D. L.
Bliss
State
Park

0   3 mi

0   3 km

Wilderness

© AVALON TRAVEL

concession. Other concessions rent boats, paddleboards, kayaks, and Jet Skis.

Spooner Lake

Heading south, NV 28 moves inland a bit to meet US 50 at **Spooner Lake** (summer $10, off-season $7), three miles northwest of Glenbrook. Park in the lot and take the easy 2.3-mile nature trail encircling the lake; it only takes an hour. Keep an eye out for ospreys prowling the shoreline for a fish dinner. Human anglers should be aware that only catch-and-release fishing is allowed, for the stocked, holdover, and native trout and chub; one barbless hook only.

A hundred feet into the lake loop, a post marks the five-mile trail through aspen-shaded North Canyon to **Marlette Lake,** which still supplies water to Virginia City, just as it has for 120 years. The moderate 10-mile round-trip trail takes about 4-6 hours to traverse. Eleven miles into the lake loop is the farther trailhead at **Hidden Beach,** where it connects with the Tahoe Rim Trail.

In summer, activities at Spooner Lake include hiking and mountain biking on the **Flume Trail,** which follows the path of the historic flume that once provided water to the silver mines of Virginia City. This exciting single track, 1,600 feet above Lake Tahoe, is one of the most scenic rides anywhere, providing spectacular views. Most mountain bike parties begin at Spooner Lake, take North Canyon Road to Marlette Lake dam (six miles, 800-foot gain), and follow the flume line 4.4 miles to Tunnel Creek Road. From there you can return to Spooner Lake, a 21-mile round-trip (3-5 hours); descend 1,600 feet (2.5 miles) to NV 28, a 13-mile one-way trip (3-4 hours); take a backcountry loop back to Spooner Lake (24 miles round-trip, 4-6 hours); or follow a different backcountry loop back to Spooner Lake via the Tahoe Rim Trail (22 miles, 2,000-foot elevation gain).

Several companies offer shuttle services that drop off and pick up riders challenging the area's backcountry and point-to-point trails. The ride from **Flume Trail Mountain Bikes** in Incline Village (1115 Tunnel Creek Rd., 775/298-2501) is free with a bike rental ($45-65 per day). Other shuttles include **Wanna Ride** (775/790-6375).

In winter, Spooner Lake has six miles of free groomed cross-country ski trails. Snowshoers are welcome to use the trails, as well, but stay to the side and away from the ski tracks. Three primitive walk-in campgrounds, at Marlette Peak, North Canyon, and Hobart,

Sand Harbor

have tables, fire rings, and restrooms. Use the bear-resistant food and trash containers.

★ Thunderbird Lodge

A spectacular example of historical preservation just south of Incline Village, **Thunderbird Lodge** (5000 NV 28, 775/832-8750, http://thunderbirdtahoe.org) is well worth taking the time to explore. The lodge was built in 1936 by the fabulously wealthy George Whittell, who earned his money the old-fashioned way: He inherited it. Noted Nevada architect Frederic DeLongchamps designed the lakeside beauty as Whittell's summer cottage, incorporating two master bedrooms, a great room with a movie screen, and extensive servants' quarters. Whittell, a colorful playboy and bon vivant of his day, entertained guests in the "Card House," a beautiful stone room that was connected to the house via a tunnel (and yes, you get to go through it!). Whittell also had a penchant for wild animals, and visitors can inspect the Elephant House, which once was home to the millionaire's pet pachyderm, Mingo.

Whittell's taste for personal indulgence is manifest in the *Thunderbird* **yacht,** a mahogany and stainless steel speedboat he commissioned in 1939 at a cost of $87,000 ($3.3 million in today's dollars). Embellished by Whittell with crystal accents, the floating palace was further renovated by subsequent owner Bill Harrah into the casino pioneer's "70-mile-per-hour speedboat."

Now under the loving care of a nonprofit association, the lodge is open for 75-minute **guided tours** (800/468-2463, Tues.-Sat. late May-mid-Oct., $39, ages 6-12 $19, including shuttle from the Incline Village/Crystal Bay visitors center) that take visitors through the servants' quarters, original kitchen, and Lighthouse Room. Walk through a 200-yard tunnel to visit the Card House and boathouse where the yacht resides. Ask about special wine, cheese, and garden tours. Waterborne tours of the mansion, its grounds, and its lavish neighbors (775/831-4386, 9am Thurs.-Sat.,

$140) leave from the Hyatt Regency Lake Tahoe hotel dock.

Skiing

The Nevada side of the lake has two smallish ski resorts, perfect for family members with varying degrees of skills. The California side, however, accommodates nearly a dozen world-class ski resorts bringing the full alpine experience to the Sierra Nevada.

★ MT. ROSE SKI TAHOE

The larger of the two resorts in Nevada, **Mt. Rose Ski Tahoe** (22222 Mt. Rose Hwy., New Washoe City, 775/849-0704 or 800/754-7673, www.skirose.com, $115, age 6-15 $75), on NV 431 11 miles north of Incline, offers 1,200 skiable acres at a base elevation of 8,260 feet and summit elevation of 9,700 feet. Six lifts and two conveyors whisk skiers to 60 runs and trails. Runs are rated for every skill level. Most are intermediate and advanced, but with several beginner and a few expert runs, as well. Snowboarders are welcome. Save a few dollars by buying lift tickets online or taking advantage of bargain Tuesdays and multiday passes. You can also rent equipment or have yours serviced and repaired. The resort offers group and private lessons, and shuttles are available daily from several of Reno's larger hotels and casinos. Many casinos offer "stay and ski" packages.

DIAMOND PEAK

Municipally owned **Diamond Peak** (1210 Ski Way, 775/831-3211, www.diamondpeak.com, $74, age 13-23 and 65-69 $54, age 7-12 and 70-79 $29, under 7 and over 79 free), two miles east of the Incline Village center, has 655 skiable acres over 30 runs—5 beginner, 14 intermediate, and 11 advanced—and a freestyle terrain park. Lessons, repairs, child care, and equipment rentals are on-site.

NORTHSTAR CALIFORNIA

As you leave Crystal Bay on CA 267, **Northstar California** (5001 Northstar Dr., Truckee, CA, 503/562-1010 or 800/466-6784, www.northstarcalifornia.com, $150, age 13-18 and 65 and over $123, age 5-12 $89, save 20% by buying online) is the first Golden State ski resort you'll encounter. Just 10 miles from Crystal Bay and the state line via CA 267, Northstar is larger than its Silver State neighbors, with 100 runs and 3,170 skiable acres. The resort also has several terrain parks, pipes, and areas for cross-country skiing and snow tubing. A true resort, Northstar offers luxury accommodations and authentic alpine-lodge dining options, both on the mountain and in the très-cool village adjacent to gondola pickup areas.

TAHOE CROSS COUNTRY SKI AREA

Taking NV 28 across the state line (it becomes CA 28) for nine miles takes you to the nonprofit **Tahoe Cross Country Ski Area** (925 Country Club Dr., Tahoe City, CA, 530/583-5475, www.tahoexc.org, $29, age 13-17 and 60-69 $25, under 13 and over 69 free). It has half-mile to three-mile loops ranging from easy, flat runs to steady climbs and curving descents, including several dog-friendly routes. Ski and snowshoe rentals are available. The nonprofit organization also operates a winter sports park in Tahoe City (251 N. Lake Blvd., 530/583-1516, $5-15 per activity), with sledding, ice skating, cross-country, snowshoeing, and biking.

SQUAW VALLEY ALPINE MEADOWS

Squaw Valley and Alpine Meadows merged in 2011 and operate as a single resort, **Squaw Valley Alpine Meadows** (1960 Squaw Valley Rd., Olympic Valley, CA, 800/403-0206, http://squawalpine.com, $159, age 13-18 and 65 and over $134, age 5-12 $98, save 25% online). With more than 25 beginner trails and an easy progression park system, Alpine Meadows caters to the inexperienced while enticing more proficient skiers with five more advanced terrain parks, seven open bowls, and plenty of steeps and chutes among its more than 100 runs. Host of the 1960 Winter Olympics, Squaw Valley boasts a peak elevation over 9,000 feet, with more than

40 beginner trails along with 16 bowls and the only funitel lift in the United States.

Even non-skiers should ride the **Squaw Valley aerial tram** (1990 Squaw Peak Rd., 800/403-0206, $44, age 5-18 $22, under 5 free). The tram climbs 2,000 feet over snow-capped granite ridges with views of plunging valleys and alpine forests. Debark at High Camp for shopping, dining, and ice skating. Squaw, home to writing and yoga retreats in summer, cultivates an attitude reminiscent of those carefree days before the tumult of the Vietnam War.

The tourism industry is about to get a major boost. County supervisors in 2016 approved a $1 billion expansion that will include new hotels, condos, employee housing, and parking structures. The planned centerpiece is a "Mountain Activity Center" with a bowling alley, rock climbing wall, simulated skydiving, and more.

DONNER

Several smaller ski resorts string along I-80 around Donner Lake. **Tahoe Donner Downhill Ski Area** (11603 Snowpeak Way, Truckee, CA, 530/587-9444, www.tahoedonner.com, $59, age 13-17 $47, age 7-12 and 60-69 $25, under 7 and over 69 free) and **Tahoe Donner Cross Country Ski Area** (15275 Alder Creek Rd., Truckee, CA, 530/587-9484, www.tahoedonner.com, $34, age 13-17 and 60-69 $25, age 7-12 $14) are perfect for budding skiers, with excellent instructors and reasonable rental rates. Six of the 15 downhill runs are rated for novices. Snowshoeing and fat biking are available at the cross-country facility.

Boreal Mountain (19749 Boreal Ridge Rd., Soda Springs, CA, 530/426-3666, www.rideboreal.com, $54, age 13-17 $44, age 6-12 and 60 and over $24) has 8 beginner runs, 11 for intermediates, and 15 for experts, along with terrain parks with pipes, jumps, berms, and more. Perfect for budget-conscious families, **Donner Ski Ranch** (19320 Donner Pass Rd., Norden, CA, 530/426-3635, www.donnerskiranch.com, $69, age 13-17 and 70 and

The Donner Party

For most on the grueling overland wagon route to California, the sight of Truckee Lake would inspire determination to complete the journey and begin a new life. But for one group of migrants from the Midwest, the snow falling on the Sierra Nevada to the west that greeted their arrival on the lakeshore in October 1846 provided a grim reminder that they were way behind schedule.

Eager to reach California, the party, led by George Donner, put its trust in a "shortcut" discovered by Lansford Hastings. The Hastings Cutoff across the Wasatch Mountains and the Great Salt Lake Desert promised to trim hundreds of miles from the journey. Instead, the new route took the Donner Party 68 days to travel from Little Sandy River, Wyoming, to Truckee (now Donner) Lake. The main California Trail was 28 days shorter and would have left them plenty of time to cross the mountains before the first snowfall.

Desperate to beat the winter storms that would close the pass until spring, the pioneers were forced to stop for several days to rest their animals and forage for food and water. The extra 100 miles spent traversing the forbidding terrain of the cutoff and along the Humboldt River, it would turn out, effectively closed their window of escape. Hopelessly snowbound, members of the party built what structures they could—cabins for some, tents made from wagon canvases for others, crude brush wikiups for others.

As those who made it across the mountains to Sutter's Fort organized rescue parties, those left behind ate the last of their provisions and turned to boiled ox hides, bones, and tree bark for sustenance. Some of the desperate tried to hike out on makeshift snowshoes. Those 10 men and five women quickly ran out of provisions, and eight died. The others made the ghastly decision to eat their fallen comrades. The seven survivors reached safety in late January. Relief parties finally arrived on February 19, 1847, finding 12 dead and 48 clinging to life. The first relief party retrieved 23 survivors, but two children died on the way out. All subsequent relief parties made their way to the various camps, often finding more evidence of cannibalism.

The tragic events claimed 41 of the 87 members of the Donner Party.

over $59, age 6-12 $29, under 6 $15) has several steeps and tree runs to please more advanced skiers and board riders and a tubing hill and lots of uncrowded beginner runs for the kids.

Sugar Bowl (629 Sugar Bowl Rd., Norden, CA, 530/427-4050, www.sugarbowl.com, $109, age 13-22 and 65-74 $89, age 6-12 and 75 and over $63) is geared more toward intermediate and advanced boarders and skiers, with 103 trails and four challenging terrain parks. Venerable **Soda Springs Resort** (10244 Soda Springs Rd., Soda Springs, CA, 530/426-3901, www.skisodasprings.com, $55, age 13-17 $50, age 6-12 $45, under 6 $5) caters to the youngsters, with Planet Kids, a snow amusement park with tubing lanes, bunny hills, snow forts, and more. The more advanced tubing hill has 20 thrilling runs. The 15 downhill trails are evenly distributed among beginner, intermediate, and advanced runs.

For something different, try the snow kiting attraction at **Royal Gorge Cross Country Resort** (9411 Pahatsi Rd., Soda Springs, CA, 530/426-3871, www.royalgorge.com, $35, age 13-22 and 65-74 $29, under 12 and over 74 free).

Casinos

The casinos in North Tahoe exude a relaxed atmosphere, as if gambling is merely an après-ski amusement—place your bet, nosh a s'more; feed the machine, sip a cinnamon-infused hot toddy. Casino entertainment also is tame compared to Reno, Las Vegas, or South Lake Tahoe—comedy clubs, lounge acts, and tribute bands. The three "big" Crystal Bay casinos are within a one-minute walk of each other. Much swankier, the Hyatt Regency Lake Tahoe Resort is in Incline Village. Nearly all offer hotel and ski packages to all the nearby resorts.

CRYSTAL BAY CLUB

Restaurants: Bistro Elise, Crystal Bay Steak & Lobster House

Attractions: arcade

Nightlife: Sports Bar, Crown Room, Red Room

Just a few hundred feet from the California border, **Crystal Bay Club** (14 NV 28, 775/833-6333, www.crystalbaycasino.com) has a laid-back, casual feel. With low minimum craps bets and liberal blackjack rules, you can while away the hours and not lose your shirt. The club does not have hotel rooms, but the two on-site restaurants are good bets. Casual and fresh, **Bistro Elise** (9am-9pm daily, $15-35) has an extensive gourmet coffee selection and a decent cellar. Try the pork gyoza appetizer. Open for dinner only, **Crystal Bay Steak & Lobster House** (5:30pm-9:30pm daily, $35-55) makes it difficult to choose between the surf and the turf. Luckily, you don't have to. Pick the 6-ounce New York and 6-ounce lobster tail. The wine list is extensive, with some pricey French selections among the reasonable but very good California vintages.

The Crown Room expanded its capacity by 20 percent in 2016 with an eye toward attracting more popular entertainers. The joint still only holds 750 concertgoers, so the intimate showroom feel is maintained. Shows have included the Revivalists, Dumpstaphunk, and The String Cheese Incident.

Completely separate from the casino, the chalet-style ★ **Border House at Crystal Bay** (24 Stateline Rd., 775/833-6333, $159-399) exudes warmth, from the in-room gas fireplaces to inviting hot showers and Jacuzzis to downy towels and plush bed linens. Big king beds and plasma TVs complete the package.

TAHOE BILTMORE LODGE

Restaurants: Bilty's, Café Biltmore

Attractions: pool, arcade, gift shop, wedding chapel

Nightlife: casino bar

Across the street from the Crystal Bay Club, the **Tahoe Biltmore Lodge** (5 NV 28, 775/831-0660, $120-135) deals blackjack, craps, and roulette on eight tables around 200-plus slot and video poker machines and a sports book. Sign up for the slot club and receive $5 in free play. Rooms are dated but big and afford nice views of the water. The pool is outdoors and suitable for summer swimming only. Fuel up with the Sunday brunch buffet at **Café Biltmore** (7am-9pm daily, $10-18, Sun. brunch $9.95, children $6.95), with all your breakfast favorites (until 1pm), plus ribs, chicken, salads, and more. The menu and operating hours at **Bilty's** (5pm-9pm Fri.-Sat., $28-50) are limited, but there's steak, burger, pasta, chicken, and fish on the menu—one choice in each category.

JIM KELLEY'S NUGGET

Restaurants: Kelley's Nugget Burgers

Nightlife: Nugget Bar

Jim Kelley's Nugget (20 NV 28, 775/831-7156), a slot shop and poker room, could be the state's only redbrick casino, which fits in nicely at the lake. **Kelley's Nugget Burgers** gets high marks for its, yes, burgers, but also chicken and jalapeno fries.

GRAND LODGE AT HYATT REGENCY

Restaurants: Lone Eagle Grille, Tahoe Provisions, Sierra Café, Stillwater Pool Bar & Grille, Lakeside Barbecue

Attractions: StayFit Gym, Stillwater Spa and Salon, private beach and pier, heated pool and whirlpools, Camp Hyatt day care

Nightlife: Cutthroat's Saloon, Pier 111

Incline Village's only casino, the **Grand Lodge** (111 Country Club Dr., 800/327-3910, www.grandlodgecasino.com, $180-280) is part of the Hyatt Regency Lake Tahoe Resort, Spa and Casino. With all those attractions packed into one footprint, the compound resembles the sprawling ski villages at the California resorts. The Hyatt is also the closest hotel-casino to forest and lakeside in Nevada. Its quaint alpine lodge exterior masks the resort's size. With 422 rooms, 24 lakeside cottages sprawling throughout the property, a massive stone fireplace in the lobby, and a full-service casino including a high-limit area, the Hyatt exudes an old-money atmosphere.

The gold, blue, and slate rooms are 400 square feet and come with coffeemakers, speakerphones, safes, mini fridges, and 37-inch flatscreens. The hotel sponsors family activities nightly—poolside movies, s'mores, and gatherings around toasty fire pits. A saltwater spa, a private beach, bike and nature trails, golf, lake jaunts on the Hyatt's private boats, and gourmet dining complete the get-away-from-it-all experience. The casino houses 250 slot machines, a sports book, and a poker room.

Big picture windows command views of the lake, beach, and bar, while substantial timbers and stone fireplaces remind diners of their lodge setting at ★ **Lone Eagle Grille** (775/886-6899, 11:30am-3pm and 5:30pm-9pm Sun.-Thurs., 11:30am-3pm and 5:30pm-10pm Fri.-Sat., $40-60). The lounge serves drinks and food between lunch and dinner seatings and throughout the day. The elk loin and quail eggs offer a just-exotic-enough break from more traditional steaks, fish, and fowl, though the beef, bison, duck, and salmon dishes are just as pleasing. While the check will not be pedestrian, the menu, atmosphere, and fare are more casual at **Sierra Café** (775/832-6675, 7am-9pm Sun.-Thurs., 7am-10pm Fri.-Sat., $18-25). Vegans will appreciate the squash stuffed with white beans, rice, and almonds, while the crab and shrimp Louie with avocado and egg ties in nicely with the water views. Not as wild as it pretends, **Cutthroat's Saloon** (5pm-midnight Mon.-Thurs., 5pm-2am Fri., 11am-2am Sat., 11am-midnight Sun., $12-20) nevertheless has friendly servers and clientele, along with traditional bar noshes and an ever-changing lineup of local and craft beers.

Food

Several eclectic eateries center on Tahoe and Village Boulevards in Incline Village. Among the best is ★ **Jack Rabbit Moon** (893 Tahoe Blvd., 775/833-3900, www.jackrabbitmoon.com, 10am-6pm Wed.-Sat., $30-50). Owner Amy Simpson cut her culinary chops in northern California, and those roots come shining through in the cuisine and wine selections. Start with a salad punctuated by fresh fruit and/or delicate cheeses, then luxuriate over perfectly seasoned beef, seafood, and Italian specialties. The menu is limited—you'll still have a tough time choosing—and changes monthly.

The **Wildflower Café** (869 Tahoe Blvd., 775/831-8072, www.wildflowercafetahoe.com, 7am-2:30pm Mon.-Sat., 8am-2pm Sun., $7-11) does solid burgers and salads, but go for one of the cold sandwiches if you come for lunch. The turkey salad or club with guacamole gets our vote. This place is no secret, and there's usually a line for breakfast. But tough it out; you'll be glad you did when your fluffy biscuits slathered in savory gravy arrive, accompanied by eggs and homemade hash.

In the Christmas Tree Center, **Mofo's Pizza** (884 Tahoe Blvd., 775/831-4999, www.mofospizza.com, 11am-11pm Mon.-Sat., 5pm-11pm Sun., $15-25) does subs and great baked pasta dishes, but the pizza's where it's at. Though it bills itself as a pub and casino, **Crosby's** (868 Tahoe Blvd., 775/833-1030, www.crosbyspub.com, 11am-10pm Mon.-Fri., 9am-10pm Sat.-Sun., $12-25), in the same shopping center, is family-friendly, serving corn dogs, chicken fingers, fries, and other kid favorites. Adult choices include sandwiches and wraps, along with steak, chicken, fish, and pork dinners.

Three tasty choices reside within a stone's throw of each other just east of Village Boulevard. **T's Mesquite Rotisserie** (901 Tahoe Blvd., 775/831-2832, www.tsrotisserie.com, 11am-8pm daily, $10-15) is well hidden, tucked away in the little shopping center beside the 7-Eleven store and the Incline Cinema, but the Villagers have ferreted it out for its big Mexican and Tex-Mex gut busters. Get the soy lime chicken or the tri-tip sandwich. Virtually next door, **Bite American Tapas** (907 Tahoe Blvd., 775/831-1000, http://bitetahoe.com, 5pm-9:30pm Tues.-Sat., $20-35) invites gastronomic exploration with small plates and snacks. Start with the garlicky, lemony white bean dip, share a cheese plate, and indulge in BLT—bacon, lobster, and tomato—sliders. Also in the center, **I.V. Coffee Lab** (907 Tahoe Blvd., Ste. 20A, 775/298-2402, 6am-4pm Mon.-Fri., 7am-3pm Sat., 7:30am-2pm Sun.) will provide your daily caffeine infusion in the form of rich, slow-drip java and espresso. They've got your sugar and carb fix covered, as well, with pastries and bagels, including dairy-free and gluten-free options.

Two spots closer to the lake deliver a more "Tahoe rustic" vibe. **Austin's** (120 Country Club Dr., Ste. 24, 775/832-7778, http://austinstahoe.com, 11am-9pm daily, $12-28) specializes in stick-to-your-ribs home cooking geared for fueling outdoor adventure or refueling after a day on the slopes or hiking trails. A big slab of balsamic-glazed meatloaf or gravy- or cheese-slathered chicken breast will have you hooked. Smack in the middle of several bike paths—including Flume Trail—**Tunnel Creek Café** (1115 Tunnel Creek Rd., 775/298-2502, http://tunnelcreekcafe.com, 8am-4pm daily, $8-12) can help you carb up with pancakes or oatmeal before mounting up. After a hard ride, check in for a cold IPA.

Crystal Bay's dining options are virtually nonexistent outside the casinos, but it's worth the short drive (or moderate walk) across the state line to **Soule Domain** (9983 Cove St., Kings Beach, CA, 530/546-7529, www.souledomain.com, 6pm-9pm daily, $22-35). Just a mile from the Tahoe Biltmore, the two-room log cabin with hand-laid stone fireplace, timbered ceiling, and rail fence posts contrasts with the sophisticated Mediterranean and American delicacies from the kitchen, such as lamb with cheese, olive, and tomato filling and fowl, beef, and seafood entrées such as seafood linguini, pork tenderloin, and curried chicken.

Accommodations

Incline Village is your only Nevada option for non-casino hotels, though there are dozens of accommodations, including $1,500-a-weekend golf, tennis, and horseback riding resorts. Incline has a few of these high-falutin' resorts, as well. They are mostly fractional ownership setups, but they accept weekend and weekly guests. The two-bedroom, two-bath units at **Hyatt High Sierra Lodge** (989 Incline Way, 775/832-0220, http://hyatthighsierralodge. hyatt.com, $309-779) include full kitchens and private verandas. The lodge is adjacent to the Hyatt Regency Lake Tahoe Resort, Spa and Casino, providing guests access to all the amenities: beach access, casino, fine dining, and more.

North of town center, the views are not as spectacular at **Club Tahoe Resort** (914 Northwood Blvd., 775/831-5750, www.clubtahoe.com, $199-229), but the price is right for what's included in each two-bedroom suite: dining area, full kitchen, CD stereo, two TVs, and a fireplace. While you won't be able to see the lake from your suite, you can stroll towering alpine forests. You could have a great time without ever leaving the property; the resort's recreational activities include basketball and tennis courts, sauna and hot tub, fitness room and racquetball, board and arcade games, billiards and horseshoes, and a bar. The three-story villas at **North Lake Lodges and Villas** (280 Glen Way, 800/821-4912, $249-329) have two full kitchens, living areas, bathrooms, and bedrooms on the first two floors, with a loft and romantic two-person Jacuzzi on the third. Studio and one-bedroom lodges are smaller, but the one-bedroom version can still sleep four.

For a more traditional but still luxurious stay, book at ★ **Parkside Inn** (1003 Tahoe Blvd., 775/831-1052, $135-190), where even the knotty-pine-paneled single rooms are a spacious 350 square feet and the indoor pool is open year-round. It's just two blocks to the Hyatt casino and recreation center, tennis courts, and gym. Complimentary Internet and continental breakfast are offered for those staying in the 38 rooms, which are decorated with outdoor equipment on the walls. **Gabrielli House** (593 N. Dyer Circle, 800/731-6222, $129-199) is the only true bed-and-breakfast in Incline Village. Each of the five bedrooms has a private bath, balcony, and television. The common-area living room is

biking the Tahoe Rim Trail

The Tahoe Rim Trail encircles Lake Tahoe for 165 miles along ridges and mountaintop, winding through national forest, state park, and wilderness lands, as well as a variety of vegetation zones. The trail offers something for everyone, with stretches ranging from easy to difficult, loop trails, and manageable segments at an average grade of 10 percent. All trail sections guarantee spectacular views of dense conifer forests, wildflower-dotted meadows, and pristine alpine lakes. Hiking, horseback riding, and skiing are allowed on all parts of the trail; mountain biking is allowed on specified portions. Motors are prohibited.

You can easily walk a part of the trail by beginning at any of nine trailheads, or if you are ambitious you can complete the whole circle and become a member of the "165 Mile Club." Camping is permitted along most of the trail, allowing extended trips into the solitude of backcountry and wilderness regions; the numerous trailheads give day users abundant opportunities to tackle smaller portions of the trail and explore the beauty of the mountains. The Nevada side has the Spooner Summit (US 50), Kingsbury (two miles north of NV 207), and Tahoe Meadows to Spooner Summit (NV 431) trailheads. California options include the Brockway trailhead (CA 267), the Tahoe City trailhead (just north of CA 89), the Barker Pass trailhead (Blackwood Canyon Rd., four miles south of Tahoe City), and, on the south side of the lake, the Big Meadow trailhead (CA 89) and the Echo Lakes and Echo Summit trailheads (US 50).

Trail maps are posted at the trailheads, but users are urged to carry maps with them on the trail. The Tahoe Rim Trail Association (128 Market St., Ste. 3E, Stateline, 775/298-4485, www.tahoerim-trail.org) carries an extensive line of maps and guidebooks. Visit their headquarters, or order online.

perfect for reading or dozing by the fire. Breakfast includes fresh fruit and muffins in addition to the hearty main dishes.

Information

The Incline Village/Crystal Bay Visitors and Convention Bureau (969 Tahoe Blvd., near the south end of town, 775/832-1606 or 800/468-2463, www.gotahoenorth.com) has all the brochures and information you'll need, including everything from hiking trails and outdoor activities to restaurants and resorts. You can download the helpful vacation planner on the website. The Incline Village library (845 Alder Ave., 775/832-4130, 11am-6pm Mon.-Fri.) is just north of the Christmas Tree Center, set back from the road a little. A sign points the way. This is a branch of the excellent Washoe County library system and has a thorough collection of Nevada history resources. Curl up with your book in front of the two-sided fireplace.

SOUTH SHORE

Singles and younger visitors probably prefer the lake's southern shore, with its gritty dive bars, throbbing nightclubs, and thriving art scene. The ski resorts stay open year-round, helping visitors take advantage of all four seasons around Lake Tahoe. Mountain biking, zip-lining, fishing, and boating attract tourists throughout the warmer months.

US 50 absorbs NV 28 south of Spooner Lake and continues west to parallel the lakeshore from south of Glenbrook, through the communities of Lakeridge, Skyland, and the tourist meccas of **Zephyr Cove** and **Stateline.** Exercise caution, however; the section between Glenbrook and Lakeridge is susceptible to high winds and slick conditions. The rain and freeze/thaw patterns also make the bluffs above unstable, often breaking loose large boulders that crash to the roadway below. Winter and spring closures are not uncommon.

Cave Rock

If the road is open, the legendary home of Tahoe Tessie, the Loch Ness Monster's distant cousin, is just four miles south of Glenbrook. One tunnel through the cave at **Cave Rock State Park** (1430 US 50, 775/588-7975, http://parks.nv.gov, $7) dates from the early 1900s. Another, according to local Native American legend, dates back to prehistory, fashioned by the Great Spirit with a spear. Just before you reach the tunnel, there's a turnoff for a parking lot, lakefront picnic area, and a boat launch ($9). Fishing is outstanding, both from a boat in warmer weather and through the ice in winter. In winter, the launch is ground zero for ice skating, and there are outstanding sledding hills nearby. Camping is available at **Elk Flat** (May-mid-Oct., $17) and **Lake View** (year-round, weather permitting, $17) campgrounds. Both have flush toilets, picnic tables, and fire pits. Fires are never allowed on the beach. Pitch your tent, then get your bearings with an easy three-mile jaunt over **Steptoe Creek Trail.** The trailhead is right at the parking area. Slightly more strenuous, Cave Springs, Cave Lake Overlook, and Twisted Pines trails are 4-5 miles each.

Zephyr Cove

Midway between Cave Rock and Stateline is the small, action-packed marina at Zephyr Cove. **Zephyr Cove Resort** (760 US 50, 775/589-4906 or 800/238-2463, www.zephyrcove.com) offers cruises aboard the *Dixie II,* which replaced a more historic forebear in 1994. The main deck has a dining area for 200; the upper deck is enclosed for dancing and cocktails and houses the captain's cabin. The "hurricane deck" is open-air and hosts the snack bar and pilothouse. On Saturday evenings, the captain hosts a dinner dance and **sunset cruise** (8:30pm, $89, children $39). The scenic, narrated **day cruise** (noon daily, $59, children $29) plies the waters between the cove and **Emerald Bay.** A costumed Mark Twain and other colorful riverboat celebrities often make the trip on Saturdays. Lunch and a full bar are available for additional charges. The resort also arranges sailing and fishing charters, sailboarding, snowmobiling, Jet-Skiing, boating, parasailing, and other adventures.

The 40-foot wood cruiser *Tahoe* (775/230-8907, Tues.-Sat. mid-May-Sept., $139, age 6-12 $59) departs from the Zephyr Cove Marina for the Thunderbird Lodge at 10am with a narrated five-hour voyage including continental breakfast, cash bar, and shoreline picnic lunch. Cave Rock, the shoreline mansions, and searches for birds of prey are included on the tour.

Be ye a landlubber? Hop on a horse at **Zephyr Cove Stables** (825 US 50, 775/588-5664, www.zephyrcovestable.com, $43-83); friendly cowpokes guide riders along the lake and over tree-lined trails on excursions of 1-2 hours. Chuckwagon meals are provided on some rides.

Round Hill Pines Beach Resort

Much of the summertime activity around Stateline is centered on **Round Hill Pines Beach Resort** (300 US 50, 775/588-3055,

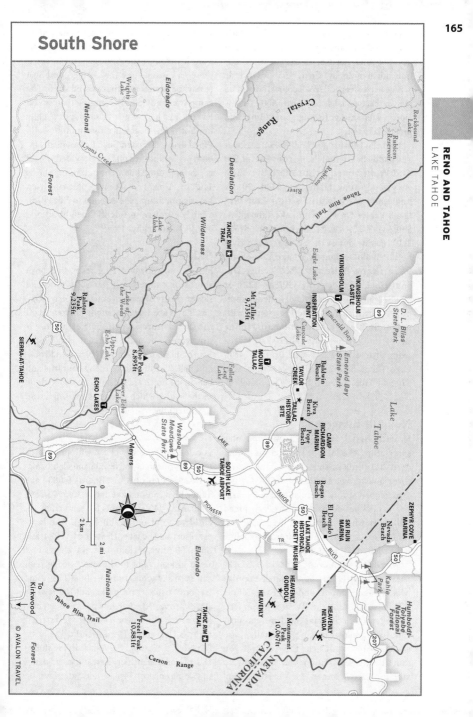

South Shore

© AVALON TRAVEL

www.roundhillpinesresort.com, $10). This half-mile-long sandy beach is on a sheltered inlet two miles north of the casinos and a half-mile north of Zephyr Cove. Facilities include a large deck area, volleyball courts, horseshoe pits, barbecues, a deli, and a bar. Activities include water-skiing, fishing, parasailing, and private lake tours.

Call the **marina** (775/588-3054) for boat and paddleboard rentals. **Borges Water Ski and Wakeboard School** (530/391-1215, www.waterskilaketahoe.com, $140-150 per hour) and **Mile High Fishing Charters** (2438 Venice Dr. E., South Lake Tahoe, CA, 530/541-5312, www.fishtahoe.com, $150-260) operate out of the area. You can fly a hot-air balloon right over Lake Tahoe with **Lake Tahoe Balloons** (2435 Venice Dr., South Lake Tahoe, CA, 530/544-1221 or 800/872-9294, www.laketahoeballoons.com) or get your thrills closer to the ground with mountain bikes, mountain boards, inline skates, and off-road and inline skateboards from **Shore Line Ski and Sports** (4100 Lake Tahoe Blvd., South Lake Tahoe, CA, 530/544-1105, and 193 Kahle Dr., Stateline, NV, 775/580-7722).

Nevada Beach

Nevada Beach is one of the most popular spots along the lake. It's also deep—more than 200 yards in some spots—and nearly three quarters of a mile long. The day-use area is open spring through fall, with parking lots ($8 per vehicle entrance fee) spread well apart, which spreads out the people, too. It's two miles north on US 50 from Stateline (take a left at Elk Point Rd.).

Nevada Beach Campground (775/588-5562, $33-39) is one of the most popular beaches and campgrounds on Lake Tahoe; this place's 54 tent and RV sites fill up fast. Make reservations as far in advance as possible (www.recreation.gov), especially if you want a primo spot near the water; if you don't have a reservation, you can show up at 9am to see if someone left early. A good

strategy is to pay the $8 for the day, hang out on the beach, then every so often take a walk through the campground to see if there's a vacancy (see the campground host to pay for first-come, first-served sites). The camp is equally popular among tenters and RVers; sites have shade or sand, but usually not both. The beach is a two-minute walk. Piped drinking water, flush toilets, picnic tables, grills, and fire pits are provided. There is a campground host. The maximum stay is 14 days. A pretty walk or aerobic run from here is north up Elks Avenue to Elk Point, a fairly exclusive residential neighborhood overlooking Zephyr Cove.

Skiing

Skiing and snowboarding resorts on both shores of Tahoe boast perfectly groomed slopes, plenty of terrain, and top-notch facilities. There are, however, subtle differences off the slopes. Après-ski on the North Shore is fine wine, gourmet dining, and jazz; on the South Shore, it's craft beer, pizza, and rock-and-roll. The crowds at the restaurants and bars in the north are sedate compared to those in the south, which often has a spring break in winter vibe.

HEAVENLY

Located right on the border, with mountaintop access from both Nevada and California, is **Heavenly Mountain Resort** (4080 Lake Tahoe Blvd., South Lake Tahoe, CA, 775/586-7000, $135-145, discounts for seniors, teens, children, and online booking). The largest resort on the lake, Heavenly has 97 trails on 4,800 acres, including several chutes that seem to lead right to the water's edge. You can even ski across the state line! The resort has only two terrain parks, but the regular slopes are varied enough to present new challenges each time down. The party gets started early as Heavenly's **Tamarack Lodge** hosts "Unbuckle" (3:30pm-5:30pm daily) with live DJs, reasonable drink prices, and go-go dancing ski bunnies on Fridays and Saturdays.

KIRKWOOD

Less a resort than an adventure, **Kirkwood Mountain Resort** (1501 Kirkwood Meadows Dr., Kirkwood, CA, 209/258-6000, www.kirkwood.com, $83-94, discounts for teens, children, and seniors), 35 miles south of Heavenly, features no on-site accommodations and little in the way of pampering amenities. It's all about the powder—and some of the most challenging double diamond runs in Tahoe. The steep drops, high elevations, and dry snow are just what adrenaline junkies ordered. Lower runs are less intense and more suitable for families, though only 12 percent of the resort's runs are rated for beginners.

HOMEWOOD MOUNTAIN

NV 28 merges into NV 89, which heads south along the lake to Homewood Mountain Resort and north to Alpine Meadows and Squaw Valley. **Homewood Mountain** (5145 W. Lake Blvd., Homewood, CA, 530/525-2992, www.skihomewood.com, $99, teens and seniors $75, juniors and super seniors $50, save 33% online) has spectacular lake views from the summit. Nearly all its 64 runs are sheltered from the wind by majestic Ellis Peak. Eight lifts take skiers and boarders to hidden powder, groomed glades, lots of intermediate, advanced, and expert runs, and the two-mile Rainbow Ridge beginner run.

Casinos

Stateline could be the quintessential California-Nevada border town, a representation not only of the economic and cultural glue that binds the two together, but also of the discrete elements that make them unique. The California side of town is an elephantine freeway exit ramp fronted by hundreds of low-rise motels, fast food spots, service stations, shopping centers, and apartment, condo, and professional developments. On the Nevada side of the border are the half dozen or so casinos, as compact and vertical as peaks in the Carson Range.

HARVEYS

Restaurants: Sage Room, 19 Kitchen & Bar, Hard Rock Café, Straw Hat Sports Bar & Grill, Carvel Ice Cream, Cinnabon, Starbucks
Entertainment: The Improv, Lake Tahoe Outdoor Arena
Attractions: wedding chapel, fitness center, pool
Nightlife: Cabo Wabo Cantina

Harvey Gross's Wagon Wheel was the first bona fide casino at South Lake, starting in the 1940s as a one-room log-cabin saloon with six

snowboarders at Heavenly Mountain Resort

slot machines, three blackjack tables, and a six-stool snack bar. Today, **Harveys** (18 US 50, Stateline, 775/588-2411 or 800/427-8397, $135-208) is a Caesars Entertainment-owned 740-room hotel with a spacious 87,000-square-foot casino.

The top of the dining lot is the casually elegant **19 Kitchen** (5:30pm-8:30pm Tues.-Thurs., 5:30pm-9pm Fri.-Sat., $40-70), with the best panoramic lake views of all the restaurants at Stateline, with two-window alcoves and three levels of tables. The **Lake Tahoe Outdoor Arena** is busy throughout the summer, with superstars such as Aerosmith, James Taylor, Stevie Wonder, and Tim McGraw among the performers. Inside, the **Cabaret Theater** hosts top names and budding comics at **The Improv.** Typical of a Harrah's property, the bars and nightlife are relatively sedate, though tequila-infused patrons of Sammy Hagar's **Cabo Wabo** have been known to whoop it up.

Interestingly, the front desk is on a level lower than the casino, under a two-story chandelier, so you don't have to lug your suitcases by the blackjack pit. The gold- or vermillion-accented rooms are the best and among the biggest—525 square feet—in South Lake Tahoe, and because Gross was first in town, they have the best mountain and lake views and are within walking distance of the Heavenly ski resort.

HARRAH'S
Restaurants: Sushi Kai, Friday's Station, Forest Buffet, American River Café, Thai Asian, Fatburger
Entertainment: South Shore Room, Center Stage Lounge
Attractions: indoor pool, family fun center, Reflections the Spa
Nightlife: Peek, Cliché Lounge, Highlander Bar

Harveys' sister property and next-door neighbor, **Harrah's** (15 US 50, Stateline, 775/588-6611 or 800/427-7247, www.caesars.com, $147-267) is luxury pure and simple: Details like blackout curtains, double soundproofing, and large, angled windows ensure a relaxing and inspiring stay. Each of Harrah's

525 sage- and maple-accented rooms has two full bathrooms, great mountain or lake views from the picture windows, and 500 square feet in which to spread out. The 65,000-square-foot L-shaped casino is isolated from most of the resort's restaurants, so the beeping of 1,900 slots and shouts of craps and blackjack players won't intrude. **Reflections the Spa** (8am-8pm daily) lets you take a trip around the world of indulgence: Turkish steam rooms, European facials, Roman baths, Swedish massage. The kids' arcade was tripled in size and is now a **family fun center** (10am-6pm daily). Families also enjoy the hotel's unique dome-covered swimming pool. Shaquille O'Neal and Paris Hilton have partied at **Peek** (9pm-3am Fri.-Sat.), where DJs spin to the enjoyment of the pretty people dressed to the nines. Lounge acts, including some pretty good cover bands, perform in the **South Shore Room. Friday's Station Steak and Seafood Grill** (5:30pm-9:30pm Sun.-Thurs., 5:30pm-10pm Fri.-Sat., $50-65), on the hotel tower's top floor, impresses with a fine cellar and the gourmet vistas visitors should expect in Lake Tahoe.

HARD ROCK
Restaurants: Park Prime, Oyster Bar, Alpine Union, Fuel
Entertainment: Vinyl, Rock On! Karaoke
Attractions: pool, fitness center
Nightlife: Center Bar, Sports Bar

Formerly the Horizon and before that the Sahara and High Sierra, the extensively renovated **Hard Rock** (50 US 50, Stateline, 800/648-3322, www.hardrockcasinolaketahoe.com, $50-120) debuted in early 2014. As you would expect from the iconic brand, the hotel celebrates music, from the gigantic metal guitar sculpture out front to the edgy rock heroes depicted with their timeless lyrics on murals throughout the property. Stop and read the rhythmic wisdom espoused by Page and Plant, Billy Joe Armstrong, and Mick Jagger. The 25,000-square-foot casino is small by South Shore standards, but there's room for 500 machines, a sports book, and all the popular tables. Slurp down a dozen at the **Oyster Bar** (11am-midnight Sun.-Thurs., 11am-2am Fri.-Sat., $15-25) before retiring to the **Vinyl** concert venue for comedy, jam bands, and intimate acoustic performances.

As some of the most recently renovated in town, the rooms at the Hard Rock include padded headboards, sleek light fixtures, and beautiful views of the mountains, trees, and pool. Even the carpet is attractive—a rarity among high-volume hotel-casinos. They've even included bedside cell phone outlets, another nice touch.

MONTBLEU

Restaurants: Ciera, Fortune, Montbleu Café, Cafe del Soul, The Buffet
Entertainment: Montbleu Showroom, Blu
Attractions: Onsen Salon & Spa, Montbleu Chapel, heated pool
Nightlife: Opal Ultra Lounge, HQ Center Bar, Craft Beer Bar

All 438 rooms at the **Montbleu** (55 US 50, Stateline, 775/588-3515, www.montbleuresort.com, $109-199) received a complete renovation in 2015, giving them a luster and vibrancy uncommon in casinos—splashes of yellow and orange in exchange for "normal" subdued hues. Montbleu's heated, indoor pool is one of the most picturesque on the lake, with boulder borders and a big rock waterfall in a secluded lagoon setting. After a day on the hiking trails or slopes and a rug-cutting evening with Blu nightclub's top DJs or live music, the Montbleu's **Onsen Salon & Spa** services will have you rejuvenated and ready to do it again. No visit is complete without sampling the fare at four-diamond **Ciera** (5:30pm-10pm Wed.-Sun., $45-60). The extensive steak, chicken, and chop menu makes it tough to choose, so opt for the prix fixe menu ($40-60). The decisions won't be any easier, but the options are more manageable.

LAKESIDE INN

Restaurants: The Timbers, Latin Soul, The Coffee Bar
Entertainment: The Tavern

Nightlife: casino bar

Small, rustically designed, locals-oriented **Lakeside Inn** (168 US 50, 775/588-7777, www.lakesideinn.com, $129-179) has pet-friendly rooms decorated with lodge paneling and comfortable bedding. The casino offers liberal odds and even conducts courses on the most popular games. Nightlife is sparse, but its location puts guests in the middle of the action. We probably shouldn't have been as surprised as we were at the tastiness of the Peruvian chicken at **Latin Soul** (8am-11pm Wed.-Mon., $10-30).

Food

The resorts are full of fine steak and seafood houses, but if you can't get enough, venture to the **Chart House** (392 Kingsbury Grade Rd., 775/588-6276, www.chart-house.com, 4pm-9:30pm Sun.-Thurs., 4pm-10pm Fri., 4:30pm-10pm Sat., $40-50) for excellent ribs and seared ahi. Better yet, go during happy hour and graze on reasonably priced fish tacos, lettuce wraps, and sliders, along with the full bar, of course.

Similar fare in a decidedly different atmosphere is the specialty at **Fox and Hound** (237 Tramway Rd., 775/588-8887, www.foxandhoundtahoe.com, 7:30am-2am daily, $12-25), just off NV 207 (Kingsbury Grade Rd.). Grab a beer, pizza, chicken wings, or whatever else that will go straight to your hips. Win a free T-shirt and meal by finishing the "You Sank My Battleship" challenge in 60 minutes: Personal pizza, two eggs, pulled pork, bacon cheeseburger, Philly cheesesteak, chicken sandwich, six wings, fries, and a salad. Competitive eater Molly Schuyler did it in less than 3.5 minutes. What are you waiting for, wimp?

Other casual meals worth leaving the slot machines for include the raw fish at **Sushi Pier** (177 Lake Tahoe Blvd., 775/588-8588, http://tahoesushipier.com, 11:30am-9:30pm Mon.-Sat., 11am-9pm Sun., $20-$35); the burgers and tots at **Lucky Beaver** (31 US 50, Ste. 104, 775/580-7770, 24 hours daily, $10-20); and the $8 lunch specials at **My Thai &**

Noodle (177 US 50, Ste. 101, 775/586-8757, www.mythainoodle.com, 11am-3pm and 4:30pm-9:30pm daily, $15-25).

Accommodations

While there must be hundreds of quaint and/or cheap motel rooms just across the California line, the pickings are much slimmer in Nevada, apart from the casinos and ski resorts.

You have your choice of three different levels of stays at **Zephyr Cove Resort** (760 US 50, 800/238-2463, www.zephyrcove. com): cabins ($155-385), lodge ($110-130), or RV park ($45-80). The resort was built in the early 1900s, and much of the original architecture and charm remains. Accommodations include six rooms in the lodge that sleep 2-6; there are also bungalows, cabins, cottages, studios, and chalets that can accommodate up to 10.

Large families will like the big units in five chalets at **Pine Cone Resort** (601 US 50, 855/833-7252, www.pineconeresort.com, $65-110). Each condo-like unit sleeps 4-6, not including the four-legged children. The resort is so dog-friendly that many units feature doggie doors that lead to enclosed runs. The resort has a heated, year-round pool and spa and lickety-split Internet. Guests can enjoy free access to a fitness club, mountain bikes, canoe, and 270-foot snow slide.

Stone fireplaces, thick timber pillars, big picture windows, and overstuffed furniture perfect for dozing greet guests to the luxurious **Edgewood Lodge** (100 Lake Pkwy., 775/773-5470, www.edgewoodtahoe.com, $350-550). Rooms appear rustic but come complete with huge-thread-count linens, plush towels and robes, and pampering tubs. If that's not enough sumptuousness, the hydro, steam, massage, and facial treatments at **Spa at Edgewood Tahoe** will have you refreshed in no time after a day on the slopes, golf course, or nature trail. The property's 18-hole course ($160-260) is as much nature commune as a game; each hole features towering pines, water views, and tee locations to suit any player's game. A fitness center, pool and hot tub, and kid-friendly **Camp Edgewood** ($150 per day), where the little ones can explore nature, create crafts, and play games, complete the experience. Two restaurants and a bar keep the experience going well into the night. Gaze across emerald fairways at pink sunsets and creamy peaks at **Edgewood Restaurant** (5:30pm-10pm daily July-Dec., 5:30pm-10pm Wed.-Sun. Jan.-June, $30-40). The fresh fish and steaks are simply prepared and complemented by sauces and flavors from around the world. The restaurant's chalet decor completes the idyllic alpine setting and seals our vote as the best non-casino restaurant on the South Shore.

Much easier on the wallet, the one- and two-bedroom suites attract families to **The Lodge at Kingsbury Crossing** (133 Deer Run Ct., 775/588-6247, www.thelodgeatkc.com, $99-129), near Heavenly Resort. En suite kitchen and laundry facilities add to the savings during longer stays. Saturday breakfast is complimentary, but be prepared to hear about vacation ownership during your meal.

Information

The **Lake Tahoe Visitors Authority** website (169 US 50, 775/588-4591, www.tahoe-south.com) is constantly updated with casino stay packages that include lift tickets, shows, dining, spa treatments, and more. Check out their blog for updates on ski and road conditions, events and holiday celebrations, etc. Access both the North and South Lake Tahoe visitors' authorities at www.visitinglaketahoe.com; www.skilaketahoe.com has up-to-date weather and ski conditions.

Central Nevada

Look for ★ to find recommended
sights, activities, dining, and lodging.

Highlights

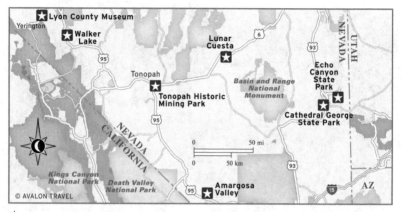

★ **Cathedral Gorge State Park:** The four-mile Miller Point Overlook trail is the perfect length for a moderate workout and a panoramic survey of haunting wash formations, while a welcome staircase allows visitors to descend to the gorge's floor for a closer look (page 181).

★ **Echo Canyon State Park:** Spire-like hoodoos spring from amid the alfalfa fields, picnic sites nestle in the shade of sheer canyon walls, and the stream-fed reservoir is stocked with crappie and trout (page 187).

★ **Amargosa Valley:** This detour en route to Death Valley is an oasis of springs, fens, and ponds, perfect for a waterside picnic (page 189).

★ **Tonopah Historic Mining Park:** Look down from a suspended cage into Jim Butler's original diggings, see a two-foot-wide exposed

silver ore vein, and experience the frisson Butler must have felt when he hit pay dirt (page 196).

★ **Lunar Cuesta:** A 430-foot-deep crater highlights this landscape strewn with lava beds and cinder cones formed in nature's volcanic crucible (page 201).

★ **Walker Lake:** Cast a fly and hang on for an epic battle against a three-pound cutthroat trout. And keep an eye out for Cecil the Serpent, a distant relative of the Loch Ness Monster (page 206).

★ **Lyon County Museum:** Look in on the lady in her kitchen, a barber, and a judge as they go about their daily activities in life-size dioramas, at this re-creation of life a century ago in the Carson River Valley (page 207).

Millions of acres have been set aside here for the enjoyment of an otherworldly landscape of lunar craters, valleys of death, and eerily quiet prairies beneath star-strewn blackness.

Explore the region along two main north-south routes: US 93 in the east and US 95 to the west. Along both routes, rustic, *Saturday Evening Post*-cover small towns, many with big-city amenities such as fine museums and first-rate hotels and restaurants, bring a touch of civilization to a rugged terrain.

Nature lovers should head down US 93, which leads to dozens of state parks, scenic drives, hot springs, and wildlife management areas. Watch hawks and eagles dive-bomb unsuspecting catfish and carp. Investigate Native American petroglyphs and experience the thrill of discovering a rich silver vein. Tumble down the "Rabbit Hole" at Cathedral Gorge State Park to experience a wonderland of weather-formed spires, turrets, and bluffs. Pack your fishing gear to try your luck with the trout.

History buffs will get their fill along US 95, where a string of ghost towns (and not-quite-given-up-the-ghost towns) provide scenic diversions. Other communities along the route are very much alive. Don't miss the haunting sculptures in Goldwell or the remnants of Gilded Age excess on display in Goldfield. Bend your elbow at the Santa Fe Saloon to conjure a bygone era. Beatty and Tonopah offer a glimpse at the everyday toil that came along with the mining boom.

This is also the location of the so-called Extraterrestrial Highway and Area 51, the infamous super-secret location where the U.S. government studies marooned aliens and develops weapons in a feeble attempt to protect Earth from space-based invasion, the details of which can only now be revealed ... (Excuse me, several men in black suits and dark sunglasses would like to have a word with me ...) Yes, the large fenced-off and heavily guarded parcel south of the Monitor Range is merely an Air Force training ground. There is nothing to see there.

Previous: ruins of a bank building in Rhyolite; Alien Research Center along the Extraterrestrial Highway. **Above:** Mesquite Flat Sand Dunes in Death Valley National Park.

Central Nevada

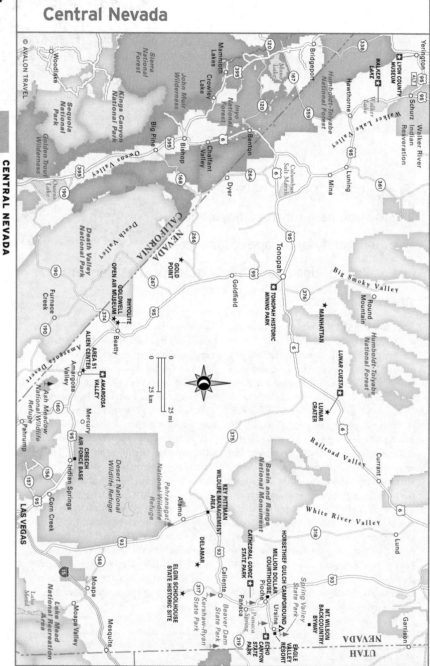

© AVALON TRAVEL

PLANNING YOUR TIME

Use Las Vegas as a base for exploration along central Nevada's two main north-south arteries, US 93 and US 95. Whichever route you prefer, you can hit the high points on a two-day excursion. Most of the major attractions in this region are located on main thoroughfares, making access a snap. These roads are well maintained and have enough traffic to quickly dissipate snow before it can accumulate.

Pahranagat National Wildlife Refuge

Lake, marsh, desert, meadow, and riparian habitats make **Pahranagat National Wildlife Refuge** (24 hours daily, www.fws.gov, free) a critical stopping ground for migratory ducks, geese, and even swans, as well as home to rodents, insects, leopard frogs—one of only a few amphibians at home in Nevada—and the iconic desert tortoise. Human visitors flock here, as well, attracted to the nonmotorized and nondisruptive outdoor activities; it's an easy 80-minute drive due north from Las Vegas via US 93.

A true oasis in a region that receives less than seven inches of rain in an average year, Pahranagat nevertheless collects water from natural warm springs into four main basins. North Marsh, Upper Pahranagat Lake, Middle Marsh, and Lower Pahranagat Lake dot the refuge's 5,400 acres and provide haven for as many as 264 bird species. Waterfowl dive for mussels and insects, and herons and egrets patrol marshlands and shorelines, spearing small fish and lizards, while wintering bald eagles and other raptors compete with human anglers for carp and catfish on Upper Lake.

Wildlife watchers and photographers find the best luck in the morning and early evening. With good timing, you might see mule deer, kit foxes, coyotes, and maybe even a mountain lion. The U.S. Fish & Wildlife Service advises to quietly approach an area where two habitats converge—meadow and marsh, for example—and wait patiently and motionlessly for wildlife to appear. Animals are attracted to these "edge" habitats because of the diverse food and shelter they present.

HIKING

Several easy walking trails connect the refuge's main water sources and habitat. The most popular is **Upper Lake Trail,** with the trailhead, information kiosk, picnic area, and restrooms on the east side of the dike separating the lake from North Marsh. The three-mile trail encircles the lake. Primitive campsites line the eastern shore, and there's a scenic overlook with magnifying view scope on the western shore. At the lake's southwestern tip, hikers have the option of veering off onto **Davenport Trail,** which leads away from the water and into high desert habitat, past several scenic overlooks, and on to the site's headquarters and small visitors center. Ask at the **visitors center** (Mile Post 32 Hwy 93, 775/725-3417, 9am-4pm Thurs.-Mon.) about scheduled or impromptu specialty hikes. Rangers and volunteers often take groups on walks to popular birding areas, or on night excursions to stargaze and find scorpions—illuminating them with ultraviolet light.

CAMPING AND BOATING

The 14 primitive lakeside campsites along Upper Pahranagat Lake are free and available on a first-come, first-served basis. A few sites are large enough for multiple tents, trailers, and RVs, though the campground has no hookups, water, or disposal facilities. Vault toilets, grills, and fire pits are on-site. Nonmotorized boats or those equipped only with electric trolling motors may be used on Upper Lake, Middle Marsh, and Lower Lake, but not on North Marsh. Boats may not be launched from trailers, and all state safety regulations apply.

HUNTING AND FISHING

Bird hunting is popular in the refuge, with ducks, geese, and quail favorite quarry. Rabbits and other birds—moorhens, coots, and snipe—can also be harvested. Hunting is allowed on Tuesdays, Thursdays, and Saturdays during the appropriate season. Dove hunting is allowed every day during the season. Hunting for deer, crows, swans, and predators is never allowed. The public hunting ground is bounded by Dove Dike the southern shore of Lower Lake. Watch for posted markings. Fishing for catfish, carp, and largemouth bass is allowed in many of the refuge's waterways, and fish are plentiful in Upper Lake. North Marsh is closed to fishing October through January. Wheelchair users can access a hunting platform on Middle Marsh area, and a fishing pier is located on Upper Pahranagat Lake. The **visitors center** (Mile Post 32 Hwy 93, 775/725-3417, 9am-4pm Thurs.-Mon.) can suggest other areas with handicap access.

Pahranagat National Wildlife Refuge

Caliente

A major division point on the Union Pacific's main line between Los Angeles and Salt Lake City, Caliente's railroad history doesn't just belong in the past; it's alive and well, continuing today. Freight trains still rattle through the middle of town carrying lumber, coal, ore, and consumer goods throughout the state. That rich early-1900s history is also on display at every turn, much of it repurposed 100 years later. The depot houses city offices, and many Union Pacific laborers' homes are occupied again. That history, along with easy access to a half dozen state parks, wildernesses, and conservation areas, has helped revive the town.

Today, Caliente (pronounced like the Spanish word but with an American West inflection: "cally," which rhymes with Sally, and "anti," as in freeze) has a vitality all its own. The streets follow an orderly company-town grid, with two main business streets downtown, one on each side of the wide railroad right-of-way. The **hot springs** for which the town was founded and named are one of the surprise treats in the state. That, along with the depot mural, Rainbow Canyon, and the singularly unstressed residents, makes Caliente an undiscovered gem in this southeastern-Nevada corridor filled with such precious finds.

SIGHTS
Railroad History Walking Tour
Start your walking tour of Caliente at the **Union Pacific Railroad Station** (100

Depot Ave., 775/726-3131, 10am-2pm Mon.-Fri.), built in 1923 for $83,000. As the steam era came to an end, the mission-style depot housed the railroad station, stationmaster's quarters, telegraph office, restaurant, and community center on the ground floor and a hotel above. A huge mural, a source of justifiable pride in Caliente, hangs in silent homage to that romantic time inside the depot. The big painting covers the history between 1864 and 1914 of the entire southern section of Nevada, from Pioche in the northeast to Las Vegas in the south and all the way up to Tonopah in the west—with a lot of detail. Locals Mary Ellen Sadovich and Rett Hastings designed and painted it. Once the nerve center of the railroad, the depot is now the nerve center of the town, housing city hall, the library (775/726-3104, 1pm-6pm Mon. and Thurs., 10am-3pm Tues.-Wed.), and an art gallery. The **Boxcar Museum** (775/726-3131, hours vary depending on volunteers' availability, $1) next door adds to the depot/mural experience, with vintage photographs and memorabilia, as well as the eponymous rolling stock.

Lots of local buildings have been standing since 1905; pick up a walking tour brochure at the depot. Wander along Clark Street past the town's iconic stone structures. A block from the depot you'll come to the **Culverwell House.** Built in the 1870s, it's one of the oldest stone houses in town. The square abode was built into a hillside, which insulates the house, keeping it cool in summer and warm in winter. Other stone houses in the area are the **Crawford House,** south on Spring Street, and the **Underhill House** at Clark and Denton. This area, the "Underhill District," includes a Mercantile Store and the Underhill Rock Apartments, built entirely of stone in 1907. After you pass the apartments (turn right off Clover Street beyond town) you'll come to the Union Pacific railroad **row houses,** standing grandly on Spring Street just north of town, which were built in 1905; notice the two choices of floor plans. Near the corner of Market and Culverwell in back of town, the **Community Methodist Church**

(140 Culverwell St., 775/726-3665) is an attractive historical and cultural structure.

Across the railroad tracks from the depot, peruse the collectibles at **Treasure Hunters Classy Consignments** (197 Clover St., 775/726-3755, 11am-5pm Tues.-Sat.) and you might spot the perfect antique knickknack or souvenir. The store also has an extensive collection of brochures and tourist information on the parks, sites, and ghost towns nearby.

Rainbow Canyon Scenic Drive

Beginning at the intersection of US 93 and NV 317, at the south end of Caliente by the Mormon church, is Rainbow Canyon, one of the most beautiful in the state. A 21-mile section of NV 317 follows an old railroad grade and wash to the ghost town of Elgin. The stretch, designated the **Rainbow Canyon Scenic Drive,** is an artist's palette of mineral-stained cliffs on either side of the road.

You'll pass under railway trestles and through a stunning wash, dry for much of the year, but with a trickling stream of runoff in early spring—enough to irrigate the teeming copses of cottonwoods on the stream bank. The cliff rock is volcanic tuff, which settled some 34 million years ago. The stunning spectrum of colors is the result of hot, mineral-carrying water flowing through and filling fissures and faults; the water seeped out or evaporated, leaving the minerals to stain the rock: rusty iron, powdery yellow calcium, acidic blue and green copper, black manganese, and white ash. Many elements combine to make this one of the most scenic and least explored roads in the state: the dips in the road in the flood zones; the many railroad trestles and bridges; the idyllic ranches, big trees, and creek; and of course the sheer and colorful canyon walls. You will have plenty of opportunities for trainspotting, as the drive parallels the bustling main line of the Union Pacific Railroad past tunnels and cuts.

As long as 10,000 years ago, Desert Archaic, Fremont, and Southern Paiute people were drawn to Rainbow Canyon. They took advantage of the seasonal water, cool

Etna Cave, and fertile floodplains, suitable for growing corn, beans, and squash. Gouged and painted **petroglyphs** are the most obvious evidence of these peoples' culture, but digs also have turned up pottery shards, stone tools, leatherwork, and basket fragments. The informative *Lincoln County Rock Art Guide* (www.piochenevada.org/maps-and-brochures.htm) explains the significance of the Rainbow Canyon artwork and gives directions to petroglyph sites throughout the area.

KERSHAW-RYAN STATE PARK

Just two miles into the Rainbow Canyon scenic drive along NV 317, a left turn leads for a mile to **Kershaw-Ryan State Park** (775/726-3564, http://parks.nv.gov, $7), named not for the dominant Major League Baseball pitchers but for an early homesteader and rancher. The entrance to this gem is a well-marked graded dirt road leading east into a box canyon off NV 317. The park is 240 acres of cliff and canyon country, liberally shaded by groves of ash and cottonwood and laced with hiking trails. The rugged cliff walls enclosing the canyon are heavily overgrown with scrub oak and wild grapevines. The sound of running water is everywhere since the end wall of the canyon has a series of seeps that send water

trickling down its face to be caught in a pond and little brook at its base. This protected canyon is early to feel spring returning and late to feel the cold touch of winter, making it a good place to visit during most of the year.

The park has 15 **campsites** ($17) and modern restrooms amid a profusion of ivy and grass. The picnic area has tables and barbecue grills. Just above the picnic area is a small wading pool for children. Above that is a beautiful seep dripping water from the canyon wall in an undercut that creates a lush hanging garden of riparian plant life including grapevines. Two short hikes (one is 1.5 miles, the other 0.25 mile) lead to other springs and verdant canyons. The 1.8-mile **Canyon Overlook Trail** leads to **Kershaw Canyon,** a favorite destination with an inspiring view.

ELGIN SCHOOLHOUSE

The canyon and its scenic route end with a historical treat. Though this area had been homesteaded and several ranches existed there as early as the 1870s, there were few children in the area until the Salt Lake, San Pedro and Los Angeles Railroad came through the valley in 1903. Several small communities popped up to serve the railroad and its passengers.

Kershaw-Ryan State Park

Many of these workers had children, and so the need for a school arose. Reuben Bradshaw, a second-generation resident, built the **Elgin Schoolhouse** (775/726-3564, tours by appointment, adults $1, 12 and under free), which educated first- through eighth-grade students here for 45 years (1922-1967). His descendants have restored the school with a neat white-with-red-trim paint job straight out of *Little House on the Prairie* and furnished it with mostly original (and some authentic period) items.

Beaver Dam State Park

One of Nevada's most remote state parks is accessed from Caliente. **Beaver Dam** (775/728-4460, http://parks.nv.gov, $7) is so irrepressibly cheerful a place that the long, dusty 90-minute drive to get there from Caliente is a small price to pay for a visit. The 2,393-acre park is set high in mountain piñon and juniper forests. Hiking trails wind under the trees and cliffs and through the canyons. Anglers may try their luck along the cottonwood-lined, beaver-dammed stream. There are picnic sites and developed campsites in the park ($14). There are no visitors centers or concessions; bring everything you'll need.

The well-marked turnoff for the state park is 5.3 miles north of Caliente on US 93. For the next 25 miles the well-graded dirt road climbs gently. However, you can't travel faster than 35-40 mph because the road twists and turns a great deal and you don't know what's coming up around the next turn or over the next hilltop. After 14 miles you come to a fork in the road. Stay on the left branch to Beaver Dam. The right branch, which rapidly becomes four-wheel-drive territory, goes to the dry remains of **Matthews Canyon Reservoir,** then winds its way through the mountains south into Utah backcountry.

After another 4.5 miles you cross the Union Pacific tracks. Four miles later you come to the beginning of a steep incline down the side of Pine Ridge into Beaver Dam State Park. While it may look like a nail-biting ride, any passenger vehicle can make it with no trouble.

From this point it's three miles to the campground. Do what the stop sign says (yes, a stop sign way out here) and register. The park is open year-round, weather permitting.

There are two campgrounds available with a total of 35 campsites. The first (to the left) is better, with tables, grills, running water, vault toilets, and camping spots for RVs as well as tents. Access the trout stream from **Oak Knoll Trail** (0.3 mile), beginning here, which intersects with **Overlook Trail** (2.2 miles). The other campground is similar but a bit more primitive, but it has nice views of abandoned Hamblin Ranch and Pine Creek. At the park's southern border, the **Waterfall Trail** (1.2 miles) takes hikers past streams, warm springs, and cascades. There's a picnic area at the trailhead.

Delamar Ghost Town

After driving 30 miles southwest of Caliente via US 93, Poleline Road, and a four-wheel-drive-recommended gravel road (about one hour), you will come upon the ghost town of **Delamar.** A booming gold-mining center in the 1890s, Delamar supported a thriving business district. As many as 120 mule-drawn freight wagons were ceaselessly employed in importing supplies from the nearest railroad in Utah. Today, you will find extensive unpreserved remnants, including mine frames, wooden and stone building walls, stone miners' huts, mine and mill debris, and a large cemetery. Many of the old tombstones have been stolen by souvenir seekers. If you're lucky, you may spy a herd of wild mustangs grazing among the rock-wall ruins. Take a page from their book and picnic among the ruins, crowded into the shallow canyon above the mine dumps.

Six miles from the Delamar turnoff you top **Oak Springs Summit** (6,237 feet). A campground a short distance off the south side of the highway has picnic tables, grills, and a green shady picnic area. It's a nice cool place at high elevation to enjoy a rest and a picnic. You may also come across trilobite fossils, remains of tiny crustaceans that lived in

Delamar's Widow-Maker Mines

Desolate and dry, the Delamar's productive hard-rock mines nevertheless attracted more than 1,500 residents to the desert outpost 30 miles southwest of Caliente. The sparsely distributed springs were barely enough to supply townsfolk with water for drinking and household needs in the 1890s. That forced the mines and mill to use dry-extraction and dry-processing methods to coax the precious gold from quartzite—an unusual bed for the lode mineral.

By 1896, the mill was processing 260 tons of ore each day, crushing the surrounding quartzite and kicking up clouds of dust—sharp, glasslike particles known as "dagger dust." Unaware miners and townspeople breathed the dust, often resulting in minute tears in their lung sacs, inflicting victims with silicosis. Hundreds of miners died from the disease, earning Delamar the ominous nickname "The Widow Maker." In fact, as many as 400 of the town's 1,500 residents fit that description, their miner husbands taken by the disease.

Near the turn of the century, the town built a pipeline to transport water from Meadow Valley Wash, 12 miles away. The water's arrival transformed the mining and milling processes, but it was too late for many who had already breathed in the deadly quartz dust. A fire destroyed the town in 1900, and although it was rebuilt, a rich ore discovery in Tonopah helped ensure the town's demise. Town founder Captain John Delamar closed up shop in 1909 after producing $15 million in gold and hundreds of corpses. A short-lived mining revival began in 1929, but Delamar itself breathed its last in 1934.

the shallow seas that covered Nevada a half billion years ago.

Key Pittman Wildlife Management Area

Named to honor a former U.S. senator from Nevada known for his vigorous support of the West's silver mining industries, **Key Pittman Wildlife Management Area** comprises two lakes. The lower lake, Frenchy, is usually dry about half the year since it's used to supply irrigation water for the farms in the area. **Frenchy Lake** is reputedly named after an old sourdough miner who worked the old Logan Mines up in the Mount Irish range to the west. North on NV 318 just under five miles is **Nesbitt Lake,** a beautiful lake that does not go dry. It's surrounded by tules, tall cottonwoods, and oak, and is inhabited by an abundance of birds and small animals. When you come to the entrance to Nesbitt Lake, stop, open the cattle gate, drive in (close the gate behind you so you don't let grazing cattle out onto the road), then take a leisurely drive around the lake. You can park at several shady areas at the beginning of the road around the lake. Nonmotorized boats are allowed on the

lake. There are no fees for picnicking or camping in this lush oasis.

Directly across from Nesbitt Lake is a barbed-wire gate to a dirt road leading 18 miles up into the Mount Irish range and the Mount Irish Archaeological District. The range and district are rich with ancient petroglyphs and other Indian artifacts. Up here you'll also find the remains of the old mining town of **Logan.** This is a dirt road and pretty isolated, so be sure to take water, a digging tool, a spare tire, and other desert survival equipment in case you get a flat or get stuck. It's a long walk back. Passenger vehicles can easily make the 18 miles to Logan, but avoid going off this road. All other access roads are strictly four-wheel-drive.

Fishing for bullhead catfish, largemouth bass, and other species is allowed year-round, except for a small area that's closed from mid-February to mid-August to give nesting waterfowl some peace and quiet.

FOOD

The best food in Caliente is of the cowboy diner variety. The **Brandin' Iron** (190 Clover St., 775/726-3164, 6am-8pm daily, $10-15) is representative. Cowboy art graces the walls, and the fare is trail-ride hearty: burgers, meatloaf, etc. Real meat and 'taters stuff, with lots of variety at any meal. The food at **Knotty Pine Restaurant** (690 Front St., 775/726-3194, 6am-9pm daily, $10-15) is filling and reasonably priced: soups, salads, burgers, and other diner fare. The bar sells promotional T-shirts so you can tell the world exactly how Knotty you have been.

Despite the name, everything is cooked to order at **J&J Fast Food** (880 Front St., 775/726-3288, 11am-8pm daily, $6-12). Still, the service *is* fast, and perfect for grabbing a meal on the go for a day at one of the area's state parks or other recreation areas. The fried finger foods—onion rings, cheese sticks, chicken nuggets, popcorn shrimp, the list goes on—are a treat for the taste buds, if not the waistline.

ACCOMMODATIONS

The **Shady Motel** (450 Front St., 775/726-3106, http://shadymotel.net, $60-70) is directly across from the depot, providing a good staging area for train photos, but you may require earplugs if you're a light sleeper. Trains do not observe quiet hours. The motel provides free hot drinks and oatmeal in the morning at reception. The **Rainbow Canyon** (880 Front St., 775/726-3291, $50-70) is on the east side of town but also near the railroad tracks. It is pet-friendly, and rooms come with 32-inch TVs.

On the other side of town, **Mull's Midway Motel** (250 Spring Heights, 775/726-3199, www.mullsmidwaymotel.com, $50-70) has strong Wi-Fi connections and free cable. Innkeeper Robert Mull will go the extra mile to ensure your stay is a pleasant one. The 52 (27 pull-through) sites at **Young's RV Park** (1350 Front St., 775/726-3418, www.young-srvparknv.com, $20) all include full water, sewer, electric, and Wi-Fi hookups. The on-site laundry and bathroom facilities are clean and modern. Tent sites are on a grassy expanse under big, shady trees.

Cathedral Gorge and Vicinity

TOP EXPERIENCE

Yet another unexpected delight on the run up US 93 (which even many Las Vegas residents have yet to discover), Cathedral Gorge is more a place to exercise the imagination than your legs and lungs. What separates these 1,578 acres from countless other washes and gulches in the state? Eons of weather and erosion have remade the landscape into a fantasyland. The walls are made of a chalky-soft suede-colored bentonite clay, which wind, rain, and melting snow have molded into gargoyles, wedding cakes, fortresses, dragons, palaces, melting elephants, and, of course, cathedrals. The baroque architectural elements—lacy, filigreed, fluted, and feathered—decorating its walls make it a must-see.

★ CATHEDRAL GORGE STATE PARK

Some 165 miles north of Las Vegas (an easy 2.5-hour drive up I-15 and US 93), **Cathedral Gorge State Park** (775/728-4460, http://parks.nv.gov, $7) knows no real visiting season. It's open year-round. A visitors center at the entrance has interpretive exhibits and park information. Be sure to check out some of the ranger programs that cover topics ranging from bird-watching to stargazing. You'll also find a campground, shaded picnic areas in strategic locations, drinking water, restrooms, and the magic of your imagination.

Park at the pullout near the signboard at the main part of the gorge. Notice the horizontal line running along the formation; the darker rock on top is compacted clay hardened by lime from decomposing limestone, while the light greenish rock below is the siltstone from the middle of the lake. The hard clay protects the soft siltstone from accelerated erosion, which is believed to have already worn away roughly 1,000 feet of deposits from the lake bed.

From here, hikes disappear into areas where the canyon walls narrow down so much that they almost create natural bridges. The **Moon Caves** formation (the "Rabbit Hole" to locals) squeezes you through a narrow opening on your belly, where you emerge Alice-like in a room surrounded on all sides by towering pillars. The best time for pictures is in the evening, as the cliffs face west.

A one-mile trail continues from the end of the paved road to **Miller Point Overlook.** The four-mile nature trail loops through the desert and around to the campground, commanding a superlative view of the whole wash. Signs along the way identify plants and animals in the lower gorge. The climb down to the gorge's floor is simple, thanks to a metal stairway erected by park managers.

The **campground** ($17) is a pleasant spot, with introduced Russian olive and locust trees. In spring, the olive trees bear a little yellow flower, which gives the susceptible locals a bad case of hay fever; birds love to eat the pea-size olives but can't quite digest them. Elevation is 5,000 feet. There are 22 developed sites for tents or self-contained motor homes up to 30 feet; the two pull-throughs can handle longer. Piped drinking water, flush toilets, showers, sewage disposal, public telephones, picnic tables, grills, and fire pits are provided. The maximum stay is 14 days. Bring your own firewood or buy it at the campground.

The historical sign for **Bullionville** stands between the entrance and Miller Point. The discovery of silver deposits spurred the founding of Bullionville in 1869, and the town's remains are still visible east of the park entrance. The Bullionville Cemetery is north of the park entrance, off US 93. Beyond Miller Point, the road begins to climb into the juniper forest on the slopes of the Highland Range. In a few miles you pass the Caselton Cutoff, then in three miles the left fork leads into Pioche.

PANACA

One mile south of Cathedral Gorge and 15 miles north of Caliente (turn east from US 93 onto NV 319) you reach desert-denying lush, irrigated fields of grains and vegetables, apple orchards, barns, and haystacks. Panaca hasn't changed much since its founding by Mormon

Cathedral Gorge State Park

missionaries more than 150 years ago. It's home to salt-of-the-earth farmers and a population that lives and dies with the fortunes of the Lincoln County High School Lynx football team. Its location within 40 miles of five of Nevada's 23 state parks makes it a good place to stop. The town's name was an anglicized version of *pan-nack-ker,* a Southern Paiute word meaning "metal" or "wealth."

Town Tour

NV 319 becomes Main Street as you enter Panaca. You're greeted by the **Panaca Heritage Center** (400 Main St., 775/728-4567), a mini museum with books, photos, and artifacts donated by local residents and descendants of people who made the town what it is today. It's open only sporadically; in hopes of raising funds to keep the center open regularly, the Panaca Heritage Center committee is selling the book *150 Years in Meadow Valley.*

At 4th Street, peek into the **Mercantile,** known to locals as the Panaca Co-op. Across the street, another adobe building, **Panaca Ward Chapel,** served as a Mormon meeting house, school, and community center. It's the oldest building in town, built in 1867. Go up a block and take a left on 5th. Notice the Italian Victorian house of brick and stone on the east corner; this was the second house of N. J. Wadsworth, a member of one of the founding families. Take the first left onto E Street, then mosey along past the high school gymnasium and ballfield (which dominate the town and are where you'll find the whole populace during a Lynx basketball or baseball game), past the schools and church, all presided over by the incongruous but striking chalk formation known as Court Rock. This public square is where Panaca's gentlemen still court their ladies.

If you continue north on 5th Street, it becomes Panaca Spring Road, which takes you to (surprise!) **Panaca Spring,** whose warm sweet water is part of Meadow Valley Wash. This Olympic pool-size spring is deep and warm, with kids swimming at all hours and a beautiful view of the valley and mountains beyond.

Practicalities

If you're looking to stay in Panaca, you've really only got one option. But what a lovely option it is: **Pine Tree Inn and Bakery** (412 N. 3rd St., 775/728-4675, http://pinetreebnb.com, $70-85). Rooms are decorated country-style, with quilted spreads on the four-posters. Indoors, choose from the big flat-screen TVs, wireless Internet, or a library full of page-turners and plenty of bright, quiet reading nooks. Outdoors, choose from horseback riding or guided ATV tours offered by the inn. The on-site bakery will grubstake you for the next leg of your journey with fresh breads, big cookies, and cakes and pies at reasonable prices. You'll need to fill up here; there are no restaurants in town.

PIOCHE

One of the more colorful and violent of Nevada's boomtowns, Pioche (pee-OACH) is said to have buried 40 to 50 men as the result of violence or accident before anyone lived long enough to die of old age. By the mid-1870s, despite the town's growth to 12,000 souls, some order had been established on the streets. One explanation credits the influx of women to the town; they married the miners and put them on short leashes. In fact, it got to the point where men were afraid of "walking down the street for fear of coming home married," and the Single Men's Protective Association was formed in 1876 to help "the bachelors withstand the wiles of the fair sex."

Pioche's boom-and-bust cycles have continued ever since. Mines and short lines came and went. Cheap power reached Pioche from Hoover Dam just before World War II. The war effort also kept the mines open, producing manganese and tungsten. Since then Pioche has managed to stay alive in large part due to highway traffic, some mining, ranching, and farming. Historical signs and sites, the visitors center and library, two museums, the tramway structure, and a couple of motels

Driving the Extraterrestrial Highway

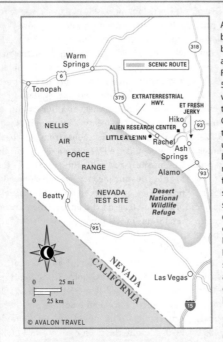

An otherwise nondescript section of blacktop, the 100-mile stretch of NV 375 between the tiny communities of Hiko and Warm Springs skirts the top-secret Air Force installation known familiarly as Area 51. While the federal government insists—when compelled by Freedom of Information Act requests—that the area around Groom Lake is merely used for research and testing experimental aircraft, self-styled ufologists, conspiracy theorists, aviation buffs, and seemingly the Nevada Department of Transportation (NDOT) beg to differ. Getting into the spirit of alleged UFO sightings and the no-nonsense security surrounding Area 51, NDOT in April 1997 designated this desolate 92-mile stretch of NV 375 the "Extraterrestrial Highway." During the ceremony, Nevada governor Bob Miller quipped that some of the signs should be placed flat on the ground "so aliens can land there." Governor Miller also commented that the designation shows Nevada has a sense of humor.

Begin your extraterrestrial journey six miles south of **Hiko,** a straight 115 miles due north of Las Vegas on I-15 and US 93.

Stop for a photo op at the junction of US 93 and NV 318 under the official "Extraterrestrial Highway" road sign, one of four erected in 1997. Previous visitors have covered it with stickers, nearly obliterating the sign's text and artwork. Across the road, alien cowboys and spaceships painted

and cafés will keep you happily occupied for an afternoon.

South of town, US 93 forks, giving you the choice of two routes: the higher, westerly road, NV 321, goes left into Pioche (6,060 feet up in the hills), and the lower, easterly one bypasses the town but leads to relics of its mining history.

Mining Relics

When US 93 forks, you can follow the lower, eastward route to explore the area's mining past. The lower road runs under the **tramway buckets** suspended on the cable between the mine and the mill. The upper road takes you

right to the headframe of the **aerial tramway** built by the Pioche Mine Company in 1923. The weight of the buckets carrying ore down to the mill helped propel the empty buckets back up to the mine. A five-horsepower engine (about the size of one that turns a large washing machine) got the whole thing going. According to the historical sign at the site, the cost of delivering ore to the mill by the tramway in the late 1920s was six cents a ton. Slide down to the 80-foot-high structure to see where the small motor turned the little pulley that turned the big pulley that hooked up to the small gear that turned the bigger and biggest gears that helped propel the cable and on the walls of **ET Fresh Jerky** (775/725-3677) tempt drivers with dried fruit, candy, flavored nuts, and over-the-top souvenirs, as well as beef, venison, elk, turkey, and other jerky products. Stock up! Abduction is possible, and we hear that Martian food is awful.

A mile of US 318 connects you to the ET Highway itself, and your next stop at the **Alien Research Center** (100 Extraterrestrial Hwy., 775/725-3750, 11am-7pm Fri.-Tues.). Don't be fooled by the quasi-official name. This Quonset hut is nothing more than a gift shop, but the tawdry T-shirts and decent selection of Star Wars collectibles and other space-y pop culture icons give it a certain charm. The opening hours are sketchy, but it's worth a stop just to take a photo of the 30-foot-tall silver alien on sentry duty.

In another 39 miles, just before entering Rachel, turn right, onto a dirt road that leads 12 miles to the perimeter of the buffer zone that protects the approach to the entrance to **Area 51**, the rumored secret location where the U.S. government hides its secret intelligence on extraterrestrial life. You'll be nowhere close to anything sensitive or unearthly, but you wouldn't know it by the half dozen warning signs on the fence. If you dare, take a picture of the "no photographs" signs. If approached by guards, do exactly what they say. They are heavily armed and have no sense of humor.

After the nice men release you from the interrogation room, hightail it to **Rachel**, gathering spot for tin-hat wearers from across the globe who are convinced that the truth is out there. The **Little A'Le'Inn** (9631 Old Mill Rd., 775/729-2515, http://littlealeinn.com, $45-60) is their clubhouse, with a flying saucer suspended on a crane, reserved parking for long-distance visitors, and Alien Burgers on the menu at the restaurant (8am-10pm daily, $8-15). The selection of alien merchandise is extensive and varied—piggy banks, cookie jars, gumball machines, and more. The motel rooms share bathrooms with others in the unit. RV spaces ($15) and a cabin ($300) are also available. The ET Highway continues for another 59 miles to Warm Springs, but this is the end of the line for alien-themed attractions.

If you don't want to drive the Extraterrestrial Highway yourself, **Adventure Photo Tours** (702/889-8687, www.vegassightseeing.com, 7am-5pm, $205) hauls vanfuls from Las Vegas. The trip includes a stop at a petroglyph site, a drive through a surreal Joshua tree forest, lunch at the Little A'Le'Inn, water, and snacks. Drivers take guests right up to the Area 51 gates, within shouting distance of the "men in black" who patrol the perimeter.

its dozens of buckets. The whole monstrous structure—including headframe, gears, cable, and buckets—is in the same place it was when the tram was shut down in the 1930s.

Town Tour

US 93's westward fork leads to Main, Pioche, and Lacour Streets, home to several historical downtown buildings. At the intersection, check out the **Commercial Club** and **Amsden Building**, at the divergence of Main and Lacour. Both by some miracle managed to survive fires, explosions, and gunfights, and are now two of the oldest buildings in Nevada. The old firehouse is next to the Amsden Building, and across the street is the **Thompson Opera House**. The interior still has the original 1873 footlights, seats, and scalloped picture frames, plus an adit to an old mining tunnel running out the back. The theater staged *Pygmalion and Galatea* on opening night, with a professional troupe from San Francisco, and hosted movies—silents and talkies—and community events during the town's boom years. Now, it's home to the Pioche Chamber of Commerce.

Down the street are the **Wells Fargo Building**, where guard Eugene Blair protected customers' valuables with a bulldog's tenacity and a trusty shotgun, and a **miner's** cabin, with local historical signs in front. Take a right on Comstock Street to get to the cemetery, with its renowned **Boot Row.** Find the grave of John H. Lynch, killed by James Harrington, according to his tombstone, in an argument over a dog on July 6, 1873. Harrington wounded three other men at the same time. Must've been one helluva dog.

Take Lacour Street from its convergence with Main to see the **Mountain View Hotel,** a mashup of shingle and classic box styles built in 1895 that's waiting for restoration. Next to the Mountain View Hotel, the **Million Dollar Courthouse** is one of Nevada's ultimate symbols of a boom-bust economy and mentality. The courthouse was designed to cost $16,000, but government graft and construction over-runs forced the price up to $26,000 when it was finally completed in 1876. Discounted bonds to finance the construction immediately put the county deep in the red, from which it took nearly 70 years to recover. By 1890, officials had yet to make a payment on the principal, and interest had accrued to the tune of $400,000—nearly 70 percent of the assessed value of the entire county! The state refused to allow the county to default, and the commissioners refinanced the debt, by then $650,000, in 1907. They finally finished paying off the bonds in 1938, four years after the building itself had been condemned, and the same year a new courthouse was constructed.

It's now home to the **Lincoln County Museum** (69 Lacour St., 775/962-5182, 10am-3pm daily May-Oct., donation). Walk in, sign in, and the volunteer will take you around the building, through the historical photo room, sheriff's office, district attorney's office, and assessor's office. The upstairs holds the fire department's room, the judge's office, and the courtroom. The judge's bench and nearby chairs are original. From there you head out the back door to the jailhouse—the middle cell has the original bunk and leg iron. The jailhouse is possibly the most graphic evidence remaining of the tough hombres that hung around this town in the late 1800s.

Recreation

Golfers are now in luck in Pioche, with the construction of **Lincoln County Links** (NV 322 at mile marker 2, 775/962-5206, donation), part of Pioche Recreation Park. The 9-hole (seven par 3s and two par 4s) dirt-and-artificial-turf course shares the park with a gun range, roping arena, and motocross course.

The **Bank Club** (723 Main St., 775/962-5116), inside a former 1860s bank building (you can still wander into the vault), offers video poker machines and refreshing cocktails. Across the street, the **Nevada Club** (738 Main St., 775/962-5170) has pizza, pool, and beer.

Food

Considering it's about the only option in town, you could do a lot worse for eats than the **Silver Café** (8am-8pm Sun.-Mon. and Wed.-Fri., $10-20) with its unpretentious and tasty offerings, such as steak sandwiches and fried seafood platters. They bake the desserts themselves, and the lunch specials are just $6.95.

Ex-Quiet Riot bassist Kelly Garni flogs his found-object art and photographs, along with pedestrian burgers and sandwiches and better gourmet coffees and desserts, at **Ghost Town Art & Coffee** (597 Main St., 775/962-5229, www.ghosttownart.com, $5-10).

Accommodations

Rooms at the **Overland Hotel and Saloon** (662 Main St., 775/962-5895, http://overland-hotelnv.com, $95-105) cater to outdoorsy types, with leather furniture, sports memorabilia, and wood-framed beds in hunting-, fishing-, Victorian-, garden-, and Southwest-themed rooms. The saloon has plenty of slots and video poker, along with one of the coolest bars anywhere. The mahogany bar top of 1868 vintage fronts a solid cherry back bar. Built in England in 1863, it is sturdy enough to have survived a trip around the Horn, the 1906 San Francisco earthquake, shipment across the Sierra, and the 1948 Pioche fire that destroyed the original Overland.

The **Hutchings Motel** (411 Lacour St. 775/962-5404, www.hutchingsmotel.com, $50-70) has lower rates and less character. The five rooms are a bit small but come with a fridge and pet friendliness. Rooms at the **Mother Lode** (378 Lacour St., 775/962-5159, $55-65) come with a coffee pot, mini fridge, and wall-mounted TV. Even more rustic, **Wright's Country Cabins** (704 Main St., 775/962-5205 or 866/810-7303, www.wrightscountrycabins.com, $65) feature two queen-sized beds, kitchenettes, cable TV, free Wi-Fi, and comfy porches. The cabins are tucked behind **Tillie's Mini Mart,** the only place in town to buy hunting and fishing licenses; it also carries food, bait, and all the camping and vacation supplies you forgot to pack.

With so many state parks in the area, it makes little sense to seek out Pioche's RV parks. If you insist, **Roll Inn RV Park** (387 Main St., 775/962-5735, $20-28) advertises full hookups and pull-through sites. You get what you pay for at city-maintained **Pioche RV Park** (462 Bush St., 775/962-3772, free, donation requested).

★ ECHO CANYON STATE PARK

Just 13 miles east of Pioche on NV 322, **Echo Canyon State Park** (775/962-5103, http://parks.nv.gov, $7) boasts some of the best fishing in the state. Stocked rainbow trout are the preferred quarry of most anglers, though hard-fighting largemouth bass and scrappy crappie are also plentiful in the 65-acre reservoir. Six picnic tables and barbecue grills form a string along the reservoir's western shore, and there's a boat launch—open only when the water's high enough—on the north shore.

Approach the park from Pioche, via NV 322 and Echo Dam Road. This narrow two-lane road winds around and then drops fast into the beautiful and inappropriately named Dry Valley, part of the Meadow Valley Wash water system. You pass by well-irrigated and verdantly green alfalfa fields, and then approach the small earthen dam stretching across Echo Canyon on the far side of the valley. When you arrive at the park, take a right to get to the ranger station and group picnic area; drive straight ahead and past the earthen dam, which is about 40-50 feet high and holds back a fairly large body of water, to get to the campground. The **campground** (775/962-5103, $17) has 33 big sites, lush with tall

Ash Canyon Trail in Echo Canyon State Park

sagebrush, plus piped drinking water, flush toilets (turned off at the end of October), sewage disposal, public telephones, picnic tables under roofed shelters, barbecues, and fire pits. Maximum RV length is 25 feet, and there are no hookups.

An amphitheater at the top of the campground hosts ranger talks and movie nights during the summer. It also marks the trailhead for **Ash Canyon Trail,** which leads into the park's backcountry. Most of the 2.5-mile trail (one way) is moderate, but the first 0.5 mile gets the thighs tingling with 300 feet of elevation gain to the rim of the valley. It's all downhill from there, with a plunge past numerous side canyons, their volcanic-ash walls eroded into dramatic bas relief. When you reach the road, you can retrace your steps or follow the pavement through Rose Valley and make it a loop.

The road continues into Echo Canyon up the wash, under big white sandstone walls—100 feet high with eroded pinnacles. It emerges in **Rose Valley,** another beautiful little basin full of alfalfa fields hemmed in by hills and canyon walls. At Rose Valley Ranch is a T intersection: To the left, the road climbs a mile back up to NV 322; head right through another lesser canyon into Eagle Valley for more of the same farm-canyon scenery. Continuing on this good dirt road takes you all the way to **Ursine,** as bucolic and pastoral a village as you could ever imagine, with huge cottonwoods and fruit trees, idyllic farmhouses, and horses and sheep along a creek. You pick up the NV 322 pavement again at the far end of Ursine; take a right. NV 322 continues onward to Spring Valley State Park.

SPRING VALLEY STATE PARK

Dozens of small washes here guarantee a reliable supply of water and make up popular **Spring Valley State Park** (775/962-5102, http://parks.nv.gov, $7), which also boasts a dam and reservoir. A canyon cliff forms about 15 percent of the dam wall. Several stone houses of a long-abandoned Mormon settlement remain here, testament to the hardships they endured and the fortitude that saw them through.

There's pretty good fishing for rainbow trout at the 65-acre **Eagle Valley Reservoir**—indicated by the large number of anglers around the lake. Stake out around the shoreline or rent a boat from **Big Fish Boat Rentals** (775/962-1405 or 775/728-4692). Docking and launching facilities are available. The muddy water precludes swimming.

Horsethief Gulch Campground (775/962-5102, $17), just west of the reservoir, has 36 campsites for tents or self-contained motor homes up to 28 feet. Shade ramadas, picnic tables, and fire pits come with each site. The campground also has flush toilets, showers, piped drinking water, a fish-cleaning station, and public telephones. The road continues along the reservoir, though the pavement ends at the dam. You'll need the *Nevada Map Atlas* to explore farther: From here the **Mt. Wilson Backcountry Byway** keeps going and going, with panoramic views of junipers and piñons, aspens and ponderosas, wildflowers and wildlife.

Just south of the park on NV 322, **Meadow Valley Recreation Area** (775/289-1800) is a good central location for spending time at both Spring Valley and Echo Canyon. It has a few campsites with fire rings, picnic tables, and primitive privies. An unexpectedly delightful creek runs through the cottonwoods.

Nearby **Eagle Valley Resort** (12555 Resort Rd., 775/962-5293, www.eaglevalleynv.com, $85-125) makes a great base camp for visitors interested in hunting and fishing in the area. Its rustic but cozy cabins sleep four and include private baths and full kitchens. The little ones will love the bunk beds in the smaller cabins. Larger lodges feature a king bed and double pullout, along with a fireplace. Barbecue facilities outside are free for the asking, and the on-site store carries all your fishing, grilling, campfire, and alcohol needs. The RV park ($21) has 50 spaces for motor homes, 36 with full hookups but no pull-throughs. Head across the road to the store and the bar for pool, video poker, and your favorite libation. Beyond the resort, you wind around Eagle Canyon past the precarious gravel- and slate-covered slopes of the White Rock Mountains until you reach Spring Valley State Park.

Las Vegas to Tonopah

The drive from Las Vegas to Tonopah, via US 95 along Nevada's southwest edge, is a journey into an old movie western, from the desolate backdrops of Death Valley to the bygone splendor of boomtown hotels. Apparitions of "soiled doves" belly up to the bar, the high society stomping grounds of Wyatt Earp and Jack Dempsey. Poignant relics have been left behind by hardscrabble miners alongside the mansions built by the fruits of their labors.

★ AMARGOSA VALLEY

Ninety minutes north of Las Vegas on US 95, you'll reach Amargosa Valley, the first of Nevada's gateways to Death Valley. NV 373 South becomes CA 127 and heads for Death Valley Junction. The same Nevada road also leads to the 22,000-acre oasis **Ash Meadows Wildlife Refuge** (610 Spring Meadows Rd., 775/372-5435, 8:30am-4pm daily, free), a vast network of springs, bogs, seeps, and small lakes ringed by walkable beaches and alluring picnic areas. More than two dozen species that don't live anywhere else on the planet exist here, making it the "most endemic" place in the country.

At **Crystal Springs,** near the refuge headquarters, a half-mile boardwalk parallels a narrow stream. The stream is a lifeline for reeds, cattails, and other riparian plants along its banks. The creek spills into a deep emerald pool, a hangout for waterfowl. No swimming, wading, or fishing is allowed anywhere in the refuge, with the exception of **Crystal Reservoir.** In the northeast corner of the refuge, **Devils Hole** is a vertical cave that dives 32 feet to the surface of a water table whose depth extends more than 500 feet. It is home to the endemic and endangered Devils Hole pupfish. Aside from the decaying scientific monitoring equipment lying around, there's

Crystal Springs in Ash Meadows Wildlife Refuge, in Amargosa Valley

not much to see at ground level (the hole itself is fenced off for safety and environmental reasons). But an overlook provides a bird's-eye view of the portal.

Practicalities

Rooms at the **Longstreet Inn and Casino** (4400 S. NV 373, 775/372-1777, www.longstreetcasino.com, $69-85), just east of the refuge, come with 42-inch TVs, but the tube cannot compare with inspiring vistas of meadows and mountains. Paying a little extra for a room with a view is totally worth it. The on-site **Jack's Café** (7am-10pm daily, $8-12) and **Nebraska Steakhouse** (5pm-10pm Fri.-Sat., $20-35) dish up reasonably priced sandwiches and rib eyes, respectively. An outdoor pool and spa amid lush landscaping and gazebos provide a relaxing atmosphere after a hard day of travel. At kitschy **Amargosa Bar** (24 hours daily), the regulars are as offbeat as the decor, spinning an inspired round of karaoke on Saturday nights, while 50 machines tempt slot aficionados. Guests at the attached **RV park** ($20) can enjoy the resort amenities. The sites are more level and the hookups more reliable at **Fort Amargosa RV Park** (US 95, 775/764-1932, $25).

At kitschy **Area 51 Travel Center** (2711 US 95, 775/372-1500, 24 hours daily), the busy gift shop, gas station, diner (7am-10pm), and even the brothel are alien-themed. The cathouse is thoughtfully located away from the more family-friendly services.

BEATTY

Another Death Valley gateway, Beatty tucks itself into the edge of Oasis Valley between the California state line and Area 51. It was founded at the turn of the 20th century to supply the Bullfrog Mining District. Today, it serves as a good stopping point for road trippers. It's also the closest town to Yucca Mountain, the on-again, off-again proposed storage site for the nation's nuclear waste. Most Nevadans oppose the project for obvious reasons.

Sights

Everyday life in a turn-of-the-20th-century mining outpost comes to life through photos, books, mining stock certificates, farm implements, children's playthings, kitchen items, and Native American artifacts at the **Beatty Museum** (417 W. Main St., 775/553-2303, http://beattymuseum.org, 10am-3pm daily, donation). The gift shop has books, apparel, and souvenirs. Many of the artifacts are donated by Beatty's residents, making the museum a repository of the town's living history.

You can find evidence of several extinct species at the **Beatty Mudmound** (2 miles southeast of town off US 95), a light gray limestone outcropping with some fossils nearly a half billion years old. Hundreds of millions of years ago, these dunes were under Nevada's shallow seas, where they captured brachiopods, gastropods, sponges, and tiny crustaceans, preserving them in the muck. Over the eons, the sediment dried and hardened into limestone and today offers up museum-quality specimens.

Food

Whether you like your French bread slathered in tomato sauce and mozzarella or surrounding thick slabs of turkey or barbecued beef, you'll be glad to get your hands around the offerings at ★ **KC's Outpost** (100 E. Main St., 775/553-9175, 10am-10pm daily, $8-12). There's a lively barroom separate from the dining room, outdoor picnic table dining, and a faux jail cell where your darling desperados can burn off some car-trip energy. The bread is homemade and the meats are roasted on-site. Most entrées include a slice of homemade cake.

Within easy walking distance of the Atomic Inn and the Death Valley Inn, **Mel's Diner** (600 US 95, 775/553-9003, 6am-3pm, $7-12) is typical Nevada diner fare: bacon, eggs, fried chicken, and burgers served with a smile. There's nothing creative or haute on the menu, but the fresh ingredients and big portions are just what Death Valley explorers need.

Omelets, skillets, and breakfast sandwiches, along with caffeine in all its glorious forms—brewed, iced, flavored, and more are available at **Gema's Wagon Wheel Cafe** (101 S. 2nd St., 775/553-9131, www.gemascafe.com, 7am-3pm Mon.-Sat., 7am-2pm Sun., $10-13). Order any of the pork dishes at **Mama Sara's** (151 S. 2nd St., 775/553-9238, 6am-9pm daily, $10-15) and you won't be disappointed. Succulent carnitas, loaded carne asada fries, spicy tamales—Mama does a pig proud.

Mismatched stools and cluttered back bar add to the rustic cantina charm of **Happy Burro Chili & Beer** (100 W. Main St., 775/553-9099, 10am-10pm daily, $5-10). Ice-cold lager provides the perfect chaser for spicy, oniony chili. Order a bowl of the good stuff or have it dumped on a burger, dog, or Fritos.

No trip through Beatty is complete without a stop at **Death Valley Nut & Candy Co.** (900 E. US 95 N., 775/553-2100, 5am-10pm Mon.-Fri., 6am-10pm Sat.-Sun.), featuring any morsel you can imagine covered in chocolate. Not to mention jerky, sodas, ice cream, coffee, and souvenirs. You'll feel like a kid in a . . . well, you'll have a good time. Enjoy your treats on the dog-friendly terrace or take them

on the road. The little oasis includes a gas station and Subway restaurant.

Accommodations

The **Stagecoach Hotel Casino** (900 US 95 N., 775/553-2419, $65-85) has all the slots and video poker variations, blackjack, poker, craps, and—never a given in rural casinos—a sports book. Rooms are larger than average with sturdy if not overly stylish furnishings. Perfectly acceptable for the price. The pool area is heavy on the deck and light on the watery diversions, but it's nice and clean. Denny's and the casino bar are open 24 hours, and the pool provides lots of deck area for sunny relaxation.

Most of the other motels also string within a block of US 95. The exception is **El Portal** (420 Main St., 775/553-2912, www.elportalmotel.com, $70-100), where some rooms contain three double beds, a convenience for large families. All have satellite TV, fridges, and microwaves in a quiet location off the main drag.

Frequented by military and Yucca Mountain workers, the **Atomic Inn** (350 S. 1st St., 775/553-2250, www.atomicinnbeatty.com, $70-80) plays up the Cold War and alien theme. A park-outside-your-room throwback to the 1950s, though it was just built in

Bottle House in Rhyolite

the 1980s, its 54 rooms got a sprucing up in 2008 and now beckon with inviting golds and honey blonde wood.

The pet-friendly **Exchange Club** (119 W. Main St., 775/553-2333, $70-90) has new 32-inch flat-screens and cold, quiet air-conditioning in every room. The 60 rooms at **Death Valley Inn** (651 US 95 S., 775/553-9400, www.deathvalleyinnmotel.com, $80-100) have satellite TV and Internet, with access to the pool, spa, barbecue area, and laundry room. Its RV park ($40-45) is the real star. It's just the right size (50 spacious spaces, 39 pull-throughs), is peacefully quiet, gives guests full access to the hotel amenities, and has hot showers.

Beatty RV Park (3 miles north of Beatty on US 95, 775/553-2732, www.beattyrvpark.com, $25-30) has no Wi-Fi or TV, but reliable hookups, friendly hosts, big, level sites, and reasonable rates make up for it. The market at **Space Station RV Park** (400 E. US 95 N., 775/553-9039, www.beattymercantile.com, $25-30) hawks fresh fruits and vegetables along with booze and lunch supplies. Burros browsing along the nearby creek is the quintessential rural Nevada sight. Don't let the location near the highway deter you; the noise is minimal.

RHYOLITE GHOST TOWN

Rhyolite was once the center of a prosperous and rough-and-tumble silver mining operation. Now a poignant and photogenic reminder of the Comstock era, it's one of the most photographed ghost towns in the country. The town boomed to sophistication and prosperity after the discovery of rich gold veins on Bullfrog Mountain in 1904. By 1907, the 4,000 residents enjoyed concrete sidewalks, electric lights, telephones, daily newspapers, an opera house, and a public swimming pool.

With more than 50 saloons in Rhyolite by the end of 1905, Tom Kelly had little trouble finding building materials for his **Bottle House,** one of three that once graced the town. Kelly embedded some 30,000 bottles, most recently emptied of Adolphus Busch

Icara by Dre Peeters at the Goldwell Open Air Museum

Beer but with a few snake oil bottles thrown in, into the adobe walls of his three-room house. Kelly never lived here; after completing the interior, he raffled it off. Renovated in 2005, the Bottle House is among the best-preserved of Rhyolite's boomtown relics. You can also imagine yourself among the crag-faced miners conducting business at the Overbury Bank or stocking up at the Porter Brothers' store, the painted ladies awaiting customers outside their cribs, and shiny-suited sharpies sizing up a mark outside the railroad depot. Ruins of all these historical buildings, along with homes, the school, and several mines, make Rhyolite a fascinating place to spend an afternoon.

GOLDWELL OPEN AIR MUSEUM

Just outside of Rhyolite, you'll find what originator Charles Albert Szukalski called an "art situation" in the middle of the vast desert. Szukalski created the original dozen artworks here at the **Goldwell Open Air Museum**

(702/870-9946, http://goldwellmuseum.org, 24 hours daily, donation), most notably *The Last Supper,* a collection of 13 ghostly plaster shrouds arranged to mirror da Vinci's masterpiece. Over the decades other artists have added to the eclectic outdoor collection, using media as diverse as native rhyolite, chrome, cinderblock, and discarded furniture. Notable additions include Hugo Heyerman's *Lady Desert: The Venus of Nevada,* a larger-than-life, pink-skinned blonde nude sculpted in Lego-like cubism, and Dre Peeters's *Icara,* a female version of the Greek mythical figure Icarus.

Artists-in-residence continually add to the collection, while earlier works succumb to wind and weather; other artists take advantage of the studio and workspace the museum provides. Pick up museum-logo merchandise, original artwork, and a self-guided museum tour brochure at the gift shop (10am-4pm most days). The visitors center sells T-shirts and keychains with photo reproductions of the museum's artwork.

GOLD POINT GHOST TOWN

About 65 miles north of Beatty, the Gold Point ghost town still breathes, thanks to its seven residents and a collection of old miners' shacks that accommodate visitors who want an authentic taste of Comstock-era digs ($110-180). With each booking, the proprietors promise breakfast, first night's dinner, a tour of the town and makeshift museum, saloon games (including pool on a 1909 Brunswick table), VCR(!) movies, access to rich fossil beds, and more. A big portion of the rate is reinvested in preserving the town's structures. Sewer, power, and water hookups come with each of the 10 RV spaces in town ($15). To get there, head north on US 95, then turn left to head west on NV 266, then take a slight left to continue south on NV 774.

GOLDFIELD

The discovery of rich silver deposits often set the pulse quickening, and Nevada owes much of its history and early prosperity to the blue-gray ore. But gold is the stuff of legend, fantasy, and irrational exuberance. When word spread in 1903 that the yellow stuff had been found just 30 miles south of Tonopah, prospectors came a-runnin'. Miners often left for the day with $250 worth of nuggets—carried in their shoes, secret pockets, hollow ax handles, and body holsters. With the pockets of Goldfield's 10,000 residents bulging with gold

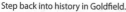
Step back into history in Goldfield.

coins, Tex Rickard, a well-known character from the Alaska gold rush five years earlier, promoted the Joe Gans vs. Oscar Nelson lightweight title fight in the summer of 1906. Gans bloodied and finally dispatched the "Durable Dane" in the 42nd round. The publicity was priceless, and prizefights have been big business in Nevada ever since.

Today, the population of Goldfield is roughly 250, though you're likely to find only a handful in town at any given time. Most of the residents mine gold in the desert or work on the highway, at the air base, or in Tonopah.

Town Tour

A tour of the historic town offers a glimpse into the rich history of the West. The **courthouse** (233 Crook Ave.), which still remains the Esmeralda County seat, has been in regular use since its grand opening in 1908. The elaborate building, constructed of native sandstone, was one of the most intricate buildings of its time and still features the original Tiffany lamps. Crook Avenue also is home to **Tex Rickard's house** and **Fire Station No. 1**, which also is still in use. Just beyond the courthouse is the original jail with three levels of metal cells. A half block west on Euclid Avenue, **Goldfield High School**, built in 1907, features a large skylight above the main entrance.

Another two blocks west is the historic—and reportedly haunted—**Goldfield Hotel**. Closed and padlocked since the last guest left in 1945, the hotel is undergoing renovations in the hopes of reopening the first two floors to visitors in 2019. When it opened in 1908, it was possibly the most luxurious hotel between Chicago and San Francisco; the stone-and-brick building was equipped with telephones, electricity, and a heating system, and was decorated with rich mahogany, black leather, gold leaf, and crystal. Soon after its opening, mining magnate George Wingfield bought the hotel and is said to still haunt the halls. His signature cigar smoke can often be smelled in his room, emanating from fresh ashes. Other reported ghosts include Wingfield's alleged mistress and illegitimate child, two guests who committed suicide in the hotel, two children and a little person who are said to pull pranks on visitors, and "The Stabber," who is said to "attack" people with a knife, although his ghostly attacks cause more fear than harm. Whether the ghosts are real or not, many people have attested to feeling strange presences in the hotel, and in room 109 cameras are said to mysteriously stop working and the room becomes intensely cold. More than one psychic has named it a gateway to another world.

A 10-minute walk north on 5th Avenue brings you to the **Santa Fe Saloon** (925 N. 5th Ave., 775/485-3431). Check out all the history on the walls. Two blocks north, the **Southern Nevada Consolidated Telephone Company** (Ramsey St. and Columbia Ave.) served as the town's communications center from 1906 to 1963.

Sights

Small-town hospitality and eclectic sensibilities are on display at the **Elite Trading Post** (430 Crook Ave., 775/485-378, 9am-5pm daily), a curiosity shop filled with antiques, coins, jewelry, books, and doodads in every corner. You could spend hours browsing this memory lane. Owners Malek and Jody Davarpanah won't mind. They seem as interested in shooting the breeze as making a sale. But buy something anyway; you're sure to find something you didn't know you needed.

Part scrap heap, part modern art gallery, the **International Car Forest of the Last Church** (Crystal Ave., about a half mile east of town) is the brainchild of artists Chad Sorg and Mark Rippie. Decrepit cars are used as canvas for portraits, landscapes, still lifes, and abstracts. The art cars are planted at odd angles, piled atop each other, and stacked against themselves in every combination imaginable.

Food and Accommodations

For a substantial meal, **Dinky Diner** (323 Crook St. 775/485-3231, 7am-7pm Mon.-Sat., 7am-2pm Sun., $8-12) is your best—and pretty much only—choice. Fortunately, the country

The **Santa Fe Saloon** (925 N. 5th Ave., 775/485-3431, rooms $50-90) advertises "Nevada's Meanest Bartender." It's probably not true, but don't cross her. The Santa Fe has been a town fixture since nearly the beginning. Constructed in 1905, the ramshackle wood clapboard structure was built outside of town to be closer to its target customers, miners in search of drink and company after dusty days in the shafts. Traveling the dusty highway makes the burnished 100-year-old bar inside just as much of a godsend today. The oldest continually operating business in town, the Santa Fe survived the big flood of 1916, the great fire of 1923, and the death of its original owner in a 1912 gunfight. The sign and front door will take you back those 100-plus years, to when Goldfield was only a few years old and this club was one of the requisite couple of dozen. It also has a handful of serviceable if plain rooms.

Your other option for libations, **Hoist House** (300 N. Columbia Ave., 775/750-7796) is across from the Goldfield Hotel. Check out the vintage bar top and even more vintage cash register behind it. Pizza ($10) is on the menu.

Tonopah Historic Mining Park

breakfasts, burgers, sandwiches, and Mexican noshes are tasty and filling. The Dinky closes early, so hurry in before dark.

Tonopah

A natural stopping point on the long drive between Reno and Las Vegas, Tonopah is a great crossroads town, a natural way station that rewards pit-stopping travelers with a hands-on history lesson and overnight visitors with one of the darkest night skies in the country. According to the apocrypha, Tonopah sprang to life when one morning Jim Butler awoke to discover that one of his burros had wandered away. He found the silly ass on what was soon to be called Mizpah Hill. Picking up a rock with which to plunk the donkey, Butler noticed the would-be projectile seemed unusually heavy. Another story, just as likely to be true, but much less imaginative, asserts that Butler

was led right to the gold vein by Indian prospectors. Butler packed a few samples in his saddlebags, and after word leaked, Tonopah soon became home to 50,000 souls, earning the title "Queen of the Silver Camps." After the mines played out in about 1915, the population began a steady decline. About 2,500 people live there now, some employed at a secure military facility, main street shops, and a molybdenum and copper mine, keeping the town's mineral traditions alive.

The **Tonopah Development Corporation,** in addition to its other duties, has commissioned a dozen murals and sculptures honoring the Butlers, the military, heroic miner Big Bill Murphy, and other

Tonopah

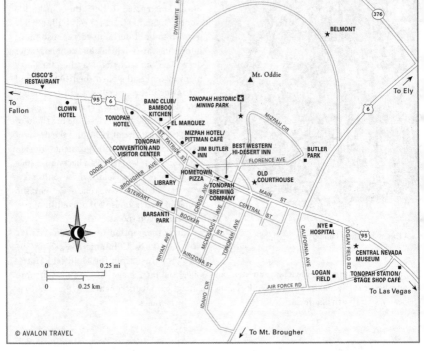

pride-instilling icons. As you drive around town, keep an eye out for these tributes.

SIGHTS
★ Tonopah Historic Mining Park

The highlight of the 70-acre **Tonopah Historic Mining Park** (110 Burro St., 775/482-9274, www.tonopahhistoricmining-park.com, 9am-5pm daily, $5, age 8-17 and over 65 $4, under 8 and active/retired military free) is poking around the former Silver Top and Mizpah mines, sorting rooms, hoists, and railroad trestles. The tour's centerpiece is the Burro Tunnel Underground Adventure where Jim Butler took some of his original samples. You'll have a bird's-eye view of a

500-foot stope as you enter the viewing cage suspended above.

Spare parts and cases of core samples sit gathering dust in buildings along the tour route, left the way they were when the mines shut down. You'll walk right across an exposed two-foot-wide vein of silver ore just like the one Jim Butler found in 1900. Peer into the 100-foot-deep crater of the Glory Hole, site of a 1922 cave-in caused by mining too near the surface. No one was killed, but only because the collapse occurred at night. Miners returned to work the next morning to find the assay office in splinters at the bottom of the pit.

Central Nevada Museum

The educational and attractive **Central**

Nevada Museum (1900 Logan Field Rd., 775/482-9676, 9am-5pm Tues.-Sat., free), just off US 95 on the south end of town near Logan Field, emphasizes the region's mining legacy. Outside, you'll find a re-created Old West town, with cabins, a saloon, blacksmith shop, and stamp mill. More mining and ranching artifacts are inside, alongside intriguing and empathetic studies of various ethnic groups' contributions to local history, culture, and art. An extensive photo collection shows local towns during the boom and abandoned mines following the bust. There's also a purple bottle collection (manganese in the glass reacts to sunlight), as well as lots of Shoshone artifacts. Another exhibit looks at the contributions of the Tonopah Army Air Field during World War II.

The research room is available for modern-day prospecting. Hundreds of books, photographs, newspapers, videos, and genealogy files can help you strike research gold. The gift shop sells the expected line of books, historical journals, postcards, and souvenirs.

Mizpah Hotel

Lovingly restored to its former glory, the **Mizpah Hotel** (100 N. Main St., 775/482-3030, www.themizpahhotel.com, $100-165) is steeped in living and—if the ghost stories can be believed—not-quite-dead history. Investors, seizing the financial opportunity afforded by the coming of the railroad in 1907, constructed this opulent 76-room gem. They spared no expense, installing an elevator, imported brass chandeliers, and stained-glass windows for the five-story building, until 1948 the tallest in Nevada. Wyatt Earp tended bar here for a time, and Jack Dempsey worked as a bouncer (according to legend, and who are we to stand in the way of a good story?). Despite the renovation and reopening, the ghosts of two murdered miners and a too-young-to-die soiled dove from the hotel's early years are said to still roam the corridors.

Tonopah Star Trails

Tonopah's nights are the darkest in America, making it the optimal spot to view the treasures of the solar system. On a clear, moonless, winter night 7,000 heavenly bodies make an appearance. Uranus and Milky Way denizens far beyond our own star system are clearly visible to the naked eye. Even simple telescopes bring into view Saturn's rings, frozen Neptune, the Ring Nebula, and even the stars of Andromeda. The **Tonopah Development Corporation**

Mizpah Hotel

Central Nevada Events

In many parts of the country parades are a lost art, but in central Nevada you can find one just about any summer weekend. As *Las Vegas Review-Journal* columnist John L. Smith noted, Nevada's small towns host more parades than Russia under Stalin. They are usually attached to quaint festivals celebrating the bygone days of a bypassed town or a patriotic holiday and are a not-to-be-missed opportunity to loosen your tie, turn off the cell phone, and sink into quaint, idyllic, pastoral times of yore.

MAY

Tonopah's **Jim Butler Days** (www.jimbutlerdays.tonopahnevada.com) are a big community fair with stock car races, a parade, a craft show, food, games, raffles, gold panning, a queen contest, and the Nevada State Mining Championships.

Walker Lake Education Day (775/945-2289, www.walkerlake.org) at Walker Lake provides the opportunity to view loons as they stop to feed and breed on their way back to their nesting grounds in Canada, along with grebes, pelicans, cormorants, and geese. Preservationists demonstrate efforts to save the lake. The event includes boat rides, water sports demonstrations, and fund-raising.

In Caliente, **Memorial Day** (www.lincolncountynevada.com) includes a huge softball tournament, parade, horseshoes and other games, art and craft fair, car show, raffle, and more. Hawthorne bills itself as "America's Patriotic Home," so of course it goes all out on **Armed Forces Day.** Events at recent celebrations included chili cook-offs, arm wrestling and golf tournaments, and, yes, a parade featuring bands and veterans and currently serving personnel from all military branches.

JUNE

Challenge yourself and your two-wheeler at Beaver Dam State Park's **49er Gravel Grinder** (775/728-4460, www.beaverdamgravelgrinder.com). Fat-tire bicyclists rumble over surfaces including asphalt, dirt, and rock while exploring the park's sloping canyons and high volcanic rock formations.

JULY

Tonopah's **Fourth of July Barbecue and Fireworks** event is good wholesome fun that in-

(775/482-9680, www.tonopahnevada.com/StarTrails) publishes *Tonopah Star Trails,* a guide to paved and unpaved roads around town that afford the best sky views. The **Tonopah Astronomical Society** (http://tas.astronomynv.org) hosts regular star parties.

CASINOS

The big-town casino is at the **Tonopah Station** (1137 Erie St., 775/482-9777 or 800/272-6232, www.tonopahstation.com, $70-90) on the south end of town. This hotel-casino was built in 1982 in the midst of the latest boom in Tonopah, next to Scolari's Warehouse Market, Tonopah's first supermarket, which opened in 1981. The compact 30,000-square-foot casino is cramped and crowded with slots and a small blackjack pit. The **Stage Shop Café** (6am-9:30pm daily, $10-17) and western saloon are standard-issue, but the memorabilia throughout offer an interesting diversion.

On the north side, the **Banc Club** restaurant/bar/casino (360 N. Main St., 775/482-5409) has slot machines and occupies a building that was once the Bank of America building. It's the site of the old Tonopah railway depot, which burned down in 1981. Though hit-and-miss, the club's **Bamboo Kitchen** (11:30am-8:30pm Wed.-Mon., $10-20) is usually a bright spot.

cludes raffles, swimming, a softball tournament, a parade, fireworks, and food. Panaca celebrates its heritage as Nevada's oldest existing community with Pioneer Days (www.tonopahnevada.com/events), featuring a parade, games, raffles, pancake breakfast, and barbecue dinner.

AUGUST

Break out your turn-of-the-20th-century garb at Goldfield Days (775/485-3560, www.goldfieldnevada.org/events) and witness Old West gunfights, street dances, tours of the historic town, games, parades, and barbecue and chili cook-offs.

SEPTEMBER

A final outdoor-activity splurge before bundling up for the winter, the Pioche Labor Day (775/962-5544, www.piochenevada.org/labor-day.htm) celebration has a parade, softball and volleyball tournaments, horseshoes, melodrama, raffles, and carnival games, along with mucking and other mining-related contests. When the sun goes down, people take to the streets for dancing to live music.

At the Silver State Classic Challenge (775/289-6900, www.sscc.us), drivers race along NV 318 for 90 miles through rural Nevada between Lund and Hiko. The two-lane course challenges drivers with speed-friendly straights, hair-raising hairpins, and ramp-like hills. Several classes of cars ensure competitive races. The Nevada Open Road Challenge in May covers the same course and has the same rules.

Transportation options old and new, airborne and terrestrial, take center stage at the Lyon County Fly-In in Silver Springs, with restored early jets, state-of-the-art fighters, and radio-controlled planes lining up with hot-air balloons, hang gliders, monster trucks, and Aston Martins. Raffle drawings, plenty of food, and gunfights in the street keep the event lively.

OCTOBER

Lincoln County's state parks are on display during the Park to Park Pedal (775/728-4460, www.parktoparkpedal.com), beginning and ending at Kershaw-Ryan State Park. The premier 100-mile race takes riders through Pioche and Cathedral Gorge, Echo Canyon, and Spring Mountain State Parks.

FOOD

Tonopah is not restaurant row, but there are a couple of standouts, especially if you're in the mood for Mexican fare. ★ El Marques (348 N. Main St., 775/482-3885, 11am-9pm Tues.-Sun., $10-20), across from the Tonopah Motel, is the best in town. The chiles rellenos are tender and cheeserrific. Service may be a bit spotty, but who's in a hurry in Tonopah?

If you *are* in a hurry but still jonesing for Mexican, hit the drive-through at Cisco's Restaurant (10am-8:30pm Mon.-Sat., $10-15), where the food ranges from Mexican to burgers to ribs and even ice cream. They have pizza, too, but leave the pie-making to the experts at Hometown Pizza (222 N. Main St., 775/482-9998, $8-20), who let you choose thin or thick crust. The $9 daily lunch buffet includes salad, soup, and breadsticks along with the pizza.

You would expect great pub food in any town along a dusty highway, and you won't be disappointed at Tonopah Brewing Company (315 S. Main St., 775/482-2000, www.tonopahbrewing.com, 11am-9pm daily, $12-25). The slow-smoked barbecue and IPAs really hit the spot after a long day of driving or traipsing around town in search of mining history, but you can make a meal of the starters and sides, as well.

ACCOMMODATIONS

The historic ★ **Mizpah Hotel** (100 N. Main St., 775/482-3030, www.themizpahhotel.com, $100-165) offers 48 suites, including custom opulence in the Lady in Red and Wagon rooms. All have big flat-screens and free Wi-Fi. The rooms are a bit small by modern standards (they were, after all, built for 19th-century-sized people). A queen bed, TV, and chair leave room for little else but the antiques, tapestries, and brass throughout. The friendly, outgoing waitstaff at the **Pittman Café** (6am-10pm daily, $10-15) serve big stacks of pancakes, crispy fish-and-chips, and other comfort food.

Tonopah has nearly 500 motel rooms, enough to accommodate most everybody at any time (except on the very busiest Saturday nights and during Jim Butler Days, the town festival that takes place the last weekend in May) and inexpensive enough that you don't have to worry about getting a good deal anywhere you go. All are located along Main Street from one end of town to the other.

The **Best Western Hi-Desert Inn** (320 Main St., 775/482-3511, www.bestwestern.com, $100-120) is second only to the Mizpah, with 62 rooms and homemade cookies at check-in. In a world of complimentary continental breakfasts, the waffles and eggs in the morning will give you a big ole happy face.

The rooms at **Jim Butler Motel** (100 S. Main St., 775/482-3577, www.jimbutlerinn.com, $80-100), next to the Mizpah, are bright and inviting, with wood furniture and faux hearths. Some rooms have fridges and microwaves; all have free Wi-Fi.

Conquer your coulrophobia and coimetrophobia at the same time at the **Clown Motel** (521 N. Main St., 775/482-5920, $40-60), which overlooks a turn-of-the-20th-century cemetery, final resting place for the victims of the 1902 Tonopah plague and 1911 mine fire. The office is crammed with jesters, jokers, and harlequins, from doll- to life-size, but the greasepaint and rubber nose motif

mill smokestack in Belmont

stops at the rooms—unless you pay extra for the clown suite. The clean, smoke-smell-free rooms have much-appreciated refrigerators and microwaves, basic twin double beds, and a decent price.

Of the other independent hostelries, only the **Tonopah Motel** (325 Main St., 775/482-3987, $50-70) is recommendable.

INFORMATION AND SERVICES

The **Tonopah Convention and Visitors Center** (301 Brougher Ave., 775/482-3558, www.tonopahnevada.com, 8am-5pm Mon.-Fri.) and the **Tonopah Chamber of Commerce** (200 S. Main St., 775/482-9680, www.tonopahchamberofcommerce.com) have all the statistics and brochures you'll need. Down the street is the third **library** (167 Central St., 775/482-3374, 10am-6pm Wed.-Sat.) ever built in Nevada, in 1912, and the oldest one still in use.

BELMONT AND MANHATTAN GHOST TOWNS

Silver indications were uncovered high up on the east side of the Toquimas in 1865. The rush was so great that 2,000 people lived in and around **Belmont** within a year. Its mines and mills produced $15 million in silver during its 15-year stint in the spotlight. Fire, vandals, souvenir hunters, and entropy took their toll for the next 60 years until Belmont was declared a National Historic District. Today, the town, 50 miles north of Tonopah, is a restored beauty with fewer than 10 full-time residents. The **Belmont Courthouse** (775/867-3001, call to arrange a tour) is open to the public. While the ruins, including the bank's brick facade and stone walls, the mill smokestack, and the Belmont Inn and Saloon, are picturesque, tramping in, around, and through them is trespassing. The town's only paid employee is a caretaker, who will no doubt check you out in his four-wheel-drive vehicle.

Shortly after Belmont's mines played out, mineral discoveries led to the founding of **Manhattan,** 50 miles farther north. Rich pay dirt was discovered in the lower levels of the hard-rock mine in 1915; by the late 1930s, advanced gold-mining technology arrived in the form of a great gold dredge. Manhattan produced $10 million in gold over its 40-year run, and a comparatively small operation continues at the site. Old headframes overlook the pit from the hill above; the company production plant is behind the pit on the other side. The town of Manhattan is up the road, with abandoned shacks, old houses, and big trees. About 60 people live in Manhattan year-round. Rather than building a new Catholic church, frugal miners relocated Belmont's then-unused St. Stephen's for rechristening as Sacred Heart Mission. It still stands today as one of the prettiest structures in town. The **Manhattan Bar & Motel** (19 Main St., 775/487-2304, $50-70) has been updated since pioneer days, but it still stands ready with cold beer and comfortable beds.

TOP EXPERIENCE

★ LUNAR CUESTA

Nevada rests on one of the most active belt of volcanoes in the world: the Pacific Ring of Fire. Driving along the Pancake Range, 80 miles east of Tonopah on US 6, you can see examples of volcanism at work in the **Lunar Cuesta.** The Apollo astronauts trained in this 140,000-acre landscape because it was the best

Lunar Cuesta

possible simulation of the moon's surface. This landscape formed during the Oligocene epoch, 40 million years ago, when a colossal eruption of white-hot steam, ash, and particulate spewed up from the depths, resulting in welded tuft or fused volcanic rock. The cinder cones, lava tongues, craters, and maars we see today are manifestations of much more recent activity, only a few thousand years old.

From US 6, take a right onto the **Lunar Loop Road** and drive three miles. Turn left at the sign to **Easy Chair Crater;** a 100-yard trail from the parking area leads up to a viewpoint. It's clear how this high-backed hole got its name: It could be God's Barcalounger. A sign points out some geology and the direction of lava flows. Just turn your head to see amazingly diverse topography: pancake buttes, mashed-potato mounds, craters, cones, the cuesta floor, and the mighty **Quinn Canyon Range** in the background.

Back on the good dirt road (35 mph, one lane), you drive another few miles and climb up to **Lunar Crater,** 430 feet deep and nearly 4,000 feet in diameter. This is a typical maar, formed when the violent release of gases reams an abrupt deep crater with a low rim. Unlike the crater behind it, which is the peak of a small cinder cone, no magma was ejected with the gases. But the old lava and ash flows were exposed by the explosion; the descriptive sign points them out.

Continuing the next eight miles toward **The Wall,** you drive on the east side of the loop along dry **Lunar Lake.** You won't wonder where or what The Wall is; Pink Floyd's eponymous double album is not only apropos, but essential.

The loop ends on the old US 6 asphalt; pick a convenient spot to four-wheel up to the highway. North of the highway is **Black Rock Lava Flow,** the most recent basalt ooze in the area, covering 1,900 acres. The lava cooled so fast that it's specked with green, red, and black glass.

Hawthorne and Vicinity

US 95 from Tonopah to Hawthorne winds through salt and borax country with not much to see or stop for throughout its 100-mile duration. The walkup **Socorro's Burger Hut** (710 Front St., 775/573-2444, Mina, 10am-6pm Thurs.-Tues., $12-20), however, is worth a stop, so time your journey so that you arrive in **Mina** at lunchtime.

Hawthorne is surrounded by thousands of thick concrete bunkers and pillboxes, filled with bullets, bombs, and missiles, all in the service of national defense. They make Hawthorne perhaps the only community in Nevada that hopes it never becomes a "boom" town. The town's ties to the military are only partly responsible for its patriotism, evidenced by red, white, and blue bunting on business exteriors and more Old Glories than a political convention. The town's memorial rose garden features many rows of roses

landscaped with paths, benches to rest on, and a babbling fountain.

Hawthorne is just a short drive from attractive Walker Lake. The views from the surrounding mountains, especially the top of Lucky Boy Pass, are spectacular, spanning 50 miles from north to south and showing the unique beauty of a desert lake. The nighttime skies are alive with stars.

SIGHTS

The big barn of a building that is the **Mineral County Museum** (400 10th St., 775/945-5142, 11am-5pm Tues.-Sat. summer, noon-4pm Tues.-Sat. winter, free) is home to numerous interesting historical displays. First check out the big painting of Hawthorne's history—everything from Cecil the Serpent to chromate-green bombs is represented. Also for the bicentennial, the townspeople created a quilt now on display. There's an apothecary exhibit from Golden Key Drugs, plus lots of firefighting, railroad, and mining equipment, including a three-piston stamp-mill crusher, as well as rock displays (this is *Mineral County*, after all) and lots of stories, including how the collection of Spanish mission bells was discovered. Recommended.

The **Hawthorne Ordnance Museum** (925 E St., 775/945-5400, http://hawthorne-ordnancemuseum.com, 10am-4pm Mon.-Fri., 10am-2pm Sat., free) highlights what was manufactured over the years at the Army Ammunition Plant. The museum showcases a few big guns, but it's mostly photos, uniforms, and newspapers, as well as torpedoes, mines, missiles, and other now-nonexplosive pieces of military history. Military buffs will find nothing more enjoyable than an afternoon spent browsing the Hawthorne Ordnance Museum. The small museum is locally run and dedicated to celebrating all things military. Visitors will find displays and exhibits of a range of ammunition dating back to the early part of the 20th century, as well as an in-depth look at the area's munitions history.

ENTERTAINMENT

It's all slots, all the time in Hawthorne. "Resort" is a bit of a stretch at the town's biggest casino, **El Capitan Resort & Casino** (540 F St., 775/945-3321, http://elcapcasino.com, $60-75). El Cap has no blackjack; it is really a 200-machine slot and video poker parlor, not that there's anything wrong with that. The old gal got a facelift in 2016, a year shy of her 75th birthday, with the facade, restaurant (24 hours daily, $10-20), bar, and casino floors all receiving upgrades including natural stone and wood to create a vintage feel. Much-needed room upgrades started before the common area changes and resumed in early 2017.

Green and picturesque nine-hole **Walker Lake Golf Club** (775/945-1111, www.golf-hawthorne.com, $15-35) features a bar serving simple snacks like hot dogs and chili. It's at the army base, about three miles north of Hawthorne, between town and Walker Lake.

FOOD

★ **Maggie's** (787 E. St., 775/945-2575, 7am-8pm Mon.-Sat., 8am-2pm Sun., $15-25) serves dinner and breakfast, but its best features are the lunch sandwiches on bread baked on the premises. Come for late afternoon soup and salad, and save room for pie! Stay a couple of hours to take advantage of the strong Wi-Fi signal and free drink refills. In summer and on not-too-breezy spring days, ask to be seated on the patio. Maggie's has won the state's Governor's Tourism Award, Business of the Year, and many other accolades.

Many choose the call-ahead takeout option at **Wong's** (923 5th St., 775/945-1700, 11am-7:30pm Sun.-Thurs., 11am-8pm Sat.-Sun., $8-15) because there's usually a bit of a wait. The Kung Pao, spring rolls, and fried rice are worth it. Nothing more than a food trailer, **Pepper's Place** (775/316-8030, 11:30am-1:30pm and 5pm-7pm Mon.-Wed., $8-12) usually sets up shop near US 93 and F Street, close to Whiskey Flats RV Park, where it slings a variety of burgers and barbecue pork and chicken sandwiches.

Great prices on Italian sandwiches, calzones, and, of course, pizza await at **Old Nevada Pizza** (497 E St., 775/945-2550, 11am-8pm Sun.-Tues., 11am-9pm Wed.-Sat., $15-20). The decor is no frills—picnic tables and plain walls. **Joe's Tavern** (537 Sierra Way, 775/945-2302, 10am-midnight Sun., 11:30am-midnight Mon.-Thurs., 11:30am-4am Fri.-Sat.) is across the street from the El Cap. It's a bar, dance club, casino (slots), pool hall, and general hangout.

ACCOMMODATIONS

The mom-and-pop ★ **Monarch Motel** (1291 5th St., 775/945-3117, $77-100) takes pride in its cleanliness and landscaping. The rooms are pedestrian, but certainly on par with anything else in town, save possibly the more expensive **America's Best Inn** (1402 E. 5th St., 775/945-2660 or 800/237-8466, www.

Side Trip to Death Valley National Park

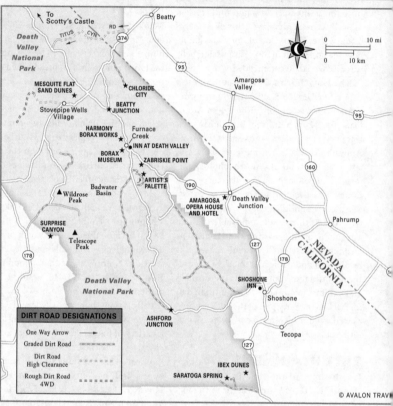

© AVALON TRAVEL

Nevada boasts more than its fair share of surreal landscapes—glaciers, deserts, caves, and dry lakes (not to mention the Las Vegas Strip). But Death Valley, just across the California state line (a small section crosses into Nevada) deserves its reputation for desolation. The lowest, hottest, and driest spot in the United States, Death Valley's unforgiving reputation obscures its pleasures—tiny pockets of beauty amid an austere landscape; thriving ecosystems defying arid plains; signs of human habitation from bygone centuries and millennia in areas with nary a drop of water in sight. The US 95 communities of Pahrump, Amargosa Valley, and Beatty, all less than two hours from Las Vegas, serve as ready-made gateways to the park.

Exploration of the southern part of the park easily begins in **Pahrump,** with a trip via NV 372 (across the state line it becomes CA 178) to Shoshone, California. Set up base camp at the **Shoshone Inn** (113 Old State Hwy. 127, 760/852-4335, http://shoshonevillage.com, $95), which boasts its own hot springs pool. The motel is within walking distance of Dublin Gulch Caves, hand-dug pits that served as a housing development for local miners. Several other hot springs gurgle up throughout the area, especially around the community of **Tecopa,** 12 miles south on NV 127. The road continues into the park proper, where guests are greeted by the **Ibex Dunes.** Farther along, **Saratoga Spring** is a veritable river by Death Valley standards and an idyllic picnic spot. Pools of life-giving water and riparian plants provide homes and nourishment for endemic fish, snails, and insects.

From **Amargosa Valley,** the popular areas around Death Valley Junction are just 24 miles south via NV 373, which becomes CA 127. The junction was the purview of the indomitable Marta Becket and her **Amargosa Opera House and Hotel** (760/852-4441, www.amargosa-opera-house. com, $65-80) until her death in 2017. Becket, a Broadway actress, discovered the shuttered hotel when her car broke down in 1962. She decided to stay. The hotel is said to harbor restless spirits.

CA 190 leads to **Zabriskie Point,** perhaps the best vantage point in Death Valley. Look down eroded basalt formations, the rust-stained Red Cathedral, and Manly Beacon, rising like a sail on a vast, rocky sea. You can hike from here through **Golden Canyon** to Red Cathedral and beyond or walk **Gower Gulch** past colorful rock formations and abandoned borax mines. The complete loop, covering both trails, is about six miles, with only mild elevation changes. It takes about four hours to complete at a moderate clip. Both routes are popular—among Death Valley's "must-do's," especially for Star Wars fans tracking down locations featured in the franchise. Most, however, start these hikes from the Badwater Road trailhead, two miles south of its junction with CA 190. Continuing on CA 190 toward Furnace Creek and turning south onto Badwater Road for nine miles leads to the nine-mile **Artist's Drive** through **Artist's Palette.** The scenic route loops through a sloping canyon wall, a kaleidoscope of greens, blues, mauves, and yellows caused by oxidizing metals in the hillside. The play of light and shadow alters the scenery throughout the day.

Furnace Creek Village, the former ranch and borax distribution center—receiving shipments via the famous 20-mule teams—has a central location and accommodations of all stripes, making it an obvious destination for visitors intending to stay in Death Valley for more than the day. Learn the history and importance of "white gold" and the Native cultures in Death Valley at the **Borax Museum** (9am-9pm daily, donation), north of Furnace Creek Ranch. Two miles north of the museum, **Harmony Borax Works** (760/786-3200) covers miners and the mining process.

Take a break from the bleak landscape at the **Inn at Death Valley** (mid-Oct.-mid-May, $375-450), on CA 190 near the Badwater Road turnoff. This luxury resort includes a spring-fed pool, spa, sauna, and golf course. The **Ranch at Death Valley** (328 Greenland Blvd., 760/786-7916, $200-270) offers rooms with patios or balconies, a huge swimming pool, and a children's play area, as well as an RV park and campground ($18-38). Other camping options include **Furnace Creek Campground** (877/444-6777, $18), open year-round, and **Sunset Campground** ($12) and **Texas Spring** ($14), open October through May.

Beatty, via NV 374 (Daylight Pass Rd. and CA 190) is the Nevada gateway to attractions in the northern section of Death Valley. Six miles southwest of Beatty, a right turn onto Titus Canyon Road skirts petroglyphs and passes Leadville ghost town before leading to the Fall and Red Wall Canyon trailheads. Sheer cliff walls tower above as you negotiate the Titus Canyon Narrows. At the end of the drive, hook up with NV 267, which leads northward to **Scotty's Castle,** a Spanish Colonial-style mansion, closed while recovering from flood damage and not expected to reopen before 2020. (The National Park Service offers a limited number of tours to witness its recovery.)

Turning south on Scotty's Castle Road from the end of the Titus Canyon scenic drive leads back to the CA 190 intersection and access to more popular attractions. Pick up NV 374 North to access the trail to **Chloride City** and **Chloride Cliff.** You'll see the ruins of a mill, circa 1916, crumbling building walls, a water tower, and crude dugouts used by silver and lead miners. Take the trail to the top of the cliff for a panoramic view.

Veering southwest on CA 190 toward Stovepipe Wells Village will take you to **Mesquite Flat Sand Dunes.** Only about 100 feet tall, they are easily climbable. Arrive before sunrise or near sunset, scale the tallest dune, and watch, mesmerized, as shifting sunlight plays on the shadows created by ripples and meandering ridgelines below.

Continuing on CA 190 you'll hit Emigrant Canyon Road, leading deep into Emigrant and Wildrose Canyons. Climb **Wildrose Peak** to commune with centuries-old bristlecone pines; surprise yourself by completing the 13-mile hike to the summit of **Telescope Peak** for spectacular valley views; submerge yourself in **mining history** at the Wildrose Charcoal Kilns and Panamint City and Skidoo boomtowns; or escape the heat with a picnic and a nap beside the gurgling creek in **Surprise Canyon.**

redlion.com, $110-140), where any of the basic rooms come with microwaves and refrigerators. Fresh cookies at check-in and the free continental breakfast are nice touches. Kids stay free. Pets can stay, too, but for an additional charge.

Bargain hunters can try the **Sand N Sage Lodge** (1301 E. 5th St., 775/945-3352, $50-75) or **Holiday Lodge** (480 J St., 775/945-3316, $60-75). At Walker Lake Village, **Cliff House Lakeside Resort** (315 Cliff House Rd., 775/945-2459, $55-100) rooms are on the beach (though the water is pretty far away these days, especially when you compare it to 30 years ago when the motel had to be closed because of flooding).

The best RV park around these parts is **Whiskey Flats** (3045 US 95, 775/945-1800, http://whiskeyflats.net, $35), with 60 big pull-through spaces, a tiny general store, strong Wi-Fi, clean showers, and plenty of peace and quiet. For cheaper, one-night stays, **Scotty's RV Park** (1101 5th St., 775/945-2079, $20) has 18 spaces for motor homes, all with full hookups; 17 are pull-throughs. Tents are not allowed.

INFORMATION

The **Mineral County Economic Development Authority** (901 E St., 775/945-5896 or 877/736-5253, 7am-5pm Sun.-Thurs.) provides demographic and business information as well as some visitor resources. The **Mineral County Chamber of Commerce** (www.mineralcountychamber.com) has no public office, but the website is chock-full of local information for visitors, as is the **county library** (110 1st St. and A St., 775/945-2778, 10am-6pm Mon.-Fri., 11am-4pm Sat.).

★ WALKER LAKE

Thirty miles long and 3-8 miles wide, this pristine high-desert limnological lodestar is actually just a piddling pond left over from ancient Lake Lahontan, which once covered 8,400 square miles of western Nevada and eastern California; Pyramid Lake, 100 miles north, is the other remnant.

The north quarter of Walker Lake is owned by the Walker River Paiute, the middle half by BLM, and the south quarter by the Army Ammunition Plant. Speedboat races, fishing and derbies, water-skiing, swimming, and camping are the main sports on the lake. Best fishing for the two- to three-pound cutthroat

Walker Lake

trout stocked in the lake is in March and April.

Sportsman's Beach is 15 miles north of Hawthorne, along the west shore below US 95. It has about 30 developed campsites ($6, $4 for undeveloped sites), outhouses, tables, and shelters. **Walker Lake State Recreation Area** (775/867-3001) is two miles south at Tamarack Point. It has 12 picnic sites, outhouses, and the lake's only boat ramp. Dry camping can be found at 20 Mile Beach nearby.

Like many lakes, Walker boasts a giant serpent. Cecil is the 80-foot-long monster that hides in the lake's ancient depths. Although he's less than benign in Paiute legends, to the children of Hawthorne, Cecil is friendly and is always well represented in local parades.

Loons visit Walker Lake on their commutes between their breeding grounds and winter home, though the water quality cannot support enough food fish for the roughly 1,400 individuals that drop in to eat and mate on their migrations. The lake also supports some 10,000 cormorants, ibis, swans, geese, ducks, and pelicans.

With the proper permits from the **Four Seasons market** on the Walker River Paiute Reservation, you can fish, boat ($8), and camp at **Weber Reservoir,** located on the reservation six miles west on the road to Yerington. The store also sells a huge variety of fireworks. Over the years the reservation acreage has been chipped away for mining and recreation, and declining water levels have left the tribe with dwindling lake frontage.

YERINGTON

Some 60 miles north of Hawthorne on US 95 is Yerington, in the Mason Valley. Two forks of the Carson River make it one of the lushest valleys in Nevada, a boon to ranchers and farmers. The standout county museum makes it a worthwhile stop along this route. The river also offers secluded recreational activities.

★ Lyon County Museum

An unexpected treasure, the **Lyon County Museum** (215 S. Main St., 775/463-6576, www.lyoncountymuseum.com, 1pm-4pm Thurs.-Sun. and by appointment, donation) documents the 150 years of settlement in the Smith and Carson Valleys. The museum comprises seven buildings, providing an overall look at valley life. The buildings include three schools, a blacksmith shop, general store, barber shop, and gas station. Some of the best displays are life-size dioramas— a parlor, a pharmacy, a court clerk's office, a dress shop, a ranch house kitchen, and a bunkhouse. Notable local residents such as the Ghost Dance prophet Wovoka; Nevada's first female doctor, Mary Fulstone; and Harry Warren, who won $1,500 from local residents by carrying a 120-pound grain sack 10 miles from Wabuska to Yerington, are honored here as well. A rotating gallery features local artists' work.

Food

Gen-u-wine home cooking awaits at **Country Sunflower** (1 Willhoyt Ln., 775/463-2054, 7am-2pm Mon.-Fri., $8-15). Locals line up before opening to get another serving of perfectly prepared bacon and eggs and biscuits as light and fluffy as throw pillows. Lunch may be even better, especially the chili, potato salad, and flaky pies. If you're in the mood for burgers, try **King's Diner** (20 W. Bridge St., 775/463-7778, 11am-8pm Mon.-Sat., $10-20). Don't forget the freshly made fries or onion rings, and top it all off with a berry milkshake. Steak dinners of every size, shape, cut, and style come off the open-flame grill at **Sherry's Stage Stop** (11 US 95A N., 775/463-3707, www.thinksherrys.com, $15-25), along with select chicken and seafood dishes. The rustic wagon wheel motif lets you know you're in the middle of cowboy country.

It's difficult for small-town joints to make a mark with Chinese food; it's either pretty good or awful. **China Chef** (415 N. Main St., 775/463-7112, 11am-9pm Mon.-Sat., $8-12) is pretty good. Nice touches include hot tea with all entrées and a selection of Chinese beer.

The Mexican choices are three times as

extensive. The happy *camarón* on the menu cover hints at the Pacific-style delights at **El Cortesz** (516 W. Goldfield Ave., 775/463-3823, www.elcortesz.com, 9am-9pm daily, $7-10). Reminiscent of a Jalisco cantina, El Cortesz's shrimp dishes—bacon-wrapped, cocktail, and an innovative ceviche—are spiced just right. The fountains, tile, and artwork give **El Superior** (215 Bridge St., 775/463-2593, $8-12) a breezy Mexican plaza feel, though it's located in a shopping plaza next to a hardware store. Fresh guacamole and salsa set the stage for typical authentic dishes. The decor isn't as interesting at **El Ateno** (615 S. Main St., 775/469-9569, $10-20), but the food is just as tasty.

There are no surprises on the menu, but the service, breakfast options, and dinner fare in the coffee shop at **Dini's Lucky Club** (45 N. Main St., 775/463-2868, www.dinisluckyclub. com, $7-10) do not disappoint. Choose from classic sandwiches, egg dishes, and more. It's inside a big slot palace. Sit at the counter and soak up the local flavor. Or come for the buffet (5pm-9pm Mon., Wed., Sat., $10.50). **Tailgaters** sports bar (517 W. Bridge St., 775/461-6027, 11am-9pm Mon.-Thurs., 11am-10pm Fri.-Sat., 11am-7pm Sun., $7-12) serves burgers and salads. But it's best for ordering a draft and noshing on bar appetizers. Save room for deep-fried peaches!

Accommodations

Motels in Yerington are marked by friendly desk staffs and lovingly maintained facilities. Ultramodern they are not, but clean, comfortable rooms are the order of the day, and they all allow pets. Formerly the Victorian Rose Inn, the bright yellow **Main Street Inn** (111 S. Main St., 775/463-2164, www.themainstreet-inn.com, $55-65) across from the courthouse offers a free continental breakfast, access to a barbecue grill, and pet-friendly rooms. A fruit-and-granola bar mini-basket greets guests. Furnishings and decor are vintage, if not classic—wood paneling, bulky TVs and easy chairs. But the technology—cable TV, wireless Internet, microwave, and refrigerator—is up to date.

Copper Inn (307 N. Main St., 775/463-2135, $60-70) is similar, though not quite as nice. Close to the casinos, **Yerington Inn** (4 N. Main St., 775/463-3144, http://yeringtoninn.com, $90-100) has more modern TVs (flat-screen LCDs), but the in-room Wi-Fi is a bit spotty. There's better coverage in the common areas. The big parking lot accommodates RVs and semi-trailers.

The Loneliest Road

Look for ★ to find recommended
sights, activities, dining, and lodging.

Highlights

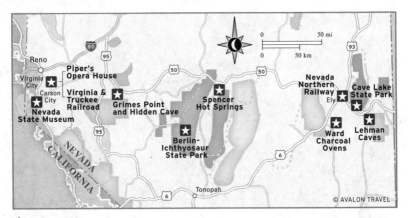

★ **Nevada State Museum:** The collection of gold and silver will have fortune hunters drooling, while exhibits on the state's frontier days offer insight into local history, geology, and fauna (page 213).

★ **Piper's Opera House:** Harry Houdini, John Philip Sousa, Lillie Langtry, and other superstars of the boomtown era played this well-preserved 1880-vintage theater (page 236).

★ **Virginia & Truckee Railroad:** The iron horse transports riders through tunnels, over bridges, and back 130 years to one of the most dynamic times in Nevada history (page 238).

★ **Grimes Point and Hidden Cave:** Petroglyphs, pictographs, and artifacts in two distinct styles shed light on the culture of Nevada's original residents (page 244).

★ **Berlin-Ichthyosaur State Park:** See the fossilized skeletons and a life-size 50-foot sculpture of prehistoric ichthyosaurs, not far from the ghost town of Berlin, which offers a glimpse into Nevada's much more recent past (page 252).

★ **Spencer Hot Springs:** The rough road

to get here will be worth it when you submerge your aching back and jarred bones into the slate-tiled pool commanding a view of the distant Toiyabe Mountains (page 253).

★ **Nevada Northern Railway:** Climb aboard Old No. 40 or one of the other powerful steam and diesel engines for a nostalgic ride through ghost towns, abandoned copper mine remains, and mountain ridges (page 257).

★ **Cave Lake State Park:** Tucked into the Schell Creek Range at 7,300 feet, wintergreen Cave Lake is the perfect subject for nature photography and an idyllic backdrop for picnicking, hiking, ice skating, and cross-country skiing (page 259).

★ **Ward Charcoal Ovens:** Well-built by true craftspeople, the kilns have survived decades of fire, wind, and rain. Nearby Willow Creek is full of rainbow and brook trout (page 260).

★ **Lehman Caves:** With stalagmites, stalactites, and all the other cool formations we think of when someone says "cave," the centerpiece of Great Basin National Park has attracted visitors since it was discovered in 1885 (page 266).

Winding its way through central Nevada, US 50 is known by several names: the Lincoln Highway, the Great Basin Highway, and perhaps most famously, the Loneliest Road in America.

This last nickname originated in a derogatory 1986 *Life* magazine article. "It's totally empty. There are no points of interest. We don't recommend it," the article quoted an AAA counselor. "We warn all motorists not to drive there unless they're confident of their survival skills."

It's true that the 400-mile blacktop strip between Carson City and Great Basin National Park was—and is—a bit desolate in stretches, but it's not the Sahara on camelback. Nevadans are nothing if not resourceful. The state quickly seized upon the article's dystopic tone, conjuring a tongue-in-cheek marketing campaign that is still going strong over 30 years later. The name breathes life into a route where plenty of historical, recreational, and cultural attractions break up the desolate landscape. Far from being apologetic about it, Nevada celebrates US 50's solitude, challenging adventuresome drivers to get off the beaten interstate and rejoice in the loneliness.

While Nevada's major tourist areas lure visitors with multimedia sensory onslaughts, US 50 engages the mind and imagination with simple pleasures. The anticipation as a trout rises from the shadows to take your fly on the Carson River. The cultural significance of a bluegrass performance at a local saloon. The surge of patriotism as Fallon's Navy aviators put their F-18s through their paces. The wonder of bristlecone pines, some of the oldest organisms on the planet, in Great Basin National Park. A spiritual awakening while watching meteors rain down from Jack C. Davis Observatory in Carson City.

Celebrate loneliness and congratulate yourself for your fortitude in tempting fate and braving this godforsaken road.

PLANNING YOUR TIME

Long stretches of little scenery and even fewer diversions punctuate this underused and underappreciated roadway. But that only helps

Previous: Ward Charcoal Ovens; Great Basin National Park. Above: Lehman Caves.

The Loneliest Road

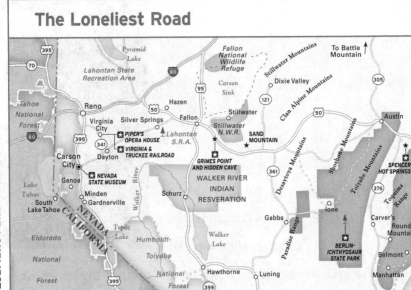

emphasize the delightful towns along the route, thoughtfully spaced about an hour apart. Carson City in the west and Great Basin National Park in the east make natural bookends for a drive across the state on US 50. You could cover the entire route in less than a day, but plan on a leisurely week to enjoy recreational activities, explore Old West sites, and bed down in quaint hotels along the way.

The Loneliest Road is best traveled in spring. The road's high mountain passes are hazardous in winter, and summer temperatures can get very hot. Turn off your cell phone (you probably won't get a signal in many of the valleys along the way, anyway), slow your roll, and engage the locals. You might learn a thing or two. You'll definitely gain a new perspective. You might be alone, but you'll be anything but lonely.

Carson City and Vicinity

TOP EXPERIENCE

Las Vegas and Reno are Nevada's financial and entertainment centers. The state's geographic center lies about 30 miles southeast of Austin, and the claim of historic center rightly belongs to Virginia City. But Carson City is the power center, where the state looks for vision, leadership, and order.

It is easy to see why *USA Today* readers voted Carson City the most travel-worthy of the country's state capitals. Carson City successfully combines a range of freewheelin' outdoor and fitness activity with rich dining and entertainment attractions. A level of quiet sophistication is embodied in rustic-elegant shops and more than a dozen art galleries.

An easy day trip from Reno or Lake Tahoe, Carson City also can serve as launching point for those intrepid souls willing to risk life and limb on the Loneliest Road. Fine restaurants will fortify adventurers, while

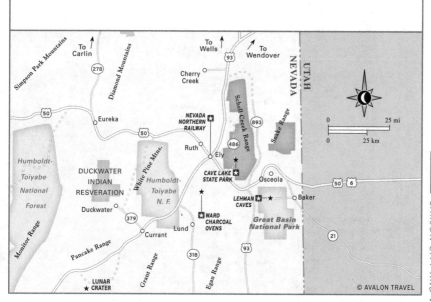

© AVALON TRAVEL

accommodations of all stripes ensure a good night's rest before setting out.

SIGHTS
★ Nevada State Museum

Nevada's premier museum, the **Nevada State Museum** (600 N. Carson St., 775/687-4810, http://nvculture.org/museums, 8:30am-4:30pm Tues.-Sun., $8 adults, age 17 and under free) is inside the famous Carson City Mint, which during its operation (1870-1893) coined 57 different silver issues, all with the very collectible "CC" mint mark. After the mint closed, the stone building, erected by town father Uncle Abe Curry, served as a federal office building until 1933, when it was abandoned. Judge Clark J. Guild mobilized a local coalition to repair the building as the site of the museum, which opened to the public in 1941.

After paying admission, head into the mint exhibit, which illustrates the entire coining process, from depositors' bullion through ingot melting to production on the likes of the huge Coin Press No. 1, on display. You can see a sample of every coin minted here—including a complete set of CC Morgan Dollars.

Nevada's Changing Earth Exhibit walks visitors through a Nevada timeline beginning millions of years ago with the climate and the geology shifting. This region of Nevada was once the Columbian mammoth's home turf, and the biggest one in the country is on display here, along with the skeleton of another old-time Nevadan, an ichthyosaur. The **Environmental Gallery** celebrates Nevada's native and endemic plants and animals. The realistic **underground mine recreation** uses reclaimed timbers, vents, and ores from once-active mines around the state, imparting a lifelike sense of working in tunnels underground.

Nevada State Railroad Museum

The success of the Virginia & Truckee Railroad in connecting Reno, Carson City, Virginia City, and Minden was partly responsible for extending the life of the Comstock Lode. Once the line connected with intercontinental service, an opulent passenger trade began as well. This history is the focus of the collection at the **Nevada State Railroad**

Carson City

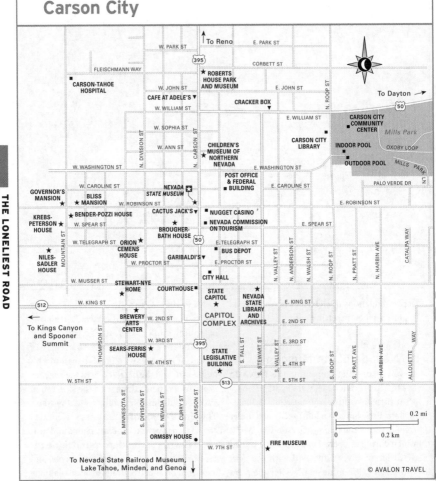

Museum (2180 S. Carson St., 775/687-6953, http://nvculture.org/museums, 10am-4pm Sat.-Sun., $8, age 4-11 $4, age 3 and under free). Of 65 painstakingly restored locomotives and cars in the collection, 40 were built before 1900, and 31 are pieces that operated on the V&T. In addition, some 15 astonishingly realistic model railroad layouts show the workings and hardships of rail trade, from both the steam and diesel eras. Some include replicas of actual pieces in the museum, allowing visitors to compare details and put the machinery into historical context. Visitors also can ride the trains and handcars.

Though not affiliated with the museum, the **V&T Railroad** (4650 Eastgate Siding Rd., 775/291-0208, www.vtrailway.com, Fri.-Sun. June-Oct., $48-54, discounts for children, seniors, and veterans) operates round-trip steam rail trips to Virginia City and through Carson River Canyon. Special trips include dinner and a melodrama, Mother's Day and Father's Day activities, wine tastings, and The Polar Express.

Nevada State Capitol

The **Nevada State Capitol** (101 N. Carson St., 775/687-4810, 8am-5pm Mon.-Fri., free) is just south of the state library between West Musser Street and West 2nd Street. Constructed of native sandstone in 1870, when it was one of only a few structures in the city, it's the second-oldest state capitol building west of the Mississippi. A fine museum on the south side of the second floor, in the old senate chambers, displays a collection of historical Nevada artifacts: William Stewart's Wooten Patent Cabinet desk, an 1862 map of the Nevada Territory, the 36-star flag, the silver trowel from the capitol's cornerstone ceremony, and the goblets used by Abe Curry and James Nye to toast statehood.

Brewery Arts Center

Brewery Arts Center (449 W. King St., 775/883-1976, http://breweryarts.org, 10am-4pm Tues.-Fri., free) sponsors more than 100 classes and workshops in visual and performing arts, art exhibits, crafts fairs, concerts, plays, storytellers, and other cultural programs throughout the year. Stop in and check the schedule; you're sure to find something that appeals to your tastes. The center is housed in a building constructed in 1865 for the Carson Brewery. For 80 years the formidable two-story brick structure produced several brands of beers, lagers, and ales, most notably Tahoe Beer. Two gallery shops showcase and sell local artists' works in paint, photography, jewelry, pottery, woodcuts, metal, and more.

Children's Museum of Northern Nevada

It took six years of fund-raising to collect $400,000 and another year of renovating to unveil the **Children's Museum of Northern Nevada** (813 N. Carson St., 775/884-2226, www.cmnn.org, 10am-4:30pm Tues.-Sun., $5 adults, $4 over age 54, $3 age 2-14). The museum is one block north of the Nevada State Museum on the opposite side of the street. There are 25 exhibits in fine arts, humanities, and science aimed at the 6-13 age group, but the hands-on, play-based learning is fun for the whole family.

Fire Museum

Chronicling the service of Warren Engine Company No. 1, the **Fire Museum** (777 S. Stewart St., 775/887-2210, www.carsoncity-firemuseum.com, 9am-5pm Mon.-Fri., donation) is housed in the city's main fire station. Warren Engine Company No. 1 began as a

Nevada State Museum

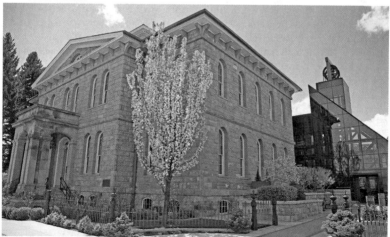

The Crookedest Railroad in the World

Bank of California owner William Ralston and his agent, William Sharon, had very nearly cornered the silver production and processing market in Virginia City by 1861. And like true entrepreneurs, they were looking to expand their holdings and vertically integrate their supply chain. Recognizing an opportunity in the nearby approach of the Central Pacific Railroad, the barons schemed to build a rail connection from Virginia City to the transcontinental line. Freight costs to and from the mines and settlements could be reduced, mining interests would beat a path to their door, and profits would soar.

Sharon started making money even before he laid a foot of track. Business owners paid him $500,000 to divert from his original plan to run the spur directly to Reno and instead choose a path through Carson City and up the Washoe Valley. The first Virginia & Truckee Railroad train arrived in Gold Hill from Carson City in December 1869. Passenger service to and from Virginia City started the next month. Winding its way from Virginia City through six tunnels, the V&T twisted its way a half mile south to Gold Hill across the vertigo-inducing Crown Point trestle and slithered through narrow canyons and steep grades to American Flat. From there, it dropped into Moundhouse and through Brunswick Canyon to Carson City. "The Crookedest Railroad in the World" was not a mere slogan. There were so many turns that the 16-mile trip required 21 miles of track.

The railroad purchased rolling stock and five engines and completed the line from Virginia City to Lakes Crossing in 1873, just as it appeared the Comstock Lode was exhausted. But the "Big Bonanza" was a windfall not only for the mine owners but for the V&T as well. Renewed activity on the Comstock Lode meant plenty of business for the railroad. Soon it had more than tripled the number of locomotives and rail cars and was making an incredible 40 runs a day, shipping ore out and supplies and timber in. At its peak in 1874, the railroad's income was $400,000 per month ($10 million in today's dollars).

volunteer firefighting fraternity in 1863 and has served Carson City uninterrupted ever since, making it the oldest volunteer company in the West; mostly professional firefighters now make up its ranks. That first year, 20 charter members of the company raised $2,000 at a firemen's ball to buy the first firefighting equipment in town: a Hunneman Engine built in the early 1800s and used by the Warren Engine Company of Boston. Later it was shipped around the Horn and worked in San Francisco and Marysville, California, before arriving in Carson City, where the company named itself for the Warren Company of Boston. In 1913, on its 50th anniversary, the company bought a Seagrave fire engine, Nevada's first motorized fire truck. Check out the Seagrave, the wild old goggles, masks, helmets, and caps, the 1870s two-wheeled hose cart, and the familiar Currier & Ives original prints of New York conflagrations.

Historical Houses

The **Roberts House Park and Museum** (1207 N. Carson St., 775/887-2714, 1pm-3pm Fri.-Sun. Apr.-Oct., donation) is Carson City's oldest house, but the Gothic Revival with its gingerbread bargeboard, lancet windows, and steeply pitched roof was not originally built here. It is believed that it was a kit house shipped from New England to San Francisco and then transported by rail and wagon to Washoe City, where it was assembled around 1859. In 1875 the house, home of James Doane Roberts and family, was moved to Carson City. Today it has been restored and contains period furniture. The park area is a pleasant spot for a picnic, with tables, grass, and mature shade trees.

The **Kit Carson Trail** leads modern-day explorers on a walking path through Carson City's historical homes district. A painted blue line and bronze medallions along the sidewalk mark the trail of Victorian-style homes, museums, and churches. Pick up the trail map at the visitors center (716 N. Carson St., 775/687-7410 or 800/638-2321). The flyer is beautifully illustrated, and the accompanying podcast (download the VisitCarsonCity app) is quite informative. The tour itself is long, with 60 stops, so you might want to rely more on the map for navigation, skipping some sites to focus on those that interest you.

Some residential highlights include the **Bliss Mansion** (608 Elizabeth St.), a two-story house built in 1879 by Duane L. Bliss, who made his fortune with the Lake Tahoe Narrow Gauge Railroad, transporting timber from Lake Tahoe to Virginia City's mines. The 1860 **Stewart-Nye home** (108 N. Minnesota St.) was built for Senator William Stewart and later sold to territorial governor James Nye. It's the oldest extant building originally constructed in Carson City. The **Governor's Mansion** (600 N. Mountain St.) has classic Southern Colonial columns and a curvilinear porch; it was completed in 1907 and completely rebuilt in 2000 with private donations.

History buffs can design their own mini tour, perhaps soaking up the creative atmosphere at the **Orion Clemens House** (502 N. Division St.). Mark Twain almost certainly slept in the two-story house that his brother built in 1863 while serving as secretary to territorial governor Nye. See the sandstone **home of city father Abe Curry** (406 N. Nevada St.), built in 1871 using materials from the state prison's quarry, formerly owned by Curry.

Other Comstock-era homes include the **Niles-Sadler House** (310 N. Mountain St.), constructed in 1878 by the Virginia & Truckee Railroad paymaster and ticket agent. It later housed Governor Reinhold Sadler, as Nevada didn't complete its governor's mansion until 1907. The plantation-style **Bender-Pozzi House** (707 W. Robinson St.) has a deep porch overlooking mature trees and an expansive lawn. It was owned by Comstock lawyer George Nourse and later by David Bender, another V&T official. The **Sears-Ferris House** (311 W. 3rd St.) was the boyhood home of George W. G. Ferris Jr., inventor of the Ferris wheel, which debuted at the Chicago World Columbian Exposition of 1893.

Homes of later Victorian vintage are represented in Carson City as well. The **Brougher-Bath House** (204 W. Spear St.) was completed at the turn of the 20th century after its owner—a state senator—struck it rich in the Tonopah boom. Notice the two-story circular porch, stained-glass windows, and circular turret. Fans of John Wayne's last movie, *The Shootist*, might recognize the **Krebs-Peterson House** (500 N. Mountain St.), built in 1914 by a surgeon and shown in the film.

Stewart Indian Boarding School

In 1890, 30 years after the complete dislocation of Nevada's Native American population, the **Stewart Indian Boarding School** (5500 Snyder Ave., 775/687-8333, http://stewartindianschool.com) opened on a 240-acre campus with three teachers and 37 students from local Washoe, Shoshone, and Paiute groups. The first students consisted of orphans, sons and daughters of tribe leaders, and children who were forcibly removed from their parents. At that time, federal policy was forced assimilation of Native Americans, carried out with military rigidity. Observing traditional customs was actively discouraged. Over the years, a more enlightened policy evolved, and the school relied less on indoctrination and more on achievement. By the time the school closed in 1980, nearly 3,000 students had completed the program. Visitors can still see the distinctive stone buildings, currently used as state offices, by following the **Stewart Indian School Trail,** a self-guided walking tour. Using your cell phone, you can hear recorded messages from school alumni and employees. In June, the annual **Stewart Father's Day Powwow** recognizes alumni and also presents traditional dancing, arts, and crafts.

Carson Hot Springs

"Gentleman Jim" Corbett trained at Shaw's

Carson City's Faded Grande Dame

As it has for nearly two decades, the **Ormsby House** (600 S. Carson St.) stands unoccupied but not neglected. It maintains a quiet dignity as its owners continue exterior upgrades while looking for a buyer. Ormsby's history, location, and still-valid unrestricted gaming license are attractive selling points for anyone game enough to return it to its former glory. The various incarnations of Ormsby House date back to 1859, when it was opened by Major William Ormsby, who was killed in the Pyramid Lake skirmish with Numaga's Paiute in 1860. Sold and expanded, by the 1870s it was regarded as one of the fanciest hotels between Denver and San Francisco. In 1880 the name was changed to the Park Hotel, and it operated into the 1920s. It was reopened in 1931 after the legalization of casino gambling by the Laxalts, possibly Nevada's most famous family. Paul Laxalt was governor of Nevada, a U.S. senator, and a close friend of Ronald Reagan, and he built the existing hotel in 1972. It was subsequently sold, expanded, went bankrupt, and was resurrected again in the 1990s, but it closed, perhaps for the final time, in 2000. Perhaps a motivated owner with deep pockets can achieve another resurrection.

Warm Springs, predecessor to **Carson Hot Springs** (1500 Old Hot Springs Rd., 775/885-8844 or 888/917-3711, www.carsonhotspringsresort.com, 7am-10pm daily, $10-15), while preparing for his prize fight with Robert Fitzsimmons in 1897. Abe Curry built his Warm Springs Hotel next to these waters and ferried the territorial legislators out here when they met at the hotel in the town's early days. Today, there's a pool ($12, seniors and children $10) with 96-98°F soft spring water containing no sulfur odor or chlorine; no city water is added, only the geothermically heated water from far belowground. The water emerges at about 127°F but is cooled by the air before guests take the plunge. Let **The Hammer**, a pounding waterfall, drive the aches and pains away. Sodium-rich waters increase buoyancy, while silica, potassium, and sulfates lend luster to nails, hair, and skin. The resort drains the pool every night and fills it up again every morning. Private in-room 95-110°F pools ($20 for two hours, seniors $15) are also available (bathing suits are optional in private rooms).

Jack C. Davis Observatory

Zoom in on other worlds with the array of telescopes at the **Jack C. Davis Observatory** (2699 Van Patten Dr., 775/445-3311, www.wnc.edu/observatory, 7:30am-11pm, free) on the campus of Western Nevada College.

The research-quality equipment, including 16-inch, 14-inch, and 10-inch scopes, can collect data from the stars, observe solar prominences, and project images onto television screens for group viewing. The public is invited to "star parties" (sunset-11pm Sat. and during solar and lunar eclipses and meter showers) for stargazing, observatory tours, and lectures on historical leaders and pop culture in addition to space and science topics.

Bowers Mansion

Live the life of the silver barons with a visit to **Bowers Mansion** (4005 Bowers Mansion Rd., 775/849-1825, 11am-4pm Sat.-Sun. mid-May-Oct., $8, age 6-17 and 62 and over $5, under age 6 free), 12 miles north of Carson City. Just like Victorian guests over a century ago, visitors to this opulent homestead can picnic, swim, and tour Sandy and Eilley Bowers's testament to the Comstock boom. Tour leaders will point out the Georgian and Italianate architecture and marble fireplaces, but the period furniture was donated by local families when the mansion was restored. The mansion is the centerpiece of **Bowers Mansion Regional Park,** available for day-use year-round, with playgrounds, picnic tables, grills, and horseshoe pits. The swimming pool and children's wading pool (noon-5pm daily, $5, age 3-17 and 62 and over $4) are fed by natural warm springs. Spectators crowd the grounds every August for the **Bowers Mansion Bluegrass Festival** ($25).

Nevada State Prison

Tours of **Nevada State Prison** (3301 E. 5th St., 775/684-3000, http://nevadastateprison. org/tours, $10 or $25 per family) take visitors inside the world's first gas chamber. Displays include cell blocks, the license plate-making room, and "The Hole," known as the most brutal solitary-confinement cell in the country. The execution chamber features rubber-sealed doors and vents used to collect cyanide gas after the deed was done. Thirty-two men met their fate in the gas chamber, the first in 1924 and the last in 1979. Eleven others died via lethal injection, the last in 2006. The prison was decommissioned in 2012 after 150 years of service. At press time, tours of the old prison were on hold. Check the website for the latest information.

RECREATION
Washoe Lake State Park

A respite from the summer heat awaits six miles north of Carson City via I-580 and Eastlake Boulevard. Visitors shed 10 degrees as their car climbs into the foothills to

Washoe Lake State Park (4855 Eastlake Blvd., 775/687-4319, http://parks.nv.gov, $7). Nonmotorized trails lead out and up into the Sierra and Carson Ranges. The Virginia Range, to the east, has motorized and non-motorized trails. Both Washoe and Little Washoe Lakes are home to catfish, white bass, perch, and wipers. Shore anglers find success all around Little Washoe Lake, as well as the North Ramp and South Beach on Washoe Lake. Motorized boating is allowed only on Washoe. Hunting is shotgun-only, and only in designated areas. There are extensive day-use facilities throughout the park, with picnic tables, sandy beaches, and grassy areas with plenty of shade.

The **Main Area Campground** ($17) can accommodate tents and RVs up to 45 feet on a first-come, first-served basis. There are no hookups, but facilities include a dump station, showers, and restrooms. With 49 tent sites and no hookups, it's not for the pampered camper, especially in winter, when nighttime temperatures routinely dip below 20°F. But what it lacks in creature comforts, the park makes up for in natural amenities: Hike the **Mount Rose Trail**, explore **Deadman's Canyon Dam**, or shoot the **Truckee River rapids**; they're all nearby. A little farther north and on

Bowers Mansion

the other side of Washoe Lake, **Davis Creek Campground** (25 Davis Creek Rd., 775/849-0684, $20) has 43 tent spaces and 19 dedicated RV spots, most with breathtaking views of the lake. There are also fine hiking trails, including **Ophir Creek Trail,** which leads past a waterfall and steep canyons on a 12-mile round-trip. **Davis Creek Park Pond** teems with stocked 10-inch rainbows. The campground is not tranquil; traffic noise tells visitors that US 395 is just beyond the tree line.

Hang Gliding

Hang Gliding Tahoe (2640 E. College Pkwy., 775/772-8232, http://hangglidingtahoe.com, 7:30am-5pm daily, $250-510) puts gliders literally on top of the action with motorized wings (and FAA-certified instructors). Lucky fliers cruise over the treetops, skim the water, race along with wild horses, and soar over the Sierras at 10,000 feet during the one-to three-hour flights. Two friends or family members can pilot their own separate aircraft, each accompanied by an instructor, while communicating with each other via radio. Buy a video or still photos to commemorate your flight.

Parks and Trails

Mills Park (1111 E. William St.), four blocks east of US 395 on US 50, is an excellent city facility with lots of recreation choices: expanses and shade trees for stretching out and napping, picnic tables, barbecue grills, and a tot lot. But it also offers basketball, volleyball, and tennis courts, horseshoe pits, a big skate park, indoor and outdoor pools, and a fitness facility next door at the **community center** (775/887-2242, $4 adults, age 4-17 and over 54 $3). Perhaps the biggest draw is the **Carson and Mills Park Railroad** (775/887-2523, www.carsoncityrailroadassociation.org, noon-6pm Sat., noon-5pm Sun., $2, under age 3 free), a one-mile, 15-minute ride in two-foot-gauge toy gondolas or covered passenger cars behind a diesel switcher.

Carson River Park (5013 Carson River Rd., 775/887-2115, 8am-dusk daily) is on both

Nevada State Prison in Carson City

sides of the Carson River about four miles out of town. Heading south on US 395 from US 50, turn left (east) on East 5th Street and drive through the middle of the grounds of the state maximum-security prison. Just the sight of the pen, roasting in the desert within high barbed-wire cyclone fencing and with gun towers at the corners, will make you appreciate the wide-open spaces and refreshing breezes that await you at the riverside park. Cross Edmonds Drive, take a right on Carson River Road, and head across the green valley down to the lazy river. Cross the little bridge and explore the network of dirt roads. Turn right (south) onto Mexican Dam Road, and in about 1.5 miles you'll come to Mexican Dam. You can't go onto the dam itself—it's private property—but there's a fine one-mile path called the **Mexican Dam Ditch Trail.** Kayakers, canoeists, and rafters can put in here for a tranquil 3.3-mile Class I and II float down the river to the new **Morgan Mill Road River Access Area,** where a concrete boat ramp provides a safe takeout point. The same ramp marks a put-in point for Class II and Class III white-water rapids through the Carson River Canyon, 9.3 miles to the Santa Maria Ranch in Lyon County. This section of river is not for beginners. Stocked 10-inch trout patrol the ramp in summer, challenging anglers. Here you can also pick up **Empire Ranch Trail,** a two-mile walk to **Riverview Park** (600 Marsh Rd., 775/887-2115), a lovely riverside park with a wetland area, exercise stops along a trail, and people walking their dogs. A Korean War veterans' memorial is next door. Reach the park by car by continuing straight on East 5th Street rather than turning onto Carson River Road toward Mexican Dam.

On the way to the river, you'll pass **Silver Saddle Ranch Park** (4901 Carson River Rd., 775/885-6000, 8am-5pm daily). The park is on the south side of Carson River Road, 0.25 mile north of Mexican Dam between the river and Prison Hill; another section of the ranch is on the east side of the river. The intention for this park is that it remains natural and undeveloped. You can walk down to the river on the old farm roads and enjoy the quiet open space.

Centennial Park (775/887-2115) is one of the largest municipal recreation facilities in Nevada. It's off US 50 east of town to the south along Centennial Drive. It boasts several softball and soccer fields, many pleasant and shady picnic sites, tennis courts, and even an archery range. This is the place for a long walk after a soak at Carson Hot Springs and a meal at Garibaldi's and before hunkering down for some craps at Max Casino.

Golf

The **Sunridge Golf Club** (1000 Long Dr., 775/267-4448, www.sunridgegc.com, $30-50), five miles south of Carson City at the north end of the Carson Valley, intersperses beautiful meadow holes, lots of water holes, elevated trees, and uncannily breaking hillside greens that will cause seasoned golfers to question their abilities and duffers to consider trading their clubs for a tennis racket. Three 9-hole courses at **Empire Ranch Golf**

Course (1875 Fair Way, 775/885-2100, www.empireranchgolf.com, $25-43) create three 18-hole combinations. The course is fairly flat and manageable, but fairways and greens are surrounded by wetlands, so it is important to keep it in the short grass. All that water attracts mosquitoes, so bring repellent.

CASINOS
Carson Nugget

Restaurants: Angelina's, The Eatery, Alatte Coffee, Wine & Deli

Entertainment: Friday Night Comedy Club

Nightlife: Cork and Bottle, Sports Bar

Interactive slot machines are all the rage in Nevada—surround sound, shell games, and other gimmicks attract players—and the **Carson Nugget** (507 N. Carson St., 775/882-1626, www.ccnugget.com) has them in spades. Most of the casino's 550 machines feature ticket in/ticket out technology. Low-limit blackjack, 5x odds on craps, live poker, and more guarantee you'll be a winner (not really). With no end in sight to the years-long "renovation" of the Ormsby House, the Nugget is the main action downtown for gaming and nightlife. This is one of four Nuggets opened in northern Nevada in the mid-1950s. This one also has a steakhouse, a café, a coffee bar, and a snack bar. All Nevada casino cafés are basically required to serve a decent prime rib, but few are better than the 12-ouncer served in **The Eatery** (6am-10pm daily, $10-20). **Angelina's** (4pm-10pm Thurs.-Sun., $10-20) is typical Italian at a reasonable price. Standard rooms at the **Carson Tahoe Hotel** up the street (800 N. Carson St., 775/882-5535, or 800/338-7760, $70-80) measure 300 square feet and come with a refrigerator and microwave if you ask. A shuttle runs regularly between the hotel and the Nugget. Ask about room, gaming, and golf packages.

Max Casino

Restaurants: Black Bear Diner, Max'd Out Coffee

Entertainment: Cabaret Lounge

Nightlife: sports bar, casino bars

Newly renovated and renamed, the former

Carson Station (and before that the Mother Lode) is now **Max Casino** (900 S. Carson St., 775/883-0900, http://maxcasinocc.com). The 12,500-square-foot gaming floor contains 200 slot machines in a variety of styles and denominations and a few blackjack and craps tables. There's also keno and a William Hill sports book. It's probably the top gambling place in town. The much-awaited **Black Bear Diner** (6am-10pm Sun.-Thurs., 6am-midnight Fri.-Sat., $15-25)—a staple of good old home cooking in the West—brings in families for hearty breakfasts, burgers, and biscuits, steak, mashed potatoes, meatloaf, and anything else that can be smothered in gravy. **Wyndham Garden** ($85-110) handles the casino's hotel portion, which as of this writing had not yet received the same renovation as the casino. The rooms, in soft mauves and robin's egg blue, are usually clean and the beds comfortable, but your mileage may vary.

Casino Fandango

Restaurants: Duke's Steak House, Ti Amo Italian Grille, Shinsen Sushi, Rum Jungle Buffet, Palm Court Grill

Entertainment: Cabaret Lounge, Galaxy Theatre

Nightlife: casino bars

More than three times as large as Max, **Casino Fandango** (3800 S. Carson St., 775/885-7000, www.casinofandango.com) jams its 40,000-square-foot gaming floor with 700 slots and 10 blackjack (player-friendly single-deck and double-deck), craps, roulette, pai gow, and three-card poker tables. William Hill runs the race and sports book. Fancy enough for date night but reasonably priced enough for family night, ★ **Ti Amo** (5pm-9pm Thurs.-Tues., $20-30) offers a strong wine list and varied, creative menu. The seafood dishes—lobster ravioli, prawn appetizers, calamari, and seafood lasagna—rule. They even have fresh sushi! Fandango also boasts Carson's best buffet. **Rum Jungle** (lunch/brunch 11am-2pm Wed.-Fri., $12; 9am-2pm Sat.-Sun., $16; dinner 4:30pm-9:30pm daily, $12-20) is nothing special by Vegas or even Reno standards, but it's filling, varied, and

fairly priced. Fridays and Saturdays are crab leg nights. **Courtyard by Marriott** (3870 S. Carson St., 775/887-9900, $125-150) is next door. The hotel's **Bistro** (6am-10am and 4pm-10pm daily, $15-25) will get you going with specialty Starbucks drinks in the morning and help you wind down with more "spiritual" beverages after dinner.

Bodines

Restaurants: Bodines Restaurant

Nightlife: Round Bar, Sports Bar

If serious gamblers prefer Fandango for its single-deck blackjack, casual players and partiers prefer **Bodines** (5650 S. Carson St., 775/885-7777, www.bodinescarson.com) for the wide selection among its 290 slot and video poker machines, cheap eats, and suave Round Bar. The sports book features row after row of high-definition, 50-inch plasmas to capture all the action. The book includes pari-mutuel bets from racetracks around the country. **Bodines Restaurant**'s (7am-10pm, $10-15) $4 breakfast and $6 lunch platter specials are quite good, and you can't beat the price.

Gold Dust West

Restaurants: Ole Ole, The Grille, Bowling Center Snack Bar

Attractions: Bowling Center, arcade, fitness center, seasonal pool and spa

The **Gold Dust West** (2171 US 50 E., 775/885-9000 or 877/519-5567, www.gdw-casino.com, $90-110) has a 32-lane bowling alley in addition to 400 slot machines and a Cal-Neva sports book outlet. You could even hit the jackpot on the Mega Bucks or dollar Wheel of Fortune machines! Play your favorite table games, including blackjack, craps, roulette, and even three-card poker. Its 142 guest rooms are a good size; amenities include a swimming pool, a fitness center, and a spa. The office center and fitness room are open all night.

The menu at Gold Dust West's top restaurant, **The Grille** (775/885-9000, 24 hours daily, $7-12), features some intriguing gourmet-like touches at budget prices, such as the

Camels in Carson Valley

As might be expected in a state whose major historical landmarks include the Sands, the Dunes, the Desert Inn, and the Sahara, camels played a role in Nevada's development. Ships of the desert first came to Nevada in 1856, when the U.S. Army took up Lieutenant Edward F. Beale's offer to train dromedaries (one-humpers) to haul military supplies throughout the arid West. Camels, after all, are bigger and stronger than horses and mules, require little water, and are accustomed to the dry heat. Beale and roughly 30 camels crossed the Colorado River into present-day southern Nevada in 1857, but his experiment eventually failed, and the army sold the stock that survived.

The army's mistake, San Francisco mining interests posited, was that it put its trust in the wrong camel: Business owners in 1861 imported several dozen Bactrian camels (two-humpers) from China and sent the beasts across the Sierra to haul salt from southern Nevada to the mines and mills in Virginia City and Austin. According to reports, the camels handled the job of toting large loads fairly well, but they had trouble negotiating rock-strewn paths, and they scared the horses. By 1875 camel-induced stampedes had become such a problem that the Nevada legislature banished them from public highways. Drovers sold their animals to traveling circuses or abandoned them to their fate in the desert. As late as the 1960s, desert rats in Nevada, California, and Arizona reported spotting feral camels roaming the playa.

While camels were a small part of the working life of the Comstock Lode, they were never raced for sport. In fact, the first reported camel race in Virginia City came 100 years after the Comstock's heyday. And true to the spirit of Western journalism, that report, as Mark Twain might have said, was greatly exaggerated: In 1959, Bob Richards, a reporter for the revived *Territorial Enterprise* in Virginia City, "reported" on the town's camel races and invited other newspapers to take up the challenge. Whether duped by Richards's story or simply calling his bluff, representatives from the *San Francisco Chronicle* and the *Phoenix Sun* showed up in Virginia City, camels in tow. John Huston, in town to direct Clark Gable and Marilyn Monroe in *The Misfits*, took the reins for the *Chronicle* and galloped (er, plodded) to victory.

After a few years' hiatus, the races returned and have been a much-anticipated annual event in Virginia City, expanding to include zebra dashes and ostrich derbies in recent years.

chicken Provençal ($8, including a side dish) and the Cajun-spiced blackened salmon Caesar salad ($10).

FOOD

Carson City seems more like a diner-and-gossip town than a gastronomic destination. The elegant fine dining establishments and authentic ethnic restaurants seem somehow deliciously, appreciatively misplaced.

Fine Dining

The best Carson City has to offer, ★ Café at Adele's (1112 N. Carson St., 775/882-3353, www.adelesrestaurantandlounge.com, 8am-9pm Tues.-Sun., $25-40) is located in the 19th-century house of Nevada attorney general and Supreme Court justice M. A. Murphy. It is extremely elegant in all its Second Empire

appointments, and you can read about it on the huge and varied dinner menu—practically anything you want that's in season is available. The bar is in the living room and several tables are in the dining room, with Victorian-style carpet, Edwardian chairs and tables, stained-glass windows, and fine lamps. The steak and seafood are magical, and renowned chef Charlie Abowd certainly knows his way around a duck.

Basque

It's all about the meat at **Villa Basque Cafe** (730 Basque Way, 775/884-4451, http://villa-basquecafe.com, 6am-3pm Mon.-Sat., $10-15), a casual but authentic breakfast and lunch spot near downtown. Pete's paella comes crammed with ham, shrimp, clams, squid, chicken, and, oh, that chorizo! In fact, Villa's rendition of this spicy sausage is so revered that the little attached shop is open two hours later than the restaurant. Spicy three-egg chorizo omelets and chorizo-stuffed burritos will get your blood flowing. Just to be clear: The chorizo is good. You should order it.

Continental

With a menu that changes weekly, **Z Bistro** (725 Basque Way, Ste. 1, 775/885-2828, www.atzbistro.com, 5pm-9pm Wed.-Sat., $15-25) keeps the locals coming back for more fresh French cuisine. Much of the menu is gluten-free, and often the menu consists of small plates, allowing for ample browsing and sampling among friends. The wine selection is as good as you would expect from an authentic French bistro. A warm, inviting, and rustic alfresco setting adds to the experience.

Right in downtown Carson City, **Garibaldi's** (307 N. Carson St., 775/884-4574, 11:30am-10pm Mon.-Fri., 5pm-10pm Sat.-Sun., $15-25) oozes old-world Italian, right down to the red-checkered tablecloths and exposed red brick. We would swim the Po for the Italian seafood dishes—especially the swordfish and wonton shrimp. The lemon-rosemary sauce makes everything that much better—even the spumoni.

Brugo's Pizza (3228 N. Carson St., 775/887-7437, http://brugospizza.com, 4pm-9pm Mon.-Tues., 11am-9pm Wed.-Sat., noon-8pm Sun., $20-30) is the informal choice for thin-crust pie, salad, and beer.

South of the Border

There are only a few tables inside ★ **The Lady Tamales** (933 Woodside Dr., Ste. 102, 775/841-6533, 10am-7pm daily, $7-12), and the decor and location add nothing to the dining experience. So unless you opt for one of The Lady's combo plates, you will want to mix and match a dozen or two tamales and tacos (beef, chicken, pork, $1 each) to go. These are little packages of heaven wrapped in corn tortillas and tied up with a bow of fresh homemade salsa.

For some of the best Mexican food anywhere, pull up an appetite at **El Charro Avitia** (4389 S. Carson St., 775/883-6261, 11am-9pm Sun.-Thurs., 11am-10pm Fri.-Sat., $12-20). El Charro opened in Carson City in 1978, the second outlet of a restaurant founded by a family of hardworking Mexican immigrants. The seafood enchiladas, burritos, and gorditas are worth the drive from Tahoe or Reno. Try the *tacos nacionales* with chicken, cream cheese, and almonds. The tamales are stuffed with barbecued pork, and the mini fajitas are a steal, as are the three-item combos; the guacamole shrimp cocktail is exquisite.

What The Lady is to tamales, **La Santaneca** (316 E. Winnie Ln., 775/301-6678, 9am-9pm daily, $8-12) is to *papusas*. Served with rice and beans, these big Salvadoran pillows are served with several fillings—pork, zucchini, cheese, etc. If you're new to Salvadoran cuisine, or just want a bit of variety, order the *típico*. It comes with a *papusa*, a stuffed banana, and a pork and yucca tamale. Lose the tortillas, add eggs, and voilà—breakfast.

Asian

Rivaling Adele's for best overall restaurant in Carson City, **The Basil** (311 N. Carson St., 775/841-6100, http://thebasilrestaurant.com, 11am-9pm Mon.-Thurs., 11am-9:30pm Fri., 5pm-9pm Sat., $15-25) specializes in fresh and authentic Thai-style fish and fowl. Tell them how much heat you want included with the ginger and soy, and enjoy your dish amid silk, rattan, and Asian art.

Top-notch sushi in Carson City? Believe it, and get some for yourself at ★ **Ming's Chinese Restaurant** (2330 S. Carson St., 775/887-8878, http://carsonmings.com, 11:30am-9:30pm daily, $8-15). The $19 all-you-can-eat sushi lunch is a real bargain. Don't let **Bamboo Garden's** (4250 Cochise St., 775/885-6868, 11am-9pm Mon.-Fri., 11:30am-9pm Sat.-Sun., $15-25) strip mall location fool you. It's casual Mandarin and Szechuan served at fast food booths, but the soft lighting, artistic and architectural accents, and tasty sizzling duck and spicy shrimp add up to a fully satisfying meal.

Casual

If breakfast is indeed the most important meal of the day, it is imperative that you stop in at the **Cracker Box** (402 E. Williams St., 775/882-4556, http://thecrackerboxdiner.com, 6am-2pm daily). This is the real diner deal, with an eight-seat counter and tables for 50 crammed into a squat box of a building. The basic $9 breakfast has slabs—not slices—of bacon, a big mess of home fries with bits of pepper and onion, and two large eggs cooked exactly the way you order them; the orange juice is freshly squeezed. Locals fill the place for lunch as well; try the soup of the day.

The few who insist the Cracker Box isn't the best breakfast restaurant in town most likely cast their lot with **Heidi's** (1020 N. Carson St., 775/882-0486, 6am-2pm daily, $10-15), which has locations in South Lake Tahoe and Fallon as well. Heidi's plate-sized omelets are as much as one person can handle, and families can dine here without taking out a second mortgage.

For dinner, the fun atmosphere, pretty good beef dishes, conversation-piece decor, and beer options on tap make **Red's Old 395 Grill** (1055 S. Carson St., 775/887-0395, 11am-9pm Sun.-Thurs., 11am-10pm Fri.-Sat., $20-30) a go-to place for locals. Women on designated nights out, softball teams, and other groups dig the patio with its gas-log fire.

Sassafras Eclectic Food Joint (1500 Old Hot Springs Rd., 775/884-4471, www.sassafrascarsoncity.com, 11am-9pm daily, $12-20) peppers its hip menu with fresh local ingredients and microbrews. Imaginative small plates and appetizers like black-and-blue shrimp fondue and sourdough loaf stuffed with a garlic and cheese medley trump the more pedestrian pizza-and-sandwich offerings.

No matter where you dine, let **L.A. Bakery** (220 W. John St., 775/885-2253, www.labakerycafe.com, 7am-5pm Mon.-Fri., 8am-3pm Sat., $7-10) handle dessert with its fruity smoothies, cupcakes, muffins, pies, and cookies. They also serve simple wraps, sandwiches, salads, and omelets.

ACCOMMODATIONS

Hotel-casinos are good places to start your search for accommodations, but there are other options. All are reasonably priced, with quiet country inns catering to more leisurely guests, while efficient hotels help business travelers and up-and-at-'em families get quick morning starts.

Wake to the aroma of new-mown alfalfa and the reflection of Sierra Nevada peaks on a tranquil pond at ★ **Deer Run Ranch Bed & Breakfast** (5440 Eastlake Blvd., 775/882-3643, $120-150). The lake attracts deer and birds while innkeeper Muffy Vhay's garden-fresh breakfasts, plush rooms, and cozy sitting room attract world-weary travelers. Thermal heating keeps the showers hot, and photovoltaic panels keep the lights burning.

Guests have access to the dining room, kitchen, and living room with its flat-screen, satellite-enabled TV at **Bliss Bungalow** (408 W. Robinson St., 775/230-0641, www.blissbungalow.com, $95-105). Built in 1914 and fully restored in 2005, this arts-and-crafts home has the original fir floors, bay windows, pine molding, and leaded-glass windows accented with intricately designed Oriental rugs in the five individually themed guest rooms. The tranquility of the rooms is matched only by the views from the front porch during balmy summer afternoons and comfortable spring and fall evenings.

Business travelers and family vacationers will especially appreciate the **Plaza Hotel** (801 S. Carson St., 775/883-9500 or 888/227-1499, http://carsoncityplaza.com, $59-89). Make the Plaza your branch office with free wireless Internet, copy, fax, and mail service, a conference room, an airport shuttle, and baggage check. Features include a location in the center of the city's attractions, free continental breakfast, in-room fridges and microwaves, and cable TV.

The location and friendly, helpful staff compensate for the less-than-pristine carpet and bathroom tile at **Hardman House** (917 N. Carson St., 775/882-7744, www.hardmanhousehotel.com, $55-85). It's geared toward early-rising business types, with continental breakfast beginning at 6am, free high-speed wireless Internet, and dry-cleaning service; there's even an evening manager's reception with wine, cookies, and coffee to help you wind down after a long day of meetings.

Camping and RV Parks

If you want to camp in town, join the numerous long-term residents at **Camp-N-Town RV Park** (2438 Carson St., 775/883-1123, $35-38). Free cable (refundable deposit) and a shade tree are included with each full-hookup gravel pad. The park is in the middle of town, so there's easy access to stores, restaurants, and casinos.

The tree-lined **Comstock Country RV Resort** (5400 S. Carson St., 775/882-2445 or 800/638-2321, www.comstockrv.com, $40-50) has a great location just south on US 395 past the junction with US 50. There are 160 spaces for motor homes, all with full hookups; 133 are pull-throughs. Tents are allowed. It is a bit pricey, but the restrooms have flush toilets and hot showers; other amenities include public phones, sewage disposal, laundry, groceries, game room, and a heated swimming pool and spa. The casinos are close.

Although it's right off the freeway, the **Gold Dust West RV Park** (2171 US 50 E., 775/885-9000 or 877/519-5567, www.gdwcasino.com, $27-33) is peacefully shady. The 47 sites might be a bit tight for larger rigs, but they have full hookups and both 30- and 50-amp service at all spaces.

INFORMATION AND SERVICES

The **Carson City Visitor Center** (716 N. Carson St., 775/687-7410, http://visitcarsoncity.com) and **Chamber of Commerce** (1900 S. Carson St., 775/882-1565) have information on local hotels and restaurants, and maps to nearby attractions.

Books and Maps

The office of the U.S. Forest Service's **Carson Ranger District** (1536 S. Carson St., 775/882-2766, 8am-4:30pm Mon.-Fri.) is a block north of the Nevada State Railroad Museum. The staff can supply good literature, maps, and information on Mount Rose, Lake Tahoe, and the Humboldt-Toiyabe National Forest, which comprises all the national forest lands in Nevada in many different places. The office also sells maps, useful books, and other items, which is unusual for a Forest Service office.

If you're serious about your maps, head to Room 206 of the **Nevada Department of Transportation** building (1263 S. Stewart St., 775/888-7000, 8am-4:30pm Mon.-Fri.) for the graphics and cartography department. Beautiful huge prints grace the foyer; beautiful huge maps are for sale upstairs. Pick up the catalog plus free mileage and public transportation maps. Huge state maps, poster-size city maps, enlarged area maps, and quad maps are available.

TRANSPORTATION

The public bus service **Jump Around Carson** (775/841-7433, 6:30am-7:30pm Mon.-Fri., 8:30am-4:30pm Sat., $1) operates four regular routes throughout town. Greyhound and the major airlines are based in Reno; no regularly scheduled flights serve this capital city. Rental car companies **Enterprise** (1063 S. Carson St., 775/883-7788, www.enterprise.com), **Hertz** (135 Clearview Dr., 775/841-8002, www.hertz.com), and **Avis** (3911 S. Carson St., 775/841-6758, www.avis.com) are open for business.

GENOA

Settled by Mormons in 1851, Genoa (juh-NO-uh) is the oldest town in Nevada. Today, the sweet smell of alfalfa is a fitting background for a visit to Mormon Station State Historic Park, commemorating the original trading post along the Emigrant Trail. Genoa was also an important stop for the Pony Express; that heritage comes alive at the city's Courthouse Museum.

Sights

The **Genoa Courthouse Museum** (2304 Main St., 775/782-4325, www.genoanevada.org, 10am-4:30pm daily May-Oct., $3 adults, $2 age 7-17, free under age 7) captures everyday working, home, and government life in the 1800s. A poignant nursery scene includes a collection of old dolls lining an exquisitely carved toddler's bed. Another display shows what the courthouse looked like from 1865 to 1916, when it handled divorces, civil suits, and the occasional murder trial. Decorated with original oak furniture from the Genoa and Minden courthouse, the display is as authentic as it gets. Don't miss the fine baskets created by the Washoe artisan Dat-So-La-Lee from roots, saplings, and willows.

Mormon Station State Historic Park (2295 Main St., 775/782-2590, http://parks.nv.gov, 9am-4:30pm daily May-mid-Oct., free) sits on the site of Nevada's first permanent nonnative settlement. The trading post established in 1851 proved a lifesaver for many emigrants on the California Trail, offering rest, food, wagon repairs, and blacksmith services for the crucial final leg of the journey. The small **museum** (11am-3pm Thurs.-Mon., $1, 12 and under free) tells the story of the pioneers who passed through. Park grounds include a wagon shed, picnic facilities, shade trees, and a replica of the log stockade.

Recreation

Two courses present contrasting challenges at the upscale **Genoa Lakes Golf Club and Resort** (2901 Jacks Valley Rd., 775/782-7700, www.genoalakes.com, $65-120). Water comes into play on 14 Lake Course holes. The water on these Peter Jacobsen co-designed links also attracts myriad wildlife, adding to the course's enjoyment. Johnny Miller co-designed the Ranch Course ($45-85) to reward long hitters who can negotiate the rugged terrain of the Sierra foothills, elevation changes, and more than 100 bunkers. All players reap the rewards of mountain and waterfall views.

Nightlife

Nevada's oldest watering hole, the **Genoa Bar** (2282 Main St., 775/782-3870, www.genoabarandsaloon.com) was built in 1853, when it operated as Livingston's Exchange. Belly up to the bar (half the bar top is original, as are the diamond-dust mirror on the back bar, the medallions on the ceiling, and a red oil lamp). The trap door by the pool table is not—as local parents sometimes claim—where naughty children will be sent to deal

Mormon Station State Historic Park

with alligators and bogeymen if they don't behave. It's actually an old ice box. Ice harvested from small lakes in the area was packed in burlap and straw to keep the bar's food fresh and drinks cool. Raquel Welch visited the bar in the 1960s and added her bra to the hundreds then hanging from the ceiling. The others have been removed, but Raquel's still occupies a place of honor.

Events

One of the oldest annual events in Nevada, **Genoa's Candy Dance** (www.genoanevada.org/candydancefaire) originated in 1919 when the town was trying to raise funds to install streetlights. The fund-raiser started out as a dance and eventually turned into a bake sale after the Genoa matriarchs mixed up batches of fudge to sell by the pound to the partygoers. The candy proved to be the star of the show, and the Candy Dance tradition began. Genoa will celebrate the 100th edition of the Candy Dance in 2019; it promises to be bigger than ever, with craft fairs, musical entertainment, dinner, and, of course, dancing and some two tons of candy for sale—plain, nut, and mocha fudge as well as nut brittles, dipped chocolates, divinity, mints, almond clusters, and more.

Food and Accommodations

The title of Genoa's best restaurant belongs to the ★ **Pink House** (193 Genoa Ln., 775/392-4279, www.thepinkhousegenoa.com, 11am-8pm Tues.-Sat., 11am-5pm Sun., $12-18), where aged cheeses, cured meats, and other old-world comfort foods take center stage. A bottle of wine with a sampler of sausages, meatballs, pork belly, and mortadella hits the spot. Or on cold winter nights, curl up with a draft beer, cup of squash bisque, and a hearty plate of macaroni and blended cheese.

The atmosphere and cuisine at **Genoa Station** (2285 Main St., 775/783-1599, 11am-7:30pm Tues.-Thurs. 11am-8:30pm Fri., 8am-8:30pm Sat., 8am-7pm Sun., $15-25) are cozy and homey, with large portions and daily theme menus (Tuesday's Mexican specials are truly special). Homemade ice cream tops off deli paninis and sandwiches at **Genoa Country Store** (2299 Main St., 775/782-5974, 8am-6pm daily, $10-15).

Nestled in the Sierra foothills is the **Genoa Country Inn** (2292 Main St., 775/782-4500, www.genoacountryinn.com, $109-129). The rooms are immaculate and feature quaint balconies but include modern creature comforts such as a wet bar, Wi-Fi, flat-screens, and microwaves. You'll be tempted to have a

the Genoa Bar, "Nevada's oldest thirst parlor"

lie-in at the **White House B&B** (195 Genoa Ln., 775/783-7208, www.whitehousebandb.us, $100-$150), but the aroma of sizzling bacon and eggs Benedict wafting from the kitchen will overcome the allure of fluffy down comforters and four-posters.

David Walley's Hot Springs Resort (2001 Foothill Rd., 775/782-8155 or 800/622-1580, www.davidwalleys-resort.com, $110-150) is just over a mile south of Genoa on NV 206. The springs, whose water reaches 160°F, have had a hotel since 1862. The original hotel burned in the 1920s and was rebuilt in the late 1980s with no expense spared and attention paid to every detail. Today it's a beautifully landscaped, luxurious, and reasonably priced hotel-spa. Rooms are decorated in white and neutral shades. Rates include the use of five springs. Non-soaking activities include massages, tennis, exercise classes, billiards, biking, and volleyball. Nonguests can use the facilities starting at $50 per day. Walley's boasts two decent restaurants: Meat, wild game, and premium liquor dominate the menu at **1862 Restaurant & Saloon** (5:30pm-9pm daily, $30-40), with live entertainment most Fridays and Saturdays till 10pm. Breakfast and lunch are dished up at **Harriet's Café** (7:30am-3:30pm daily, $12-20).

MINDEN

The middle jewel in Carson Valley's triple crown, Minden is 15 miles south of Carson City. Built with Danish, Basque, and German influences, Minden celebrates wholesome Americana with art exhibitions, musical performances in the park, crafts fairs, and community picnics.

Town Tour

Entering town from the northwest on US 395, you will first pass the **Carson Valley Inn** at the stoplight. Notice the buildings, which have been renovated to function as an estate distillery, now owned by Bently Nevada Corporation. The **flour mill** (1609 US 395 N.) is straight out of a 1910 model railroad layout with a faded brick facade, stately 45-foot steel silos, and old-time signs. Next door, the brick **butter company** (1617 US 395 N.) replaced the original wood structure in 1916 to increase production and pasteurize the butter, as mandated by a then-new California law.

Pick up a map and start a **Walking Tour** at the **Carson Valley Improvement Club** (1602 Esmeralda Ave., 775/782-5078), which has served Minden since 1912 as a church, movie theater, basketball court, and morgue, among other roles. Down the street in old downtown is the **C.O.D. Garage** (1593 Esmeralda Ave.), founded in 1910 as a Model-T dealer by Clarence O. Dangberg (C.O.D.). Its Union 76 sign is a great retro photo op. Across the street, the county office building is the former **Minden Inn** (1594 Esmeralda Ave.), designed by Frederic DeLongchamps. The classy inn, completed in 1916, was frequented by Clark Gable, Jean Harlow, and other Hollywood biggies. Follow Esmeralda Avenue northwest a few more blocks to **Minden Park.** The **courthouse** (1616 8th St.) was another DeLongchamps creation.

Recreation

Wannabe sky jockeys can take their pick of wild blue yonder excursions in Minden. **Soaring NV** (1142 Airport Rd., 775/782-9595, www.soaringnv.com, 9am-6pm Thurs.-Mon. Apr.-Aug., $169-600) gives passengers bird's-eye views of Lake Tahoe and Carson Valley via glider. Choose serene cruises and graceful turns or pulse-quickening rolls, loops, and inverted flying. You can also learn to pilot your own glider. If you find gliders too confining, you can jump out of a perfectly good airplane with **Skydive Tahoe** (1128 Airport Rd., 775/790-7602, www.skydivelaketahoe.com, $230). On the way up, you will command outstanding views of the lake and mountains. On the way down, you'll hit speeds of 120 mph as you freefall for nearly a minute before your tandem instructor deploys the chute for a five-minute drift to a soft landing. Both companies offer photo and video add-ons to commemorate your flight.

If water is more your element, head over to **Carson Valley Swim Center** (775/782-8840, http://cvswim.com, 9am-7:30pm Mon.-Thurs., 9am-8:30pm Fri., 11am-6pm Sat.-Sun., $5, over age 60 and under 18 and disabled $3), boasting two cool waterslides, diving boards, a competition pool, a family pool, water toys, and a climbing wall.

Casinos

The gaming action is at **Carson Valley Inn** (1627 US 395, 775/782-9711, www.carsonvalleyinn.com, $100-120), a modern casino with 600 slots and video poker, live poker, pari-mutuel horseracing, and a sports book, as well as the requisite casino steakhouse and coffee shop. The showroom books regional bands and comedians, while an outdoor stage attracts more accomplished acts. You can save 20 percent or so by staying in the 74-room motor lodge ($75-85) rather than the hotel. The RV resort ($32-56) has 59 sites (26 pull-throughs) with full hookups.

Food

Lightning-quick service with a smile enhances the standard-but-tasty Mexican at **Francisco's** (1588 US 395, 775/782-6496, 11am-9pm daily, $8-14). **Cowboy Café** (1679 US 395, Ste. A, 775/782-8800, 6am-2pm Tues.-Sun., $8-12) is a breakfast institution in Minden, serving buckaroo-size pancakes and crispy, oniony home fries.

Monochromatic photos at each booth complete the arts-and-crafts interior architecture at **CV Steak** (Carson Valley Inn, 1627 US 395, 775/783-6650, www.carsonvalleyinn.com, 4:30pm-10pm Wed.-Sun., $20-30), formerly Fiona's. The remodeled restaurant is just as classy as the old space. A fine wine selection complements the pasta, seafood, and top-notch beef dishes, which include salad, vegetables, and potato. Even if you're not a fan of au gratin, order the au gratin.

GARDNERVILLE

While Minden luxuriates in tranquil European charm, Gardnerville, just two miles away, focuses on its farming and commercial traditions.

Town Tour

Continuing the Minden-Gardnerville sightseeing trip along US 395, you pass the **Carson Valley Museum and Cultural Center** (1477 US 395, 775/782-2555, 10am-4pm Mon.-Sat., $3 adults, $2 age 7-17), originally the 1915 high school building, designed by Frederic DeLongchamps. Inside you'll find exhibits on the life of a Basque sheepherder in the desolate Pine Nut Mountains, Washoe art, and state-of-the-art medical equipment circa 1880. The area's history lesson continues up the road at the Basque **French Hotel and Bar** (1437 US 395), which hosted traditional *pelota* tournaments in the 1930s. Next door, **Buckaroo's Saloon** (1435 US 395, 24 hours daily), home to fierce dart competitions, pool, and Saturday night karaoke, is in the old **Adaven Building,** which still sports original granite blocks made by the Carson City Penitentiary on one exterior wall. The Adaven ("Nevada" spelled backward) has served as the Odd Fellows hall, post office, soda fountain, hotel, and restaurant.

Recreation

Big trees and the Carson River dominate the **Carson Valley Golf Course** (1027 Riverview Dr., 775/265-3181, www.carsonvalleygolf.com, $26-30). The short (6,022 yards) par-71 layout challenges players with small greens and well-placed greenside bunkers.

Float along the river and valley below with **Balloon Nevada** (775/790-7572, prices vary), which takes two or three passengers up to 5,000 feet high to survey all they command. Private marriage proposal and wedding flights also are available. The experience is more down to earth but no less thrilling at **Sheridan Creek Equestrian Center** (551 Centerville Ln., 775/265-7371, www.sheridancreekequestriancenter.com, $40 per hour). In addition to dressage lessons, boarding, and other services, the proprietors lead trail rides and supervise children's birthday parties that include pony rides and picnics.

Wink's Silver Strike Lanes (1281 Kimmerling Rd. #8, 775/265-5454, www.winkssilverstrike.com, 11am-8pm Sun.-Mon., 11am-9pm Tues.-Thurs., 11am-11pm Fri.-Sat.) has 26 lanes, including four in a private party room. With cocktails, pub food, pool, darts, foosball, and sports on TV, there would be really no reason to ever leave if they didn't close.

Casinos

Sharkey Begovich has been gone since 2002, but **Sharkey's** (1440 US 395 N., 775/782-3133, 6:30am-midnight Sun.-Thurs., 6:30am-4am Fri.-Sat.) is open again after some much-needed 2015 renovations. Some of the building—notably an exposed brick wall and hardwood floors—has been restored to its former glory, while other features, such as the old facade sign, now occupy places of honor among the memorabilia. Upgrades included relocating the Silver Dollar Bar and installing 200 of the most modern machines (along with a neat display of vintage slots). Sharkey's also has a sports book and bingo lounge. While prime rib remains the house specialty, the **Jackpot Café** (24 hours daily) surprises with its "superfood" salad.

The Washoe Tribe runs **Wa She Shu** (1001 US 395 N., 775/265-8690, www.washeshucasino.com), with 130 machines over a 4,600-square-foot gaming floor. The facility also includes a bar, restaurant ($8-$15), and travel plaza.

Food

For such a small town, Gardnerville boasts a surprising number of terrific eateries. Two of the best are in the same otherwise nondescript strip mall. The seafood and steak dishes prepared with a Mexican flair at **Julio's** (1328 US 395 N., #303, 775/783-8232, 11am-2pm and 4:30pm-8:30pm Tues.-Fri., 4:30pm-8:30pm Sat.-Sun., $20-25) are worth tracking down. Chef Julio Hernandez and his partners make a special effort to keep the prices reasonable. A few doors down, perfectly spiced vegetable

and fruit curries (the pumpkin is the best, we think) and authentic flavors highlight a visit to **Thai Jasmine** (1328 US 395 N., #204, 775/783-8625, $10-15).

Healthy, light lunches are the specialty at **Café Girasole** (1483 US 395, 775/782-3314, http://cafegirasole.com, 10:30am-5pm Mon.-Tues., 10:30am-7pm Wed.-Fri., 10:30am-3pm Sat., $10-12). It's worth the effort to find this spot, especially if you're a fan of California-fresh sandwiches and grilled veggies, caramelized onions, artichokes, and sun-dried tomatoes.

Jethro's Oven, Grille & Sports Bar (1281 Kimmerling Rd. #A3, 775/265-2215, www.jethrosbarandgrill.com, 9am-midnight Sun.-Thurs., 9am-2am Fri.-Sat., $10-25), next to the bowling alley, has a menu as long as your arm: omelets and breakfast sandwiches, pub appetizers, pizza, burgers and sandwiches, Mexican, and barbecue. It's all good, and made even better when chased by cold beer and a touchdown by your favorite team on the big screen.

Gardnerville is blessed with two terrific Basque restaurants. Both serve traditional picon punch. You'll barely feel the first punch, but the second is a real haymaker, and the third might send you down for the count! ★ **J.T. Basque Bar and Dining Room** (1426 US 395 N., 775/782-2074, www.jtbasquenv.com, 11:30am-2pm and 5pm-9pm Mon.-Sat., $26-30) has been serving locally raised potatoes, onions, and beef for well over 50 years. Family-style meals of soup, salad, beans, French fries, and wine complement exotic entrées like pig feet, tripe, and rabbit, or more traditional top sirloin, lamb, and chicken. The menu is slightly different at **Overland Restaurant & Pub** (1451 US 395, 775/392-1369, www.overlandrestaurant.com, 11:30am-8pm Sun.-Thurs., 11:30am-9pm Fri.-Sat., $20-40): pasta, boar, and elk in addition to the steak.

Pick up some on-the-road energy at **Chocolate Shoppe by Sweet Images** (1363 US 395 N. #7, 775/267-1002, www.chocolateshoppe.us, 11:30am-8pm Mon.-Thurs.,

11am-10pm Fri.-Sat., 9am-8pm Sun.). The confectioner makes creamy truffles, thick fudge, crispy peanut brittle, and more every day. The little pieces of heaven are a bit expensive, but it's not every day you can treat yourself to homemade decadence.

Accommodations

Several mom-and-pop motels provide clean, comfortable rooms. The best is **Historian Inn** (1427 US 395 N., 775/783-1175 or 877/783-9910, http://historianinn.com, $120-220), with Western- and Nevada-themed artwork and wood floors and a salon and spa on-site. It's right on US 395/Main Street, so weekday commuter traffic noise can intrude into rooms facing the road. The Historian serves a free light breakfast and allows pets for a modest per-stay fee. Other options include the **Westerner** (1353 US 395, 775/782-3602 or 800/782-3602, $70-100), whose rooms have small fridges and big TVs and which is close to shopping and restaurants; and the **Sierra Motel** (1501 US 395, 775/782-5145 or 800/682-5857, $70-90), with views of snow-dusted peaks.

Information

The **Carson Valley Chamber of Commerce and Visitors Authority** (1477 US 395, Ste. A, 775/782-8144 or 800/727-7677, www.carsonvalleynv.org, 8am-5pm Mon.-Fri.) has information on the entire Carson Valley. The website is more insightful and helpful than most.

TOPAZ LAKE

Like its big sister to the north, this underappreciated trinket 20 miles south of Gardnerville via US 395 (three miles south of the intersection with NV 208) sits half in Nevada and half in California. It's also fringed by the mighty Sierras and has a state-line lodge with gambling just across the border. Unlike Tahoe, however, Topaz is an artificial water-storage basin that impounds water from the West Walker River for recreation and irrigation. It's also a treeless desert compared to forested Tahoe. Fishing, water-skiing, and picnicking are other popular diversions.

It's stocked with 40,000 trout per year, and recently introduced largemouth and small-mouth bass populations are thriving. Fishing season runs January-September. The browns and rainbows can reach seven pounds, and 3-4 pounders are not uncommon.

Topaz Lake Park (775/782-9828, camping $25, $35 with hookups), on the northeast side of the lake near the boat launch (head south on US 395 past NV 208; turn left at the sign for a mile), is a perfect base for the outdoor enthusiasts the lake attracts. It's a big spot with a mile of beachfront. The 15 RV hookup sites come with electricity, water, and dump stations. Tenters can make use of 40 developed campsites or camp just about anywhere in the park. There's a grassy playground for the kids. The maximum stay is 14 days, and reservations are required.

If you're not fond of roughing it, Super 8 handles the lodging at **Topaz Lodge** (1979 US 395 S., 775/266-3338, www.topazlodge.com, $75-100), which includes a free continental breakfast. Most rooms and the casino bar command striking views of the lake. The small casino floor is heavy on slots and video poker, but other options include keno, bingo, blackjack, and three-card poker. **The Steak House** (5:30pm-10pm Wed.-Sun., $25-35) grills a mean elk chop along with its more traditional beef, chicken, and seafood menu. The specials and the vistas at the **Lakeview Coffee Shop** (6am-10pm daily, $10-15) can't be beat. The views aren't as spectacular at the **RV Resort** ($22), but the price is right and includes a coupon book for cocktails and meal discounts.

DAYTON

US 50 runs through the middle of Dayton. Stopping along the trail to the California gold fields, Abner Blackburn scraped around some outcroppings in Gold Creek near Dayton in 1849 and found a bit of color. It was the first gold discovered in the Silver State. Today, Dayton bills itself as a town of firsts, claiming to be the state's oldest permanent settlement as well as the site of Nevada's first marriage and, alas, its first divorce.

The **Dayton Museum** (Shady Ln. at Logan, 772/246-6316, 10am-4pm Sat., 1pm-4pm Sun. Mar.-Nov. and by appointment, free), located in an 1865 schoolhouse, chronicles all this early history with artifacts from the town's peak years of gold prospecting, railroading, mining, and ranching. The museum also has maps for a half-hour walking tour of the town, covering Nevada's oldest cemetery, the first depot for the Carson & Colorado Railroad (currently under restoration), the famed Odeon Hall & Saloon (where,

contrary to a plaque's assertion, Ulysses S. Grant did not make a speech in 1879), and much more.

North of town, the Carson River (raging with spring runoff or a muddy trickle in the arid summer) and US 50 cut through **Dayton State Park** (US 50, 775/687-5678, http://parks.nv.gov, $7), which provides picturesque and easily accessible spots for picnicking, fishing, bird-watching, and camping ($17) at 10 non-reserved sites. You might see hawks, deer, porcupines, and waterfowl near the river. Rangers often lead interpretive hikes to the remains of the Nothing but the Rock Point Mill, the largest stamp mill in these parts.

Virginia City

TOP EXPERIENCE

Starting as early as 1851, a backwash of disillusioned California gold seekers filtered east to search Nevada's high desert for the precious metal. One pair of miners on Sun Mountain optimistically called their gopher hole the Ophir Mine, after the biblical land where the wealth of King Solomon was located. Yet they remained unaware of the real riches

right beneath their feet. The more they dug, the more they got bogged down by blue-gray mud. The miners flung it aside until a visitor carried a chunk down to Placerville in July 1859 and had it assayed. The mud was found to contain $875 per ton in gold and an incredible $3,000 per ton in pristine sulfuret of silver. The news spread and some 10,000 fortune seekers flooded the ragged settlement on Sun

Virginia City

Mountain. The Comstock Lode and Virginia City were about to explode.

Today, more than three million visitors a year drive up beautiful Geiger Grade or Devil's Gate to recapture a piece of Virginia City's boomtown glory. While small-scale prospecting operations continue near here even today, Virginia City has staked its claim in the travel industry, mining deep-pocketed tourists. Despite its occasionally kitschy souvenirs, the town's attractions are authentic and as close as you're likely to come to imagining yourself a miner on payday, eager to soak up all the entertainment, culture, whiskey, and social accompaniment your money can buy. Get a feel for those heady Comstock days, from the sweltering, claustrophobic working conditions endured by miners to the tools of the sex trade at the Red Light Museum to the opulent mansions of the silver kings. Virginia City may be a tourist trap, but it's one you won't mind being caught in.

SIGHTS
Underground Mine Tours

The Comstock Lode was Virginia City's heart and soul. Two mine tours allow you to get under the ground to see what the miners saw. The **Chollar Mine** (615 S. F St., 775/847-0155, www.chollarminetours.com, 1pm-3:30pm Sat.-Thurs. May-Oct., $10 adults, $2 age 5-12), the last of the Comstock's old original mines, is the most authentic. The Chollar was the fifth highest in production, producing more than $18 million in gold and silver, and this tour shows you the real thing, with the square-set timbering, ore, and old tools and equipment as well as knowledgeable, experienced guides. The 30-minute guided walking tours go over 400 feet into the mountain. The Chollar Mine is not far from the center of town; you can get there by going downhill from C to F Street, turning south on F, and continuing for about a half mile; or head south from town on C Street, turn east onto the truck route just past the Fourth Ward School, and follow the road around.

Virginia City's other underground tour, of the **Ponderosa Mine** (106 S. C St., 775/847-7210, 11am-5pm daily summer, noon-5pm daily winter, $7 adults, $2 age 5-12), departs from the rear of the Ponderosa Saloon. The mine tunnel snakes 315 feet from the rear end of the saloon into the Best and Belcher diggings, whose pay dirt yielded 55 percent silver and 45 percent gold. Displays include gold-rich ore, the powder room where "monkeys" (young boys) worked, square-set timbering, minerals under black light, and all the heavy buckets, drills, winches, and rods the miners used to muck the rock, tunneling 6-8 feet per day. The guide enumerates myriad dangers: the perpetual threats of cave-ins, fire, scalding steam and water; the terrible heat and bad air; not to mention the back-breaking, head-knocking, bone-crushing work itself. At $4 per day, the equivalent of $232 today, the miners were well paid, considering that most hard-rock miners around the world earned less than $1 per day; still, this tour is graphic evidence that the Comstock miners earned every penny. At the far end, the guide might light two candles and kill the overheads. If he blows out the candles, an early-warning signal of gases or a lack of oxygen, you'll feel like you're back in 1873. The only inconsistency is the 52°F temperature; you could take a jacket, but it isn't really necessary.

Comstock Gold Mill

Virginia City offers several chances to see how miners got the ore out of the mines, but the **Comstock Gold Mill** (F St. at the railroad crossing, 775/742-9694, 11am-3pm Thurs.-Mon. May-Oct., $10 adults, $5 age 5-12) is a chance to see how they got the gold out of the ore. Stamp mills crushed the ore, and the slag was placed on a steel table, where mercury was added, attracting the gold pieces. Burning drove off the mercury and left the gold. Mercury is toxic, however, and millers died from working with it, so the process changed in the 1880s. The new process screened the ore and then washed away the small rocks and dirt, leaving the heavier gold. Narrated tours explain it all.

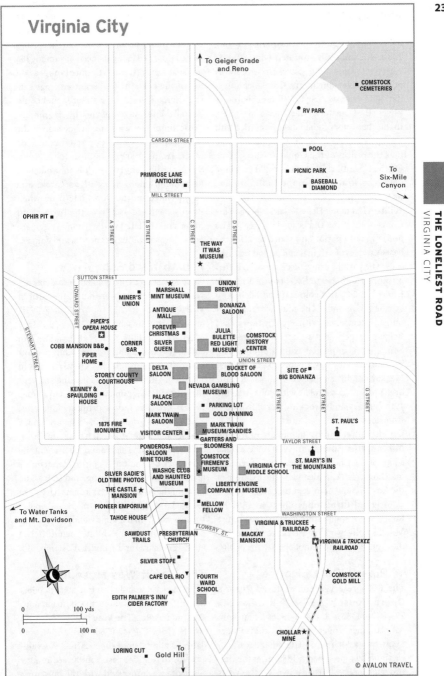

Virginia City

To Geiger Grade and Reno

COMSTOCK CEMETERIES

RV PARK

CARSON STREET

POOL

PRIMROSE LANE ANTIQUES

PICNIC PARK

BASEBALL DIAMOND

To Six-Mile Canyon

MILL STREET

OPHIR PIT

A STREET

B STREET

C STREET

D STREET

THE WAY IT WAS MUSEUM

SUTTON STREET

HOWARD STREET

MINER'S UNION

MARSHALL MINT MUSEUM

UNION BREWERY

ANTIQUE MALL

BONANZA SALOON

STEWART STREET

PIPER'S OPERA HOUSE

FOREVER CHRISTMAS

CORNER BAR

SILVER QUEEN

JULIA BULETTE RED LIGHT MUSEUM

COMSTOCK HISTORY CENTER

COBB MANSION B&B

PIPER HOME

UNION STREET

STOREY COUNTY COURTHOUSE

DELTA SALOON

BUCKET OF BLOOD SALOON

SITE OF BIG BONANZA

KENNEY & SPAULDING HOUSE

NEVADA GAMBLING MUSEUM

PALACE SALOON

PARKING LOT

E STREET

F STREET

G STREET

1875 FIRE MONUMENT

MARK TWAIN SALOON

GOLD PANNING

ST. PAUL'S

VISITOR CENTER

MARK TWAIN MUSEUM/SANDIES

GARTERS AND BLOOMERS

TAYLOR STREET

PONDEROSA SALOON MINE TOURS

COMSTOCK FIREMEN'S MUSEUM

ST. MARY'S IN THE MOUNTAINS

SILVER SADIE'S OLD TIME PHOTOS

WASHOE CLUB AND HAUNTED MUSEUM

VIRGINIA CITY MIDDLE SCHOOL

THE CASTLE MANSION

LIBERTY ENGINE COMPANY #1 MUSEUM

PIONEER EMPORIUM

TAHOE HOUSE

MELLOW FELLOW

To Water Tanks and Mt. Davidson

WASHINGTON STREET

FLOWERY ST.

VIRGINIA CITY

SAWDUST TRAILS

PRESBYTERIAN CHURCH

MACKAY MANSION

VIRGINIA & TRUCKEE RAILROAD

VIRGINIA & TRUCKEE RAILROAD

SILVER STOPE

CAFÉ DEL RIO

FOURTH WARD SCHOOL

COMSTOCK GOLD MILL

EDITH PALMER'S INN/ CIDER FACTORY

0   100 yds

0   100 m

CHOLLAR MINE

LORING CUT

To Gold Hill

© AVALON TRAVEL

© AVALON TRAVEL

Mackay Mansion

The **Mackay Mansion** (129 S. D St., 775/847-0373, www.uniquitiesmackaymansion.com, 10am-4:30pm daily summer, winter hours vary, free) reigns as the best way to see how the other half lived during the Comstock's heyday. John Mackay, heir to William Sharon as king of the Comstock Lode, lived and worked in this three-story Italianate-style edifice with a wraparound veranda and a large deck, using it as the offices of the Gould & Curry Mine Office. Up until 1950, visitors could purchase gold bars straight from the vault. Mackay occupied the home after George Hearst—William Randolph Hearst's father—made his Comstock fortune and headed back east. The house's grand parlor and staircase offer the best examples of original and period furnishings. The parlor's centerpiece, an overstuffed burgundy-upholstered set, fronts a mirror framed in 24-carat gold leaf and backed by crushed diamonds. The Mackay family indulged themselves with French tapestries, Belgian carpets, and a James Broadwood & Sons piano, imported from London. The tour includes the upstairs bedrooms used by Mackay and his children as well as the children's play area, complete with dolls from the 19th century and a rocking horse from the Comstock era.

Other silver barons' homes are nearby on **Millionaires Row.** While you're here, take a look at the Chollar, Bowers, and governor's mansions. You can also view the exterior of the Castle, a 16-room gem that still contains all-original furnishings. Built in 1868 by Robert Graves, superintendent of the Empire Mine, its olivewood shutters are visible, but the exquisite interior is not open to the public.

★ Piper's Opera House

The well-preserved and restored **Piper's Opera House** (12 B St. and Union St., 775/847-0433 or 888/422-1956, 11am-4pm daily summer, winter hours vary, guided tours 11am-1pm and 3pm, $5 adults, age 6-12 $2) was built by John Piper in 1885, after the first two opera houses burned down. Canvas walls to aid the acoustics, balconies and chandeliers designed to throw patterns on the ceiling, the original round-backed chairs, and the spring-loaded floor (a dance enhancer) are among the unusual features. Advertisements appear on top of the curtain. Three slotted stage sets (a parlor, a forest, and a street scene) could be rolled into and out of view by stagehands. Proscenium box seats are on one side of the stage. Performers who appeared here include Mark Twain, Harry Houdini, John Philip Sousa, Lillie Langtry, Al Jolson, and John Barrymore, among many others. Circles and keys painted on the floor date from when Piper's was used as a basketball court and roller rink in later years. Today the opera house hosts weddings, concerts, and dances.

Fourth Ward School

Once educating as many as 1,000 students per year (the classrooms were huge), the **Fourth Ward School** (537 S. C St., 775/847-0975, http://fourthwardschool.org, 10am-5pm daily May-Oct., $5 adults, $3 age 6-12), at the south end of town, was one of four public schools in use during Virginia City's heyday. Built in 1876, it boasted newfangled heating and ventilating technology and water piped to all four floors, including indoor drinking fountains. The last class graduated in 1936, and today the Nevada State Museum has set up an excellent exhibit on the ground floor about the Comstock community's culture, letter-press printing technology, mining, and education. Some of the 16 original classrooms have been restored with original desks, maps, and books. Visitors can sit in the same wooden desks students in 1876 used. Exhibits include a 3-D viewing machine and a model of a stamp mill.

The Way It Was Museum

With the largest and most impressive collection of Comstock mining artifacts, maps, minerals, and photos, **The Way It Was Museum** (113 N. C St., 775/847-0766, 10:30am-4:30pm daily, $3 adults, under age 12 free) is a valuable link to Nevada's past. You can see how the silver ore was processed with the museum's working scale models of stamp mills, mine reproductions, and Cornish pumps, all built by J. E. Parson of Oroville, California. Three videos with Charlie Jones and Merlin Olsen discuss the Comstock, Piper's Opera House, and Mark Twain; they alone are worth the price of admission.

Marshall Mint Museum

More mint than museum, but more gift shop than anything, the **Marshall Mint Museum** (96 N. C St., 775/847-0777 or 800/321-6374, www.marshallmint.com, 10am-5pm daily, free), located in the 1861 assay office building, sells Christian-themed medallions, hand-crafted gold jewelry, collectible coins, and silver-cast currency reproductions.

Mark Twain Museum

The **Mark Twain Museum** (53 S. C St., 775/847-0525, 10am-5pm daily, $5, children $2) was once the pressroom for Nevada's oldest publication, the *Territorial Enterprise,* which started up in Genoa in December 1858, moved briefly to Carson City, then in October 1860 settled down into a long and profitable run in Virginia City, with writers like Mark Twain and Dan DeQuille keeping things lively. The museum displays 19th-century printing technology, such as an 1894 lino-type, an old binding machine, and a hot-type cabinet. Twain's original desk is on display, along with some of his books and journals and even his commode! The press area, where Twain's desk was spared from the great 1875 fire, was insulated from the conflagration by the debris from the charred offices above. The current office was built around the press area the next year, and continued to publish until 1893. Also called the Territorial Enterprise Museum, it's in the center of town, in the basement of a gift shop.

Comstock Firemen's Museum

Located in Virginia City's original 1864 fire-house, the **Comstock Firemen's Museum** (117 S. C St., 775/847-0717, www.comstock-firemuseum.com, 10am-4pm daily May-Oct., donation) is one of only a few buildings that survived the big fire of October 1875. As Virginia City grew, its fire department also grew to include a hook-and-ladder company, six engine companies, and seven hose companies. An 1874 Clapp & Jones steam fire engine has been restored to operating condition and is one of the coolest artifacts in the collection. Nevada's oldest piece of fire equipment is also here: an 1839 four-wheel hose carriage

Twain's desk, on display at the Mark Twain Museum

Cradle of Journalists

For most, life on the Comstock Lode was a dusty, lonely existence. Prospectors who ventured west with visions of stuffing their pockets with silver to bankroll a life on easy street for their families often found frontier life a bitter reality. A few of these disenchanted would-be silver barons, such as Mark Twain, quickly learned:

the real secret of success in silver mining—which was, not to mine the silver ourselves by the sweat of our brows and the labor of our hands, but to sell the ledges to the dull slaves of toil and let them to the mining!

Twain found wielding a pen more enjoyable and lucrative than wielding a shovel, and became the most famous journalist to make his name on the Comstock. His dry observations—many self-deprecating—earned him a spot on the *Territorial Enterprise* in Virginia City, where he never let the facts get in the way of a good story. Twain became a master at hoax journalism, fabricating tales of petrified men and bloody shootouts.

California gold rush journalist William J. Forbes got his start in Nevada. The hard-bitten and hard-drinking Forbes did not suffer fools lightly, especially when those fools were running the territory. When Governor James W. Nye's pet project, a dam and a mill, ran way over budget and ran out of money with the job half completed, Forbes noted that "Governor Nye has a dam by a mill site, but he has no mill by a dam site." Forbes eked out a living in several Nevada boomtowns before opening a saloon, writing that "of 20 men, 19 patronize the saloon and one the newspaper. I'm going with the crowd." While the gin joint may have been the only profitable business Forbes ever owned, ink ran in his veins. He soon sold out and returned to his rattletrap press.

Twain's friend and mentor in Virginia City, William Wright, under the pen name Dan DeQuille, was king of the hoaxes, though his serious accounts of life in the mining camps, especially *The Big Bonanza,* are still considered classics of mainstream reporting and are often credited with establishing the criteria for modern journalism.

Affectionately known as "Lying Jim," James Townsend's tales were tall. When he came to work at one newspaper, he introduced himself to readers by telling his "life story." According to Jim's biography, his shipwrecked mother had been captured by cannibals. After his birth, Jim was fattened for a dozen years in anticipation of being the main course at a tribal feast. He escaped, became a successful businessman, and ran up a considerable fortune. Then disaster struck. He became a journalist, squandered his fortune, and was reduced to continuing to write for his supper.

Other notable writers who cut their teeth or honed their trade on the Comstock include Myron Angel, Fred Hart, and Jock Taylor of the *Reese River Reveille.* Angel wrote the definitive Comstock-era chronicle, the *1881 History of Nevada.* Wells Drury edited the *Gold Hill News* for a dozen years. When he applied for a job with Alf Doten, he was informed that citizens of the rough-and-tumble frontier didn't settle their differences with lawyers and libel suits. "You write what you please. Nobody censors it," Doten told Drury. "But you must defend yourself if anybody has a kick."

originally used in Philadelphia and bought for use in Virginia City in 1870.

Comstock History Center

Mining and railroad history are on display at the **Comstock History Center** (20 N. E St., 775/847-0419, 11am-4pm Thurs.-Sun., free), including Engine No. 18 of the historic Virginia & Truckee Railroad. The center also contains railroad and other historical photos and reference material.

★ Virginia & Truckee Railroad

Free your imagination as you spy exposed silver ore veins along a ride on the **Virginia & Truckee Railroad** (165 F St., 775/847-0380, www.virginiatruckee.com, 10:30am-4pm daily late May-late Oct., $10-12.50 adults, age 5-10 $5-6). This historic railroad route shuttled rich Comstock ore to quartz reduction mills while the return trip supplied the richest city on earth with lumber, mining timbers, and cord wood for fuel. The 35-minute narrated tour, on steam and diesel locomotives in summer, diesel only in winter, takes passengers from the F Street depot past several famous mines and through Tunnel No. 4, one of five burrowed through rock walls for the line's 1,600-foot change in elevation. As they chug past the Chollar, Potosi, Yellow Jacket, Crown Point, and other historic mines, passengers can spot the telltale blue-gray veins still exposed.

The V&T also offers one-way and round-trip rides from Virginia City to Carson City. The one-way voyage is through a 566-foot tunnel, over the highway via a dramatic bridge crossing, past a scale and water stop that serviced 40 trains a day during Virginia City's heyday, and through American Flat, a contender for the state capital until the ore ran out and the town disappeared. Round-trips (90 minutes each way) from Carson City include a three-hour layover in Virginia City. Special trains run throughout the year: the haunted Pumpkin Train in October, the Santa Train in December, and other themed rides for Memorial Day and Independence Day.

St. Mary's in the Mountains Catholic Church

St. Mary's in the Mountains (Taylor St. and E St., 775/847-9099, 10am-4pm daily, Mass 4pm Sat. and 11:30am Sun., donation) is Nevada's oldest Catholic church. Burly Paddy Manogue built the church after the 1875 fire and ministered to the Irish-Catholic miners of Virginia City for almost 20 years. Volunteers offer free tours of the museum and wine cellar. The sanctuary's Victorian and Gothic architecture features a 17th-century Florentine canvas over the altar and a four-by six-foot depiction of the Virgin Mary done in needlepoint by nuns who spent five years creating it. **St. Paul's Episcopal Church** (87 F St.) and **First Presbyterian** (196 S. C St.), which survived the great fire, are also worth checking out for their architectural and spiritual inspiration.

Julia Bulette Red Light Museum

Julia Bulette, Virginia City's prostitute with a heart of gold, became prosperous plying the world's oldest profession and popular by supporting the fire department and many other civic and charitable causes. The **Julia Bulette Red Light Museum** (5 N. C St., 775/847-9288, 11am-9pm Wed.-Sun. May-Oct., 11am-9pm Thurs.-Sun. Nov.-Apr.), in the basement of the Mustang Ranch Steakhouse, has only a nebulous connection to the world's oldest profession as practiced by Bulette, who was murdered in 1867. The exhibits are more sophomoric than serious—old condom wrappers and sexual aids, snake oils, a walking stick made from an elephant's penis, and nudie shot glasses.

Washoe Club and Haunted Museum

Named the most haunted place in the most haunted town in Nevada according to the, um, experts, The **Washoe Club and Haunted Museum** (112 S. C St., 775/847-4467, www.thewashoeclub.com, noon-6pm Mon.-Fri., 11am-9pm Sat., noon-7pm Sun., $8, age 5-16 $5), built in 1875 after the great fire, was the hangout of local millionaires and celebrity visitors such as Ulysses S. Grant, Thomas Edison, and Wyatt Earp. The posh upstairs digs were accessed by the spiral staircase, still viewable in the back, which is listed by Ripley's as the longest spiral staircase without a supporting pole. Hourly tours of the top two floors include the infamous Millionaires' Club, piano room, and pitch-black room 12. Visitors claim to have experienced cold drafts, feelings of unease, and brushes with ethereal beings—some captured as ghostly digital images. Some say these sightings were the work of the spirits served in the full bar on the ground floor. Tour tickets include admission to the small haunted museum, which includes "the crypt," where, during one particularly brutal winter, officials stored dozens of bodies until the ground thawed enough to allow for burial. Hard-core ghost hunters can opt to be locked in overnight ($1,000 for up to eight people).

NIGHTLIFE

No visit to Virginia City is complete without a stop at the **Bucket of Blood Saloon** (1 S. C St., 775/847-0322, www.bucketofbloodsaloon.com, 10am-9pm daily), if only to get the conversation-starting T-shirt. Built just after the big fire atop the destroyed Boston Saloon, the origin of the Bucket's name is the subject of some debate. There are several plausible stories, but our favorite is that miners sweated a bucket of blood daily, justifying their indulgence in a few cold ones. The Bucket is well-populated with cowboy hat-wearing tourists. It's light and airy thanks to the big picture window in back overlooking Six-Mile Canyon. Belly up to the old-fashioned bar with its ornate woodwork and brass accents and groove to the country, rock, and bluegrass acts on stage most weekends.

The **Delta Saloon** (18 S. C St., 775/847-0789, www.thedeltasaloon.com, 10am-5pm Mon.-Thurs., 10am-11pm Fri., 7am-midnight Sat., 8:30am-6pm Sun., $10-20), a half dozen doors north, used to be the closest thing to a casino Virginia City had to offer, with 125 slots and video poker machines (there are no table games in town). But in 2015 the new owner failed to qualify for a gaming license. The Delta is open for bar patrons and diners, and the restaurant does steak, pulled pork, and chicken fingers right. Go to the back of the Delta and read the display explaining the macabre (and maybe even partially true!) history of the suicide table. The old faro layout is said to have caused three gamblers to take themselves off to the big casino in the sky following large gambling losses.

Up the block is the **Ponderosa Saloon** (106 S. C St., 775/847-0757), in the old Bank of California building. The highlight is the original bank vault, with a half-inch steel-plate cage surrounded by two-foot-thick walls. Study the historical photos and the portraits of the early celebrities (Julia Bulette, James Finney, Henry Comstock, and Mark Twain)

while enjoying a strong belt, live bands, and karaoke performances.

Ruby's Chicago-style pizza sets the **Red Dog Saloon** (76 N. C St., 775/847-7474, http://reddogvc.rocks, 11am-9pm Sun.-Thurs., 11am-11pm Fri., 11am-11:30pm Sat., $8-16) apart. The full bar, jazz on Sundays, and rock-and-roll most weekends don't hurt, either. The **Mark Twain Saloon** (62 C St., 775/847-0599, http://marktwainsaloon.com) is the only 24/7 party place in town. Of course, "party" is a relative term in rural Nevada, but the Twain has 70 video poker machines, and the pizza ovens are always hot. The spicy chili, tangy barbecue, tasty sausage, and cheese dips at **Mellow Fellow** (171 C St., 214/914-9155, www.mellowfellowpub.com, noon-8pm Thurs.-Fri., 11am-8pm Sat., 10am-4pm Sun.) are just the ticket on a cold northern Nevada day. And the hot food demands a cool draft beer or two.

With live music and karaoke most nights, **Red Light Lounge** (5 N. C St., 775/847-4188, 10am-9pm Wed.-Sun.) in the Mustang Ranch Steakhouse's basement makes a splash with its appetizers, especially its blue cheese sliders and Irish nachos. Next door to and forever associated with Piper's Opera House, the **Old Corner Bar** (12 N. B St., 775/847-4900, 11am-9pm Mon.-Thurs., 11am-midnight Fri.-Sun.) maintains the same subdued hospitality that Lillie Langtry and Mark Twain once enjoyed. A bit removed from the C Street tourist throngs, the Corner Bar attracts more local residents with its blazing fire in winter and outdoor people-watching perches in more clement weather. Local country and soft rock bands perform on most weekends, and wannabe stars take the karaoke stage weekly.

SHOPPING

While much of Virginia City is authentic, it's also a tourist town, full of kitschy souvenir stores, ice cream parlors, and old-time photo studios. Despite the shtick, many of the wares are unusual and nostalgic. A half-dozen jewelry and mineral shops dot Virginia City's main drag, including the **Silver Stope** (58 N. C St., 775/847-7900, http://thesilverstope.

com, 10am-7pm daily), specializing in Native American-inspired silver and turquoise pieces, and **Stone Age Quarry** (81 S. C St., 775/847-0706, 9:30am-9pm daily), with a large selection of meteorites, crystals, specimens, and Eastern and New Age spirituality stones.

Recent finds at **Primrose Lane Antiques** (182 S. C St., 775/847-0775, 11am-5pm daily) include a vintage wooden telephone and console radio straight out of Hooterville and a hardwood china cabinet complete with a full set of porcelain tableware for eight. Primrose Lane seems to specialize in unusual and didn't-know-I-wanted-it items. Items at **Virginia City Antique Mall** (54 N. C St., 775/847-0511) run the gamut from the sublime to the ridiculous. Stalls lining the boardwalk give off a flea market air and inspire the same hopefulness that an undiscovered treasure awaits at the next booth.

No less than six general stores carry candy, soda, postcards, T-shirts, and all the other traditional souvenirs you could want. Our favorite is **Grant's General Store** (59 S. C St., 775/847-7245, 9am-7pm daily), but **Sawdust Trails** (166 S. C St., 775/784-0106, 10am-7pm daily) serves the same purpose.

Specialty stores include **Sandie's** (53 S. C St., 775/847-7950, 10am-7pm daily) for fairies, swords, dragons, armor, and all things fantasy and medieval. **Pioneer Emporium** (144 S. C St., 775/847-9214, 10am-5pm daily) offers custom-crafted cowboy and Western-style hats, and **Forever Christmas** (88 N. C St., 775/847-0110, http://4everchristmas.net, 10am-6pm daily) handles holiday decorations and gifts.

The best thing about the toys and games at **Little City Items** (145 S. C St., 775/847-4200, 10am-5pm daily) is that you don't have to hook them up to the television to play them—they are vintage, classic, and just plain good old-fashioned fun toys.

Virginia City offers a handful of old-time photo shops: **Silver Sadie's Old-Time Photos** (116 S. C St., 775/847-9133), **Priscilla Pennyworth's Photographic Emporium** (203 S. C St., 775/847-0333), and **Garters &** **Bloomers** (63 S. C St., 775/847-7979). The props and costumes turn you into practically any kind of character from the roaring 1870s that you'd like to be: a barmaid, a piano player, a cocktail waitress, a cowboy or cowgirl, or a gunslinger. Get an 8-by-10 for about $20.

FOOD

The homemade salsa gives ★ **Café Del Rio** (394 S. C St., 775/847-5151, http://cafedelriovc.com, 11:30am-8pm Fri.-Sat., 10am-7pm Sun. fall-spring; 11:30am-8pm Wed.-Sat., 10am-7pm Sun. summer, $10-15) the title of best Mexican and Southwestern joint in northern Nevada. Anything in the tacos, enchiladas, and carnitas line will serve you right, especially the steak fajitas and steak tacos. The interior and decor are modern and inviting, although the exterior maintains the Old West feel.

The former site of the *Territorial Enterprise* went from slinging ink to slinging hash with the opening of **Palace Restaurant and Saloon** (54 S. C St., 775/847-4441, 8:30am-4pm Tues.-Thurs., 8:30am-8pm Fri.-Sat. and Mon., 8:30am-6pm Sun., $7-12) in 2000. The corned beef is sublime. Try a breakfast hash with a bacon bloody Mary or a lunchtime Reuben paired with one of the 10 beers on tap.

Much more than dried and smoked beef, **Virginia City Jerky Company** (204 S. C St., 775/847-7444, www.vcjerky.com, 11am-4pm daily, $9-12) serves thick lunch slabs of pork, steak, ribs, and pastrami with bread and picnic sides. Of course, you will want to pick up a pound or two of the pepper-, teriyaki-, cayenne-, or chili-spiced top round signature product.

The **Firehouse Restaurant & Saloon** (171 S. C St., 775/847-7744, 11am-8pm Wed.-Sat., 11am-6pm Sun., $10-15), at the south end of town, is a coffee shop and bar that serves inexpensive breakfasts and lunches. Have the barbecue if you're here at lunchtime.

It's not your average joe at the **Roasting House** (55 N. C St., 775/847-0708, www.theroastinghouse.com, 7:30am-4pm daily, $7-10). In addition to serving breakfast, sandwiches, soups, salads, and ice cream, Roasting House roasts its own beans. It's the former home of the Brass Rail Saloon, and the rail counter remains, inviting you to belly up to the bar for a different kind of brew. You'll certainly see, probably smell, and maybe even taste the fudge being slopped around on tables in the picture windows in front of **Grandma's Fudge Factory** (20 N. C St., 775/847-0770, 10am-5pm Mon.-Fri., 10am-6pm Sat.-Sun.).

ACCOMMODATIONS

Reflecting the era it keeps alive, Virginia City is home to hotels and inns of every stripe, from quaint and rustic to regal. For the latter, we suggest the Victorian sophistication and charm of ★ **Edith Palmer's Country Inn** (416 S. B St., 775/847-7070, www.edithpalmers.com, $110-160). Chintz wallpaper, satin pillows, and downy comforters in the eight rooms nestled in two houses on the property ensure comfort, and mountain, courtyard, and sunrise views offer welcome respites from workaday lives. Built in 1863 and used as a cider factory, the property opened for overnight trade in 1948 and reopened in 2003 after extensive expansion and renovation. A stone outbuilding, originally used to produce cider and vinegar during the Comstock, is now the **Cider Factor Restaurant** (noon-9pm Sat.-Tues., $18-25). Dine outside or enjoy a steak and cocktails in front of the big stone fireplace at the copper and cherrywood bar.

More Victorian elegance can be found at **Cobb Mansion Bed & Breakfast** (18 S. A St., 775/847-9006 or 877/847-9006, http://cobbmansion.com, $99-199), which offers six rooms appointed in period antiques in a mansion setting. Once owned by a prosperous Comstock-era merchant, the three-story mansion, open spring-fall, overlooks the Carson River. Start each morning with a full breakfast in the opulent dining room.

For a more *High Plains Drifter* feel, you can't beat the ★ **Silver Queen Hotel and Wedding Chapel** (28 N. C St., 775/847-0440, www.silverqueenhotel.net, $55-125), with authentically restored Old West rooms, including old-fashioned claw-foot bathtubs and excluding televisions and telephones. Many rooms feature 16-foot ceilings or views of the Sugarloaf Mountains or bustling C Street. Like seemingly everywhere else in town, the hotel is said to be haunted. At the back of the huge and ornate back bar is a small wedding chapel. The Captain and Tennille tied the knot here in 1975. The shop has reproductions of vintage clothing so you can get your Butch and Sundance on and get yer picture took. At the 1861-vintage **Gold Hill Hotel** (1540 Main St., Gold Hill, 775/847-0111, www.goldhill-hotel.net, $130-210), just down the hill from Virginia City, you can stay in one of the oldest hotel rooms in Nevada or, if you prefer more modern accommodations and enough room to turn around, a spacious queen room with attached patio. Larger families can bed down in the Miner's Cabin, a two-bed, two-bath lodge with a full kitchen, or one of the lodges and guesthouses across the street. Wherever you stay, patronize the slope-roofed saloon. Sign a dollar bill and staple it to the ceiling. Fair warning: Both the Gold Hill and the Silver Queen are said to be haunted—rumors that the owners encourage.

Antique furnishings and Victorian elegance grace all 14 rooms at the **Tahoe House Hotel** (162 S. C St., 775/847-5264, www.tahoehousehotel.com, $120-180). The garden and great room, with its potbelly stove, hardwood bar, and honky-tonk piano, are terrific gathering spots for families, friends, and soon-to-be-friends.

The 15 rooms at the **Virginia City Inn** (675 S. C St., 775/847-0282, www.virginiacityinn.com, $90-150) all celebrate the history and culture of the area and the Comstock era, from buckaroos and cowboys to immigrants and Native Americans. The **Comstock Lodge** (875 S. C St., 775/847-0233, $60-80) has 14 rooms, all done in period antiques. The **Sugarloaf Mountain Motel** (430 S. C St., 775/847-0551 or 866/217-9248, www.sugarloafmountain-motel.com, $90-120) was an 1878 boardinghouse, but the bright and airy rooms of today contain no bunkhouse connotations. Rooms include cable TV, microwaves, and refrigerators. Coffee and teakettles are on by 7am along with breakfast snacks in the trading post. The 66 rooms at **Silverland Inn & Suites** (100 N. E St., 775/847-4484, www.silverlandusa.com, $135-175) are more contemporary, with modern furnishing, console televisions, an indoor pool and Jacuzzi, fitness room, and business center.

The best part of a stay at **Virginia City RV Park** (355 N. F St., 775/847-0999, http://vcrvparknv.com, $38-44) is that it's next to a town park with tennis and basketball courts and a seasonal outdoor swimming pool. The RV park's sites are smallish, and not the most level. It's the only one in town, so beggars can't be choosers. The market is well-stocked, and there's a tent area and a few cabins for rent.

INFORMATION

The **Virginia City Tourism Commission** (86 S. C St., 775/847-7500 or 800/718-7587, www.visitvirginiacitynv.com) is on the northwest corner of C and Taylor Streets.

Fallon

The marshland that attracted early Native American nomads, beaver hunters, and salt miners now irrigates endless rolling alfalfa fields and draws duck hunters from around the world to Fallon, "The Oasis of Nevada." The contrasts are stark: lush green fields in the middle of the dry beige desert; delicate ecosystems existing amid (and often actually assisted by) dams and other human interference. The town boasts several historic sites, a top-notch museum, and a thriving downtown. The calendar is full of wholesome annual events, and the summers are full of Saturday night diversions like farmers markets, bandstand concerts, antique shopping, and stock car racing.

SIGHTS

Fallon's seeming incongruities extend to its attractions. Visitors can commune with the simple yet poignant petroglyphs created by ancient civilizations at Grimes Point or feel the adrenaline rush as fighter pilots put their powerful aircraft through their paces across the road.

Lahontan State Recreation Area

Just about midway between Carson City and Fallon on US 50 is the **Lahontan State Recreation Area** (16799 Lahontan Dam Rd., 775/867-3500, http://parks.nv.gov, $7), a camping, catch-and-release fishing, water-skiing, and swimming spot. Lahontan boasts 25 picnic, camping, and swimming beaches at three different locations. From Lahontan Dam, follow the gravel shore road southwest past 10 separate beaches; the 7th has wheelchair access. There are 40 campsites ($15) for tents or self-contained RVs up to 30 feet long, along with piped water, flush toilets, showers, picnic tables, grills, and fire pits. Primitive on-the-beach camping is permitted anywhere along the shoreline except the day-use areas and boat ramps. The 17-mile-long reservoir invites shore and boat anglers to try their luck for walleye, catfish, trout, and wipers.

Fort Churchill

Seven miles south of Lahontan State Recreation Area, just off US 95A a few miles south of Silver Springs, is **Fort Churchill State Historic Park** (10000 US 95A, 775/577-2345, http://parks.nv.gov, $7), which was built in 1860 to protect early settlers. Its ruins are preserved, along with remnants and interpretive displays about the garrison, the Pony Express, and the Overland Telegraph, whose routes ran through the area. A haven for outdoors lovers, the park

Fallon

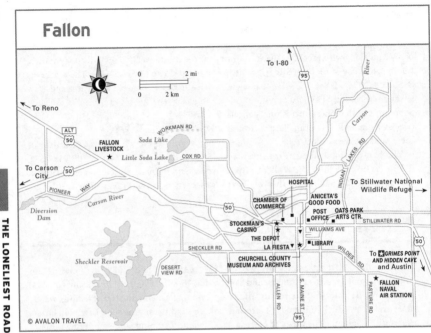

© AVALON TRAVEL

contains a **campground** ($17) with 20 cottonwood-shaded spots big enough for most motor homes, as well as tents and trailers. Reservations are not accepted. It has a dump station but no hookups. Attractions include hiking and horseback trails and access to the Carson River for canoeing and kayaking. Visitors also can tour several former working ranches between the fort and Lahontan State Recreation Area.

Churchill County Museum and Archives

Despite surprisingly stiff competition, we are inclined to agree with the **Churchill County Museum and Archives** (1050 S. Maine, 775/423-3677, www.ccmuseum.org, 10am-5pm Tues.-Sun. Mar.-Nov., 10am-4pm Tues.-Sat., 10am-3pm Sun. Dec.-Feb., free), which bills itself "The Best Little Museum on the Loneliest Road in America." Along with a collection of mineral specimens and mining equipment required by state law to display (kidding!), the museum interprets the Native

American and pioneer life. The Indian collection includes hand-woven baskets, a tule hut, arrowheads, duck decoys, and other necessities. The pioneer section shows a turn-of-the-20th-century kitchen complete with cast-iron stove, a family room with pianos, cameras, telephones, dolls, and other luxuries, a quilt and embroidery display, and feminine accoutrements like those sold in the Bluebird Hat Shop in the 1920s. The museum also chronicles the excavation of **Hidden Cave,** 12 miles east of town, with **tours** (9:30am, second and fourth Sat. each month, excluding holidays, free) starting from the museum. The museum gift shop is housed in **Woodliff's Novelty Store,** one of Fallon's oldest commercial structures.

★ Grimes Point and Hidden Cave

Take US 50 west out of town and south around the naval air station for 10 miles to **Grimes Point** to see remarkable petroglyphs, believed to have been carved sometime between

5000 BC and AD 1500. This prehistoric rock art site, one of the largest and most accessible collections in Nevada, contains about 150 basalt boulders covered with carvings. Pick up an information booklet at the trailhead; it identifies the eight signed stations on the mile-long trail.

Two types of petroglyphs are visible along the trail: primitive "pit and groove" formations, created by striking the boulders heavily with a sharp stone; and "Great Basin pecked" creations, in which flat stones were used to sand the shapes into the rock. There are also two distinct styles, curvilinear and rectilinear, basically meaning lazy eights and stick figures. Some of the artwork's symbolism is obvious—the sun, snakes, and people—but you'll also see petroglyphs that resemble mushrooms, butterflies, tadpoles, and even fire trucks. Petroglyphs had religious and cultural significance: The carvings were traditionally performed by a shaman before a hunt or ceremony. By the end of the trail, you'll have had enough petroglyph exposure to invent your own theories about their shapes, meanings, ages, and scientific descriptions.

Four schoolboys stumbled upon **Hidden Cave**, a mile northeast of Grimes Point, in the 1920s. In excavations that continued through the 1970s, it yielded 2,500 Native American artifacts, including leatherwear, basketry, carved wooden and stone tools, arrow shafts and points, and stored food.

Two signs near the trailhead point you in the right direction. The Bureau of Land Management has installed an information kiosk at the trailhead parking lot for Grimes Point and Hidden Cave. The interpretive loop includes petroglyphs, tufa, and obsidian. Signs along the trails make it harder to get lost. The cave itself is accessible only via tours offered from the **Churchill County Museum** (1050 S. Maine, 775/423-3677, www. ccmuseum.org, 9:30am, second and fourth Sat. each month, free). Inside, lamps light the yawning cavern.

Fallon Naval Air Station

Just across US 50, you might be able to see the Navy's F-18 Hornets engaging each other in mock dogfights over the training area east of the Stillwater Range. The area's 300 days of crystal-clear skies, an extensive training facility that includes 13,000 miles of airspace and four live-ordnance target ranges, and a 14,000-foot-long runway make it an ideal location for practicing combat scenarios.

For an even better view, take Maine or

Hidden Cave

South Taylor Street for about five miles down US 95 until you see the sign for the **Fallon Naval Air Station** to the left on Union Lane. Go another few miles on Union Lane until you get to the south gate. Then take a right on Pasture Road and a left on Berney Road to view the takeoffs and landings on the other side of the high cyclone fence.

The Top Gun air combat school arrived in May 1996, and 25 pilot trainers are stationed at the base year-round. An aircraft carrier's entire fighter wing can train together here at the same time using realistic fight scenarios and comprehensive air combat tactics. Ten trainees at a time are assigned to the school for 10-week flight and air-combat classes offered four times a year.

Sand Mountain

About 25 miles east of Fallon, a paved access road delivers visitors to **Sand Mountain** (www.blm.gov, $40 weekly use fee). When the wind is just right, this 600-foot-tall singing sand dune emits whistles and roars that can reach more than 100 decibels. These "songs" can last for several minutes. Bikes and four-wheelers equipped with whip flags can speed along a few marked trails and ride the ridges, while sandboarders hurtle down steep 500-foot dunes. Some parts of the mountain are closed to protect the habitat of the endangered and endemic Sand Mountain blue butterfly. There are also designated nonmotorized areas for hikers and bicyclists. Dry camping is allowed in a designated area at the mountain's base. Vault toilets are provided, but campers must bring their own water and firewood. Warm spring and fall weekends can see several thousand off-roaders crawling over the mountain like ants. A few days later, the shifting grains erase all traces. Midsummer is especially hot at Sand Mountain; always bring plenty of water.

RACING

Speed freaks can have their time in the spotlight and the cockpit, competing at the **Top Gun Raceway Motor Sports Complex** (15550 Schurz Hwy., 775/423-0223 or 800/325-7558, www.topgunraceway.com, 6pm Fri., 9:30am Sat.-Sun. mid-Mar.-mid-Oct., $10 adults, $5 age 6-12, free under age 6), 11 miles south of Fallon on US 95. The track has state-of-the-art staging and timing equipment, lights for night racing, and a concession stand. Another option is the **Rattlesnake Raceway** (2000 Airport Rd., 775/423-7483, http://rattle-snakeraceway.org, 6pm Sat., $8 adults, $4 age

ATVs on Sand Mountain

6-15, free under age 6), which holds events for Karts and dwarfs. It's three miles northwest of Fallon: Go west on US 50, then north on Cemetery, Indian Lakes, and Airport Roads.

CASINOS

Stockman's Casino (1560 W. Williams Ave., 775/423-2117, www.stockmanscasino.com) is the full-service gambling and entertainment place in Fallon, with liberal blackjack rules (low minimum, doubling down on any two cards, re-splitting, jackpot options), a table-game variation of Texas Hold 'em, live keno, 260 TV show-, movie-, and pop culture-themed slots, and a William Hill sports betting kiosk. True to its generic name, **Stockman's Steakhouse** (5pm-9pm Tues.-Sat., $20-30) runs out the typical steak-chops-seafood lineup common to casino fine dining restaurants statewide, though the reasonably priced chicken Monterey ($18) is tasty. The blue crab-stuffed mushroom appetizer ($12) is a worthwhile splurge. **Stockman's Café** (7am-11pm daily, $10-20) has diner fare and the best milkshakes in town. **Holiday Inn Express** ($110-125) handles the casino's hotel operations with the same professionalism, friendliness, and amenities you would expect from the chain. You will appreciate the hot breakfast and indoor pool/hot tub.

Depot Casino & Restaurant (875 W. Williams Ave., 775/423-2411, www.depotcasino.com), located in the town's original 1907 railroad depot (although the building itself has been relocated a few times), has almost as many gaming machines as Stockman's but no table games. Bingo is upstairs. Big, filling breakfast portions, sandwiches, and pasta dishes are the highlight at the **Depot Diner** (775/423-3233, 8am-9pm, $10-20), which boasts cool railroad signs and memorabilia. The bar, full of big-screen TVs, is the place to be during football season.

Fallon Nugget (70 S. Maine St., 775/423-3111, www.nuggetcasinos.com) features the only full-service sports book (9am-6pm Mon.-Wed., 8am-6pm Thurs.-Sun.) in town, courtesy of William Hill. But its greatest claim to awesomeness is ★ **Aniceta's Good Food** (775/423-5440, 6am-2pm Tues. and Sun., 6am-9pm Wed.-Sat., $6-12), with burgers, fries, chicken, and bacon and eggs in all their greasy (in a good way) glory.

There are more slots at **Bonanza Inn & Casino** (855 W. Williams Ave., 775/423-6031), where the Super 8 ($50-65) rooms are clean and quiet, and the **Silver Springs Nugget** (1280 US 95A, Silver Springs, 775/577-4263, www.nuggetcasinos.com).

ENTERTAINMENT AND EVENTS

Every Tuesday at 11am, the **Fallon Livestock Exchange** (2055 Trento Ln., 775/867-2020, www.fallonlivestock.com) auctions sheep, goats, pigs, cattle, calves, and horses at its facility eight miles west of town on US 50. A real throwback to the Old West, modern auctions use technology (live Internet streaming video) to link stock buyers from around the world to the local sale, which is conducted in a 200-seat ring corral. The country-fried steak gravy at the stockyard's **Running Iron Café** (775/867-2031, 7am-2pm Mon.-Fri., 8am-2pm Sat.-Sun., $8-12) is so good it will make you forget your manners. If you prefer sugary over savory, the sweet cream pancakes are the way to go.

Housed in the renovated former Frederic DeLongchamps-designed school, the **Oats Park Arts Center** (151 E. Park St., 775/423-1440, www.churchillarts.org) hosts theater and live music performances and classic movie screenings. Three galleries display paintings, sculpture, and photography by artists from throughout the West. It also has a gift shop and the well-stocked Art Bar.

FOOD

Slanted Porch (310 S. Taylor St., 775/423-4489, www.slantedporch.com, 11am-3pm Mon.-Sat., $12-18) has our vote for the best lunch in Fallon, offering green salads and hot or cold sandwiches.

JD Slingers (855 W. Williams Ave., 775/423-3050, www.jdslingers.com, 7am-9pm daily, $10-20) has a menu almost as thick as the Fallon phonebook, with extensive breakfast items, steaks, salads, chicken, and salmon, and anything you can think of that fits between two slices of bread, including 16 burgers and six—count 'em, six!—grilled cheese offerings!

The roadhouse-style **Middlegate Station** (42500 Austin Hwy., 775/423-7134, 7am-9pm daily, $7-15), 47 miles west of town, also does tacos, breakfast, and cold beer. But burgers, Wild West relics, and rustic ambiance are the stars. Sign a dollar bill and tack it to the ceiling, then get all *Man vs. Food* and challenge the Monster Burger. You win a free T-shirt if you can finish the 20-ounce Angus burger on a big sourdough bun with cheese and all the fixin's, along with a pile of fries.

Though it doesn't rate as fine dining, ★ **La Fiesta** (60 W. Center St., 775/423-1605, 11am-10pm Sun.-Thurs., 11am-11pm Fri.-Sat., $10-15) challenges Slanted Porch for best overall eatery in town. It serves huge platters of traditional south-of-the-border fare, and the service is so fast that the carnitas and cheesy enchiladas are still steaming when they reach your table. In a world where if you've tasted one, you've tasted them all, the white salsa and tortilla chips at La Fiesta really stand out. You can find cheaper Mexican fare in plenty of other places, but life is too short.

Don't be put off by the open, austere dining room at **Azteca Grill & Bakery** (1740 W. Williams Ave., 775/423-4964, 7am-8:30pm daily, $7-10). The storefront taqueria needs every inch of table space to accommodate its adoring fans. The proprietors put as much love into their homemade salsas, sauces, chips, and side dishes as they do their scrumptious after-dinner sweets.

All-you-can-eat sushi draws a crowd, but the authentic Chinese entrées keep us coming back to **The Wok** (255 S. Maine St., 775/423-5588, http://thewokfallon.com, 11am-9pm Mon.-Thurs., 11am-10pm Fri.-Sat., $10-20; sushi buffet 11am-8pm Mon.-Thurs., 11am-9pm Fri.-Sat., $16-22). We think the steamed rice is better than the fried variety, especially with pork lo mein or lemon chicken. The brothy soup, of course, is the draw at **Vn Pho** (1770 W. Williams Ave., 775/428-5858, http://vnphofallon.com, 11am-9pm Tues.-Sun., $8-12), but the pot stickers and egg rolls—not to mention the reasonable prices—are as good as you will find this side of Hanoi.

Other worthy choices include **Maine Street Café** (810 S. Maine St., 775/423-1830, www.mainestreet.cafe, 7am-2:30pm Mon.-Wed., 7am-8:30pm Thurs.-Sat., $10-20), for American beef dishes and Italian-themed dinners such as fettuccine and chicken piccata, and **Courtyard Café** (55 E. Williams Ave., 775/423-5505, www.courtyardcafefallon.com, 7:30am-2:30pm Mon.-Sat., $10-15), for sandwiches, salads, and quiche.

ACCOMMODATIONS

Most of Fallon's motels are of the chain variety. **Holiday Inn Express** (1560 W. Williams Ave., 775/428-2588, www.ihg.com, $100-133) is the Stockman Casino's hotel option. Clean and fresh in a chain-hotel way, it attracts families with its indoor-outdoor swimming pool and free continental breakfast. Williams Avenue also hosts **Best Western** (1035 W. Williams Ave., 775/423-6005, http://bestwesternnevada.com, $70-90), **Comfort Inn** (1830 W. Williams Ave., www.choicehotels.com, $70-90), and **Econo Lodge** (70 E. Williams Ave., 775/423-2194, www.choicehotels.com, $65-75).

Budget options include **Gold Star Inn and Suites** (1051 W. Williams Ave., $55-70) and **Value Inn** (180 W. Williams Ave., 775/423-5151, www.valueinn.net, $50-65), with lightning-fast Internet, microwaves, fridges, and peace and quiet. The room rates make it worth putting up with a few inconveniences, such as slightly frayed towels and nicked furniture.

For local color, try the **Overland Hotel** (125 E. Center St., 775/423-2719, www.theoverlandhotel.com, $45-65), its rooms restored to their 1910s grandeur. Soundproofing apparently hadn't been invented when the hotel was built in 1908. The draws are the history and local rusticity, especially the old jukebox and just-as-old 45s playing on it in the kitschy, memorabilia-strewn barroom. If you plan to do your gambling or socializing at Bonanza Casino, or if you're bringing Fido and Fluffy, you may prefer to stay close by at the **Super 8** (855 W. Williams Ave., 775/423-6031, www.wyndhamhotels.com, $45-65).

RV Parks

Of the two standard RV parks west of Fallon on US 50, **Fallon RV Park** (5787 US 50, 775/867-2332, www.fallonrv.com, $40-45, $29 tents) is the nicer. The trees are larger—especially at the sites close to the market—the grass is greener, and the spaces are wider. Cable and Wi-Fi are free. There are 44 spaces for motor homes, all with full hookups; 20 are pull-throughs. Tents are allowed.

You could opt to save a few bucks and pull into **Sage Valley RV** (4800 US 50, 775/867-3636, $27-30), but even though it's a mile closer to town, you'll probably wish you hadn't. The Sage is showing its age, and the sites can be cramped if your rig is of any size. In fact, there's a lot about the place that seems small: the pads and the restrooms, for example. The one advantage the Sage has over Fallon RV is that the noise from the highway doesn't seem to carry to the sites. **Bonanza Inn**'s RV park (855 W. Williams Ave., 775/423-6031, $15) is a better budget option, especially if you will be spending most of your time in the casino. The sites are big, but there's no shade and not much to look at, although you can't beat the price, which includes access to the casino's amenities. **Churchill County Fairgrounds** (99 Sheckler Rd., 775/423-7733, $15) has 48 full-hookup sites, a dump station, and showers. People attending the livestock shows fill the place quickly, but if there are no events, you can have your pick of prime sites, which are level and shady.

For scenery and non-gambling activities, keep driving toward Austin on US 50. About 60 miles outside Fallon (or 50 miles from Austin, if you are driving west) you will happen upon **Cold Springs Station** (52300 Austin Hwy., 775/423-1233, $30-35). The 25 gravel sites are level, if a little tight. Dozens of hiking and ATV trails traverse dry lake beds and creeks both dry and flowing. Markers denoting Pony Express routes and the local station's location add historical significance. In addition to the full-hookup (including Wi-Fi) RV park, this traveler's rest boasts a small motel, rental cabins, a bar, restaurant (8am-8pm, $12-20), gift shop, and laundry facilities. All are top-shelf and reasonably priced, considering they're the only game within 50 miles.

INFORMATION AND SERVICES

Fallon Chamber of Commerce (85 N. Taylor St., 775/423-2544, www.fallonchamber.com) has all the statistics and information on the area, as well as hotel and restaurant deals. The **Churchill County Library** (553 S. Maine St., 775/423-7581, 9am-6pm Mon. and Thurs.-Fri., 9am-8pm Tues.-Wed., 9am-5pm Sat.) has a Nevada room overflowing with interesting books and reports.

Austin and Vicinity

The 110 miles between Fallon and Austin are perhaps the loneliest along the Loneliest Road. While Austin is far removed from its boomtown years, it's still a mighty welcome sight for the weary traveler. With the Toiyabe Mountains serving as inspirational backdrop, outdoor activities await: hunting, fishing, camping, mountain biking, and even land sailing.

SIGHTS

Coming from the west into town, turn right on Castle Road and follow a precipitous road about a half mile around to **Stokes Castle.** This curious attraction is a rare three-story stone structure built by mining baron Anson P. Stokes, who admired the castle towers he saw on a visit to Italy. This reproduction was built of hand-cut native granite, the huge blocks hoisted into place with a hand winch and held in place with rock wedging and clay mortar. Incredibly, after all that work, it was only occupied for a month or two in the summer of 1897 before Stokes sold his Austin business interests and never returned. Today, the castle is a fine place to have a picnic or stretch your legs in the piñon forest up the hill, which has a great overlook of Reese River Valley. You can't go inside, but you could camp here in a pinch.

Typical of the breed, the **Austin Historical Museum** (180 Main St., 775/238-4150, by appointment, donation) houses a smattering of mining, ranching, railroad, and Native American artifacts lent or donated by the area's residents.

On the east side of town, **Gridley Store** (247 Water St., 775/964-1202, by appointment) was opened in 1863 by Rueul Gridley, whose name lives on in conjunction with a 50-pound sack of flour. Gridley paid off a losing bet by carrying the flour from his store to a bar across town, then auctioning it off for a donation to the Sanitary Fund. The highest bidder auctioned it off again, then again, and again. Townsfolk raised $6,000 by the end of the afternoon. From there, Gridley took the sack to Virginia City and repeated the process, then on to California and eventually the East Coast, raising $275,000 for Civil War relief. Gridley himself died penniless six years later. Some believe his restless soul still haunts the building, toting the famous flour sack on his shoulder. The house next to Gridley's store was originally the town brothel.

RECREATION

Mountain bikers come to this corner of the Toiyabe Mountains for its lung-searing hill climbs, heart-stopping downhills, and killer views for off-road bikers of any ilk. Beginners and younger riders will appreciate **Castle Loop,** a 4.5-mile relatively flat trail that gives a gentle sample of what the sport can offer, with twisting turns, a few jumps, and one or two short climbs. More seasoned cyclists may want to test their mettle on **Gold Venture Loop.** There are plenty of steep climbs as the trail gains 4,500 feet over 27.5 miles. But it rewards riders with an exhilarating spin through a mine road and the rollercoaster ride down to Birch Creek. The **Austin Ranger District** (775/964-2671) and the **Austin Chamber of Commerce** (775/964-2200) can provide information and directions to the trailheads for these and dozens more mountain rides.

Land sailing enthusiasts rave about the smoothness of the Smith Creek dry lake bed, which can propel their wind-powered yachts at up to 100 mph. Each summer, as many as 200 land sailors from around the world converge on this glassy sheet of dirt 30 miles west of Austin to put their three-wheeled contraptions through their paces at the **Holy Gale,** sponsored by the **North American Land Sailing Association** (775/355-7035, www.nalsa.org/events.htm).

FOOD

Austin has two places to eat, each with unique charms. At **Toiyabe Café** (150 Main St., 775/964-2220, 6am-8pm daily Apr.-Oct., 6am-4pm daily Nov.-Mar., $10-20), try the green chili and Swiss or Spanish omelet or bacon and eggs for breakfast. Lunch and dinner fare includes good soup and burritos, burgers, steak sandwiches, and fish; beer and wine are available.

The **International Café and Bar** (59 Main St., 775/964-1225, 6am-8pm daily, $8-12), on the west side of town, is in the second-oldest hotel building in Nevada and makes a mean bacon-topped sirloin with all the fixings for $11 along with traditional breakfasts for under $8.

ACCOMMODATIONS

There are 39 hotel rooms in Austin, none of which could be considered luxurious. Call for reservations, as Austin is a popular overnight stop for tour buses. One busload of tourists can monopolize all the rooms in town.

The most up-to-date accommodations in Austin await at the **Cozy Mountain Motel** (40 Main St., 775/964-7433, $55-75), a string of 12 recently remodeled "modular" units that resemble mobile homes or construction-site mobile offices. It's more inviting and attractive than it sounds, with flower boxes, hanging lanterns, clean restful beds, and flat-screen TVs with premium channels, although the rooms aren't terribly large and Internet is spotty. The rooms at the Cozy Mountain are positively palatial compared to those at the 17-unit **Lincoln Motel** (60 Main St., 775/964-2698, $50-60). The Lincoln somehow manages to fit a queen bed, a TV, a dresser, and a tiny bathroom into its standard 8- by 10-foot guest rooms, which were renovated in 2007. However, larger rooms, even a few with three queen-size beds, are available. Fresh coffee at the front desk takes the edge off a tedious drive even before you check in. There are 10 plank-built guest rooms in the shade of some tall trees at the **Pony Canyon Motel** (Main St., 775/964-2605, $45-65). Following

town tradition, the guest rooms are small and utilitarian.

A converted and renovated 1860s boardinghouse, **Union Street Lodging** (69 Union St., 775/964-2364, www.unionstreetlodging.com, $75-95) is Austin's first full-service bed-and-breakfast. The bigger guest rooms feature four-poster beds. All guest rooms are tidy and snug, with Nevada-themed artwork. Coffee is on in the wee hours, and the full breakfast is of the appropriately hearty variety, served at 8am. Treat your significant other like a queen or king by booking at **Paradise Ranch Castle** (440/781-8768, www.paradiseranchcastle.com, $100-110), a real Arthurian keep just 15 miles from Austin. In addition to the free hot breakfast, guests have the run of the castle, including a rec room with jukebox and pool table, cash bar, and DVD collection. There's plenty of space for off-roading and horseback riding, and you can stargaze from the castle turrets. Fishing creeks and lakes and hot springs are nearby. Take NV 722 west out of Austin for 13 miles to Road 215 north.

RV Parks

Austin RV (244 Water St., 775/964-1011, $25), at 6,900 feet in elevation, has good shade, although the pull-through sites can be a bit uneven. Fee collecting is somewhat based on the honor system (read the signs on the information board and drop the night's payment in the drop box on the front of the office). There are 15 RV sites and four tent sites. **Pony Express RV Park** (260 Main St., 775/964-2005, $22) offers six gravel RV sites with basic hookups. It's close to a town park and public swimming pool. No tents. Dry, no-hookup camping is available 25 miles east of Austin on US 50 at Hickison Petroglyph Recreation Area (free). Big rigs may find the sites a bit too snug for comfort.

INFORMATION

The **U.S. Forest Service Station** (100 Midas Canyon Rd., 775/964-2671), on the west side of town overlooking the junction of NV 305, sells

The Toiyabe and Toquima Ranges

The Toiyabe Range is the preeminent stretch of mountains in central Nevada, anchoring a vast network of mountains and valleys, busted boomtowns, and dusty outposts. They are home to Austin, which bathed in the radiant glow of silver mining in the 1870s, and Eureka, whose brick structures were built to survive boomtown floods and fires and still stand today. The Toiyabe—a Shoshone word variously translated as "black mountains," for the thick piñon, juniper, and mahogany cover, or "big mountains," for their length, height, steepness, and ruggedness—stretch from Toiyabe Peak near Austin to Mahogany Mountain opposite Carvers. This mansard roof tops the middle of the state in a thin straight line more than 10,000 feet high for 50 miles. The southern slope extends for another 20 miles, hooking up with the Shoshone Range to the west and gradually squeezing off the Reese River Valley in between. Numerous tributary creeks converge here to create the mud-puddle Reese River and fertile ranch land.

The upper range elongates for another 50 miles, rising to a head at mystical Mount Callaghan, paralleled by the Toquima Range to the east across Big Smoky Valley. Austin, at 6,500 feet one of the highest towns in Nevada, sits on the western slopes of the Toiyabes. Monitor Valley and the Monitor Range, with their adjoining mining towns and ghost towns, complete the pattern.

Three peaks in the Toiyabes tower over 11,000 feet, with **Arc Dome,** near the convergence of the Shoshone and Toiyabe Ranges, the highest at 11,788 feet. Another four peaks in the range rise over 10,000 feet. The top of mighty Mount Jefferson of the Toquima Range right across the valley actually looks down 200 feet at the crown of Arc Dome. This is one of the finest mountain scenes in the state.

Arc Dome is the largest U.S. Forest Service wilderness area in Nevada at 115,000 acres. *Hiking the Great Basin,* by John Hart, covers a baker's dozen hikes here in detail, including two for Arc Dome, several for Twin Rivers and Jett Canyon, and the 65-mile **Toiyabe Crest National Recreation Trail.** *Nevada Wilderness Areas,* by Michael Rose, covers seven hikes here, including two Twin River loops; Cow, Tom's, and Jett Canyons; and the Toiyabe Crest Trail. If internal combustion is more your style, the roads down Big Smoky from Austin to Tonopah and up Reese River Valley from Ione Canyon to Austin provide two of the most breathtaking scenic cruises in the West.

detailed maps and can advise you on hikes in the area.

The **Austin Chamber of Commerce** (122 Main St., 775/964-2200, www.austinnevada.com/chamber) has a large rack of brochures in the foyer of the courthouse; the chamber office upstairs is open most weekday mornings.

★ BERLIN-ICHTHYOSAUR STATE PARK

Austin is the starting point for exploring the valleys west of the Toiyabe Range. Taking NV 722 and NV 21 along the Reese River between the Shoshone and Toiyabe fingers and crossing to the Shoshone Range's western slope via NV 844—a 60-mile, two-hour drive from Austin—brings you to **Berlin ghost town,** one of the best-preserved in Nevada. It

owes its early history to mining claims begun in 1863 by prospectors from Austin. At the turn of the 20th century, the Nevada Mining Company built a large mill here that operated for nearly two decades. The town didn't last much longer than that; Berlin's post office closed in 1918. It has been a state park since 1955. Today, Berlin is preserved in a state of arrested decay.

The **Berlin-Ichthyosaur State Park office** (775/964-2440, http://parks.nv.gov) is in the former mine superintendent's home, where you can pay the $7 park entry fee and pick up a brochure with a good map; the office keeps irregular hours. If it's closed, just up the road is a sign with a map of Berlin in 1905. Park and walk the well-trod trails and explore the ghost town remnants and marine fossils, explained by helpful plaques. Up the hill are the ruins of the assay office, a stagecoach stop, a machine shop, and the hoist building over the main mine shaft. Tours of the mine itself are no longer offered due to safety concerns.

The biggest building in Berlin, down by the road, is one of the last original mills in Nevada. Check out the tongue-and-groove joints and wooden pegs holding the whole thing together. Four big steam engines on the floor powered 30 stamps, and you can easily imagine the deafening din of metal on rock. For all that, Berlin produced less than $1 million worth of precious metals between 1900 and 1907.

Take (gravel) Primitive Road up from Berlin and turn right into the **campground** ($17), which has 14 sites, some suitable for RVs up to 25 feet, among pines and junipers; there are fire rings, good outhouses, and running water (spring-fall).

A trail from site 8 leads 0.5 mile to the **fossil shelter,** or you can drive up to it on Primitive Road. Rangers lead 40-minute **tours** (10am and 2pm Mon.-Fri., 10am, noon, and 2pm Sat.-Sun. Memorial Day-Labor Day, $3 adults, $2 children). Try to imagine what it might've looked like when ichthyosaurs swam in the warm ocean that covered central Nevada 225 million years ago. Fossils of

these giant marine creatures were first found in 1928. Extensive excavations in 1954 uncovered partial remains of 40 individual ichthyosaurs. These creatures were great predators 50-60 feet long and weighing 50-60 tons, with 10-foot heads, 8-foot-wide jaws, and foot-wide eyes. Outside the shelter is a sculpted relief of the creatures dating to 1957. If the shelter isn't open, descriptive signs and big picture windows provide a self-guided "tour" of the skeletal features of the fossils.

★ SPENCER HOT SPRINGS

Eleven miles east of Austin, turn right onto NV 376; a dirt road (National Forest 001) immediately heads off east (left) toward the Toquimas. Follow it to where a left turn (unmarked, but easily recognizable) leads up to **Spencer Hot Springs.** Far from a resort spa, the springs nevertheless combine fine views—the Toiyabes stretch into the background, and the Monitors reach out in front—with a soothing hot soak. But while the setting is desolate, the springs are likely to be well-trafficked. It seems locals, visitors, and nature-lovers of all stripes know about the twin cowboy tubs situated along this lonely dirt road. These springs are surprisingly quite

ghost town of Berlin

civilized, expertly "developed" by helpful previous visitors. The big main pool at the top ledge is sandbagged, tastefully tiled with slate, and offset by a little wooden deck. Toward the road a bit is a big galvanized tub. The metal cattle troughs collect *very* hot water directly from the source, via a moveable pipe. Push the pipe out of the trough to let the water cool, pull it back in when you're ready to steep. Lie back, breathe deeply, and offer up a prayer of thanks from your frayed nerve endings. Other pools along the stretch are ringed with stone and are cooler than the first 105-degree metal troughs. The resident herd of burros may come take a peek while you're bathing. Dry camping is allowed around the springs; please camp well away from the water so others may enjoy the spa treatments.

TOQUIMA CAVE

Eleven miles farther south past Spencer Hot Springs along the dirt road, **Toquima Cave** is full of ancient Native American pictographs. More overhang and rock shelter than cave, the grotto is gated to prevent vandals from disturbing the sacred Shoshone artwork. But you can still see and photograph the designs left between 1,400 and 700 years ago. A campground is a half mile away, offering five non-reserved spots. One is big enough to handle a 25-foot RV. A vault toilet is the only concession to civilization. An easy trail leads to the cave. Stone stairs make the final climb a dawdle.

KINGSTON AND BEYOND

If you forgo a dip at Spencer Hot Springs, stay on NV 376 southbound. You'll spy Toiyabe Peak (10,793 feet) and Bunker Hill (11,474 feet) as you approach the first ridgeline. About 15 miles south of the US 50 junction is a turnoff into **Kingston.** In the late 1960s, a developer attempted to transform the ranch land around present-day Kingston into a tourist destination, with cobblestone streets, outdoor cafés, and upscale boutiques; it never took off. Today there's a little gold mining, supported by a small settlement, the third-largest population center in Lander County after Battle Mountain and Austin. **Miles End Bed & Breakfast** (107 Del Dr., 775/964-1046, www.milesendbnb.com, $120-175) puts guests up in luxury cabins with access to a wood-fired hot tub, games, and free, full breakfast. All cabins have private baths and king or queen beds. Dinners can be arranged; there's a full bar, and the Kingston general store is across the road.

soakers at Spencer Hot Springs

The pavement continues through Kingston but ends on the way into **Kingston Canyon** (Kingston Canyon Rd.) and **Kingston Campground,** five miles from town, and **Big Creek Campground** 13 miles farther along. In between, you will find ample opportunities for primitive camping and trout fishing in Groves Lake and the numerous small streams nearby.

You'll also find access to the **Toiyabe Crest Trail.** Only hardened hikers should attempt to conquer the five-day, 72-mile undertaking along the ridgeline and through the **Arc Dome Wilderness,** which consistently reaches 10,000 feet in elevation. The access window for the full trail is short: tackle it in June or July, after the snow has melted but the water sources have not yet evaporated. Pack in everything you will need for dry camping, and pick up the north trailhead just past Groves Lake. Less arduous but just as scenic day hikes embark from near the Toiyabe Crest Trail's **South Twin River trailhead,** 25 miles south of Kingston on NV 376: **Stewart Creek Trail** (five miles out and back), **Cow Canyon Trail** (five miles), and **North Twin River Trail** (eight miles).

Eureka

Miners began to notice Eureka when silver turned up in 1864, but the difficulty processing the lead-laden ore dampened the interest. The complex refining required the ore be sent overseas for processing, cutting deep gouges into potential profits. In the 1870s, smelters sprung up in Eureka, greatly simplifying the process and spurring renewed mining interest—in the lead more than the silver—in the remote town. By 1879, large-scale exploitation of the deposits was underway, and Eureka was on its way to earning the nickname "Pittsburgh of the West." The town grew to 9,000 residents, but the 1880s saw the once-lucrative mines peter out. In addition to mining, which is still susceptible to boom-and-bust cycles, agriculture remains a vital part of Eureka's economy, along with outdoor recreation.

Dozens of striking stone and masonry buildings dating from the 1880s and 1890s are still in use in Eureka, making it easy to imagine life in a turn-of-the-20th-century mining town. For a guided itinerary, get the town tour brochure at www.rainesmarket.com/eureka.

Outside of town, Barrick Gold Corp. operates the **Ruby Hill Mine** (US 50 and NV 278, 775/401-6435). Tours of the open-pit heap-leach operation that recovers 4,000 ounces of gold per year are offered by appointment.

SIGHTS

Eureka is a charming town with many well-preserved 19th-century buildings. To mitigate the damage from frequent floods and fire, boom-era residents built many structures out of brick. Today, several of these intriguing structures, many still in use, can be seen.

Eureka Opera House

Originally intended as a union hall, the unfinished building that became the **Eureka Opera House** (31 S. Main St., 775/237-6006, 8am-5pm Mon.-Fri., free) was purchased for a song when the striking union needed emergency funds. A regular stop for touring operas and other professional productions, the opera house also hosted boxing matches, debates, school functions, and the Nob Hill Fire Company's annual New Year's Eve masquerade balls. Later, silent films and talkies were shown here until 1958. Sadly, a carelessly placed lantern ignited the magnificent Italian hand-painted stage curtain in 1923, but the "new" curtain, brought in from Minneapolis in 1924, is just as striking. Fully restored, the opera house today is a venue for cultural events and conventions.

Eureka County Courthouse

The **Eureka County Courthouse** (10 S. Main St., 775/237-5530) continues to mete out frontier justice as it has since 1880. The great fire of 1879 burned the original wooden courthouse to the ground around the iron jail and fortified vault. The county constructed the current brick structure around these two fireproof elements. Architecture and design fans will enjoy the details of the vaguely Italianate building: a second-floor balcony, brick pilasters, cornices, a filigreed parapet wall outside, and an imported Spanish cedar judge's bench and balustrade, gilded accents, a 19-foot pressed metal ceiling, and a suspended spectator gallery inside the courtroom.

Eureka Sentinel Museum

The town newspaper is no longer functioning, but the press equipment in a back room of the **Eureka Sentinel Museum** (10 N. Monroe St., 775/237-5010, 8am-noon and 1pm-5pm Tues.-Sat., free) looks like it could do the job if anyone has the urge to start it up again. The paper kept residents in the know from 1879 to 1960; posters printed at the office during the run adorn the pressroom walls. Virtually every aspect of boomtown life is depicted, including residents' work (mining tools and stock certificates) and their leisure (a re-created parlor, kitchen, and barber). Finish your tour at the gift shop, which sells soap and pottery made in Eureka along with books, postcards, and souvenirs.

FOOD

The few restaurants in Eureka are surprisingly good. Pick one depending on what you're in the mood for. At **Owl Club Bar & Steakhouse** (61 N. Main St., 775/237-5280, 10:30am-2am Mon.-Thurs., 8am-2am Fri.-Sun., $15-25), steak—especially the Basque-style grilled sandwich—hits the spot. The establishment has a few dozen slots, a bar, and a gift shop. For gourmet coffee and pastries, **The Roost** (110 S. Main St., 775/237-5002, 6am-noon Mon.-Fri., 8am-noon Sat.-Sun., $5-10) rules. For lunch subs, head to **Pony Express Meats and Deli** (101 Bullion St., 775/237-7665, 6am-2pm Mon.-Sat., $6-12). **Urban Cowboy Bar and Grill** (121 N. Main St., 775/237-5774, 11am-9pm daily, $12-20) touts its Mexican and American cuisine, but the former is the draw, especially the tamales and carne asada, with rice and beans, of course.

ACCOMMODATIONS

Clean, comfortable, and cheap are about all you can ask along this stretch of desolate desert highway. Thankfully, a couple of family-owned establishments hit the mark on all counts. The **Eureka Gold Country Inn** (251 N. Main St., 775/237-5247, www.eurekagoldcountryinn. com, $102) has shed its affiliation with Best Western and gone independent. It has maintained a standard for service and cleanliness, however, with free breakfast and more modern decor and amenities (spa, exercise room) than the town's other choices. But we're sure the **Sundown Lodge** (60 N. Main St., 775/237-5334, $50-60) gets its share of sticker shock-weary travelers who opt for rooms at half the competitor's price, especially if all they really want is a roof and a bed for the night. The Sundown is also within sight of a market and the Owl Club, the only place in town that passes as a night spot. With nightlife almost nonexistent, the Sundown's large flat-screen TVs are a godsend for passing the time.

If you don't need TV or a phone, microwave, or coffee pot, spend an authentic 19th-century luxury-free night at the ★ **Jackson House Hotel** (701 N. Main St., 775/237-5247, www.eurekagoldcountryinn.com, $79). Its nine rooms give a taste of how the well-heeled traveled at the turn of the 20th century. Grand Victorian-style furnishings, claw-foot tubs, crystal, cherrywood, and gilt grace the rooms and the elegant dining room and bar.

With just 15 spaces and few amenities, **Silver Sky Lodge** (US 50 S., 775/237-7146, $25) is not a long-term prospect, but the hookups are strong and universal.

Ely

Ely has certainly benefited from the US 50 "Loneliest Road" campaign. But this town is much more than a mere whistle-stop on an old highway. Indeed, there's much to do in and around Ely. The town's connection to mining is evident everywhere: the open copper pits, charcoal ovens to produce fuel for smelters, and the painstakingly restored Nevada Northern Railway short line. Nature lovers will find much to appreciate here too, from picturesque Murry Canyon to the elk herd that returns year after year to share habitat with bald eagles and ravens. For another type of wild life, there are some 500 slot machines and a dozen lively watering holes.

SIGHTS

★ Nevada Northern Railway

While most historic sites offer a glimpse into the past, the **Nevada Northern Railway National Historic Landmark** (1100 Ave. A, 775/289-2085 or 866/407-8326, www.nevadanorthernrailway.net,

8am-5pm daily, $8 adults, $4 age 4-12, free under age 4) transports visitors back more than a century to relive it. The site encompasses the entire Nevada Northern railyard, its facilities, and the rolling stock. The tour, one of the most thrilling in the state, takes you through the most complete and authentic working remains of any short-line railroad in the country—and then you get to ride on it.

Altogether there are more than 30 buildings from the 1906-1907 era, including an old water tower and sand and coal bins. Start your exploration of this workhorse operation at the old depot, built in 1907 with local sandstone and restored to its original grandeur. Check out the ticket office and big black-and-white historical photos.

From the depot, walk by the 1905 freight barn, the oldest building in the complex, past the bus barn and master mechanics offices, and then into the engine house, where most of the equipment is stored, including

Nevada Northern Railway National Historic Landmark

Ely

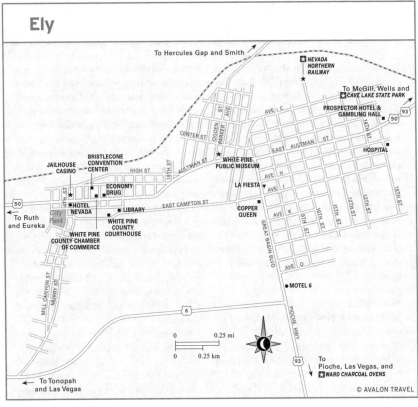

To Hercules Gap and Smith

NEVADA NORTHERN RAILWAY

To McGill, Wells and CAVE LAKE STATE PARK

PROSPECTOR HOTEL & GAMBLING HALL

AVE L C

CENTER ST

OGDEN ST

PARKER AVE

AULTMAN ST

EAST AULTMAN ST

HOSPITAL

BRISTLECONE CONVENTION CENTER

JAILHOUSE CASINO

HIGH ST

WHITE PINE PUBLIC MUSEUM

15TH ST

16TH ST

14TH ST

ECONOMY DRUG

AVE H

LA FIESTA

AVE I

HOTEL NEVADA

LIBRARY

EAST CAMPTON ST

COPPER QUEEN

AVE K

13TH ST

12TH ST

11TH ST

10TH ST

9TH ST

WHITE PINE COUNTY COURTHOUSE

WHITE PINE COUNTY CHAMBER OF COMMERCE

City Park

To Ruth and Eureka

GREAT BASIN BLVD

AVE O

MILL CANYON ST

MURRY ST

MOTEL 6

PIOCHE HWY

0   0.25 mi
0   0.25 km

To Pioche, Las Vegas, and WARD CHARCOAL OVENS

To Tonopah and Las Vegas

© AVALON TRAVEL

locomotives, cabooses, and a passenger coach. Next stop is the rip-track building, or car-repair shop, which houses the Old No. 40 steam engine, restored in 1939.

By now you're itching to fire up a train and light out for the territory. From March through mid-November (except most Tuesdays), steam engines (weekends) or diesels (weekdays) pull passengers on the 90-minute routes ($31 adults, $15 age 4-12, free under age 4, surcharge to ride in the caboose or the cab with the engineer) through tunnels and along mountain grades. A snack bar in the last car sells drinks and snacks. The museum also offers special-event train rides, including the popular Polar Express at Christmas, Winter Photo Shoot, Stargazing, a Fourth of July Fireworks and Barbecue Train, Train Robbery Adventure, and Haunted Ghost Train. Advance reservations often are required.

Bristlecone Convention Center

The remains of the world's longest-lived organism are on display at the **Bristlecone Convention Center** (150 6th St., 775/289-3720 or 800/496-9350, 9am-5pm Mon.-Fri.)—depending on your viewpoint, a testament to advances in climatology or to the willful destruction of the earth's precious resources. A cross-section of the 5,000-year-old bristlecone pine, dubbed Prometheus, occupies a framed place of honor. It was cut down by a graduate student studying climate history with the approval of the U.S. Forest Service. He had no reason to believe the tree was the oldest in existence. It had lived at the tree line on Wheeler Peak, a focal point of Great Basin National Park. The felling remains controversial among scientists and environmentalists alike. The story is recounted in Jim Sloan's excellent *Nevada—True Tales from the Neon Wilderness.*

White Pine Public Museum

Bring your clan to see the cave bear skeleton model and other eclectic stuff at the **White Pine Public Museum** (2000 Aultman St., 775/289-4710, www.wpmuseum.org, call for hours, donation). Outside is Nevada Northern rolling stock, a drilling rig, and the original Cherry Creek depot, which was transported to the museum in 1991. Cherry Creek, like much of the area around Ely, was an important mining district in the 1870s and 1880s. The museum pays tribute to this legacy with a comprehensive 300-specimen mineral collection. Other displays include a large collection of Hesselgesser dolls, Indian baskets, and turn-of-the-20th-century furniture.

Murals and Sculpture

The White Pine Public Museum proudly displays the first of two dozen **murals** (www.elyrenaissance.com/muralmap.html) commissioned by professional artists or undertaken by local residents. Pick up a map at the convention center. The museum's mural, on an outside wall, depicts an early Fourth of July celebration. Other realistic murals, mostly along Aultman and Clark Streets between Mill and 10th Streets, also pay homage to Ely's past. There are tributes to Basque sheepherders, the Pony Express, copper mining, Italian immigrant labor, railroading, and small-town life. **Sculptures** are interspersed with the murals, giving another artistic perspective on Nevada history. Check out the sculpture of the Shoshone woman gathering pine cones (Clark St. and 8th St.).

Conclude your tour with a look at the restored homes in **Renaissance Village** (6th St. and Ely St., June-Sept.) that explore the cultures of the various people that built the town. Most Saturdays in fall, the village hosts a farmers market; cultural demonstrations,

art festivals, concerts, and more find a home here throughout the summer.

Success Summit Loop

This scenic drive starts just off US 93, six miles north of McGill. Turn onto NV 486 and head through **Gallagher Gap,** on the other side of which the road cuts south. Picturesque **Duck Creek Ranch** is three miles off to the right, and **Bird Creek** Forest Service campground is off to the left, up into the Schell Creeks. This is a classically beautiful eastern Nevada ranching valley, with **Timber Creek** Forest Service campground four miles east and **Berry Creek** campground five miles east from the junction at the end of the pavement. Any of these campgrounds (June-Sept., $8) provide access to productive elderberry and chokecherry bushes and trout streams in the area. The fruit is free for the picking, but if you try your fishing luck, make sure you have a Nevada license and trout stamp. Haul in your own firewood and boil the creek water before you drink it.

The road now turns rocky and rough and can support speeds of only 20 mph, in some places 10 mph. In a few miles, there is an unmarked fork in the road—go right. You descend into **Boneyard Canyon** then climb to aptly named **Success Summit** (if you haven't slid off the road, ruined your suspension, or had a flat tire), which has great views. The growing season is short, but if you've timed it right, you'll be rewarded with the sight of vibrant wildflowers. This is also where Nevada's largest elk and deer herds are found, most often seen in the early morning and evening. From here the road switches back about a dozen times and descends along Steptoe Creek to Cave Lake State Park, where the pavement resumes after 25 miles of rough road.

★ Cave Lake State Park

Beautiful mint-green **Cave Lake** is perched at 7,300 feet in the Schell Creek Range. Rainbow and German brown trout are available for catching year-round. **Cave Lake State Park** (off NV 486, 775/867-3001, http://parks. nv.gov, $7) has a full roster of summer water activities, while winter means ice fishing, cross-country skiing, sledding, snowshoeing, and snowmobiling. **Steptoe Creek Trail** parallels the road for three miles from the park entrance to the lake. **Cave Springs Trail,** a moderate five-mile hike, meanders throughout the surrounding hills.

Two campgrounds have a total of 36 sites: **Elk Flat** (May-mid-Oct., $17) and **Lake View** (year-round, $17) also have heated showers and flush toilets. With more than 100,000 visitors to this park yearly, these sites fill up fast.

★ Ward Charcoal Ovens

Heading south of Ely on US 93/50/6, go past NV 486 a few miles to the sign for **Ward Charcoal Ovens.** Turn right (west) onto a well-graded gravel road, which can support speeds of 40 mph, and go six miles to Cave Valley Road. Turn left and enjoy the view of the beehive-shaped ovens lined up in the desert, hemmed in by a broken ridgeline.

The Ward Mining District was founded in 1872, and a San Francisco company began digging in 1875. These six charcoal ovens, the largest in Nevada, were built in 1876 to supply smelters with superhot-burning fuel to refine the complex lead-silver-copper ore. The mills shut down in 1879, a big fire razed the town in 1883, and the post office closed in 1887. Only $250,000 in silver was reportedly recovered. The kilns, however, built by a master mason, survived it all, lasting another 100 years and counting.

Each oven is 30 feet high and 27 feet wide at the base, with a door, window, and chimney hole. Each oven held 35 cords of piñon and juniper wood stacked inside; the openings were shut with iron doors, and a fire was started. By controlling the fire and using small vents around the base of the ovens to limit and regulate the amount of oxygen feeding it for 13 days, tenders charred the wood to perfection and then smothered the fire by closing all the vents. Each oven yielded 300 bushels of charcoal per batch.

Ward Charcoal Ovens State Historic Park (775/867-3001 or 775/289-1693, http:// parks.nv.gov, $7) has camping, ATV and interpretive hiking trails, and access to Willow Creek, a tiny stream with cagy rainbow as well as brown and brook trout. **Willow Creek Campground** ($14) has two pull-throughs and 12 smaller sites for rigs or tents. Water is available May-September.

Ely Elk Viewing Area

Heading south from Ely for 11 miles on US 93 brings you to this mile-long corridor where you can pull off the highway to view a diverse variety of wildlife, including the largest herd of elk in Nevada. They return here year after year during both the March-April and October-November seasons to feed and rut. The area is also home to golden eagles, ravens, black-tailed jackrabbits, and chipmunks. Bald eagles arrive in late fall and spend the winter here as well.

CASINOS

Casino action centers on the corner of Aultman and 5th Streets.

Hotel Nevada

The ★ **Hotel Nevada** (501 Aultman St., 775/289-6665 or 888/406-3055, www.hotel-nevada.com, $59-69) ranks among the oldest hotels in the state and has an appropriate exterior with neon slot machines and a big die-cut Unknown Prospector, a combination of the two most enduring and recognizable images of the state's identity. This 67-room piece of Nevadiana was the tallest in the state (a sky-scraping six stories) when it was built in the 1920s. It's still the tallest structure in town. The Nevada is your only option in White Pine County if you're interested in hold 'em or blackjack. More than 200 slot machines will happily gobble your pocket change. The full-service sports book helps ensure lively crowds around the big-screen TVs throughout the bar area on fall football weekends. The hotel's guest rooms are small but charming. Diner fare with premium coffee is available anytime in the **café** (24 hours daily, $10-17). The food is simple, but the selection is huge.

Jailhouse Motel and Casino

The **Jailhouse** (211 5th St., 775/289-3033 or 800/841-5430, www.jailhousecasino.com, $56-70) is on the site of the original city hall and jail. It's all machines: 146 of them in denominations from a penny to a dollar, along with games from traditional reel slots and video poker to keno, spin poker, and multigame machines. The casino sports bar is tuned to all the action, so you can toast your team's good fortune or drown your sorrows, as the case may be. The motel's 60 "cells" come with access to a small weight room and spa. You're in for a new experience (we hope!) when you dine in your own prison cell in the **Cell Block Steak House** (5pm-9pm daily, $20-30). Hardly bread and water, this is chops, seafood, and beef at reasonable prices in a fun and unstuffy atmosphere. Plan to do a little hard time when you're in town. Parolees can opt for **Outlaw BBQ and Café** (7am-9pm daily summer, 6am-6pm daily winter, $10-15) for ribs, chicken, burgers, and breakfast.

Copper Queen

Out on the Pioche Highway, the **Copper Queen** (805 Great Basin Blvd., 775/289-4884, www.elyramada.com, $75-120) has slots, both vertical and horizontal, but no table games. It's the only casino in the state that shares a room with the motel pool. The heated pool, whirlpool, and 80 slots are housed in a 9,000-square-foot atrium area behind the front desk. Guest rooms by Ramada are warmly decorated in burgundy and navy; bathrooms are utilitarian, but other amenities lend a touch of home: free Wi-Fi, a complimentary continental breakfast and windshield wash, and free cookies and bottled water in the room. Despite the extensive American and Italian selections, stick with the pizza at **Evah's Restaurant** (11am-9pm daily, $10-20).

Prospector Hotel & Gambling Hall

An ox and cart, motorcycles, staghounds, and other eclectic accoutrements greet visitors to the **Prospector** (1501 E. Aultman St., 775/289-4607 or 800/750-0557, www.prospectorhotel.us, $99-120), which opened in 1995 and has expanded to 100 slots. Lithographs and mementos of Nevada's past decorate hallways and public areas. The namesake cocktails at **Margaritas** (5:30am-11pm, $12-25) perfectly complement the authentic fajitas, huevos rancheros, and other common but well-prepared Mexican dishes.

FOOD

This is Southwestern cowboy country, so you won't find much radicchio salad or soy mousse on the menus. That's part of the reason locals love ★ **La Fiesta** (700 Ave. H, 775/289-4114, 11am-10pm daily, $12-17), for Mexican food with some authentic kick. They serve their homemade tortilla chips with a spicy cabbage salsa—hot and cool. Other safe bets in town include **Twin Wok** (700 Park Ave., 775/289-3699, 11am-9pm daily, $10-15) for garlicky shrimp and other Chinese delights in huge portions. The hot and sour soup and fried wontons make a fine lunch.

It's neck-and-neck in the competition for best burgers in town. **Racks Bar & Grill** (753 Aultman St., 775/289-3131, www.racksnevada.com, 11am-11pm Mon.-Sat., 11am-6pm Sun., $10-20) has the more extensive menu: hot and cold sandwiches, seafood, chops, steaks, salads, and pasta in addition to a dozen burger choices. The **Silver State** (1204 Aultman St., 775/289-8866, 6am-8pm Mon.-Sat., 6am-3pm Sun., $10-15) is more geared toward fried meats and potatoes, though the wraps and other cold sandwiches share the spotlight.

Finally, for a real old-fashioned treat, stop in at ★ **Economy Drug** (696 Aultman St., 775/289-4929, www.economydrugely.com, 9am-6pm Mon.-Fri., 9am-5pm Sat.) and pull up a stool at the soda fountain. The milkshakes, floats, sodas, and malts are heavenly, and the lunchtime sandwich specials are pretty good too. Feeling adventurous? Try the marshmallow lemonade.

ACCOMMODATIONS

Nearly two dozen lodging options in Ely offer more than 650 rooms at quite reasonable rates. Most of the older and less expensive places are bunched along Aultman Street between 3rd and 15th Streets; some newer ones are on US 93 South (Pioche Hwy.).

For motels, our picks in Ely include the weathered-brick and wood-shingled **Rustic Inn** (1555 Aultman St., 775/289-2800, www. countryrusticmotel.com, $55), which despite the rustic look is quite modern and spacious, reflecting authentic pride of ownership; and the **Bristlecone Motel** (700 Ave. I, 775/289-8838 or 800/497-7404, www. bristleconemotelelynv.com, $69-79), which is spotless with country quilt-like bedspreads and a Western motif. Close-to-the-casinos options include **Four Sevens** (500 High St., 775/289-4747, $40-60), behind the jailhouse and across from the Bristlecone Convention Center, and **Motel 6** (770 Ave. O, 775/289-6671 or 800/466-8356, www.motel6.com, $56-70), across from the Copper Queen, one of the largest in town with 99 rooms.

Other fine examples of chain hotels in town include **La Quinta** (1591 Great Basin Blvd., 775/289-8833, www.laquintaely.com, $125-140), which will send you on your way with a killer free hot breakfast. Its 100 rooms are decked out in gold and maroon and come with free Internet, mini fridges, and microwaves. The indoor pool area and fitness center are immaculate. Formerly a Best Western, the **Magnuson Hotel Park Vue** (930 Aultman St., 775/289-4497 or 888/297-2758, www. magnusonhotels.com, $53-65) offers a complimentary breakfast. As in nearly all motels in this part of Nevada, small pets are welcome.

For infinitely more atmosphere, book in at the **All Aboard Cafe & Inn** (220 E. 11th St. E., 775/289-3959, $120-150), just up 11th Street from the Nevada Northern depot. Built in 1907 to house the Ely City Grocery, the inn still reflects that dusty Old West era. Inside,

Victorian paint, wood trim, tile, marble, fixtures, and glass details stand out from the 1990 full restoration. All rooms come with satellite television, Wi-Fi, balconies, and en suite bathrooms. Stroll the grounds under Victorian gaslights, past the gazebo, swings, and gardens. In the morning enjoy a hearty breakfast in the big, airy room separate from the café dining room. The **café** (7am-9pm Tues.-Sat., 7am-2:30pm Sun., $12-23) serves a bit of everything for dinner—steak, chicken, seafood, and Italian specialties. The large and varied soup-and-salad bar is perfect for lunch.

RV Parks

KOA of Ely (Pioche Hwy., 3 miles south of Ely, 775/289-3413 or 800/562-3413, www.ko-aofely.com, $32-42) is the largest RV park in all of eastern Nevada. Mature cottonwoods rim the perimeter, and Chinese elms line the sites. Ward Mountain in the Egan Range broods directly behind the park, which sits up above the valley a little, so at night you can look down at the lights of town. There are 80 spaces for motor homes, most with full hookups; 38 are pull-throughs. The overnight RV sites are set on dirt or gravel pads. Tents are allowed in a separate grassy area. Groceries, a playground, and dog park are available, as well as basketball, volleyball, and horseshoes, but there is no pool.

Valley View RV Park (40 US 90 N., 775/289-3303, www.valleyviewrvelynevada. com, $32) has mature landscaping—tall trees and a thick, lush, grassy central park—a definite advantage. On the other hand, the sites, though level and large enough, could use a facelift. It is friendly, convenient, and usually quiet. There are 46 spaces for motor homes, all with full hookups, and 12 pull-throughs. No tents. Accessible and private restrooms have flush toilets and hot showers; public phones are available. Reservations are recommended spring-fall, especially for the pull-throughs.

A level but mostly treeless lot, the RV park at **Prospector Hotel & Gambling Hall** (1501 Aultman St., 775/289-8900, www.prospectorhotel.us, $22), on the east side of town, has strong hookups and satellite reception in its 22 spaces, six of them pull-throughs. You can't beat the rate, and guests are welcome to use the hotel's swimming pool. All the spaces are first-come, first-served; the park often fills up by early afternoon. Nearby road traffic noise can be a nuisance, but things generally quiet down at night.

INFORMATION AND SERVICES

The White Pine County **Chamber of Commerce** (636 Aultman St., 775/289-8877, www.whitepinechamber.com) can point you in the right direction and answer questions. The **library** (950 Campton St., 775/289-6900) is next to the courthouse.

Great Basin National Park

TOP EXPERIENCE

The air is fresh, the views are grand, and the vibe is reverent in this hallowed temple of the wilderness. One of the smallest national parks and the only national park in Nevada, Great Basin National Park was created to preserve and showcase a preeminent example of the vast ecosystem, which covers 20 percent of the lower 48 states, including almost all of Nevada. The Snake Range packs a more diverse ecology into a discrete mountain range than any of the other 250 ranges in this vast western desert. All five Great Basin biological zones occur in the roughly 8,000 feet from the valley to Wheeler Peak, the second-highest point in Nevada. The range contains the only permanent glacier-like ice in the state. It boasts a large forest of 4,000-plus-year-old bristlecone pines, the oldest living organisms on the planet. Within the quartzite limestone are corridors of caverns that have been carved by water over millions of years.

Great Basin receives an average of 80,000 visitors per year. It gets crowded on weekends during the short peak season, when late arrivals can be turned away from the cave and campgrounds. All the park's campgrounds are first-come, first-served, but you can make advance reservations by phone for the cave tours—a wise idea on summer weekends. Many visitors treat the park as a day-trip detour and view the caves, drive to the

Great Basin National Park

Great Basin National Park

peak overlook, and then continue on their way. Since it's extremely remote from urban areas and interstate highways, there is little of the carnival atmosphere that pervades many other national parks in the West. Tiny Baker (population 382), five miles from the park entrance, is the nearest settlement. Ely, the largest nearby town, is 70 miles by road.

SIGHTS
Driving Tour

Leaving Ely and heading east, US 50 dips south and climbs into the piñon pines and junipers of the **Schell Creek Range.** Right over **Connors Pass** (7,780 feet) the very big **Snake Range** comes into view, and **Wheeler**

Peak (13,063 feet), with permanent snow at its crest, towers above the tree line. For a short distance, as you cross **Spring Valley** toward the Snake Range, you're heading right at Wheeler.

US 50 meets US 93 at Majors Junction; follow US 6/50 left. Continuing east, the road drops into Spring Valley between the Schell Creeks behind and the Snakes ahead. The road up Spring Valley is worthy of an afternoon's scenic drive on its own.

An alternative route is a right turn at the sign for **Osceola.** This very rough gravel road is passable, though just barely, with a low-clearance vehicle. The road climbs straight up into the Snakes and past a cemetery and old gold pit. Some rusty mining junk and ramshackle shells of buildings are scattered around near the top. Placer gold was discovered here in 1872, and hydraulics were used to sluice out the nuggets and dust. Prospectors brought in primitive grinders and later built a small stamp mill. In order to supply enough water for sluicing, a ditch was dug in 1889 around the mountain from Lehman Creek on the west side of the Snakes. The rough road rejoins the highway on the east side of the mountains.

If you don't take the Osceola detour and stay on the main highway, you make a big loop north, through the low point of the Snakes, **Sacramento Pass** (7,154 feet). To the north, **Mount Moriah** rises to an apex 1,000 feet lower than Wheeler Peak. Nevada's fifth-highest peak, Mount Moriah is now a designated wilderness area, one of 14 created in 1989. Its 82,000 acres feature The Table, a one-square-mile rolling-tundra plateau at 11,000 feet, bordered by bristlecone pines. Hampton Creek Trail is a steep 15-mile round-trip hike to the summit of Mount Moriah that requires a four-wheel-drive vehicle; Hendry's Creek Trail is a 23-mile round-trip backpack hike up to The Table.

Turn off US 6/50 at the boarded-up Y Truck Stop onto NV 487 and take a look-see around **Baker.** At a site just north of town, archaeologists have discovered the ruins of a settlement of the Fremont Indians, who were based in central and southwestern Utah around the time the Ancestral Puebloans (Anasazi) were predominant in southern Nevada. The Fremonts had the largest population of any native civilization in the area, about 10,000 people at its height. The Baker site is believed to be a western outpost of the agricultural Fremont. Like the Puebloans, they disappeared from their western frontier around 1270 because of a 20-year drought. Three pit houses, pottery, arrowheads, and artifacts have been found.

Visitors Centers

The **Great Basin Visitor Center** (57 N.

NV 487, Baker, 775/234-7331, www.nps.gov/grba, 11am-5pm daily Apr.-Oct.) sells tickets for the **cave tour** ($8-10 adults, $4-5 age 5-15 and over age 54), if you haven't already bought tickets in advance (do yourself a favor and buy in advance at www.recreation.gov). Allow time to study the exhibits on park flora, fauna, and cave formations and to enjoy the 3-D Landsat thematic image. You could easily spend an hour just looking at the books, slides, and videos.

The real adventure starts six miles west at the **Lehman Caves Visitor Center** (5500 W. NV 488, 775/234-7331, ext. 242, www.nps.gov/grba, 8am-5:30pm daily summer, 8:30am-4:30pm daily winter). Stock up on quality artwork and books as well as T-shirts and other take-homes. Quite a bit of the inventory comes from Nevada, some from the immediate area. Borrow a trail guide from inside and take the **Mountain View Nature Trail** at the side of the building. Stop first at **Rhodes Cabin** to see the historical exhibit on the caretaking of the national monument. Then stroll the gentle 0.3-mile trail, stopping to read about juniper and piñon pine, mountain mahogany and mistletoe, limestone and marble, and cave entrances.

Giant apricot trees that were planted more than 100 years ago still reach for the sky in front of the visitors center and down the hill slightly toward the parking lot. They produce a ton of very fine sweet and juicy fruit the second week of August. Help yourself; they're better than candy.

Inside the visitors center, at **Lehman Caves Cafe** (8:30am-4pm daily Apr.-May and mid-Sept.-Oct., 8am-5pm daily June-mid-Sept., $10-20) the food is gratifyingly good, and considering it's a monopoly, it is pretty reasonably priced. Breakfast and lunch are served, and homemade soups are distinctive and well-seasoned. Try the "incredible ice cream sandwich," a double scoop crammed between a giant pair of oatmeal cookies, easily big enough for two.

The Western National Parks Association

Bristlecone Pine FAQ

Are bristlecone pines really the oldest living things on Earth?

In 1964, only six years after Edmund Schulman of the Arizona Tree-Ring Research Group published an article in *National Geographic* announcing the discovery of bristlecone pines, a scientist doing research on Wheeler Peak found the tree called Prometheus, later determined (when it was felled by a graduate student and the Forest Service) to be 4,900 years old. This ancient organism was older, by more than 1,000 years, than the largest California sequoia. It predated the pyramids in Egypt by 1,200 years.

How do they live so long?

In his excellent and lyrical *Trees of the Great Basin,* Ronald Lanner comments that in the case of the bristlecones, "Adversity breeds longevity." Because these trees inhabit such a harsh environment—at the highest elevations, on exposed and rocky slopes, bearing the full brunt of the elements—they enjoy a suitable lack of competition; only limber pine and Engelmann spruce keep these tim-

bristlecone pine

berline ancients company. Also, since bristlecone stands are somewhat sparse, fire presents less danger. Finally, these slow-growing trees produce an extremely dense wood, which is highly resistant to infection, parasites, and decay.

How do they die?

A very little at a time. Even 3,000-year-old trees continue to be reproductively active and bear cones. Incredibly, the inexorable forces of erosion finally overtake their mountain habitat and expose the root system, which dries out and rots or becomes susceptible to fungus or parasites. The upper limbs connected to the lower roots then die off one by one. Next, the wind and rain scour off the bark, leaving a bleached and polished trunk. Still, 90 percent of a bristlecone pine can be dead while, in Lanner's words, "a single sinuous strip of living bark connects the occasional live limb to the occasional live root." Also, an old bristlecone can stand for 1,000 or so years after dying off completely.

What does science learn from the mighty memories of these trees?

Thankfully, scientists have developed core-sampling techniques that enable them to "read" the rings without having to cut down the whole tree to do it (although Prometheus wasn't so lucky). Bristlecones are sensitive to drought conditions, which restrict their ring formation. In this way, these trees provide dendrochronologists a natural calendar of climatic events dating back nearly 9,000 years using long-dead trees. When you consider that scientific weather records have only been kept for the last 100 years, it becomes clear that the bristlecones add immeasurably to our knowledge. In addition, the trees can help us measure the action of erosion itself.

operates the **bookshops** at both visitors centers.

★ Lehman Caves

Five hundred million years ago, Nevada was a shallow sea, teeming with creatures like the ichthyosaur (now Nevada's official state fossil). The eons of pressure changes, incessant heating and cooling cycles, erosion, and calcification acted on that primordial seabed, pushing into mountain ranges, changing sandstone into marble, and cutting deep gashes in the rock. The result, countless calcite dribbles later, is the **Lehman Caves,** with ornate and incredible stalagmites, stalactites, and other features.

Depending on which legend you believe, either Absalom Lehman, his brother, his hired hand, or his horse may have discovered these caves in 1885—though bones found in the cave suggest Native Americans likely found it first, perhaps 800 years earlier. Today, cave tours ($8-10) of varying length (60-90 minutes) depart the **Lehman Caves Visitor Center** (5500 W. NV 488, 775/234-7331, ext. 242, www.nps.gov/grba) every two hours 8:30am-4pm daily in summer, twice daily 9am-3pm in spring and fall, and at 1pm winter weekdays and 9am and 1pm winter weekends. Reserving space in advance is a good idea on weekends.

Forty other caves and rock shelters are scattered throughout the park between the 8,000-foot and 12,000-foot levels. One of these "wild caves," **Little Muddy** (775/234-7561, Oct.-Mar.), is open to experienced and environmentally aware cavers via permit. Other wild caves containing sensitive bat habitats are off-limits.

HIKING AND CAMPING

The park has five developed first-come, first-served **campgrounds** (775/234-7331, $12) with vault toilets and picnic tables and tent pads at each site. There are no hookups, and few sites are level. **Lower Lehman Creek Campground** is open year-round. Those at higher elevations—**Baker Creek, Strawberry Creek, Upper Lehman Creek,** and **Wheeler Peak**—are open generally May-October, although water may not be available early and late in the season. Claim your site early on summer weekends. Upper Lehman, Wheeler Peak, and Baker Creek each have one wheelchair-accessible site. At the time of writing, the Strawberry Creek site was closed for repairs. The park also has primitive camping facilities (free) along Snake Creek. Campsites have fire grates and picnic tables but no water. They're open year-round but are often muddy in spring and snow-covered in winter. These sites are difficult to reach and are definitely not for RVs.

Lehman Creek and Wheeler Peak

Turn left off the main park road (Lehman Caves Rd./NV 488) just before the visitors center onto **Wheeler Peak Scenic Drive** (open June-Oct., weather permitting) and switchback your way along the creek toward the peak. You will pass **Lower Lehman Creek Campground** at 7,500 feet, with 11 sites used mostly by trailers and RVs. **Upper Lehman Creek Campground,** a quarter-mile ahead at 7,800 feet, has 22 tent sites and better scenery. The **Lehman Creek Trail** starts here and leads seven miles to Wheeler Peak Campground. If there's no water at the campsites, get it from the Lehman Caves Visitor Center, 3.5 miles down the road.

Continuing up this extraordinary road (RVs or vehicles over 24 feet not recommended), at around 8,500 feet there are a couple of curves and then the peak, from tree line to summit, takes your breath away. At 9,000 feet the views get even better. The road keeps climbing, with the peak ahead and the vast valley behind, until you get to the parking lot for the **Summit Trail,** taking you four miles in distance and a gasping 3,000 feet in elevation up to the top of 13,063-foot Wheeler Peak. Start early to avoid getting caught in midafternoon thunderstorms, which are common and treacherous on the mountain. The scenic drive ends a mile later at **Wheeler Peak Campground.** The campground is 13 miles from the visitors center at a breath-sucking 10,000 feet. It has 37 sites.

Before tackling the 8-mile out (and up!) and back Summit Trail or the 13-mile Baker and Johnson Lakes Loop, warm up your hiking boots and cardiovascular system on the **Alpine Lakes Trail.** Starting 0.25 mile from **Wheeler Peak Campground** and passing **Theresa and Stella Lakes,** the 2.7-mile trail can be conquered in an aerobic hour or a lethargic two hours. The grades are easy, the lakes are pretty, and the peaks are mighty.

After acclimating on this loop, walk the **Bristlecone and Glacier Trail,** 2-3 hours round-trip (4.6 miles) and not especially strenuous. Signs point the way at the forks and intersections with the other trails. An interpretive trail 1.4 miles from the trailhead circles the bristlecone sanctuary, where these ancient beings cling to life with a precarious yet tenacious grip. The spirituality here is palpable, and hikers unconsciously adopt a light step and a reverent tone as they move in awe through this divine forest. Don't be shy about caressing the trees—the barkless wood, burnished by thousands of years of wind, rain, snow, and sun, invites touch. The bottlebrush needles are soft, sensual, and surprisingly young feeling. The living parts of the trees are triumphal, but even the dead parts are beautiful. This forest is exquisite proof that wood can remain attractive long after death and does not demand to be buried.

Past the temple of the pines, the trail becomes steep and rocky, but your perseverance over the next mile will be rewarded. In no time you enter the cirque, a valley carved by the extant glacier and bookended by sheer cliffs, with Wheeler Peak in view. Political skirmishes during the effort to create a national park focused on whether the ice field was a true glacier or simply a "snow field." Park supporters rallied behind the little patch of ice, insisting it was Nevada's only glacier and thus needed protection. Wheeler's ice does move, so technically it is a glacier. But anyone who has seen larger glaciers farther north might think it looks more like an ice cube.

Baker and Johnson Lakes

A bit past the Wheeler Peak Scenic Drive turnoff, Baker Creek Road leaves the main road to the right and runs south, then west, up to 7,000 feet. It's a good gravel road that supports speeds of 25 mph through piñons and aspens and past massive stone outcrops. A little less than three miles from the main road you will pass **Baker Creek Campground.** Three miles beyond the campground brings you to the trailhead for the steep, 13-mile

Baker Lake and Johnson Lake Loop Trail. Both lakes are five miles from the trailhead with one mile between them over the Johnson Pass (10,800 feet) of Pyramid Peak (11,921 feet). Much of this area in the central and southern part of the park is generally accessible to high-clearance vehicles on dirt roads from NV 487 near Garrison, Utah. Several points on the trail provide 360-degree vistas, including inspiring looks at Baker Peak and Wheeler Peak.

Just short of Johnson Lake, you'll see the remains of a mining camp. Johnson Lake Mine has been reduced to the ruins of a few cabins, some discarded mining equipment, and a 1,000-foot aerial tramway that transferred tungsten ore from the mine to a packing station, where it went by mule to the on-site mill. Tungsten was important during World War I, when it was alloyed with steel for use in radio transmitters.

A well-graded gravel road heads into the southeast corner of the park from south of Garrison. At the end, a 1.7-mile trail brings you to **Lexington Arch,** a six-story natural limestone arch. Ask at the visitors center about the **Big Wash** hike. No permits are required for backcountry hiking or camping, but the National Park Service strongly encourages you to fill out a voluntary backcountry registration form.

FOOD AND ACCOMMODATIONS

The tiny town of **Baker** (population 55), five miles from the park entrance, has a couple of options for accommodations and a bite. The **Stargazer Inn** (115 Baker Ave., 775/234-7323, www.stargazernevada.com, $72-98) has cleaned up since 2017, when it transformed from its previous life as the Silver Jack Inn and LectroLux Café. It's now more boutique and less bohemian. The inn also rents RV spots ($25) with water and electricity connections. The inn's restaurant, **Kerouac's** (7am-10am and 5pm-10pm Wed.-Mon. mid-Apr.-mid-Nov., $15-30), serves breakfast and dinner.

The 29 guest rooms at **Border Inn**

Loneliest Road Events

JANUARY

Ice and snow sculptures, both imposing and dainty, are on display as Cave Lake State Park hosts the **Fire and Ice Festival** (800/496-9350, www.elynevada.net/fire-and-ice). Enjoy sledding, skating, ice bowling, train rides, and ice golf all weekend. On Saturday night, spectacular fireworks—detonated from a moving train—illuminate the hauntingly stark white landscape.

MAY

Vintage models, muscle cars, and classic roadsters vie for attention at the **Show What Ya Brung Car Show** (775/883-0927, www.visitcarsoncity.com) in Eureka, along with food vendors, a rummage sale, and kiddie rides. Judging for best in 22 classes and best in show is conducted during a Friday night musical concert and cruise-in along Main Street, with prizes awarded on Saturday.

JUNE

Cave Lake State Park's **Cocktails and Cannons** (775/289-4325, www.elynevada.net/bathtub-boat) is actually a pretty tame family event with bathtub races, a barbecue, fireworks, and yes, cannon shots. The racing tubs are studies in creativity and engineering, and the barbecue includes steak and seafood. Afterward, relax with beer, wine, and cocktails as fireworks explode over the lake.

Carnival rides, A-list musical performers, cooking and craft contests, and big and handsome livestock and agricultural products from around the state highlight the **Nevada State Fair** (877/916-3247, www.nevadastatefair.org) at Mills Park in Carson City.

Chrome-clad raw horsepower is on display at the **Silver Dollar Car Classic** (775/230-6750, www.silverdollarcarclassic.com) in Carson City. Mills Park is ground zero for the '50s dance party, carnival, and food trucks. But the real attractions are the 400 or so American muscle cars shined up to make an impression. Whether you're a Ford fan, a Chevy shill, or a Mopar maniac, you'll find plenty of kindred spirits willing to swap hotrod stories.

Amateur and professional chefs compete in Dayton's **Oodles of Noodles** (775/246-7909, www.daytonareachamberofcommerce.com) to see whose linguini, macaroni, and fettuccini recipes can "pasta" test as best noodle dish in town. A crafts fair gives attendees a chance to work off all the carbs.

AUGUST

Most events are free at **Jazz & Beyond** (775/883-4154, www.jazzcarsoncity.com), held at multiple public and private venues throughout Carson City. Performers from throughout the West polish up their brass to bring everything from big band and jumpin', jivin' swing to smooth, downtempo rhythms and a little rockabilly and blues.

SEPTEMBER

Small-town celebrating at its best, **Dayton Valley Days** (775/301-9567, www.daytonvalleydays.org) in Dayton brings together community members for a pet parade, crafts fair, musical entertainment, an art show, silent auction, games, Civil War encampment, and good ol' American fun.

(US 6/50, 13 miles east of the park entrance on the Utah-Nevada line, 775/234-7300, www.borderinncasino.com, $50-60) are paneled and plain. The bunkhouse-like hotel also has a restaurant (6am-10pm, $10-20), a bar, slots, a pool table, RV parking, and gas. The gas pumps are in Utah, where transportation taxes are lower, making it about 15 cents cheaper than in Nevada. The slot machines, of course, are on the Nevada side. The RV park's 20 spaces ($25) are big and level, with full hookups but no other frills; Wi-Fi, cell, and satellite TV reception is spotty.

Similar remodeled guest rooms and a bar can be found at **Whispering Elms** (120 Baker Ave., 775/234-9900, http://camptheelms.wixsite.com, $62-67), which has horseshoe pits and satellite TV. It also has RV parking ($25-30) and tent camping ($17).

Hidden Canyon Retreat (2000 Hidden Canyon Pkwy., 15 miles south of Baker, 775/234-7175, www.hiddencanyonretreat. com, $149-225) is a complex with lovely lodge rooms and suites surrounding an idyllic courtyard. The rolling grounds comprise stands of juniper and piñon pine, meandering streams, pastureland, and habitat that attracts golden eagles, wild turkeys, mule deer, and other wildlife. The resort rents ATVs, has a small game room, and allows catch-and-release fishing. Other activities include horseback riding, hiking, fossil hunting, and stargazing.

Northern Nevada

Look for ★ to find recommended sights, activities, dining, and lodging.

Highlights

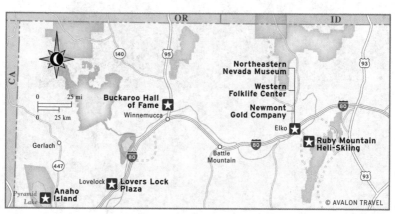

★ **Anaho Island:** Awkward on the ground but majestic in flight, thousands of pelicans feed and raise their hatchlings on this Pyramid Lake refuge. The island is off-limits to humans, but you can see the birds from a boat with binoculars (page 278).

★ **Lovers Lock Plaza:** Devoted couples symbolize their iron-clad commitment by fastening their love lock to a chain and throwing away the key. It's an Americanized version of an ancient Chinese custom. For lovers who decide to make their attachment more formal, the courthouse is next door (page 287).

★ **Buckaroo Hall of Fame:** Nevada's ranch hands have turned ridin', ropin', and wranglin' into an art form. Their individualism and style in the face of hardship are celebrated at this Winnemucca museum (page 292).

★ **Northeastern Nevada Museum:** Two-million-year-old mastodon bones are the highlight of this eclectic museum in Elko. Other exhibits include works by renowned Western artists Edward Borein, Will James, Ansel Adams, and Edward Weston (page 298).

★ **Western Folklife Center:** The Great Western Songbook and the renowned National Cowboy Poetry Gathering celebrate trail philosophy, cowboy sagacity, and ranch culture at this top-notch museum, gallery, and performance venue (page 300).

★ **Newmont Gold Company:** With nary a pick in sight, Newmont is one of the world's largest producers of gold, with strip mines all along the lucrative Carlin Trend. Tours reveal the entire process (page 300).

★ **Ruby Mountain Heli-Skiing:** Drop nearly 40,000 feet in six daily runs over unblemished powder on perhaps the most beautiful mountains in Nevada (page 306).

Built on the backs of hardened hard-rock miners, tireless Basque sheepherders, flinty-eyed cowboys, and grizzled mountain men, northern Nevada has always been an irresistible challenge to rugged adventurers.

Today, the region surprises the stalwart souls and independent spirits who confront the majestic peaks and ice-blue alpine lakes. Remnants of a massive, Pleistocene-era lake dot the landscape, providing stunning vistas and recreational venues. Primitive trails parallel I-80 with flashes of inspiration, unexpected beauty, and a touch of romance. In spring, riotous wildflowers bravely peek out from the craggy mountain crevices.

During the 51 weeks a year it's not hosting the alternative arts festival called Burning Man, the Black Rock Desert in Nevada's northwest corner rewards self-reliant campers with a forbidding, windswept moonscape perfect for introspection and contemplation. On the other side of the state, the Ruby Mountains dare hikers of all abilities with a network of trails. The most ambitious can tackle the 35-mile Ruby Crest route, which takes hikers' breath away both figuratively, with picture postcard views of verdant canyons and

snow-covered summits, and literally, as it drifts upward to Wines Peak, at an oxygen-depleted 10,893 feet. Sights and activities here are just as evocative as their names: Purgatory Peak, the Royal Peacock Opal Mine, the Bloody Shins Trail.

In between, you will encounter small-town inhabitants who maintain a Spartan dignity punctuated by neighborliness and humor. Winnemucca's Buckaroo Hall of Fame celebrates the dust-encrusted ranch hands and trail bosses who tamed the Wild West. Meanwhile, the Western Folklife Center in Elko keeps that spirit alive, connecting traditional cowboy art, music, and poetry with their rightful place in the American zeitgeist.

PLANNING YOUR TIME

For a true taste of rugged northern Nevada, take a leisurely weeklong drive along I-80, starting from Reno. It's best to travel in the summer. Winter storms can be fierce and

---

Previous: mustangs in northern Nevada; Pyramid Lake. **Above:** Anaho Island.

Northern Nevada

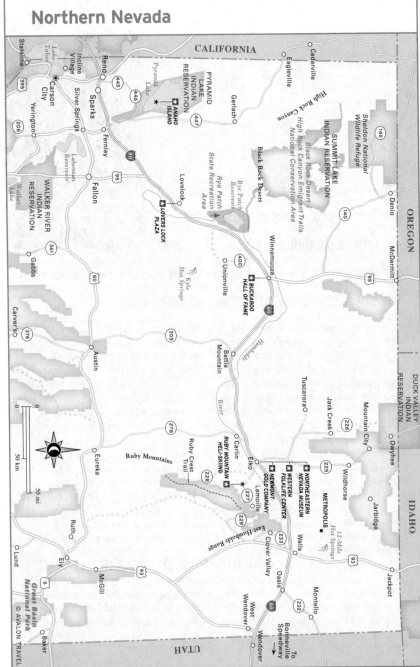

CALIFORNIA

Stateline
Lake Tahoe
Incline Village
Reno
395
Carson City
Silver Springs
Sparks
445
446
Yerington
208
Walker Lake
WALKER RIVER INDIAN RESERVATION
Fernley
80
95
Fallon
Lahontan Reservoir
361
Gabbs
50
Carver's
376
Austin
Eureka
Ruth
Lund
Ely
6
McGill
93
Baker
Great Basin National Park
© AVALON TRAVEL

Pyramid Lake
PYRAMID LAKE INDIAN RESERVATION
447
★ ANAHO ISLAND
Gerlach
High Rock Canyon
Black Rock Desert
High Rock Canyon Emigrant Trails National Conservation Area
Black Rock Desert
SUMMIT LAKE INDIAN RESERVATION
Cedarville
Eagleville
Sheldon National Wildlife Refuge
140
140
Denio
McDermitt
95

Lovelock
★ LOVERS LOCK PLAZA
Rye Patch Reservoir
Rye Patch State Recreation Area
Winnemucca
Kyle Hot Springs
Unionville
400
★ BUCKAROO HALL OF FAME
80
Humboldt
305
Battle Mountain
Humboldt River
278
Carlin
Ruby Mountains
Ruby Crest Trail
RUBY MOUNTAIN HELI-SKIING
228
227
229
East Humboldt Range
233
Clover Valley
93
Tuscarora
Jack Creek
Mountain City
226
225
Elko
Lamoille
NEWMONT GOLD COMPANY
WESTERN FOLKLIFE CENTER
NORTHEASTERN NEVADA MUSEUM
METROPOLIS
12-Mile Hot Springs
Wells
Owyhee
Wildhorse
Jarbidge
Jackpot
Oasis
Montello
232
West Wendover
Wendover
Bonneville Speedway
To Bonneville Speedway
80

OREGON
DUCK VALLEY INDIAN RESERVATION
IDAHO
UTAH

0   50 km
0   50 mi

snow-covered mountain passes treacherous when temperatures dive. Plan on a day or two in the "big" cities along the route—Winnemucca, Elko, and Wendover—depending on your interests, but also take advantage of the small towns, back roads, and wilderness attractions in between them. Getting off the main road offers opportunities for discovery and adventure. Consider spending a mind-clearing night in Black Rock Desert, hot tubbing, stargazing, and meditating. Talk to a buckaroo, break bread with a Basque sheepherder, tour a gold mine, or climb a peak in the Ruby Mountains.

Pyramid Lake

TOP EXPERIENCE

The stark desert oneness gives way to a pewter-blue vision. Its meandering inlets, treeless shoreline, and glassy surface notwithstanding, Pyramid Lake is no mirage, though the perfect pyramid rising from its shallow center seems as incongruous as those emerging from the sands of Giza.

Pyramid has been called the most beautiful desert lake in the world. It's one of the largest freshwater lakes in the western United States: 27 miles long, 9 miles wide, 370 feet at its deepest, 3,789 feet above sea level, with a water temperature a swimmable 75°F in summer and a forbidding 42° in winter. Its source, the Truckee River, leaves Lake Tahoe and travels 105 miles down the east face of mighty mountains, through thirsty cities, and across reclaimed desert before trickling into the southern delta of the lake, which has no outlet. Anaho Island juts up off the eastern shore slightly south of the pyramid, providing breeding grounds for the American white pelican and other shorebirds.

The east shore is restricted to day use. If you're here to boat, fish, or camp, you need to access the lake area from NV 446, which parallels the west shore (turn left on NV 447 just south of Nixon or take NV 445 from Sparks and merge with NV 446 at the lake).

Stopping at the **Pyramid Lake Paiute Tribe Museum and Visitors Center** (709 State St., Nixon, 775/574-1088, 10am-4:30pm Tues.-Sat., free) will shed light on the tribe's culture and why it holds Pyramid Lake and the surrounding area sacred. Learn about the Pyramid Lake War of 1860, the largest battle between American Indians and whites in Nevada's history. Read about and see photos of the **Great Stone Mother**—a tufa rock formation at the lake that looks remarkably like a shrouded Indian woman seated with an open baby basket next to her. The sacred formation is off-limits to all but tribal members. Other exhibits detail the habits of the fish and birds that live here.

FISHING AND BOATING

Monster **Lahontan cutthroat trout** lurk in Pyramid Lake, just waiting for you to cast a fly their way. Ten-pounders are not uncommon, and a half dozen trophies of 20 pounds or more are documented each **trout season** (Oct.-June). Few species have adapted to the lake's high alkalinity. In addition to the Lahontan cutthroat, the **Sacramento perch** maintain a thriving population. Though they can be fished year-round, most are caught in spring and early summer. Anglers can keep as many as they like. Catch them with tube baits and jigs. Spoons and flies catch the two species of **tui chub,** the favorite cutthroat prey. Anglers who happen upon a large school often can make a catch with nearly every cast until it passes. Big, hard-fighting **carp** are here, too, but since organic bait is not allowed, they generally are only caught by accident. Pyramid Lake is the only place the endangered **cui-ui** sucker fish can be found. If you are unlucky enough to hook one, release it immediately and carefully.

Anglers can launch boats to go after the

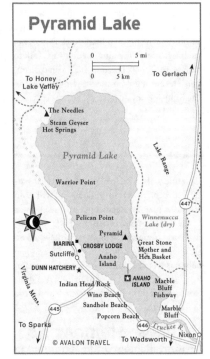

Pyramid Lake

0   5 mi
0   5 km

To Honey
Lake Valley

To Gerlach

The Needles
Steam Geyser
Hot Springs

Pyramid Lake

Lake Range

Warrior Point

Pelican Point

Winnemucca
Lake (dry)

447

Pyramid

MARINA   CROSBY LODGE
Sutcliffe

Anaho
Island

Great Stone
Mother and
Her Basket

DUNN HATCHERY

★ ANAHO
ISLAND

Indian Head Rock

Marble
Bluff
Fishway

Virginia Mtns.

Wino Beach
Sandhole Beach
Popcorn Beach

Marble
Bluff

445

Truckee R.

446

To Sparks

To Wadsworth

Nixon

© AVALON TRAVEL

fish or wade into the water. Waders often employ modified stepladders—some equipped with seats and platforms anchored in the sandy lake bottom—to increase their casting distance, elevate them out of the frigid water, and improve their visibility when scanning for cutthroats near the surface.

The lake is located on Paiute Indian reservation land. The tribe, not the local, state, or federal government, makes the rules. State fishing licenses are not needed; however, anyone dropping a line will need to purchase a **permit** ($11 one day, $88 for the season) either online (https://plpt.nagfa.net/online) or at one of the stores that ring the lake. Boaters and day-users are charged similar fees. Fishing from a boat requires both the fishing fee and the boating fee. Personal watercraft users pay higher fees ($26 per day, $208 for the season). Bring your own boat and other watercraft or rent from the marina. Discounts for seniors, active military and veterans, and children under 18 apply. See the website for details. Camping is allowed ($15 per vehicle per night, $38 for three nights).

Several experienced charter captains can put anglers onto big cutthroats. They all provide expertise and equipment, but customers are responsible for their own Pyramid Lake permits. **Cutthroat Charters** (29555 Pyramid Hwy., Sutcliffe, 775/476-0555, www.fishpyramid.com, $125-$175) also offers shore fishing (waders, rod, flies, etc. included) and year-round perch charters. With 50 years of experience on the lake, Gary Bonanno is so confident that he offers a partial refund if clients fail to hook a cutthroat on his **Pyramid on the Fly** shore fishing excursions (775/560-7935, www.pyramidonthefly.com, $200-300 for 1-2 people). **Pyramid Lake Guide Service** (545 Harbin Ln., Reno, 775/722-2267, www.pyramidlakeguideservice.com, $375 for 1-2 people, $75 each additional) also offers fly-fishing clinics ($150 per person).

If you visit in spring, call for a tour of the **Dunn Hatchery** (63 Sutcliffe Dr., Sutcliffe, 775/476-0500) on the lake's west side to see how the tribe's four hatcheries help ensure healthy populations of cutthroats and cui-ui. The tour includes demonstrations of artificial spawning, fertilized roe collection, incubation, hatching, rearing, tagging, and release. Displays and artifacts show fishing's role in Paiute history and culture.

CAMPING

Unless posted, tent and RV camping is allowed everywhere along the west shore (pitch tents at least 100 feet from the water). Rates are $15 per night. Pay at any store at the lake or buy a permit purchased on-site or at https://plpt.nagfa.net/online. **Pelican Point,** a couple miles north of Sutcliffe, is a popular choice not only for camping, but also for shore and float tube fishing. There's a boat ramp nearby. For a little more seclusion, keep going north on NV 445 and pick any dirt road that leads to the water. If you get to the end of the pavement, you've found **Warrior Point,** another perfectly acceptable camping option.

Cui-ui Fish

The endangered cui-ui (pronuounced "KWEE-wee") is a sucker fish that lives only in Pyramid Lake. A prehistoric species, cui-ui inhabited Lake Lahontan for tens of thousands of years; as the inland sea slowly evaporated, these fish of the deep were able to survive at the bottom of the little Pyramid Lake remnant. Cui-ui grow as large as seven pounds and can live 40 years. They spawn between the ages of 12 and 20, as early as April and as late as July, when they swim upstream as far as 12 miles west to lay their eggs.

These fish were so much a part of the Native American culture that the local Paiute tribe was known as the "cui-ui eaters." In the old days, before the Derby Dam water diversion lowered the lake's level, the Paiute spearfished and snagged them at the mouth of the Truckee River during the spawn.

The Works Progress Administration's 1940 *Nevada—A Guide to the Silver State* reported that because of Derby Dam, "the flow into the lake has been curtailed [and] the fish runs have practically ceased. Cui-ui schools circle through the shallows near the river mouth, searching in vain for spawning grounds, and pelicans step in and gorge themselves."

The cui-ui were nearly extinct by the 1940s. They managed to recover slightly in 1952 with one of the largest spawning runs (120,000 fish) in recent history, but compared to the millions of cui-ui that spawned in the past, the population was decimated, prompting the federal government to list the fish as an endangered species in 1967. Another large run was recorded in 1969 (110,000 fish), but only a handful of cui-ui spawned between 1976 and 1982, and a census in 1984 counted only 150,000 of them. No cui-ui spawned between 1987 and 1992. The Paiute members voluntarily stopped eating them in 1979.

In the early 1970s, federal courts directed that water in Stampede Reservoir be used exclusively to benefit the cui-ui. A small pulse of fresh reservoir water is released as early as January to tickle the spawning instinct; the pulse reaches its peak by April, which helps the fish reach the spawning grounds. The fresh water also incubates the eggs and helps the microscopic larvae to swim back to the lake.

The Marble Bluff dam and fishway were built in 1976 to stop the erosion of the riverbank, which threatened the stability of Nixon, just upstream. The dam also protects critical cui-ui spawning habitat. Some cui-ui will use the three-mile clay-lined fishway, which resembles an irrigation canal with a number of terraces known as ladders, but many won't. During large spawning runs, the fish jam the entrance to the fishway, and some are smothered before they can be gathered onto a large elevator platform, which raises them up to the river and washes them into it. In 1993, after one of the wettest winters and springs in the 20th century, so many fish struggled onto the elevator that it couldn't lift them, and 3,000 died. Officials had to load nearly 5,000 cui-ui into trucks, drive them past the fishway, and drop them back into the river.

After the failure of the fish elevator, the federal government in 1996 allocated $2.5 million to redesign the Marble Bluff dam, fishway, and elevator. Aided by high water and other factors, more than 250,000 cui-ui spawned in the spring 1997 run, a 50-year high. The Cui-ui Recovery Team now estimates the total adult cui-ui population at 1 million. John Jackson, director of water resources for the Paiute reservation, says down-listing the cui-ui on the Endangered Species List from endangered to threatened status is under consideration.

Today, anglers sometimes land cui-ui when fishing for Lahontan cutthroat trout at Pyramid. The fish remain on the endangered species list, and there is a zero-kill policy. This policy, the Paiute hatcheries, and timed water releases from Boca and Stampede Reservoirs work to ensure the cui-ui's survival.

With 44 spaces two miles from the Pelican Point boat launch, **Pyramid Lake Marina and RV Park** (2500 Lakeview Dr., Sutcliffe, 775/476-1155, $25, or $15 for beach sites with no hookups) is clean and convenient, with a small store. **Crosby Lodge** (30605 Sutcliffe Dr., 775/476-0400, www.crosbylodge.net, 6:30am-8pm Mon.-Thurs., 6:30am-9pm Fri., 6am-9pm Sat., 6am-8pm Sun., $60-120) offers rooms and trailers, as well as groceries, fishing gear, alcohol, souvenirs, and boat storage.

★ ANAHO ISLAND

A national wildlife refuge, **Anaho Island** floats in Pyramid Lake like a giant stingray, its wide, flat wings spreading out to gradually meet the water. It's home to large breeding colonies of California gulls; double-crested cormorants; great blue, snowy, and black-crowned egrets; and Caspian terns as well as one of the world's largest colonies of American white pelicans.

Anaho Island is completely **off-limits** to visitors, and boats are prohibited from coming within 1,000 feet. However, **bird-watchers** can anchor outside the restricted area, settle down with a pair of binoculars, and observe avian behavior. Migrating birds begin arriving in February, nest in March and April, rear chicks throughout the summer, and head south for Mexico and Central and South America in September.

Pelicans are the easiest birds in the world to recognize. Clumsy and comical on the ground, majestic and dignified in the air, pelicans have such sensitive nesting instincts that they have long been considered a measure of this landscape's wildness. Their creamy white feathers, black-tipped wings with 10-foot spans, and huge orange bills cause them to stand out in the crowd of cormorants, herons, terns, ducks, geese, gulls, hawks, owls, and smaller species that, several months a year, call Anaho home. Tens of thousands of birds set up a makeshift pelican city each spring. Pelicans pair off and settle into a nest, barely a hole in the ground, softened perhaps with some dry grass and sage twigs. Into it the female lays two eggs, incubating them for a month with the webs of her feet. The male flies off every day to bring back a fish dinner. After hatching, the chicks mature quickly, reaching flight growth in two months and full growth (15-20 pounds) in time to migrate in the fall.

Black Rock Desert

TOP EXPERIENCE

The edge of a shimmering lake seems to be hurtling toward you but always remains just ahead—out of reach. It's the same body of water that enticed gold rush pioneers to struggle onward, hoping in vain to slake their crushing thirst. Like them, you'll never reach it, because it doesn't exist. Welcome to Black Rock Desert, where even the illusions are on a grand scale. Encompassing a million acres, Black Rock comprises the largest playa in North America, a collection of remote wildernesses, and a conservation area that bears witness to the country's dreams of manifest destiny. Today, it serves as a magnet for off-roaders, speed demons, rock hounds, stargazers, solitude seekers—and revelers at the Burning Man festival that each year signals the end of summer.

The Black Rock Mountain Range bisecting the desert was once a landmark along the California and Oregon Trails, with an estimated 30,000 emigrants crossing through between 1849 and 1870. Because of its remote location and hard surface, this is the best-preserved section of the route west. Wagon wheel ruts are still visible in the dried mud. The 800,000-acre **High Rock Canyon Emigrant Trails National Conservation Area** and 10 adjacent designated wilderness areas covering

750,000 acres make this area the largest conservation area in the Lower 48.

PLANNING YOUR TRIP

The **Black Rock Visitors Center** (205 Transfer Station Rd., 775/557-2503, 9am-5pm Thurs.-Mon. Apr.-Oct.) provides safety tips along with interpretive signs about the area's wildlife, history, recreational activities, and natural resources. Take County Road 447 northwest out of Gerlach. In less than a mile, turn right on Transfer Station Road.

Occupying the southwest corner of the wilderness area, the playa is the 200-square-mile bed of long-evaporated Lake Lahontan. It's so flat that a person standing in the middle of it can easily discern the curvature of the earth. Unless you're coming specifically to attend Burning Man, it's best to steer clear of Black Rock in the weeks leading up to and following the alt-art festival (held in late Aug.-early Sept.). **Late spring** and **early fall** are the best times to visit. Temperatures are moderate and the sun-baked playa is dry and firm enough for automobile travel, supporting even heavy RVs and four-wheel-drive vehicles, the preferred mode of transportation here. Relentless summer sun adds several degrees to the temperature of the area's hot springs, nudging them from soothing to unbearable. Damp heavy winters and early spring showers soften and sometimes flood the playa. When this occurs, long-dormant fairy shrimp and water flea eggs hatch, providing a smorgasbord for passing birds but creating nightmares for drivers who defy the wet playa and find themselves axle-deep in mud and silt. Some are stranded for days.

Be careful! This place is treacherous, and people die out here every year. It's easy to get lost, and if your car breaks down, you might not make it home. If you're planning to explore the Black Rock in any depth for an extended period, plan ahead and **pack wisely,** with wilderness survival in mind. Carry detailed **topographic maps** and a **compass;** five gallons of **water** per person per day and **emergency food** for a week. Also bring sunblock, a first-aid kit, warm clothes, and some portable shade; two spare tires, tools, a hand winch, rope and chain, shovel, and axe; extra gas, belts, hoses, and fluids; and a CB radio. Many people actually tow in an extra car.

Starry skies, unspoiled nature, and solitude—not modern facilities—are what make **camping** in this backcountry so special. While some primitive established campsites exist at **Soldier Meadows,** feel free to pitch

Black Rock Desert playa

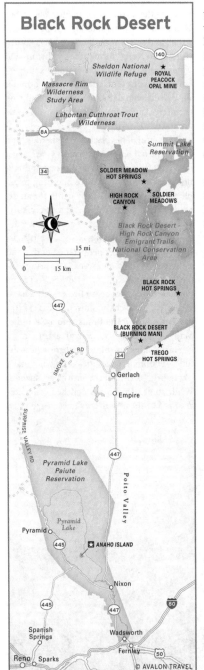

Black Rock Desert

Sheldon National
Wildlife Refuge

ROYAL
PEACOCK
OPAL MINE

Massacre Rim
Wilderness
Study Area

Lahontan Cutthroat Trout
Wilderness

140

8A

Summit Lake
Reservation

34

SOLDIER MEADOW
HOT SPRINGS

HIGH ROCK
CANYON

SOLDIER
MEADOWS

*Black Rock Desert –
High Rock Canyon
Emigrant Trails
National Conservation
Area*

0   15 mi

0   15 km

BLACK ROCK
HOT SPRINGS

447

BLACK ROCK DESERT
(BURNING MAN)

34

TREGO
HOT SPRINGS

Gerlach

Empire

Pyramid Lake
Paiute
Reservation

447

Poito Valley

Pyramid
Lake

Pyramid

445

ANAHO ISLAND

Nixon

445

447

80

Spanish
Springs

Wadsworth

Reno   Sparks

Fernley

50

SMOKE CRK RD

SURPRISE VALLEY RD

© AVALON TRAVEL

---

your tent in the middle of the playa. Many visitors prefer to use areas their predecessors have cleared in order to minimize human impact on the desert. Previously used or dispersed campsites can sometimes be found along the playa's edge, steps off the desolate dirt roads and near the many **hot springs** in the area. Camping within 300 feet of any open water is prohibited. All fires must be contained or elevated off the ground to avoid scorching the playa.

First-timers may feel more comfortable exploring Black Rock with the experts at **Friends of Black Rock High Rock** (320 Main St., Gerlach, 775/557-2900, http://blackrockdesert.org, 8am-4pm Thurs.-Mon.). This volunteer conservation group leads hikes, geocaching hunts, and stargazing expeditions throughout the year.

ORIENTATION

Approach Black Rock Desert by heading east on I-80 and taking exit 44 toward Wadsworth on NV 447. The dry bed of Lake Winnemucca and the Nightingale Mountains beyond are evident on your right, and the Lake Range rises on your left. In 80 miles, exit onto County Road 34 in Gerlach to reach the two main entrances to the playa. Check on conditions in Gerlach—you're looking for dry, dry, dry, because when it's wet, the playa is an impassable sump. The first entrance, just a few miles past Gerlach, is rough and suitable only for four-wheel-drive vehicles. Passenger cars and RVs can negotiate the second entrance, some 10 miles farther on, with little difficulty. Whichever exit you take, check to ensure the playa is dry before driving on it.

GERLACH

Heading north on NV 447 past Pyramid Lake, the valley narrows as you come upon the modern ghost town of Empire. The gypsum mine and plant here closed in 2011, taking 100 jobs and the heart of the region with it. More than 1,000 people lived in Empire and Gerlach during the facility's heyday. Fewer than 200 remain. Those who are left depend on tourism,

Burning Man

What started in 1986, when Larry Harvey expressed himself by burning a human effigy in San Francisco as a dozen of his neo-hippie friends watched, has evolved into a $10 million annual festival of individualism for 50,000 free spirits. Burning Man, the weeklong celebration in **Black Rock Desert,** is part avant-garde art show, part rebellion against commercialism and societal mores, part self-actualization, and whatever else each participant wants it to be.

The climax comes at the end of the week with the burning of the Man, a towering sculpture of a person. His immolation also represents something different for everyone in attendance. Perhaps it's a statement about the precariousness of life, or the futility of clinging to material possessions, or rebirth after destruction; or maybe it's just a really cool bonfire.

Whatever Burning Man is, it certainly has grown. In 1998 the gathering attracted an estimated 15,000 participants, and by 2010 there were 51,000. In recent years the community known as **Black Rock City** that springs up on the playa outside **Gerlach** is temporarily one of the 10 largest towns in Nevada. Huge art installations, bizarre art cars, ornate costumes, all-night music parties, lights everywhere, and, of course, lots and lots of fire are the hallmarks of the party in the playa. So too are nudity, alcohol, and drugs.

Since no commerce is allowed except at the café and ice station, "Burners" have to haul everything they need in and out with them, although everyone is encouraged to share with others. And there is a lot of infrastructure. The city is mapped out on arcs of streets in which theme camps and individual participants set up elaborately decorated sites. Black Rock City also has its own constabulary (the Black Rock Rangers), radio stations, daily newspapers, and village lamplighters as well as fire, emergency, and sanitation departments. Bicycles are the primary mode of transportation.

Still, taking the leap at Burning Man provides a lesson in survival: Scenes from the parched playa often resemble the film *Mad Max Beyond Thunderdome*. Everything and everyone is constantly covered in a thin brown coat of alkaline dust. Most participants carry dust masks and goggles with them at all times; dust storms blow through the city without warning, knocking over tents and installations. Daytime temperatures can soar to over 100°F, and it has been known to freeze at night.

The event takes place on federal Bureau of Land Management land. There's a **hefty admission fee** ($425-950 in 2017), part of which goes to the Bureau of Land Management.

Organizers promote the festival as an experiment in temporary community, where participants can shed the fetters of society and stretch the ordinary limits of life. They put a lot of effort into trying to make Burning Man a peaceful and safe experience; although police are present, citations are rare. Participants are required to take away everything they brought in, and volunteers stay for weeks to return the Black Rock Desert to its pristine condition. After a while, it's as though the event never took place . . . until next year.

Burning Man (https://burningman.org) happens the week around Labor Day (late Aug.-early Sept.) outside Gerlach.

so if you have time to spare, check out **Empire Store,** the last place for provisions before Black Rock. Its deli sandwiches are the perfect picnic food.

It's 10 more miles to Gerlach, at the foot of 9,000-foot **Granite Peak.** Gerlach may appear a sleepy hamlet known only as base camp for Burning Man, but it is in fact one of the few places in northwest Nevada with a motel, gas station, and slot machines, all courtesy of Bruno Selmi, "The Emperor of Gerlach." The local legend passed away in 2017 at age 94, but his family-owned empire lives on, including the restaurant at **Bruno's Country Club** (445 Main St., 775/557-2220, 7am-8pm, $10-15). We doubt that Selmi's Italian homeland produces ravioli with red sauce any better. Breakfast and lunch fare is standard, but good and filling, and the bar is open late. Half of the 40 rooms at **Bruno's Motel** ($50-90) were destroyed in an October 2016 fire. The survivors are small and basic, though they have satellite TV and some come with kitchenettes. Up the street from Bruno's, **Water Tower Park** offers a cool, shady picnic spot away from the desert sun. The park centers on a restored 1909-vintage redwood water tower once used by the railroad.

Stock up, fuel up, and drink up, then continue north out of town for less than a mile to a fork in the road. Take the right leg—Old Highway 34—for two more miles to find the turnoff to **Guru Road.** Lovingly restored by volunteers after a 2005 mudslide, Dooby Williams's drive-through art experience contains rock sculptures, life-size dioramas made from desert flotsam, and wise and witty aphorisms scrawled on boulders.

A more traditional art gallery can be found by backtracking to the Y and taking the left leg for 14 miles to **Planet X Pottery** (8100 NV 447, 775/442-1919, 10am-4pm most days—call to be sure), where artist John Bogard creates porcelain and stoneware pottery designed to be as practical as it is beautiful.

HOT SPRINGS

Geothermal activity abounds in the magical mountains and valleys around Black Rock. Formed by watershed drainages and heated by the same magma that helped shape the landscape, these springs vary from very warm to boiling hot. Watch your footing around the pools to avoid slipping into a scalding cauldron, and always test the water before wading in.

Trego Hot Springs

Hot Springs Etiquette

Relaxing in a hot spring has a way of mellowing a person's outlook, but bathers still get a bit piqued when newbies fail to follow the proper etiquette. Safety and courtesy are the watchwords. Keep the following tips in mind and you won't find yourself in, ahem, hot water.

- No glass near the springs.

- Clean up after yourself (and pick up a few things less conscientious visitors have left).

- Take turns.

- Don't be a prude. Nude soaking is common, so don't be surprised if you happen upon a pool of people in the altogether.

- Don't be an exhibitionist. On the other hand, if a family or church group has arrived at the spring before you, don't assume they will be okay with you stripping down. Bring a suit, just in case.

- Camp at least 500 feet away. Camping next to a spring gives the impression you're laying claim to it.

Trego Hot Springs

One of the best and most accessible springs is **Trego Hot Springs,** due east across the playa from the main turn into Black Rock Desert off Country Road 34 from Gerlach. Most years, you can simply follow other vehicles' tire tracks, taking care when crossing two sets of railroad tracks. Or you can pick up Old Highway 49 between Empire and Gerlach. The Y-shaped spring is large enough for swimming and group outings. Because the hot water from the source mixes with cooler water farther away, you can easily find the section where you feel most comfortable. Much of the bottom is covered with fine silt, ideal for a mud bath. While the water is too tepid in most places to sooth away the aches, the fine, sulfuric silt on the bottom is nature's facial mask and exfoliant. Lesser-known **Frog Springs** is four miles to the west, near a stand of large trees.

Black Rock Springs

You will need four-wheel-drive to confidently reach the springs farther north. At the northern tip of the playa near Black Rock Point, **Black Rock Springs'** clear, aqua water is beautiful, inviting, and dangerously hot. Under no circumstances should you enter the main pool. The water cools as it flows into shallower pools suitable for soaking. It's usually accessible only in summer and fall when the playa is dry. Follow the tread marks north on Soldier Meadows Road (a right turn 13 miles north of Gerlach). This area is part of the Applegate-Lassen section of the California Trail. Interpretive signs chart the 49ers' progress and hardships. An old tumbledown sheepherder's wagon lends atmosphere to the springs. Don't climb on it. Six miles due north, **Double Hot Springs** is doubly dangerous, at 180 degrees. At least one person has been killed by jumping or falling in. A fence surrounds the hottest, deepest pool, but even the runoff is hot enough to cause third-degree burns. Some 50 yards downstream, volunteers have piped water into a large tub. This is the only safe place to soak at Double Hot.

Soldier Meadows Hot Springs

If you continue to follow Soldier Meadows Road, you'll wind up in . . . Soldier Meadows, naturally. Though a few of the pools are on private property, **Soldier Meadows Hot Springs** itself and dozens of small warm, hot, and cold springs dot the troughs between rolling hills on public land. Native Americans,

Oregon- and California-bound immigrants, cavalry soldiers, and prospectors have all been drawn by the life-giving water. Test the water in the pools before wading in; some are hot enough to cook beans in a can, so they also can scald unwary bathers.

HIGH ROCK CANYON

Graffiti left by Oregon-bound emigrants making their way through High Rock Canyon documents life along the Applegate-Lassen Emigrant Trail. The trail remains unchanged since John C. Frémont explored it and wagon trains traversed it. And High Rock Canyon remains unchanged since volcanic eruptions and tectonic action formed it, enticing hardcore adventurers with backcountry adventure.

A rough four-wheel-drive trail leads to the main canyon and serves as the "trunk" to several branches of dirt roads that beckon mountain bikers, hikers, hunters, and campers who can do without such on-site luxuries as food, water, and shelter. The canyon rewards them with inspiring jaunts through chokecherry- and aspen-dotted valleys and rambles through slot canyons so narrow only a sliver of sky is visible above. At **Mahogany Creek** you can touch 800-foot sheer walls on both sides of the trail as you squeeze through monochromatic monoliths—black basalt on top, a layer of scorched red soil below, followed by beige ash from older volcanic eruptions and sage, rust, yellow, and green lichens at the base. The craggy peaks above are perfect homes for nesting golden eagles, prairie falcons, hawks, and owls.

A corrugated metal cabin at **Stevens Camp** at the north end of High Rock Canyon was built by hunters to rescue their brethren who might find themselves lost and stranded in the freezing wilderness. Over the years, it has served its purpose, with grateful users replenishing firewood before leaving and returning in better weather to replenish the store of canned goods. There's a stove, pots and pans, and bunk bed frames and springs. It has been so well maintained by users that the BLM has not only allowed its continued existence but even helped develop primitive tent camping sites nearby with a vault toilet, picnic tables, fire pits, and a grill. The tent sites (and in summer, the cabin itself) are available for free on a first-come, first-served basis. It is a popular choice, so bring a tent in case someone already has claimed the cabin.

Getting There

The road through High Rock Canyon can be accessed off County Road 34, 62 miles north of Gerlach. Actually, "road" is giving this cursed trail too much credit; again, if you're not in a high-clearance, heavy-duty-suspension, four-wheel-drive vehicle, you shouldn't be here. The road is closed from February to mid-May to give nesting raptors and lambing bighorns some peace.

A pullout in the middle of the first (and most spectacular) canyon has firewood, campfire rocks, and a cozy carbon-covered cave. Your pace will slow down to about one mile an hour because of the rocks, dips, ruts, and creek crossings.

The hard driving continues. If you're really into this country, you can carry the appropriate topo maps, which will let you know about side trips to historic sites, such as cabins, pioneer graffiti, and old emigrant camping grounds. Along the main track is a lone cabin, where there's a pullout if it gets dark and you need to stop for the night. The surface improves around 25 miles from the entrance to the canyon; it's back up to 20 mph, with some cattle around.

At the next fork in the road, go straight; you'll have to open and close a wire gate behind you. From there you climb up to Stevens Camp, the only place on the road with potable water. At Stevens, cut around to the northwest and drive at around 25 mph until you come out on County Road 8A—wide, smooth, allowing 45 mph, a bit slippery and washboardy from the gravel, but black velvet compared to the past 35 miles.

Access is easier if you're coming from Vya, via County Road 8A, which runs east for 25 miles to Stevens Camp Road. It's 15 miles to the camp.

SOLDIER MEADOWS

Soldier Meadows is one of the most popular areas for **camping** in the Black Rock Desert. There are five designated sites at **Hot Creek Campground,** one at **Hidden Spring,** and one **primitive cabin;** all have fire pits and vault toilets. There is no charge to camp, but space is limited. No reservations are needed; find an open site and claim it as your own.

More plush digs, homemade meals, and other luxuries can be found at **Soldier Meadows Ranch and Lodge** (Soldier Meadows Road, Gerlach, 775/849-1666, $120-175), a working cattle ranch carved among steep canyons and rolling meadows stretching nearly to Nevada's northwest corner. Accommodations run from the bedroll and bunkhouse ranch hand experience to cattle baron suites with kitchen, dining room, and private bath. The main lodge also offers queen and bunk bed rooms with shared bathroom and shower facilities. Tent ($12) and RV ($15) sites are first-come, first-served. The proprietors rustle up stick-to-your-ribs breakfasts (7am-8am, $13) to fuel your day's adventure and family-style dinners (6pm-7pm, $25)

featuring the ranch's own beef. Sack lunches ($10) can be ordered the night before. Horses and well-behaved dogs are welcome.

SHELDON NATIONAL WILDLIFE REFUGE

The 350,000-acre **Sheldon National Wildlife Refuge** (headquarters at NV 140, 14 miles west of Denio, 775/941-0200, www.fws.gov/refuge/sheldon) supports 270 animal species, diverse plant life, and a variety of habitats. It's the winter home to nearly 4,000 pronghorn antelope. Though the pronghorn disperse in the summer, there's a good chance you can spot some in early morning. They're very fast and will keep their distance, but once they feel safe, they'll resume their camel walk, occasionally bouncing over the sage as if on springs. You may also see bighorn sheep, grouse hiding in the sagebrush, and golden eagles canvassing the high basalt mesas.

Virgin Valley Campground, near the refuge headquarters, is a good starting point for your visit. Maintained by a group called Friends of the Refuge, this free campground has about eight loosely defined spaces with fire pits and tables, pit toilets, and a tap for drinking water. The stone-rimmed **hot pool** has a fresh gravel bottom, and the adjacent

spring-fed hot pool at Sheldon National Wildlife Refuge

showers, in an old stone building, are clean and in good repair. At about 85°F, it's more of a warm spring, but welcome nonetheless. A colony of guppies lives in the lightly mineralized water. Some are fantails with orange, yellow, and blue spots. In summer, you'll fall asleep to a bullfrog serenade. All in all, it's a nice place, marred only by the halogen lights outside a nearby ranch house and the minimal privacy afforded by the open campsites.

Fishing for bass, crappie, perch, and other warm-water species is allowed in the **Dufurrena Ponds.** Trout fishing is good when water levels are high in **Big Springs Reservoir,** six miles west on NV 140, and **Catnip Reservoir,** 12 miles farther west via County Roads 8A and 34A. Five miles south of Catnip, a scenic overview commands the flats surrounding **Swan Lake** and **Swan Reservoir,** favorite gathering spots for hundreds of pronghorns.

Other activities allowed throughout the refuge include **hiking** and **backcountry camping** (permit required, designated areas only), **horseback riding** (pelletized feed only, no hay), **rock hounding** (seven pounds per day, no digging, obtain permission if collecting on mining claims), and **hunting** for sage grouse, waterfowl, pronghorn, and bighorn. Permits and/or tags are required; other restrictions apply. More information is available at the **Nevada Department of Wildlife** (www.ndow.org/Hunt).

Opal Mines

Fortune hunters can drive southwest from Virgin Valley Campground on Virgin Valley Ranch Road to **Royal Peacock Opal Mine** (10 Virgin Valley Rd., Denio, 775/941-0374, www.royalpeacock.com, 8am-4pm daily mid-May-mid-Oct., $65-190), in search of the elusive fire opals. Volcanic ash, silica chips, buried organic material, superhot water, and a few million years combined to create these light-refracting gems. Kids can dig free with paying adults in the mine tailings. Sifting through the bank diggings is more expensive but potentially more rewarding. On-site **RV camping** ($40) includes electrical, sewer, well water, and Internet, as well as shower, restroom, and coin laundry facilities. **Tent sites** ($10 per person), a furnished **cabin** ($75) that sleeps three, and a **trailer** ($75) that sleeps two are also available.

Other pay-to-dig opal mines in the area include **Bonanza** (43255 Sagebrush Creek Rd., 775/375-5955, www.bonanzaopals.com, 8am-4pm Wed.-Sun. Memorial Day-Labor Day, $70) and **Rainbow Ridge** (Denio, 775/941-0270, www.nevadaopal.com, 8am-4pm Fri.-Tues. late May-mid.-Sept., $100, age 10-15 half price).

I-80 East to Elko

Paralleling the Truckee and Humboldt Rivers, I-80 cuts a swath through some of the toughest stretches faced by the Oregon- and California-bound pioneers during the mid-19th century. As you journey across the 40 Mile Desert between Wadsworth and Lovelock, take solace in knowing that your trip will be immeasurably more pleasant than the journey of those traveling westward via covered wagon during the gold rush, or even via the first transcontinental railroad, completed along this route a couple decades later.

Several interesting and historic small towns dot the rugged mountains and open plains along the route from Reno. The looming forms of Lovelock, Winnemucca, and Battle Mountain are especially welcome on this long drive. The friendly people who live here confirm that these towns are real, not mirages.

LOVELOCK

A microcosm of Nevada's economic past, present, and future, Lovelock lets visitors experience all the state's most important industries—gaming, ranching, farming, mining, and outdoor recreation—all in one place. Though Lovelock capitalizes on its romantic name, marketing itself as a wedding and vow-renewal locale, it's really named for George Lovelock, a Welsh quartz miner who bought donated land for the railroad station.

The Humboldt River and lush grazing land that made the area a welcome respite for California and Oregon Trail trekkers now sustain a thriving ranch community. Rye Patch Reservoir, created with the completion of the dam in 1936, irrigates 40,000 acres and draws boaters, anglers, and campers throughout the year. Couer Rochester, the second-largest silver mine in the country, operates just south of the recreation area in the Humboldt Mountain Range. EP Minerals' Colado Plant is the world's largest producer of diatomaceous earth.

★ Lovers Lock Plaza

Stop at the **Pershing County Chamber of Commerce** (350 Main St., 775/273-7213) for brochures and information. You're already at your first downtown attraction. **Lovers Lock Plaza** (400 Main St.), adjacent to the circular courthouse, carries on the Chinese tradition of symbolizing unbreakable love by affixing a lock to a chain, then throwing away the key. More than 1,000 locks adorn the Lovelock chain, an American version of the links that wind their way around the Great Wall of China and the Yellow Mountains. Most shops in town can supply the lock; put it on any available link on the chains snaking around and among the pillars in the plaza. If you're ready to formalize your iron-clad love, Lovelock has a few quaint churches and a justice of the peace who can officiate. Get a marriage license right here at the **county clerk's office** (8am-5pm Mon.-Fri.). The **Pershing County Courthouse,** designed by prolific Nevada architect Frederic DeLongchamps, recalls the Roman Pantheon. Completed in 1921, it's the only circular courthouse still in use in the country. Get married here, and you can start going round and round with your spouse right away. Why wait till the honeymoon's over?

Town Tour

The plaza is a great place to start a self-guided tour of Lovelock's historical buildings. Next door, the **post office** (390 Main St., 775/273-7862, 8:30am-5pm Mon.-Fri.) was built in 1938 in the Starved Classicism style. Inside, Ejnar Hansen's mural, *The Uncovering of*

Lovers Lock Plaza in Lovelock

Ranch outside of town, the fully restored structure was transported to its current location, where it showcases historical relics, including mining equipment, a relocated assay office, and vintage stock certificates. You'll also find items associated with early Native Americans and the Emigrant Trail.

Lovelock Cave

At the Marzen House Museum or the chamber of commerce, pick up a map about the 20-mile drive known as the **Lovelock Cave Backcountry Byway.** It begins at the Marzen House and heads through town, irrigated fields, and along the Humboldt River. The road traces the base of the West Humboldt Mountains and follows a section of the California National Historic Trail to Lovelock Cave.

Lovelock Cave (NV 397/S. Meridian Rd., 22 miles south of Lovelock) can be considered the beginning of civilization in Nevada. Discovered by teenagers in 1887, the horseshoe-shaped cave achieved archaeological significance after a company began excavating its bat droppings in 1911 for use in fertilizer. Basketry, intricate tule duck decoys, and other objects signifying human occupation were uncovered under 250 tons of bat scat. Unfortunately, treasure hunters and vandals looted or destroyed many relics before archaeologists reached the site. The nearby **Leonard Rock Shelter,** protected by petroglyph-decorated tall tufa, yielded relics and other evidence of continual though sporadic occupation from about 4000 BC to AD 1400.

Food

Shame on you if you expect anything other than ranchland diner grub in Lovelock. Duck into the **Cowpoke Café** (995 Cornell Ave., 775/273-2444, 6am-9pm Mon.-Fri., 6am-3pm Sat., $10-15) for the best pie in town. Folks also rave about the veggie burger (in cattle country?!). From Mexican chiles rellenos to rib-sticking breakfasts, **La Casita** (410 Cornell, 775/273-7773, 7am-8pm daily) has it all. **Temptations** (395 Main St., 775/273-1921,

the Comstock Lode, completed in 1940, is a prime example of the WPA public art initiatives implemented under President Franklin Roosevelt. Continue east for a block to reach the 1880 **Union Pacific Depot** (1005 W. Broadway), the only remaining in a series of residential No. 2 style, two-story station houses built along the Southern Pacific Railroad. Politician and noted orator William Jennings Bryan spoke here in 1915. The building, which retains its yellow-and-brown color scheme, was added to the National Register in 2004.

Across the street, stop in at the **Longhorn Saloon** (925 W. Broadway Ave., 775/273-7015) and gaze at the intricate beauty of the murals on the walls. A 15-minute walk south on Broadway and Marzen Lane brings you to the **Marzen House Museum** (25 Marzen Ln., 775/273-4949, 1:30pm-4pm Wed.-Sat. May-Sept., donation). Built in 1874 on Colonel Joseph Marzen's 3,400-acre Big Meadow

7am-8pm Mon.-Fri., 9am-8pm Sat., $10-15) offers a wide selection of panini, but try the chicken salad or Mediterranean wrap. The location inside a gas station doesn't do much for the atmosphere, but the pie and calzones are the draw at **Pizza Factory** (365 Cornell Ave., 775/273-3232, http://pizzafactory.com, 11am-9pm Mon.-Sat., noon-8pm Sun., $12-20).

Accommodations

I-80 through northern Nevada wasn't completed until 1983; for decades the traffic light at Main Street and Cornell Avenue was the only one on the highway between New York and San Francisco! This accounts for the motels along Cornell Avenue, which enjoyed a prime location on the route.

On the north side of town, **C Punch Inn** (1420 Cornell Ave., 775/273-2971, www.cpunchinnandcasino.com, $65-75) is the closest thing to a casino, with a roomful of slot and video poker machines. It's also a working cattle ranch and alfalfa farm, so you know the on-site **Black Rock Grill** (24 hours daily, $10-17) serves terrific steaks and burgers. Some rooms are pet-friendly.

Freight trains might rouse light sleepers at the quaint **Cadillac Inn** (1395 Cornell, 775/273-2798, $60-65), but that's just part of the charm. The building is old, but management takes justifiable pride in the motel's cleanliness.

Families will appreciate the small kitchenettes in the rooms at **Royal Inn** (1435 Cornell Ave., 888/950-5062, $60-70). Other choices are the **Lovelock Inn** (55 Cornell Ave., 775/273-2900, www.lovelockinn.com, $50-75), closer to the center of town, and **Lovelock Nugget** (515 Cornell Ave., 775/273-7023, $50-65), on the south end. RVers can find level, shady spots at **Lazy K Campground and RV** (1550 Cornell Ave., 775/273-7090, http://lazy-k-campground.business.site, $30-35).

RYE PATCH STATE RECREATION AREA

The designated purpose of **Rye Patch Reservoir** (2505 Rye Patch Reservoir Rd., 775/538-7321, $7), 22 miles north of Lovelock on I-80, was irrigation of farms and ranchlands in Lovelock Valley. However, its 72 miles of shoreline and 11,000 acres of surface water have also created a multi-species fishing opportunity and a sublime recreation complex.

Crappie, walleye, and black bass can be caught best in spring and early summer, using jigs and small plastics. Wipers prefer live minnows. Fall is the time for catfish, with most

Rye Patch Reservoir

caught on night crawlers, liver, or stink bait. A boat ramp near the most popular fishing spots is near the Westside Campground, along with a dump station. A smaller boat launch is at Pit Taylor Cove, 10 miles north via I-80 exit 138.

This is an ideal spot for camping and picnicking, with two designated day-use locations, complete with restrooms. Two no-hookup campgrounds ($14), the 22-site **River Campground** below the dam and the 25-site **Westside Campground** on the reservoir's (you guessed it) west side, have flush toilets and showers. Primitive camping is allowed along the water, with some sites accessible by rough roads, others by boat only.

UNIONVILLE

A little over an hour's drive from Lovelock, Unionville sits in the aptly named Buena Vista Canyon. During the Civil War, Confederate sympathizers founded the site and named the town Dixie. When northerners, arriving to work the mines, outnumbered the southerners, they quickly voted to rename the town to show support for Lincoln's government. While there are still a few remnants of those roaring times in the 1860s, there is no formal preservation effort afoot. A couple dozen folks still live among the ruins, which include a schoolhouse and the shack where Mark Twain lived for a few weeks while his dreams of mining fortunes glimmered and died. Visitors can relax in Unionville's tranquil, scenic canyon locale, taking advantage of the hiking, hunting, and fishing spots nearby.

Establish a base at the **Old Pioneer Garden Bed & Breakfast** (2805 Unionville Rd., 775/538-7585, www.oldpioneergarden. com, $110-160), the only commercial operation in town. The owners have restored one of Unionville's first structures, the Hadley House, incorporating its original stone walls. The restored home now includes six guest rooms; a second restored home has additional rooms for rent. To get there, take I-80 to exit 149 between Lovelock and Unionville. Driving south on NV 400 will bring you to a

crossroads, with Unionville to the west and Kyle Hot Springs to the east.

KYLE HOT SPRINGS

Once a haven for the rich, now abandoned, **Kyle Hot Springs** is still a pleasant spot for a soak. A soothing 90°F, the pool may not be enough to defeat the chill on autumn or winter nights, but in summer, it's a fine spot from which to survey the remnants of the erstwhile resort. A strong sulfur odor prevails as the hot water travels via cattle trough into the pool. Don't submerge silver jewelry in the sulfuric water; it will tarnish. A short walk brings you to the bathhouse, where the Comstock muckety-mucks could steam their way to better health. To get there, take I-80 to exit 149. Drive south on NV 400 to a crossroads; go east for Kyle Hot Springs.

WINNEMUCCA

A crossroads for Indians, trappers, pioneers, miners, and maybe—just maybe—one of the most infamous outlaw bands in history, Winnemucca was a road trip stop even before the place had a name. It still is today, as transportation continues to shape the town's identity. An extensive trail system supports avid ATV and mountain bike riders. Classic cars and motorcycle rallies highlight several fairs and festivals throughout the year. And on many weekends, bronc busters, barrel racers, and bull riders can be found hanging on for dear life.

After the discovery of silver nearby, Winnemucca became a boomtown. In the 1870s, it won the county seat and the railroad was completed. A large Chinatown sprouted up, and Basque shepherds settled in to labor on the surrounding ranchlands. The Chinese were hounded away and little remains of their time here, but the Basque influence is still evident in the town's restaurants and cultural events. Many residents still make their livings in the livestock trade.

Town Tour

Start at the site of Winnemucca's main claim

Winnemucca

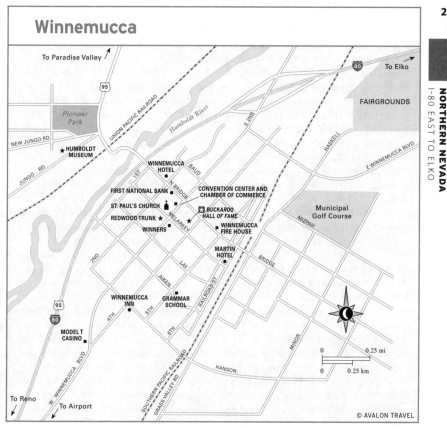

To Paradise Valley

UNION PACIFIC RAILROAD

Humboldt River

To Elko

80

FAIRGROUNDS

95

Pioneer Park

NEW JUNGO RD

JUNGO RD

★ HUMBOLDT MUSEUM

1ST

N BRIDGE

BAUD

E 2ND

HASKELL

E WINNEMUCCA BLVD

WINNEMUCCA HOTEL

FIRST NATIONAL BANK

CONVENTION CENTER AND CHAMBER OF COMMERCE

ST. PAUL'S CHURCH

MELARKEY

BUCKAROO HALL OF FAME

Municipal Golf Course

REDWOOD TRUNK ★

★ WINNEMUCCA FIRE HOUSE

MIZPAH

WINNERS

MARTIN HOTEL

2ND

LAY

BRIDGE

AIKEN

WINNEMUCCA INN

GRAMMAR SCHOOL

RAILROAD ST

5TH

4TH

6TH

MINOR

95

80

MODEL T CASINO

SOUTHERN PACIFIC RAILROAD

GRASS VALLEY RD

HANSON

0   0.25 mi

0   0.25 km

To Reno

To Airport

© AVALON TRAVEL

to fame, George Nixon's **First National Bank** (352 Bridge St.). While Butch Cassidy's role in the town's most famous bank robbery is unclear, it's certain that members of Butch's gang were responsible, one of the robbers even holding a knife to Nixon's throat. Understanding the value of a good story, Winnemuccans insist Butch masterminded and directed the robbery. From here, head west to Nixon Park at the main intersection downtown. At the corner of Winnemucca Boulevard (locally known as Main Street) and Melarkey Street is an eight-foot-diameter cross-section of a **redwood tree trunk,** which washed ashore in Crescent City, California, in 1964. The good people of Crescent City presented it to mark the beginning of the Winnemucca-to-the-Sea Highway, which ends in Crescent City.

The **Winnemucca Convention Center** (50 W. Winnemucca Blvd., Ste. 1, 775/623-5071) houses the **Chamber of Commerce** (30 W. Winnemucca Blvd., 775/623-2225, www.humboldtcountychamber.com), which can provide you with a free visitors guide and map that will help navigate the rest of the tour. Go up a block to Bridge Street and turn east. A restored commercial building (355 S. Bridge St.) used to house the **Turin Brown Mercantile,** which was built in 1898. Continue on to 5th Street to the **Humboldt County Courthouse,** a pillared dispensary of justice constructed in 1921 from the designs of Frederic DeLongchamps. On the same corner is the art deco **Winnemucca Fire House,** completed in 1935.

Cut over the southeast quadrant of town. Head south for two blocks. If school's not in session, peek in at the 1927 **Winnemucca Grammar School** (522 Lay St.), just as lovely and Rockwellian as ever. While you're in the neighborhood, sidle on over to the busy **Martin Hotel** (94 W. Railroad St.); the Basque cuisine at its restaurant is some of Nevada's best. **St. Paul's Catholic Church** (350 Melarkey St.) brings you full circle from your wanderings around town. It was constructed in 1924 on the original site of the town's first Catholic mission. Its striking Spanish Colonial architecture makes it one of the most photographed structures in town.

★ Buckaroo Hall of Fame

At the Winnemucca Convention Center, pay tribute to the working ranch hands who built this part of Nevada with calloused hands and strong backs at the **Buckaroo Hall of Fame and Western Heritage Museum** (30 W. Winnemucca Blvd., 775/623-5071 or 800/962-2638, www.buckaroohalloffame.com, 8am-4pm Mon.-Sat., free). Remember, they're buckaroos (a bastardized, anglicized pronunciation of the Spanish *vaquero,* or skilled horseman). They get touchy if you call them cowboys. Buckaroos have flair—form as well as function. In 1927, Charles Russell, chronicler of all things Western, made the distinction, noting that buckaroos "were generally strong on pretty, usin' plenty of hoss jewelry, silver-mounted spurs, bits, an' conchas. . . . These fellows were sure fancy."

Displays not only honor the vaqueros inducted so far but also present the rugged lifestyle they led through artwork, song, and other media. Buckaroo Hall of Famers must have been born in the 19th century and worked as a cattleman within a 200-mile radius of Winnemucca. Next door, well-shaded **Riverview Park** is a fine place for a picnic.

Humboldt Museum

Across the river at Pioneer Park is the **Humboldt Museum** (175 Museum Ave., 775/623-2912, http://humboldtmuseum. org, 9am-4pm Wed.-Fri., 10am-4pm Sat., donation), housed in the former St. Mary's Episcopal Church building (1907). It showcases the courage of Native Americans and westward emigrants, the wonder of Hollywood and the automobile, and the region's history from the Ice Age to today. You'll see Winnemucca's first piano, brought here in 1868; Indian relics from Lovelock Cave; and a scrapbook from *The Winning of Barbara Worth,* filmed 30 miles west of Winnemucca at the edge of the Black Rock Desert in 1926. The newer rear building boasts a mural of what downtown looked like around the turn of the 20th century. Its antique auto collection includes a 1901 Merry Oldsmobile, the county's first car.

Biking

The provocatively named **Bloody Shins Trail** actually consists of a collection of mountain bike trails east of town. There's a trail for every level of biker, along with facilities for horseback riding and hiking. Conveniently located but usually not crowded, the trails are one- and two-track dirt paths, 7- to 24-mile loops with no gates to open or close. Biking at an elevation of 4,500 to 5,200 feet, you can expect inspiring views and adrenaline-pumping turns, drops, and rises to take your breath away. For information on Bloody Shins or the more remote **Blue Lakes Trail,** contact the BLM's **Winnemucca Field Office** (5100 Winnemucca Blvd., 775/623-1500).

Casinos

Winners (185 W. Winnemucca Blvd., 775/623-2511 or 800/648-4770, www.winnersinn.com, $60-90) is the only place in town to find craps and roulette. It also has blackjack, three-card poker, and a couple hundred slots, of course, as well as a bingo parlor. The lounge hosts standup comedians, vintage rockers, and cover bands most weekends. The hotel and its early 1980s decor have a frayed-around-the-edges feel.

Alexander von Humboldt

As you've probably gathered by now, the area around Winnemucca is Humboldt Land: Humboldt County, the Humboldt Mountains plus the East and West Humboldt Mountains, Humboldt National Forest, Humboldt Sink, Humboldt Mining District, Humboldt Trail, and of course the Humboldt River. So who was Humboldt, anyway, and how did his name become attached to so many important features in northern Nevada?

Surprisingly, for all his accomplishments in Europe, Russia, and Latin America, Alexander von Humboldt not only never discovered anything in Nevada, he never even set foot in the state! Still, his résumé apparently made enough of an impression on John C. Frémont that when he happened upon an unpretentious northern Nevada stream in 1844, he designated it the Humboldt River.

Alexander von Humboldt was born in Berlin in 1769. He received a college education in mining technology and advanced quickly in his field. At the age of 27 he inherited a substantial sum of money, with which he embarked on a scientific expedition that ranged from Venezuela, Cuba, and Colombia to Mexico and the United States. He collected botanical, zoological, geological, and astronomical data and studied Pacific Ocean currents, the Cuban plantation economy, and pre-Columbian cultures. He climbed to 18,000 feet in the Andes, surveyed the headwaters of the Amazon, followed ancient Inca trails in Peru, and sipped mint juleps with James Madison in Washington, D.C.

Humboldt settled in Paris in 1808 and began publishing the reports and results of his travels and inquiries. The subsequent 30-volume, 12,000-page encyclopedia earned him an international reputation as a "one-man institution" at the same time that it ruined him financially. Humboldt then embarked on several years of diplomatic missions for Frederick William III of Prussia, traveled through Siberia at the invitation of Czar Nicholas I, and finally settled down to a position as lecturer and author in Frederick's court in Berlin.

For the last 30 years of his life, Humboldt concentrated on his five-volume *Kosmos*, an epic survey of the earth and the rest of the universe. In it, he attempted to determine, through scientific knowledge, the place of humanity in the cosmic order. Alexander von Humboldt died in Berlin in 1859 at the age of 90.

With plenty of red and blue neon outside and opulent decor, the compact slot palace **Winnemucca Inn** (741 W. Winnemucca Blvd., 800/633-6435, www.winnemuccainn.com, $90-110) feels bigger than it is. A rowdy sports bar complete with high-def big screens, a William Hill sports book, and a sedate coffee shop are all stuffed into a space the size of a Harrah's Tahoe ladies room. The hotel has a few suites to accommodate families and strong sound- and light-proofing for anyone who needs a good night's (or day's) sleep after a long drive.

The **Model T** (1130 W. Winnemucca Blvd., 775/623-2588, http://modeltcasino.com, $55-70) is a casino, hotel, and RV park with gaming options that include more than 200 slot machines. The large rooms, pool, and good free hot breakfast at the on-site Quality Inn are pluses, but gamblers and drivers who need a place to rejuvenate will have all their needs met. Families should probably look elsewhere.

Pete's Gambling Hall (1985 W. Winnemucca Blvd., 775/625-1777 or 800/465-4329, www.petesgamblinghall.com), next to the Holiday Inn Express, has 176 slots, blackjack, three-card poker, and a Dos Amigos Restaurant inside. The **Sundance Casino** (33 W. Winnemucca Blvd., 775/623-3336), across from the Chamber of Commerce at Bridge and Main, is all slots and video poker, all the time.

Food

Any discussion of food in this part of Nevada must start with Basque cuisine. It's usually served family-style, with course after glorious course tempting your taste buds. Choices range from steak, lamb, pork, and shrimp to more exotic fare like rabbit, tripe, pig's feet, and beef tongue, often generously slathered in garlic or pepper. Traditional sides include pinto beans and salad (mix them together like a real Pyrenean), stocky soup, mashed potatoes, green beans, and French fries. Wash it down with potent picon punch. One of the state's best Basque restaurants is at the ★ **Martin Hotel** (94 W. Railroad St., 775/623-3197, http://themartinhotel.com, 11:30am-2pm and 4pm-9pm Mon.-Fri., 4pm-9pm Sat.-Sun., $25-40). With all the sides, a couple of platter-sized entrées—with three, count 'em three, pork chops and a hunk of lamb shoulder—can feed a family of four.

Ambrosia takes the form of shredded beef flautas at **Chihuahua's Restaurant** (71 Giroux St., 775/403-9200, www.chihuahuasgrill.com, 7:30am-10pm daily, $12-18). Tender and perfectly seasoned, the beef is a carnivore's dream and a vegetarian's potential downfall (they have vegetarian entrées, so if you fall off the wagon, it's your own fault). Dine in front of a trompe l'oeil arch opening onto a Mexican village courtyard. Start with a cerveza in the bar; finish with fried ice cream.

A Winnemucca institution for a half century, **The Griddle** (460 W. Winnemucca Blvd., 775/623-2977, www.thegriddle.com, 6am-2pm daily, $10-15) serves the best breakfast in town, from basic bacon and eggs to the haute-ier tomato and basil omelets, all delivered fast and friendly. They serve a tasty grilled meatloaf sandwich and other sandwiches for lunch, but breakfast is where this place shines.

Wonderful House (105 W. 4th St., 775/623-5997, 11am-9pm daily, $7-12) delivers good service and substantial Chinese dishes served with steamed or fried rice. The chicken dishes, especially the sesame, sweet and sour, and Hunan, never disappoint.

At the **Flying Pig** (1100 W. Winnemucca Blvd., 775/623-4104, 11am-9pm daily, $10-20) the sauce is so tangy, with a touch of honey sweetness, that you'll want to buy a bottle to take home. Ribs are fall-off-the-bone perfect, but it's the lunchtime pulled pork sandwich with that spicy sauce that keeps us coming back. Don't overlook the on-tap microbrew selection.

Accommodations

This crossroads town boasts more than 1,000 hotel rooms and hundreds of RV spaces. Booking in advance may save a few bucks.

Other than the casinos, the best budget choice is the **Town House Motel** (375 Monroe, 775/623-3620 or 800/243-3620, http://townhouse-motel.com, $70-80). Tom and Ana Marie Smith have been running this clean, comfortable motel since 1980, and their pride shows in crisp linens, sparkling bathroom tile, and sparkling swimming pool. The rooms, especially those at the back, are far enough off the beaten path to be relatively quiet. A perfect family option, **Scott Shady Court** (400 1st St., 775/623-3646 or 866/875-3646, www.scottshadycourt.com, $50-80) has a cozy setting off the main drag, a luxurious indoor pool, and a safe, grassy playground area. It stands on the Scott family's old dairy farm, converted to cabins in 1928. It's worth driving by just to see the cool art deco sign.

Chain outlets include **Motel 6** (1800 W. Winnemucca Blvd., 775/332-0878, www.motel6.com, $50-70); a big-roomed Best Western, the **Gold Country Inn** (921 W. Winnemucca Blvd., 844/243-9761, www.bestwestern.com, $130-160); a very good **Holiday Inn Express** (1987 W. Winnemucca Blvd., 775/625-3100 or 800/465-4329, www.ihg.com, $125-180); and **Candlewood Suites** (460 E. Winnemucca Blvd., 877/660-8543, www.ihg.com, $110-130), which is geared for business travelers with full kitchens, big desks, and plenty of outlets for laptops and cell phone chargers.

RV PARKS

With four parks ranging from solid to downright luxurious, Winnemucca is an RV gold mine. Heck, you don't even have to bring your rig with you. The **New Frontier** (4360 Rim Rock Rd., 775/621-5277, www.newfrontier-rvpark.com, $34-38), in the northeast part of town, will rent you a turnkey RV ($65) with two TVs, cable, and everything else you need, with discounts for weekly and monthly rentals. They also offer wide, paved pull-throughs and back-ins and strong 30- and 50-amp hookups. The minimarket, lounge, laundry, and showers are clean and modern, and the site is away from I-80 road noise. Tents are not allowed.

Nearly as good, **Winnemucca RV Park** (5255 E. Winnemucca Blvd., 775/623-4458 or 877/787-2755, www.winnemuccarvpark. biz, $32) has been in the same location, about a mile east of downtown Winnemucca, for more than 20 years. The trees are mature, and there's plenty of green space, including a very nice grassy tenting area. There are 132 spaces for motor homes, 83 with full hookups and 70 pull-throughs. The seasonal pool is heated, and the on-site owners provide a shuttle service to casinos and restaurants.

Kids will love the water balloon fight catapults and kidney-shaped pool at **I-80 KOA Winnemucca** (5575 E. Winnemucca Blvd., 800/562-7554, http://koa.com, $28). A putting green, shuffleboard court, and dog run make sure everyone gets their exercise. No tenters need apply at the paved **Model T RV Park** (1130 W. Winnemucca Blvd., 775/623-2588, http://modeltcasino.com, $30), in the parking lot of the Model T Casino. There are 58 spaces for motor homes, all with full hookups, all pull-throughs. Restrooms have flush toilets and hot showers; a laundry, convenience store, and seasonal pool are available.

Information and Services
Park Cinemas (738 W. Winnemucca Blvd., 775/623-4454, $7-9) is the only theater between Sparks and Elko. The duplex shows first-run features weeknights and matinees on weekends. Winnemucca has a fine **library** (85 5th St., 775/623-6388, 9am-5pm Thurs.-Sat. and Mon., 9am-9pm Tues.-Wed.). The Nevada Room has lots of primary sources;

local newspaper indexing cuts hours off research time. The **Greyhound** office (www. greyhound.com) is at **City Gas and Liquor** (240 W. Winnemucca Blvd., 775/623-4464). **Amtrak** (209 Railroad St., 800/872-7245, www.amtrak.com) blows through town once daily in each direction.

BATTLE MOUNTAIN
Natural attractions and outdoor adventure draw visitors to this quiet Nevada town. It's well located to offer access to public land bursting with opportunities for wildlife viewing, hiking, fishing, hunting, and biking. Opportunities for motocross, mountain kart and stock car racing, and off-roading will get your heart pounding. Unlike other towns along the I-80 corridor, Battle Mountain's downtown hasn't budged for over 120 years. Front Street still fronts the railroad yards, with businesses and full storefronts lining the opposite side. Broad Street bisects the business district.

Sights
Housed in an authentically restored 1920s ranch house, the **Battle Mountain Cookhouse Museum** (905 Burns St., 775/635-8548, www.cookhousemuseum. org, noon-4pm Tues.-Sat., donation) offers a glimpse into what life was like here some 100 years ago. Exhibits include everyday 19th-century household items and rotating local art displays. Poetry readings, musical performances, and a history library make this a one-stop cultural experience.

Twelve miles southwest of town, **Phoenix Mine** (1080 Chukar Ln., 775/635-6640, 9am-noon, free) is one of several Nevada pits owned by Newmont Gold Corporation, producing more than 200,000 ounces of gold and nearly 50 million pounds of copper each year. Tours are available the third Thursday of the month, April through October.

One of the many boomtowns that went bust when the mines played out, **Galena** is slowly receding into history and the surrounding canyon. Dilapidated homesteads,

Thunder Mountain

Frank Van Zant, a member of the Creek Nation who renamed himself Chief Rolling Mountain Thunder, is responsible for the **Thunder Mountain Monument** (www.thundermountain-monument.com), an eclectic folk art collection near Imlay, 33 miles southwest of Winnemucca on I-80. Using abandoned car parts, scrap metal, concrete, and treasures salvaged from junkyards, over 30 years the chief built what is described as "a monument to the American Indian, a retreat for pilgrims aspiring to the pure and radiant heart," according to a website maintained by his son, who is working to restore the roadside museum and art gallery.

Van Zant created the five-acre site along I-80 after serving in World War II and careers in law enforcement and the ministry. He retired, remarried for the third time, and set out for rural Nevada—where he reinvented himself as Chief Rolling Thunder Mountain. The chief at times said his inspiration came in a dream that a giant eagle swooped down from the sky and told him "this is where I should build his nest." Other times, he claimed a less spiritual beginning: His truck broke down, so he set up camp and started foraging.

Whatever the origin, the monument soon took on a life of its own, growing into a monument to the American Indians' struggle, a plea to take care of the environment, and other ideals. In the 1970s, the monument's messages attracted rebellious young people who helped in the art's creation and added a hostel house, underground hut, and even a playground. The hippies looked to Rolling Thunder as a spiritual guru. Though he never claimed mystical powers, some believers claimed Rolling Thunder could teleport objects, create rain, and heal wounds and diseases. The interfaith community thrived in the 1970s, serving the spiritual needs of such notables as Buckminster Fuller and the Grateful Dead, and remained in operation until 1985. A lifelong addiction to cigarettes caught up to Van Zant in the 1980s; his wife left and took their children with her; and fewer counterculture allies visited to help with the site. He committed suicide in 1989, and his life's work fell victim to fire, vandalism, and neglect.

Thankfully, Frank's son and an old friend have taken on the responsibility to restore Thunder Mountain Monument. There is plenty to spark interest and imagination in what's left of the hostel and playground and to contemplate in the art created from civilization's castoffs.

Rolling Thunder's grandson, Sidian Morning Star Jones, is a founder of Open Source Religion, which explores and melds beliefs and rituals of various religious traditions, including those preached by Rolling Thunder.

mine outbuildings, and the shells of once-prosperous mercantiles still invite adventurers and photographers. The ghost town is 10 miles south of Battle Mountain on NV 305. Turn west, following the dirt road for three miles into Galena Canyon.

Recreation

Well-marked single- and double-track loops with a variety of elevation changes, lengths, and terrain make the **Copper Basin Mountain Bike Trails** accessible to bikers of all skill levels. Put your cardiovascular system to the test with steep climbs, then coast down through sage-covered ravines and past Pony Express routes. Reach the trailhead by

heading south on NV 305 for three miles and turning west on Copper Basin Road.

Those who prefer horsepower to pedal power should head to the **Shoshone Off-Highway Vehicle Trails System,** 25 miles south of Battle Mountain. Spanning 8,000-foot mountains and traversing pine forests and high desert ecosystems, the family-friendly 60-mile trail system has a flat staging area for easy loading and unloading of OHVs. The trails eventually will expand to 184 miles of tracks suitable for jeeps and trucks as well as ATVs. In town, Kart, IMCA modified, and stock drivers meet their need for speed around the quarter-mile dirt oval of the **Battle Mountain Raceway** (Airport

Way, 775/635-5060, www.battlemountain-raceway.org, gates 5pm, racing 7:30pm, $10, students $5, under 5 free) a couple weekends a month, spring through fall. Just past the raceway, ATVs and motorcycles are welcome at **Battle Mountain Motocross** track.

Battle Mountain is smack in the middle of mule deer territory, which are coveted by hunters. Pronghorns are prolific as well, and a few tags for mountain lions and recently re-introduced California bighorns are available each season. Hunting jackrabbits, ground squirrels, and other small game does not require a license. Bird hunters will find targetable grouse and chukar, though waterfowl generally bypass ponds and casual water in favor of the Humboldt River north of town. Permits are required for trapping red, gray, and kit foxes, mink, and otter.

Stocked rainbow trout and yellow perch thrive in **Willow Creek Ponds,** 22 miles southwest of Battle Mountain. The two reservoirs are the perfect size for float tubes and portable boats. Many streams in the area accommodate native rainbow and brook trout.

The nine-hole **Mountain View Golf Course** (205 Fairway Dr., 775/635-8488, $13 nine holes, $20 18 holes) is tucked into the desert just south of town. The USGA-rated links challenge players of all skill levels with tight doglegs and narrow fairways. Water hazards have been enlarged, more greenside bunkers added, and some holes lengthened, putting a premium on pinpoint approach shots. A driving range, putting green, cart rental, bar, restaurant, and pro shop complete the experience.

Casinos

More restaurant than casino, the **Owl Club** (72 E. Front, 775/635-2444) has a variety of slots—81 in all. The restaurant (6am-10pm Sun.-Thurs., 6am-11pm Fri.-Sat., $10-15) gets high marks for its fried chicken and sandwiches. The bar gets even higher marks for its potent cocktails. Ditto for the **Broadway Colt Casino** (650 W. Front St., 775/635-3278)

in the Flying J Travel Center. Expect about 70 older slots and good diner food—especially the ranch-style breakfasts.

Food

The steaks at the **Hide-A-Way** (872 Broad St., 775/635-5150, 11am-9pm Tues.-Sat., $15-30) are so big and juicy that ordering shrimp tacos would be heresy—spicy, delicious heresy. **El Aguila Real** (254 E. Front St., 775/635-8390, 11am-9pm daily, $10-20) has all the flavor of a resort restaurant without the pretentious atmosphere and pricing. Don't forget the fried ice cream. **Mama's Pizza** (515 E. Front St., 775/635-9211, 11am-9pm Mon.-Sat., 11am-8pm Sun., $10-20) has good pizza and killer cheesy breadsticks. **Ming Dynasty** (146 E. Front St., 775/635-8698, www.mingdynasty-battlemountain.com, 11am-9pm Mon.-Fri., noon-9pm Sat., $12-20) is good for takeout; get the Szechuan beef.

Accommodations

Most motels are on or near Front Street (NV 304). The best is ★ **Big Chief Motel** (434 W. Front St., 775/635-2416, www.big-chiefmotelbmnv.com, $60-80), with beds and pillows like clouds, a pool, and free Wi-Fi and continental breakfast. The remodeled standard rooms at the back of **Battle Mountain Inn** (650 W. Front St., 775/635-5200, www.battlemtninn.com, $55-80) are larger and quieter, with more subdued decor than the older versions. All rooms have free Wi-Fi, refrigerators, coffeemakers, and microwaves. The casino cashier doubles as the front desk clerk at the **Nevada Hotel** (72 E. Front St., 775/635-2444, $32-40), the hostelry wing of the Owl Club casino. You can't beat the price. Big TVs and showers seal the deal.

The **Super 8** (825 Super 8 Dr., 775/635-8808, www.wyndhamhotels.com, $75-90) is right on the freeway, but thanks to sturdy walls, good insulation, and double-paned windows, you'd never know it. The rooms are quite large; most include a sofa bed, making this a good choice for large families.

CAMPING AND RV PARKS

The 50 spotless RV sites at **Clark Park** (625 W. Humboldt St., 775/635-9600, $35) are pull-through. All are clean, with gravel pads and little greenery. It's within walking distance of convenience stores and restaurants, and there's a laundry on-site. An extension of the parking lot at Flying J Plaza, **Colt RV Park** (590 W. Front St., 775/635-5424) has 96 full-hookup spaces for motor homes; 79 are pull-throughs. Accessible restrooms in the truck stop have flush toilets and hot showers; public phone, laundry, and, of course, groceries and fuel are available. For more greenery and scenery, but no amenities, head to the **Mill Creek camping area** ($5), 22 miles south of Battle Mountain off NV 305, toward Austin. The former Civilian Conservation Corps camp, at an elevation of 5,000 feet, has a small, shady, secluded camping area for tents and small RVs amid cottonwoods beside Mill Creek.

Information and Services

Check with the **Chamber of Commerce** (625 S. Broad St., 775/635-8245, www.battlemountainchamber.com) inside the Civic Center for information on Western, Native American, cultural, and recreational activities, including gold mine tours. The **library** (625 S. Broad St., 775/635-2534, noon-5pm Tues. and Fri., 1pm-6pm Wed., 3pm-8pm Thurs., 10am-4pm Sat.) is next door. For sundries, stop in at **Mills Pharmacy** (990 Broyles Ranch Rd., 775/635-2323, 9am-7pm Mon.-Fri., 9am-2pm Sat.).

Elko

This booming town has a brash, modern frontier energy all its own. It's easy to slip into Elko's strong stream of hustle and bustle, which seems to keep pace with the traffic on the superhighway, the freight and passenger trains chugging right through town, and the planes landing at and taking off from the airport. Yet Elko also has a warm, homespun vitality to it. Coming into Elko after a long drive from any direction is like stepping up to a blazing campfire on a cold desert night. Elko speaks to you, forever tuggin' your sleeve and calling you home. Elko is the largest town between Salt Lake City (237 miles east) and Sparks (nearly 300 miles west), and between Las Vegas (400 miles south) and Twin Falls (173 miles north)—an area roughly comparable in size to New England. So you may find yourself returning to Elko again and again.

Elko has been gentrified and citified over the last quarter century, but it remains dedicated to its ranching and mining heritage. Indeed, it's still the same place local vaqueros come to on a Saturday night and where Basque sheepherders flock (see what we did there?) to wallow in their unique history and culture. It also boasts one of the finest museums in the state, the National Cowboy Poetry Gathering, and some of the most irresistible outdoor recreation anywhere.

SIGHTS
★ Northeastern Nevada Museum

The remarkable **Northeastern Nevada Museum** (1515 Idaho St., 775/738-3418, http://museumelko.org, 9am-5pm Tues.-Sat., 1pm-5pm Sun., adults $8, discounts for children, students, seniors, and military) is one of the largest, most varied, and most interesting collections in the state. Galleries include works by renowned Western artists Edward Borein, Will James, Ansel Adams, and Edward Weston.

The animal collection—with 300 specimens—is a veritable safari to "Nevada Mountain," a peak covered with Great Basin critters in their re-created natural habitat. The two-million-year-old bones of Murray the Mastodon, dug up at nearby Spring Creek

Elko

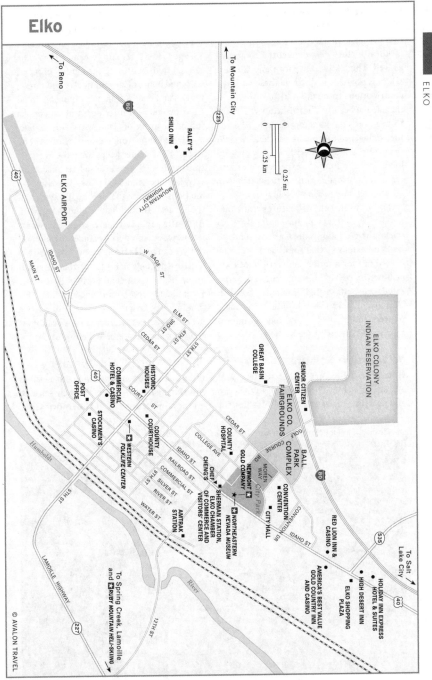

© AVALON TRAVEL

in 1994, get their own separate place of reverence. Other vignettes show animals from all over the world in natural settings.

Local history gets reverential treatment as well. The Native American and Chinese sections poignantly describe these cultures' contributions throughout history. Artifacts include the beautiful burnished bar salvaged from an early gin joint that dated to 1916 and the original printing press from the *Elko Daily Free Press*. The art gallery hosts traveling exhibits that run from the expected desert watercolor landscapes and rustic sketches to abstract oils and urban photographs.

The mining exhibit features multimedia displays explaining how companies retrieve the gold along the Carlin Trend, so rich and extensive that some say it won't be mined out for another generation. Marvel at how the ore is blasted, scooped, separated, crushed, settled, leached, cyanided, charcoaled, acid-treated, inductothermed, poured, and bricked—all to recover microscopic gold specks.

★ Western Folklife Center

Housed in the former Pioneer Hotel (1913) and anchored by a 40-foot mahogany, cherry, and pearl bar, the **Western Folklife Center**

(501 Railroad St., 775/738-7508, www.westernfolklife.org, 10:30am-5pm Mon.-Fri., 10am-5pm Sat., $5, seniors and students $3, age 6-12 $1) remains a centerpiece. The ground floor houses a gift shop full of tapes, CDs, and books of cowboy poetry and music; posters and photos from the annual National Cowboy Poetry Gatherings; and songbooks full of the music of Gene Autry, Roy Rogers, and Dale Evans from the heyday of cowboy culture. The center keeps alive the Western spirit and cowboy code of self-reliance, honesty, fair play, and hard work. Traveling exhibitions celebrate the cowboy lifestyle from the western United States, South America, Australia, and Europe through artwork, leatherwork, and performances throughout the year. The **National Cowboy Poetry Gathering** began in 1985 when a small group of folklorists and poets organized an event that has become an annual tradition for thousands of people who value and practice the artistic expressions of the American West and work hard to preserve their future.

★ Newmont Gold Company

Witness Elko's boom firsthand with a visit to a working gold mine. There's a new sense of urgency and prosperity at **Newmont Gold**

wildlife diorama at the Northeastern Nevada Museum

Company (775/778-4068, 9am-noon 2nd Tues. each month Apr.-Oct., free), since the precious metal has skyrocketed to $1,300 an ounce. Reservations for tours are first-come, first-served; reserve at least a week ahead. Children 6 and older are welcome, accompanied by an adult. Tours leave from the Northeastern Nevada Museum; transportation is provided to the mine, where visitors can see the pit, dump leach, and milling facilities. Newmont revolutionized gold mining by using processes to recover specks of gold almost invisible to the naked eye. It has developed strip mines all along the Carlin Trend, one of the most lucrative gold deposits in the world. The company's sophisticated, clockwork operation is a far cry from the hit-and-miss attempts by Nevada's earliest prospectors to strike it rich. Free samples are sometimes handed out, but not on the day you'll be visiting.

California Trail Interpretive Center

Part museum, part virtual reality, the **California Trail Interpretive Center** (1 Trail Center Way, 775/738-1849, www.californiatrailcenter.org, 9am-4:30pm Wed.-Sun., free), eight miles west of Elko on I-80, makes westward expansion and the hardships of the trail interesting even for kids. Interactive displays focus on Native Americans; packing for the five-month wagon trip; forts, way stations, and natural landmarks along the journey; and more.

City Tour

Mature trees invite picnickers and frolickers to 21-acre **Elko City Park** (1435 Idaho St.), between Sherman Station and the Northeastern Nevada Museum. Before it was a park, in the 1870s, this area was known as China Ranch for the big vegetable patches the Asian railroad workers planted here. The gardens fed residents and miners for miles around. Nine blocks south, you'll come to the 1910 neoclassical **Elko County Courthouse** (571 Idaho St.), which incorporates a dome and a two-story portico with pediments and cornices. It was here, outside that original brick courthouse, where Nevada executed its only woman. Elizabeth Potts and her husband, Josiah, were hanged in 1890 for the murder and dismemberment of neighboring rancher Miles Faucett. Interestingly, the judge who presided over the Pottses' trial was unconvinced of Josiah's culpability and pleaded with the board of pardons to commute their sentences. Take Court Street (one block north of Idaho) back downtown to view some **historical houses;** the oldest is on Court Street near 4th, refurbished and now inhabited by Chilton Engineering. The shop next door on the corner was the **first schoolhouse** in Elko, built in 1869.

RECREATION

Rodeos, equestrian events, and other Western activities have a home at the **Horse Palace** (670 Bronco Dr., 775/753-6510 or 775/753-6295, www.springcreeknv.org, 10am-dusk summer, 8am-dusk winter, $7-18) in Spring Creek, at the foot of the Ruby Mountains. It has a 1,500-seat indoor arena surrounding a 150- by 300-foot show floor. There are warm-up rings, dressage rings, hunt rings, miles of trails for riding, and boarding facilities.

With a north-facing slope, a base elevation of 6,200 feet, and a maximum elevation of 6,900 feet, **SnoBowl Ski & Bike Park** (1992 Snobowl Rd., 775/777-7707, 9am-3pm Sat.-Sun. and holidays, $20) offers good skiing even when there's no snow in the valley. The ski hill is served by two rope tows and a chairlift. The tube and sled area is free. Warm winter weather and rudimentary snowmaking equipment have caused several unplanned closures in the past, but the volunteers who run the nonprofit slope, give lessons, and rent equipment do everything in their power to get you on the powder. Call first to make sure it's open.

Stock cars of various classes compete at the **Summit Raceway** (Errecart Blvd., call for directions, 775/778-6622, www.raceelko.com, 6:30pm Fri.-Sat. Apr.-Sept., adults $10, age 6-12 $5, under 6 free). Watch from the grandstand or set up camp chairs in the bed of your pickup truck.

An hour north of Elko on NV 225, 120-acre **Wild Horse Recreation Area** (775/385-5939, http://parks.nv.gov, $7) offers abundant **fishing** year-round. Ice fishers have easy access via flat terrain to find abundant brown trout and yellow perch. Those species, as well as wiper, catfish, and smallmouth bass, are active in warmer months. Shore and boat fishing are allowed. Winter visitors find miles of **cross-country ski trails** with views of the reservoir and the mountains beyond. **Snowmobiling** is gaining in popularity in the area as well, with a variety of conditions. Summer is peak time for viewing wildlife and wildflowers. Hunting is not allowed in the recreation area, but other areas near the reservoir attract pronghorn, mulies, chukar, grouse, and waterfowl. The **campground** ($14) with showers and restrooms is open year-round. No other facilities are available.

Whatever your prey of choice—big game, duck, turkey, bass, trout—**Bill Gibson of Elko Guide Service** (775/744-2277, www.elkoguideservice.com) and his expert guides put you on the right track. They also organize summer horseback pack trips and cabin camping adventures. Other local licensed outfitters include **Mountain Man Outfitters** (775/625-1717, http://nevadaoutfitter.com), **Nevada High Desert Outfitters** (775/738-4082, www.nhdo.com), and **Secret Pass Outfitters** (775/304-1560, www.secretpassoutfitters.com).

CASINOS

The heart of downtown is the **Ramada Elko Hotel at Stockmen's Casino** (340 Commercial St., 775/738-5141, www.wyndhamhotels.com, http://stockmenscasinoelko.com, $55-85). Try your luck with 150 slot machines and a few blackjack, craps, roulette, and three-card poker machines over an expansive 8,000-square-foot casino floor. The showroom hosts a regular lineup of standard musical and comedy entertainment.

The coffee shop is friendly and attentive. Remodeled in 2016, the 133 rooms come with all the amenities, including microwave and mini fridge. Pets are welcome, and full breakfast is included. A heated pool, business center, and on-site restaurant complete the package.

Across the street from the Ramada, **The Commercial** (345 4th St., 775/738-3181, http://stockmenscasinoelko.com) ushered in the time-honored Nevada tradition of mixing big-time entertainment with high-class gaming when Ted Lewis and his band took the stage on April 26, 1941, for a free show. Even earlier, in 1937, the casino unveiled a small dance floor and band alcove in the bar, creating one of the first lounges in Nevada. Turning 150 in 2019, The Commercial is showing its age. Give the 140 or so slots a miss, but stop in to visit White King, the largest polar bear exhibited in Nevada (which isn't saying much) and probably the country (which is). This guy stands 10 feet, four inches, and weighs more than a ton.

Farther east, the **Red Lion Inn & Casino** (2065 Idaho St., 775/738-2111 or 800/545-0044, www.redlion.com/elko, $100-130) is a roomy 17,000-square-foot resort with a Vegas-style pit of eight table games (blackjack, three-card poker, craps, and roulette). The only poker room in town, a sports book, keno, and row after row of slots are packed in as well. The Show Lounge hosts live bands (8pm-midnight Tues.-Thurs., 9pm-1am Fri.-Sat.) and karaoke (Mon. night). The rooms boast bathrooms accented with imported granite vanities and ceramic tile floors. Microwaves and refrigerators come with upgraded accommodations. The pool (open spring through fall), fitness center, and gift shop round out the all-inclusiveness.

At the **Gold Country Inn & Casino** (2050 Idaho St., 775/738-8421 or 800/621-1332, www.goldcountryinnelko.com, $70-90), high-tech video slots coexist with venerable reel varieties. The rooms are decorated with Native American motifs. Big rooms include premium channels on flat-screen TVs, microwaves, and mini refrigerators. Some have kitchenettes; others welcome pets.

On the west side, near the airport, the **Gold Dust West** (1660 Mountain City Hwy., 775/777-7500, www.gdwcasino.com) has slots and a few table games, along with a café and lounge, but no hotel. It's more of the same at **Roadhouse Casino** (1165 E. Jennings Way, 775/777-9300, 11am-11pm), next to Winger's Roadhouse Grill. Players enjoy free drinks and big-screen TVs.

SHOPPING

Get into the Western spirit with authentic, handmade (and pricey!) leatherwear, saddles, silver spurs and buckles, lariats, and more at **J.M. Capriola** (500 Commercial St., 775/738-5816 or 888/738-5816, 9am-5pm Mon.-Sat.). Check out the artwork on the stairway and the craftspeople hard at work upstairs. Just as if it had been plucked from 1880, false-fronted **Anacabe's General Merchandise** (416 Idaho St., 775/738-3295, 10am-6pm Mon.-Fri., 9:30am-5:30pm Sat.) offers more mundane Western attire: workaday boots, moccasins, jeans, anoraks, hiking gear, and souvenirs.

FOOD

Not surprisingly, the main theme in this cow town is beef: Burgers, T-bones, prime rib, carne asada, and other bovine blessings are on the grill.

The **Star Hotel**'s Basque restaurant (246 Silver St., 775/738-9925 or 775/753-8696, www.elkostarhotel.com, 11am-2pm and 5pm-9:30pm Mon.-Fri., 4pm-9:30pm Sat., $25-45) opened in 1910 as a Basque boardinghouse. Since then, the Star has been owned by a succession of Basque innkeepers. Typically, the seating is family-style and the soup, salad, beans, veggies, fries, and bread are bottomless. Entrées include trout, pork, lamb, steaks, and even rock lobster.

The name **Toki-Ona** (1550 Idaho St., 775/778-3606, http://eattokiona.com, 6am-9:30pm daily, $15-30) is translated as "come to this place," and who are we to argue? The Basque dinner options include seafood dishes

just as good as the beef and lamb. All come with soup, salad, green beans, spaghetti, rice, and choice of fries or baked potato. Breakfast and lunch, including non-Basque sandwiches, are also served.

The mole-topped enchiladas are the highlight at **Dos Amigos** (1770 Mountain City Hwy., 775/753-4935, www.dosamigosrestaurante.com, Sun.-Thurs. 11am-9:30pm, Fri.-Sat. 11am-10pm, $15-20). Locals recommend the extravagant brunch buffet (11am-3pm, $14, children $7). At **La Fiesta** (780 Commercial St., 775/738-1622, $10-15), the chiles rellenos combination and a margarita will have you set for the evening. Although it's fast food, the quality ingredients and careful preparation at **9 Beans and a Burrito** (2525 Argent Ave., 775/738-7898, 7:30am-9:30pm Mon.-Sat., 7:30am-8:30pm Sun., $10-15), in the Raley's plaza, make it a worthy stop; big burritos are the specialties, but we're partial to the hard-shell tacos.

★ **Chef Cheng's Chinese Restaurant** (1309 Idaho St., 775/753-5788, 11am-9pm daily, $15-20) is consistently ranked among the best in the country. Cheng has quite a knack for seafood. His walnut prawns are the equal of anything in San Francisco, and we can't get enough of his crab Rangoon and seafood hot pot. If you're more turf than surf, opt for the salt-and-pepper pork.

Ravioli like mama used to make awaits you at **Luciano's** (351 Silver St., 775/777-1808, www.lucianosnv.com, 11am-2pm and 5pm-9pm Mon.-Fri., 5pm-9pm Sat., $20-30)—if your mama is a Paris-trained culinary expert in Italian-fusion cuisine, that is. If not, let chef Luc Gerber show you what you missed. White linen, dark wood, and local art create a cozy setting. The casual **Tomato's Italian Grill** (245 3rd St., 775/753-9100, www.elkotomatos.com, 11am-9:30pm Mon.-Thurs., 11am-10:30 Fri.-Sat., $15-25) dishes out huge slabs of lasagna and other favorites. Bread and olive oil for dipping, terrific sides like stuffed mushrooms, and a decent wine selection make for full bellies.

While the bar side of **Matties Sports Bar**

& Grill (2535 Mountain City Hwy., 775/753-3877, www.mattiesbar-n-grill.com, 11am-8pm Sun.-Thurs., 11am-9pm Fri.-Sat., $10-20) goes in for biker rallies and body paint contests, the restaurant side is family-friendly. Burgers, fries, and a game room will tempt the tykes, while a full slate of sandwiches, steaks, and healthier choices satisfies diners of all ages. Similarly named **Machi's Saloon & Grill** (450 Commercial St., 775/738-9772, www.machissaloon.com, 11am-2pm and 5pm-9pm Mon.-Fri., $15-30) boasts an extensive menu of seafood and Italian specials.

Expect a hearty breakfast—biscuits and gravy, hotcakes, eggs, bacon, and sausage— at the **Coffee Mug** (576 Commercial St., 775/738-5999, http://coffeemugelko.com, 6am-9pm daily, $10-15), a local favorite for more than 25 years. The waitstaff is friendly and the kitchen is lightning fast. Lunch and dinner combine comfort food with surprises like grilled halibut and bacon-wrapped prawns. The breakfast menu at **McAdoo's** (382 5th St., 775/777-2299, www.mcadooselko.com, 7am-3pm daily, $10-15) is adventurous: meat-and-egg sandwiches flavored with aioli, vinaigrette, or parmesan. Lunch offerings are more extensive, with soups, sandwiches, and quiche of the day. Fruit-infused "ades" (prickly pear limeade!) and teas top it all off.

There is a bar at **JR's Bar & Grill** (Gold Country Inn, 2050 Idaho St., 775/778-0515, www.goldcountryinnelko.com, 24 hours daily, $10-20), and some of the food is grilled, but it's really more of a family restaurant where you can always find dependable belly fillers. The Red Lion Inn & Casino (2065 Idaho St., www.redlion.com/elko) offers the 24-hour **Coffee Garden Restaurant & Buffet** (775/738-2111, $10-20) and **Aspens** (775/753-0562, 4pm-9pm Sun.-Mon., 4pm-10pm Tues.-Sat., $20-40), a first-class dining room.

ACCOMMODATIONS

Elko can be a tough place to get a room, especially in the summer and on weekends year-round, but if you call even a day or

two in advance, you'll probably be able to come up with an adequate place to stay in your price range. Idaho Street is motel/inn/motor lodge central.

High Desert Inn (3015 E. Idaho St., 775/738-8425, www.highdesertinnelko.com, $50-75) is within easy walking distance to the Red Lion and Gold Country Inn casinos. The big, warm, indoor pool is open year-round but closed on Sundays. The fitness center is well maintained and contains both cardio and weight machines. The **Thunderbird** (345 Idaho St., 775/738-7115, $70-85) hooked us with its iconic art deco sign and keeps us coming back with clean rooms, a cool pool, and western-sage decor. The rooms at the **Esquire** (505 Idaho St., 775/738-3157, www.motelinelkonv.com, $60-70) are more pedestrian, with less subdued color schemes.

Despite a location in the middle of a fast food jungle, the smoke-free **Shilo Inn Suites** (2401 Mountain City Hwy., 775/738-5522 or 800/222-2244, www.shiloinns.com, $80-120) is perfect for business travelers, with a fitness facility, pool, and the usual in-room necessities. **Oak Tree Inn** (95 Spruce Rd., 775/777-2222, www.oaktreeinn.com, $65-105), on the other side of Mountain City Highway, is a little cheaper and almost as convenient, with an airport shuttle, free breakfast, blackout curtains, and noise-reducing materials for restful nights.

You know what you're going to get at chain options: **Hilton Garden Inn** (3650 E. Idaho St., 775/777-1212 or 855/618-4697, $110-150), **Quality Inn** (3320 E. Idaho St., 775/777-8000, $70-100), **Motel 6** (3021 E. Idaho St., 775/332-0879, $40-55), **Holiday Inn Express** (775/777-0990 or 844/291-6679, $95-120), **Best Western Elko Inn** (1930 Idaho St., 775/738-8787, $100-130), **Travelodge** (1785 Idaho St., 775/753-7747, $60-80), **Super 8** (1755 Idaho St., 775/738-8488, $50-60), and **Days Inn** (1500 Idaho St., 775/738-7245, $50-60). Just west of town and north of Idaho Street and I-80, **Ledgestone** (2585 E. Jennings Way, 775/738-2200, http://ledgestonehotel.com/elko, $100-120) offers extended stay packages and bright, airy, contemporary rooms with full kitchens.

RV Parks

The grassy sites at **Iron Horse RV Resort** (3400 E. Idaho St., 775/777/1919 or 800/782-3556, www.ironhorservresort.com, $40-55) are a welcome change from the pavement often found in urban parks. Though the swimming pool is tiny, campers have access to the pool and other amenities at the Hilton Garden a stone's throw up the road (as well as discount meal coupons). **Double Dice RV Park** (3730 E. Idaho St., 775/738-5642, www.doubledicervpark.com, $35-40) is a full-scale urban RV park atop a hill in East Elko, with its own sports bar and lounge, complete with pool tables, big TVs, and sandwiches and burgers for sale. There are 140 gravel spaces for motor homes, all with full hook-ups, and 75 pull-throughs. Reservations are recommended in summer. Free continental breakfast is included in the rate. There's not much scenery at the concrete **Gold Country RV Park** (2050 Idaho St., 775/738-8421 or 800/621-1332, www.goldcountryinnelko.com, $25) at the east end of Elko, which has 26 spaces for motor homes, all with full hookups.

INFORMATION AND SERVICES

Next door to the Northeastern Nevada Museum, **Sherman Station** (1405 Idaho St., 775/738-7135), a group of five buildings all built of logs between 1880 and 1903, houses the Elko Chamber of Commerce and visitors center. The bookstore (9am-5:30pm Mon.-Fri., 9am-5pm Sat.) is worth a look, too.

TUSCARORA

Fifty miles from Elko (north via NV 225 North and NV 226 West), this tiny ranching community is the unlikely home and studio of some of the most accomplished pottery instructors in the country. **Tuscarora Pottery School** (775/756-5526, www.

tuscarorapottery.com) accepts novices and seasoned pros alike for intensive summer training sessions using locally sourced clay. Call to schedule a tour to see state-of-the-art throwing equipment and handmade kilns. While you're here, drop in for a cold beer, dinner, or a night's RV stay at **Taylor Canyon Resort** (NV 226, 775/756-6500), a mecca for area hunters and anglers. A trout stream runs right through the property, and they will put your kills in cold storage until your adventure is over. A bar, camping supplies, and hot showers all come in handy.

JARBIDGE

Some of Nevada's best elk hunting and the only place in the state to land a bull trout draw outdoors types to the Silver State's remote northeast corner. Jarbidge is home to a score of hardy souls and is surrounded by 113,000 acres of the **Jarbidge Wilderness,** amid raging rivers, towering peaks, and wildflower-festooned forests. Roughly 100 miles (a bit more than three hours) north of Elko via NV 225, the community is a mere 10 miles from the Idaho line. The townsfolk maintain a gas pump, saloon, hotel, general store, and post office. Stock up on supplies and pick the likeliest looking dirt road (there's not a mile of blacktop within 15 miles). You're sure to find the perfect trout stream, mule deer herd, bike track, or hiking route.

History buffs will want to stroll around town. Don't miss the old jail, built in 1911, with the preserved cell once occupied by Ben Kuhl, the "mastermind" behind the country's last stage robbery. Prosecutors won conviction in part because of a bloody palm print Kuhl left on a piece of mail during the holdup and stage driver's murder. It was the first instance in the United States in which fingerprint evidence was admitted in court. Other preserved buildings in town include prostitutes' cribs, miners' cabins, and the community center, circa 1910, which serves as an impromptu museum.

The Ruby Mountains

TOP EXPERIENCE

Punctuated by frost-fringed alpine lakes and 10,000-foot peaks (Ruby Dome actually measures 11,387 feet), the Ruby Mountains may be Nevada's most stunning backdrop. Visitors are awestruck simply driving along this inspiring scenic byway. A short walk from the roadway leads to easy walking trails to surprising natural wonders—a riotous patch of wildflowers here, a waterfall of spring runoff there, a majestic bighorn lording over the canyon from a rocky precipice above.

The Rubies—named for the garnets prospectors mistook for more precious stones—really cast their magic spell on adventurers who blaze their own trail. These mountains are home or migratory stop for some 200 species of birds, huge herds of mule deer and other large game, feisty brook trout, and more recreational opportunities than you could enjoy in a lifetime. Hike, hunt, fish, bike, and ride through these "Alps of Nevada" during the summer. Routine winter snowfalls of 10 feet set the stage for backcountry skiing on pristine powder so remote it can only be reached by helicopter.

★ RUBY MOUNTAIN HELI-SKIING

With access to open bowls, chutes, couloirs, tree runs, steeps, and other terrain, the guides at **Ruby Mountain Heli-Experience** (775/753-6867 or 775/397-1215, www.helicopterskiing.com, late Jan.-mid-Apr., $1,450-1,716 pp per day) have been creating tailor-made backcountry ski and snowboard trips since 1977.

The company's 10,000-square-foot **Ruby 360 Lodge** is perched at 7,000 feet up with commanding views of the surrounding mountains and Great Basin. The lodge has room for 20 guests, who enjoy a full bar, massage services, and great grub. Jump in the copter right outside the door. The popular three-day option includes an 18-run guarantee, guide service, ski rental, meals, and lodging. Single-day trips, available only on Thursday, include six runs, guide service, breakfast, and lunch. The company will fly non-skiers into (and out of)

entrance to Lamoille Canyon in the Ruby Mountains

the most remote parts of the range. Guided hikes cost $1,600 for up to four people.

For a top-of-the-world getaway, Ruby Mountain Heli-Experience can put you up in **Ruby High Yurt** ($250 up to four guests, $50 each additional guest, two-night minimum) at 9,700 feet. A traditional round tent favored by the nomads of the Central Asian steppes, the yurt is fully furnished and includes solar-powered lights and outlets. Heated by a propane fireplace, guests at the yurt can cook using the supplied two-burner propane stove and cookware. Up to six additional guests can bunk down in two insulated weather ports adjacent to the yurt.

Spring, summer, and fall guests can hike along Conrad and Talbot Creeks, which flow nearby. In winter, tour skiing will take guests throughout the area. The company provides many additional fee-based services for yurt guests, including helicopter access to avoid the two-hour uphill hike to the yurt location, mule-team packing, guides, and even chef-prepared provisions.

LAMOILLE

This idyllic foothill village makes a compelling case as a base camp for Ruby Mountain adventures. The first homesteaders settled here in 1865 and the post office arrived in 1883, but it took another 50 years for an actual road to reach the valley. Established in 1905, the **Little Church of the Crossroads** might be the most heavenly located house of worship in the state—very close to God. Stop and gaze at the deer grazing on the grounds, then venture inside to see the stained glass and learn more about the church's history and architecture.

Hotel Lamoille (925 Lamoille Hwy., 775/753-6871, $50-70) is a bargain, with its three quaint suites. Sit on the back porch and sip a sweet tea or enjoy a picnic under cottonwoods along the creek bank across the street. Next door, the **Pine Lodge Dinner House** (915 Lamoille Rd., 775/753-6363, 4pm-9pm Mon.-Sat., 4pm-8pm Sun., $30-40) serves hearty steaks and ribs with a full

bar. Farther along Main Street, **O'Carroll's** (833 Lamoille Hwy., 775/753-6451, 11am-8pm Mon.-Fri., 9am-9pm Sat., 9am-8pm Sun., $10-15) serves breakfast and lunch; the onion rings are a must.

If you're traveling with a large party, you can rent the entire lodge at **Red's Ranch** (1337 Country Lane Rd., http://redsranch.com, $2,500): 10 themed one- and two-bedroom suites with private baths and antique furnishings. Common areas include a great room with a large stone fireplace, a 12-seat dining room, and seasonal swimming pool. Belly up to the bar for nightly libations and the cheese board. Call to inquire about individual room rentals.

LAMOILLE CANYON SCENIC BYWAY

This byway, also known as National Forest Road 660, takes visitors deep into picturesque Lamoille Canyon, a microcosm of the entire

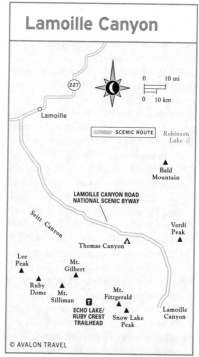

Lamoille Canyon

© AVALON TRAVEL

Ruby Mountain range. It's an accessible introduction, with wonderful trails, lake and ridge views, and diverse animal and plant life. Called the Yosemite of Nevada, the deep canyon features high peaks dusted with snow year-round and crystal-clear waterfalls created by spring runoff.

Access the scenic byway by taking NV 227 (Lamoille Hwy.) south from Elko for 19 miles. Turn right onto the byway a mile outside the hamlet of Lamoille. Look for the sign. In less than three miles, you will pass the **Powerhouse Picnic Area** (day use, $5), site of family reunions and weddings, and **Camp Lamoille,** a group camp site available for rent from the local Lions Club. Drive through the camp to the cattle guard. At the back of the camp is the trailhead to **Echo Lake,** the largest and deepest in the Rubies (155 feet). The trail is quite difficult, disappearing completely for long stretches on its 3,500-foot rise to a gasp-inducing 10,400 feet. Still, a reasonably fit and motivated hiker can cover the 11.3-mile round-trip in a day. An overnight trip with the fly rod and float tube is worth the effort—the trout angling is among the best and most scenic in Nevada.

The byway crosses and parallels Lamoille Creek for three miles to **Glacier Overlook,** a view of the gash glaciers carved into the mountains, complete with signs describing glacial formations and movements. Two miles farther, **Thomas Canyon Campground** (early May-late Sept., 877/444-6777, $17), with tall aspens and cottonwoods and a gurgling creek full of rainbow and brook trout, makes for ideal conditions for both tents and trailers and a good base for hikers at 7,600 feet. The easy, four-mile **Thomas Canyon Trail** leaves from here, taking hikers past waterfalls, wildflowers, and beaver ponds. Bighorns and mule deer are common, but the trail is heavily used. Wildlife sightings are more probable along more remote trails.

At 8,000 feet, **Terraces Campground** (mid-June-mid-Sept., 775/752-3357, $17), surrounded by aspen and wildflowers, is often reserved for group events like weddings and church camps. When not reserved, the nine tent-only sites are available first-come, first-served. Here you will find the trailhead for the leisurely one-mile round-trip **Nature Trail** through aspen shade and along the rock-strewn creek bed.

For a more challenging hike, head up **Verdi Peak.** It's only two miles round-trip, but you'll gain 1,700 feet in elevation, reaching an exhilarating 10,800 feet. There is no trail. Follow the access road until you find an opening. Cut over as soon as you see a drainage, and follow it as far as possible. From here, turn around, catch your breath, and admire the view of Lamoille Canyon. Then, look up and find a saddle ridge. That's your destination. Pick your way parallel to the saddle, then head up. As you crest the ridge, ice-covered, cobalt-blue **Lake Verdi** comes into view. Hike down (steep, but not difficult) for a closer look, or admire the lake from afar before retracing your steps to the campground. Adrenaline junkies may want to continue on to **Robinson Lake,** seven miles ahead, or **Soldier Lake** and the photo-worthy **Hidden Lakes** beyond. Beware, though: The three-mile section between Verdi Lake and Thorpe Creek is not for softies.

Two miles past Terraces Campground, the byway loops back on itself.

RUBY CREST TRAIL

The parking lot at the end of the Lamoille Canyon Scenic Byway is a perfect jumping-off point for more terrific hikes, focusing on the lakes and prominent peaks at this end of the 37-mile **Ruby Crest National Scenic Trail.** The hiking season starts mid-June and lasts roughly 12 weeks. Weekdays you'll meet a few more people, but weekends you're fending off crowds, especially on the first few miles. Backpackers, however, can leave the crowds far behind on any number of explorations to high-country lakes (many filled with trout) and isolated canyons. The following passages describe hiking the Ruby Crest Trail from south to north.

From road's end, it's an easy-to-moderate

two-mile hike along the creek to **Lamoille Lake,** crossing three creeks (bridges supplied by the U.S. Forest Service) and passing **Dollar Lakes** along the way. The track reserved for hikers is steep at the beginning but shadier and more scenic than the horse trail. Bring your rod, as the trout bite is outstanding here.

Continuing south, you can make out the head, beak, and wings of **Bald Eagle Crest,** with late summer snow defining the feathery wingtips. After another mile, when you reach **Liberty Pass,** at 10,450 feet, you're rewarded with a view of the other side of the mountain, which is even more beautiful than the side you just climbed up. From here, lakes line up like sapphires on a necklace: After **Lamoille Lake,** it's a mile to **Liberty Lake** and another mile to **Favre Lake.** Less than a mile farther looms **Castle Lake,** and **North Furlong Lake** is a mile and a half beyond Castle, for those with the stamina and drive to continue. **Wines Peak,** the highest point on the trail at nearly 11,000 feet, looms another mile to the southeast (a full six miles from Lamoille Lake).

The nine miles between Wines Peak and **Overland Lake** are some of the most secluded on the trail, as only those hiking the whole 37 miles of the Ruby Crest Trail should venture this far in. It's also the most rugged leg of the journey. Water is scarce, so it is best to start early and push on until you reach the lake. The rest of the trail leads through aspen stands, creeks, and wildflower meadows. It's beautiful, but not as majestic as the first half, showing why many prefer to hike the trail from south to north (starting at the other end, at **Harrison Pass,** the full trail takes several days, but saves the best scenery in this area for last).

The road's end also marks the beginning of the four-mile round-trip trail to **Island Lake.** The well-maintained trail meanders through hillsides covered with phlox, larkspur, and other wildflowers and across a wooden bridge. You will gain significant elevation, but 10 switchbacks make for an easy climb.

RUBY DOME

The tallest peak in the Rubies at a nosebleed-inducing 11,387 feet, **Ruby Dome** challenges hikers with a 4,800-foot elevation gain over the six miles from trailhead to summit. The 12-mile round-trip takes about 10 hours. If you're hiking in summer, get an early start to beat the heat.

The **Spring Creek trailhead** is on private property, so hikers must visit the Spring Creek Association headquarters (451 Spring Creek Pkwy, Spring Creek, 8am-noon and 1pm-5pm Mon.-Fri., 775/753-6295) to pay the $10 per person day-use fee and a $25 deposit for a gate key. To reach the campground and trailhead, turn south from NV 227 onto Pleasant Valley Road, about three miles west of the town of Lamoille. Continue for three miles to the end of the road.

From the end of the road, hike southeast through aspen-shrouded **Hennen Canyon.** If you lose the trail (which is easy to do, especially early in the season before it gets well-trodden), follow **Bufferfield Creek.** You will notice a change in ecosystem and terrain as you near **Griswold Lake,** approximately halfway to the summit. You can press onward or camp here to prepare for the arduous second half of the hike. Walk to the back side of the lake and continue on the trail. Cresting the next ridge will put you face to face with Ruby Dome, its summit a tantalizingly close 1,200 feet up.

If you can stomach the sheer rock faces falling off below you, a ridge to the left of the trail is a pretty direct route to the top. Otherwise, negotiate the snow-filled (at least until early summer) chute to the right. Emerging from the chute or the ridge, you will see two cairns bookending the summit. Enjoy the view, pat yourself on the back, and sign the book to commemorate your accomplishment.

SPRING CREEK MARINA

The Spring Creek Association also runs the 32-acre **Spring Creek Reservoir** (sunrise-dark, 775/753-6295) and the parkland surrounding it. Take Lamoille Highway

(NV 227) southeast out of Elko for 10 miles to the roundabout at Spring Creek Parkway. Go east for three miles to the marina. Shore, pier, and nonmotorized boat fishing is good for planted trout and bass. Nevada fishing regulations apply for nonresidents: limit three per person or seven per family. Swimming is allowed when weather permits; there is no lifeguard, so exercise caution. Ditto when skating or ice fishing in winter. The park includes covered picnic tables, barbecues, a playground, a baseball diamond, and heated restrooms.

SOUTH FORK RESERVOIR

The **South Fork Reservoir** is surrounded by 2,200 acres of wildlife-filled meadowlands and rolling hills. Swimming, boating, fishing, hunting, wildlife viewing, camping, and picnicking are popular activities. It's 16 miles south of Elko on NV 228 (roughly 10 miles south of the intersection with NV 227). The South Fork Dam, constructed between 1986 and 1988, is made up of a million cubic yards of earth, which dammed South Fork Creek roughly 10 miles from the Humboldt River. The reservoir, when full, stretches 3.5 miles, covers 1,650 surface acres, and impounds 40,000 acre feet of water.

The Nevada Department of Wildlife stocks trout and bass; the park is known for its trophy-class trout and bass fishery. The 25-site **campground** (early May-mid.-Oct., 775/744-4346, $14, maximum 14 days), with showers and running water but no hookups, is on the reservoir shore, about two miles from the dam. Open camping is also available along the southwest shore ($5); you can come to the campground to shower. The smaller of two boat ramps is on this side of the reservoir. It can accommodate boats up to 15 feet. Float tube enthusiasts are encouraged to use this area. The main boat launch has ample parking and a non-flush restroom. The park is open year-round, but winter access may be difficult. Call 775/744-4346 if there are any doubts.

A mile from the South Fork Reservoir, the **Ruby Crest Guest Ranch** (197 Western Hills #13, Spring Creek, 775/744-2277, $150-300) is also the home of the **Elko Guide Service** (www.elkoguideservice.com), which offers a wide variety of activities, including nature tours, horseback trail riding, summer horseback pack trips, fishing, and hunting (the rifle, muzzleloader, and bow-hunting trips for big game are quite popular). Winter activities include cross-country skiing, snowmobile trips, ice fishing, and chukar hunting. Ranch vacations are a specialty, with accommodations ranging from a room at the ranch to rustic log cabins at the base of the Ruby Mountains to tent camps. Guided trips usually include lodging, meals, and most equipment.

RUBY LAKE NATIONAL WILDLIFE REFUGE

Just over 60 miles south of Elko on NV 228 is an unusual sight for the Great Basin Desert: a freshwater bulrush marsh, host to a large variety of wildlife. The **Ruby Lake National Wildlife Refuge,** a.k.a. Ruby Marshes, is open every day from an hour before sunrise until two hours after sunset. Within the 38,000-acre refuge, created in 1938, is a network of ditches and dikes built to manage the riparian habitat. More than 220 species of birds, including trumpeter swans, canvasback and redhead ducks, cranes, herons, egrets, eagles, and falcons, are found in the refuge in a normal year, along with five types of introduced trout and bass. In summer, rattlesnakes and garter snakes take in the sun, stretching out along the roadsides (and sometimes right in the traffic lanes). You might see one feeding on a leopard frog, the refuge's only amphibian. The wheelchair-accessible viewing platform at **Narciss Boat Landing** provides an elevated perch, and photo blinds scattered throughout overlook popular birding spots. For a general overview of the refuge, drive over the dikes in a loop punctuated by 13 interpretive displays describing the flora, fauna, and natural environment playing out before you.

Hunting with non-toxic shot is permitted for most waterfowl, including ducks, dark geese, coots, snipe, and common moorhens.

All other species of wildlife are protected. Fishing is allowed year-round except where posted. Largemouth bass can be caught primarily in the **South Marsh** and the marsh units north of **Brown Dike,** with summer fishing your best bet. Rainbow trout, and to a lesser extent brown and tiger trout, are mostly found in the **Collection Ditch** and the spring ponds along the southwest side of the refuge. Angling for trout peaks in the spring and fall. Be aware of special regulations, as boating and bag limit rules vary by location and date. Use of baitfish—live or dead—crayfish, and amphibians is prohibited.

Camping is not allowed inside the refuge, but if you head south on County Road 767, you'll reach the **South Ruby Campground** (877/444-6777, $15) at 6,200 feet. It has 33 gravel sites shaded by juniper and piñon, water, toilets, and an RV waste dump. Sites at lower elevations are open all year. Winter camping offers fewer amenities but a lower fee. Most sites have tent pads. The host sells firewood and has a handy trolling motor charging station. Near the **Gallagher Fish Hatchery,** sites are on a rise overlooking the marsh. Primitive camping is allowed on Forest Service land 300 feet west of County Road 767 and on BLM land east of the refuge.

Wells

The same waterways and wildlife habitat that made this area a bountiful hunting ground for the Western Shoshone and a welcome respite for the westward pioneers continue to lure travelers seeking small-town hospitality and outdoor exploration. Wells's most intriguing attractions are the surrounding hills, valleys, forests, and mountains. Its man-made sights exist to interpret its history and natural environment.

Located at the intersection of I-80 and US 93 and an easy drive from Elko, Boise, Twin Falls, and Salt Lake City, Wells is also a crossroads town with a wide range of accommodations and amenities. It's a good place to wait for the sun to go down if you're heading west. The interstate aims directly toward the fiery orb in late afternoon, making driving a challenge—all blinding light and dark shadow.

SIGHTS AND RECREATION

Artifacts, documentation, and dioramas inside the **Trail of the 49ers Interpretive Center** (436 6th St., 775/752-3540, 9am-5pm daily, donation) tell the story of this important section of the California and Oregon Trails. Displays include a covered wagon, arrowheads, and Native American clothing. The center also houses the Wells Chamber of Commerce, which distributes an informational brochure and directions to **Metropolis ghost town,** via 8th Street and Metropolis Road. Built as a planned community of 7,500 in 1910, Metropolis is not a victim of depleted gold and silver deposits, but rather a lack of water. Today, the school's grand entrance arch, concrete hotel ruins, and a poorly marked cemetery are all that remain.

Well-groomed and challenging, nine-hole **Chimney Rock Golf Course** (408 Vetosa St., 775/752-3928, Apr.-Oct., $15) is only 3,064 yards, making accuracy and iron play king. The course has a pro shop, carts, range, putting green, bar, and teaching pro.

FOOD

Bella's Restaurant & Espresso (143 US 93, 775/752-2226, www.bellasrestaurant.us, 5am-9pm daily, $15-25) is famous for miles around for its chicken-fried steak breakfast; the corned beef hash and smoothies also get top marks. After the filling breakfast, you can skip lunch and come back for the fish-and-chips dinner. Visitors amazed to find touches of civilization in rural Nevada appreciate the gourmet coffee and pick up cinnamon rolls and espresso for the road. They often have a different reaction when they discover the owner also runs Bella's Hacienda Ranch, a legal brothel. Parents can be assured that the businesses are nowhere near each other.

Located right at the junction at the TA Petro truck stop, the **4 Way Casino** complex (1440 6th St., 775/752-2000, 24 hours daily) includes an Iron Skillet restaurant, a Dunkin' Donuts, and more than 100 slots in all denominations up to $1. At **Luther's Bar & Grill** (479 6th St.), you can try your luck at bar-top video poker while noshing pizza, wings, Mexican dinners, and finger foods. Friday is karaoke night. You also can't go wrong at **ChinaTown** (755 Humboldt Ave., 775/752-2888, www.wellschinatown.com, $12-25). The softball-size egg rolls are a must. The homemade lo mein, sweet and sour, and curry are hot, tasty, and plentiful.

ACCOMMODATIONS

The best part about the motel rooms in Wells is the price. There are few in-room frills outside mini fridges and microwaves, but the places listed here offer clean sheets and towels, comfortable beds, and quiet nights.

Two of the best options bookend the town. On the west side, **ChinaTown Motel** (755 Humboldt Ave., 775/752-2888, www.wellschinatown.com, $55-65) offers studio and one- and two-bedroom suites with a kitchen featuring an oven and stovetop. The RV park ($15-20) is just a hard-pack lot, but it has electric, water, cable, and Wi-Fi. On the east side, the hospitable staff at **Rest Inn Suites** (1509 6th St., 775/752-2277, www.restinnsuitesmotel.net, $60-70) are a fount of local knowledge. Each suite includes a 50-inch flat-screen TV, perfect for unwinding after a hard day at play.

Several locally owned motels dot 6th Street. You can't go wrong with **Sharon** (635 6th St., 775/752-3232, $50-60), where Paul Mayes carries on the friendly, funny, customer-comes-first service established by his father, Fred.

The red art deco sign of **Lone Star** (676 6th St., 775/752-3633, $50-60) was featured in the 2001 film *Joy Ride*.

Camping and RV Parks

Not to be confused with Angel Lake Campground, **Angel Lake RV Park** (124 S. Humboldt St., 775/752-2745, www.angellakerv.com, $32-35) just south of I-80 has pull-throughs long enough for any size rig plus Internet and TV rooms to supplement full hookups and Wi-Fi. Tent sites are available. Well north of the interstate, **Mountain Shadows** (807 Humboldt Ave., 775/752-3525, $25-30) is older, smaller, and a bit more cramped, but the hookups and Internet service work. It's quiet at night, but weekday mornings are a different story, as the permanent residents leave for work. Big patches of grass and mature shade trees highlight a stay at **Welcome Station RV Camp** (I-80, exit 343, 775/752-2736, $18-25). Mountain views, a stream, and a pond complete the idyllic setting. The 21 sites are suitable for trailers and rigs up to 35 feet.

INFORMATION AND SERVICES

The **Wells Chamber of Commerce** (436 6th St., 775/752-3540, www.wellsnevada.com) has extensive though sometimes outdated information. You can also stop in at **City Hall** (525 6th St., 775/752-3355) to read the bulletin boards and rifle the info rack. The **library** (208 Baker St., 775/752-3856, 11am-5pm Mon.-Wed. and Fri., 11am-7pm Thurs.) has Internet service for public use.

12-MILE HOT SPRINGS

12-Mile Hot Springs (also known as Bishop Creek Hot Springs) is not easy to find, but that's the beauty of it. Once you arrive, you can count on peace and solitude. From Wells, take Metropolis Road northbound eight miles through fragrant farm country. Turn left at the not-so-helpfully named County Road for a bumpy six miles to the parking area. Don't risk tire or suspension damage; if the going gets rough, pull off the road, park, and hoof it to the parking lot. From there, it's less than a half mile to the springs. The trail passes through narrow canyons and past an old iron bridge, making for an interesting hike, especially in the snow. Your destination is a 40-foot concrete pool, which collects water oozing from the canyon wall. Temperatures in the three-foot-deep, gravel-bottomed pool range from a tepid 99° F opposite the source to a barely bearable 105° F.

ANGEL LAKE SCENIC BYWAY

Angel Lake is a Bob Ross painting come to life. On calm winter days, it throws a perfect mirror image of the snowcaps towering above, disturbed only by canoers and anglers looking for rainbows, tigers, and brookies. The 13-mile **Angel Lake Scenic Byway** from Wells makes a lovely drive, especially in spring when the fields are full of wildflowers. The road is well paved, but it's narrow enough to create a few white-knuckle moments. It can be treacherous or closed in winter. Piñon pine, mountain mahogany, and aspen dot the lower elevations, while the surrounding mountain scarps and pinnacles pierce the sky before parting to reveal the lake after a 3,000-foot climb.

On the way to the lake, set up camp at one of the 19 sites at 6,800-foot **Angel Creek** (775/752-3357, May-Sept., weather permitting, $15), with trailheads into the aspen-strewn Humboldt Wilderness two miles to the west on Forest Road 500. Campers in large mobile homes will have to stop here. The final four miles of the loop are too steep for big rigs. Smaller RVs can continue to the top of the road to **Angel Lake Recreation Area** (775/752-3357, July-Sept., $27), a 26-site campground and picnic site at 8,500 feet. Aspens separate campsites, but they are too short to offer much shade. You can pick up the **Smith Lake trailhead** here and hike into the northern section of the East Humboldt Wilderness. Pack your gear, as the largemouth and striped bass may be biting. The eight-mile **Winchell Lake** trail picks up just southeast of the campground. Its alpine waters are just as beautiful as Angel Lake's, but much less crowded on summer weekends. There's a good chance you'll catch a glimpse of pronghorns, mule deer, bighorns, or mountain goats. Both campgrounds have potable water and restrooms. Keep an eye out for **Chimney Rock** on the eastern horizon. There's no stopping

Angel Lake

along the byway; either pull into the last campground or turn around immediately at the summit and head back down.

HOLE IN THE MOUNTAIN

Along the remarkable eastern scarp of the Humboldts, 6.4 miles south of Wells on US 93, a distinct right turn onto NV 232 leads into Clover Valley and past **Ruby Mountain Brewing Company** (free tours by appointment, 775/752-2337). Continue nine miles to a four-wheel-drive track on the right. Follow this rugged "road" three miles into Lizzie's Basin, just below the East Humboldts' highest mountain (11,276 feet). The phenomenon from which the peak derives its name accounts for one of the strangest and most compelling summits in the west: a large (30- by 25-foot) natural window in the thin marble of the mountaintop. This cyclopean eye, staring east and west, was known as Taindandoi (Hole in the Top) to the Shoshone and as Lizzie's Window to the early settlers, named after the first local to mention the aperture.

Wendover

Passing through the Pequop and Toano Mountains on I-80, you'll sight the Pilot Range and its most prominent, eponymous peak. Pilot Peak served as a beacon to pioneers along the Emigrant Trail, who focused on it during their brutal ordeal crossing the blazing Great Salt Lake Desert.

Next stop: Wendover, a booming border town, located on the state line between Nevada and Utah. Its backyard is a shimmering, carbon-arc-white expanse of earth, so white that even in the summer's scorching heat, the surface remains cool. The heat waves and blinding silver reflection do strange things to radio and TV signals. Fierce thunderstorms are caused by the rising heat, but then everything dries and brightens in a matter of minutes. Another oddity: The bases of telephone poles on the flats become permeated with salt water; when the water evaporates, the salt crystals expand, swelling and splitting the poles.

The cause? Wendover sits on the western side of what was once Lake Bonneville, which covered a large area of northwestern Utah to a depth of 1,000 feet. With no outlet, the lake shrank, leaving behind a smooth layer of salt and other minerals here at the lowest point of the Bonneville basin—where the salt flats are now—roughly 16,000 years ago. The eastern stretch of this massive prehistoric lake survives today as the Utah's Great Salt Lake.

Against such a surreal backdrop, the bright lights and big hotels of Wendover are as inviting to modern-day travelers as Pilot Peak, on the western horizon, ever was to the pioneers of the past. Note that it's more properly called West Wendover—the town of Wendover is across the state line in Utah. The white state line is painted across Wendover Boulevard between the Stateline and Silver Smith; Wendover Will points at it with two moving arms. The big hotels are on the Nevada side, and the low-rise services line the main street of the state next door in Utah. Wendover is on mountain time; move your watch ahead one hour.

BONNEVILLE SPEEDWAY

In 1914, Wendover lost its anonymity forever when speedsters discovered the ideal conditions of the salt flats. Teddy Tezlaff set the first land-speed record driving a Blitzen Benz just under 142 mph and put Wendover on the map, but it did not become popularized as the **Bonneville Speedway** until the 1930s. Speed freaks kept coming back with hotter and faster wheels. Craig Breedlove's famous *Spirit of America* set and reset records; he was the first to break the 600-mph mark.

Today, three weeks of official races are held

on the flats. The Southern California Timing Association (www.scta-bni.org) hosts **Speed Week** the third week in August, attracting 400-plus cars and motorcycles in various classes, including some land missiles that exceed 500 mph, and the **World Finals** in late September or early October. In between, the Utah Salt Flats Racing Association (www.saltflats.com) presents **World of Speed** in mid-September. All events are subject to cancellation if the salt is too wet or thin. Hardcore gearheads probably prefer Speed Week, while World of Speed hosts some novelty events in a party atmosphere. When you're finished getting your speed on, remember to wash your car's undercarriage to prevent the salt from eating it away.

To drive on the **salt flats,** take I-80 into Utah and get off at exit 4. Go north for a mile on Leppy Pass Road and take a right on Bonneville Speedway Road. When the road ends, the flats begin. Make sure the surface is dry, and stay away from the edge of the salt crust lest you break through and become stuck in the underlying mud. Access is limited during racing events and filming of the dozens of car commercials and end-of-days movies for which the salt flats are an impressive backdrop.

Where the salt flats end, the Silver Island Mountains begin. A 54-mile loop encircles the volcanic range that once formed the shoreline for ancient Lake Bonneville—you can see coral formations in the rock face. Several pull-outs and scenic vistas provide opportunities for viewing the mountains in contrast with the perfect pancake of the salt flats below.

CASINOS

As you might expect, the casinos are the big hotel players in town. The Peppermill family's three entries (Montego Bay, Peppermill, and Rainbow) are the best of the bunch and the biggest players in terms of both entertainment and accommodations.

Montego Bay

Restaurants: Romanza, Oceano Buffet, Paradise Grille, Coffee Corner
Attractions: Spa Montego, seasonal outdoor pool, fitness center, gift shop
Nightlife: Romanza Bar, Casino Bar

The casino, guest rooms, and café at **Montego Bay** (680 Wendover Blvd., 775/664-4800, www.wendoverfun.com, $100-175) are brightly lit and airy, the bedrooms in creams and golds. The gaming floor is packed with 27 tables—blackjack, craps, pai gow, roulette,

Bonneville salt flats

Northern Nevada Events

The towns of the Humboldt Valley celebrate every aspect of their culture and history, and there's plenty to celebrate. The region has been at the forefront of mining milestones, farming and ranching breakthroughs, military successes, and Western heritage.

JANUARY

Elko's **National Cowboy Poetry Gathering** (775/738-7508, www.nationalcowboypoetrygathering.org) is a weeklong celebration of the rural West through modern and traditional arts born of the land. Elko overflows with thousands of cowboys and cowgirls, poets and musicians, artisans and scholars, ranch hands and city dudes who value and practice the artistic traditions of the region and are concerned about the present and future of the West.

FEBRUARY

Smoke and steam billow from Nevada Northern Railway locomotives as 100-year-old passenger cars and boxcars rattle along the iron ribbon at Ely's **Winter Steam Photo Spectacular** (775/289-2085, www.nnry.com). Rail fans and shutterbugs can capture breathtaking images of trains backdropped by snow-covered peaks and rolling plains.

MARCH

Winnemucca's **Ranch Hand Rodeo** (775/623-5071, www.ranchrodeonv.com) has 30 teams from Nevada's vast ranches competing for bragging rights and prizes in saddle bronco riding, calf roping, wild mugging, team roping, ranch doctoring, and team branding.

One of the region's most prestigious photography events, Winnemucca's **Shooting the West** (775/623-3501, www.shootingthewest.org) brings some of the world's greatest photojournalists and nature photographers to lead hands-on workshops on professional technique, editorial submission, and more.

MAY

Run-A-Mucca (775/623-5071, www.runamucca.com) is Winnemucca's big motorcycle rally that tempts riders with big prizes. In addition to free live music, barbecue feasts, and vendors, bikers can win $1,000 in the burnout contest or poker run. And some lucky raffle-ticket holder goes home with a new ride.

JULY

Hot rods and cool cats roll into Wells for the **Fun Run Classic Car Show** (775/752-1153, www.

and Let It Ride, along with 500 slots and video poker machines. They deal hold 'em and stud in the cozy poker room. Sweat out the tension in the casino's fitness room, then soothe it away at **Spa Montego Bay** (10am-4:30pm daily), next to the outdoor pool (seasonal) and hot tubs (year-round).

Wendover Nugget

Restaurants: Nugget Steakhouse, Nugget Buffet, Golden Harvest Café, Starbucks, Trino's Tacos, Dreyer's Creamery

Attractions: gift shop, arcade, outdoor pool, atrium

Nightlife: Nugget Sports Bar, Martini Bar, Cigar Bar, Billiards Bar

The 47,500-square-foot **Wendover Nugget** (101 Wendover Blvd., 800/848-7300, www.wendoverresorts.com, $60-120) is attractive and classy. The table game pits deal blackjack, Royal Match, roulette, craps, three-card poker, and pai gow poker, automatically tracking your play, so comps accrue quickly. The sports book has 18 large TVs and three mammoth projecting screens. The 830 machines include all denominations, including plenty of penny slots. The rooms are a bit worn, but wellsfunrun.org), a chrome-filled party with street dances, "show & shine," a poker run, and more. Lovelock's **Frontier Days** (775/442-1336, www.lovelockfrontierdaysnv.com) feature old-fashioned fun including feats of strength (arm wrestling), speed (bicycle races), and daring (a scavenger hunt) along with clowns, cribbage, tractor pulls, parades, poetry, and music.

Since 1964 the Elko Euzkaldunak Club has organized the **National Basque Festival** (775/934-5552, www.elkobasqueclub.com), an annual celebration of Basque musical, historical, and artistic culture. The celebration typically includes folk dancing, Basque songs, art, and traditional games such as weightlifting, tug-of-war, and wood-chopping. Nevada's oldest rodeo, Elko's **Silver State Stampede** (775/934-2392, www.silverstatestampede.com) challenges the best working cowboys in Nevada and neighboring states with traditional rodeo events. Live musical entertainment follows each evening's go-around.

AUGUST

Multiple tracks and classes challenge the limits of man and machine at **Speed Week** on the Bonneville Salt Flats near Wendover. Speeds over 400 mph are possible on the ultra-smooth surface. A similar event, the **Bonneville World Finals** (559/528-6279, www.scta-bni.org) is held in October.

SEPTEMBER

In the Black Rock Desert, **Burning Man** (415/863-5263, www.burningman.org) sees tens of thousands of workaday slobs shed their inhibitions (and often most of their clothes) to live on the fringe for a week of self-expression, art appreciation, environmental stewardship, and rebellion against The Man, commercialism, consumerism, government oppression, and anything else that sticks in their craws.

OCTOBER

Fallon's **World Cowboy Fast Draw Championship** (775/575-1802, www.cowboyfastdraw. com) has modern-day Doc Hollidays face off against the stopwatch to earn the title of fastest gun in the world. Between the high noon showdowns, celebrities try their hand at wielding the six-shooter.

Fallon's Lattin Farms hosts a **Fall Festival** (775/867-3750, www.lattinfarms.com/fall-festival), complete with a corn maze, hay rides, pumpkin patch, kiddie rides, and a scarecrow-building station. Food trucks and an arts and crafts fair make for a full day.

clean, with blonde furnishings contrasting with darker maroon. **Trino's Tacos** (10am-late Wed.-Mon.) and **Dreyer's ice cream shop** (10am-late Wed.-Mon.) are just steps away from the sports book, so you'll hardly have to move while watching football all weekend—just like home! Four bars, all with different vibes; a seasonal pool; fine dining; and Wendover's only video game arcade complete the resort experience. DJs and local bands perform in the sports bar on weekends.

Peppermill

Restaurants: Pancho and Willie's, Café Milano, Café Espresso

Entertainment: Peppermill Concert Hall, Peppermill Cabaret

Nightlife: Pancho and Willie's Cantina, Poker Bar

The 36,000-square-foot casino inside the Italianate **Peppermill** (680 W. Wendover Blvd., www.wendoverfun.com, 775/664-2255, $100-130) has more than 900 machines. There's no poker room, but guests can bet and follow all the sports and racing action on big-screen sports book TVs. Spacious

356-square-foot rooms are decorated in rich chocolates and cool creams. Every seat at the **Peppermill Concert Hall** is within 100 feet of the stage, putting fans within high-five range of country, vintage rock, and soul acts, as well as A-list comedians.

Rainbow

Restaurants: Steak House, Primo, 2nd Street Deli, Coffee Bar, Bimini Buffet
Entertainment: Rainbow Cabaret
Attractions: year-round indoor pool
Nightlife: Bimini Bar, Primo Bar, Sports Book Bar

The gaming floor at the **Rainbow Casino** (1045 W. Wendover Blvd., 775/664-4000, www.wendoverfun.com, $100-130) is the biggest of the three Peppermill Group properties, with an eight-table poker room and nearly 1,000 machines. **Rainbow Cabaret** (7pm-2am Tues.-Sun.) serves up cold cocktails and hot rock and country bands playing cover tunes into the wee hours. Rooms in the west wing are almost identical in size and decor to Peppermill rooms. East wing rooms have the same color scheme but are smaller and about $10 cheaper.

Red Garter

Restaurants: Beans and Brews, Prospector Café, The Italia
Nightlife: Stage Bar, Sports Bar

At the intimate **Red Garter** (1225 Wendover Blvd., 775/664-2111 or 800/982-2111, www.wendoverresorts.com, $75-90), more than two-thirds of the 500 machines are of the penny, nickel, and quarter variety. You can usually find low-limit craps, blackjack, and roulette. The rooms are furnished with attractive mauve fabrics and mahogany-colored furniture.

FOOD

The casinos are the epicenter of dining in Wendover. All have a variety of options, including buffets and 24-hour cafés.

Fine Dining

If you call your restaurant simply the **Steak House** (Rainbow Casino, 1045 W. Wendover Blvd., 775/664-4000, www.wendoverfun.com, 5pm-9pm Sun. and Wed.-Thurs., 5pm-10pm Fri.-Sat., $30-55), the beef had better be amazing. Mission accomplished! Both the prime rib (medium rare, of course) and Black Angus sirloin are always cooked to perfection. Bread and salad are much more than afterthoughts. Enjoy the modern, yet classy atmosphere with white linen and leather.

The steak is always in play at **Romanza** (Montego Bay, 680 W. Wendover Blvd., 775/664-4800, www.wendoverfun.com, $25-40) as well, but Italian specialties rule. The chicken piccata with mushrooms and zucchini is a masterpiece of Tuscan simplicity. The decor is an amalgam of dark wood, soft, noise-absorbing drapery, and large video screens projecting landscapes and street scenes.

Beef is again the star at the **Nugget Steakhouse** (Wendover Nugget, 101 W. Wendover Blvd., 775/664-2221, www.wendoverresorts.com, 5pm-10pm Sun. and Wed.-Thurs., 5pm-11pm Fri.-Sat., $25-40), but the seafood offers viable options. The house specialty lobster bisque or credible oysters Rockefeller would be a terrific start to a meal in the steakhouse's rustic yet chic setting.

Buffets

Wendover's buffets seem intent on simply fueling guests for another session in front of the slot machines. The food may be better than mediocre, but it's never memorable, varied, or inspired. If you're a crab legs fan, Friday night's seafood buffet at **Bimini** (Rainbow Casino, 680 W. Wendover Blvd., 775/664-4000, www.wendoverfun.com, 11am-3pm Mon.-Fri., 9am-3pm Sat.-Sun., 4pm-9pm Sun.-Thurs., 4pm-10:30pm Fri.-Sat., $14-24) is a buck cheaper than its twin at Montego Bay. The Mongolian barbecue and other Asian dishes, as well as several types of cheesecake, make a weekday trip a filling bargain.

It's more of the same at **Oceano** (Montego Bay, 680 W. Wendover Blvd., 775/664-4800, www.wendoverfun.com, 11am-3pm

Mon.-Fri., 9am-3pm Sat.-Sun., 4pm-9pm Sun.-Thurs., 4pm-10:30pm Fri.-Sat., $15-25), though it's a step below Bimini's. Landlubbers should go when it's cheaper, loading up on fried chicken, carving station ham and roast beef, and desserts.

The **Nugget Buffet** (101 W. Wendover Blvd., 775/401-6840, www.wendoverresorts. com, 11am-3pm Mon.-Fri., 9am-3pm Sat.-Sun., 5pm-9pm Sun.-Thurs., 4pm-11pm Fri.-Sat., $13-28) calls the others' Friday night seafood bet and raises a Saturday evening steak night.

Mexican

Wendover boasts a few good Mexican restaurants, with varying degrees of authenticity. Upscale **Pancho and Willie's** (Peppermill, 680 W. Wendover Blvd., 775/664-2255, www. wendoverfun.com, $20-35) is the best in town. Order the sombrero-size chimichangas and you won't have to buy breakfast the next day. Saguaro and yucca decorations lend just the right Sonoran atmosphere.

From the outside, **Los Compadres** (85 E. Skyhawk Dr., 735/249-6002, $8-12) looks like you've stumbled onto the wrong side of the tracks. But inside, the smells from the kitchen will have you salivating before you order. The burritos (order the adobada) aren't as big as at Pancho and Willie's, but it doesn't matter. They could be twice as large and there still wouldn't be any to take home. Similarly unpretentious, **Salt Flats Café** (85 E. Skyhawk Dr., 435/665-7550, 10am-9pm daily, $7-10) heaps on the portions. May we suggest the chile verde?

ACCOMMODATIONS

Wendover has some 1,500 hotel and motel rooms, with another 500 or so on the Utah side. If you aren't interested in the amenities

or the hustle and bustle at the casinos, chains such as Motel 6, Best Western, Knights Inn, Days Inn, and more are standing by.

Wendover KOA (651 N. Camper Dr., 775/664-3221, www.koa.com, $40-50) is the only noncasino RV park, though even it is right out the Red Garter's and Rainbow's back doors. It can accommodate rigs up to 80 feet. The park is hard dirt with scrubby trees. Only a few sites have trees tall enough to provide shade. The pool is open Memorial Day through Labor Day, and there are basketball, volleyball, and tetherball courts, plus a miniature golf course and playground. **Wendover Nugget's RV Park** (101 W. Wendover Blvd., 775/664-2221, www.wendoverresorts.com, $30-40) consists of 18 paved spaces with barebones on-site amenities but access to the casino's facilities.

INFORMATION AND SERVICES

The **West Wendover Tourism and Convention Bureau** operates the Nevada Welcome Center (735 Wendover Blvd., 775/664-3138 or 866/299-2489, 9am-5pm Mon.-Fri.). Staff not only hand out brochures but also share insiders' tips for making the most of your visit. The Tourism and Convention Bureau promotes Wendover's citywide annual festivals, such as Cinco de Mayo and Independence Day. The Wendover branch of the **Elko County Library** (590 Camper Dr., 772/664-2510) is open weekday afternoons. **Hertz** (775/664-4887, www.hertz. com) maintains a rental counter at Montego Bay, and the **Greyhound station** is at the Pilot Travel Center (1200 W. Wendover Blvd., 775/664-3400, www.greyhound.com). **Toana Taxi** can be reached at 775/664-4400 (Nevada) or 435/665-8294 (Utah).

Background

The Landscape

Half a billion years ago, Nevada rested underwater. For roughly 150 million years, the shells and skeletons of brachiopods, primitive trilobites, tiny spiny starfish, single-celled radiolaria, and algae accumulated on the shallow ocean floor and were pressurized into limestone. Great upheavals then raised the land, draining the sea and leaving towering mesas, alluvial plains, and sunken basins into which seawater rushed back. Then, at the end of the Permian period, a collision of supercontinents forced the ocean into retreat again and triggered a near-global extinction.

This mass extinction of plants and animals ("The Great Dying") freed massive quantities of oxygen that had been bound up by carbon in living organisms. The oxygen rusted the ubiquitous ferrous iron in Nevada's newly exposed seabed and limestone deposits, turning them red. Millennia of sandstorms, rain, and temperature extremes eroded and sculpted the sediments into the spires, ridges, caves, and other geologic features that make Nevada unique.

Erosion continues to litter Nevada's valleys with mountain material. Some ranges have been whittled down over the past 15 million years to a mere 12,000 feet. Others have been completely buried in their own shavings. Still other ranges are growing as their blocks tilt more steeply. Some hills are really the peaks of mountains that extend thousands of feet below the surface, iceberg-style, resting on bedrock. Nevada is home to some 200 named mountain ranges, 90 percent of them oriented northeast-southwest. The other 10 percent constitute what's known as a discontinuous fault zone—hooked, curved, folded toward all points on the compass. Collectively referred to as the Walker Lane Belt, these individually scrambled mountains at the same time occur in a line, northwest-southeast, roughly 400 miles long along the geologically uneasy California-Nevada state line.

TWO STATES IN ONE

Unlike Nevada's next-door neighbor to the west, where the demarcation between its northern and southern zones is based as much on states of mind as on geography, northern and southern Nevada can be pinpointed fairly specifically. Simply stated, Nevada's two deserts separate the state into its two distinct parts. Northern Nevada is usually considered to include everything within the Great Basin Desert, while southern Nevada occupies the Mojave Desert. The differences in the field probably wouldn't be immediately apparent to the untrained eye, but the two primary and related factors are elevation and vegetation.

The base elevation of the Great Basin Desert ranges 4,500-6,200 feet, where the predominant vegetation is sagebrush. The Mojave's elevation in Nevada starts at 490 feet (the lowest and southernmost point in Nevada at the Colorado River near Laughlin) and ascends in elevation northward to the Great Basin; the predominant vegetation below 4,000 feet is creosote.

Although the northern part of the state accounts for 80 percent of the land, the southern part accounts for 80 percent of the population. As for climate, the farther south you travel in Nevada, the hotter and drier it gets. Las Vegas has some of the lowest precipitation and the lowest relative humidity of any metropolitan area in the country; Laughlin, at the extreme southern tip of the state, is second only to Laredo, Texas, for having the most record-high temperatures in the country.

Previous: Joshua trees in the high Nevada desert; petroglyphs in Valley of Fire State Park.

Great Basin Desert

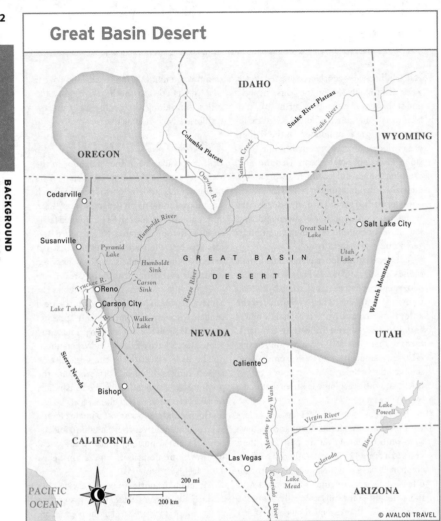

© AVALON TRAVEL

Nevada's 110,000 square miles, or 70,264,320 acres, make it the seventh-largest state. The federal government owns nearly 60 million of those acres, or 85 percent of the total land area. Of the federal acreage, nearly 50 million acres are managed by the Bureau of Land Management, with just over 5 million acres controlled by the U.S. Forest Service. The military has over 4 million acres, which it uses for bases, training grounds, and test sites; that number is growing.

Native American reservations, national wildlife refuges, and wilderness areas account for the remainder of the federal land total. Twenty-four state parks preserve roughly 50,000 acres, and the rest is privately owned.

THE DESERTS
Great Basin

The Great Basin Desert is one of the major geographic features in the United States. It stretches 500 miles between California's Sierra

Nevada and Utah's Wasatch Mountains, up to 750 miles between Oregon's Columbia Plateau and southern Nevada's Mojave Desert, and makes up a large part of the Basin and Range physiographic province. John C. Frémont named the Great Basin in 1844 for a curious and unique phenomenon: internal drainage. The rivers here have no outlet to the sea. They meander for various distances through arroyos and canyons before emptying into lakes, disappearing into sinks, or just evaporating.

The Great Basin is not a bowl-shaped depression between the two major mountain ranges; it is more like a square of corrugated cardboard inside a shallow box. Some of the interior ridges—the mountain ranges—rise higher than the sides of the box. All the ranges, no matter what their height, have troughs between them. There are upward of 300 separate mountain ranges, resembling "an army of caterpillars crawling northward out of Mexico," according to early explorer C. E. Dutton. The Great Basin Desert covers roughly 75 percent of Nevada, and Nevada contains roughly 75 percent of the Great Basin Desert. Only a few thousand years ago, huge lakes left over from the wet Pleistocene covered much of this desert. The earth is highly mineralized: Copper, lead, iron, gypsum, salt, magnesite, diatomaceous earth, silver, and gold have all been mined in large quantities. But this desert's most unmistakable characteristic is the basin-and-range corrugation. The average base elevation (where the basins meet the ranges) is 5,000 feet above sea level. The overwhelmingly predominant vegetation is sagebrush, the state flower. Piñon pine and juniper, mountain mahogany and aspen, fir, pine, and spruce inhabit the higher life zones, where many creatures, from field mice and jackrabbits to pronghorn and bobcats, reside.

Mojave Desert

At the southern tip of Nevada, the Mojave Desert borders the northern boundary of the great Sonoran Desert, which encompasses southwestern Arizona, southeastern California, Mexico's northwestern state of Sonora, and nearly the entire Baja California Peninsula. The Mojave Desert is a basin, sluicing south into the main drainage, the Colorado River. Elevations begin to plummet south of Goldfield on the west side and Caliente on the east, down to around 2,000 feet at Las Vegas, then down to around 500 feet at Laughlin. The Mojave is not only lower but also hotter and drier than its northern Nevada counterpart. Its prevalent vegetation consists of creosote, yucca, and Joshua tree. Snakes, lizards, and bighorn sheep predominate.

THE MOUNTAINS

Depending on who's counting and how, 150-300 mountain ranges have been counted within Nevada's borders. Most were created by the tectonic pressure exerted on the western continental crustal surface from the strain of the Pacific Plate edging north against the North American Plate at the San Andreas Fault. This colossal jostle has fractured the crust at numerous places; at the cracks, some chunks have sunk down, some have lifted up, and some have listed over. A typical Nevada range is 50 to 150 miles long and 10 miles wide. Each range is slanted, a long gentle slope on one side and a sheer scarp on the other. Boundary and Wheeler, the two highest peaks, reach just over 13,000 feet. Mount Moriah, Mount Jefferson, Mount Charleston, Arc Dome, Pyramid Peak, and South Schell Peak hover around 12,000 feet. A score of others rise higher than 10,000 feet.

Limestone ranges occur primarily in eastern Nevada, from the Tuscarora Mountains to the Las Vegas Range. The Schell Creeks, Egans, and Snakes around Ely are the best known and best representatives of the limestone massifs. The sandstone ranges occur in the southern Mojave: the Spring and Muddy Mountains outside Las Vegas. The granite ranges mostly cluster in the west-central part of Nevada around the most magnificent granite mountains of them all: the Sierra Nevada. The volcanic ranges are the youngest and most active of Nevada's various types of ranges and mark the eastern edge of the famous Pacific Ring of Fire. The Virginia Range is one of the older, more eroded, and most mineralized of the volcanic ranges and has yielded hundreds of millions of dollars in gold and silver. The Monte Cristos, west of Tonopah, are an anomaly in the Great Basin—crescent-shaped, containing badlands, and brightly colored. The Pancake Range is only a few thousand years old, and the Apollo astronauts used its Lunar Cuesta to simulate the craters, lava flows, and calderas of the moon.

The rest of Nevada's many mountain ranges are composites, exhibiting a great variety of granite, sedimentary, volcanic, and metamorphic signs. The Humboldts, Santa Rosas, Stillwaters, and Toiyabes are composite ranges, and the Toiyabes have been called "the archetype of Nevada ranges."

THE RIVERS

Ten rivers of note snake around Nevada. The Truckee, Carson, and Walker Rivers flow in while the Bruneau, Owyhee, and Salmon Rivers flow out. The Humboldt and Reese Rivers are born and die in the Great Basin. The state's southeast boundary is formed by the Colorado River, which meanders for 150 miles along the edge. The Amargosa River rises in the Nuclear Test Site, slightly waters Beatty, then flows underground to Death Valley. Seven of the 10 rivers are dammed.

The Humboldt

Originating in northeastern Nevada, the Humboldt River flows southwest, picking up runoff from the East Humboldts, the Rubies, and a half dozen other mountain ranges north and south of it between here and Beowawe. It cuts northwest up to Winnemucca and back southwest into the Rye Patch Reservoir. Beyond the dam, it disappears into its own sour sink. Pioneer migrants cursed its foul water and harvested all the vegetation from its banks, and reclamation projects dammed it to irrigate Pershing County. A railroad, a U.S. defense highway, and an interstate highway have been built next to it.

aerial view of the Hoover Dam and the Colorado River

The Colorado

Nevada got lucky in 1866 when, only two years after its boundaries were surveyed, the state was allowed to extend its southern borders into Utah and Arizona Territories. Nevada annexed 150 miles of the west bank of the Colorado River along with Las Vegas Valley, the Muddy and Virgin Rivers, and Meadow Valley Wash. The Colorado is one big river that had made its own destiny for countless eons until the federal Bureau of Reclamation took on the Hoover Dam project in the 1930s. Davis Dam, 80 miles south of the Hoover Dam and built in 1954, further controls this now-docile dragon in Nevada.

The Sierra Three

The Truckee, Carson, and Walker Rivers all flow east out of the Sierras and fan out northeast, east, and southeast, respectively, into western Nevada. The northernmost of the three, the Truckee River, emanates from the edge of Lake Tahoe and flows northeast. It provides all the water for Reno-Sparks and some water for the reclamation projects in Fernley and Fallon. Derby Dam, which diverts Truckee River water to Lahontan Reservoir, was the Bureau of Reclamation's first dam, built in 1905. The rest of the river water reaches its original destination at Pyramid Lake.

The Carson River, which flows north to Carson City, then east between the Virginia Range and the Pine Nut Mountains, at one time spread out into the desert within the large Carson Sink. Today, a dozen or so miles west of the sink, the Carson is backed up by Lahontan Dam and then sent by canals and ditches to irrigate Fallon. For years little water reached the Carson River marsh at Stillwater National Wildlife Refuge, but that is beginning to change.

The Walker River flows north from two forks into idyllic Mason Valley. It passes Yerington and then makes a big U-turn around the Wassuk Range and heads south into Walker Lake. Bridgeport Lake in California is where the East Fork is dammed early on, and Topaz Lake is where the West Fork is dammed early on; Weber Reservoir backs up the Walker River on the east side of the Wassuks a little north of Walker Lake, its final destination.

The Idaho Three

The Bruneau, Owyhee, and Salmon Rivers flow north from the area where the Snake River Plateau protrudes into the Great Basin. They empty into the Snake River, which empties into the mighty Columbia River. The headwaters of the Humboldt cascade south from the Great Basin side of the plateau. This is a very active corner of Nevada for water, a real slice of the Pacific Northwest. The Owyhee River is dammed at Wildhorse, and the Snake River is dammed in Idaho.

THE LAKES
Artificial Lakes

Lake Mead is the largest artificial lake in the country, created by 7 million tons of cement poured 700 feet high to hold back the raging Colorado River. Lake Mojave is restrained by an earth-filled 200-foot dam. Both Rye Patch (on the Humboldt River) and Wildhorse (on the Owyhee River) Reservoirs are popular with anglers, boaters, and campers; South Fork Dam, completed in 1988, is the newest dam in Nevada, impounding 40,000 acre-feet of South Fork Creek 10 miles south of Elko; the state's newest park is also here. Lahontan Reservoir (on the Carson River) also has lots of campsites in addition to the amazing network of ditches and canals through Fallon between it and the Carson Sink.

Altered Lakes

The overflow from the Truckee River once drained out of Pyramid Lake and into Winnemucca Lake. It took only 30 years for large Winnemucca Lake to dry into a playa after the Truckee Canal diverted some river water to Lahontan Valley. Today, 100 years later, Pyramid Lake may be headed for a similar fate, having dropped to uncomfortably low levels. But now it appears as if almost everyone—the feds, the state, the hatcheries, the power company, and the conservationists (although not the farmers, entirely)—are starting to agree on how to satisfy the various conflicting water requirements for the lakes, refuges, irrigation systems, and urban populations.

Ruby Marsh has dikes and causeways around and through it; Pahranagat is less changed. Walker Lake, like Pyramid, has had its water diverted and its fishery devastated; this lake could be one of the most endangered in the West.

For sheer beauty, Lake Tahoe—logged out, fished out, dammed, silted, but now slowly returning to a fairly pristine condition—is unsurpassed, except maybe by a few of those backcountry lakes way up in the Ruby Mountains.

Plants and Animals

PLANTS

Creosote

The Mojave Desert covers the southern quarter of Nevada, and the creosote bush covers the Mojave. Because of the extremely arid environment, these shrubs, which grow 2-10 feet tall and sprout dull-green resinous foliage, are widely scattered over the desert sand, occupying only about 10 percent of the available surface. Their presence generally indicates conditions unsuitable for agricultural cultivation. They grow in the 450- to 3,000-foot elevation zone in Nevada, mostly limited to the Mojave in the south and the lowest points in the lowest valleys in the Great Basin.

Joshua Tree

This picturesque tree, also known as the tree yucca or yucca palm, can grow to 30 feet tall with a stout body and boldly forking branches. It blooms bright yellow March-May. The Joshua tree was named by Mormon pioneers who imagined the big yucca's branches to be imploring, slightly grotesque "arms" pointing the way to the promised land.

Sage

Sagebrush is the state flower. It's also possibly the most memorable and enduring image of Nevada, along with neon, that travelers take home with them. Covering a third of the desert surface, sage protects the earth from wanton erosion. It also gives shelter to snakes and small rodents that burrow under the bush, and it feeds sage hens, squirrels, jackrabbits, and other fauna that eat the spring buds. Sheep, cattle, and pronghorn also nibble on the young leaves.

Juniper

Utah juniper is the most common tree in the Great Basin. It grows on every mountain range and in some basins. Juniper is also the first tree that takes to a particular microenvironment; piñon follows later. Junipers grow to 20 feet and are sometimes as round as they are tall. They produce blue-green juniper berries (bitter but edible), pale green needles, and yellowish pollen cones. You'll normally see them at 6,000-8,000 feet.

Piñon Pine

Piñon is a Spanish word for pine nut. The tree's nuts feed small and large rodents, birds, deer, and even bighorn sheep and bears. It was the staple food for Great Desert Native Americans, who harvested the nuts from groves that they considered sacred and ground them into flour, which they baked into biscuits, cakes, and a type of breadstick. Today the Paiute and Shoshone continue to celebrate piñon harvest festivals in the early fall.

Cottonwoods, willows, aspens, sagebrush, rabbitbrush, and Mormon tea, among other trees and plants, also grow in the piñon-juniper zone.

Other Trees

Starting at around 7,500 feet and going up to 11,000 feet or so are the trees that most people relate to the forest. In the Great Basin, the higher you go, the wetter the environment and the bigger the trees. Ponderosa, Jeffrey, and sugar pine; white fir; and incense cedar occupy the lower reaches of the forest. Lodgepole and white pine along with mountain hemlock inhabit the middle zone at about 9,000 feet. Douglas fir, white fir, blue spruce, and Engelmann spruce top off the thick growth up to 10,000 feet. Limber and bristlecone pine trees survive and thrive at or above the usual tree line in the harshest environment known to trees of the Great Basin.

ANIMALS

Fish

Contrary to popular perception, Nevada is not just a great desert wasteland. In fact, nothing dispels the myth quite so forcefully as the fact that Nevada has more than 600 fishable lakes, reservoirs, rivers, streams, and creeks.

The biggest fish are found in the biggest lakes. Mackinaw, a variety of Great Lakes trout, averages 20 pounds (the record is a monster 37-pounder); catch mackinaw deep in Lake Tahoe.

Rainbow trout, channel catfish, and big, tasty striped bass prowl Lake Mead. The big linesides feed on planted trout fingerlings below Hoover Dam at Willow Beach.

Lahontan cutthroat, the "trout salmon" that so impressed John C. Frémont, grow to 15 pounds in Pyramid Lake; a 41-pounder is on display at the State Museum in Carson City, but it's a member of the original species, which is now extinct. The ancient cui-ui sucker fish is native to Pyramid Lake. Lake Mead boasts an abundance of striped bass and a regenerating population of the popular largemouth bass.

Seven-pound cutthroats, five-pound browns, and three-pound rainbows are fished from Topaz Lake and a number of ponds and streams in Nevada. One-pound golden trout are catchable in the lakes (especially Hidden Lake) high up in the Ruby Mountains.

Lizards

Nevada has 26 species of lizards, about 15 of them in the Mojave Desert. Of the 3,000 lizard species worldwide, only two are poisonous, and Nevada has one of them. The banded Gila monster is found in Clark and Lincoln Counties between the Colorado and Virgin Rivers.

The chuckwalla, a 16-inch vegetarian, is found in Clark and Nye Counties. The desert iguana is another vegetarian. The Great Basin whiptail is found at 2,000-7,000 feet. It's easy to identify, since its tail is twice as long as its body. Another species with a distinctive tail is the zebratail, which is banded with black and white stripes. It wags its tail as it flees, hoping to distract its predators. If another animal gets the tail, the zebratail grows

another. Zebratails are extremely fast and zig-zag when they run.

The collared lizard has a black-and-white band around its neck. It's generally seen around rocky terrain, hunting for grasshoppers, cicadas, and leopard lizards. It bites if handled. Leopard lizards are extremely common in northern Nevada. They're easy to recognize, with thick spots all over their bodies and very long thin tails.

The horned lizard is an unusual creature of the desert Southwest. It is black and tan and grows horns on the back of its head. Small spines cover the rest of its body. Ants are its favorite food. It relies on camouflage for protection but will puff up and hiss if threatened.

The most common lizard of Nevada is the Western fence lizard. It's brown with bright blue stomach patches. Like the zebratail, it can shed its tail to escape danger, then grow another.

Snakes

Like lizards, most snakes in Nevada are found in the Mojave Desert. Several varieties of rattlers inhabit the Las Vegas area. The Panamint has a wide range (from Las Vegas to Tonopah) and a bad bite. The Southwestern speckled likes the mountains and washes around Lake Mead. Western diamondbacks are easy to identify, as their name implies, and it's a good thing since they're especially ill-tempered as well as being the largest of the seven species of Nevada rattlers. The Mojave rattler is sometimes mistaken for the diamondback, although it has distinctive black and white tail rings. The Mojave rattler is less nasty, but its venom is 10 times more poisonous. The sidewinder is a small rattlesnake, around two feet long, known for the S-curve trail its slithering motion leaves in the sand. The Great Basin rattlesnake has the largest range, covering more than half the state at 5,000-10,000 feet in elevation.

The mountain king snake is not poisonous, likes river bottoms and farmlands, and eats rattlers for breakfast; it's immune to the venom. Because it displays red and black bands, it's often confused with the highly poisonous **Arizona coral snake,** with its red and yellow bands. Though they're not supposed to exist in Nevada, coral snakes have been identified as far north as Lovelock and as far west as Carson City. The **Great Basin gopher snake** is probably the most common and widely distributed serpent in Nevada and is active during the day. It's not poisonous; it kills small mammals by constriction.

Desert Tortoise

The desert tortoise is the state reptile. It's unmistakable with its hard shell and fat legs. The front legs are larger than the rear, for digging burrows that protect them on hot summer days and when they hibernate through the winter. These tortoises eat grasses and blossoms in the early morning and late afternoon. In June, females lay 4-6 eggs in shallow holes and then cover them with dirt. The eggs hatch late September-early October. The tortoises can live to be 100 years old.

Birds

Nevada is one of the best places in the West to look for raptors—eagles, hawks, falcons, and ospreys. The Goshute Mountains, specifically, between Ely and Wendover, are on the flyway of up to 20,000 migrating raptors every year.

Both bald and golden **eagles** are found in Nevada. Golden eagles stay year-round, mostly in the northern part of the state; bald eagles migrate here for the winter and like well-watered and agricultural areas.

Ospreys have wingspans approaching those of eagles and are related to vultures. Since they feed entirely on fish (they're also known as fish hawks), ospreys are mainly observed feeding in the rivers and lakes of the Reno-Tahoe area on their migration south for the winter.

Accipiters include **goshawks,** fairly large birds about the size of ravens; **sharp-shinned hawks,** about the size of robins; and **Cooper's hawks,** similar to sharp-shins. Since accipiter habitat is mostly in forests and

heavily wooded areas, HawkWatch has found their populations to be on the wane because of extensive logging in the Pacific Northwest and western Canada.

Buteos are the hawks normally seen soaring above the desert. Among them are **ferruginous hawks,** which live in the juniper of eastern Nevada year-round. Common **red-tailed hawks** prey on lizards in the Mojave. **Rough-legged hawks** winter in Nevada, while **Swainson's hawks** prefer Nevada in the summer and then fly to South America for the winter, although they're fairly uncommon these days.

Sharp-eyed bird-watchers can also spot marsh hawks, kestrels, merlins, and peregrine falcons.

Pelicans have traditionally nested in large numbers at Anaho Island in Pyramid Lake. Other shorebirds also nest at Anaho. The wildlife refuges at Ruby Marsh, Stillwater, Pahranagat Lakes, Railroad Valley, Kirch (south of Ely), and others are also prime bird-watching locales.

Mountain Lions and Bears

Populations of pronghorn, elk, deer, sheep, wild horses, and burros have all revived in the past 50 years, and mountain lions and bears have become more common in both the remote and inhabited mountains.

Mountain lions aren't particularly shy of humans, but they're so elusive that they're not often seen. When one is, especially in a populated area, it's trapped and relocated, and it makes pretty big news. Attacks on humans are rare but not unknown. Also known as cougars, panthers (or painters), and pumas, mountain lion males weigh up to 160 pounds and females 100-130 pounds. As such, they're second in size only to bears as North America's largest predators. They hunt at night, taking coyotes, mule deer, bighorn sheep, beavers, and even porcupines.

Likewise, **black bears** are more common in Nevada than most people think. A Department of Wildlife study a few years ago concluded that up to several hundred bears of humans and are occasionally seen in towns looking for cats and dogs. They prey voraciously on domestic stock, killing an estimated 10,000 sheep and cattle each year in Nevada. The federal Animal Damage Control (ADC) hunts them all over the West, killing nearly 100,000 coyotes in 17 western states every year.

Bighorn Sheep

The desert (or Nelson) bighorn is the state animal. It is smaller than its cousins, the Rocky Mountain and California bighorns, but has bigger horns and is therefore highly prized as a big-game trophy. In fact, hunters have stalked this animal since records of such activities have been kept; petroglyphs and pictographs, including those in Valley of Fire State Park northeast of Las Vegas, illustrate bighorn hunting. It's even believed that sheep were a larger part of the Native American diet than deer. More than 2,000 hunters apply for the 100 or so sheep tags distributed every year to Nevadans; 1,000 nonresidents compete for the dozen out-of-state tags.

Wild Horses and Burros

One of the great wildlife controversies in Nevada is over wild horses, also known as mustangs, a nonnative species introduced by Spanish colonists. Since the Wild Free-Roaming Horse and Burro Act was passed in 1971, the Bureau of Land Management (BLM) has protected these horses and burros—estimated at 45,000—"as a symbol of the history and pioneer spirit of the West."

The policy has been the bane of ranchers and farmers whose livelihoods the beasts threaten. For nearly 50 years rival interests have fought over rounding up the horses for slaughter. Animal advocates won most of the latest battles, and the horses still run free.

Bighorn sheep roam throughout Nevada.

live in Nevada, most in the Sierras and the rest in the Pine Nut and Sweetwater Ranges in western Nevada and around Jarbidge in northeastern Nevada. These bears can be any color from blond to cinnamon to jet-black; nearly all have a white patch on their chests. The males can be six feet long and weigh 300-400 pounds; the females are about five feet long and up to 200 pounds.

Coyotes

Smart, patient, and fast, coyotes reproduce readily and in large numbers, and they're utterly opportunistic, taking advantage of bumper crops of rabbits or vulnerable deer, even supplementing their diet with pine nuts. Coyotes have also pretty much lost their fear

Environmental Issues

WILDERNESS

To many Nevadans, *wilderness* is a dirty word, a negative concept. It means controlled access and use: reduced grazing, road and dam building, and mining—in short, general commercial restraint of the activities that most rural Nevadans rely on for their livelihoods.

The federal government owns more than 80 percent of Nevada, most of it in the hands of the Bureau of Land Management (BLM). In the final days of his administration, President Obama designated some 300,000 Nevada acres as the Gold Butte National Monument, a move cheered by Democrats and environmentalists and panned by Republicans and agribusiness interests.

Traditionally, mining and ranching interests have been far too strong to be overcome by any wilderness proposals. Recently, however, the mass migrations into Nevada's two urban areas and the increasing importance of tourism to the state's economic well-being have turned the tables. The 1964 Wilderness Act empowered states to set aside peaks, canyons, forests, streams, and wildlife habitats in parks, and by 1989 the political stars were aligned properly for the federal government to designate wilderness areas in Nevada; 733,400 acres of national forest lands were protected as wilderness areas in 14 separate locations around the state.

NUCLEAR ISSUES
Nevada Test Site

This 1,350-square-mile chunk of the southern Nevada desert is a Rhode Island-sized area that's off-limits to the public—but you probably wouldn't want to go there even if it weren't. Between 1951 and 1962 there were 126 atmospheric tests of nuclear weapons conducted within the test site's boundaries. Another 925 underground explosions rocked the desert 1962-1992, and the federal government has admitted to another 204 secret detonations.

It all started after U.S. scientists and military planners found that nuclear test explosions over the Marshall Islands in the central Pacific were politically and logistically inconvenient, and they went looking for a more suitable location on the U.S. mainland. Nevada already had the enormous Las Vegas Bombing and Gunnery Range, and there was nothing out there anyway, right? The first bomb, a one-kiloton warhead dropped from an airplane, was detonated in January 1951, initiating another bizarre episode in southern Nevada history, not to mention a deadly "nuclear war" against atomic veterans and downwinders that continues to this day.

Set off just before dawn, the tests sometimes broke windows in Henderson, 100 miles away. The fireballs could be seen in Reno, 300 miles away, and the mushroom clouds tended to drift east over southern Utah. A silent majority certainly worried which way the wind blew, the Atomic Energy Commission erected realistic "Doom Town" sets to measure destruction, and thousands of soldiers were posted within a tight radius to be purposefully exposed to the tests. Livestock dropped dead fairly soon after exposure, and people involved with or in proximity to the tests have been dying of cancer and leukemia ever since.

Still, far from disturbing the local health consciousness, at the time Las Vegas turned the blasts into public-relations events, throwing rooftop parties to view them. A vocal minority seemed to contract a strange "atom fever," marketing everything from atom burgers to nuclear gasoline and appointing a yearly Miss Atomic Blast.

The Nuclear Waste Repository

In the 1980s the state was chosen to play host to yet another aspect of the nuclear industry—radioactive waste. Yucca Mountain, 100 miles northwest of Las Vegas, was the only site considered to become the nation's permanent high-level radioactive waste storage site. After reviewing mountains of data—some allegedly sugarcoated and even outright falsified by the Department of Energy—the site in 2002 was approved to become the nation's nuclear waste dump. The state of Nevada filed lawsuits challenging the science, safety, and constitutionality of forcing one state to accept the nation's nuclear waste, but the Yucca Mountain recommendation was quickly approved by the Bush administration. In 2009 the Obama administration said the Yucca Mountain site was no longer an option, and the project was effectively canceled when its funding was left out of the federal budget.

But wait! Under the Trump administration, the site is undergoing additional scrutiny to determine its suitability as a waste repository.

LAND USE
Mining Reform
The General Mining Act of 1872, still in effect today, came under serious fire from the Clinton administration. The law, designed to hasten the 19th-century exploration of the West, gives miners the right to prospect hundreds of millions of acres of land that is ostensibly owned by the government, lease it for $2.50-5 per acre (the 1872 prices were never raised), and dig up the minerals on the land without paying the government any royalties.

Since 1994 the BLM has not accepted new patents on mining claims, and attempts in Congress to end new patent claims and impose federal royalties on mining profits have failed.

Range Reform
Farming and ranching are no different from mining when it comes to changing perceptions of land use based on environmental values versus lifestyle and economic considerations. The argument goes that alfalfa farming, for example, produces 1 percent of Nevada's gross state product while using more than 85 percent of the available water. On the other side, ranchers argue that federal lands are owned and used by the people, more often than not third- and fourth-generation ranchers on the same land who have a strong vested interest in the health of the land for continuing their livelihoods and lifestyles. Farmers, ranchers, and miners all believe that their way of life is under attack and will soon be legislated out of existence by the powerful forces of urban environmentalism that hold an almost religious conviction to return the land to their vision of nature, an early-18th-century ideal.

These are tough issues anywhere, but out here in a state that's owned almost entirely by the federal government, they are profound and divisive concerns that will affect the future of the state.

History

INDIGENOUS PEOPLE
Excavation and carbon dating of artifacts discovered in caves around the state have supplied evidence that Native Americans occupied the region now encompassed by Nevada as early as 11,000 BC. Bones taken from a cave near Winnemucca Lake and spear tips unearthed at Leonard Rock Shelter, south of Lovelock, attest to a human presence along the shoreline of great Lake Lahontan between 10,000 and 7500 BC. Basket remnants from

the rock shelter are thought to have been woven around 5600 BC.

At Tule Springs, an archaeological site near Las Vegas, indications are that Paleo-Indians also lived in shoreline caves at the tail end of the wet and cold Wisconsin Ice Age and hunted Pleistocene mammals such as woolly mammoths, bison, mastodons, and caribou as early as 11,000 BC.

The Lovelock Cave was a treasure trove for archaeologists, who excavated darts and fishhooks, baskets, domestic tools, tule duck decoys, shell jewelry, and human remains dating from roughly 2000 BC.

Ancestral Puebloans

At about the beginning of the Common Era, Native Americans in Nevada's southern desert began to develop the first signs of civilization. By AD 800 their civilization was at its peak: They cultivated beans and corn in irrigated fields, lived in grand 100-room pueblos, fashioned artistic pots and baskets, mined turquoise, and generally enjoyed a sophisticated lifestyle in the fertile delta between the Muddy and Virgin Rivers in what is now southeastern Nevada. Around 1150, however, the Ancestral Puebloans migrated from their homeland. No one knows for sure why, but speculation includes drought, overpopulation, disease, collapse of the economic underpinnings of the culture, or warring neighbors.

Paiute, Washoe, and Shoshone

The Southern Paiute claimed the territory that the Ancestral Puebloans had fled, but they never regained the advanced elements of their predecessors' society. In fact, for the next 700 years, the Paiute remained nomadic hunter-gatherers. The Northern Paiute migrated north to populate the high desert, where they encountered the Washoe and Shoshone. All settled into a basically peaceful coexistence, adapting to the arid land. For hundreds of years, the Washoe of western Nevada, the Shoshone of eastern Nevada, and the Paiute of northwestern and southern Nevada developed and maintained cultures perfectly adapted to their difficult environments. Within 40 years of contact with Europeans, the Native American lifestyles had been destroyed.

EXPLORERS AND PIONEERS

The first Europeans to enter what is now Nevada were Spanish friars surveying a trail to connect missions in New Mexico and on the California coast. Two expeditions in 1776—one led by Francisco Garcés, the other

by friars Silvestre Vélez de Escalante and Francisco Atanasio Domínguez—explored the region, but only Garcés touched the far southern tip of Nevada. Escalante and Domínguez, however, discovered a couple of large rivers running west from Utah and postulated a great waterway flowing from there to the Pacific. Thus the mythical San Buenaventura River, a great river that flowed from the Rocky Mountains to the Pacific Ocean, was introduced into the frontier imagination. It took almost 70 years to bury the myth.

In 1826, Jedediah Smith led a party of fur trappers through the same country that Garcés had crossed and spent that winter in California. In the spring he crossed the central Sierra Nevada and discovered the Great Basin Desert—the hard way. Smith's party struggled through the sand and sage with no water for days at a time, crossed a dozen mountain passes, stumbled into Utah, and reached the Salt Lake Valley an agonizing month and a half after leaving the coast.

A year later, Peter Skene Ogden entered Nevada from the north and trapped beaver along the Humboldt River. In 1829 Ogden returned to the Humboldt and then continued south, becoming the first nonnative to cross the Great Basin from north to south. Meanwhile, Kit Carson and company were following parts of the route laid out by the Franciscans, thereby helping to establish and publicize the southern Spanish Trail trade route. In 1830, Antonio Armijo, a Mexican trader, set out from Santa Fe on the Spanish Trail. An experienced scout in Armijo's party, Rafael Rivera, discovered a shortcut on the route by way of Las Vegas's Big Springs, thereby making him the first nonnative to set foot on the land that only 75 years later would become Las Vegas.

In 1841 the famous Bidwell-Bartleson party became the first migrants to set out from Missouri and enter California. Through a combination of dumb luck and good guides, these pioneers managed to follow Walker's route along the Humboldt River, Carson Sink, Walker River, and over the Sierras. With

Virginia City, Nevada's first boomtown

survive, slowed migration temporarily. But in 1848 the United States emerged victorious from the Mexican-American War and appropriated the rest of the West; fortuitously, only two weeks earlier, the country's first major gold deposits had been discovered at Sutter's Mill, sending settlers westward.

Genoa and Las Vegas

Over the course of the next few years, the population of the country around Mormon Station—Washoe and Carson Valleys, Johntown, and Ragtown—started to grow. Traders, prospectors, wagon drivers, and homesteaders moved in. In 1855 this far-western corner of Utah Territory, administered from Salt Lake City, was designated Carson County and put under the direct administration of local Mormon officials and colonists. Mormon Station was renamed Genoa and became Nevada's first county seat.

Missionaries were also dispatched from Salt Lake City to southern Nevada at a rest stop along the Spanish Trail known as Las Vegas, or The Meadows. They built a stockade similar to the one in Genoa, befriended the Paiute, nourished the migrants, and even began mining and smelting lead nearby. But tensions between the Mormon colonists and miners, meager rations, and the hardships and isolation of the desert caused the mission to disband.

In addition, Mormon leader Brigham Young, concerned with the possibility of going to war with the U.S. Army over autonomy, bigamy, and manifest destiny, recalled the missionaries from Genoa. Their places were taken by the people who would soon become the first official Nevadans.

The Comstock Lode and Virginia City

Prospectors and gold miners had been crawling all over the Carson River and its tributary creeks for almost a decade by 1859, when two Irish gold miners dug a hole around a small spring high up on Sun Mountain and struck gold. The respectable quantities of gold,

them were the first cattle, wagons, and white woman and child to enter Nevada. Their success encouraged a few more staggered wagon trains to attempt the long journey across the uncharted western half of the country and stimulated the first official mapmaking expedition through the Great Basin.

Frémont and the Forty-Niners

In 1843, John C. Frémont, a lieutenant in the U.S. Army's Topographical Corps, was assigned the job of exploring and mapping much of what would become Nevada; he also hoped to finally locate the elusive San Buenaventura River. Guided by Kit Carson, he marched west through the Columbia River Basin, then cut south into far northwestern Nevada. He came across and named Pyramid Lake, followed the Truckee River for a spell, turned south and "discovered" the Carson River, and glimpsed Lake Tahoe.

The famous Donner incident, in which an ill-fated pioneer party became snowbound in the Sierras and resorted to cannibalism to however, were encased by a blue-gray mud, a peculiar rock that polluted the quartz veins, fouled the sluice boxes, and diluted the quicksilver. But when a visitor to the diggings carried a bit of the mud down and had it assayed in Placerville, it was found to be nearly pure sulfuret of silver.

The Comstock is still one of the largest silver strikes in the world, and Virginia City remains one of the most authentic and colorful boomtowns in the Wild West. The enormous impact of the riches, power, and fame of this find meant that within a year Nevada had become its own territory.

Meanwhile, trading posts were established all along the Humboldt Trail, at Lovelock, Winnemucca, and Carlin, among others. Boomtowns such as Aurora, Austin, and Unionville were mushrooming up in the desert. Gold was also discovered at Eldorado Canyon on the Colorado River, a short distance from Las Vegas. But Virginia City was the lodestar, the ultimate boomtown. In 1864, a mere five years after its discovery, the Comstock had earned Nevada its statehood. It also helped finance the Union Army during the Civil War, and Nevada's two new senators cast the deciding votes to abolish slavery. The unearthing of tons of silver affected monetary standards worldwide.

Carson City and Reno

In 1858, Abraham V. Curry and his partners bought the 865-acre Eagle Ranch for $1,000. Curry put $300 down, but the seller, his own creditors about to catch up with him, bolted town, never bothering to collect the other $700. Curry bought out his partners, laid out the town, offered free and low-cost lots to permanent settlers, and plotted his strategy to make his town the state capital. Although discovery of the Comstock was still more than a year away and the "ranch" was little more than sand and sage, Curry had found the spot where he'd base his empire.

The ambitious New Yorker promoted the desolate valley as the eventual site of the state capital, which he named Carson City, after

the nearby Carson River. Carson City boasted wide city streets, a four-square-block area known to settlers as the Plaza and to Curry as Capitol Square, and a few buildings constructed of adobe bricks. He also discovered a large limestone outcrop near a warm spring on the property, which he used as a quarry; he dammed the spring and built a bathhouse, which attracted prospectors and travelers.

Curry not only got his capital city, he got the state prison and a federal mint as well, but Myron Lake won a 10-year contract to collect tolls on his bridge over the Truckee River at a bustling little site soon to be known as Reno. The new state's eastern and southern boundaries were pushed outward, swallowing a few chunks of Arizona and Utah Territories, including 150 miles of the Colorado River. Alfalfa was on its way to becoming the star crop of Nevada agriculture. The miners of the Comstock, digging to more than 500 feet, were greedily devouring virtually every tree within 50 miles for timber supports. And Virginia Town was quickly turning into Virginia City, the largest and loudest metropolis between Salt Lake City and San Francisco.

Silver was located at Eureka, 70 miles east of Austin, and at Hamilton, 70 miles farther east. Gold and silver were mined in Robinson Canyon as well as Osceola, just west of the Utah border around today's Ely. The silver at Tuscarora opened up the northeast. A gold miner from Eldorado Canyon named O. D. Gass homesteaded Las Vegas Valley, squatting in the ruins of the Mormon fort. But the big news, in 1868, was the arrival of the Central Pacific Railroad—at Reno in May, Winnemucca in September, Elko in February 1869, and Promontory Point, Utah, in May. It also hatched Lovelock, Battle Mountain, Carlin, and Wells as it went.

The Railroads

The transcontinental railroad across northern Nevada stimulated the building of numerous wagon roads to the north and south, interconnecting the whole top half of the six-year-old state. The Virginia & Truckee Railroad connected the mines at Virginia City to the mills at Carson City and the main line at Reno. The railroads abandoned thousands of Chinese workers after construction was completed. After numerous skirmishes and several major battles, the Native Americans were finally subdued, then left to fend for themselves both on and off the few reservations set up to contain them.

A disastrous fire in 1875 temporarily muffled Virginia City's boom, and although Big Bonanza silver restored it even beyond its previous splendor, the Comstock mines played out in the next few years. By then Eureka was producing enough silver to rate its own railroad connection, but the demise of Comstock silver mining quickly forced Nevada to its knees.

SINCE 1900

In 1900 Jim Butler located some very rich rock in the wilds of south-central Nevada. Butler's silver strike at Tonopah was the first news of prosperity in a generation. Two years later, Goldfield began booming even more loudly 25 miles south of Tonopah.

The railroads reached their prime, with the Western Pacific Railroad traversing Nevada in 1909, from Oakland, California, across the Black Rock Desert, along the Southern Pacific route from Winnemucca to Wells, and then along a northern route to Salt Lake City. Short lines ran from Tonopah into California, from Searchlight to Las Vegas, from Pioche to Caliente, from Carson to Minden, from near Yerington to Wabuska, and elsewhere around the state.

The Road

A company with the auspicious name of Nevada Rapid Transit had already built a road especially for automobiles between Rhyolite and Las Vegas in 1905. Floods in 1907 and again in 1910 knocked out hundreds of miles of track on both the northern and southern routes. And in 1913, the designation of Nevada Route No. 1 along the Humboldt, the first state auto road, spelled an end to the railroads' monopoly on automated transportation.

Nevada passed its first motor vehicle law in 1913; the license fee was based on the horsepower (any auto with more than 20 hp needed a license). In 1914 a highway between Los Angeles and Salt Lake City through Las Vegas was begun; it took 10 years to build. The Federal Aid Road Act of 1916 allocated funds to stimulate rural road building, which sent Nevada on such a road-building binge that it had to establish a Department of Highways less than a year later. In 1919, this state agency laid a road down on top of the defunct Las Vegas and Tonopah Railroad right-of-way, the first stretch of the Bonanza Highway (US 95).

The Federal Highway Act of 1921 invested more money in building long-distance connectors. Over the next several years, the Highway Department improved old Nevada Route No. 1 by widening and grading it and laying down gravel. By 1927 the transcontinental Victory (US 40) and Lincoln (US 50) Highways were complete; a national exposition was held in Reno to celebrate, for which that city's first arch was erected over Virginia Street. The roads had an immediate negative impact on the railroads, and the downtowns along the tracks began their inexorable migrations, relocating along the highways.

The Crash

The stock market collapse of 1929 took Nevada's banks with it. The Great Depression had begun, but three events in the following two years significantly shaped Nevada's urban history: divorce residency requirements were lowered to a scandalous six weeks, wide-open casino gambling was legalized, and Hoover Dam was built. Divorces and gambling combined to focus a national spotlight on Reno, Biggest Little City in the World and the biggest city in Nevada. Unhappily married celebrities waited out their six weeks for a divorce in the spotlight of newspaper society pages around the country—dateline Reno. Raymond and Harold Smith, veteran carnies and fledgling casino operators, embarked on a national advertising campaign to polish the image of gambling; their "Harold's Club or Bust" billboards attracted gamblers and thrill-seekers in droves. Las Vegas also hit the front pages: "Best Town by a Dam Site." Construction workers from the dam flooded the Fremont Street clubs and Block 16 cribs on payday; after the Hoover Dam was topped off, many stayed. And when the first turbine at the dam turned, Las Vegas had as much juice as it would need to do what it was destined to do.

Midcentury and Beyond

A big Naval Air Station went in at Fallon, and an Army Air Base opened at Stead Field outside Reno. When the Army Airfield was installed near Las Vegas in 1941, it supplied the growing town with a steady stream of soldiers and prompted the opening of El Rancho Vegas and the Last Frontier Hotel on what would soon be known as the Strip. Basic Magnesium began mining metals at Gabbs and built factories and a town for 10,000 people at Henderson between Las Vegas and Boulder City. After the war, Mafia money and muscle, supervised by a "charming psychopath" named Benjamin Siegel, built the ultimate one-stop pleasure palace. Bugsy Siegel expanded the Las Vegas Strip, furthered the modern tourism industry, and ushered in a 20-year underworld siege of southern Nevada. Embattled state officials, caught in an unexpected squeeze play between federal heat and its growing casino revenues, slowly legislated systems to regulate the casinos.

Otherwise, the conservative moral sensibilities of the country in the 1950s did little to prevent Nevada from marching to its own unconventional drummer. In 1951, for example, Nevada welcomed the Nuclear Test Site to the state, enjoying the fireworks for 10 years until they went underground. The hotel-casinos kept opening one after another, year after year, and the brothels were left the way they've always been. Divorces were granted as routinely as ever, and the Freeport Law, instituting tax-free warehousing, was passed.

Finally, Howard Hughes rode into Las Vegas on a stretcher and bought half a dozen of the most troublesome Mafia-owned hotels. This put the seal of corporate respectability on them and paved the way for Hilton, Holiday Inn, Ramada, MGM, and other publicly traded companies to run the industry. Nevada's gambling revenues have never looked back.

Decades later, with the construction of the Mirage in 1998, casino mogul Steve Wynn began Las Vegas's transformation from a gambling destination to a vacation destination. His insistence on resort-class hotel amenities such as gourmet restaurants, nightclubs, and your-wish-is-our-command spas has been envied—and since then emulated—in just about every Nevada town with more than one stoplight.

Today, entrepreneurs have set their sights on Nevada as a technological and infrastructure hub. Venture capitalist Tony Hsieh revolutionized marketing, employee relations, and customer service as CEO of Zappos, the Nevada-based online shoe-seller. In 2016, Elon Musk opened Gigafactory near Reno to produce lithium ion batteries for his Tesla electric car company. Nevada continues to expand its economy, with blossoming industry leaders in drone technology, solar power, distribution facilities, data centers, and more.

Economy

TOURISM AND GAMBLING

Tourism is by far the state's largest employer, accounting for 32 percent of all jobs; in southern Nevada it's closer to 40 percent. More than 400,000 casino workers cater to Nevada's 54 million tourists; both numbers have rebounded significantly since the Great Recession. Given these statistics, it's amazing to think that the state Commission on Tourism wasn't created until 1983. In 2016 Nevada's casinos accepted $114 billion in wagers.

MINING

Mining is Nevada's second-largest revenue-generating industry. At $1,260 per ounce, gold is the most sought-after nowadays, even in the Silver State. Nevada's mines annually ferret 5.6 million ounces of the yellow metal from the earth. More gold has been mined in Nevada in the past five years than was mined at the height of the California, Comstock, and Klondike rushes combined. The Klondike, Goldfield, and Montana mines produced 5 million ounces between 1900 and 1910, and the Comstock produced 8.3 million ounces of gold between 1864 and 1889.

Silver production is significant as well, but with prices trending not much above $20 per ounce, silver production is merely a byproduct in the search for its flashier cousin, with production in the range of 22-28 million ounces annually. This is a reversal of production in the Comstock Lode era, when gold was a byproduct of the silver mining. Just under 200 million ounces of silver were wrested from the Comstock. Today Nevada has just one mine, the Coeur-Rochester mine near Lovelock, that is primarily a silver mine.

Nevada is the country's largest gold and silver producer, producing a whopping 74 percent of the nation's gold and 11 percent of the world's gold each year. If Nevada were a separate country, it would be the third-largest gold-producing nation in the world after South Africa and Australia. North America's largest gold mine, the Barrick Gold Strike Mine north of Carlin, is one of several Nevada mines that each produce over 1 million ounces of gold every year.

AGRICULTURE

Nevada farms produce alfalfa and to a lesser extent wheat and barley, alfalfa seed, garlic, onions, and potatoes. Hay crops as a whole account for well over half of all harvested acreage in Nevada. There are approximately 1,700 cattle ranches in Nevada. Cattle production dropped dramatically in the 1980s, primarily because of reduced red meat consumption, but it has seen a resurgence since 1990, with about 500,000 head of cattle in production. Nevada ranchers are largely dependent on public grazing lands, primarily federal Bureau of Land Management lands, for at least part of their forage needs.

Nevada is also home to 95,000 sheep and 7,500 hogs, figures that have decreased dramatically from previous years. In the early 1930s Nevada had 1.3 million sheep, but sheep ranching declined as it became less profitable.

Local Culture

DEMOGRAPHICS

According to official statistics, in 2000 Nevada's population topped 2 million for the first time, and in 2018 it reached 3 million. The ninth most sparsely populated state, Nevada is nevertheless the third most urbanized—94 percent of residents live in cities. Las Vegas's Clark County is home to 2.3 million souls, while the population of Reno's Washoe County tops 440,000.

NATIVE AMERICANS

At the beginning of the 19th century, four groups of Native Americans lived in what is now Nevada. The small population of Washoe lived in the west-central region around Carson City, Lake Tahoe, and the eastern Sierras. The Northern Paiute made a large section of western Nevada their home, ranging from today's Humboldt County to Esmeralda County. The Southern Paiute occupied all of Clark County and the southeastern section of Lincoln County. The Shoshone were found in the east, from Elko County to southern Nye County.

These groups shared many customs and lifestyles. They spent so much of their time gathering and preparing food in the harsh environment that they had little time for war. The only time the small bands gathered into larger groups was for cooperative hunting or harvesting efforts or to skirmish with neighbors or encroachers; otherwise each band, a single-family unit or a group of no more than 100 individuals, was mostly autonomous. The resources of the local environment tended to dictate the size of bands. The Pyramid Lake Paiute, for example, were a large group with abundant resources. Its chiefs were famous, and the band was able to hold its own against the more warlike Pitt River bands from the north. Bands had headmen as well as shamans, who were found to possess powers of prophecy, healing, or magic.

Family Life

Native Americans enjoyed extended family arrangements, usually including the maternal grandparents. Variations might consist of two wives and a husband (the second woman was adopted if she found herself alone through widowhood or some other reason) or two husbands and a wife.

The never-ending search for food dictated daily and seasonal activities. Native Americans had little need for shelter (except for shade) or clothing (except for a breechcloth and skirt) in the summer. In winter they stayed in a kind of tepee with a framework of poles and branches; grass or reeds made up the roof, which had a hole in it for smoke from the fire. In winter they wore animal-skin robes, hats, moccasins, skirts, or sage-bark sandals and caps, and slept under rabbit-fur blankets.

Mostly nomadic, they had to carry everything during their frequent moves; a sophisticated basket technology evolved. Woven from split willow twigs, grasses, and cattail reeds (tule), conical baskets were used for transporting possessions or served as women's caps. Natives even developed large clay pots for cooking and boiling water, using pitch from piñon pines to keep them from leaking. Decoys and snares fashioned from willow and tule twigs aided hunting. Cradleboards attained a level of art. Properly shaped stones provided mortar-and-pestle tools for grinding, and drums, rattles, and flutes were used. The Indians were particularly ingenious in their knowledge and use of local plants. Everything had a use, and everything was sacred. They also fished and hunted rabbits, squirrels, antelope, mountain sheep, deer, ducks, and birds.

Religion

Spirits embodied everything in nature, animate or inanimate. Fire, fog, even rocks were alive and required an empathy equal to that for a wolf (a good influence), a coyote (a bad influence), or a wife or husband (either). Dreams, omens, seasonal cycles and unnatural variations, prayers, and the powers of the medicine man all figured into Native American spirituality, which was as integral a part of their daily routine as eating and sleeping.

Contact

The first Anglo-Europeans who came into contact with the Shoshone, Paiute, and Washoe Indians considered them to be only slightly better off than wildlife. They had no possessions, no houses, and hardly any clothes. The Native Americans were on peaceful, even friendly terms with the first trappers and traders, but the coming wagon trains quickly turned the Indians and the whites against each other. The pioneers' migrating cattle ate all the Indians' grasses, loggers cut their sacred piñon pines, and large areas were denuded of all the living things that the native people had used to survive. Although the Nevada Paiute and Shoshone had no real organizational structure for waging war, and Nevada histories usually only describe the largest armed confrontations (Pyramid Lake, Paradise Valley, Black Rock Desert, and Battle Mountain), there were many skirmishes with some loss of life on both sides. Within 25 years of the first wave of nonnative migrants, the Indian spirit had been broken, self-reliance was shattered, and dependence became their way of life.

Reservations

"The early history of Indian reservations in America is generally one of confusion and mismanagement," E. A. Hoaglund writes in *Washoe, Paiute, and Shoshone Indians of Nevada*. A near total lack of direction, financing, facilities, equipment, education, understanding of the Native American experience, and compassion for their cultural dislocation colored a full 70 years of relations. The reservations were usually too small, the land too poor, and the populations too large.

In 1887 the Dawes Act tried to disenfranchise the reservations in an attempt to ease assimilation into nonnative culture. In June 1934 the Indian Reorganization Act began a process of redressing this tragic part of American history by giving more money, land, cattle, and irrigation systems to the reservations. Self-government was made official by way of Tribal Councils. The 1978 Indian Self-Determination Act addressed the need for economic development. Slowly, the federal government has untangled the complex questions of land issues and begun to show some responsiveness to the simple question of human rights.

A good way to observe Indian traditions and customs in action is to attend a powwow put on by one of the tribes.

BASQUES

The Basque people are the oldest ethnic group in Europe. Evidence of their continuous existence dates to 5000 BC, a full 3,000 years before Indo-European people arrived. There are roughly 3 million European Basques, their homeland occupying the Pyrenees mountain region of France and Spain.

Basques migrated to Argentina and many made their way north, especially in the 1850s to the California gold rush. Following the silver exodus east to Washoe, they mined in Nevada until that work dried up. They then returned to a skill familiar from the old country: sheepherding. Basque sheepherders readily took to the pastoral life of the American West, particularly in northern Nevada. For nearly 50 years, Basque ranchers ran the largest bands of sheep in the country. They imported relatives, friends, and neighbors to herd sheep. Contract shepherds often took payment in lambs and sheep, with which they started their own ranches. Herders remained in the backcountry alone with their flocks all through the summer. It was an arduous and lonely life in a strange and barren country, but a prevalent aspect of the Basque national character is the ability to endure: Hard work, loneliness, and physical strength are part of the measure of their self-worth.

Sheepherding was seasonal, and while many shepherds remained on the ranches in the off-season, others drifted into towns and the hotels run by fellow Basques. These boardinghouses quickly became the center of Basque culture in rural Nevada.

Oso Garria!

The Basque hotel is a legacy that endures. The Winnemucca Hotel, for example, is the second oldest in the state. Gardnerville's Overland Hotel dates from 1909, Elko's Star Hotel from 1911, and the Ely Hotel is from the 1920s. No traveler to Nevada should leave without experiencing a meal at a Basque hotel.

A Basque meal, especially dinner, is never taken lightly, nor is it a light meal. It consists of a multitude of courses served family-style: soup, salad, beans or pasta, French fries, and usually an entrée of chicken, beef, or lamb. Make sure to try a picon punch, made with Amer Picon (a liqueur), grenadine, and a shot of brandy. Few northern and central Nevada towns are without Basque restaurants, where you're guaranteed a fine filling meal and a social experience. Raise your glass of picon punch and toast the house: Oso garria!

The Basque festival is the other enduring cultural tradition. Festivities include mass, folk dancing, strength and endurance competitions, a sheep rodeo, and the consumption of enormous quantities of red wine from the bota (wineskin). The Basques are known for their world-class wood chopping, and contestants compete in areas of strength and will. Soka and tira are the popular tugs-of-war.

Pelota is handball, of which jai alai is an offspring. Weightlifting and carrying are the real crowd pleasers. Annual festivals take place in most of the larger towns in northern Nevada; check the events section of Nevada magazine in summer.

THE ARTS

People have been creating Nevada-themed art for longer than Nevada has been a state. In fact, Native Americans who haunted the sunbaked sandstone of the south and the crystal lakes of the north used sharp stones to gouge records of their never-ending search for food well before Columbus. Still, it's true that Nevada got a late start in developing European-influenced art. Few miners speeding to stake claims on the latest silver strike bothered to bring their easels and watercolors; Basque sheepherders, concerned with eking out a living, gave little thought to focal points and forced perspective.

But the state's artistic environment has been expanding exponentially. Once those pioneers found a moment of spare time, they found inspiration everywhere they looked. Nevada still boasts unspoiled views of mountains, rivers, canyons, and forests, as well as art deco, beaux arts, modern, and classical architecture and signage to tempt today's painters and photographers. Many who have flocked to the state contribute to the thriving arts districts that serve as centerpieces for impressive urban renewal projects in both Las Vegas and Reno. Reno's Riverwalk district and Las Vegas's 18b arts district feature contemporary eateries and stylish boutiques in addition to bohemian galleries, studios, and artists' lofts.

Ely is the leader but certainly not the only Nevada city to chronicle its history through an ambitious series of historical murals throughout the town. In southern Nevada, Boulder City has commissioned not only several murals but also brass statues depicting raptors, playing children, and mythical figures. Henderson commissioned J. Seward Johnson to cast bronzes of everyday life in the bedroom community along Green Valley Parkway. Johnson's works include children frolicking with a garden hose to beat the summer heat (in front of the Green Valley Library), friends on their way to play a set of tennis, and a mother stooping to tie her daughter's shoelace.

Other artists didn't wait around for

municipal patronage. Michael Heizer has spent 30 years creating *City* near Garden Valley. This massive undertaking, like Heizer's *Double Negative* near Overton, is one of several striking pieces of sculpture (or, if you prefer Robert Smithson's term, "earthwork") in Nevada. *City* uses native boulders and caliche, among other materials, to depict a juxtaposition of ancient and modern sites. The unbounded souls who prowl the Black Rock Desert for Burning Man also have felt the urge for self-expression. Among the most notable is Jim Denevan, who "draws" geometric designs by dragging fencing behind a small plane. Many of Denevan's pictures (think crop circles in the sand) cover dozens of square miles. It was around here too that the muse told "the Guru of Gerlach," Doobie Williams, to adopt a dusty back road, name it Guru Road, and adorn it with witticisms, earthy wisdom, and Elvis tributes.

Nevada's history and eclectic citizenry have provided raw material for writers and poets as well. More than one masterpiece has been set in or focused on Nevada: Hunter S. Thompson's *Fear and Loathing in Las Vegas,* Mark Twain's *Roughing It,* Nicholas Pileggi's *Casino,* and *Moon Nevada,* to name a few.

Essentials

Transportation

GETTING THERE
Flying to Southern Nevada

As befitting major tourist destinations, the big airports in Las Vegas and Reno are convenient and efficient. More than 47 million passengers moved through Las Vegas's **McCarran International Airport** (LAS, 5757 Wayne Newton Blvd., 702/261-5211, www.mccarran.com) in 2016. Only seven airports in the world boast more takeoffs and landings than McCarran.

Terminal 1 welcomes most domestic flights, while Terminal 3 is for international traffic and a few domestic travelers. If you're flying in for a vacation anywhere in Nevada, consider touching down in Las Vegas first. McCarran International is one of the easiest airports in the country to access, and with a little research and planning, it can also be one of the cheapest. Reno is an hour by air from Las Vegas. The airport provides easy transfers to the Las Vegas Strip using **shuttle vans, buses,** and **rental cars.** Limousines are available curbside for larger groups.

To ensure plenty of time for checking luggage, passing the security checkpoint, and arrival at your departure gate, plan to arrive at least two hours before takeoff—three hours for international flights. If you don't download to your phone or print your boarding pass before arrival, you can use self-service kiosks and skip the line at the counter. If you are flying out of Terminal 1's A, B, or C gate, you can walk to your boarding area. D Gate is in a separate location; arrive there via monorail. Follow the signs.

Citizens Area Transit routes 108 and 109 service Terminal 1. The bus stop is on level 0, down one level from baggage claim and across the pedestrian crossing. Look for the covered Regional Transportation Commission shelter. Route 108 runs up Swenson Street. Though it never quite reaches Las Vegas Boulevard, it comes close at the corner of Paradise Road and West Sahara Avenue. But you can connect with the Las Vegas monorail at several stops for Strip access. If you're headed downtown, take the bus to the end of the line. Route 109 runs east of route 108 up Maryland Parkway. To get to the Strip, you have to transfer at the large cross streets onto westbound buses that cross the Strip. There are stops at Charleston Boulevard, Sahara Avenue, Desert Inn Road, Flamingo Road, and Tropicana Avenue. Route 109 also ends up at the Downtown Transportation Center.

The bus stop at Terminal 3 is on level 2, up the escalator from baggage claim. Exit the terminal building and cross the pedestrian crossing. The shelter is at the Departures curb across from door 44. The Westcliff Airport Express stops here as well as at Terminal 1. It stops on the Strip at Tropicana Avenue (Excalibur, New York New York, Tropicana, and MGM Grand casinos) and downtown's Casino Center. The Centennial Airport Express also picks up at Terminal 3, stopping on the Strip at Spring Mountain Road (Wynn, Palazzo, and Treasure Island casinos) and downtown, near the D casino.

Bus fare is $2 for a single ride, $6 for two hours, $8 for 24 hours. Children under age 5 are free when riding with a guardian.

You can take a **Gray Line** airport shuttle van to your Strip downtown hotel ($18.50 round-trip). These shuttles run continuously, leaving the airport about every 15 minutes. You'll find the shuttles outside the baggage claim area. You don't need reservations from the airport, but you will need reservations

---

Previous: sign welcoming visitors to the Little A'Le'Inn in Rachel; gambling sign on Fremont Street in Las Vegas.

from your hotel to return to the airport. Call 702/739-5700 to reserve a spot on an airport-bound shuttle 24 hours in advance.

Except for peak periods, **taxis** are numerous and quite readily available, and drivers are good sources of scuttlebutt (not always accurate) and entertainment suggestions (not always wholesome). Of course, Las Vegas operates at peak loads most of the time, so if you're not in a taxi zone right in front of one of the busiest hotels, it might be tough to get one. Cab companies are adapting, however, and visitors now can hail rides on apps such as Curb. The 16 companies plying the streets of Las Vegas charge $3.50 for the flag drop and $2.76 per mile.

A taxi ride from McCarran International Airport to the Strip (15 minutes) runs about $25; from the airport to downtown (25 minutes) about $45, including the $2 surcharge assessed for pickups from the airport, and there is a $3 credit card processing fee. You can join the taxi line right outside the airport terminal. **Lyft** and **Uber** can get you there for about half the price under normal demand conditions; however, both Uber and Lyft employ surge pricing, which can easily double the fare during peak usage. You'll have to hoof it to the special pickup and drop-off area in the airport parking garage.

The **Laughlin/Bullhead International Airport** (IFP, 2550 Laughlin View Dr., Bullhead City, AZ, 928/754-2134) is on the east side of the Colorado River. It is a full-service regional airport with daily American Airlines flights to Phoenix. The airport also welcomes commercial charter flights from more than 100 cities arranged through Harrah's Laughlin and the Riverside Casino.

Flying to Northern Nevada

Every year, about 3.7 million people pass through the 23 passenger gates at **Reno-Tahoe International Airport** (RNO, 2001 E. Plumb Ln., 775/328-6400). Alaska, Allegiant, American, Delta, JetBlue, Southwest, United, and Volaris transport passengers between Reno and West Coast and Midwest destinations, including non-stop flights to Chicago, Dallas, Denver, Las Vegas, Los Angeles, Phoenix, Salt Lake City, San Diego, San Francisco, and Seattle. Conveniently located, the airport is only a 10-minute drive from downtown, right off US 395 (a.k.a. I-580) south to the airport exit.

Arrive at least 90 minutes before your flight is scheduled to depart.

The city bus service, **RTC Ride** (775/348-7433) provides weekday-only service from the airport to downtown via route 19, leaving from the north end of the median just outside the exit doors from baggage claim.

Reno's complimentary **hotel shuttles** run from about 5am to midnight, stopping along the curb outside the D doors north of baggage claim, with stops at the Atlantis, Circus Circus, Grand Sierra, Harrah's, John Ascuaga's Nugget, the Peppermill, Sands, Silver Legacy, and more. Contact the hotel directly. A few companies staff booths near the terminal's A, B, C, and D doors, offering paid shuttle service from the airport: **Airport Mini Bus** (775/786-3700), **North Lake Tahoe Express** (866/216-5222), and **South Tahoe Airporter** (866/898-2463).

Eleven **taxi companies** service the Reno area, with pickup at the airport just outside the D doors near baggage claim. A trip from the airport to the university campus or the Virginia Street casinos is about $15. The Reno airport's rideshare pickup location is right outside baggage claim, in the North Lot. Rates are about the same as for a cab.

If your itinerary calls for mostly backcountry adventures in the mostly rural northeast quadrant of the state, **Skywest Airlines** (775/738-5138), the Delta connector, operates two flights daily to and from Salt Lake City from **Elko Regional Airport** (975 Terminal Way, 775/777-7190) on Mountain City Highway at the west end of town. **El Aero Services** (775/738-7123) offers charter fixed-wing and helicopter service out of the airport for business and leisure travelers. Historical artifacts and black-and-white photos and captions line the wall behind the airport's luggage carousel. Services include a restaurant, ATM, vending machines, business center with free charging stations and work tables, and **Avis** (775/738-4426), **Enterprise** (775/738-2899), and **Hertz** (775/738-5620) car-rental counters. A computer dispatch system ensures prompt pickups from the airport or anywhere else around town from **Elko Taxi** (1104 W. Main St., 775/738-1400).

Train

Amtrak runs cross-country rail service on the transcontinental line laid through Nevada in 1869. Its California Zephyr passes right through the middle of downtown Reno (blocking traffic twice a day for 5-10 minutes). The train stops in Reno once daily in each direction, heading west to Emeryville, in the east San Francisco Bay area, and east through Salt Lake City, Denver, and Omaha to Chicago. Nevada stops include Reno, Winnemucca, and Elko. Amtrak also operates several buses daily between Reno and Sacramento, to connect with other trains there. There is no direct service from Reno to Las Vegas. In fact, no Amtrak trains stop in Las Vegas. If you need to rail it between Reno and Las Vegas, you'll have to take the Zephyr to Salt Lake then a bus the rest of the way.

Bus

Greyhound bus routes connect terminals in Las Vegas, Winnemucca, Wendover, Reno, Lovelock, Elko, and Battle Mountain. Popular routes into the downtown **Las Vegas terminal** (200 S. Main St., 702/383-9792) originate in Los Angeles, Phoenix, San Francisco, and Salt Lake City, with stops in between and connections to cities farther afield.

Buses arrive in **Reno** (155 Stevenson St.) every few hours from San Francisco, and there are two or three departures between Reno and Las Vegas each day. Most other routes require transfers in northern California, Salt Lake City, or through another hub.

Car

Five main roads crisscross Nevada, three east-west and two north-south. **I-80** takes the long northern route west across the shoulder of Nevada from Wendover through Reno and into California. **US 50** cuts across the shorter waist of the state from Ely and joins up with I-80 at Fernley, then splits off to Reno or Carson City. **US 6** travels along with US 50 from the Utah line to Ely before cutting south to Tonopah and out toward Fresno in California. **US 95** zigzags south, then southwest, then south, and finally southeast for nearly 700 miles from McDermitt at the north edge of the state to Laughlin at the south. **US 93** travels between Jackpot and Boulder City for 500 miles in a fairly straight line.

Reno is 15 miles east of the California border. The Reno-Sparks area is served by two major highways: **I-80,** which crosses the country from San Francisco to New York, bisects the region from east to west; and **US 395** runs from southeastern Oregon briefly through Nevada (from Reno to Topaz Lake), then heads south through California down to near Los Angeles. Be aware that severe winter storms can make road travel treacherous, especially through mountain passes. And road closures due to inclement weather are not uncommon in winter.

Downtown **Las Vegas** crowds around the junction of I-15, US 95, and US 93. **I-15** runs from Los Angeles (272 miles from Las Vegas, 4-5 hours) to Salt Lake City (419 miles from Las Vegas, 6-8 hours). **US 95** meanders from Yuma, Arizona, on the Mexican border, up the western side of Nevada, through Coeur D'Alene, Idaho, all the way up to British Columbia, Canada. **US 93** starts in Phoenix and hits Las Vegas 285 miles later, then merges with I-15 for a while only to fork off and shoot straight up the east side of Nevada and continue due north all the way to Alberta, Canada. **I-215/515** makes an oval around the Las Vegas Valley, alleviating some traffic snarls.

Southwest Driving Distances

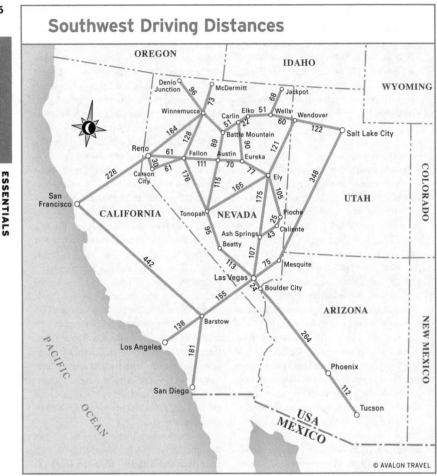

© AVALON TRAVEL

GETTING AROUND
Bus

Citizen Area Transit (CAT, 702/228-7433, www.rtcsnv.com) runs 39 routes all over Las Vegas Valley. Fares are $2 for a single ride, $6 for two hours, $8 for 24 hours daily, free under age 5 when riding with a guardian. Access the route guide online for stops and times. Bus service is pretty comprehensive, but even the express routes with fewer stops take a long time to get anywhere.

RTC Ride (775/348-7433, $2, 24-hour pass $5) serves the Reno/Sparks area with 26 routes that operate approximately 6am-11pm. The most popular routes run 24 hours; others, such as routes to ski areas or business centers, run less frequently depending on the season, time, and day of the week. The main terminals are at 4th Street in Reno and Centennial Plaza in Sparks. Routes and schedules are available in the Regional Transportation Commission's Bus Book. RTC Ride bus route 19 operates weekdays between the airport and the downtown Reno terminal. Travelers to other destinations can connect at the terminal.

Car

Your own car is the best way to get around the state. Buses don't reach half the state. Distances are long, and services are few and far between. Even the good city bus routes take a long time, and taxis are expensive; with a car you can find yourself on a lot of gravel, if you're adventurous, and if your steed is trusty you can really get out there. That's the idea, isn't it? If you do plan on some off-asphalt exploring, remember that desert driving is hot, dusty, bumpy, and hard on tires and suspensions. Make sure your ride has ample fuel and fluids, a spare tire and jack, and a recent tune-up. Carry plenty of spare water (for both your traveling party and your radiator), a flashlight and flares, spare belts and hoses, a tool kit, and a shovel; baling wire, duct tape, and superglue often come in handy. Don't forget a rag or two and a pair of gloves. The passes in, around, and through Lake Tahoe function as wind tunnels and often require snow chains.

Commonsense maintenance consciousness is required on the road. If the car gets hot or overheats, stop for a while to cool it off. Never open the radiator cap if the engine is steaming. After it has sat, squeeze the top radiator hose to see if there's any pressure in it; if there isn't, it's safe to open. Never pour water into a hot radiator—you could crack your block. If you start to smell rubber, your tires are overheating, and that's a good way to have a blowout. Stop and let them cool off. In winter in the high country, a can of silicone lubricant such as WD-40 will unfreeze door locks, dry off humid wiring, and keep your hinges in shape.

Updates on Nevada road conditions are available by calling **Road Condition Report** (877/687-6237).

More and more Las Vegas casinos are charging nonguests for parking, raising the ire of locals. Rates are comparable or less than those charged by most California resort hotels, and you can still find free parking most nights if you're willing to walk a few blocks.

RULES OF THE ROAD

The speed limit on most of the interstate and U.S. highways (I-80, I-15, US 95, US 93, plus a few state roads) outside of the cities and towns is 75 mph. On I-80 it's 80 mph most of the way between Fernley and Lovelock. You can drive 65 mph on the interstates in Reno and Las Vegas. Most passers-through drive 80-85 mph without worrying about being noticed by the highway patrol. Since the superhighways are two lanes in each direction, road courtesy isn't much of a problem; anyone wanting to go faster than you can zip around on the left.

Passing is generally not a problem on the two-lane highways through rural Nevada; the solid and dotted lines are well maintained, and long straight stretches through the valleys are conducive to safe zipping.

There are only a few curvy roads and long climbs up mountains on main roads in Nevada, and here passing can be a problem. The good news is that turnouts are common. The bad news is that some flatlanders and RV drivers don't know what turnouts are for. If you're pulling a heavy load, are nervous about mountain driving, or just have a slowpoke car, pull over and let the drivers behind you pass.

CAR RENTAL

Most of the large car-rental companies have desks at the **McCarran Rent-A-Car Center** (702/261-6001). Dedicated McCarran shuttles leave the main terminal from outside exit doors 10 and 11 about every five minutes bound for the Rent-A-Car Center. International airlines and a few domestic flights arrive at Terminal 3. Here, the shuttle picks up outside doors 51 through 58. Taxicabs are also available at the center. Companies represented at the center include **Advantage** (800/777-9377), **Alamo** (800/462-5266), **Avis** (800/331-1212), **Budget** (800/922-2899), **Dollar** (800/800-4000), **E-Z** (800/277-5171), **Enterprise** (800/736-7222), **Hertz** (800/654-3131), **National** (800/227-7368), **Payless** (800/729-5377), **Thrifty** (800/367-2277), and **Zipcar** (866/494-7227). Others will pick up customers at the center.

All the standard rental car companies operate out of the Reno airport, as well, which makes it convenient if you're flying in and out, though you'll have to join the throngs there if you're not. If you don't want to deal with the airport, most of the rental car companies also have offices in town. Rent a Car Now.Com (www.rentacarnow.com/city/reno.html) offers a convenient service that allows you to compare models, rates, and locations.

When you call around to rent, ask what the *total* price of your car is going to be. With sales tax, use tax, airport fees, and other miscellaneous charges, you can easily pay as much as 60 percent over and above the quoted rate. One recent online search found a six-day economy rental in Las Vegas for $76.28; fees and taxes added another $75.26! Typical shoulder-season weekly rates in Las Vegas run from about $150 total for economy and compact cars to $280 for vans and $450 for luxury sedans. Prices increase by one-third or more during major conventions and holiday periods.

Check with your insurance agent at home about coverage on rental cars; often your insurance covers rental cars (minus your deductible), and you won't need the rental company's. If you rent a car on most credit cards, you get automatic rental-car insurance coverage. Las Vegas rental-car rates change as fast as hotel room rates, depending on the season, day of the week, and convention traffic.

RVs

Travelers using Las Vegas as their base or departure point can rent virtually any type of recreational vehicle, from conversion vans to 40-foot Class A rolling mansions.

El Monte RV has two locations in southern Nevada (3800 Boulder Hwy., 702/269-8000; and 13001 Las Vegas Blvd. S., Henderson, 702/269-0704 or 888/337-2214). They deal primarily in Class C "cab-over" models and Class A rock-star tour bus behemoths. Base prices for the Class C cab-overs start at about $1,600-2,000 per week, but miles—bundled in 100-mile packages—and incidentals such

as kitchenware, pillows, coffeemakers, and toasters can easily increase the total by 25 percent. El Monte's big dog, an AC37 Slideout that sleeps five, goes for more than $3,000 per week before mileage and extras.

Cruise America (551 N. Gibson Rd., Henderson, 702/565-2224) touts its exclusively cab-over fleet as having more ready-to-use sleep space and maneuverability. Its RVs range 19-30 feet, suitable for parties of 3-7 people. Seven-night rentals average $1,200-1,700. The company adds a mileage estimate (at about 35 cents per mile) at the time of rental and adjusts the charges based on actual miles driven when you return the vehicle. Common extra charges include linens, kitchen equipment, and generator use.

Jucy (5895 Boulder Hwy., 800/650-4180) rents conversion vans with two double beds, mini fridge, gas cooktop, and sink for about $800 per week, all the necessaries included. **Sahara RV Center** (1518 Scotland Ln., 702/384-8818) makes things simple, with daily peak-season rates of $190-220 for Class C RVs, $365-425 for Class A. Three-day minimums apply. Rates are about 20 percent less off-season, but prices and minimums rise during holidays and special events like NASCAR weekend and Burning Man.

Reno RV renters have more limited options. **El Monte RV** (2575 Kietzke Ln., 775/825-0100) is the best bet. It offers a fleet similar to and rates identical to the Las Vegas stores. Other options include **Compass Campers** (866/425-0307), with cab-overs in the $1,900-2,100 range and Class A options starting at $2,700.

TOURS

Several companies offer the chance to see the sights of **Las Vegas** by bus, helicopter, airplane, or off-road vehicle. The ubiquitous **Gray Line** (702/739-7777 or 877/333-6556, www.graylinelasvegas.com) offers air-conditioned motor coach tours of the city by night as well as tours of Hoover Dam and the Grand Canyon. **Vegas Tours** (866/218-6877, www.vegastours.com) has a full slate of outdoor, adventure, and other tours. Tours of the Grand Canyon and other nearby state and national parks are available as well. **Pink Jeep Tours** (702/895-6778 or 888/900-4480, www.pinkjeeptourslasvegas.com) takes visitors in rugged but cute and comfortable 10-passenger ATVs to such sites as Red Rock Canyon, Valley of Fire, and Hoover Dam. For history, nature, and entertainment buffs looking for a more focused adventure, themed tours are on the rise in Las Vegas, with offerings such as **Haunted Vegas Tours** (702/677-6499, www.hauntedvegastours.com) and the **Las Vegas Mob Tour** (www.vegasmobtour.com).

Several tours explore the beauty and history of the **Reno/Lake Tahoe** area. The knowledgeable guides at **Sierra Comstock Tours** (775/997-8649) lead small groups on sojourns around the region, stopping for a couple hours in Virginia City and Lake Tahoe during its signature seven-hour tours. Other themed tours focus on Native American history, gourmet food, shopping, and railroad/boomtown history. More active tours are the specialty of **Sierra Adventures** (775/323-8928): Peavine Peak single-track biking, Truckee River rafting, ballooning, motorized hang gliding, horseback riding, and more. Cost per person is based on group size and includes pickup from area hotels. The **Lake Tahoe Visitors Authority** (https://tahoesouth.com/tours) publishes a comprehensive list of lake-based tours ranging from sleigh rides to winter and summer wilderness survival courses.

Recreation

Some two-thirds of Nevada is owned by the federal government, and pretty much everything that's not used for secret research or weapons testing can be used for some recreational purpose.

STATE PARKS

The **Nevada Division of State Parks** (775/684-2770, http://parks.nv.gov) manages and maintains 24 parks in four regions: Carson-Tahoe, Fallon, Panaca, and Las Vegas. Entrance fees are generally $7 per car, and camping fees are $14-17 per site. Discounted annual passes are available at the parks and by contacting the headquarters.

U.S. FOREST SERVICE LANDS

The **U.S. Forest Service** (775/331-6444, www.fs.fed.us/r4/htnf) oversees the **Humboldt-Toiyabe National Forest,** which encompasses all of Nevada and the far eastern edge of California. The "Humboldt" part of the name is in honor of German naturalist Baron Alexander von Humboldt. Although Humboldt never visited the area, he was something of a hero to the explorer John C. Frémont, who named the East Humboldt Mountain Range and the Humboldt River after him. *Toiyabe* is an ancient Shoshone word meaning "mountain." The Humboldt-Toiyabe is the largest forest on the U.S. mainland. The Forest Service's website contains information on the forest's archaeology, history, and geology; snowmobiling, hiking, biking, and horseback riding trails; camping locations; and wilderness areas.

NATIONAL PARKS

Great Basin National Park (775/234-7331, www.nps.gov/grba), administered by the National Park Service, is the only national park located exclusively in Nevada. It charges no entry fee, though guided group tours of Lehman Caves are offered for $8-10 per adult, with discounts for children and seniors. The park has various campsites available for $12-25.

A sliver of **Death Valley National Park** (760/786-3200, www.nps.gov/deva) cuts through Nevada. The $25 per-car entry fee is good for seven consecutive days. Camping at

Furnace Creek Campground is $22; it's $14-16 at most other campgrounds and free in a few at higher elevations. The below-sea-level campgrounds are open from mid-October to mid-April only, with extended seasons as the elevation rises.

OUTDOOR PURSUITS

Whether you prefer alpine lakes, desert washes, or expansive playas, you'll find ample opportunity to hike, bike, and ride on the state's extensive network of paths and trails. Nevada is a magnet for hunters, with a variety of waterfowl; big game and predator species such as mountain lions, elk, mule deer, and whitetails; and fur-bearing animals like mink, foxes, and bobcats. Southern Nevada attracts anglers with its rainbow trout, striped bass, catfish, and black crappie, while the northern half of the state offers white crappie, perch, walleye, and several species of trout.

Find information on seasons, licenses, limits, and more from the **Nevada Department of Wildlife** (800/576-1020, http://ndow.org).

Lee Canyon (6725 Lee Canyon Rd., 702/385-2754, www.skilasvegas.com/winter) is the Las Vegas area's go-to (only) ski resort, while Reno and Lake Tahoe visitors who want to stay in Nevada have their choice between **Diamond Peak** (1210 Ski Way, Incline Village, 775/832-1177) and **Mt. Rose Ski Tahoe** (22222 Mt. Rose Hwy., Reno, 775/849-0707, www.skirose.com). Of course, anyone in northwestern Nevada has a choice among dozens of some of the best powder in the country just across the state line in California's Sierra Nevada. For a unique experience, **Ruby Mountain Heli-Experience** (775/753-6867, www.helicopterskiing.com) promises several runs per day over pristine powder in the beautifully rugged Ruby Mountains.

Gambling

Gambling and Nevada are inseparable in the national consciousness. The state's reputation since casino gambling was legalized has been predicated on Americans' image of gambling: The media, authorities, moralists, and sore losers have accused the Silver State of being a haven for organized crime, petty criminals, vice run amok, and lowlifes in general. The height of the heat centered on the 20-year period from 1946, when Benjamin Siegel, Las Vegas's most notorious gangster, built the seminal Flamingo Hotel, to 1966, when Howard Hughes introduced corporate respectability. Since then, Nevada's image has taken a turn for the better. Sixty percent of the state's massive gambling revenues come from the losses of out-of-staters. Hospitality jobs account for 28 percent of employment in Nevada, and taxes on casino profits make up 45 percent of state general fund revenues. The indirect impact of massive gambling tourism on the state's economy is incalculable. It is the major reason Nevada has no state income tax.

THE QUESTION OF HONESTY

In this cash-crazy business, everyone is afraid of everyone. The casinos have always been afraid of cheating customers and dishonest dealers and have evolved some of the most sophisticated security and surveillance technology, not to mention some of the heaviest private muscle, this side of the military. As the benders, crimpers, hand muckers, and past-post artists of yesteryear have turned into today's sleight-of-hand artists, card counters, and computer-equipped players, the catwalks and one-way glass above the casino ceilings have given way to video cameras and recorders in addition to all the bosses in the pit, the house guards, and outside security contractors.

Nevada started with little to no regulation

of casinos when gambling was legalized in 1931, and it took more than 50 years to reach a middle ground where the regulation was sufficient to keep things honest but also allow the industry to prosper. The Nevada Gaming Control Board, by way of announced and unannounced inspections, owner and employee screening, and customer-complaint services, has dealt with the state government's two main fears. The first is the house cheating the state by underreporting the action, skimming cash, and various other nefarious scams. The second is the house cheating the players. The conventional wisdom is that with the astronomical number of people playing, the small amount of money that they're risking and losing, and the profits that are accruing, the casinos don't need to cheat players; indeed they'd be crazy if they did. They'd risk losing what amounts to a license to take money thanks to the house advantage.

CASINO PSYCHOLOGY

Millions of people sample the excitement and temptations of Las Vegas every year, and the number of visitors continues to grow. Inside the casinos are a dozen different table games and scores of gambling machines, free drinks, acres of dazzling lights, expert come-ons—in short, limitless choices designed to sweep you off your feet and empty your pockets. Decades of marketing history and a distinct mathematical disadvantage work against you. Every inch of neon, every cocktail waitress, every complimentary highball shares the same purpose: to confuse you, bemuse you, and infuse you with a sense of saloon-town recklessness. And that's where the house advantage kicks in.

The house, of course, holds the advantage in every game it offers. The house accrues this edge either by paying out winners less than the odds dictate (35-1 on a 37-1 single-number roulette bet, for example) or by charging players a fee when they win a zero-expectancy game (raking the pot in poker, or charging vigorish on sports bets). Dozens of books are available outlining optimal blackjack and live, tournament, and video poker strategies. Reading a few probably won't turn you into a professional gambler, but they can make the games more fun and your bankroll last as long as possible.

ATTITUDE

Don't ever let anyone tell you differently: In a casino, it absolutely *is* whether you win or lose. You can beat the casino, but not with any of a thousand superstitions or "systems"; not with being cool, knowing all the rituals, or looking like James Bond; not even with an above-average degree of competence at the games. The only way most of us will ever turn a significant profit is to get very lucky in the short term and quit before we give it all back.

The gambling professionals (there are maybe a few thousand true pros, defined as people who make their entire living at gambling, mostly in Las Vegas) are part mathematician, part accountant, part actor, and part psychologist. They play high-level blackjack or Texas hold 'em; they pounce on progressive video poker machines when the meter goes positive; they capitalize on every tiny advantage; and sometimes, they cheat. They subscribe to the unlimited-bankroll school, which holds that "money management" is a crock. They take the big losses in stride and the big wins for granted. They eat, sleep, and dream gambling theory; they spend all their time in casinos; they carry a lot of cash and flash it when necessary; they throw big bucks at small edges; and sooner than later they publish books about how to win at gambling, where the real money is.

The rest of us are rank amateurs. We're supposed to be in it for the fun, the recreation value, and to some extent the dream of the once-in-a-lifetime jackpot although that's only possible at bad-odds games such as keno and slots, which take your money only a bit more slowly than a pickpocket. For us it's about spending the same money on gambling that we'd use to buy tickets to a ballgame, a concert, or an amusement park. It's about maximizing our vacation budgets by taking advantage of the rock-bottom room, food, beverage, and entertainment prices in Nevada. It's about risking our gambling bankrolls for the excitement and adrenaline of the casino, the camaraderie with fellow players.

In this case, the way to play is to set a limit and not go over it. Never play with money that you can't afford to lose; that's one of the sure signs of gambling addiction. And never try to chase your losses—another sign of the onset of problematic or compulsive gambling. Be a good loser, be a good winner, have some fun, and tip your dealers and waitresses. Oh, and good luck.

GAMBLING 101

Though it has lost some of its shininess recently, thanks to Nevada's great shows and restaurants and other states legalizing casinos, gambling is still a big reason people come to Nevada. Dream of winning big but expect to lose, and make it a goal to lose only a certain amount. Set aside a certain amount of money each day for gambling, and stop when it's gone. Remember, the only way to end a gambling session with a small fortune is to start with a large one. Here's how to play Nevada's most popular games.

Baccarat and Mini-Baccarat

Baccarat is played with eight decks of cards. It tends to be a high-stakes game, with minimums starting at $20. It's usually played in an upscale area of the casino, with dealers wearing tuxedos. Before cards are dealt by the players, players bet on the player or the banker, and each gets two cards. Aces are worth one point, face cards are worth zero, and others are face value. Depending on the totals of the first two cards, either the player, the banker, or both may draw a third. The hand closest to nine is the winner.

Mini-baccarat is played at a blackjack-style table with smaller minimum bets. It's played like baccarat except the dealer deals the cards. Wagers can be made on the player, the banker, or for a tie.

Big Six Wheel

The Big Six Wheel is the game you are least likely to win. Looking like a big carnival wheel with dollar bills inserted, it offers players a chance to bet $1 or more on $1, $2, $5, $10, and $20 symbols. You may also place a bet on the joker and house symbols. If your number comes up after the spin, you win that amount. In the unlikely event you happen to hit a joker or house logo, it pays 40 to 1. Big Six—along with keno—offers some of the worst odds in the casino.

Blackjack

Also called 21, blackjack is the most popular casino table game. The object is to have your cards total closer to 21 than the dealer, without going over. Players play against the house rather than against each other. It's one of the best games to play since your odds of winning are greater than if you play a slot machine, roulette, or most other games of chance. According to "optimal" strategy, if the dealer has 7, 8, 9, 10, or ace showing on his or her hand, it's advisable to hit (take additional cards) until your hand reaches 17 or more (or you bust). If the dealer has 2, 3, 4, 5, or 6 showing, stand (don't hit) unless your hand is 11 or less, because no matter what card comes, you can't bust. If you are dealt a pair (two 7s, two 9s) you can split them and play two separate hands if you choose. Again, the conventional wisdom is to split 8s and aces. This doubles your stake so that you have two separate bets on each hand. Usually you can "double down" on certain two-card hands. Always do this with 11, and almost always (unless the dealer shows an ace) with 10. Simply turn your hand over and place another stack of chips equal to your original wager. The dealer will give you one card to complete your hand. For example, you put a $25 green chip in the betting circle. You're dealt a 6 and a 5, and the dealer's "up" card is a 9. Flip your cards over, confidently put another greenie next to its sibling in the circle, and smile knowingly as the dealer "paints" your hand with the queen of diamonds, giving you 21.

Craps

Craps is one of the more social games in the casino, as groups of players gather around a table and whoop and scream as numbers come up on the dice. A shooter rolls two dice, and if the dice total 7 or 11 on this "come-out" roll, everyone who has a bet on Pass wins automatically, and everyone with a bet on Don't Pass loses. (Betting on the Don't Pass Line is the opposite of betting on the Pass Line; these pay 1-to-1 odds.) If the come-out roll is 2, 3, or 12, the shooter and all Pass bettors lose. Don't Pass bettors win on 2 or 3. Any other come-out roll becomes "the point," and a marker is placed in that position on the table. The shooter must then throw the point again before throwing a 7. If the shooter succeeds, Pass wins and Don't Pass loses. If the first roll is a 12, no one wins. After the come-out roll, players can also bet on Come and Don't Come. The next throw becomes the Come number, and a Come bet wins if the thrower throws that number before throwing a 7.

To fully understand Pass Lines, points, and other rules, it's best to take one of the instruction courses offered by the casinos. There are lots of betting options, which makes craps one of the more interesting table games. Laying or taking "odds" on or against the point is the only bet in the casino where the player gets fair odds. If the point is 4, there are three ways the shooter can make his point (1-3, 2-2, and 3-1) and six ways to lose by rolling a 7. An odds bet on four, therefore, pays 2 to 1 (or 6 to 3). Lots of places let you take 5x or even 20x odds, shrinking the casino's advantage even further. This refers to the maximum you can bet at the fair odds. At a 5x table, if you bet $5 on the pass line, you can bet up to $25 on the odds. In this case (say the point is 4), if you take full odds and the shooter rolls another 4 before he "sevens out," you'll win even money on your line bet ($5) and fair odds, or 2 to 1 on your odds bet ($50).

Keno

Keno may be played in the casino or in most Las Vegas coffee shops. Every 10-15 minutes a machine selects 20 out of 80 possible winning numbers. To play you must fill out a form for each game you wish to play and pick the numbers you hope will turn up on the keno board. A keno ticket is divided into numbers 1 to 40 on top and 41 to 80 on the bottom. You can pick 1 to 15 numbers on a straight ticket. Depending on what the payout table indicates, you could win $9 on a $1 bet if five out of eight numbers match, and more matching numbers mean more winnings. (The higher value you place on your bet, the more you win if your numbers come up.) A replay ticket simply uses the same numbers you played on the previous ticket. With a split ticket, you can bet different amounts on two or more groups of numbers. The amount you bet is divided among the number of groups you are playing. A keno runner will take your bet and return with your winning or losing ticket. Many people play $2 or $4 bets while they are having breakfast or lunch. The odds are heavily in favor of the house, but it can be a fun way to pass the time. There are myriad ways of picking numbers, splitting your bet, and so on. The rules are posted at all tables along with keno forms.

Let It Ride

Growing in popularity, Let It Ride can be played on tables with a dealer or at some video machines. Players play a basic five-card poker hand with the goal of getting the best possible hand. (In this game the dealer doesn't have a hand.) A player places three chips of equal value on the table and is dealt three cards. Two community cards are placed face down in the center. If you like your three cards you can place them under the first chip. If you are not happy with your cards, you can indicate to the dealer that you are taking back your bet by scraping the cards on the table toward you, or making a brushing motion with your hand. When all players have made a decision on their three cards, the dealer flips over the first community card, which counts as each player's fourth card. The procedure is repeated with the second community card, completing everyone's hand. A pair of 10s pays even money, two pairs 2 to 1, and so on. A royal flush pays 1,000 to 1.

Poker

Television has made poker one of the most popular casino games, and it's played much the same as you may play with your friends. But in Vegas the stakes are usually quite a bit higher. The dealer handles shuffling and dealing, and the house takes in a few dollars from each pot. Variations of poker include seven-card stud, Omaha, and Texas hold 'em; the latter, especially the no-limit variety, is the most popular variation. Any casino with a poker room deals this game—both in tournaments, where all you have to lose is your entry fee, and "ring games" (cash games), where your whole bankroll could be at stake on every hand.

Race and Sports Book

Sports betting in Vegas is huge. Bets on the Super Bowl alone account for $80 million annually. Most of the major casinos have large areas where players can bet on horse races and sports events. Horse and greyhound races are broadcast live from many tracks, and fans can root for their horse or dog on large-screen televisions.

Roulette

One of the simpler games, roulette features a big wheel with numbers 00 through 36 marked in red and black. It's possible to bet on 0 or 00 but neither counts as red or black, or odd or even, so they are colored green on the wheel. Players can bet on individual numbers, groups of numbers, red or black, or odd or even, small (1-18) or big (19-36). Choosing the right number pays at 35 to 1. Choosing a pair of numbers pays 17 to 1, a block of three pays 11 to 1, and so on. Experts advise against betting on 0, 00, 1, 2, and 3, which pay 5 to 1 and offer the worst odds on the table. Many gamblers say it is better to take part in fewer spins, place what you can afford to risk on an even money bet (odd-even or red-black), and walk away whether you win or lose. While that makes statistical sense and applies to any game where the odds are against you, it's not much fun. Roulette chips are purchased in stacks of 20, and when you buy your chips you tell the dealer if you want the value to be $1, $5, $20, and so on. Most roulette tables have a minimum value of each chip, such as $1.

Slots

Every casino has rows and rows of slot machines, and they've become even more popular since slot manufacturers introduced interactive games with bonus rounds based on popular games, TV shows, and other themes. Reel-type machines, where you line up one or more symbols to win, have also been modernized to include multiple pay lines and gimmicky bonus features. Penny and two-cent slots are becoming hugely popular, though most people bet multiple pennies on each of several lines, making them cost more than 1 cent per spin. Nickel, quarter, and dollar machines are still widely played. Casinos also set aside high-roller slot areas for those willing to pay $5 and up per spin. The odds of winning at a slot machine are set by the casino and vary widely depending on the establishment and machine. Your chance of hitting the jackpot at a quarter slot machine is likely to be 1 in 10,000 or smaller. The house advantage on slots ranges 2 to 25 percent. Generally, dollar machines pay back at a higher percentage than quarter or nickel machines, but you may win smaller sums (like $50-100) more frequently on nickel and quarter slots. Progressive machines are linked to networks of other machines throughout Nevada and have the potential to pay off in millions of dollars but offer payouts less frequently; a fraction of every coin bet goes into the progressive jackpot pool (you can see the amount increase on a display over the slot cluster until someone hits it).

If you plan to play the slots, take the time to join each casino's slot club. Even if you aren't a heavy gambler or big winner, the time you play can earn points toward free meals, free rooms, and other promotions that you will receive in the mail.

Video Poker

Video poker is played like regular draw poker, except you are playing against a machine and receive set payoffs for specific hands. Several variations include Jacks or Better, Deuces Wild, and a slew of bonus machines that pay off more for four of a kind and less for the more common and mundane winners such as three of a kind and straights. Many of the machines allow players to choose the denomination played—a nickel to a dollar per hand. Basically you are dealt a hand, choose which cards to keep or discard, and rack up winnings or losses depending on the cards you are dealt. One of the appeals to this game is that there isn't as much pressure playing a machine as sitting at a table with a bunch of other players, and it's a good way to get more familiar with the game.

Conduct and Customs

ADULT ENTERTAINMENT
Prostitution and the Sex Industry

In Nevada, like everywhere else, sex sells, and outside the Reno and Las Vegas areas, sex is sold. Brothels opened in Virginia City long before any grocery stores and not long after the first saloons. At its peak 150-300 dens of ill repute were operating, and just as the miners fanned out from the Comstock Lode to discover mineral riches across the vast state, the women followed right behind.

Today, 20 licensed and regulated brothels operate in the rural parts of the state. Prostitution is still illegal in Las Vegas and Reno. Of course, that doesn't mean it doesn't happen, often under the guise of to-your-room strippers and massage parlors. Both the client and the prostitute can go to jail if arrested in a street prostitution sting, and although the prostitutes are arrested more often than the clients are, clients are taking a risk when they engage in illegal prostitution.

The "gentlemen's clubs" work hard to walk the fine line between creating fantasies and fulfilling them, adopting strict no-nonsense policies against prostitution. If found guilty of encouraging the world's oldest profession, they risk losing their liquor licenses or being shut down (in reality, both amount to the same thing). Still, the strippers (most prefer to be called "exotic dancers") are independent contractors, not employees. While bouncers keep a pretty close eye on the action, even in the clubs' VIP rooms, they can't monitor conversations. Assignations and negotiations could be going on anywhere.

More innocent but hardly subtle use of sex appeal can be found all over Nevada, from topless showgirls and tanned beefcake reviews to corseted cocktail waitresses and model-like blackjack dealers.

SMOKING AND DRINKING

The drinking age in Nevada is 21. If you're of age, you can drink more readily and cheaply than anywhere else in the country. Every casino in the state and many bars remain open 24 hours, and every casino serves free drinks to players. The easiest way to get free booze is to plop down at a video poker bar, stick in $20, and tip the bartender well. You don't even have to play: Simply buy in, get your comp drink, and cash out.

Like most of the country, Nevada prohibits smoking in areas that serve food. While the law is not universally observed in bars, most have erected barriers between their drinking areas and their dining areas. It's not uncommon to see signs proclaiming, "Smoker-friendly bar; smoke-free dining." Smoking is part of the deal in casinos. Some have adopted smoke-free areas, usually an area with a few slot machines and a section of the race and sports book. But they're usually separated from the tobacco users by empty floor space, with nothing to prevent the smoke from wafting over.

As of July 2017 anyone over 21 in Nevada may legally possess up to one ounce of marijuana. Driving under the influence of marijuana is a crime, however, and public consumption of the drug is not allowed. The state government still has not promulgated laws for retail pot sales.

Travel Tips

INTERNATIONAL TRAVELERS

Foreign travel to Las Vegas, as is the case anywhere in the United States, requires a passport and a tourist visa. Visas are available from the U.S. embassy in your country at an average cost of $160. It is recommended that you apply for a visa several weeks before your anticipated travel date to allow ample time for processing. Holders of Canadian passports do not need a waiver, and citizens of many other countries can apply through the Electronic System for Travel Authorization. Check with the U.S. Department of Homeland Security to see if you qualify.

Eighteen countries maintain consulates in Las Vegas: Armenia, Bulgaria, Chile, Czech Republic, El Salvador, France, German, Guatemala, Ireland, Japan, Lithuania, Mexico, Monaco, Namibia, Poland, Romania, Sweden, and Switzerland. They can assist their visiting citizens with replacing lost passports, legal representation, support for crime and accident victims, and even emergency financial assistance.

TRAVELERS WITH DISABILITIES

All the casinos and almost all the major tourist attractions in Nevada are fully compliant with Americans with Disabilities Act requirements. Most hotels have plenty of wheelchair-accessible rooms and ramps and have at least a few low roll-up gambling tables and machines. Taxis and buses are equipped to ease entering and exiting. Even some nature attractions have built boardwalks, transportation, or viewing platforms to make them fun for everyone. Still, casino properties are huge and often crowded, so people with limited mobility may have difficulty maneuvering around and among the casinos, especially on the Las Vegas Strip.

Some Nevada attractions are valued for their historical significance or natural beauty, making them inaccessible by people using wheelchairs. Many buildings associated with mining, being built more than 150 years ago, were not constructed with wheelchairs or service animals—or even today's large-bodied Americans—in mind. Tight corridors, winding staircases, and uneven floors can make negotiation difficult.

TRAVELING WITH CHILDREN

No one under 21 can participate in—or even watch—casino gambling in Nevada casinos. But they can walk through. Older kids on their own and younger kids with their parents must be moving along toward some destination—the arcade, movie theater, or restaurant. If you're with your kids and stop somewhere in the casino for some reason, security guards not far behind will ask you to continue on your way. The guards will tell you that both you and the casino can be fined for having youths in a gambling area. You and your kids can stop in a gambling area only if you're standing in a line to see a show or enter a buffet that winds through the casino.

What about 19- or 20-year-olds who sit down to play? That depends on the casino. The unwritten rule used to be that minors could play but they couldn't win. In other words, 20-year-olds could feed the slots until they were broke, but if one hit a jackpot that required a slot host to fill out IRS paperwork (anything more than $1,200), for which seeing identification is required, the underage player not only wouldn't get paid, they'd get the bum's rush out the door to boot. Court case after court case has upheld the casino's right to refuse to pay; in fact, if the casino did pay, it could get fined or lose its license. These days, with more and more kids roaming around Las Vegas, some joints check ID religiously; others don't.

GAY AND LESBIAN TRAVELERS

Nevada—especially the rural areas—is about as libertarian as they come, and Las Vegas is proud of its long-nurtured "if it feels good, do it" philosophy. However, only recently has the state lived up to its promise regarding LGBTQ tourists. Everyone is protected by anti-discrimination laws, and same-sex couples have been legally marrying since 2014.

Both Vegas (Sunset Park) and Reno (Wingfield Park) host pride festivals.

Gay, lesbian, and transgender travelers will find themselves at home in casinos, showrooms, and nightclubs in Las Vegas, Reno, and

Lake Tahoe, which also contain their share of gay bars. The pickings are much slimmer in rural areas. Gay-friendly bars can be found all over Las Vegas, but the biggest concentration lies around Naples Drive and Paradise Road near UNLV. The queen of the "Fruit Loop," as it's affectionately called, is **QuadZ** (640 Paradise Rd., 702/733-0383, 24 hours daily). Unpretentious and maybe even a little divey, QuadZ serves up strong, cheap drinks and music videos on the big screen. While you're in the neighborhood, check out **FreeZone** (610 E. Naples Dr., 702/794-2300, 24 hours daily) for the best drag shows in town. There's a dearth of dedicated lesbian bars, but women are welcome and often out in force at the gay establishments in town.

A few casinos actively court gay patrons. Luxor, for instance, hosts **Temptation Sunday** pool parties throughout the summer. A resident DJ, celebrity cameos, stiff drinks, and lots of exposed flesh highlight the gathering.

Gay bars aren't as concentrated in Reno, though most are within several blocks north of the Truckee River. The **5 Star Saloon** (132 West St., 775/499-5655, 5pm-5am daily) runs the gamut depending on which night you visit; it's part neighborhood hangout, part dance club, part karaoke lounge, and part go-go bar.

Health and Safety

WEATHER

Two generalizations apply to Nevada's weather: It's hot in the summer and dry year-round. Always carry water; it's a desert out there. If you're hiking, have a canteen on your belt and a gallon jug in your pack.

The prevailing winds in the southern part of the state are southerlies, which have crossed the fierce Sonoran Desert and hold little moisture. Las Vegas is the driest metropolitan area in the United States, receiving an average of just 3-4 inches of precipitation a year. On top of that, the southern

part of the state gets scorched 7-8 months of the year. Temperatures in Las Vegas that reach 110°F are not uncommon in May and September; highs can rise to 115°F in July-August. Laughlin can hit 120°F and usually registers over 20 days per year of the country's highest temperatures. A record-high temperature for the state was recorded in Laughlin in June 1994: a sizzling 125°F. If you're driving, a five-gallon container of water will get you or someone you happen upon through almost any emergency. Any supermarket will sell gallon jugs of spring water; don't run out. You might also buy canned or boxed juices.

Cloudbursts and thunderstorms can strike anywhere in the state but happen mostly in the south. They can dump more rain in an hour than many places receive in six months. These torrential downpours tend to be extremely localized and dangerous, giving rise to raging and roiling water that surges down gullies, washes, and drainages that might have been dry for a decade. The "wet" season is December-March; summer storms and flash floods, known in Las Vegas as "monsoon season," occur June-August.

Since most of the state is around a mile high, winters can be surprisingly severe. The harshest locations for this season are northeastern Nevada from Jarbidge to Ely, with temperatures regularly dropping below zero and the snow remaining for 4-5 months and even longer in some places. Central Nevada is similar. The western and southern sections from Reno to Laughlin have milder and shorter winters, one reason that 80 percent of Nevada's population lives in this "sun belt."

CRIME

The transience and low economic status of many people attracted to Nevada by a boomtown mentality are evident in a number of ways. Nevada has the highest rate of high school dropouts in the country and one of the lowest proportions of college-educated citizens. This makes for a large population of undereducated and economically challenged people. Add to that lots of cash floating around and hordes of unwary tourists, and it's no wonder Nevada's crime rate is among the highest in the country. One study ranks the state as the fifth-most litigious, based on the number of lawsuits filed. Crimes inside casinos are rare, but alcohol flows freely, so brawls on the street are not. Common sense is to stay in well-lighted areas and travel in groups, which will go a long way toward ensuring you don't become a victim.

Information and Services

TOURIST INFORMATION

The best general source of information about the state, *Nevada Magazine* (401 N. Carson St., Ste. 100, Carson City, 775/687-5416, www.nevadamagazine.com), has been financed by the state government since the 1930s. The "Nevada Events and Shows" section provides comprehensive listings of things to do around the state; the website provides contact information for convention and visitors bureaus, chambers of commerce, events hotlines, and more.

Visitor information is also available through state and federal agencies:

• **Nevada Commission on Tourism** (401 N. Carson St., Carson City, 775/687-4322 or 800/638-2328, www.travelnevada.com)

• **Nevada Division of State Parks** (901 S.

Stewart St., 5th Fl., Ste. 5005, Carson City, 775/684-2770, www.parks.nv.gov)

• **Great Basin National Park** (100 Great Basin National Park, Baker, 775/234-7331, www.nps.gov/grba)

• **Lake Mead National Recreation Area** (601 Nevada Hwy., Boulder City, 702/293-8906, www.nps.gov/lake)

• **Bureau of Land Management** (1340 Financial Blvd., Reno, 775/861-6400, www.nv.blm.gov/nv/st/en)

• **Humboldt-Toiyabe National Forest** (1200 Franklin Way, Sparks, 775/331-5644, www.fs.fed.us/r4/htnf)

• **Nevada Division of Wildlife** (1100 Valley Rd., Reno, 775/688-1500, www.ndow.org)

• **State Library and Archives** (716 N.

Carson St., Ste. 6, Carson City, 775/687-8393, www.nevadaculture.org)

- **Road Condition Report** (877/687-6237)

Every major library in the state has a Nevada room or a special collection of local-interest titles. The three main libraries for researching specific aspects of the Nevada experience are the **Getchell Library** on the University of Nevada, Reno, campus (1664 N. Virginia St., 775/784-1110), the **Lied Library** on the University of Nevada, Las Vegas, campus (4505 S. Maryland Pkwy., 702/895-2286), and the **State Library** (100 N. Stewart St., Carson City, 800/922-2880).

MAPS

The biggest, most beautiful, and most informative Nevada landscape map is produced by **Raven Maps** (800/237-0798, www.raven-maps.com). It's available for $30 (paper) or $50 (laminated). The Nevada **Department of Transportation** (1263 S. Stewart St., Carson City, 775/888-7627, www.nevadadot.com/traveler/maps) also has wall-size maps of the roads, counties, and natural features. In addition, it publishes an indispensable *Nevada Map Atlas* of 127 quadrangle maps of the state, which include all the unpaved roads.

ESSENTIALS
INFORMATION AND SERVICES

Resources

Gambling Glossary

call: In poker, to match a previous player's bet.

double down: In blackjack, the player's option to double the amount bet and receive one (and only one) additional card to complete the hand.

expectation: The statistical profit or loss that would accrue if a bet were made thousands of times. If you won $1 every time a coin came up "heads" and lost $1 every time it was "tails," your expectation would be $0. But if you won $2 for every head and lost $1 for every tail, your expectation would be $0.50 (50 heads = $100, 50 tails = -$50, for a profit of $50; $50/100 iterations = $0.50). Expectation can be positive or negative (almost always in casino games).

field: In craps, an even-money bet that the shooter's next roll will total 2, 3, 4, 9, 10, 11, or 12. There are 16 dice combinations that come up winners and 20 that are losers.

flop: The first three shared cards that are revealed all at once in poker games with five community cards. The next card is called "the turn" or "fourth street"; the final community card is "the river" or "fifth street."

odds: The potential payout for a winning bet; 2-to-1 odds means the winner will receive $2 for every $1 bet (the bettor also gets the original $1 wager back). Also, a craps bet made after the come-out roll, in which the player receives true odds that the shooter will (or will not, if the bettor played the "don't pass" line) make his or her point before rolling a 7.

pari-mutuel: The pools of money from which winning bets are paid. Under this system, used by North American racetracks, the odds are determined by the amount bet on each entrant in the race. A horse with $20,000 worth of bets on it out of the $100,000 total wagered in the race would pay 4-to-1 because four times more money was bet on the other horses ($80,000) than was bet on it.

reel machines: Mechanical slot machines with three or more wheels with symbols on them. Line up the right combination of symbols to win.

ring game: In poker, a game played for cash rather than for tournament prize money.

toke: A tip given to a casino dealer or cocktail waitress. Short for "token of appreciation."

Suggested Reading

The **University of Nevada Press** (775/784-6573, www.unevadapress.com) is the best source for current books about Nevada. Gambling-related reading material is the focus of Las Vegas-based **Huntington Press** (702/252-0655 http://huntingtonpress.com) and **Gambler's Book Club** (702/382-7555, www.gamblersbookclub.com).

A visit to any bookstore specializing in Nevada themes will turn up many books on interesting Nevada-related topics, including the California Trail, the Pony Express, Native Americans, the Basques (check out the University of Nevada Press's Basque series), ghost towns, and the natural history and geology of the Great Basin. Larger museums in the state usually offer a good selection of Nevada-related books.

For an exhaustive bibliography on Nevada and gambling, see *Nevada—An Annotated Bibliography,* by Stanley Paher (Las Vegas: Nevada Publications, 1980). Although published nearly 40 years ago, it's still the most comprehensive general bibliography available.

TRAVEL AND DESCRIPTION

Glass, Mary Ellen, and Al Glass. *Touring Nevada: A Historic and Scenic Guide.* Reno: University of Nevada Press, 1983. An excellent guide, well organized into specific "circle tours" for those interested in the historical significance of the sights of Nevada.

Tingley, Joseph V., and Kris Ann Pizarro. *Traveling America's Loneliest Road: A Geologic and Natural History Tour through Nevada along U.S. Highway 50.* Reno: University of Nevada Press, 2000. A guide to geologic features and other points of interest along US 50 between Lake Tahoe and Great Basin National Park.

Toll, David W. *The Complete Nevada Traveler: The Affectionate and Intimately Detailed Guidebook to the Most Interesting State in America.* Virginia City, NV: Gold Hill Publications, 2008. Short histories and quick stops on a voyage around the Silver State.

GEOLOGY AND ENVIRONMENT

DeCourten, Frank, and Norma Biggar. *Roadside Geology of Nevada.* Missoula, MT: Mountain Press, 2017. A guide to the minerals, mines, dry lake beds, and outcroppings right under our feet in Nevada.

Floyd, Ted, et al. *Atlas of the Breeding Birds of Nevada.* Reno: University of Nevada Press, 2007. Nevada is an important winter home and migratory rest stop for raptors, songbirds, and waterfowl. Birders will appreciate this indispensable guide.

Kavanaugh, James J. *Nevada Trees & Wildflowers: An Introduction to Familiar Species.* Chandler, AZ: Waterford Press, 2008. A companion for photographers and horticulturists.

RECREATION

Dickerson, Richard. *Nevada Angler's Guide—Fish Tails in the Sagebrush.* Portland, OR: Frank Amato Publications, 1997. A handy, useful, and authoritative guide to 116 of the most accessible fishing spots in Nevada.

Hauserman, Tim. *Cross-country Skiing in the Sierra Nevada: The Best Resorts & Touring Centers in California & Nevada.* Woodstock, VT: Countryman Press, 2007. Say "Nevada skiing" and most people think of rushing down pristine powder. Hauserman gives Nordic fans their own reason for embracing the state.

Papa, Paul. *Mountain Biking Las Vegas and Southern Nevada: A Guide to the Area's Greatest Off-road Bicycle Rides.* Guilford, CT: Falcon Guides, 2017. Maps and directions to where to pedal in the Las Vegas area.

HISTORY

De Quille, Dan. *History of the Big Bonanza: An Authentic Account of the Discovery, History, and Working of the World-renowned Comstock Lode of Nevada.* New York: Crowell, 1947. Effectively combines scholarly history, personality sketches, and the humor for which De Quille became legendary.

Ford, Jean, Betty Glass, and Martha Gould. *Women in Nevada History: An Annotated Bibliography of Published Sources.* Reno: Nevada Women's History Project, 2000. An excellent resource for finding out everything you ever wanted to know about women in the Silver State's history.

Gibson, Elizabeth. *It Happened in Nevada: Remarkable Events That Shaped History.* Guilford, CT: Globe Pequot Press, 2010. Little-known details enliven Gibson's lively retelling of familiar events in Nevada's history.

James, Ronald M. *The Roar and the Silence: A History of Virginia City and the Comstock Lode.* Reno: University of Nevada Press, 1998. This lively, thoughtful book chronicles the area's history from its earliest days through the early 20th century, when the lode finally gave out and the Comstock sank into silent decay, up to the present, when Virginia City and its environs found new life, first as a community of bohemians and artists and more recently as a tourist attraction.

Land, Barbara, and Myrick Land. *A Short History of Las Vegas.* Reno: University of Nevada Press, 2004. A lively history, illustrated with historical and recent photographs, telling the story of the Las Vegas area from the earliest visitors 11,000 years ago up to the present.

Land, Barbara, and Myrick Land. *A Short History of Reno.* Reno: University of Nevada Press, 1995. An entertaining and anecdotal history of Reno's colorful past and the larger-than-life characters who left their mark on the city, illustrated with dozens of black-and-white photos.

Laxalt, Robert. *Nevada—A History.* New York: W. W. Norton, 1977. A very personal, lyrical, and selective account of the history and shape of the state by one of Nevada's best-known and best-loved writers.

Merlin, Peter W. *Nevada Test Site.* Mt. Pleasant, SC: Arcadia Publishing, 2016. How this hunk of desolate desert helped shape America's defense policy.

Moe, Al W. *Nevada's Golden Age of Gambling: The Casinos, 1931-1981.* North Charleston, SC: Createspace, 2012. Lots of photos complement a walk down memory lane with Howard Hughes, Bugsy Siegel, and their colorful contemporaries.

Pileggi, Nicholas. *Casino: Love and Honor in Las Vegas.* New York: Simon & Schuster, 1995. The basis for the film *Goodfellas* is a gripping account of how the mob ran and eventually lost control of Las Vegas.

Reid, Ed, and Ovid Demaris. *The Green Felt Jungle.* New York: Pocket Books, 1964. A classic book in the diatribe style describing Las Vegas as "a corrupt jungle of iniquity."

GAMBLING

Anderson, Ian. *Turning the Tables on Las Vegas.* New York: Vintage Books, 1976. Ian Anderson was a pseudonym for R. Kent London, a highly successful and anonymous card counter, who goes into extraordinary detail about playing and betting strategies, camouflage, interaction with the pit personnel, and maintaining a winning attitude. Required reading for aspiring counters.

Nelson, Titus. *Las Vegas Insider's Guide: Save Money, Keep Safe, Operate and Survive in Sin City.* Henderson, NV: Silverview Publishing, 2014. Focuses on "adult" Vegas and Nevada—brothels, gambling, booze, etc.

BIOGRAPHY

Canfield, Gae Whitney. *Sarah Winnemucca of the Northern Paiutes.* Norman, OK: University of Oklahoma Press, 1983. Biography of the daughter of Chief Winnemucca, whose book *Life Among the Piutes* became a classic.

Garrison, Omar. *Howard Hughes in Las Vegas.* Secaucus, NJ: Lyle Stuart, 1970. Everything about this troubled, mysterious billionaire is gripping, but this book, centered around the four years Hughes spent sequestered on the ninth floor of the Desert Inn, is especially eye-opening, shedding light on the public events and private life of the recluse as he set about to buy and redesign the city that may well have been "his true spiritual home."

Hillyer, Katharine. *Mark Twain: Young Reporter in Virginia City.* Reno: Nevada Publications, 1997. Tells the story of Twain's life as a young reporter in Virginia City, which was the beginning of his literary career.

Swanson, Doug. *Blood Aces: The Wild Ride of Benny Binion, the Texas Gangster Who Created Vegas Poker.* New York: Viking, 2014. The story of the Binion's Casino founder and the creation of the World Series of Poker.

LITERATURE

Glotfelty, Cheryll, ed. *Literary Nevada: Writings from the Silver State.* Reno: University of Nevada Press, 2008. A variety of styles and voices capture the quintessential Nevada viewpoint, with all its complexities and contradictions.

McLaughlin, Mark. *Sierra Stories: True Tales of Tahoe.* 2 vols. Carnelian Bay, CA: Mic Mac Publishing, 1997-1998. Stories about Lake Tahoe and the Tahoe area.

McMurtry, Larry. *The Desert Rose.* New York: Simon & Schuster, 1983. An affectionate and poignant little character study of an aging showgirl and her ties—men, daughter, neighbors, friends, and coworkers—that McMurtry wrote over a three-week period during a lull in the writing of his epic *Lonesome Dove.*

Thompson, Hunter S. *Fear and Loathing in Las Vegas.* New York: Random House, 1998. Thompson's classic drug-addled novel popularized his subjective blend of fact and fiction, which became known as gonzo journalism.

Internet Resources

VISITOR INFORMATION

Nevada's cities and regions maintain visitor information sites with links to area hotels, amusements, and recreational facilities. Many also produce online or print visitors guides. See these sites for specific information about the happenings during your visit:

- **Las Vegas:** www.visitlasvegas.com, www.vegas.com
- **Laughlin:** www.visitlaughlin.com
- **Reno and Lake Tahoe:** www.visitrenotahoe.com, www.renotahoe.com
- **Carson City:** www.visitcarsoncity.com
- **Virginia City:** www.virginiacity-nv.org
- **Humboldt Valley:** www.cowboycountry.org
- **Great Basin:** http://ponyexpressnevada.com

Travel Nevada
http://travelnevada.com
The official site of the Nevada Commission on Tourism, with hotel deals, travel packages, and tourist attractions listed by town.

Las Vegas Convention and Visitors Authority
www.lvcva.com
The authority works to fill southern Nevada's 150,000 hotel rooms with vacationers, conventioneers, and business travelers. It runs the massive and technologically advanced Las Vegas Convention Center.

Nevada Department of Transportation
www.nevadadot.com
The site has traveler information, speed limits, weather conditions, maps, and highway safety information.

RECREATION

Nevada Division of State Parks
http://parks.nv.gov
A wealth of information on state parks, including fee schedules, hunting, fishing, camping, day-use facilities, special events, and conservation efforts.

Bureau of Land Management
www.blm.gov/nv/st/en.html
The state field office for the Bureau of Land Management has a nifty brochure on conservation efforts and the bountiful opportunities that public lands provide, as well as information on hunting, camping, and off-roading on federal land.

CULTURE

Indian Territory
www.blm.gov/nevada
Works to advance the political and economic causes of Nevada's Native Americans and to foster understanding of Indian ways by presenting cultural and artistic displays of their lifestyles and history. Download the beautiful brochure from the site.

University of Nevada
www.unlv.edu
www.unr.edu
The sites have enrollment statistics, applications, and sporting event schedules for Nevada's four-year universities. In addition, you'll find links to the university libraries and on-campus museums, art galleries, and gardens.

NEWSPAPERS

Las Vegas Review-Journal
www.lvrj.com
Vegas's major newspaper is the *Las Vegas Review-Journal*. Its "Neon" section profiles

the weekend's hottest events and lists the entertainment options for the coming week. Margo Bartlett Pesek's Sunday "Trip of the Week" chronicles interesting places to visit and day trips from Las Vegas.

Las Vegas Sun
www.lasvegassun.com
Las Vegas's second daily newspaper, smaller and more liberal, reports on big issue events, with less focus on day-to-day news and events.

Reno Gazette-Journal
www.rgj.com
Click the "Metromix" tab on the home page for information on restaurants, nightclubs, bars, and concerts.

Index

List of Maps

Photo Credits

page 1 © Lokinthru | Dreamstime.com; page 4 © Fabio Formaggio | Dreamstime.com; page 5 © Ktom32 | Dreamstime.com; page 6 (top left) © Chris Moran | Travel Nevada, (top right) © Photoquest | Dreamstime.com, (bottom) © Rinus Baak | Dreamstime.com; page 7 (top) © fyletto | 123RF, (bottom) © Sandra Foyt | Dreamstime.com; page 8 © Hotaik Sung | Dreamstime.com; page 9 (top) © Ritu Jethani | Dreamstime.com, (bottom left) © Kojihirano | Dreamstime.com, (bottom right) © Chris Moran | Travel Nevada; page 10 © Littleny | Dreamstime.com; page 13 (top) © Heavenly Mountain Resort, (bottom) © Kaitlin Godbey | Travel Nevada; page 14 © Neillockhart | Dreamstime.com; page 15 © Chris Moran | Travel Nevada; page 16 (top) © Kwiktor | Dreamstime.com, (middle) © Kwiktor | Dreamstime.com, (bottom) © Foster Eubank | Dreamstime.com; page 17 © Sandra Foyt | Dreamstime.com; page 18 © Vinsphoto | Dreamstime.com; page 21 © Rudi1976 | Dreamstime.com; page 24 © neillockhart | 123RF; page 27 © trekandshoot | Dreamstime.com; page 29 © Natalia Bratslavsky | Dreamstime.com; page 31 (top) © Nito100 | Dreamstime.com, (bottom) © Kobby_dagan | Dreamstime.com; page 33 © Chris Moran | Travel Nevada; page 39 © Steve Collender | 123RF; page 42 © Kobby_dagan | Dreamstime.com; page 46 © Littleny | Dreamstime.com; page 49 © Rabbit75 | Dreamstime.com; page 55 © Brian Jones | Las Vegas News Bureau; page 56 © Brian Jones | Las Vegas News Bureau; page 57 © Darrin Bush | Las Vegas News Bureau; page 58 © Sam Morris | Las Vegas News Bureau; page 61 © Brian Jones | Las Vegas News Bureau; page 65 © Diegograndi | Dreamstime.com; page 70 © Brian Jones | Las Vegas News Bureau; page 99 © Kobby_dagan | Dreamstime.com; page 102 © Wangkun Jia | Dreamstime.com; page 104 © Sunnywood | Dreamstime.com; page 112 © Brian Jones | Las Vegas News Bureau; page 117 (top) © Mblach | Dreamstime.com, (bottom) © Vinsphoto | Dreamstime.com; page 119 © Spvvkr | Dreamstime.com; page 123 © Weezybob5 | Dreamstime.com; page 126 © Victorianl | Dreamstime.com; page 131 © Photoquest | Dreamstime.com; page 135 © Neillockhart | Dreamstime.com; page 140 © Travel Nevada; page 152 © Matthewtrain | Dreamstime.com; page 156 © VisitRenoTahoe.com; page 163 © VisitRenoTahoe.com; page 167 © Yue Liu | Dreamstime.com; page 172 (top) © Chris Boswell | Dreamstime.com, (bottom) © Kaitlin Godbey | Travel Nevada; page 173 © Jason P Ross | Dreamstime.com; page 176 © Kkistl01 | Dreamstime.com; page 178 © Sydney Martinez | Travel Nevada; page 182 © Fernley | Dreamstime.com; page 187 © Travel Nevada; page 189 © Chris Moran | Travel Nevada; page 191 © Sydney Martinez | Travel Nevada; page 192 © Karin Van Der Laan | Dreamstime.com; page 193 © Sydney Martinez | Travel Nevada; page 195 © Neillockhart | Dreamstime.com; page 197 © Travel Nevada; page 200 © Coopls | Dreamstime.com; page 201 © Sydney Martinez | TravelNevada; page 206 © Neillockhart | Dreamstime.com; page 209 © Arlene Hochman Waller | Dreamstime.com; page 211 © Daniel Larson | Dreamstime.com; page 215 © Sydney Martinez | TravelNevada; page 219 © Fernley | Dreamstime.com; page 220 © Larry Gevert | Dreamstime.com; page 227 © Travel Nevada; page 228 © Sydney Martinez | Travel Nevada; page 233 © Chris Moran | TravelNevada; page 237 © Scott Smith; page 245 © Sydney Martinez | Travel Nevada; page 246 © Sydney Martinez | Travel Nevada; page 253 © James Feliciano | Dreamstime.com; page 254 © Sydney Martinez | TravelNevada; page 257 © Terence Mendoza | Dreamstime.com; page 263 © Rinusbaak | Dreamstime.com; page 266 © Adonis84 | Dreamstime.com; page 271 (top) © Neillockhart | Dreamstime.com, (bottom) © Kaitlin Godbey | Travel Nevada; page 273 © Dtfoxfoto | Dreamstime.com; page 279 © Chris Moran | Travel Nevada; page 281 © Kringsj | Dreamstime.com; page 282 © David N. Braun | Dreamstime.com; page 285 © Sydney Martinez | Travel Nevada; page 287 © Travel Nevada; page 289 © Travel Nevada; page 300 © Chris Moran | Travel Nevada; page 306 © Larry Gevert | Dreamstime.com; page 313 © Sydney Martinez | Travel Nevada; page 315 © Daniloforcellini | Dreamstime.com; page 320 (top) © Pancaketom | Dreamstime.com, (bottom) © Kojihirano | Dreamstime.com; page 324 © Photoquest | Dreamstime.com; page 329 © Brian Jones | Las Vegas News Bureau; page 333 © Larry Gevert | Dreamstime.com; page 342 (top) © Kevin Grant | Dreamstime.com, (bottom) © Jacek Sopotnicki | Dreamstime.com

MOON ROAD TRIP GUIDES

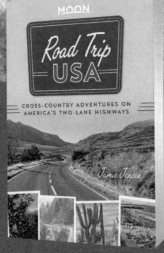

Road Trip USA

Criss-cross the country on America's classic two-lane highways with the newest edition of *Road Trip USA!*

Packed with over 125 detailed driving maps (covering more than 35,000 miles), colorful photos and illustrations of America both then and now, and mile-by-mile highlights

Advice on where to
sleep, eat, and explore

Detailed driving
directions including
mileage and
drive times

Itineraries for a
range of timelines

Moon Travel Guides
are available from your
favorite bookseller.

MOON
PACIFIC
NORTHWEST
Road Trip

SEATTLE, VANCOUVER, VICTORIA,
THE OLYMPIC PENINSULA, PORTLAND,
THE OREGON COAST & MOUNT RAINIER

ALLISON WILLIAMS

MOON
ROUTE 66
Road Trip

MIDPOINT
CAFE

CANDACY TAYLOR

MOON
SOUTHWEST
Road Trip

LAS VEGAS, ZION & BRYCE, MONUMENT VALLEY,
SANTA FE & TAOS, AND THE GRAND CANYON

TIM HULL

MOON
VANCOUVER &
CANADIAN ROCKIES
Road Trip

VICTORIA, BANFF, JASPER, CALGARY,
THE OKANAGAN, WHISTLER &
THE SEA-TO-SKY HIGHWAY

CAROLYN B. HELLER

Join our travel community!
hare your adventures using #travelwithmoon

MOON.COM
@MOONGUIDES

MOON NATIONAL PARKS

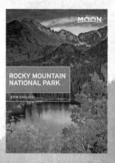

In these books:

- Full coverage of gateway cities and towns
- Itineraries from one day to multiple weeks
- Advice on where to stay (or camp) in and around the parks

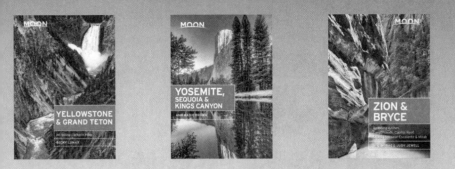

Craft a personalized journey through the top National Parks in the U.S. and Canada with Moon Travel Guides.

Join our travel community!
Share your adventures using **#travelwithmoon**

MOON.COM
@MOONGUIDES

Wander through the Southwest and Texas with Moon Travel Guides!

Guides for City Escapes

Trips South of the Border

MOON.COM | @MOONGUIDES

MAP SYMBOLS

═════	Expressway	○	City/Town	✈	Airport	♨	Golf Course
─────	Primary Road	◉	State Capital	✕	Airfield	P	Parking Area
─────	Secondary Road	⊛	National Capital	▲	Mountain	▲	Archaeological Site
┄┄┄┄	Unpaved Road	★	Point of Interest	✦	Unique Natural Feature	⛪	Church
────	Feature Trail	•	Accommodation	⚐	Waterfall	⛽	Gas Station
------	Other Trail	▼	Restaurant/Bar	♠	Park		Glacier
········	Ferry	■	Other Location	ⓣ	Trailhead		Mangrove
═════	Pedestrian Walkway	▲	Campground	✕	Skiing Area		Reef
▥▥▥▥	Stairs						Swamp

CONVERSION TABLES

$°C = (°F - 32) / 1.8$
$°F = (°C \times 1.8) + 32$
1 inch = 2.54 centimeters (cm)
1 foot = 0.304 meters (m)
1 yard = 0.914 meters
1 mile = 1.6093 kilometers (km)
1 km = 0.6214 miles
1 fathom = 1.8288 m
1 chain = 20.1168 m
1 furlong = 201.168 m
1 acre = 0.4047 hectares
1 sq km = 100 hectares
1 sq mile = 2.59 square km
1 ounce = 28.35 grams
1 pound = 0.4536 kilograms
1 short ton = 0.90718 metric ton
1 short ton = 2,000 pounds
1 long ton = 1.016 metric tons
1 long ton = 2,240 pounds
1 metric ton = 1,000 kilograms
1 quart = 0.94635 liters
1 US gallon = 3.7854 liters
1 Imperial gallon = 4.5459 liters
1 nautical mile = 1.852 km

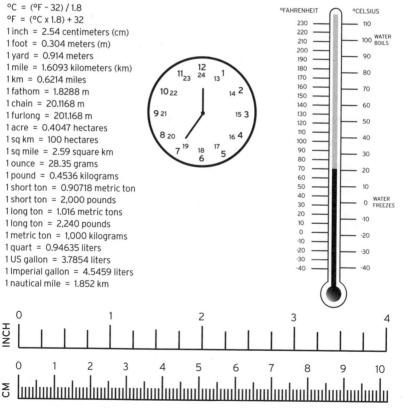

MOON NEVADA

Avalon Travel
Hachette Book Group
1700 Fourth Street
Berkeley, CA 94710, USA
www.moon.com

Editors: Kathryn Ettinger, Kevin McLain
Series Manager: Kathryn Ettinger
Copy Editor: Deana Shields
Graphics Coordinator: Krista Anderson
Production Coordinator: Krista Anderson
Cover Design: Faceout Studios, Charles Brock
Interior Design: Domini Dragoone
Moon Logo: Tim McGrath
Map Editor: Kat Bennett
Cartographers: Brian Shotwell, Austin Ehrhardt
Indexer: Greg Jewett

ISBN-13: 978-1-63121-732-6

Printing History
1st Edition — June 2018
5 4 3 2 1

Text © 2018 by Scott Smith.
Maps © 2018 by Avalon Travel.
Some photos and illustrations are used by permission and are the property of the original copyright owners.

Hachette Book Group supports the right to free expression and the value of copyright. The purpose of copyright is to encourage writers and artists to produce the creative works that enrich our culture. The scanning, uploading, and distribution of this book without permission is a theft of the author's intellectual property. If you would like permission to use material from the book (other than for review purposes), please contact permissions@hbgusa.com. Thank you for your support of the author's rights.

Front cover photo: road into the east entrance of Valley of Fire State Park © Dennis Maisel/ TandemStock.com

Back cover photo: Las Vegas neon lights © Soleilc/ Dreamstime.com

Printed in Canada by Friesens

Avalon Travel is a division of Hachette Book Group, Inc. Moon and the Moon logo are trademarks of Hachette Book Group, Inc. All other marks and logos depicted are the property of the original owners.

All recommendations, including those for sights, activities, hotels, restaurants, and shops, are based on each author's individual judgment. We do not accept payment for inclusion in our travel guides, and our authors don't accept free goods or services in exchange for positive coverage.

Although every effort was made to ensure that the information was correct at the time of going to press, the author and publisher do not assume and hereby disclaim any liability to any party for any loss or damage caused by errors, omissions, or any potential travel disruption due to labor or financial difficulty, whether such errors or omissions result from negligence, accident, or any other cause.

The publisher is not responsible for websites (or their content) that are not owned by the publisher.